Since reading Law at Oxford, A. J. Davies has worked as a tutor in adult education for the Workers' Educational Association and for London and Cambridge Universities' Extra-Mural Departments. Between 1982 and 1986 he was Librarian of the Marx Memorial Library in London. As Andrew John Davies he now writes for the *Independent* on social history and architecture, and he also runs two organisations specialising in leading people on historical walks, 'All About Britain' and 'All About London'.

A frequent contributor to radio and television programmes on politics, he is also in demand internationally as a lecturer and has toured both Germany and Australia.

His published work to date includes several acclaimed books on the history of London, a political and social study of the 1940s, and *We, The Nation: The Conservative Party and the Pursuit of Power*, which is also available in Abacus.

A.J. Davies lives in London.

*Also by A.J. Davies from Abacus*

WE, THE NATION
The Conservative Party and the Pursuit of Power

# TO BUILD A NEW JERUSALEM

The British Labour Party
from Keir Hardie to Tony Blair

A.J. Davies

An *Abacus* Book

First published in Great Britain by Michael Joseph in 1992
This revised edition first published by Abacus in 1996

A CIP catalogue record for this book
is available from the British Library.

ISBN: 0 349 10809 9

Typeset in Bembo by
Palimpsest Book Production Limited,
Polmont, Stirlingshire
Printed and bound in Great Britain by
Clays Ltd, St Ives plc.

Abacus
A Division of
Little, Brown and Company (UK)
Brettenham House
Lancaster Place
London WC2E 7EN

*To George, Henry and Jessica —*
*the new generation*

# Contents

# Acknowledgements

Many institutions and people have helped me prepare both the 1992 and 1996 editions of *To Build A New Jerusalem*. I owe much to the British Library, the London Library, the Cambridge University Library, the House of Lords Records Office, the Bodleian in Oxford, the Marx Memorial Library, the Public Records Office, the National Museum of Labour History, the Fawcett Library, the William Morris Gallery in Walthamstow, the Labour Party, the British Library of Political and Economic Science, Worcester College, Oxford, the former Communist Party Library and finally the public libraries in Westminster, Islington, Saffron Walden and Liverpool. The dedication and long hours which their staff put in refute the assertion that nowadays people are 'only in it for the money'. Here are thin cats who deserve to be a lot fatter.

Various draft chapters were read and discussed at conferences at the University of North London, at the Imperial War Museum, at the Australian Studies Centre, at an economics seminar organised at Cambridge University by Bob Rowthorn and others, and in front of innumerable adult education classes. Thanks for everyone's comments.

As for individuals, the list could indeed be as long as this book. Collectively, I want to thank the scores of people who contacted me after the first edition of *To Build A New Jerusalem* with information, praise and criticism. Individually, I want to single out some very good friends, colleagues and sparring partners: Ross Lidstone, David Coubrough, Chris Sheppardson, Mike Hill, Jamie Baird, Mike Chanan, John

Kavanagh, Jeremy Newsum, Alan Day, Cowpe, Charles Freeman, Graham Goulding, Simon de Galleani, Phil Sissons – in fact the entire team and supporting cast of 'The Packer Rejects' cricket team which, year after year, rather like Glamorgan, Watford and the New England Patriots, threaten to take the sporting world by storm but never quite make it. But we will.

Mind you, sceptics suggest that a better and more politically aware XI would comprise the wonderful Victoria Coubrough, Janie Hill, Fiona Baird, Gillian Newsum, Suzie Kavanagh, Linda Freeman, Sue Day, Bronwen Goulding, Pauline Cowpe, Solette Sheppardson, Shona Lidstone, Pauline de Galleani and Louise Sissons. Thank you too to Simon and Frances van der Borgh.

At a crucial moment Jatin Oza nurtured my sick computer Adrian and returned him to full health, while accountant Peter Thompson strives hard to make sense of my financial approximations. I owe a great deal to Dr Arthur Brown, who started me off in adult education; and, of course, thanks to Chris and Lesley Lintott.

I also want to mention Louise Haines and Susan Watt for their work on the 1992 edition, together with Garron Baines, David Barrs, Sarah Birdsey, Simon Blanchard, Roy and Ann Collingsworth, Max and Sadie Egelnick, Fran Hazelton, Kevin Jordan, Mark Jordan, Andrew Lorenz, Charles Poulsen and, finally, Charlie Revitt, the real salt of the earth.

Janet Ravenscroft edited this book, as she did my history of the Conservative Party, with stunning efficiency. Likewise, Patricia Hymans provided both volumes with excellent indexes. At Little, Brown, many thanks to Alan Samson, who commissioned this book, to Andrew Gordon for his relentless but exceedingly friendly attention to detail and to the delectable Claire Holt, not least for our shared Southwoldian enthusiasm.

Andrew Lownie, nominally my agent, is in reality a good

friend, adviser and catalyst. Here is an agent who genuinely cares for books as books, not as 'deals' or financial units on a balance sheet.

I relish my loving family: Libo and Charles Toghill for their unfailing devotion to an errant nephew; Simon and Julia, Emma and Dominic for being such good pals; and of course Mum and Dad, who despite their understandable puzzlement that I never did become a lawyer have always cared.

I salute the memory of Robert Montgomery, the nicest guy of them all.

This list is in danger of resembling a cringe-making Hollywood acceptance speech in which everyone everywhere is mentioned, including the cat (thank you, Tootsie). But enough. There are several personal friends whose love, encouragement and example has always meant that life is wonderful. To Liz, Margaret, Jane, Margaret (a distinguished long service medal) and finally Jean Collingsworth – who as always goes through draft after draft of my books with love and a stiletto-like pen, even though her university duties are onerous.

Thank you.

**A.J. Davies**

And did those feet in ancient time
Walk upon England's mountains green?
And was the holy Lamb of God
On England's pleasant pastures seen?

And did the Countenance Divine
Shine forth upon our clouded hills?
And was Jerusalem builded here
Among these dark Satanic mills?

Bring me my bow of burning gold!
Bring me my arrows of desire!
Bring me my spear! O clouds, unfold!
Bring me my chariot of fire!

I will not cease from Mental Fight,
Nor shall my Sword sleep in my hand,
Till we have built Jerusalem,
In England's green & pleasant Land.

WILLIAM BLAKE
Preface to his poem 'Milton'
(c. 1800–04)

# Beginnings

'In writing upon this, as upon every subject, I speak a language full and intelligible. I deal not in hints and intimations. I have several reasons for this: first, that I may be clearly understood. Secondly, that it may be seen I am in earnest; and thirdly, because it is an affront to truth to treat falsehood with complaisance.'

THOMAS PAINE, *EXAMINATION OF THE PROPHECIES*, 1806

'Politics is about power. Power is about people. People are personalities.'

JAMES MARGACH, *THE ANATOMY OF POWER* (1979)

'Workers of the world forgive me.'

THE WORDS PRINTED UNDER A POSTER OF KARL MARX IN EAST BERLIN IN THE SUMMER OF 1990

More adults play the National Lottery each week than bother to vote once every four or five years. Surveys have shown that one person in three has no idea which party their own MP belongs to. In 1986, one in three company heads could not identify Nigel Lawson as the Chancellor of the Exchequer, even though he had been in that post for no less than three years.

Holiday tour operators traditionally report a doubling in bookings when the date of a general election is announced as people flee the country in order to escape the political saturation which overwhelms the media. Fewer than one in twenty of the people questioned in a European poll take an active interest in politics. Young people, in particular, seem especially dismissive of organised politics. More people belong to the Royal Society for the Protection of Birds than the combined membership of the Conservative, Labour and Liberal Democrat parties.

In view of such findings, why should anyone in their right mind devote a large chunk of their life to researching and writing a book of political and social history? Why spend years exploring the British Labour Party in an attempt to discover why it is as it is?

In my case, it is because of a job I once had.

Clerkenwell Green in London can boast many radical associations. In 1381 Wat Tyler's peasants camped nearby on their way to London to complain about the poll tax. In later years the Green was the best-known of all open-air forums until the creation of Speaker's Corner in Hyde Park towards the end of the nineteenth century.

On the north side of the Green stands an elegant and compact house of 1737 which was built on the site of a medieval nunnery whose arches can still be glimpsed in the basement. Number 37 Clerkenwell Green was used as a Welsh Charity School until 1772 when it was taken over by a variety of businesses including a pub, cobblers, dressmakers. In 1872 it became a radical working men's club and was notable for being open to women. In 1893 Britain's first socialist publishing house, the Twentieth Century Press, moved in here. The poet, designer and socialist William Morris guaranteed the first year's rent of £50.

It was to this building that Lenin came between April 1902 and May 1903 to edit the Bolshevik paper *Iskra* which was printed on special wafer-thin paper and then smuggled back into Czarist Russia. The Twentieth Century Press moved out during the 1920s and in 1933 the Marx Memorial Library moved in. Its foundation was both a memorial to Karl Marx on the fiftieth anniversary of his death and an act of opposition to the burning of books then taking place in Nazi Germany.

This Georgian side of Clerkenwell Green was nearly demol-ished in the mid-1960s but a campaign led by John Betjeman and others ensured its survival. In 1983 an appeal to raise money was sponsored by both the leader of the Labour Party, Michael Foot, and the soon-to-be leader, Neil Kinnock. I was Librarian of the Marx Memorial Library from 1982 to 1986.

The Marx Library is a registered charity, open to all whatever their political views. One of the most regular users when I was there was the *Daily Telegraph* whose journalists were scrupulous in telephoning to check facts and news items. Often television companies came to film, making use in particular of the archives of the International Brigade, those men who had fought in the Spanish Civil War in the 1930s. The Library contains a wonderful collection of rare pamphlets, books and periodicals dating back to the English Civil War of the 1640s. There is also a remarkable range of material on American politics assembled by a former Librarian, John Williamson, who had been deported from the United States during the McCarthyite era in the 1950s.

It was a pleasure, too, to organise public lectures held at the Library and during my time speakers included historians Asa Briggs, Eric Hobsbawm, Christopher Hill, Stuart Hall and John Saville as well as politician Tony Benn. The lecture hall vibrated to the sound of many divergent beliefs and opinions – a striking contrast to the monolithic stance of the so-called 'Left' in Eastern Europe. In fact it was the Marx Library which in 1978 sponsored Eric Hobsbawm's lecture 'The Forward March of Labour Halted?' which sparked off much controversy.

As Librarian, one of my most important jobs was to lay a wreath on Karl Marx's grave in Highgate Cemetery at exactly 2.15 each 14th March, the very moment of his death. I also spent much of my time showing people around the tiny Lenin Room inside the Library where *Iskra* ('The Spark') had been edited. 'Around' is perhaps the wrong word since the room with its single desk, chair and filing cabinet barely holds five people at any one time. When dealing with the frequent parties of Soviet visitors, I had to talk to them in batches: 'Next, please'; 'Move along there'; 'Right down inside'. Some of these groups were attentive but others desperately wanted to go shopping in Oxford Street. For them I speeded up my talk.

From time to time, showing someone the Lenin Room could be a curiously moving experience. One afternoon a black South African socialist arrived and asked to have a look. When I explained to him that this was indeed the very room in which his idol Lenin had worked, he began to weep. It brought home to me that for some people allegiance to their beliefs, whatever they may be, really is a matter of life and death and not just a political game. We also had a long talk about the chances of release for his other idol, a certain Nelson Mandela, then still incarcerated in a South African prison.

The most famous visitor during my time as Librarian was Mikhail Gorbachev who came over with his wife Raisa to meet Mrs Thatcher in December 1984. On arrival in London, his first call was to the Marx Memorial Library. Everyone could feel his great vitality charging up the atmosphere around him. Remarkable too was his spontaneity; not generally a feature of Soviet visits. We sat downstairs in the lecture hall and, as usual, the Soviet party organised itself hierarchically into rows – most Russian groups were very status-conscious. The Gorbachevs sat in front, the interpreter behind, then the Soviet Ambassador in the third row and so on. Raisa was having none of this and she insisted that the interpreter should sit in the front row with them.

One of the fascinations of working at the Library was talking to the other people involved there. The Library's President was an old Balliol man who had been introduced to Lenin by his father. The Library Chairman, Chairwoman or possibly Chairperson – no one could ever agree on the ideologically correct terminology – had been educated at a convent school and was now chief executive of the *Morning Star* newspaper. The Library Secretary had begun his working life as an East

End tailor during the 1930s and took part in the Battle of Cable Street in October 1936. Members of the Committee included university lecturers, film editors, librarians, trade unionists, a former general secretary of the national Labour Party (Jim Mortimer), the retired and the unemployed.

And me? I went to public school and then read Law at Oxford. I had been a moderately active member of the Saffron Walden Labour Party with a tiny claim to political fame and a footnote in the history books through having organised a 'one member, one vote' ballot of the local membership for the deputy leadership contest between Tony Benn and Denis Healey in 1981 – one of the first times this was ever done and several years before Messrs Kinnock, Smith and Blair took up the idea. I was also asked to stand for Parliament but soon realised I was too (over) sensitive to put up with the inevitable buffetings from opponents and supporters alike.

As for users of the Library, I soon learnt to discount popular stereotypes that dismiss political activists as being either dull and boring or loud and abrasive – though it must be said that some were fairly intense. One group of six people used to meet regularly at the Library to plot the overthrow of world capitalism. While waiting for this to happen, they produced a series of pamphlets of impenetrable complexity and occasionally expelled a former comrade for 'bourgeois revisionism' or some other mortal sin.

Most people, however, were generous, thoughtful and with an overwhelming interest in the world around them, showing a concern for others which I thought and still think was admirable, however much I might disagree with some of their political opinions. Virtually all of them, for instance, devoted a large part of their free time to raising money for charities or helping the sick and elderly.

Working at the Library did give me the opportunity to read my way through shelves of books about the history of the labour movement. How dull many of these publications were, almost as if unreadability was a sign of political virtue.

I was sometimes cheered to find that I was not alone in these critical thoughts when Library members returned volumes with despairing marginal annotations or comments such as 'Boring', 'Couldn't get into it' and so on. Most of these dutiful histories were painstakingly stuffed with committee reports and acronyms while being completely devoid of that passion and commitment that had led so many people to give up their time and sometimes even their lives for a great political cause.

In his essay *The English People*, published in 1947, George Orwell claims that the English language is peculiarly prone to jargon. How he would have hated the language of exclusivity which has characterised much recent writing produced by the British Left. The irony is that writers supposedly representing or supporting the working class should employ a style comprehensible only to academics. To give one example. Before his untimely death in May 1994 the left-wing academic Ralph Miliband wrote several influential and usually lucid studies of the Labour Party, British society and so on. Turn to his *Marxism and Politics* (1977), however, and you frequently come across passages such as this:

> As for 'state monopoly capitalism', the designation is misleading inasmuch as it tends to suggest something like a symbiotic relation between the contemporary capitalist state and monopoly capitalism. This is inaccurate and opens the way to an over-simplified and reductionist view of the capitalist state as the 'instrument' of the monopolies. In reality, there is the capitalist state on the one hand and 'monopoly capitalism' on the other. The relation between them is close and getting ever closer, but there is nothing to be gained, and much by way of insight to be lost, by a reductionist over-simplification of that relation. 'State monopoly capitalism' does not leave enough space, so to speak, in the relation between the two sides to make the concept a useful one: in so reducing this space, it renders the relation too unproblematic, at any level.

Raymond Williams was another much-respected commentator

who similarly tortured the English language in ways that would have driven Orwell to despair. One leading socialist writer remarked on television a few years ago that those who attack complexity are guilty of 'reverse snobbery'. In which case I have tried to ensure that *To Build A New Jerusalem* contains an inordinate amount of reverse snobbery.

The decline in the radical tradition of writing for all in clear and direct language is shown by the increasing use of a 'depersonalised' vocabulary. Indeed, in some quarters this has become a mark of whether a book is sufficiently 'serious' and 'rigorous' enough to merit critical attention. It is surely no coincidence that many of the best political books published recently have been biographies, diaries or memoirs in which the personal simply cannot be omitted: Ben Pimlott's studies of Hugh Dalton and Harold Wilson, Anthony Howard on Richard Crossman, Susan Crosland on her husband Tony, Philip Ziegler on Wilson, Hugo Young on Margaret Thatcher, Kenneth Morgan's *Labour People*, Denis Healey's *The Time of My Life*, Noel Annan's *Our Age*, sections in the diaries of Beatrice Webb, Barbara Castle, Richard Crossman and Tony Benn, the essays of E.P. Thompson and so on.

I left the Marx Library in 1986 because I wanted more time to write and research my books on the history of London, to give lectures and to lead walks around the capital and the rest of Britain. But, more importantly, my political opinions had become so uncertain that I found it impossible to say quite what 'socialism', 'the Left' and so on were all about. I felt I could not give the job of Librarian the commitment it needs. I will always have fond memories of the Library, its wonderful volunteer workers, its priceless materials and the wide range of visitors I encountered, especially the kind Soviet groups who gave me painted Russian dolls, LPs of peasant music and, on several occasions, the selected works of Lenin.

It was because of my political uncertainty as well as my determination to produce something about British politics which would be accessible to all that I have spent several years researching and writing this book. I have explored the history and development of the British Left, hoping to answer some of the questions that have bothered me and others for several years.

*Jerusalem* was of course researched and written at a time when the Conservative Party and the ideas of the 'New Right' ruled the political and intellectual roost in Britain. As an organisation which by its very nature favoured collectivist and public solutions to economic and social problems, the Labour Party was systematically denigrated and written off. The last Labour administration under James Callaghan was tarred with the phrase 'Winter of Discontent', Harold Wilson was portrayed as a shifty failure and the Attlee governments of 1945–51 were attacked by historians such as Correlli Barnett for their incompetence and cowardliness.

In other words, the Labour Party was the villain of the piece in Britain's apparent fall from Victorian grace. But surely it was not all so simple and two-dimensional as this, and one important reason for wanting to explore the British Left was to probe this stereotype. What were the successes and failures? What values and ideas had animated the Labour Party in the past? Were they relevant today? Why had the Conservatives proved so successful at winning elections? These and many other questions deserve a more thoughtful answer than that provided by the New Right.

The first edition of *To Build A New Jerusalem* was completed in the summer of 1991 and published in early 1992, in the run-up to what proved to be a general election held in April 1992. The reviews were uniformly favourable and I received many fascinating letters from readers all over the country. But although the book was intended to be read by everyone of all political persuasions and none, the palpable sense of deflation experienced by most Labour Party members and supporters after the Conseratives unexpectedly won that election meant the book got rather pushed to one side. Not many people could bear to think about, let alone read, anything 'political'.

If a week is a long time in politics, then four years is an eternity. In 1992 Neil Kinnock was leader but now, in 1996, Tony Blair stands supreme. Tragically, John Smith has also been leader. The Labour Party has been radically changed and altered, to the extent that the present leadership often prefers to call it 'New Labour'. Clause Four is no more and the alliance with the unions, which had created the Party in the first place, has come under continuing and sustained attack.

Looking back at the first edition, I am chuffed that many of the changes which I predicted in my last chapter – including the Party's name – have come about. I also remain convinced that the three-phase history of the Party (formation; power and breakdown; regrouping) still holds true. Mind you, I also got a couple of dates wrong.

This new edition has allowed me not only to bring *To Build A New Jerusalem* right up to date but to rewrite and expand it enormously, covering in detail some of the themes which originally I just touched upon. For example, there is much more material on the key topics of money, of Labour's relationship with the unions and of the Party's grassroots and regional differences.

Although a few of the more iconoclastic members of Tony Blair's entourage apparently think that New Labour represents an entirely new beginning – that Mr Blair's election as leader in July 1994 constituted some kind of 'Year Zero' – it seems to me that many of the problems which Labour is grappling with in the 1990s are not in fact new. The relationship between power and principle, the issues of public ownership, taxation, welfare and constitutional reform, the best way to win elections – these topics and many others dogged Ramsay MacDonald, Clement Attlee and Harold Wilson in the past just as they do Tony Blair at present.

This new edition has also given me the opportunity to incorporate some of the excellent research published since I finished writing in autumn 1991, such as the recent biographies of Harold Wilson, William Morris, Manny Shinwell, Michael Foot, Harry Pollitt, George Brown, Arthur Scargill, John Smith and Tony Blair, Peter Hennessy's *Never Again*, Anthony King and Ivor Crewe's account of the SDP, various academic studies and so on.

As for myself, in the intervening years I have published a lengthy study of the British Conservative Party, called *We, The Nation: The Conservative Party and the Pursuit of Power*. Sadly, it is generally Conservatives who study the Conservative Party and socialists who concentrate on the Labour Party. This is very limiting. You simply cannot understand either party in isolation from its main rival. In fact, I have probably learnt as much about the British Labour Party from sitting in the Bodleian Library, Oxford and wading through the archives of the Conservative Party as from any other source.

In effect, therefore, this is a brand new book – for a start, it is over five hundred pages long rather than the first edition's three hundred – but I hope it has amplified on the virtues, such as they were, of the original.

I am still not part of any group or 'magic circle', whether it be around the *Spectator*, *New Left Review* or the *Guardian*. I do not want to be an MP, spin doctor or obtain an academic post. I have 'called' this book exactly as I see it: a personal interpretation of British history over the last hundred years.

Throughout I have tried to integrate the lives and person-alities of Labour leaders, members and supporters with the context of events in Britain and abroad. If it is thought that the book is sometimes concerned too much with individuals, well, Kenneth Morgan has pointed out that although the British labour movement is supposedly against 'excesses of individualism [it] can go to extreme lengths to perpetuate the cult of personality':

More than the Conservatives have ever done, Labour draws constant inspiration from the ideas and achievements of key individuals, in both the political and industrial spheres. Indeed, it could be argued that, since Labour necessarily arose to represent the poor and inarticulate, its need for charismatic individuals has been all the greater than that of its better-endowed opponents.

In any case, I find people both past and present infinitely fascinating.

It would be foolish to pretend that a history of the British Left can ever be a swashbuckling romance: a kind of 'Indiana Jones Meets The Transport and General Workers' Union'. Committees, reports and the minutiae of administration have always been important to the way any political organisation operates. But it seemed to me then at the Marx Library, and still does today, that any history of the Left, or the Right for that matter, should try to woo and win potential readers rather than make them face some kind of political assault course. If a thing is worth saying then surely it is worth saying clearly.

The justification for the title is not only that the hymn 'Jerusalem' is often sung at the memorial services of influential Labour politicians from George Lansbury to Clem Attlee to Tony Crosland, but the British labour movement is and always has been different in important ways from its European counterparts – although, of course, Blake's poem is not exclusive to British socialism: the verses are printed on the programmes of Women's Institutes all over the country.

*To Build A New Jerusalem* is selective, as any history book must be if it is to avoid becoming an antiquarian exercise. In the preface to *Eminent Victorians*, Lytton Strachey discusses how the 'explorer of the past' should work:

> He will attack his subject in unexpected places; he will fall upon the flank, or the rear; he will shoot a sudden, revealing searchlight into obscure recesses, hitherto undivined. He will row out over that great ocean of material, and lower down into it, here and there, a little bucket, which will bring up to the light of day some characteristic specimen, from those far depths, to be examined with a careful curiosity.

I have not treated the people or events in this book as 'specimens' but it is clear what Strachey meant. He was certainly right about 'that great ocean of material', much larger now than when he was writing. Ramsay MacDonald's papers, for instance, amount to no fewer than 1,600 files which are stored at the Public Records Office. The *Warwick Guide to British Labour Periodicals 1790–1970* lists a grand total of 4,125 separate titles and it is estimated there have been 6,000 different trade unions in Britain since systematic records were first kept from the 1890s.

Hugh Dalton's diaries amount to nearly two million words whilst Richard Crossman's diaries were published in four weighty volumes which total 1,136, 688, 851 and 1,039 pages respectively. And pity the poor biographer of Tony Benn; quite apart from the six hefty volumes of diaries so far published – in themselves a rigorous selection – and his thousands of speeches and articles, apparently he receives 2,000 to 3,000 letters each week. That publishers feel it is worthwhile bringing out so much material confirms how the labour movement has 'arrived'; in the Victorian period it was generals and churchmen whose works appeared at such length. However, more can sometimes mean less.

But if the book mountain is daunting, then what about newspapers? I once sat in the Cambridge University Library and blithely ordered up all the copies of the *Daily Herald* newspaper for the 1930s. Half an hour later I noticed staff struggling with scores of heavy-bound volumes. To my horror, I realised that I had asked them to fetch several hundredweight of material.

With so many thousands of publications in print it is often difficult to distinguish the wood from the trees. In many ways, therefore, this books represents a kind of personal map, trying to provide an up-to-date overview of what has happened so far and might happen next.

What is 'right' and who is 'left'? The terms derive from which side of the hall groups sat in the French Assembly two hundred years ago, but since then many layers of different meaning have attached themselves to both these words and to others such as 'conservative', 'liberal' and 'socialist'. It is, I think, clear in the following pages who stands for what, but an excellent shorthand definition has been provided by Ben Pimlott:

> Labour is known to be against privilege, social hierarchy, capitalism, personal wealth, inequality, unregulated markets, the powerful, the Establishment, the upper classes, nationalistic fervour, military might; and in favour of equality, civil rights, state intervention, democracy, the working class, internationalism. Little in either list has changed in a hundred years, which is why the attitudes are so readily identifiable with the Left (and why Labour finds it so hard to disassociate itself from them).

One final problem: footnotes. These immediately repel many general readers and one sometimes feels that the notes are designed to show off the author's dedicated research rather than to help the reader. What one historian has called 'the pleasures of the past' can easily become submerged in ostentatious display. On the other hand, if you don't support assertions and claims then critics will correctly reach for the devastating words 'lightweight' and 'insubstantial'.

I have therefore included notes together with a select bibliography at the end of the book, which is the least I can do to acknowledge the excellent work of the scholars and academics on which I have drawn. To find the source of a quotation or statement, just identify the key words or statistic and turn to the back.

Where should *To Build A New Jerusalem* begin . . .?

# Part One

*From Keir Hardie to Clement Attlee*

'SOCIALISM IS MUCH MORE AN AFFAIR OF THE HEART THAN OF THE INTELLECT.'

Keir Hardie, March 1906

# 1

## Who Cares About Keir Hardie?

'I know what I believe to be the right thing, and I go and do it.'
KEIR HARDIE

'A mere abstraction, be it ever so demonstrable scientifically, will never move masses of people.'
KEIR HARDIE

'Light is a more important factor than heat.'
REPORT ON FABIAN POLICY, TRACT 70

Early on the morning of 3 August 1892, an unusual procession set out from Canning Town in East London to make its exuberant way to the Houses of Parliament. The noise was provided by an out-of-tune trumpet player, who lustily accompanied the singing of fifty men following a wagonette. Inside this vehicle was a Scotsman called Keir Hardie, the newly elected MP for West Ham South, on his way to take up his seat in Westminster. He was the first ever Labour Member of Parliament.

At the end of the seven-mile journey, the trumpeter launched into the 'Marseillaise', a song associated with French Revolutions but adopted for the present occasion in the absence of any suitable British revolutionary songs. Bystanders and MPs alike were horrified at what was happening; 'The Mother of Parliaments' had never seen anything like this before.

Even more shocking was the fact that Keir Hardie, MP, was proposing to enter the House 'unsuitably dressed', wearing not the frock coat and silk top hat hitherto considered obligatory when attending what was effectively the best gentlemen's club in the world, but instead a tweed suit and something which looked very much like a deerstalker. Next morning an outraged press lambasted the new MP with a vehemence which, over the next twenty-five years, would become customary.

Acutely aware of the symbolic value of clothes, Hardie realised that his arrival in an ordinary working outfit was tantamount to challenging the Establishment. As his friend and companion in the procession, Frank Smith, observed: 'The man who did not change his garb, simply because of his change in social status, was not likely to change his principles.' And yet, out of the thousands of words written on or about Hardie's arrival in Parliament, only one contemporary journalist, the Liberal A.G. Gardiner, seems to have recognised what 3 August 1892 might ultimately lead to:

> I am not sure that when the historian of the future discusses our time he will not find the most significant event on that day in 1892 when James Keir Hardie rode up to Westminster from West Ham, clothed in cloth cap, tweed suit, and flannel shirt, and accompanied by a band. The world scoffed at the vulgarity, or shuddered at the outrage, according to its humour; but the event was, nevertheless, historic. It marked the emergence of a new force in politics.

Within fifteen years of his election, Hardie had broken the stranglehold of the Conservative and the Liberal Parties by creating a new political organisation, the Labour Party, which was rooted in the trade union movement. By the 1920s this youthful body had replaced the Liberals as the main rival to the Conservatives and had even formed its own government. In 1945, less than forty years after Hardie had founded the new party, a Labour government came to power with a huge majority. A.G. Gardiner lived to see his prophecy come true. He died in 1946 at the age of eighty.

★     ★     ★

Keir Hardie is the undisputed father of the modern British labour movement, a pioneer who worked unceasingly for 'the Cause'. He has a secure and honoured place in any socialist pantheon. Yet people seem to know his name and little else. This complex and fascinating man has been submerged beneath layers of ritual hero-worship. Hardie's early biographers, for instance, were in fact hagiographers, glossing over uncomfortable incidents and events in his life in their eagerness to portray a difficult but essentially saint-like individual.

What kind of man was this Scot who devoted his life to the early socialist movement? What forces drove him on so that he rarely slept more than three or four hours a night, always looked at least ten years older than his real age, and died almost of a broken heart after the outbreak of the First World War shattered his faith in mankind?

Hardie himself gave posterity little help in answering these questions. Few personal remarks or feelings appear in his letters, and unlike most Labour leaders he never found the time or inclination to write his memoirs. But we do have photographs of him and for once perhaps the camera does not lie. They show an upright, uncompromising, bearded man whose path is not lightly to be crossed. Always unsmiling, he stares out of the photographs like some minor Old Testament prophet about to summon up fire and brimstone to hurl at his enemies. His stubborn and bloody-minded independence is obvious.

Hardie's friend Bruce Glasier wrote that he was able to 'stand alone, fight alone, win alone, bear defeat alone.' Hardie himself once remarked that, 'Companionship is good, solitude is best.' And yet this was also the married man who enjoyed a long, passionate relationship with the suffragette Sylvia Pankhurst who was less than half his age.

The sense of determination and grievance often necessary to be a pioneer was derived largely from the circumstances of Hardie's upbringing. Born illegitimate in a one-room cottage in Legbrannock, Lanarkshire, in August 1856, he spent just a few days at school before starting work at the age of eight in order to supplement the family income. He was sent down the mines at ten and could barely write until his late teens. In his early twenties he was sacked from his job and blacklisted by the mine owners because of his trade union activities.

This summary of Hardie's early years sounds as if it comes straight from a Victorian melodrama. He did later refer to his upbringing with some bitterness – 'I am of the unfortunate class who never knew what it was to be a child – in spirit, I mean' – and only rarely mentioned his illegitimacy. His mother was a farm worker called Mary Keir but it is unclear who the father was. The name of a collier appears on the birth certificate of 1856, yet there is some suspicion that this was done in order to hide the identity of the local doctor. It is remarkable that three of the British labour movement's most influential figures – Hardie, Ramsay MacDonald and Ernest Bevin – should all be illegitimate.

Hardie's mother eventually married a ship's carpenter called David Hardie, but his difficulty in finding work meant that the large family – Keir had six half-brothers and sisters – was often on the move all over Scotland as the stepfather sought employment. The latter's frequent drinking, when apparently he used to taunt Keir's mother with the existence of 'the Bastard', led the young boy to a lifelong commitment to the temperance movement.

It was Keir's dismissal from one of his jobs that helped fuel his driving determination. He was employed by a baker who was a pillar of the local community, God-fearing and upright – which did not stop him sacking the ten-year-old boy for being marginally late for work and then refusing to pay him his last week's wages. It was an act of spite with terrible consequences for the family with David Hardie out of work.

After the Hardie family left Glasgow, Keir was sent down the mines, working as the trapper responsible for keeping supplies of fresh air on the move. This job entailed long hours on his own but it was now that the young man showed his ambition to get on in life. He taught himself shorthand, using a pin to scratch out the figures on a slab of stone.

While working at another pit in charge of his pony Donald, an accident to the cage which brought the miners to the surface meant the boy was trapped below ground along with other miners. They were eventually rescued without mishap, but the hazards of this occupation as well as the offhand and penny-pinching attitude the coal owners displayed towards safety made a lasting impression on Hardie. As late as 1918, 1,300 miners were killed in accidents every year. Hardie was later to write of his time as a boy down the mines:

> For several years as a lad I rarely saw daylight during the winter months. Down the pit by six in the morning, and not leaving it again until half-past five meant not seeing the sun, and even on Sunday I had at that time to spend four hours down below. Such an experience does not develop the sunny side of one's being.

In later life Hardie never forgot these bitter, early experiences. But the crucial thing about Hardie was that he determined to do something about it, to try and improve these primitive working and living conditions. The only possible way was to set up a trade union. This was very much easier said than done because, in the middle of the Victorian period, trade unions catered almost exclusively for the skilled workers.

The first attempts to set up trade unions in Britain were hampered by the passage of the Combination Acts in 1799 and 1800 which outlawed the formation of working men into organised groups in order to press for better working conditions. The Acts were not finally repealed until 1824. The rapid onset of both industrialisation and the factory system meant that large numbers of men and women were thrown together as employees, often labouring in appalling conditions for meagre pay. The only way the weak could defend themselves in a so-called 'free labour market' was by banding together into collective bodies, namely trade unions. In the 1820s the Tory statesman Sir Robert Peel had justified the existence of trade unions: 'Men who . . . have no property except their manual skill and strength, ought to be allowed to confer together, if they think fit, for the purpose of determining at what rate they will sell their property.'.

In 1833 the philanthropist and factory owner Robert Owen formed an organisation called the Grand National Consolidated Trades Union. Within a year it could boast a membership of over one million. The union's weaknesses lay in its federal structure which meant that it was difficult to co-ordinate action. Its lack of money ensured that strike pay was out of the question. In 1834 the union miscalculated its strength and called a strike that ended in disarray and its own collapse. At the same time the authorities launched a legal counter-attack against union activities, shown at its most virulent in the transportation of the six Tolpuddle Martyrs of Dorset who were sent to Australia simply for joining a trade union.

The disintegration of these early attempts at industrial organisation led to a lull in activity for the next decade and a half. But when attempts were made to establish unions in the 1850s, the industrial climate was very different. Britain was now 'the Workshop of the World' and possessed a 'labour aristocracy' – that is, skilled workers such as engineers, mechanics, carpenters and 'railway servants' who felt that they had a stake in the expanding capitalist system. Whereas the members of Owen's Grand National Consolidated Trades Union had been fighting to overthrow the new system, groups such as the Amalgamated Society of Engineers, formed in 1851, were more interested in trying to improve their status within it.

These 'New Model Unions' rigorously excluded the unskilled by charging high subscriptions and often drawing up rules which specified that they were for craftsmen only. Like the twenty-eight 'Rochdale Pioneers' who had each subscribed £1 in 1844 and begun the Co-operative movement, the New Model Unions were thoroughly respectable bodies. Photographs of their leaders such as Robert Applegarth and William Newton and their colleagues on the Trades Union Congress, which first met in 1868, show men who clearly value moderation and sobriety above all else. They were quite content to work patiently and slowly within the parliamentary system for legal reform.

Their strategy seemed to work: trade unions were given legal recognition in 1871 and in 1875 the right to peaceful picketing. As far as possible the leaders of the New Model Unions worked hand in hand with employers. Robert Applegarth claimed that he never 'had a wrong word with an employer in my life, either as a workman or as a representative of working men.' These men were stalwart supporters of William Gladstone's Liberal Party. With their acute sense of social status, they looked down on the miners as distinctly inferior workmen and for being supposedly so anarchic in their habits as to be incapable of recruitment into trade unions.

This attitude guaranteed that when Keir Hardie tried to establish a miners' union he could expect little or no help from the existing unions. A further difficulty was that the only work available in most mining districts meant going down the pits. If sacked by the owner, it was almost impossible for a miner to find alternative work. Any organised protest among the miners was countered with lock-outs by the owners who knew that eventually the men would be starved back to work. 'Blacklegs' were imported from outside the district if the strike action looked serious.

Hardie began work in Hamilton, Lanarkshire. His Christian evangelicalism meant that he believed each person was responsible for their own salvation. He therefore never hesitated to criticise the miners themselves, pointing out that it was partly due to their own failure to organise that the owners got away with often callous behaviour. His attitude was rather different from that of some later labour leaders for whom 'the lads' could do no wrong. But Hardie also maintained that, in the words of a later Scottish socialist James Maxton, 'poverty was a man-made thing' and therefore open to change.

In 1879 came the blow that Hardie must have been expecting. At the age of twenty-three he was sacked from the pit, along with two of his half-brothers, and blacklisted because of his trade union activities. It could not have happened at a worse time as he had recently married a Miss Lillie Wilson. Hardie managed to support himself over the next few years by accepting a modest salary for his work as the agent for several small miners' unions and by various pieces of journalism.

In fact, it was his talent as a journalist which in 1882 brought him the opportunity to edit his local newspaper, the *Cumnock News*. He accepted the offer. That the *Cumnock News* was a Liberal newspaper suggests Hardie still hoped that the changes he was seeking could be brought about under the aegis of the Liberal Party.

Formed in the 1860s, the Liberals were a strange amalgam of elements: wealthy landowners jostled with Nonconformists and Jewish people, trade unionists and Irish Home Rulers with out-and-out radicals. What held them together as the main opposition to the Tory Party was their hostility to vested interests and unnecessary privilege. Often a radical force, the Liberals had reformed the educational system, the army, the civil service and the drink trade as well as recognising trade unions and introducing the secret ballot. In 1884 they extended the vote by means of the third Reform Act. The electorate increased from three to five million male voters, constituting about half the adult male population in Britain.

Nevertheless, it was clear that on this issue the Liberals were being expedient rather than principled. John Vincent has put it bluntly: 'The Liberals, flatly, were not democrats, their Reform Bill of 1866 was an exclusion Bill, and when they adapted democracy after 1867 for political purposes, they knew neither its feelings nor its justifications.'

It was also apparent by the 1880s that the Liberal Party's attachment to the idea of *laissez-faire* or of market forces was sacrosanct and beyond challenge. They therefore opposed the government action which, in the view of many observers, was the only way to deal with the widespread poverty and squalor that disfigured parts of the country.

The virtues of private enterprise were of no help to the hundreds of thousands of people whose low wages and lack of any accident or employment insurance condemned them to a knife-edge existence. The workings of the free market economy ensured that the 'have-nots' would experience destitution and perhaps the ultimate degradation of the workhouse. There was no welfare state and only the fortunate few could rely on the 'friendly societies' or workmen's clubs that had been legally recognised in 1855 and which catered for the better-off workman.

In the face of overwhelming social problems, charitable gestures, however laudable, were not enough. As the slogans on early socialist banners sometimes declared: 'Damn your charity; we want justice.' Government action was urgently needed. But the Liberal Party was opposed to such intervention.

Hardie brought a hardhitting edge to the *Cumnock News*. For instance he published a 'Good Pits Guide' praising owners who had introduced safety measures but condemning those who had not. He also spent much of the 1880s trying to set up miners' unions in Scotland, often in the face of opposition from men who were loyal supporters of the Liberal Party. Hardie began to realise that industrial action needed to be backed up by political change and yet the Liberal Party was not sufficiently radical for this.

The Party hierarchy, for its part, was very grateful for the votes of the newly enfranchised electorate but was unwilling to put forward working-class candidates for safe Liberal seats. The handful of so-called 'Lib-Lab MPs', usually miners, were no more than a strategic figleaf. Hardie's growing dissatisfaction was increased by his contacts with socialists such as Henry George, who advocated sweeping land reforms, and with Friedrich Engels and Eleanor Marx.

In 1888 a by-election helped to crystallise Hardie's views. The sitting Liberal MP for Mid-Lanark resigned his seat on the grounds of ill-health. Hardie argued that in this miners' constituency a miners' candidate should surely be nominated to take his place. His own name was put forward. It was rejected by the Lanark Liberals in favour of a 'safe' candidate, namely a London barrister. With typical obstinacy Hardie decided to stand anyway. It was a decision which culminated nearly twenty years later in the establishment of the Labour Party.

The Mid-Lanark Liberals suddenly realised that Hardie's candidature threatened their hopes of retaining a safe seat. Wouldn't he split the anti-Conservative vote? Wasn't he a poor man, with a growing family? Surely he could be bought off. Hardie therefore found himself summoned to a meeting with Sir George Trevelyan, a Liberal grandee and treasurer of the national Party. Hardie tells what happened:

> Sir George was very polite, and explained the unwisdom of Liberals and Labour [Hardie was calling himself a National Labour Party candidate] fighting each other. They wanted more working men in Parliament, and if only I would stand down in Mid-Lanark he would give me an assurance that at the General Election I would be adopted somewhere, the party paying my expenses, and guaranteeing me a yearly salary – three hundred pounds was the sum hinted at – as they were doing for others (he gave names). I explained as well as I could why his proposal was offensive, and though he was obviously surprised, he was too much of a gentleman to be anything but courteous. And so the fight went on.

Hardie might have found the proposal 'offensive'; many others would not have done. As a miner, he would have earned about £70 or £80 a year, so the offer of £300 was a substantial one. There must have been pressure too from his wife Lillie who was never keen on her husband's political activities. Keir Hardie was in effect fighting on both personal and political fronts – which only made

him the more determined to do what he was convinced
was right.

At the by-election in April 1888, Hardie polled just 617
votes out of a total cast of 7,381, several thousand behind the
victorious Liberal. His comparative lack of success underlined
what a huge task lay ahead of him. But the decisive break
from the Liberal Party had been made, the first faltering steps
taken towards the creation of a new political party – and it was
Hardie who had taken those steps.

The next task was to create some kind of organisation and
political machinery. Ever since the Birmingham Liberal Joseph
Chamberlain had first introduced the paraphernalia of political
organisation in the 1860s, which ranged from membership lists
to canvassing, it was clear that the days of the independent
candidate were swiftly coming to an end. In May 1888, a
month after the Mid-Lanark contest, twenty-seven people
met in Glasgow to found the Scottish Labour Party. Hardie
was elected secretary.

The president of this new body was R.B. Cunninghame
Graham, an extraordinary character who had already been a
Radical MP, a writer, an international traveller, adventurer
and a gaucho in Latin America. He was the maverick son of
a Scottish laird and claimed a right to the Scottish throne. An
expert horseman, Graham loved to gallop flamboyantly around
Hyde Park with his beautiful Spanish wife.

Cunninghame Graham's involvement was significant in
demonstrating that any new venture would not be an exclusively proletarian grouping. Although insistent on the need to
create a new party, Hardie was pragmatic enough to realise
that he must work alongside sympathetic allies from whatever
background. As he himself succinctly put it in September
1888: 'If, therefore, anyone, peasant or peer, is found willing
to accept the programme and work with the party, his help
will be gladly accepted.'

This generous approach explains why the Labour Party, for
instance, has always welcomed into its ranks recruits from

privileged positions in society. The desire to be inclusive rather than exclusive lay behind Hardie's decision to call it the Scottish Labour Party rather than the Scottish Socialist Party: in the 1880s, the word 'socialist' was generally regarded as a foreign and rather frightening label.

He was also shrewd enough to understand that creating a new party in Britain would be no overnight job – which is one reason why he cautiously started in Scotland. But Hardie was not starting completely from scratch. By the late nineteenth century Britain had been transformed into a predominantly urban and industrial society, the first in the world. E.J. Hobsbawm has noted that Britain then was:

> . . . first and foremost, a country of workers. R. Dudley Baxter, calculating the size of the various British classes in 1867, reckoned that over three quarters – seventy-seven per cent – of the 24.1 million inhabitants of Great Britain belonged to the 'manual labour class'; and he included among the 'middle class' all office-workers and shop-assistants, all shopkeepers, however tiny, all foremen and supervisory workers, and the like.

Firmly rooted within this urban working class were the trade unions, trades councils, co-operatives and friendly societies which formed 'a world of labour', a sort of alternative network of loyalties offering members mutual assistance. Though working class, this world was not opposed to the existing system but was, in fact, supplementary to it. This frame of mind reflected the largely consensual and pragmatic character of the British political system.

The historian Henry Pelling has commented that the most important feature of British socialism is the belief that it is possible to achieve a transfer of power without resorting to violence. Hardie decided that Parliament had to be the focus of this transition. He was hostile towards abstract dogma and Marxist theory because, in his own words, 'it does not touch one human sentiment or feeling . . . it entirely leaves the human element out of account.' As proposed by Hardie, British socialists were to work for piecemeal change within the system. This tradition was strikingly different from that propounded by most other socialist parties elsewhere in Europe. Marxist historians have dubbed it 'labourism' and usually berated its unspectacular and limited ambitions.

In particular there were two organisations that Hardie hoped would form the bedrock for any new political body. The first were the Nonconformists who opposed the established Church of England and so traditionally had been tied to the Liberal Party. In order to detach as many Nonconformists as possible, Hardie presented socialism as an ethical and moral gospel. This desire 'to build a New Jerusalem' fitted in with his own evangelical beliefs. As he wrote later in his book *From Serfdom to Socialism* (1907): 'Socialism, like every other problem of life, is at bottom a question of ethics or morals. It has mainly to do with the relationships which should exist between a man and his fellows.'

Yet fine thoughts and beautiful words alone would never be enough to create the New Jerusalem. Hardie also required trade union support, even though the leaders of the New Model Unions were happy enough to stay within the fold of the Liberal Party. But without trade union assistance in terms of both finance and membership any new party would simply be a small and insignificant sect without influence.

Within just two months of his stand at Mid-Lanark, a strike took place in London which was to herald the break-up of the old order and give added strength to Hardie's ideas.

On 23 June 1888 an article appeared in a small circulation weekly magazine called *The Link*. Titled 'White Slavery in London', it was written by a journalist, Annie Besant, and highlighted the terrible working conditions of the matchgirls employed at the Bryant and May factory in Bow in the East End of London.

The directors of Bryant and May – prominent supporters

of the Liberal Party and instrumental in the erection of the statue of William Gladstone which still stands outside St Mary's church, Bow – promptly sacked the girls suspected of giving Mrs Besant her information. She had written about their low wages, the regular fines and deductions to which they were subject, and also the horrors of 'phossy jaw' caused by the phosphorus used in the match-making process which slowly ate away the girls' faces. To the directors' anger, the girls did not just meekly accept the sackings but instead, at the urging of Mrs Besant, walked out en masse. Equally surprised by this unanimity were the New Model Unions.

The campaign waged by these 1,400 matchgirls soon enlisted public sympathy and over £400 was received in donations. Six hundred of the girls were sent fruit-picking in Kent to swell the strike fund. Within a few days a report on the dispute by the impartial Toynbee Hall, a settlement established in Whitechapel four years before, confirmed almost all the girls' assertions. Bryant and May were forced to capitulate. Within a fortnight the matchgirls had won their dispute and returned to work.

Their triumph sent shock waves through the labour movement. If one group of unorganised workers – and women at that – could take on their employers, why shouldn't others? The following month the gasworkers in East London managed to get their working day reduced from twelve hours to eight without having to go on strike. Then, in 1889, came the dispute that marked this 'New Unionism' as a decisive political force which would underpin Hardie's efforts to establish a working-class party.

Conditions on the London docks were unbelievably savage. Too many men chasing too few jobs meant that a foreman could pick out those he wanted with all the arrogance of a rich man at a slave market. Herded together into what was called 'the Cage', grown men fought and struggled with each other to attract the foreman's attention. One of the dock leaders, Ben Tillett, described in his pamphlet *A Dock Labourer's Bitter Cry* how the foreman: 'Walks up and down with the air of a dealer in a cattle-market, picking and choosing from a crowd of men who, in their eagerness to obtain employment, trample each other under foot, and . . . like beasts they fight each other for the chance of a day's work.'

The wives of these desperate men sometimes even offered sexual favours to contractors in the hope that this would secure employment for their husbands.

As with the miners and the matchgirls, the New Model Unions had always regarded the dockers as being beyond the pale of trade union organisation. Once more they were proved wrong. In August 1889 a dispute at the South-West India Dock escalated and the men walked out. Their main demand was for 'the dockers' tanner' – that is, payment of sixpence an hour – but they also wanted employment of not less than four hours at a stretch rather than bits and pieces here and there.

Well led by John Burns, Ben Tillett and Tom Mann, the dockers conducted a highly organised campaign and made sure that, like the matchgirls the year before, they gained and then held public support. Marches from East London to the dock companies' headquarters in the City were always held in co-operation with the police and passed off peacefully. One socialist who was on the strike committee, H.H. Champion, stressed in his account of the strike just how vital this air of order and calm was:

. . . though there was little public sympathy shown in the earlier days of the strike, as soon as it became widely known that thousands of the strikers had marched through the City without a pocket being picked or a window being broken, and that at the head of the procession was a man whose public position was a guarantee that 'the mob' had a responsible leader [John Burns], the British citizen felt he might go back to his suburban villa when his day's work was done full of confidence that his warehouses would not be wrecked in the night, and that he could afford to follow his natural inclination and back the poor devils who were fighting with pluck, good humour, and order against overwhelming odds.

However it would be a mistake to exaggerate public sympathy for the dockers. The attendants at Madame Tussaud's wax-works, for instance, regularly found needles stuck in the heart of the effigy of John Burns.

The dockers also received international support, including a donation of £50,000 from the Australian trade unions. Finally, like the matchgirls and gasworkers before them, the dockers were successful. These industrial disputes gave a surge of confidence to this New Unionism and the number of trade unionists doubled between 1888 and 1892.

Similar developments were taking place all over Europe. New working-class organisations were being created which reflected the new collective spirit of 'all for one and one for all' that had developed out of the massing together of factory workers in towns and cities. For example, working-class parties were formed in France in 1882, in Italy in 1883, in Belgium and in Spain in 1885; they complemented the German Social Democrats founded the previous decade and Keir Hardie's Independent Labour Party which was to be established in 1893. It is no coincidence that socialists now began to use the word 'masses' or that the failure of Sir George Trevelyan's intervention over the Mid-Lanark by-election symbolised the decline of the 'politics of personal influence'.

Nevertheless, in Britain many workers were still unrep-resented by labour organisations. Few women joined trade unions (even less provision was made for them) and in rural districts the pioneering union organiser Joseph Arch fought long and hard but often in vain to represent agricultural workers. In Scotland, too, trade union representation remained patchy whilst political activists continually bemoaned the stoi-cism of their colleagues. For instance, a young and idealistic socialist called Rowland Kenney noted of his fellow cotton operatives in Lancashire that they wanted 'neither revolution nor rebellion of any kind.' Instead their limited aims in life could be summed up in the phrase:

> Eight hours work, eight hours play,
> Eight hours lie-a-bed, and eight bob a day.

But whatever the disappointments, the underlying trend was undoubtedly in Hardie's favour. The Liberal Party had been conspicuous by its absence from the above industrial disputes – except where, as in the Bryant and May case, it was prominent Liberals themselves who were the unpopular employees.

Yet life remained difficult for Hardie. Year after year he stood up at the annual Trades Union Congress conferences to argue the need for a political party in Parliament which would represent organised labour. There was still much snobbery among the older unions and at the 1890 conference the representatives of skilled labour jeered those representing the unskilled. At the next year's conference, only eleven delegates voted in favour of setting up a Parliamentary Fund to support an independent party. But in the summer of 1892, Keir Hardie's own election as MP for West Ham South helped to give a focus to his arguments.

What was a Scot doing as the MP for an East London constituency? Not even Hardie's bitterest opponents denied the man's extraordinary energy which took him propagandising for the Cause all over the country. Just reading a list of his weekly commitments makes one feel exhausted. His efforts were helped by the skills he had gained through his training as a lay preacher. His oratory was simple and direct and he never used notes, preferring to respond to the mood of the crowd. Hardie's speeches and imagery still have a compelling power today. To give two examples:

> The nation is yours when there is debt to pay, it is yours when there is blood to shed; but if you attempt to rule it, you are told that you are interfering with what does not belong to you.

And, when attacking the idea of monarchy:

> Either the British people are fit to govern themselves or they
> are not. If they are, an hereditary ruler is an insult; if they are
> not, they should not be entrusted with votes.

In an age without microphones – one contributory reason why
so few women were able at this time to make their mark on
the British labour movement – Hardie's powerful voice was
able to inspire and control his audiences. Gradually he became
a national and not just a local figure. The change was reflected
in the title of the monthly magazine that he also found the
time to edit and most of whose contents he wrote. The
*Miner* was first published in January 1887; in 1889 it became
the *Labour Leader*.

It was his growing national reputation as both organiser and
inspirer which prompted Hardie's supporters to put forward
his name in West Ham. Fortunately for him the Liberals
failed to decide on a candidate and so gave Hardie their tacit
support. He stood as an independent Labour candidate against
the Conservative, a Major Banes. Inevitably, the press called it
a battle between 'the Major and the Miner'. Victory came in
July 1892 when Hardie was elected by over a thousand votes –
and so on 3 August 1892 he went in procession to Westminster
to take up his seat.

Hardie was not the only independent Labour candidate
elected to Parliament at that 1892 general election. Battersea
in South London returned John Burns who had been one of
the leaders of the dock strike; for Middlesborough there was
the seamen's leader, J. Havelock Wilson. In contrast to Hardie,
both these men soon began to display all the characteristics
of the old trade union MPs, hanging on to the coat-tails of
the Liberal Party and sucking up to its leaders in the hope
of political preferment.

So why was Hardie different? He never forgot nor forgave
the early privations he had experienced, and this gave him the

courage to do only what he believed to be right. Impervious to the blandishments of Parliament with its sense of ease and self-importance which often blunted the edge of many once fiery MPs coming after Hardie, he did not like the House of Commons: 'I feel like a bird with its wings clipped when I am there.' He always remembered the ordinary people outside Westminster and his persistent campaigning on behalf of the jobless earned him the label 'Member for the Unemployed'. His unconventional arrival at Parliament had shown the metal of the man. But the outrage which greeted his actions on that day was as nothing compared with the abuse heaped on his head over 'the Royal baby' incident.

On 23 June 1894, 260 people died in a terrible mining tragedy at Cilfyndd in South Wales. That same week President Carnot of France was assassinated and the then Duchess of York had a baby. Parliament sent a telegram to the French Assembly deploring the President's death. No telegram was sent to the mourners in South Wales. The House of Commons also decided to dispatch a message of congratulations to the Duchess.

Hardie asked the Liberal Leader of the House what message was to be sent to South Wales. Sir William Harcourt replied offhandedly that of course the House sympathised with the Welsh people but there the matter must rest. Hardie was incensed and decided to oppose the motion congratulating the Duke and Duchess. The reaction of his fellow MPs was extreme. Throughout his speech he was interrupted, jeered and hissed. All around him there was commotion. One observer described the scene: 'They howled and yelled and screamed, but he stood his ground.' Hardie never minded being a minority of one, but he was gratified to receive over a thousand letters of support from the public after this incident.

At the general election of 1895 the Liberals put forward their own candidate at West Ham South and, not unexpectedly,

Hardie lost his seat – although the extent of his influence was seen three years later in 1898 when West Ham became the first council in Britain to have a Labour majority. By the time of his defeat, he had set up the Independent Labour Party (ILP) which was founded in Bradford in January 1893. Hardie, Burns and Wilson had stood as individuals without any organised party backing. The ILP was designed to provide this back-up and to draw together British socialists into a national party.

Not everyone, however, accepted the invitation. H.M. Hyndman's Marxist Social Democratic Federation argued that the ILP was not left-wing enough. But nothing would budge Hardie from his strategy of 'labourism', of working carefully and slowly for change. He knew that anything too extreme would either frighten off the trade unions, which were to be the keystone of the new party, or else risk splitting the movement on religious or regional lines as had happened in several European countries.

Hardie was instrumental in founding the Labour Representation Committee (LRC) in 1900, a tentative first step by the unions in the direction of parliamentary representation. That same year he was returned as MP for Merthyr Tydfil, a seat he retained until his death in 1915. He still had few colleagues in the House of Commons but again fought his corner with vigour.

In 1901 the House of Lords' decision in the 'Taff Vale Case' held that union funds were at risk from any employer who suffered loss through a strike; a judicial ruling that completely hamstrung the unions. Virtually every union now realised that a political voice in Parliament was vital if their interests were to be properly defended. The major unions began to turn their backs on the Liberal Party and to affiliate instead to the Labour Representation Committee, supporting it financially. At the 1906 general election twenty-nine MPs were elected on the LRC ticket and it was renamed the Labour Party. Keir Hardie was elected its first chairman.

★    ★    ★

So at last Hardie had achieved what he had been working towards. But at what cost? Journalist A.G. Gardiner described him as 'The Knight of the Rueful Countenance' and Hardie himself observed, 'I have few friends and cannot, somehow, enter into the healthy and legitimate light side of life.' One socialist who had once worked for Hardie, S.G. Hobson, wrote that laughter was at a discount.

There was certainly no disjunction between Hardie's political views and his private opinions. His obstinacy and independence were not political camouflage but true aspects of his personality. He was impervious to bribes or corruption. He had turned down Sir George Trevelyan's offer of money and a safe seat years before, and his integrity did not waver when success finally arrived. 'High Society' wooed him in vain. In *From Serfdom to Socialism*, published in 1907, Hardie scathingly referred to 'the vicious tastes and luxurious habits of the idle rich . . .' Gardiner was correct to write that 'You will never find a dress shirt under the red tie of Keir Hardie. He will never be petted by Princes and Peers.'

His emotional life was rather more complicated. Separated for long periods from his wife Lillie who remained in Scotland with their three children, Hardie took rooms just off Fleet Street. London to him was 'a haunting horror' which no doubt contributed to his melancholy. When Parliament was sitting he allowed himself only a few hours of sleep each night in order to cope with his voluminous correspondence. Everyone worried that he did not eat properly and smoked too much.

Hardie always paid generous tribute to his wife Lillie's support. At the 1914 ILP Conference, for instance, he said 'never has she reproached me for what I have done for the cause I love . . .' But a friend who knew them both well, Katherine Glasier, thought that Lillie was 'temperamentally unfitted for the storms and vicissitudes of her husband's public life . . .' It is evident too that despite the moral and puritan exterior of Hardie, he was fiercely attracted to other women. In the 1890s he fell in love with a young woman called Annie Hines, although it is unclear whether they ever became lovers.

There is no uncertainty over his relationship with Sylvia Pankhurst, an affair which lasted for six years between 1906 and 1912. Hardie at forty-seven was more than twice the age of the twenty-two-year-old Sylvia. She was one of the daughters of Emmeline Pankhurst, founder of the Women's Social and Political Union, the main suffragette organisation. Clearly the relationship, which was probably more emotional than physical, brought much happiness to both sides but it eventually petered out. The affair suggests that Hardie was a more complicated man than his early biographers claimed.

Elected chairman of the Labour Party at the age of only fifty, most observers thought that Hardie was set fair for many more political triumphs. In fact, from this point onwards his career declined. He was above all a loner who preferred to stand defiant against the whole world. Never a good 'Party man', Hardie disliked the slog of committee work and lacked the flexibility to acquire the necessary skills to lead a party in the House of Commons. 'I am an agitator,' he once claimed, before going on to declare in a memorable phrase, 'My work has consisted of trying to stir up a divine discontent with wrong.'

In 1907 Hardie gave up the Labour Party chairmanship with relief and devoted himself to what he was best at, namely stumping around the country and putting across his political beliefs. The zeal and courage of the pioneer were to be superseded by the more slippery skills of the parliamentarian: Keir Hardie gave way to Ramsay MacDonald.

What kind of men were the first twenty-nine Labour MPs elected at the general election of 1906? Photographs show a widely contrasting group of individuals. There was Keir Hardie, of course, bewhiskered and stern, and the handsome Ramsay MacDonald. There was Will Crooks, the former docker who had held open-air meetings outside the gates of the East India Dock in London each Sunday. Called 'Crooks' College', they functioned as something like a Victorian Open University.

Also present were Will Thorne who never went to school, began work at the age of eight and and was taught to read and write by Eleanor Marx, Karl's daughter; and Philip Snowden, crippled in a bicycle accident as a young man and renowned for the invective he directed at political opponents. Defeated candidates included the dockers' leader Ben Tillett, a fine orator who had managed to overcome his terrible stammer by laboriously reading out the novels of Dickens to his wife every evening.

Later on in life, comfortably ensconced in the House of Lords, several of these veterans wrote memoirs with smug titles on the lines of 'From Rook Scarer to Peer'. These books helped generate an interpretation which has been dubbed 'the forward march of Labour', namely the theory that the British labour movement's progress was evolutionary, gradual, peaceful, inevitable: a sort of radical counterpart to the Whig Theory of History.

Not only does this approach overlook the fact that Labour's progress was certainly not inevitable – during the 1930s, the 1950s and the 1980s, for example, many despaired that the Party would ever govern again – but it ignores too the hard graft and struggle which accompanied attempts to build up trade unions in particular. Most employers were resolute that their semi-feudal right to hire, fire and determine rates of pay as well as conditions at work should not be fettered in any way. They were prepared to resort to intimidation and violence if necessary.

Between 1880 and the outbreak of the First World War in 1914 numerous bitter industrial disputes involved the naked use of force. Several employers' organisations were formed to combat the new unions. Perhaps the most determined of these groups was the Shipping Federation, set up the year after the Dock Strike of 1889. The Federation's historian wrote that 'From the first the Federation was founded as a fighting machine to counter the strike weapon, and it made no secret of the fact'. If necessary, use was made of a fearsome-sounding bunch called the 'Eye-Ball Buster Gang' and in 1893 a strike in Hull saw two gunboats moored in the Humber and the city turned into an armed camp.

On an individual level, veteran unionist Tom Mann's party-piece was showing off the scars and bumps on his skull whilst the dockers' leader Ben Tillett had his nose broken, ribs cracked and hernia ruptured in the course of his union career. Tillett and his colleagues were generous in turning the other cheek; he once declared in a speech that 'They did not want to rob anyone. If they did, they would be adopting the malpractices of the people who robbed them.'

Another characteristic uniting these first Labour MPs was the extraordinary efforts they had made to educate themselves. Take J.R. Clynes, the Oldham mill-worker who began work at just ten years of age. He spent his spare time reading a dictionary: 'I became like a character from an old romance, my body walking and talking by day, but my soul coming to life only at nights under the potency of the magic words I culled from my sixpenny dictionary.'

Another common feature was their sex; they were, of course, all men. Women did not get the vote until 1918, and even then on unequal terms. Twenty-three of the twenty-nine were trade unionists, confirming just how successful Hardie's strategy of wooing union support had been. Half had links with Nonconformist religion and several were associated with the temperance movement.

All were working class, reflecting the solid roots of this new organisation. By 1900 no less than three-quarters of the workforce were manual labourers, and although there were obviously gender and regional differences this relatively unified class formed the heart of Hardie's party. Yet it was clearly a Labour and not a socialist party, made up of moderates rather than revolutionaries. The middle-class Marxist H.M.

Hyndman criticised these 1906 MPs for exhibiting 'a dull and deferential respectability.'

What ideas animated them? In 1906 the magazine *The Review of Reviews* asked the new MPs as well as the thirteen 'Lib-Lab' MPs – mostly miners who eventually joined the Labour Party – what books had led them to become socialists. Their eclectic replies show a startling range of influences. Richard Crossman once claimed that the British labour movement was not 'bookish'; he was wrong. Books have been important, but not those books which are most obviously considered 'socialist'.

For example, the Bible was mentioned by several MPs as a powerful motivator; as *The Review* pointed out, 'For a party pledged to secular education this fact is noteworthy indeed.' The novels of Charles Dickens came up several times as did writers like Shakespeare, Milton, Shelley, Bunyan and Thomas Carlyle. Karl Marx was named only twice, which would not have been the case if a similar survey had been taken of contemporary French and German socialist MPs. One critic pointed out that none of the writers mentioned, bar John Bunyan, was a representative of manual labour. All the works were very general and lacked any economic detail or proposals.

Of course this was no coincidence. Elsewhere in Europe socialists zealously drew up and debated manifestoes, programmes and statements of aim. In Britain, however, Hardie and his colleagues were little interested in theoretical discussion – which certainly didn't mean they had doubts as to what they were against.

In 1902 the American writer and socialist Jack London visited the capital. Instead of concentrating on the West End like most tourists, he actually lived in the East End for several months. His book *The People of the Abyss*, published the next year, provided a horrifying picture of what life was like for hundreds of thousands of people in what he called 'the City of Degradation', supposedly the richest city in the world and the centre of a mighty empire. London detailed the widespread drunkenness, the wife beating, the hundreds of prostitutes. Take this description of a horrific 'pass the parcel':

> When a child dies, and some are always bound to die, since fifty-five per cent of the East End children die before they are five years old, the body is laid out in the same room. And if they are poor, it is kept for some time until they bury it. During the day it lies on the bed; during the night when the living take the bed, the dead occupies the table, from which, in the morning, when the dead is put back into the bed, they eat their breakfast. Sometimes the body is placed on the shelf which serves as a pantry for their food. Only a couple of weeks ago, an East End woman was in trouble, because, in this fashion, being unable to bury it, she had kept her child three weeks.

Outrage at such conditions, and at both the Conservative and Liberal Parties that had governed the country between them for the previous fifty years, explains why individuals such as Hardie spent most of their lives trying to bring about radical change.

Their anger did not necessarily mean that their socialism could readily be defined, as is clear today when reading the speeches and writings of the twenty-nine Labour MPs. The word 'socialism' itself had first been used nearly eighty years before, in the Owenite *Cooperative Magazine* of November 1827, but no one had ever specified exactly what this word meant or implied. Instead there were just vague references to 'the socialist commonwealth' or 'the New Jerusalem'.

Keir Hardie in particular always bathed his New Jerusalem in a warm, heavenly glow: 'I come from a race of seers, and I see clearly in prophetic vision the day, not fifty years ahead, when the cause for which we stand will be triumphant.' He never did manage to flesh out his vision.

Hardie's colleagues rarely proved more forthcoming but there was one tenet that they would have agreed on, namely the imperative need for collective control rather than private ownership. It was this feeling which inspired the famous Clause Four of the Constitution, drawn up in 1918, calling for 'the Common Ownership of the Means of Production'.

This looseness in spelling out what socialism meant was matched by the Labour Party's lack of organisation. It was, in fact, more a grouping of like-minded individuals than an efficient and relatively disciplined political party as we know it today. There were no local Labour Parties or even individual membership, let alone any defined policies.

One major problem was money. Even though political organisation was not as expensive as it later became, a predominantly working-class party without backing from industrial, commerical or landed interests inevitably found it difficult to pay its way. Labour was not in power and therefore unable to profit from the 'sale of honours' practised by both Conservative and Liberal administrations.

Money mattered. Even though the Corrupt and Illegal Practices Act of 1883 had placed restrictions on how much candidates could spend in the run-up to parliamentary elections, nothing was said about the lengthy intervals between elections. Take the behaviour of the wealthy Tory William Harvey Du Cros in Hastings in 1905:

> Du Cros had turned the ground over thoroughly in preparing for his candidature over the past year – fifty pounds to be shared among the slate clubs; supporters working round the pubs with the free beer; school teas at the schools and teas for the 'old people'; and good advice about Empire and 'Imperial Destiny' (the new catch-phrase) and promises of jobs in his London factory for the workless.

Robert Tressell described the electioneering tactics of Du Cros in his masterpiece *The Ragged Trousered Philanthropists*.

Sometimes wealthy individuals gave donations to hand-picked Labour figures, particularly Keir Hardie who received funds from the Cadbury family and the steel magnate Andrew Carnegie. Countess de la Warr provided vital financial support for the fledgeling newspaper the *Daily Herald* whilst from time to time the Conservative Party itself discreetly supplied funds – the infamous 'Tory Gold' – in the hope that Labour candidates would draw off votes from Liberals.

There was in fact only one solution to the money problem. The unions had created the Labour Party, and it was the unions which must pay for it. If the industrial arm of the labour movement wanted a political voice, then they had to put their hands in their pockets – or at least in those of their members. They duly established political funds, automatically deducting small sums from members on a weekly basis. In 1909 this method was declared illegal by the courts but a Liberal government, dependent on Labour support, overturned the ruling by means of the Trade Union Act of 1913. Trade unionists could indeed choose not to contribute but this involved the effort of 'contracting out' and few did so.

As the historian of party finances, Michael Pinto-Duschinsky, has accurately observed, 'In finance, as in so much else, the emergent Labour Party relied almost entirely on the organised support of trade unions.' Of course this reliance had enormous implications for the Labour Party in every respect – organisation, policy, the background of MPs – and will recur frequently throughout this book. Paying the piper as they did allowed the unions to select most of the tunes.

It was also trade union money and influence which impelled the Labour Party to start organising on national and modern lines. At the Party Conference held at Nottingham in January 1918 a Constitution was drawn up which, in historian Margaret Cole's words, finally 'implied that the Party was now set to become an adult political organisation, ready to challenge either or both of the two older parties.'

The man who drew up this Constitution as well as the statement of policy which followed it, *Labour and the New*

*Social Order*, was Sidney Webb. His name will always be inextricably linked with that of his wife, Beatrice.

People sometimes laugh at the Webbs and they were, in some respects, figures of fun. There was their obsession with facts and yet more facts which, like socialist Gradgrinds, they incorporated into heavy tomes read nowadays only by insomniacs or Ph.D students. They are well known too for their distinctly unromantic marriage. The honeymoon, for instance, was spent researching trade union records in Dublin. The Webbs' ascetic life-style and frugal housekeeping encouraged shrewd dinner guests to eat beforehand. Kingsley Martin, for many years the editor of the *New Statesman*, attended one gathering and tentatively asked the Webbs if he could use their lavatory; apparently they seemed surprised that their guests actually possessed bodily needs.

Yet this summary neglects the Webbs' many virtues, foremost among them being their remarkable disinterestedness: they laboured for many years towards the general good without hope or expectation of financial reward. Both wore rings inscribed with the words '*Pro Bono Publico*'. They were never malicious or self-seeking, always generous, dedicated simply to the service of others. And, not least, they enjoyed a happy marriage which is movingly depicted in Beatrice's *Diaries* and her book *Our Partnership*.

Beatrice Potter was born in January 1858 into a family whose ancestors had done well in business. Her grandfather had been in the cotton industry while her father had prospered in railways and the timber trade. Richard Potter and his wife had nine daughters. Eight of them went on to marry men who became pillars of the Establishment. Margaret Cole has listed some of these husbands. Among them were:

R.D. Holt, merchant of Liverpool; Leonard Courtney, who became Lord Courtney of Penwith and narrowly missed the Speakership of the House of Commons; Arthur Payne, mill-owner; Alfred Cripps, barrister and subsequently Lord

Parmoor; Henry Hobhouse, member of a great Liberal political family, MP for Somerset and Chairman of the Somerset County Council; Arthur Dyson Williams, barrister.

Beatrice, the youngest daughter, was to be different. Childhood illness meant she had little in the way of a formal education but proved healthy enough to be launched into the London season, 'coming out' in 1876. This upper-class social institution supposedly ensured that girls found suitable husbands of their own class. It had the opposite effect on Beatrice, turning her against the conspicuous waste and extravagance of High Society.

She did however meet and fall in love with the rising politician Joseph Chamberlain, whose talents in running his home city of Birmingham in the 1860s and 1870s were now being demonstrated on the national stage. Several years older than Beatrice, he had already been widowed twice and was looking for a companion to be his political hostess and help further his career.

Beatrice was astute enough to realise what such a marriage would entail: 'I shall be absorbed into the life of a man, whose aims are not my aims, who will refuse me all freedom of thought in my intercourse with him; to whose career I shall have to subordinate all my life, mental and physical.' Miss Potter once asked Chamberlain if it was true that in his household only one view on any subject was allowed: his own. He replied simply, 'That is so.'

Nevertheless, despite his authoritarian nature, Beatrice was deeply drawn towards Chamberlain, both intellectually and physically. After much heartbreak on her side she finally turned down his proposal of marriage, although at great cost to her own happiness. 'Will the pain never cease?' she asked herself, and at one point even contemplated suicide. 'If Death comes it will be welcome – for life has always been distasteful to me.'

Beatrice kept herself occupied, first by rent-collecting for a charitable organisation in the East End of London and then by helping her cousin Charles Booth on the research for his multi-volume *The Life and Labour of the People of London*; books which did much to stir the late-Victorian conscience. Her zeal for detailed research replaced the religious faith she had lost. It was at this point in her life that she met Sidney Webb, a high-flying civil servant.

Webb was a mine of information on almost every social and political question of the day. He was a leading figure in the Fabian Society, the group established in 1884 which brought together a miscellaneous body of individuals ranging from the aspiring playwright George Bernard Shaw to the philandering journalist Hubert Bland who was married to the writer Edith Nesbit, later to be famous for *The Railway Children*. Most radicals at this time were involved with the Fabians, including many people who will bulk large in this book: Keir Hardie, Ramsay MacDonald who sat on the Executive for several years, Annie Besant, H.G. Wells, Dr and Mrs Pankhurst, the Reverend Stewart Headlam and the playwright and theatrical producer Harley Granville Barker.

The Fabians took their name from the Roman general Fabius Cunctator whose policy of caution had gradually worn down and defeated Hannibal. The moderation of the Fabian Society in working for reform within the parliamentary system – what Sidney Webb was later to describe as the inevitability of gradualness – seemed ideally suited to British conditions. The Fabians eschewed revolutionary rhetoric in favour of detailed investigation of the facts, and these facts revealed the inequalities and injustices emanating from the *laissez-faire* and individualist philosophy that influenced successive governments.

They argued that 'every man for himself' should be replaced by a collectivist emphasis on the public good requiring a much greater role for government. Instead of being a spectator on the sidelines, the state should roll up its sleeves and get into the action as a player. *Fabian Essays* of 1889 was both an indictment of late Victorian society and a constructive call to arms. The Society proved adept at publicising its ideas; more than 10 per cent of the membership were journalists, so that the loud and articulate trumpeting of their doctrines disguised a small membership.

It was because she admired Sidney Webb's contribution to *Fabian Essays* that Beatrice arranged a meeting. He seems to have fallen in love almost at first sight with the beautiful and gifted Miss Potter but she was less enchanted, still bearing the emotional wounds of her relationship with Chamberlain. In her *Diary* Beatrice was brutally frank in her description of Sidney: 'I am not sure as to the future of that man. His tiny tadpole body, unhealthy skin, lack of manner, cockney pronunciation, poverty, are all against him.'

But gradually, over a period of months, she warmed towards him, although making it clear that she was attracted by Sidney's mind and nothing more. After their engagement, Sidney boldly sent his fiancée a photograph of himself. Beatrice replied, 'Let me have your head – it is the head only that I am marrying.' Sidney had to recognise that public-spirited research formed the basis for their marriage: 'One and one,' he remarked, 'placed in a sufficiently integrated relationship, make not two, but eleven.' And yet, despite this unpromising beginning – and the fact that some friends like Charles Booth and his wife dropped Beatrice because they felt she had married beneath her – the Webbs' marriage, celebrated in the summer of 1892, turned out to be enormously happy on both sides.

Over the next fifty-one years they devoted themselves to their work, researching and writing many books together. They agreed not to have children in case it unsettled their work routine. Beatrice once asked in her *Diary*: 'Are the books we have written together worth (to the community) the babies we might have had?' On the whole, the answer for Beatrice seems to have been yes.

Each Webb book was laboriously constructed from mountainous piles of file-cards, every card recording one 'fact' which was then placed in order. Such an accumulative method squeezed out any human dimension to their books, and it is no coincidence that their most readable works today – Beatrice's letters, diaries and *Our Partnership* – retain a personal and engaging touch absent from the couple's more 'serious' historical researches. But their solid work did provide ammunition for early labour leaders as they argued the case for the trade unions and the Labour Party.

However the Webbs were not just ivory-tower academics. Instrumental in founding both the London School of Economics and the *New Statesman* magazine, Sidney also worked extensively for the London County Council and sat as a Labour MP during the 1920s. Beatrice was a formidable member of the Poor Law Commission of 1908 and her Minority Report heralded the disintegration of the old Victorian assumptions towards poverty which maintained it was your own fault if you were poor.

There is still argument about the extent both of their influence and that of the Fabians. Like Hardie, the Webbs initially wanted to work through the Liberal Party until they realised that the trouble with Gladstonian Liberalism was that it 'thinks in individuals': 'We have become aware, almost in a flash, that we are not merely individuals, but members of a community, nay, citizens of the world.'

Eventually their disillusion with the individualistic Liberals convinced them that only the new Labour Party offered a suitable vehicle for their policies. That Sidney should draw up the Constitution of the Labour Party in 1918 demonstrated how successfully the Fabians established their beliefs as the ideology of 'labourism'.

It was a reminder, too, that the Labour Party was not an exclusively working-class body. In many ways the Webbs and the Fabians acted as the brains of the Labour Party and their influence grew stronger from the 1930s onwards when the Party grappled with the problems of administration and government.

But, of course, a heart is also vital to any living body. And here one returns to the lonely, difficult, courageous figure of Keir Hardie as he makes his way to Parliament in August 1892. It was Hardie who recognised that millions of people were not adequately represented by the Conservative or Liberal Parties and that a political organisation was needed which would mitigate the consequences of a capitalism based on market forces. It was Hardie who more than any other person created the Labour Party and so dramatically influenced the course of British society and politics over the next hundred years. Or, in the more extravagant language of Ramsay MacDonald: 'He will stand out for ever as the Moses who led the children of labour in this country out of bondage . . .'

That is why one should care about Keir Hardie.

# 2

# The Mild-Mannered Desperadoes

## Revolutionaries in Britain and British Revolutionaries

'Marx himself . . . did not wish to be called a "Marxist" and ridiculed the "Marxists" to his heart's content.'

WILHELM LIEBKNECHT

'We'll ask the man, where do you stand on the question of revolution? Are you for it or against it? If he's against it, we'll stand him up against a wall.'

V.I. LENIN

French Revolutions, American Revolutions, the European Revolutions of 1848, Russian Revolutions – recent world history seems to be one revolution after another. Why hasn't Britain had one? A possible answer is that it did, over three hundred years ago. Why then has it not had another, more recent revolution? Because, paradoxically, the English Revolution – the Civil War of the 1640s followed by the execution of Charles I – led to the Restoration and then the so-called 'Glorious Revolution' of 1688 which ushered in a political system under which change usually takes place gradually and in piecemeal fashion with a minimum of bloodshed.

There was, however, one occasion in the nineteenth century when it did look as if a modern 'British Revolution' might indeed take place. In the 1830s and 1840s the authorities were deeply scared of the Chartists, the movement which took its name from the six points of the Charter, the programme drawn up in a London pub. The Charter demanded the extension of the vote to all men over the age of twenty-one, for constituencies to be the same size, for an end to the property qualification for MPs, for the payment of MPs, and for the secret ballot. Ironically, these five points are now law; the only point missing is the call for annual Parliaments.

Chartist demonstrations sometimes displayed lurid slogans such as 'Fight to the knife for children and wife' and 'More pigs and fewer priests'. Even though an abortive 'Rising' in Newport, Wales led to the deaths of fourteen people, on the whole the Chartist agitation had been peaceful and law-abiding. However when the Chartist leaders announced their plans for a meeting on Kennington Common in South London on 10 April 1848, the government thought this might very well be the English '1789'. They panicked.

Queen Victoria and her family fled London for the safety of the Isle of Wight. The seventy-nine-year-old Duke of Wellington was put in charge of the capital's defences while 150,000 'Special Constables' – more men than he had commanded at the Battle of Waterloo against Napoleon – were rapidly sworn in. Troops were stationed in churches and 1,500 Chelsea Pensioners guarded the bridges at Battersea and Vauxhall.

Heavy gun batteries were even brought up from Woolwich whilst huge bound volumes of *The Times* blocked up the ground floor windows of the Foreign Office. Cannons were placed on the roof of the Bank of England and gunsmiths ordered to make their weapons unusable in the event of looting. The government commandeered the national electric telegraph system and also rushed through Parliament a Gagging Act imposing a penalty of seven years' transportation for seditious speeches.

On the morning of 10 April, 1848, observers noted that

inhabitants of the capital seemed edgy and nervous – and none more so than Feargus O'Connor, the Irishman who was MP for Nottingham and accepted as the leader of the Chartists. Though a fine journalist and orator – one eyewitness claimed that his voice was so powerful that it '. . . made the vault of Heaven echo with its sound' – O'Connor was already exhibiting that manic streak of vanity which eventually saw him spend the last few years of his life incarcerated in a mental asylum. He called himself 'the Lion of Freedom' and his delusions of grandeur even extended to signing his letters 'Feargus Rex'.

One reason for O'Connor's nervousness on 10 April was that he and the other Chartist leaders had no idea how to push forward the Chartist cause. Previously they had concentrated on drawing up petitions in favour of the six points, hoping to pressure the House of Commons into debating them. The 1839 Petition had carried the signatures of one million people; the 1842 Petition had been signed by over three million. Six miles in length, this second petition was taken to Parliament in a huge wooden frame requiring thirty men to carry it. Neither petition was debated by the House of Commons, and by 1848 the Chartist leaders were expected to make sure that the third petition met with a better fate than the first two.

O'Connor arrived at Kennington Common to find a much smaller crowd than anticipated. Estimates vary but a figure of about 100,000 seems approximately right. He discovered that the Commissioner of Police had banned the proposed mass march to Westminster. Only a small delegation was to be allowed to accompany the petition. O'Connor had to decide whether to challenge this decision, by force if necessary. Here was the moment when discontent might have burst into something more.

It didn't. O'Connor meekly accepted the police decision. Several revolutionary speeches were delivered to the crowd, but it all proved an anti-climax. The weather was unsympathetic too. The rain came down and most people went home to tea. The Queen returned to London, the Duke of Wellington retired once again to the House of Lords and the Specials were stood down. When scrutinised at the Houses of Parliament this third petition was found to contain thousands of false names, including those of the Queen and the Duke. Although the Chartist movement continued, never again did it constitute a threat to the British state.

Contrast 10 April 1848 in London – no injuries, no deaths, few arrests – with events elsewhere in Europe: the crumbling of governments, the overthrow of monarchs, troops firing wildly on crowds in the streets.

A few months after the crushing defeat in mainland Europe of the 1848 Revolutions, a penniless German arrived in London where he was to spend the remaining thirty-four years of his life. As a young man Karl Marx had been a typically Romantic and wild student, fighting duels, drinking too much and writing three passionate volumes of poetry dedicated to Jenny von Westphalen, later to become his wife. While at university in first Berlin and then Jena, Marx became interested in politics. He subsequently edited a newspaper called *Rheinische Zeitung* which soon fell foul of the authorities because of its radical views and was shut down by the censor in March 1843.

Marx's ideas were still unclear but he was beginning to stress the economic or materialist basis of human society. He also suggested that the onset of industrialisation would inevitably generate a proletariat or working class which in turn would wage war on class society. The ensuing struggle would lead to the replacement of capitalism by socialism and eventually create a classless society.

In February 1848 Marx and his friend Friedrich Engels published *The Communist Manifesto*. It began with the bald assertion, 'A spectre is haunting Europe – the spectre of communism' and contained a stirring call to arms: 'Workers of the world, unite. You have nothing to lose but your chains.' Not even Marx, always confident in his own judgements, could have expected such an instant response. Over the next few months uprisings took place all over Europe, appearing to confirm his analysis. But he had failed to realise that the European middle classes, and none more so than the British, would at the death prefer social order to social justice. They sided with the forces of law and order and the revolutions were defeated.

Marx was now a marked man. By August 1849, exiled from France, Germany and Belgium and harrassed by the police, scarcely a country in Europe was prepared to accept him other than Britain, the traditional sanctuary for fugitives and refugees. For virtually the rest of his life Marx was dogged by money problems and, in fact, within a few weeks of his arrival he and his family were evicted from their Chelsea lodgings for not paying the rent. Jenny, who over the next thirty years proved to be a faithful and loyal partner to her husband, described in a letter to a friend how humiliating it was to have their difficulties witnessed by 'two or three hundred persons loitering around our door – the whole Chelsea mob' who had gathered to watch the eviction.

The Marx household moved to Dean Street in Soho, then one of the most overcrowded and unhealthy parts of London. Without the financial support of Engels, who was based at his family's textile firm in Manchester, things would have been even more perilous. Even so, the Marx family, together with their devoted maid Helene Demuth, known as Lenchen, shared two small rooms, which can still be seen today, above a smart and expensive Italian restaurant. Only many years after Marx's death did Engels reveal that a relationship between Karl and Lenchen had produced a son. Mrs Marx bore children too and once, when their child Guido died (Guido because he was born on Guy Fawkes' Night), Marx had to beg in the streets in order to pay for the coffin.

Marx tried to support himself by odd pieces of journalism but his command of English was initially shaky and there was not much of a market either for his ideas or the difficult style in which he expressed them. Once, in desperation, he tried for a job as a clerk on the Great Western Railway but was promptly turned down because of his appalling handwriting. This scrawl caused many problems for Engels and Marx's daughter Eleanor when they came to transcribe his work after his death.

Marx mixed mainly with his fellow German exiles in London, though they seem to have spent most of their time bickering and squabbling. He was particularly jealous of the art historian Kinkel because of his heroic part in the 1848 Revolution in Prussia when he had led an uprising. Few of these exiles had much contact with the native British labour movement and Marx himself haunted the British Museum conveniently situated nearby. His personal isolation reflected the political isolation of socialists all over Europe as a period of reaction set in after the 1848 Revolutions.

This conservative mood left Marx and his associates rather like beached whales, waiting desperately for the political tide to turn. He never found it easy to come to terms with the dilemma of being a revolutionary in a decidedly non-revolutionary situation. Only once was he involved in day-to-day practical political activity. In 1864 a group of individuals gathered in London to set up an international body called the International Working Men's Association (later to be known as the First International). Marx was invited at the last moment to the inaugural meeting held in Covent Garden in September 1864 and did not speak. But he was elected to the General Council and drew up the rules, the first of which called for 'the protection, advancement and emancipation of the working classes'.

Marx's force of character and certainty about his own ideas meant that he quickly dominated proceedings. But not even he could overcome the disunity plaguing the International from the start – over one hundred different organisations from many countries had affiliated, and none was prepared to concede a shred of autonomy. The disputes at meetings became so acrimonious that on one occasion an irate Spanish delegate brandished a pistol at his comrades.

In the absence of modern communications it was difficult to know precisely about labour disputes abroad, although some foreign 'blacklegging' was prevented. Nationalist preferences predominated over internationalist concerns, a portent of what happened within the European labour movement on the outbreak of war in 1914. The International did achieve some notoriety during the Paris Commune of 1871 when the authorities blamed them for helping to forment this uprising. But the Commune was crushed and the International soon forgotten.

Its comparative impotence led to renewed bickering, especially when anarchists, who distrusted any form of organisation or discipline, grew in influence, threatening Marx's control. In the early 1870s Marx moved its nominal headquarters to New York, where he knew it would expire. He preferred to kill off the International rather than let it fall into anarchist hands. It was formally dissolved in 1876. Once again Marx retreated to his study.

There is much irony in Marx's devotion to economics in view of his own poverty. As he once ruefully acknowledged, 'Never, I think, was money written about under such a shortage of it.' He was a terrible manager of his own household affairs; not only was he unable to support himself or his family but unexpected windfalls were also soon squandered. A double inheritance received in 1864 was quickly dissipated and later he could not live on an income of £300 per annum, in Victorian terms a substantial sum.

Without Engels' financial help, the Marxes would have ended up in the workhouse. They were not, however, always very grateful to their benefactor. Engels lived happily with a factory girl called Mary Burns (when she died, her sister moved in). Although Mrs Marx was prepared to accept Engels' money, she stoutly refused to visit Manchester because she disapproved of Engels' liaison with Mary.

Photographs of Marx show him as a heavily bearded and stern-looking patriarch, but he did possess a more appealing side. He always carried with him photographs of his mother, wife and eldest daughter. A Prussian police spy, reporting on the Marx household in 1853, left this report:

> Sitting down is quite a dangerous affair: here is a chair with but three legs; there another, which by chance is still intact where the children are playing at being cooks. Courteously this is offered to the guest, but the children's cooking is not removed and you sit down at the risk of ruining your trousers. None of this occasions Marx or his wife the slightest embarrassment. You are received in the most friendly manner, cordially offered pipes, tobacco or whatever else is available. In any case the clever, agreeable talk compensates to some extent for the domestic shortcomings and makes the discomfort endurable . . .

This is a charming portrait by an observer whose job did not make him sympathetic towards the Marxes.

One of their daughters, Eleanor, claims that her parents had a great sense of humour:

> Assuredly two people never enjoyed a joke more than these two. Again and again – especially if the occasion were one demanding decorum and sedateness, have I seen them laugh till tears ran down their cheeks, and even those inclined to be shocked at such awful levity could not choose but laugh with them. And how often have I seen them not daring to look at one another, each knowing that once a glance was exchanged uncontrollable laughter would result.

The Marx family outings to Hampstead Heath each Sunday were highlights of the week as they and their friends ate, played and slept. There is also the famous occasion of Marx's pub crawl down Tottenham Court Road. Having decided to take a drink at each pub along the way, on leaving the eighteenth Marx and his friends shattered a number of street-lamps with a volley of stones – whereupon they found themselves chased by four policemen. Their long and hard run ended only when Marx's detailed knowledge of London's alleys and passages enabled them to elude their pursuers.

Marx's relative isolation from the world around him, and his lack of English friends, helps explain why he never properly analysed the traditions and institutions of the country in which he now lived. Why, for example, did Britain lack the revolutionary tradition of neighbouring France? One of the specific features he might have investigated was British rulers' avoidance of violent repression. British socialism remembers the Peterloo 'Massacre' of 1819 as a horrific battle, and indeed six people died. Yet compare both this and 'Bloody Sunday' in Trafalgar Square in 1887 after which one person died with elsewhere in Europe where the most violent repression was practised and massacres were common. British riots had a peculiarly national quality: in 1886 the unemployed lustily bellowed out 'Rule Britannia' as they smashed shop windows.

The British ruling class seems to have had a shrewdness not always displayed by its European counterparts. For instance, the suffrage was gradually extended throughout the century – in 1832, 1867 and 1884 – before protest could become even pre-revolutionary. In France, revolution was almost commonplace. In Britain, it was difficult to see what form a rising might take. The murder of Queen Victoria? Stringing up MPs in Parliament Square? Ransacking St Paul's and Westminster Abbey? Even to pose such questions reveals their absurdity.

In his search for the non-existent spirit of British revolution, Marx might also have examined the continuity of national institutions; a continuity which derives from the fact that Britain has not been invaded since 1066 or suffered the traumatic shock of defeat in a major war. Moreover the traditional moderation of the Church of England prevented any upsurge of the anti-clericalism that provided the basis for several European socialist movements. The Nonconformist influence too, which Hardie had recognised and accommodated when he formed the Labour Party, gave the British labour movement a distinctive heritage deeply hostile to the materialist Marxist philosophy.

Above all, British moderation, empiricism and the inclination to 'mind one's own business' is thoroughly unconducive to the development of a politically dynamic and informed society. Several commentators have noted the strength of the British non-participatory political tradition whereby 'politics is left to the politicians'. The British are not lazy; just that our enthusiasm and voluntary spirit is usually directed towards sport, flower clubs and a myriad of other non-political activities.

So what was Marx writing about? His detailed research into British capitalism, buttressed by the mountain of facts contained in the government 'Blue Books' which he purchased second-hand in Long Acre, Covent Garden, confirmed his bleak assessment that the rich were getting richer and the poor poorer. Sooner rather than later, this growing polarisation would lead to revolution. A passage towards the end of the first volume of *Das Kapital*, published in German in 1867, forecast what would happen:

> Along with the constantly diminishing number of the magnates of capital who usurp and monopolise all advantages of this process of transformation, grows the mass of misery, oppression, slavery, degradation, exploitation; but with this too grows the revolt of the working class, a class always increasing in numbers, and disciplined, united, organised by the very mechanism of the process of capitalist production itself. The monopoly of capital becomes a fetter upon the mode of production, which has sprung up and flourished along with, and under it. Centralisation of the means of production and socialisation of labour at last reach a point where they become incompatible with their capitalist integument. This integument is burst asunder. The knell of capitalist private property sounds. The expropriators are expropriated.

His materialist philosophy insisted that people were the products of their own society. Although this tenet must presumably also apply to Marx himself, later Marxists often claimed that the great man had, in fact, discovered the 'laws' of human society and that his writings were, as a Soviet textbook dealing with *Das Kapital* once put it, *For All Times and All Men*. It is extraordinary how many modern Marxists, in flagrant violation of Marx's own approach, maintained that his ideas, formed in the very different circumstances of the nineteenth century, still held true and were valid in the twentieth century.

In particular, Marx often formulated his ideas in terms characteristic of the melodramas dominating the Victorian stage: Capital is implacably opposed to Labour; the rich face the poor; workers battle against owners; class struggle and conflict is inevitable. Practical detail is conspicuously absent from his work – 'If I but knew how to start a business . . .' he once wrote despairingly to Engels. In retrospect Marx appears more of a Romantic figure struggling in a garret than the 'scientific socialist' his supporters claim him to be.

One paradox of his writing is that a man claiming to show how and why the working class would eventually triumph should write in a language so difficult for anyone to understand, even though he himself stressed the value of clarity. In part this reflects Marx's unflattering view of the working class; as his friend Wilhelm Liebknecht commented, 'The masses were to him a brainless crowd whose thoughts and feelings were furnished by the ruling class.'

Certainly this limitation partly explains the lack of English translations of his writings. The first volume of *Das Kapital* was not issued in English until 1887, four years after his death. The other volumes were not published until 1907. *The Communist Manifesto* itself did not appear in book form in English until 1888. Marx's work was much more widely published in France and Germany – the Continental taste for abstract thought contrasting with English 'feet on the ground' empiricism.

★　　★　　★

Since so little of Marx's work was available in English, few British socialists could be familiar with his writings except for those who spoke foreign languages. George Bernard Shaw, for instance, read *Das Kapital* in German whilst studying in the British Museum. Another initiate was H.M. Hyndman, the powerful and egocentric individual who can plausibly claim to be the pioneering British Marxist. As the first person to try and create a British revolutionary party, Hyndman's tenets of sweeping and possibly violent change were very different from the approach favoured by Keir Hardie and the Fabians.

Henry Mayers Hyndman was born in 1842 into a comfortably well-off family which had prospered from trade with the West Indies. He was educated privately and then at Trinity College, Cambridge, where his chagrin at not winning his cricket blue still rankled when he came to write his memoirs:

> I declare that I feel at this moment, fifty years later, my not playing for Cambridge against Oxford in the University Cricket Match as a far more unpleasant and depressing experience than infinitely more important failures have been to me since.

This failure did not stop Hyndman from playing county cricket for Sussex for several years, frequently against H.G. Wells' father Joseph who represented Kent. In one historic match between the two counties in June 1862 Wells senior achieved the notable feat of taking four wickets in four balls. Hyndman also qualified at the Bar and began work as a journalist for the *Pall Mall Gazette*.

Hyndman's social conscience was first stirred whilst investigating living conditions in the East End. His socialism was confirmed in 1880 when he read a French version of Marx's *Das Kapital* during a voyage to America. Returning home a convinced Marxist, Hyndman was certain in his own mind that Britain was poised to enter a period of class warfare. He proclaimed his beliefs in an article of 1881 called 'The Dawn of a Revolutionary Epoch' which predicted the inevitability of upheaval and revolution.

That same year Hyndman set up a loose political body called the Democratic Federation, hoping it would build upon the success of London's many radical working men's clubs founded at the time which functioned, in the words of one historian, as 'workers' universities'. He also published a book titled *England for All* which drew upon Marx's work but tactlessly did not actually mention 'the German doctor' by name because he felt that this would alienate possible supporters.

Naturally such an outrageous act of plagiarism – and what was worse from Marx's point of view, incorrect plagiarism – did not endear him to either Marx or Engels and they quarrelled bitterly. It revealed too an anti-German streak in Hyndman which proved so significant in 1914 when he was one of the most rabid 'war mongers' of them all.

By 1884 Hyndman's Marxist convictions had hardened and the name of his organisation was changed to the Social Democratic Federation (SDF), thus linking it with the social democratic organisations on the Continent. If this sounds decidedly moderate and rather like the forerunner of the party founded by Roy Jenkins, Dr David Owen and others in the 1980s, it wasn't. In the nineteenth century the phrase 'social democracy' was equated with Marxism and militancy. The SDF also established its own printing press, the Twentieth Century Press, which produced a weekly paper called *Justice*. Its circulation was always meagre – in his memoirs Hyndman remarked sadly, 'We did not meet a long-felt want, that's certain' – and later he regretted the time and money spent on it.

What did Hyndman and the SDF stand for? They emphasised the importance of the class struggle rather than any brand of ethical socialism with its 'love thy neighbour' approach. The SDF – opponents sometimes said this acronym stood for 'Silly Damned Fools' – was deeply sceptical about the possibilities of parliamentary change. Hyndman's friend Edward Carpenter wrote in his autobiography that 'We used to chaff him [Hyndman] because at every crisis in the industrial situation he was confident that the Millennium was at hand' – an optimism imitated by far-left groups in Britain to this day.

Hyndman also reputedly carried around with him a list of the intended members of his first revolutionary cabinet, once remarking that 'I could not carry on unless I expected the revolution at ten o'clock next Monday morning.' He was to endure a great many frustrated Monday mornings.

At first glance, Hyndman certainly does not fit any stereotype of what a Victorian revolutionary should be like. He lived for many years in Hampstead, one of the smartest parts of London, and his house now carries a memorial plaque. He always wore a frock coat and top hat, even when thundering out bitter denunciations of capitalism, and earned his living from speculating in ventures which ranged from gold-rushes in Australia and the United States to Colt guns and pencils. In his private life he was caring and considerate. Beatrice Webb once referred to British revolutionaries as 'the mild-mannered desperadoes'.

Hyndman's biggest failing was his authoritarian and egotistical personality. He liked to get his own way, which explains why he was on bad terms with Marx, Engels and also William Morris. But this self-righteousness also meant that he never wavered in the decision to turn his back on a traditional career in Establishment politics that might have led him to a position in the Cabinet. Instead he dedicated himself to tramping up and down the country in order to propagate what was a distinctly unfashionable and minority cause.

His courage was evident too after the so-called 'West End riots' of 1886 when demonstrators marching along Pall Mall stoned the windows of the smart gentlemen's clubs. Because he had delivered a speech just before the riot began, Hyndman found himself on trial at the Old Bailey for sedition. Helped by his training as a barrister, he defended himself with great persuasiveness and secured an acquittal.

The SDF's membership remained small, reaching only 3,250 at its height in 1897. Although size is not everything, this figure contrasted unfavourably with, say, the German Social Democrats whose power appeared so threatening to the authorities that an 'anti-Socialist Law' was in force in Germany between 1878 and 1890. As soon as the ban was lifted, the party gained nearly one and a half million votes and thirty-five seats in the parliamentary elections. The SDF's vote in British elections, on the other hand, was numbered in tens rather than millions.

Why was the SDF so small? Once more we are back with the inescapable fact that British life and culture is not really happy with the theoretical and political philosophy of Marxism. Hyndman in particular believed in a thoroughly dogmatic and arid Marxism, arguing that Marx's 'scientific laws' were immutable. Such an approach completely devalued the idea of human agency – if something was bound to happen, then there was little incentive to help it on its way.

In particular, the SDF never surmounted the obstacle that in Britain the trade unions had preceded Marxism, whereas in mainland Europe it was generally the other way around. But instead of trying to propagate Marxist ideas within the unions, Hyndman dismissed them as 'mere palliatives'. The great Dock Strike of 1889 was written off as 'a waste of energy'. Keir Hardie's attitude, of course, was very different. He argued that the unions, whatever their defects, were the essential roots out of which any significant labour movement in Britain had to grow.

Without these trade union links the SDF was bound to remain small in size and therefore prone to the sectarianism and squabbling which then and now has been such a feature of parts of the British Left. William Morris, for one, attacked the SDF's 'pedantic tone of arrogance and lack of generosity which is disgusting'. Not that Hyndman, with his absolute belief in his own correctedness, minded this: 'The reproach of sectarianism carries with it no odium for us.

Truth must ever be sectarian: error alone can afford to be catholic.'

The SDF's uncompromising purism was confirmed by its unwillingness to enter into alliances with other groups. In 1901 it made the crucial mistake of withdrawing from the newly formed Labour Representation Committee, the body which in 1906 became the Labour Party. This decision ensured that Marxism would remain on the fringes of the labour movement. It forms one of the 'might-have-beens' to ask whether the history of the British labour movement might not have been very different if the SDF had stayed put.

But somehow it is difficult to believe that Marxism would ever have ousted cautious and pragmatic labourism. In many ways the SDF's actions prefigured the split between moderates and militants which occurred within the British labour movement after the Russian Revolutions in 1917. Hyndman's prickly personality often expressed itself in scathing abuse of the working classes. He once referred to them as 'manifest degenerates', echoing Marx's 'brainless crowd' – primarily because they simply would not do what he told them to do. The music hall and the rise of mass sport were two popular activities which the SDF also blamed for diverting the workers' political energy into trivial pursuits.

Unable to accept the near unanimous support for existing political institutions, the SDF's propaganda often took on a bleak and gloomy tone. Robert Tressell's *The Ragged Trousered Philanthropists*, published posthumously just before the First World War, is a compelling example of this. The house-painter Tressell lived in Hastings and was an active member of his local SDF branch.

Written in his free time, Tressell's novel depicts with unsparing candour the ways in which 'the bosses' manipulate their compliant and stupid employees. For example, he describes a parliamentary election contested by two equally unsavoury candidates, Adam Sweater and Sir Graball D'Encloseland (the William Harvey Du Cros we met in the last chapter). Sheep-like, the voters do exactly as they are told. Tressell is brutal in his comments:

> In the face of such colossal imbecility it was absurd to hope for any immediate improvement. The little already accomplished was the work of a few self-sacrificing enthusiasts, battling against the opposition of those they sought to benefit, and the results of their labours were, in many instances, as pearls cast before the swine who stood watching for opportunities to fall upon and rend their benefactors.

Tressell's 'swine' inevitably reminds one of Hyndman's 'degenerates' and Marx's 'brainless crowd' and his book graphically conveys the frustration and isolation which many early socialists must have felt, struggling in the face of widespread antagonism and indifference. *The Ragged Trousered Philanthropists* does contain humour and passion too, but to Tressell the domination exercised by the authorities seems as total as in George Orwell's later *1984*. It is difficult to see how any kind of dissent or opposition could make itself effective. Tressell himself died penniless in a Liverpool workhouse in 1912.

It would be wrong to dismiss the SDF as of no importance. Some of their members were extraordinarily innovative in the methods utilised to put over their case to the public. They were the first organisation to hold unemployed marches – later revived in the 1920s and 1930s – as well as introducing 'Church Parades' in which crowds of the jobless attended church services on a Sunday in order to shock the consciences of the well-off. The SDF was prominent too in holding open-air meetings all over the country, often in the face of police obstruction.

The SDF's assertions about the extent of London poverty in the 1880s also prompted the Liverpool shipowner Charles Booth to launch his own investigations into the state of the capital's poor. Booth confidently expected to disprove what he dismissed as Hyndman's alarmist claims. In fact, as he explicitly recognised, Hyndman had if anything under-estimated the position. Booth's series *The Life and Labour of the People of London*, which appeared in seventeen volumes between 1891 and 1903, helped to shift public opinion towards a more radical frame of mind which favoured government intervention in order to improve work and living conditions.

It is notable, too, just how many influential people passed through the SDF's ranks. According to the German socialist Edouard Bernstein, no fewer than 100,000 individuals had at some stage of their life been members of the British party. William Morris, Eleanor Marx and Edward Carpenter will be discussed in the next chapter, but other members of the SDF (and its successors the Social Democratic Party and the British Socialist Party – left-wing groups have always been fond of name changes) included Ernest Bevin, Tom Mann, Ramsay MacDonald, Herbert Morrison, George Lansbury, John Maclean, Harry Pollitt and Willie Gallacher, all of whom will be mentioned frequently in the following pages.

Two other, totally different, SDF members were Jim Connell and Frances, Countess of Warwick. Connell was a huge Irishman who sported an enormous moustache and large red hat. Apart from writing the words to the internationally famous song 'The Red Flag', he also set up a Poachers' Union in which members' subscriptions helped pay the fines. His pamphlet of 1898, *The Truth about the Game Laws*, ends: 'The poacher is the incarnation of the spirit of revolt against oppression and injustice. He dares to fling his naked hand against the bayonets that guard the land monopoly.'

Connell also loved to deliver a lecture entitled 'From Protoplasm to Man', but legend has it that he never managed to progress beyond the opening two-hour introduction.

The Countess of Warwick on the other hand, reputedly the most beautiful woman in England, had inherited no less than 30,000 acres. A long-standing mistress of the Prince of Wales, later Edward VII, her husband was a Conservative MP. In 1895 he inherited his title of Earl of Warwick and Frances therefore became a Countess. To celebrate this event, she planned a huge ball at Warwick Castle. Hiring an eminent French dressmaker to design her costume she went as Marie Antoinette. The outfit alone cost more than a hundred guineas, approximately twice what the average worker then earned in a whole year.

Two days after the event, the Countess' attention was drawn to an article in the socialist weekly *Clarion* which vigorously condemned the extravagance of this ball. She was so incensed that she left her guests at the Castle and caught the first train to London in order to remonstrate with the editor of the paper, Robert Blatchford. Coming face to face with him, she claimed that the festivities had in fact given employment to hundreds of people in Warwick. She described in her autobiography what happened next:

> And then Robert Blatchford told me, as a Socialist and a Democrat, what he thought of charity bazaars and ladies bountiful. He made plain to me the difference between productive and unproductive labour. One phrase still lingers. He said that labour used to produce finery was as much wasted as if it were used to dig holes in the ground and fill them again.

Blatchford and the Countess talked for several hours. Afterwards she paced up and down Paddington Station mulling over what he had said. By the time of her return to Warwick she had decided Blatchford was right. 'Next day I sent for ten pounds' worth of books on Socialism. I got the name of an old Professor of Economics, and under him I started my period of study without delay.'

From that day onwards the Countess was a staunch supporter of the SDF and of other socialist causes, giving up much of her wealth to fund them. This took courage – most of her friends 'cut' her because of her new allegiance. Occasionally there were incongruous moments. She once hired a private train to take her home after an SDF Conference in 1902, and perhaps the Countess was behind the decision of the SDF to send a loyal address to Edward VII on his coronation that same year – not an action one would have expected from a Marxist party!

That Lady Warwick should be so vehement a left-winger helps explain the fascination of the history of British socialism, particularly the way in which it repeatedly contradicts stereotypes and confounds expectations. Similarly, of course, the British Conservative Party also resists easy generalisations.

One SDF member who blazed meteorically in the political firmament but then faded away was Victor Grayson, elected as the socialist MP for Colne Valley at a by-election in July 1907. Even Grayson's opponents admired his oratory, which drew thousands of people to his meetings – married women sold their wedding rings to help pay Grayson's election expenses. His election address was typically uncompromising and began, 'I am appealing to you as one of your own class. I want emancipation from the wage-slavery of Capitalism.' It went on, 'We must break the rule of the rich and take our destinies into our own hands.'

Grayson scraped home to victory by fewer than two hundred votes. He travelled to Westminster resolute, like Hardie fifteen years before, not to be muffled by the parliamentary proprieties. Within a few months he interrupted a debate in the House of Commons to demand that something be done about unemployment. Although rebuked by the Speaker, Grayson refused to give way. Finally, he shouted out that this was 'a House of murderers' and passed several withering comments on the timidity of his colleagues, who ironically enough included Keir Hardie himself.

But Grayson's revolt was very much that of an individualist and the unrelenting pressures of being a political rebel soon got to him. He always scorned the puritan, 'hairshirt', strain within the labour movement embodied by Hardie and some sections of the Independent Labour Party. Edward Carpenter, an admirer of Grayson, wrote of him, 'His fund of anecdotes was inexhaustible, and rarely could a supper party of which he was a member get to bed before three in the morning.' Robert Blatchford likewise said that 'I have never met a man so utterly full of the joys of life.'

Sadly these 'joys' embroiled him in a complicated private life – he was bisexual – and his heavy drinking sometimes caused him to miss meetings or else to speak when drunk. Grayson lost his seat at the 1910 general election. He then wrote for Blatchford's paper *Clarion*, but his health was continually breaking down. Marriage to an actress brought no relief from debts and drink. In 1916, while in Australasia, he joined the New Zealand Army and was wounded fighting in the trenches in France. His wife Ruth died in childbirth.

In September 1920 Grayson suddenly vanished from the face of the earth. There were various supposed sightings of him over the next thirty years, yet never anything definite. There has been some speculation that he got caught up in Lloyd George's 'honours for sale' scandal and fell foul of the mysterious tout J. Maundy Gregory, but no one knows for sure. It was a sad and squalid end to a briefly very promising career – 'Labour's lost leader' as one biographer has called him.

'A fiery socialist, without any principles and given to mere phrases.' This damning indictment of Grayson was penned by a man who as both a revolutionary and a human being proved to be very different from Grayson: Lenin.

In Tom Stoppard's play *Travesties*, a number of famous individuals are shown meeting in Zurich where they all lived during the First World War. There is Lenin, James Joyce and the Dadaist poet Tristan Tzara. The three men might have met each other, but almost certainly didn't. Yet in reality an equally disparate group of later-to-be-famous figures did actually once meet, in May 1907, at a 'socialist church' in Islington, north London. As well as Lenin, there was Leon Trotsky, Maxim Gorky, Joseph Stalin and the revolutionary Rosa Luxemburg. English observers included two future leaders of the Labour Party, Ramsay MacDonald and George Lansbury.

Why were they meeting and what were the Russians doing in London in the first place? The answer lies yet again in Britain's traditional role as a refuge for exiles and outcasts. Twenty years before, the anarchist Prince Kropotkin had been on the run from the Czarist police. He described in his autobiography how he boarded a ship, not knowing its nationality nor where he might end up: 'Then I saw floating above the stern the union jack – the flag under which so many refugees, Russian, Italian, French, Hungarian and of all nations have found an asylum. I greeted that flag from the depth of my heart.'

British tolerance was not just a cosy myth. Unlike virtually every other country in the world, newcomers could not be prevented from landing. The Special Branch, founded in 1887, did keep an eye on suspects and a statute of 1905 allowed the authorities to restrict the arrival of 'aliens', although in practice they rarely did.

Russian revolutionaries knew of Britain as a safe haven and in 1907 the Russian Social Democratic and Labour Party, under pressure from the Czarist secret police, decided to hold their 5th Congress in London. Delegates moaned about the inhospitable weather and commented scathingly on the small size and influence of their British revolutionary counterpart, the SDF, led by Hyndman. They no doubt contrasted the activities of the law-abiding SDF with their own perilous experiences. Assassination, suicide, terrorism, torture and imprisonment were simply to be expected as part of a Russian revolutionary's life. If union leaders such as Ben Tillett dismissed the 'chatterers and magpies of continental revolutionists', the Russians in turn scorned people like Grayson as effete and irresponsible.

Take Lenin himself. His older brother had been summarily executed by the Czarist authorities for his part in a suspected terrorist plot. Lenin abandoned his legal studies and became a full-time revolutionary. Anything that got in the way of this was discarded. He stopped listening to classical music because, he said, it made him feel too benevolent towards his fellow human beings. A very good chess player, that too had to be dropped as it was squandering energy which should have been devoted to politics.

Somewhat surprisingly he found the time to marry Nadia Krupskaya, but her account of their life together, *Memoirs of Lenin*, is largely devoid of personal detail. Instead it catalogues furtive meetings, the relentless exposure of political heresy (that is, anyone whose views did not coincide with Lenin's) and attempts to get around the Russian censors by means of invisible inks and aliases.

Although Lenin, like Marx and Hyndman, came from a comparatively privileged background, he was bolstered by his confidence that Marxism was scientific and 'true'. Therefore he knew exactly what the working classes wanted, even if they didn't know it yet themselves. Everything and anything was a means to one single end: revolution. 'We say that our morality is entirely subordinated to the interests of the proletariat's class struggle,' he once chillingly remarked.

The difficulty for Lenin was that the working classes showed little inclination to bring about the revolution themselves. His solution was to build a political party which, as an élite or vanguard, would guide and lead the masses. Highly centralised and controlled from above, this party would be completely different from the British SDF. For Lenin 'the Party' not only had a monopoly of the truth but it also, as he made clear in his tract *What is to be Done?* – much of which was written in London – came before everything else: health, honesty, happiness, life even. The revolutionary '. . . must be ever ready to do anything'. This doctrine was later called 'Marxism–Leninism'.

Lenin knew London well. He had lived there for eighteen months between 1902 and 1903, learning English at Speaker's Corner in Hyde Park and editing the Russian Social Democrat paper *Iskra* at the SDF's printing press on Clerkenwell Green. Other Russian exiles preferred Paris as a refuge because the weather was generally better, but at least London offered the

British Museum whose Reading Room had always been a place of sanctuary for penniless refugees. George Bernard Shaw once referred to 'British Museum Socialism' and, many years later, in July 1939, Louis MacNeice wrote a poem called 'The British Museum Reading Room' which ends:

> Between the enormous fluted Ionic columns
> There seeps from heavily jowled or hawk-like foreign faces
> The guttural sorrow of the refugees.

These exiles also congregated at the Communist Club in Charlotte Street, near Tottenham Court Road in London, which contained a library, billiard room and cheap restaurant. The Club was always full of tobacco smoke and the babel of foreign tongues as the émigrés interminably argued and disputed, just as Marx and his German colleagues had bickered at the Communist Club fifty years before when it was based in Soho. The Club was eventually closed down by the police on the outbreak of war in 1914 and became instead a furniture depository. The building was bombed in 1940.

Despite Lenin's prolonged stay in London he participated little in the British labour movement. Again like Marx, his circle of English friends was miniscule. It was almost as if he feared contamination by the native socialists. Hyndman once said of himself that he was '. . . a Socialist unarmed with revolvers or any other dynamite other than mental dynamite.' For Lenin, any kind of dynamite was legitimate in the class struggle. The differences between the Russian Social Democrats and the British were encapsulated by the 5th Congress of 1907.

The Russians met in the Brotherhood Church, Islington, because the minister in charge, a Reverend Swann who was to be one of Victor Grayson's full-time supporters at the forthcoming Colne Valley by-election, was a Christian Socialist. The interior of the church was plain and simple. Gorky thought it 'unadorned to the point of absurdity'. The

320 delegates, amongst them Stalin and Trotsky, were greeted by Ramsay MacDonald. Then, courtesies over, the Russians got down to the serious business of creating a revolutionary party. Lengthy theoretical debate and argument followed as the correct party line was hammered out. One delegate plaintively remarked that 'The speeches of the leaders lasted for hours . . .'

Sometimes proceedings were interrupted by the need for the English to hold services but otherwise the delegates kept relentlessly at it, even taking their meals on the spot at a makeshift kitchen run by Gorky's wife. A full two days were spent just finalising the agenda for what they were to discuss and then a further week passed in organisational wrangling. The split between those who became Bolsheviks and those who became Mensheviks was developing – and Lenin wanted to clarify the differences between what were essentially militants (Bolsheviks) and moderates (Mensheviks).

Lenin always maintained that to the English all foreigners were alike, and they regarded the Russian émigrés 'with a native perplexity'. One or two newspapers tried to stir up hostility against what the *Daily Mail* called 'a congress of undesirables'. From time to time a few people gathered outside the Brotherhood Church to hurl abuse but nothing more substantial. As always, Londoners went about their own business.

Quite apart from their un-English preoccupation with theory, the Congress represented a political philosophy completely at odds with that of the new British Labour Party formed only the year before. Keir Hardie's Labour Party was a reformist and constitutional body wedded to parliamentary change. Lenin and the Russian Social Democrats regarded this 'labourist' approach as mistaken and dangerous. Only true believers could be admitted to the revolutionary vanguard, and at this 1907 Congress a resolution calling for a 'broad [Russian] Labour Party' rather than a revolutionary Marxist party was defeated by 169 votes to 94.

But, however passionate or learned the debates, the delegates still had to pay for their food and lodging. As the weeks passed, a number of them began to return to Russia. Lenin and the other leaders hoped to raise money in London, but only Gorky with his international reputation as a writer had access to wealthy Englishmen and he was not prepared to use his contacts because of his unease at the political direction of the Congress.

Help finally arrived in the unlikely shape of Joseph Fels, an American based in England who had made a fortune out of laundry soap. Beatrice Webb was very snobbish about him – 'a decidedly vulgar little Jew with much push, little else on surface' – which did not stop her trying to wheedle money out of Fels for her own political projects.

Fels looked upon the Russian delegates as victims of Czarist repression and he was taken to see the Congress in action by his unofficial adviser, George Lansbury. Although agreeing to make a loan of about £1,700 to the Russian Social Democrats, he insisted that the conference end because of his worry that the Russian delegates might give British socialists a bad name.

Fels stipulated, too, that the remaining delegates should sign the agreement to accept the money – not all of them did – and that the loan should be repaid by or on 1 January 1908. It wasn't. Joseph Fels died in 1914. Eight years later, in 1922, the repayment was made to Fels' widow by the Soviet Trade Delegation in London.

Much had happened during those fifteen years in which the loan had been outstanding. In 1907 the Russian Social Democrats had been small and divided, facing the powerful Czarist regime. By 1922, Lenin's Bolsheviks controlled one of the largest countries in the world.

Who could have guessed that this same party and its leaders, for whom London had been such an important venue, would in the years after 1917 exert an immense influence on the development of the British Left?

# 3

# Socialism and the New Life

## Standards and Double Standards

'In looking into matters social and political I have but one rule, that in thinking of the condition of any body of men I shall ask myself "How could you bear it yourself? What would you feel if you were poor against the system under which you live?"'

WILLIAM MORRIS, IN A LETTER OF 1883

'The aim of socialism is to substitute the word "ours" for the words "mine" and "thine".'

ROBERT BLATCHFORD

'I do not want the movement to be a depository of old cranks, humanitarians, vegetarians, anti-vivisectionists and anti-vaccinationists, party-craftys and all the rest of them, we are scientific socialists and have no room for sentimentalists. They confuse the issue.'

H.M. HYNDMAN

In January 1889 a young woman called Marjorie Davidson, a member of the Fabian Society, was planning to set up home with another Fabian. It was a venture fraught with difficulty for a young, self-conscious and wealthy socialist. She asked George Bernard Shaw for his advice: 'We want to know what is the ideal Socialist home – I don't think we ought to have servants but that is an open question.' Another Fabian, Sidney Olivier, suggested that 'the [house] work should be done by unmarried relations.' The Oliviers themselves kept servants but insisted that they ate together with the family – apparently to the acute embarrassment of all.

The problems of everyday life troubled many of Britain's pioneer socialists. How should their high political ideals be translated into their personal lives? How to create a 'Fellowship of the New Life', as the Fabians had originally been called? Some, such as the Webbs, H.M. Hyndman and Edward Carpenter, possessed substantial private incomes and often felt guilty at their affluence, particularly when so many of the working class whose cause they championed lived in abysmal physical conditions. No one seems to have emulated St Francis of Assisi and simply given away their money.

William Morris was another well-off socialist who was often confronted with this question at public meetings. He replied:

> I am not a rich man, but even if I were to give all my money away, what good would that do? The poor would be just as poor, the rich, perhaps, a little more rich, for my wealth would finally get into their hands. The world would be pleased to talk about me for three days until something new caught its fancy. Even if Rothschild gave away his millions tomorrow, the same problems would confront us the day after.

No doubt Morris has a point – but, even so, I suspect that the moral standing of socialism would rise no end if there were a few more 'three-day wonders'.

A further problem was that the burning desire to bring about social justice often made individuals difficult to live with. John Trevor, the founder of the Labour Church in 1891, commented upon the paradox in his autobiography:

> What fate is it that makes some of us so uncomfortable to live with and work with; and, by burdening us with ideas [of making the world a better place], makes us such a burden to those who look to us for support and comfort? Is it not possible to reform the world without all this sacrifice of peace and happiness?

Trevor went on to answer his own question: 'No. There is no other way.'

But what did socialists see as being so wrong with 'the Old Life'? In 1916 Edward Carpenter received an address on his seventieth birthday which had been signed by many distinguished friends. In his reply, he looked back and identified everything that he deplored in the nineteenth century. He lambasted:

> ... the Victorian Age, which in some respects, one now thinks, marked the lowest ebb of modern civilised society: a period in which not only commercialism in public life, but cant in religion, pure materialism in science, futility in social conventions, the worship of stocks and shares, the starving of the human heart, the denial of the human body and its needs, the huddling concealment of the body in clothes, the 'impure hush' on matters of sex, class-division, contempt of manual labour, and the cruel barring of women from every natural and useful expression of their lives, were carried to an extremity of folly difficult for us now to realise.

This is certainly a pretty comprehensive list of failings! Carpenter's complaints covered both society and 'the human heart'. But how did socialists propose to change matters?

None of the left-wing traditions discussed so far offered any guidance about moral issues. Neither Keir Hardie's 'labourism', nor Hyndman's Marxists, nor Lenin's revolutionary élite showed much interest in the personal or subjective characteristics of political activity. Instead they all tended to argue that political power was the overwhelming necessity, coming well before the need to sit around debating individual morality. 'For the greater good' (of whichever party or group) could easily sanction all kinds of appalling human behaviour. Each of these traditions was associated with 'bigness', with the large and often difficult concept of 'class', 'mass' and 'state' – none of which gave a meaning to people's existence or offered much practical help. 'Socialism' could often seem alien and intimidating.

Some groups advocated 'the religion of socialism', the title of several books and pamphlets published in the 1880s and 1890s. In his newspaper, *Clarion*, Robert Blatchford explained the impulse behind this phrase: 'If Socialism is to live and conquer, it must be a religion . . . If Socialists are to prove themselves equal to the task assigned to them, they must have a faith, a real faith, a new faith.'

This faith centred above all on the building of 'a New Jerusalem', a new, fair and just society for everyone. It is no coincidence that many socialists spoke of their 'conversion' to socialism or, in William Morris' even more striking phrase, crossing 'the river of fire'. John Trevor likewise described the effects of Blatchford's book *Merrie England* in making converts to 'a new life': 'Their eyes shine with the gladness of a new birth.'

This faith has sometimes been called 'Christian Socialism' but, comprising so many different ideas and beliefs, it defies labels. Some claimed inspiration from Jesus Christ – Keir Hardie, for example, thought that Christ's Sermon on the Mount summed up communism. Others looked back to the radical priest John Ball, one of the leaders of the Peasants' Revolt in 1381, who wrote:

When Adam delved and Eve span
Who was then the gentleman?

In other words, because there were neither servants nor classes in the Garden of Eden these must therefore be man-made and, if so, could be 'man unmade'. The clarity of John Ball's language was echoed in the lengthy struggle to have the Bible translated from Latin into English. This campaign gave the radical movement, until recently, a longstanding association with plain speech.

In the late nineteenth century socialist churchmen began to form themselves into groups and organisations. One of the most important was the Guild of St Matthew, founded in 1877 by Stewart Headlam. He had experienced a traditional

Establishment education at Eton and then Trinity College, Cambridge. At university he came under the influence of F.D. Maurice, an early Christian Socialist, who had lost his professorship at London University because he doubted the doctrine of everlasting damnation for sinners. Headlam's early years in the church were spent in the poorer parts of London, and it was while he was at St Matthew's, Bethnal Green, that his ideas began to coalesce. He stressed the practical aspects of Christianity:

> I have always deprecated other-worldliness, as it is called, morbid concern about self, hysterical visions of Heaven, as though earth were a place to be despaired of. I have always talked of the Kingdom of Heaven being fulfilled here and now on earth, and deprecated too much dwelling on a future life, fortified by the fact that Christ Himself said very little about the other world, and very much about this.

To Stewart Headlam, the New Jerusalem was a living, realistic possibility.

In 1884 the Guild of St Matthew adopted more explicitly socialist aims. As this was some months before Hyndman founded the Social Democratic Federation (SDF), the Guild can claim to be Britain's first socialist organisation. A resolution passed by the Guild at a meeting in Trafalgar Square in October 1884 reveals the trenchant thrust of its policies:

> Whereas the present contrast between the great body of the workers who produce much and consume little, and of those classes which produce little and consume much is contrary to the Christian doctrine of brotherhood and justice, this meeting urges on all Churchmen the duty of supporting such measures as will tend – a) To restore to the people the value which they give to the land; b) to bring about a better distribution of the wealth created by labour; c) to give the whole body of the people a voice in their own government; d) to abolish false standards of worth and dignity.

This was strong meat for Headlam's superior, the Bishop of London. Headlam made himself even more unpopular by setting up the Church and Stage Guild in order to foster closer relationships between the two professions. At a time when the Church still regarded actresses and music-hall performers as little better than prostitutes, Headlam's licence to preach was promptly withdrawn. In other words, he was sacked.

The only prominent public figure to stand by Oscar Wilde during the dramatist's trial and imprisonment, Headlam devoted the rest of his life to his work as a London County Councillor and a member of the London School Board, struggling to improve the capital's standard of education. He died in 1924. Although the Guild of St Matthew was never large numerically – at its peak in 1895 it had no more than 364 members – it was important in attempting to relate socialism to everyday life.

At the same time, other churchmen also began to question the direction of the Anglican church. Many were 'ritualists' or from the High Church wing and they stressed the importance of the sacraments. More importantly for society as a whole, these priests were determined to share the suffering of their parishioners and so they moved to poor urban districts. Among them were Father Lowder who built a church in Wapping, London, and Father Dolling at St Agatha's in the slums of Portsmouth.

Several socialist groups expressed themselves in religious terms while remaining outside the organised churches. For example, the Labour Church had its own rituals and conduct and was likened to 'a kind of Socialist Salvation Army'. Likewise the Socialist Sunday School movement founded in 1892; their activities included much singing and dancing as well as the learning off by heart of the Socialist Ten Commandments. The First Commandment, for instance, read: 'Love your schoolfellows who will be your fellow-workmen in life.' Singing was regarded as particularly important in the early days because, as one socialist remembered, it 'made us feel that we were not solitary but in the great accord of the brotherhood of mankind.'

This tradition of Christian Socialism often surfaced in meetings of the first Labour Party branches, some of which started or ended with the hymn 'When Wilt Thou Save the People, Lord?' The labour movement's subsequent immersion in electoral politics, winning parliamentary and council elections and raising the money to run a party machine, did dissipate this 'religion of socialism'. The practicalities of day-to-day organisation often elbowed out the spiritual dimension.

But not entirely. Certainly when comparing the British labour movement with its European counterparts, one striking difference is the British emphasis on ethical rather than purely materialist issues. William Blake's poem *Jerusalem* is one of the most quoted of them all. Hugh Gaitskell, leader of the Labour Party in the 1950s and early 1960s, once lamented that he was the head of a religious movement rather than a political party.

The controversy over Gaitskell's attempt to drop Clause Four from the Labour Party constitution following the election defeat of 1959 was, as his biographer noted, 'studded with biblical terminology'. Participants talked of Tablets of Stone, the Ark of the Covenant, the 39 Articles, the Old and the New Testaments and so on. Even Harold Wilson, shortly to put himself forward as the technocrat par excellence, felt moved to describe Clause Four as the Party's 'Book of Genesis'.

Tony Benn is another leading figure who continually emphasises the religious contribution to the British labour movement, once claiming in the House of Commons that socialism emanated from the passage in Genesis when Cain asked: 'Am I my brother's keeper?' More recently, as we shall see, both John Smith and Tony Blair have been explicit in their avowal of Christian Socialism.

It is impossible to understand the British Left without recognising how this important spiritual heritage has moulded native radicalism. As a result, 'labourism' has a character and set of values different from those that prevail in most other European countries.

Although the religion of socialism offered many telling moral criticisms of Victorian capitalism, it was rather less convincing when portraying what kind of society might take its place. Generalised benevolence and exhortations to 'love thy neighbour' were often about as far as it went. This lack of precision was evident in books by two influential late-Victorian socialists, William Morris and Robert Blatchford.

Both the works, *News from Nowhere* (1890) and *The Sorcery Shop* (1907), are categorised as 'Utopias', members of the tradition established by Thomas More's original book *Utopia*, written in the early sixteenth century. More's book depicts an idealised society some time in the future, implicitly criticising the contemporary reality which surrounded him. The word 'utopia' itself comes from the fusion of two Greek words meaning 'no place', suggesting that More had a fairly realistic estimation of the likelihood that such a society would ever be achieved.

Karl Marx disliked Utopias for being unscientific and a waste of time. William Morris was more perceptive in realising that most people, working on the theory of 'better the devil you know than the devil you don't', are unlikely to welcome widespread social and political change unless it offers them something appreciably better than the present. His *News from Nowhere* was written in the hope of inspiring people to work for radical improvements in society. As Fiona MacCarthy, his most recent biographer, has commented, 'Morris releases the imagination by suggesting that another form of society is *possible*. For people suffering political stagnation – then and now – it points to a way out.'

However it is noticeable that Morris skates over some of the problems which have plagued human life from the beginning. In *Nowhere*, for instance, we are simply told that the instinct for 'manslaughter' and crime has been bred out of human beings. There are no laws, no buying or selling, no paid work, no government, no prisons and no private property. Morris explains in his story that 'the great change' came about in 1952 (ironically enough, one year after a Labour government was in fact turned out of office by Winston Churchill's Conservatives).

A prohibited march sparks off a train of events that leads to a massacre in Trafalgar Square, a General Strike and the eventual assumption of power by the ominously named Committee of Public Safety. From then on, we are told, people simply cast off their antisocial attitudes and behaviour prevalent under the previous regime. Morris gleefully describes a London in which the Houses of Parliament contain a dung market (he was never a great believer in parliamentary change!), apricot trees grow in Trafalgar Square, and the East End has been cleared of its slums.

The egalitarian society depicted in *News from Nowhere* is, on the face of it, a surprising fantasy to have been created by a Victorian whose early life was a pattern of nineteenth-century bourgeois respectability. Morris was born in Walthamstow, London, in 1834. His father was a City stockbroker who sent his son to Marlborough public school and then Oxford, where he originally intended to enter the Church.

At Oxford, however, Morris was influenced by the writings of the critic John Ruskin and rebelled against what he thought of as the ugly and philistine Victorian machine-made culture. In reaction, he looked back towards the sense of community and wholeness which in his imagination characterised fourteeth-century England – it is no coincidence that the inhabitants of Nowhere wear medieval costume.

Morris started to write poetry, displaying a fierce Romantic spirit in such works as *The Life and Death of Jason* and *The Defence of Guenevere* whose aspirations and ideals seemed at odds with Victorian gentility and commericalism. His growing hostility towards his own part of society did not remain simply as words on a page. He was, above all, a man of action whose remarkable energy drove him to explore many different fields of activity, as poet, designer, artist and socialist. In his own words, 'To do nothing but grumble and not to act – that is throwing away one's life.' As Asa Briggs once commented, 'He was an angry young man and an angry old man, but he always knew what he was angry about.'

In part Morris' abundant energies were a displacement from his unhappy marriage. The beautiful Jane Burden, archetypal model for so many Pre-Raphaelite paintings, produced two daughters but she and Morris were clearly out of sympathy with each other, as almost every visitor to their home noticed. The vivacity of Morris, always talking, his hands never still, was in no way compatible with the self-absorption of Jane. She subsequently fell in love with the painter and poet Dante Gabriel Rossetti, a liaison which Morris accepted but which brought him much pain. Clearly the idealised figure of Ellen in *News from Nowhere* has a great deal of wish fulfilment about it.

Everyone respected Morris' seeming omniscience, but equally admirable was his sincere desire to share his insights. A workman once charmingly said of a boat trip down the Clyde with Morris that it was 'as good as a university education'. Neither was he an intellectual snob. George Bernard Shaw described visiting a police station where Morris was bailing out colleagues arrested during a free speech demonstration. Amid the inevitable delays, Morris, oblivious to the noise and bustle about him, sat on the floor reading Dumas' novel *The Three Musketeers* 'for the hundredth time or so'.

By no means a saint, Morris was renowned for his volcanic outbursts of temper. He once threw an employee guilty of bad workmanship into a vat of dye. One sympathetic critic suggests that the explanation for these rages may lie in some form of epilepsy. It is also reassuring that Morris could not do everything brilliantly. He was a poor public speaker and sometimes vented his frustration in scornful comments about his audience. In his diary for January 1881, for example, he gave a talk at the Hammersmith Radical Club and called the audience 'a very discouraging set of men'. He then went on to castigate 'the frightful ignorance of English workmen'.

Morris' experience of shoddy Victorian workmanship first came in 1856 when he and his friend Edward Burne-Jones shared a flat together in Red Lion Square, London. So dissatisfied was Morris with the quality of furniture available for sale that he designed his own. When he married Jane in 1859, Morris asked another friend, the architect Philip Webb, to build him a house in Bexley Heath, Kent. It is known as the Red House because of Webb's lavish use of red brick. Again Morris designed his own furniture and two years later, in 1861, founded the firm which later became Morris and Co.

Morris wanted this firm to be run on the lines of the old medieval guilds so that workers could participate in every aspect of production, rather than experiencing the division of labour characteristic of capitalism under which labourers repeated the same tasks over and over again. He deliberately did not expand the company beyond about one hundred employees and led the firm with such success that its stained glass, furniture, embroidery and patterns for wallpapers are still much admired in homes today. This practical achievement gives even more force to Morris' economic and political ideas, proving that he was not simply an armchair theorist.

Similarly Morris never forgot that his privileged position entailed duties and obligations: '. . . it was my good luck only of being born respectable and rich, that has put me on this side of the window among delightful books and lovely works of art, and not on the other side, in the empty street, the drink-steeped liquor shops, the foul and degraded lodgings.' His active political involvement began in the 1870s when he became increasingly disenchanted with the Liberal Party's imperialist foreign policy. In January 1883 Morris joined Hyndman's Democratic Federation, becoming its treasurer and collaborating with Hyndman on the book *England for All*, published the next year.

Despite his best intentions, however, Morris' restless individualism meant that he was never really a party man, as is shown by his unsuccessful record in terms of practical politics. He soon clashed with Hyndman and in late 1884 left to form the Socialist League which, even at the height of its influence, never had more than seven hundred members.

Much of the League's time was spent debating the question whether socialists should actually work through the parliamentary process at all. He spent a lot of money – up to £500 a year – on the weekly magazine *Commonweal*. Within a couple of years the Socialist League was taken over by the anarchists and Morris left his own creation. In the opening pages of *Nowhere* he satirises the sectarian rivalries and squabbles which preoccupied the League (and much of the British Left): 'there were six persons present, and consequently six sections of the party were represented . . .'

Morris carried out this political work entirely selflessly. He had nothing to gain from the undertaking and much to lose, especially as 'I dread a quarrel above all things . . .' His name was proposed in 1892 as a possible Poet Laureate to succeed Tennyson, but his socialist views ruled him out. It took courage to argue for his convictions in a society where socialism was derided and often provoked physical attack. Morris' letters are full of reports of his being heckled, jeered and manhandled. He even called for 'some organised body guard round the speaker when we speak in doubtful places.'

From 1892 Morris confined his political activities to the Hammersmith Socialist Society which met in the converted coach house of his beautiful home, Kelmscott House, overlooking the Thames. This Society was intended to be a debating group, and it attracted G.B. Shaw, H.G. Wells, who typically flaunted his radicalism by wearing a bright red tie, Oscar Wilde and W.B. Yeats. Morris also showed he was not one to bear grudges by helping out his former rival, Hyndman, advancing the £50 guarantee for the first year of the Twentieth Century Press, the SDF's printing press, when it moved into 37 Clerkenwell Green in 1893.

What was Morris' legacy to future generations? Well, it is certainly diverse and wide ranging – his daughter May once observed that 'My father never takes any recreation, he merely changes his work.' Engels might have referred to Morris as 'hopelessly muddle-headed' and 'a settled sentimental Socialist' but later Marxists have claimed him as one of their own. So too have ethical socialists. And in 1935 an article actually appeared in the *Fascist Weekly* asserting that Morris was a forerunner of fascism because he was supposedly 'imbued with the Viking spirit'!

Leaving aside his political influence, he had a profound effect on British and European design. He was concerned too with the environment. In 1877 Morris formed the Society for the Preservation of Ancient Buildings (SPAB) which tried to prevent the wholesale vandalism that some Victorian architects wreaked on old buildings. SPAB can be seen as the first of the conservation bodies which subsequently included the National Trust, the Georgian Society, the Victorian Society and English Heritage. A striking passage from a speech given at SPAB's annual meeting in 1889 summed up his position:

> It has been most truly said . . . that these old buildings do not belong to us only; that they have belonged to our forefathers and they will belong to our descendants unless we play them false. They are not in any sense our property, to do as we like with them. We are only trustees for those who come after us.

In another lecture Morris inveighed against 'litter bugs' with heavy irony: 'When we Londoners go to enjoy ourselves at Hampton Court, for instance, we take special good care to let everybody know that we have had something to eat: so that the park just outside the gates (and a beautiful place it is) looks as if it had been snowing paper.' Like William Blake, he hated 'dark satanic mills' and invited his readers to 'dream of London, small, and white, and clean . . .'

His insistence that work should be fun rather than some sort of punishment for the privilege of living also strikes a modern chord. Morris and Co. emphasised that, wherever possible, workers should experience the whole production process as they had done in the Middle Ages. Morris was not 'Luddite' in his attitude towards machines; he never rejected them entirely but believed they should be the slaves and not the masters.

The drawback of this ideal – and it is one which still remains – is that beautiful, hand-made items are inevitably expensive so just the wealthy can afford them. Only mass production can supply enough commodities for mass consumption. He once mischievously claimed that 'There are no greater fools than the rich who buy my wall-papers – except for those who don't!' At least Morris' workforce was better treated than in most Victorian businesses (except perhaps for the workman thrown into the vat).

Morris also stressed the quality of life: what he called 'the art of living', deriving his views from Ruskin's dictum that 'There is no wealth but life'. He loved laughter and fellowship and scorned puritanism. This question of just how human beings should treat each other is one which has interested few socialists before or since. Whereas the legacy of some early British socialists seems today to be of marginal importance only, the ideas of Morris have grown in relevance since his death in 1896. Time and time again, Morris' name will crop up in the following pages.

Robert Blatchford's book *The Sorcery Shop* was subtitled 'An Impossible Romance'. It depicts a world with no money or guns, no government, no meat, no alcohol, no tobacco, no schools, no political parties, no army, no legal system, no religion. In the absence of all these activities, it is difficult to see quite how Blatchford's Utopian inhabitants occupy themselves, other than by playing cricket – one of his own passions.

Like *Nowhere*, there is a complete absence of conflict and no sense of how either Utopia planned to deal with individual differences, whether it be in terms of intelligence, appearance, strength and so on. But it is less this book that made Blatchford so influential than a work with the quaint title *Merrie England*.

Today, Robert Blatchford is a forgotten figure. No plaques or statues commemorate the man who was probably the most successful British socialist spokesman of all time. 'For every convert made by *Das Kapital*, there were a hundred made by *Merrie England*' was the *Manchester Guardian*'s verdict on Blatchford's most famous book, which sold a staggering total of over two million copies in Britain and around the world. It has recently been described as perhaps 'the most effective ever [socialist] propaganda'.

Remarkably, this success was achieved without any advertising and with few reviews. The book consists of a series of letters addressed by Blatchford to 'John Smith', an imaginary factory worker in Oldham, 'a hard-headed workman, fond of facts', explaining why he should be a socialist. It was an unlikely publication for a man who had had little schooling and spent seven years as a regular soldier in the British Army.

Blatchford was born in 1851, the son of unsuccessful actors. The early death of his father meant that the family was always perched on the breadline. Apprenticed to a brush-maker in Halifax, he stuck the job for six years but then ran away, ending up in the army. He left after seven years, married his childhood sweetheart and worked in a factory. Writing articles in his spare time and painstakingly copying out a dictionary in order to expand his vocabulary, he immediately displayed a strong gift for journalism and joined the group of newspapers run by Edward Hulton. Blatchford then researched and wrote a series on the slums of Manchester, and what he saw made him a socialist.

The increasingly radical tone of Blatchford's articles caused mounting friction with Hulton and in October 1891 he left to set up his own newspaper, the *Clarion,* a weekly which became one of the British Left's most influential and best-loved publications. It was a risky project. Blatchford, his artist brother Montagu and two fellow journalists, A.M. Thompson and Edward Fay, only just managed to raise the necessary £400 capital.

From the first the *Clarion* dispensed with heavy theory and abstract language. Written in a style which welcomed rather than alienated readers, the newspaper's slogan was 'instructive without being dry, and amusing without being vulgar'. Its brand of socialism extolled happiness; as Margaret Cole once noted, 'it made Socialism seem as simple and universal as a pint of bitter.'

The *Clarion* represented the adventurous and devil-may-care strand within British socialism, very different from the puritan and earnest stance of Keir Hardie's *Labour Leader.* The *Clarion's* wide range of interests is vividly shown by its own advertisement which called the paper 'an illustrated weekly journal of Literature, Politics, Fiction, Philosophy, Theatricals, Pastimes, Criticism, and everything else'. There's not much left out there! As Blatchford once declared: 'If I desired to rouse a people, the figures I should deal in mostly would be figures of speech. Economics are for the very few, God's love is for the many.'

The *Clarion* also created its own powerful cultural movement. Like William Morris, Blatchford was keen on the idea of 'fellowship' and he initiated Clarion Scouts, Clarion Vocal Unions, Clarion Glee Clubs, Clarion Clubhouses, Clarion Handicraft Guilds, Clarion Field Clubs and a National Clarion Cycling Club. Clarion Vans travelled the country – six were in existence by 1908 – setting up in market squares and on village greens and trying to convert bystanders to the joys of socialism. The movement even had its own language dubbed 'Clarionese'. Crucially, the Clarion Fellowship exhibited a tolerance and humour that has not always characterised the British Left.

Blatchford's writings proved all the more powerful because of the clarity and simplicity of his style. He never forgot his readers, always imagining them to be the soldiers with whom he had shared army life. In 1925 he published an excellent book called *English Prose and How to Write It*, advising writers 'never to use a long word if a short one will do. The one-syllable words are the backbone of our language.' He went on, 'clear writing requires clear thinking' and urged 'Study the comfort of your reader.' Unfortunately, Blatchford's suggestions were disregarded by many later socialist writers.

But style without content is not much good either, and the quality of Blatchford's writing does not disguise the fact that the Clarion movement was stronger on emotion and rhetoric than analysis or prescription. Blatchford admitted as much in *Merrie England*: 'The establishment and organisation of a Socialistic State are the two branches of the work to which I have given least attention.'

Take the vagueness of his reply to the question of how socialism will come about. 'Let people desire it,' said Blatchford, 'and I am sure we may safely leave them to secure it' – not a very helpful response. To the enquiry how this socialist state will operate in practice, Blatchford returns an answer which reminds one of the bureaucratic élitism of some Fabian plans: 'Just get a number of your cleverest organisers and administrators into committee and let them formulate a scheme.' This shows a touching faith in committees, but Blatchford actually loathed them.

The *Clarion*'s circulation settled at about 60,000 copies a week. The newspaper very much reflected Blatchford's personality and his patriotic support for the British Army during the Boer War alienated some readers, as did his campaign against orthodox religion. But until 1914 *Clarion* remained a distinctive and important mouthpiece for British socialism. Blatchford's hostility towards the German Army led him, like Hyndman, to support the First World War and in effect destroyed his left-wing standing.

The *Clarion* limped on until 1934 with dwindling influence and readership. His adored wife Sally died in 1921. Blatchford lived in retirement in Sussex, writing novels and an attractive autobiography titled *My Eighty Years*. He died in 1943, aged ninety-two.

Despite his many admirable qualities, Blatchford's writings remain very much of their period and do not have the universality which would make them of lasting value. It is this, perhaps, which explains his long neglect. Nevertheless, in his life and in his work he exemplified immediacy, humour, toleration and fun – qualities which will win more hearts than the most rigorous theory is ever likely to do.

The labour movement has always been split between those who argue that socialism should first and foremost be about freedom and happiness, and those who maintain that pleasure is a diversion until radical political and economic change has been implemented. This division is best illustrated by comparing two contemporaries, Victor Grayson and Keir Hardie. It is hardly surprising that they disliked each other. As we have seen, Grayson was all for enjoying life and had nothing but 'contempt for the crank socialists who believe that collectivism means living on cabbages and carrots and drinking cold water'.

Hardie, on the other hand, thought that 'Socialism is a serious task, demanding serious work at the hands of its advocates, and anything which introduces levity or frivolity into the movement is hindering, not helping, its progress.' Following his example, in 1918 the Scottish conference of the Labour Party actually voted for the prohibition of alcohol.

Tension between the two camps was even more apparent over sexual questions. Many socialists naturally rationalised their own experiences. H.M. Hyndman and Robert Blatchford both enjoyed happy marriages and were strongly in favour of monogamy. H.G. Wells delighted in making love to different women and so he argued in his novel *The New Machiavelli* (1911) that the élite (which naturally included himself) should be allowed to enjoy the pleasures of free love.

Double standards were endemic. Most Victorian socialists argued, at least in theory, for equality between the sexes, but somehow this demand often got lost. An early draft for the Charter in the 1830s had called for the vote for both men and women over the age of twenty-one, but more cautious voices claimed that this was impractical and so 'male persons' only appeared in the Six Points – even though the Chartist and historian R.G. Gammage thought that women were even more enthusiastic for the Charter than men.

Others had no standards at all, reflecting the masculinity of the labour movement. Raphael Samuel once accurately commented that 'Socialism, after all, was conceived as a movement of working *men*, and it is evident that male bonding, and the exclusion of women, was one of the very principles of trade unionism.' Women were seen largely as passive beings whose main role was domestic; their grievances were deemed secondary to the concerns of male trade unionists.

Marked inequality existed in the home too. Not until the Married Women's Property Act of 1870 did a wife retain ownership of her own property on marriage. Or else women and girls were sex objects. Child prostitution was rife – only in 1885 was the age of consent raised from thirteen to sixteen. Precisely what this narrow role meant for women in personal terms is conveyed by Edward Carpenter whose autobiography gave a chilling picture of the futility of his sisters' lives in Victorian England:

> . . . there were six or seven servants in the house, and my six sisters had absolutely nothing to do except dabble in paints and music as aforesaid, and wander aimlessly from room to room to see if by any chance 'anything was going on'. Dusting,

cooking, sewing, darning – all light household duties were already forestalled; there was no private garden, and if there had been it would have been 'unladylike' to do anything in it; *every* girl could not find an absorbing interest in sol-fa or water-colours; athletics were not invented; every aspiration and outlet, except in the direction of dress and dancing, was blocked; and marriage, with the growing scarcity of men, was becoming every day less likely, or easy to compass. More than once girls of whom I least expected it told me that their lives were miserable 'with nothing on earth to do'. Multiply this picture by thousands and hundreds of thousands all over the country, and it is easy to see how, when the causes of misery were understood, it led to the powerful growth of the modern 'Women's Movement'.

A handful of women did challenge this convention of passivity, encouraged by Ibsen's play *A Doll's House* which was first performed in this country in June 1889 and showed Nora slamming the door on her past life and going her own independent way. But the path of a pioneering woman in the late nineteenth century was not helped by the behaviour of many socialist men who acted more like traditional Casanovas or predators than comrades and helpmates. H.G. Wells, for instance, formed relationships with several women until they had children, whereupon he quickly fled back to the domestic comforts provided by his long-suffering wife Jane.

Similarly the Fabian Hubert Bland also had several affairs and actually founded an organisation which he called the Anti-Puritan League. Nevertheless when he learnt of his daughter's plan to elope with Wells, he pursued them like the typical outraged father and ended up punching Wells on the nose at Paddington Station!

SDF member, university lecturer and failed playwright Edward Aveling was another energetic philanderer, in spite of his somewhat unprepossessing appearance. Hyndman said that Aveling 'needed but half an hour's start of the handsomest man in London . . .' to make a woman fall in love with him. He lived for several years with Eleanor Marx, youngest daughter of Karl and herself an active participant in the Dock Strike of 1889, systematically filching her inheritance. When she found out that Aveling had in fact secretly married another woman, she killed herself.

One woman who did remain true to her own star was Annie Besant, organiser of the matchgirls' strike in 1888. A fascinating character, Besant's energy and curiosity led her to sample virtually every philosophy of life then available, as Yvonne Kapp has marvelled: '. . . she ran the whole gamut from established religion, through High Church Anglicanism, the Oxford Movement, Theism, Atheism, Malthusianism, Radicalism, Science, Philanthropy, Fabianism, Feminism and Socialism to Theosophy.' In a ten-year period she produced fifty-one books and pamphlets as well as giving hundreds of lectures. That many of the philosophies Besant embraced were seen as heretical by the orthodox was symptomatic of the growing revolt against conventional thought.

She was born Annie Wood in 1847. Her father died when she was a young girl and Annie developed a fierce determination to work things out for herself. Yet in her youth she held romantic Victorian views on the appeal of clergymen as marriage partners: 'To me a priest was a half-angelic creature, whose whole life was consecrated to heaven . . .' Unfortunately, the clergyman she chose to marry after a whirlwind courtship, a Reverend Frank Besant, was in reality a thoroughly unappealing man 'with very high ideas of a husband's authority and a wife's submission.' She was horrified to discover the sexual aspects of marriage, writing in her autobiography that she had 'no more idea of the marriage relation than if I had been four years old instead of twenty.'

Though they had a son and a daughter, the marriage was unhappy almost from the start. When their baby girl Mabel fell seriously ill, Annie nursed her but the sight of the small child's pain turned her decisively against the idea of a God: 'There had grown up in my mind a feeling of angry resentment against the God who had been for weeks, as I thought, torturing my helpless baby.' She left both the Church and her husband. He kept custody of the son, she of the daughter.

Annie Besant then met the popular free-thought lecturer Charles Bradlaugh who was separated from his alcoholic wife. Bradlaugh and Besant were simply good friends, though inevitably the gossips and scandalmongers got to work. As Annie put it, 'the mere fact that a woman is young and alone justifies any coarseness of slander.' She and Bradlaugh spent the next few years touring the country lecturing on secularism, which in the 1870s was yet another ingredient in the revolt against conventional Victorian thought. Stick-wielding and stone-throwing mobs sometimes broke up their lectures.

In 1877 she and Bradlaugh found themselves in court on the charge of selling an obscene pamphlet. Called *Fruits of Philosophy*, this publication had been published forty years before by an American called Dr Knowlton. One section contained some elementary suggestions about birth control, such as withdrawal before ejaculation. Bradlaugh and Besant favoured birth control, as they explained in their *Preface* to Knowlton's pamphlet: 'We think it more moral to prevent the conception of children, than, after they are born, to murder them by want of food, air, and clothing.'

After a celebrated trial, both of them were found guilty of publishing a book calculated to deprave public morals but the verdict, a severe one carrying a fine and imprisonment, was quashed on appeal over a technicality. This did not stop Reverend Frank Besant, Annie's estranged husband, from seizing custody of their daughter Mabel on the grounds of Annie's way of life: 'the little child was carried away by main force, shrieking and struggling, still weak from the fever, and nearly frantic with fear and passionate resistance.' Both son and daughter returned to Annie when they came of age.

In the 1880s Annie helped Bradlaugh in his struggle to take up his seat in the House of Commons as the Radical MP for Northampton. As a free-thinker, he claimed the right when taking his seat to affirm rather than swearing the oath. The Speaker refused to allow this and excluded Bradlaugh from sittings. On one occasion, in 1881, ten policemen were required to remove the burly Bradlaugh. Four times he was excluded, but three times the electors of Northampton returned him. Finally, in 1886, Bradlaugh was allowed to take up his seat by a new Speaker and in 1888 the Oaths Act permitted affirmation in both the House of Commons and in the law courts.

By the middle of the 1880s Annie had become a socialist, which Bradlaugh was not – he once referred to the socialist movement as being made up of 'poets and fools' – and their friendship cooled, although forty years later Annie still kept many photographs of him on the walls of her home. She sat on the executive of the Fabian Society and agitated on behalf of sections of the workforce such as the matchgirls. Interestingly enough Besant's socialism, like that of Hyndman and Blatchford, was precipitated by her shock on visiting England's slums.

To her mind, however, socialism lacked a vital spiritual dimension. In 1889 she reviewed two books by Madame Blavatsky, the leader of the Theosophy movement, a creed popular in the late nineteenth century. Annie visited India and found its peace and tranquillity so affecting that she decided to move there permanently. This was by no means the end of her public career. She dedicated herself to the Indian independence movement and was briefly interned by the British authorities in 1917 because of her activities. Annie Besant died in India in 1933.

Outstanding women in public life such as Annie Besant might have been exemplary but they were, of course, exceptions. It was essential to develop a strong collective voice. One who tried was Emma Paterson, the founder of the Women's Trade Union League in 1874. The TUC voted in favour of female suffrage from 1884 and its Congress four years later stated that 'where women do the same work as men they shall receive equal pay.' On the Left, Hyndman's Social Democratic Federation (SDF) and the Independent Labour Party (ILP) at its 1894 Conference also demanded votes for women.

However, there was a marked reluctance to go beyond resolutions on paper and to incorporate 'women's issues' into their programmes and day-to-day activities. Some leading socialists strongly opposed such ideas. Belfort Bax, for instance, was an important figure within Hyndman's SDF. Not content with being a member of the Men's Anti-Suffrage League, he actually argued that women were inferior beings because they had smaller brains. Hyndman himself held that women advocating emancipation 'ought to be sent to an island by themselves'. Even William Morris thought that, 'Of course we must claim absolute equality of condition between women and men, as between other groups, but it would be poor economy setting women to do men's work (as unluckily they often do now) or vice versa.'

The scale of the inequality is graphically shown by comparing the wages of men and women before the First World War. In Sheila Rowbotham's words:

> In 1906 the average wage of the male worker in Britain was around 30s a week. Women's rates were well below this. Textile workers were among the best-paid women, and had a long tradition of unionisation. They earned about 18s 8d in this period. But women in the linen and silk trades, in glass making and in printing earned only half this amount. Below these came the home-workers. A woman carding hooks and eyes at home could earn 5s a week if she worked eighteen hours a day.

Much early union activity centred on the struggle to organise women shopworkers, a particularly exploited group of workers. This is how the gifted Mary Macarthur began. In 1903 she became the secretary of the Women's Trade Union League and in just two years raised its membership from 14,000 to 70,000, as well as finding the time to edit the *Woman Worker*.

But it was always an uphill struggle, as one contemporary study of women made clear when it listed six obstacles to organising women into trade unions: the character of women's work; low wages; the delay in recognising women on the part of men's trade unions; antagonism on the part of employers; the 'broken term' of industrial life; and, finally, tradition.

Frustration at the male socialist groups' indifference was one reason why Mrs Emmeline Pankhurst, a member of both the Independent Labour Party and the Fabians, set up the Women's Social and Political Union (WSPU) in 1903, the main suffragette body. The suffragettes were noted for the extraordinary range of their activities, from colourful marches and rallies to bands, theatre groups and art exhibitions as well as their weekly newspaper *Votes for Women*.

Male support for the suffragette movement, especially from many men associated with active suffragettes, seems to have been patchy. Hannah Mitchell noted in her autobiography that her husband was a sympathiser, but only up to a point:

> . . . men are not so single-minded as women are; they are too much given to talking about their ideas, rather than working for them. Even as socialists they seldom translate their faith into words, being still conservatives at heart, especially where women are concerned. Most of us who were married found that 'Votes for Women' were of less interest to our husbands than their own dinners. They simply could not understand why we made such a fuss about it.

Hannah Mitchell's words could be quoted in every chapter of this book and be relevant to each of them.

The work of the WSPU was later overshadowed by their tactics of stone-throwing, arson and hunger strikes – emulating Mrs Pankhurst's belief that 'The argument of the broken window pane is the most valuable argument in modern politics.' Labour MPs were not averse to votes for women; Keir Hardie and George Lansbury in particular proved strong advocates of the cause. But in a two-party system where both major parties were against reform – the Conservatives on principle, the Liberals because they feared giving the vote to those they thought would vote Conservative – it was impossible for the suffragettes to succeed. Women (and even then not all of them) did not get the vote until after the First World War.

If life was difficult for women, it was certainly no easier for homosexuals. Not only were homosexual acts illegal but the full ferocity of Victorian feeling erupted during the trial of Oscar Wilde in 1895. Wilde's plays continued to run in London, but with the playwright's name stripped out. When George Bernard Shaw tried to put together a petition demanding the reprieve of Wilde, only the Reverend Stewart Headlam was brave enough to sign. It was Headlam who stood bail for Wilde and met him on his release from prison in May 1897. Wilde's long article *The Soul of Man under Socialism* was a typically idiosyncratic attack on some worrying tendencies in the labour movement: '. . . I confess that many of the socialistic views that I have come across seem to me to be tainted with ideas of authority, if not of actual compulsion.'

Some socialists abhorred homosexuality. Engels, for example, wrote of homosexual acts as 'gross, unnatural vices'. Others like George Bernard Shaw, despite his support for Wilde, counselled caution, urging that socialism should not get associated with this 'sex-nonsense' and that 'It doesn't help us in the movement to be mixed up with every new fangled idea.'

These Shavian remarks were expressed in letters to Edward Carpenter, one Victorian socialist who did advocate homosexual love. Like Robert Blatchford, Carpenter's name today is almost forgotten, but in his own time he was something of a guru, if only because he had the courage to try and live out his ideals in his own life rather than just writing about them. William Morris, for example, was a great admirer.

Born in 1844, Edward Carpenter spent an unhappy childhood in Brighton before going to Cambridge where he became a Fellow of his college and entered the Church. After several years of this cloistered existence, Carpenter's growing awareness of his own sexual preferences started to turn him against academic life and 'the ever-lasting discussions of theories which never came anywhere near actual life . . .'

Carpenter spent the next seven years as a university extension tutor in the north of England, lecturing mainly on astronomy. In 1883 he bought a cottage outside the village of Millthorpe in Derbyshire where he lived life as naturally as possible, growing his own food, dressing simply, writing in the mornings and making sandals for his friends. Millthorpe was not a successful commercial venture and without the legacy of £6,000 from his father's will Carpenter would never have survived.

He lived with a working-class man called George Merrill, his life-long companion until Merrill's death in 1928. It was brave of Carpenter to set up home with Merrill – several of his friends were horrified by the arrangement. Even more courage was needed to write the books he did, arguing there was no single type of male sexuality. Several publishers ran scared of his work after Oscar Wilde's trial and conviction, and sometimes Carpenter was forced to write in a deliberately oblique way. For instance, his book *Iolaus* (1902) is subtitled 'An Anthology of Friendship' but concentrates solely on male friendship.

One of Carpenter's most attractive qualities was his dislike of fixed rules. He was a vegetarian and teetotaller but not fanatically so. His friend Charles Sixsmith noted his feeling that, 'if rigid vegetarians and teetotallers would occasionally have a good fling and devour beef and drink beer it would do them a lot of good.' He also prized tenderness and sincerity, celebrating values which contradict the macho image of strength and brute force popular in some circles.

Carpenter embodied, too, the tolerant questioning of convention typical of much British socialism before 1914. He recognised by the 1920s, however, that the labour movement had taken a more orthodox and rigid path. His friend

E.M. Forster wrote a touching memorial after Carpenter's death in 1929: '. . . perhaps he never understood that for many people personal relationships are unimportant for the reason that their hearts are small. His own heart was great, and made him a great man.' The great-hearted Carpenter believed that at its core socialism must be about how human beings behave towards their fellow human beings.

The 'New Lifers' never really got to grips with two major problems. The first was how best to put across their ideas in an often hostile world. Blatchford, Carpenter and many others argued for simple persuasion and argument, for writing, lecturing, debating and personal example. But such methods reached only small numbers of people compared with, say, the mass circulation of the *Daily Mail* founded in 1896.

The other difficulty was that the New Lifers never specified how they would bring about change, nor what these changes in fact entailed. In part this arose from the almost bewildering variety of their ideas. This chapter alone has looked at individuals ranging from Stewart Headlam, William Morris and Robert Blatchford to Annie Besant, Charles Bradlaugh and Edward Carpenter, while the ideas and movements have included Christian Socialism, the Clarion movement, feminism, secularism and so on.

But in the face of sometimes vociferous public hostility, these New Lifers courageously highlighted various issues which today are far more acceptable. Take animal rights, for instance. In 1906 a handful of anti-vivisectionists put up a statue in Battersea Park in honour of a brown mongrel terrier which had been killed during experimental tests. The statue was promptly attacked by medical students during what were called the 'Brown Dog Riots'. The rioters succeeded in stealing the statue and then melting it down. In 1985, a new statue to the Brown Dog was erected.

Similarly the New Lifers tried to uphold the ideals of internationalism in the face of jingoist 'Little Englander' frenzies promoted by some sections of the popular press.

When writer and radical exile Sergius Stepniak was killed on a level-crossing in West London in 1895, his cremation drew such figures as William Morris, Keir Hardie and Eleanor Marx – and, even more impressively, tributes were paid to Stepniak in six different languages.

One characteristic common to these disparate ideas was the sense of fellowship they gave to often small groups of people: 'social-ism'. A future Labour Party leader and Prime Minister, Clement Attlee, an active member of the ILP in the East End of London before the 1914–18 war, once claimed that 'this spirit of exaltation' arose because 'We were crusaders in enemy-occupied country.'

W. Stephen Sanders, an early socialist, paid a lovely compliment to the unheralded members of these bodies in his autobiography *Early Socialist Days* (1927):

> I desire to pay a personal tribute to the unknown men and women, the rank and file of those early days, who gallantly played their parts in preparing the way for the great movement which now counts its adherents by the million. Recognition is due to those who formed the tiny nuclei at the open-air meetings, held the flag around which the audiences gathered, sold literature, made the modest collections, and cheerfully performed the arduous tasks of electioneering. They never spoke of burdens or self-sacrifice: to them work for the movement was a means of self-expression. In spite of quarrels, bitterness, weakness, personal failings – we were very human – and inadequacy of many kinds, their faces were towards the light, and they produced examples of courage in disheartening surroundings, unselfishness and loyalty to a cause, without expecting or receiving material reward: a firm faith in the abundant capacity of human nature to act from idealistic motives. To them, and the movement they helped to build, I owe a further gain: the discovery of a meaning and a purpose in the tangled medley of events we call life.

Sadly, after 1918 this tradition of pluralism, tolerance and of building a movement from the bottom up was largely, but not completely, squeezed between the pincer movement of labourism, concerned above all with electoral politics and the smooth running of a party machine, and Communism which sacrificed personal considerations to the demands of 'the Party'. The insights of individuals such as Stewart Headlam, Robert Blatchford and Edward Carpenter were forgotten.

Even the very idea of 'the New Life' was often scorned. In 1937 George Orwell, hardly the most conventional man himself, felt impelled to write in language similar to Hyndman's dismissive remarks quoted at the beginning of this chapter: 'One sometimes gets the impression that the mere words "Socialism" and "Communism" draw towards them with magnetic force every fruit-juice drinker, nudist, sandal-wearer, sex-maniac, Quaker, "Nature-cure" quack, pacifist and feminist in England . . .'

This was a sad and unjust comment. In the last twenty years several concerns which Orwell disparaged – the environment, natural medicine, women's issues – have forced themselves back into public consciousness. The whole 'New Age' movement has encouraged people to delve back into the past and discover that many of the ideas and individuals consigned to the dustbin of history by writers such as Orwell do in fact have a contemporary relevance.

As yet, Tony Blair's Labour Party, understandably motivated by the need to acquire political power, has paid only brief and passing attention to these hidden traditions. In which case, 'New Labour' is treading closely in the footsteps of Old Labour.

But this may well change. Tony Blair himself does not shy away from discussing ethical issues; his biographer John Rentoul recently observed that 'the redefinition of socialism as to do with moral rather than the material relationships between people is perhaps the most important philosophical change in the Labour Party since it was last in office. It was a change completed and made explicit by Blair.'

No one can be certain what the relationship should be and will be between libertarianism, economic growth and so on. These issues are discussed later, but it is revealing that they are now on the agenda. The New Lifers discussed in this chapter would feel exonerated.

# Tho' Cowards Flinch and Traitors Sneer

## The Rise and Fall of Ramsay MacDonald

'"I always feel proud, Tommy, that we knew him [Hamer Shawcross, the character based on Ramsay MacDonald] in Ancoats. It's marvellous to think that he sprang from the people."

Sir Thomas patted Polly's stout arm. "Yes, my dear. And while he was about it, he took care to spring a good long way from 'em."'

HOWARD SPRING, *FAME IS THE SPUR*

'When the buggers [his own members] are giving you trouble, give 'em a mass meeting. That gets it out of their system.'

JIMMY THOMAS, LEADER OF THE NATIONAL UNION OF
RAILWAYMEN

In 1947 the Boulting brothers produced a film version of Howard Spring's popular novel *Fame is the Spur*. Novel and film depict the growing conservatism of a once fiery radical as personal ambition and vanity make him turn his back on his working-class roots. At the end of the film Lord Shawcross (played by Michael Redgrave) dies alone, but not before he realises what an empty and unprincipled man he has become. Spring called his protagonist Shawcross, but everyone knew that he had modelled him on Ramsay MacDonald, the first Labour Prime Minister who died in 1937, just three years before Spring's book was published.

In the course of his long political career, Ramsay MacDonald had once been revered by his colleagues in the labour movement but heartily detested by the Conservatives for his semi-pacifist stance during the First World War. Horace King, a socialist who eventually became Speaker of the House of Commons in the 1960s, recalled that MacDonald had been 'the god, the god of the whole Labour Party in Britain.' In similar vein a German observer noted on the eve of the 1929 general election that '. . . in the slums of the manufacturing towns and in the hovels of the countryside he [MacDonald] has become a legendary being – the personification of all that thousands of downtrodden men and women hope and dream and desire.'

But after August 1931, when MacDonald as Labour's Prime Minister unexpectedly ditched his Cabinet and formed a National Government which promptly trounced his old party at a general election, positions were reversed. MacDonald was now lauded by Conservatives but reviled as a traitor by socialists. One trade union branch even plucked out the eyes from the portrait of MacDonald embroidered on their banner.

MacDonald's career was full of such paradoxes – here, above all, was a man who had struggled to create and unify the Labour Party but then split it from top to bottom. How can the life of the best-hated and most-loved of politicians be explained? What does it reveal about the British Left?

James Ramsay MacDonald was born in 1866 in a two-room cottage in Lossiemouth, north Scotland, a small fishing village. His parents, Anne Ramsay, a farmworker and dressmaker, and John MacDonald, the head ploughman at a nearby farm, never married. His illegitimacy was something MacDonald never forgot and which explains in large part his often over-sensitive and prickly character.

His father soon vanished from the scene and the boy was brought up by his maternal grandmother. He developed a love of reading, devouring the books given to him by a neighbouring watchmaker whilst the local schoolmaster proved to be an inspirational teacher. MacDonald left school at eleven intending to be a fisherman; instead he worked as a farm labourer until the schoolmaster appointed him a pupil teacher.

After four years as a teacher MacDonald left Lossiemouth in search of wider horizons and travelled to Bristol. Although he was there for only a few months, Bristol had a tremendous impact on him. Virtually the only city in Britain outside London that had an organised socialist movement in 1886, MacDonald joined the local SDF branch. Helped by a gift of £5 from Edward Carpenter, he set up its library. Like many other pioneering socialists of the 1880s, the zeal of these British socialists compensated for their small numbers. As MacDonald wrote later, 'We had all the enthusiasm of early Christians in those days. We were few and the Gospel was new.'

Returning briefly to Scotland, MacDonald next made his way to London, desperately searching for work. A job addressing envelopes for the Cyclists' Touring Club at ten shillings a week was followed by a post as a warehouse clerk. In his spare time he read voraciously in the Guildhall Library, hoping to win a scholarship to one of the science schools in South Kensington. But he overworked, as he was prone to do throughout his life, and collapsed. He went back to Scotland once more, but returned to London after a period of recuperation.

This time MacDonald was employed as the secretary of the aspiring Liberal politician Thomas Lough, holding this post for several years. He gave it up in favour of freelance journalism and research work for Sir Leslie Stephens, novelist Virginia Woolf's father, who edited the *Dictionary of National Biography*. Apparently, he worked on the entries from the letter 'M' onwards. In his spare time he joined socialist societies, speaking on innumerable and draughty street corners. MacDonald's character and opinions were formed by his mid-twenties and in fact they changed little over the rest of his life.

Hardworking, determined, sensitive, a fine speaker and organiser, the handsome MacDonald often displayed contradictory sides to his personality. On the one hand, there was the dreamy idealist and romantic who became secretary of a group called 'The Fellowship of the New Life' (from which the Fabian Society had initially grown) and enthusiastically ran its commune in Doughty Street in London. The Fellowship's objective was 'the cultivation of a perfect character in each and all'. On the other, there was the cautious, pragmatic and ambitious man keen to play a conspicuous part in building up a powerful labour movement. Even in these early days, he once declared his aim was eventually to become Prime Minister.

A member of both the Fabians and the Social Democratic Federation, in 1894 he also joined the Independent Labour Party (ILP). This revealed not only the flexibility of socialist organisations at this period, but also MacDonald's feeling that Keir Hardie was right to set up an independent working-class party distinct from the Liberal Party. In the 1895 general election he stood unsuccessfully as an ILP candidate for Southampton. A passage in MacDonald's election address neatly sums up why he and many others were deserting the Liberals:

> . . . I ceased to trust in the Liberal Party when I was convinced that they were not prepared to go on and courageously face the bread-and-butter problems of the time – the problems of poverty, stunted lives, and pauper-and-criminal-making conditions of labour.

In 1895 MacDonald met and fell in love with Margaret Gladstone, a young Fabian from a well-off family. They became engaged on the steps of the British Museum in the summer of 1896 and were married soon afterwards. Margaret was crucial to her husband in two ways. First of all, their happy marriage gave him a stability and happiness which he had never known before, removing some of his earlier remoteness. Her sociability meant that their flat at 3 Lincoln's Inn Fields became a kind of socialist salon, introducing MacDonald to a huge circle of friends which later proved invaluable.

Secondly, Margaret's private means allowed Ramsay to devote himself fully to the labour movement, enjoying as he did an economic security known to few of his colleagues. He was therefore uniquely placed to build himself a formidable position, and with his capacity for hard work he duly seized the opportunity. In 1900, for instance, he was appointed secretary of the new Labour Representation Committee (LRC) and concentrated on acquiring trade union affiliations to the new body. This arduous task required all MacDonald's qualities of patient persuasion.

MacDonald also understood the need to have several LRC representatives in Parliament, thereby providing a focus for the new organisation's efforts. His success in establishing the LRC allowed him to negotiate a secret electoral agreement with the Liberal Chief Whip, Herbert Gladstone, who wanted to maximise the anti-Conservative vote. As a result a handful of Liberal and LRC candidates were given clear runs against Conservatives. At the 1906 general election twenty-nine LRC candidates won seats in Parliament, among them MacDonald himself who was successful in Leicester. At their first meeting, the successful LRC MPs renamed themselves the Labour Party.

Although Keir Hardie was the prime founder and creator of this political party, MacDonald's administrative abilities proved crucial in giving it a shape and structure. Hardie disliked the House of Commons and from 1907 MacDonald was effectively the leading personality within the party.

In a series of books and speeches MacDonald tried to explain what British socialism was all about, seeking to give it a moral and political basis distinct from *laissez-faire* liberalism. The difficulty is that his writings were extraordinarily abstract and unspecific, and reading them was rather like wading through an ocean of cotton wool. Winston Churchill once said of MacDonald that no man could pack such a number of words into so small a space of thought. To give just one example of his writing style:

> Though economic creeds are torn to tatters, though the habits and ways of men disappoint the hearts of reformers, though the bright-eyed enthusiasm of youth fades into the yearning disillusionment of age, the guidance of the world will not be left to cynicism and pessimism, for the music of love and beauty will still be heard over faithless sadness, and chivalrous idealism will save us from selfishness and sleep.

This is all one sentence – and you can take your pick as to quite what he is on about.

However, two important points do emerge from MacDonald's work, namely the emphasis on community- rather than class-consciousness, and his belief that communal and collective effort was morally superior to individualism. He insisted too, and this is an issue still relevant to sections of the British Left, that suffering and deprivation were unlikely to bring about socialist change:

> I know that there is a belief still fairly prevalent amongst one School of Socialist theorists that the more Capitalism fails, the clearer will the way to Socialism be, that from the misery of the people the Socialist future will arise. I have never shared that faith. For with depression has not come more strenuous thinking, but more despairing action. Poverty of mind and body blurs the vision and does not clarify it . . .

Missing from MacDonald's books and speeches is any detail sketching out what a Labour government might actually do in office. They show clearly what MacDonald is against, in broad terms: greed, poverty, suffering and so on. But aren't most people? MacDonald fails to answer the question 'what is

distinctive and unique about socialism and what has it to offer?'
Love thy neighbour as thyself is an excellent moral imperative
but not much of a recipe for political administration. His ideas
could mean everything, or nothing.

Even MacDonald's sympathetic biographer, David Marquand,
concluded that 'In place of the revolutionary utopianism of
Marx, he offered, in effect, evolutionary utopianism – a kinder,
but not in practice a more useful creed.' His colleague Philip
Snowden thought that MacDonald's speeches at this time
suffered '. . . from a failing which has grown upon him with
advancing years, of being unable to make a speech which was
not open to any interpretation a person chose to place upon
it.' It was a characteristic well caught by Howard Spring in
*Fame is the Spur*.

When it came to the vital area of economics, the Labour
Party's approach was one of 'leave it to Snowden'. Snowden's
reputed expertise was apparently based on the two years he
had spent as a young man working as a tax collector in the
Orkneys. But once again a study of Snowden's ideas reveals
much evangelical zeal and many uplifting versions of a New
Jerusalem, but a corresponding absence of financial detail.
'Leave it to Snowden' – paralleling Keir Hardie's claim that
'Socialism . . . is not a system of economics' – was a decision
which later had disastrous consequences.

Despite, or perhaps because of this deliberate policy which
gave few hostages to fortune, the labour movement was
growing in strength. Local election results showed that the
Labour Party was a powerful presence all over the country. In
addition, the 600,000 members of the Co-operative movement
in 1890 had increased to over three million by 1914, whilst
the *Daily Herald* newspaper, originally a strike sheet produced
by London printers in January 1911, had become a national
newspaper. The growth of factories, towns and cities fomented
the collective environment and culture in which the labour
movement sunk its roots.

However there were complaints, and not just from the left

wing, that MacDonald's Labour Party was too timid. The Liberal government led by Campbell-Bannerman and then from 1908 by Herbert Asquith, modified their party's historic attachment to *laissez-faire*, passing a series of important social measures which included the introduction of old-age pensions, unemployment insurance, unemployment exchanges, trade boards setting a minimum rate of pay in certain industries, and from 1911 the payment of MPs.

Stimulated by the energy of Lloyd George and Winston Churchill, the Liberal administration exhibited a reforming zeal that the small number of Labour MPs could only applaud from the sidelines. MacDonald, who had been formally elected chairman of the Labour Party in 1911, stuck to his cautious policy of establishing a respectable image for his group. The Parliamentary Labour Party in particular was criticised for contributing little to the wave of strikes launched between 1911 and 1913, particularly in the mining and transport industries.

Influenced by syndicalist ideas which called for workers' control rather than parliamentary speeches, these disputes were marked by the violence of the clashes between the strikers, police and troops. In November 1910 a miner was killed at Tonypandy in Wales and during the rail strike in 1911 signal boxes were attacked, track torn up and telegraph systems damaged. At Chesterfield the railway station was set on fire and the crowds dispersed only after bayonet charges by the army. Two people were killed at Llanelli when soldiers opened fire.

'Labour unrest' in the years leading up to the First World War provides one partial exception to the generally non-violent nature of the British labour movement. It certainly alarmed MacDonald as much as it did the authorities. For him, any activity which hampered the slow, gradual work of building a strong Labour Party in Parliament was counter-productive.

MacDonald's task was made much harder by the unexpected

death of his wife Margaret in September 1911. She herself had been an active socialist, playing a major part in the National Union of Women Workers founded by Mary Macarthur in 1906. She loved research – her husband noted of Margaret's family that 'A Blue Book was second in rank of sacredness only to the Gospels.' They would work side by side at 3 Lincoln's Inn Fields, desks awash with reports, books and pamphlets, surrounded by their five children. Domestic life was chaotic – MacDonald seems to have existed on a staple diet of bananas – but rewarding. For recreation, the MacDonalds enjoyed walking and foreign travel.

Her death ended all this and MacDonald was inconsolable. He wrote a touching memoir, later expanded into a full-length book, and a fine memorial was erected in Lincoln's Inn Fields near to their flat, where it remains today. MacDonald never recovered from his wife's death. Many years later someone asked him why he had never remarried. His reply was simple: 'My heart is in the grave . . .' Without Margaret, his over-sensitive and often difficult personality returned in force, and he had to endure the personal and political traumas of the First World War alone.

The outbreak of war in August 1914 was a shattering blow to both MacDonald and Keir Hardie. Just seven years earlier, Keir Hardie had boasted of the decline of the war spirit: 'It would, for instance, be a difficult task, and one yearly becoming more so, for the rulers of say France and Germany, to again embroil these two nations in war with each other.' The ILP's *Manifesto on the War*, issued on 11 August 1914, was simply headed 'German Workers Our Comrades'.

Most British workers did not, in fact, feel this to be the case. Hardie himself was hooted and mobbed in his own Merthyr constituency. He never recovered from this shock to his deeply held belief in the brotherhood of man. As his daughter put it, 'he had not the strength to go on'. Keir Hardie died in September 1915.

As one might have expected, MacDonald's position was less

clearcut. He had a shrewd view of the power of nationalism: 'Race, patriotism, nationality – these are by far the strongest forces actuating the human heart and mind. I doubt if socialism will ever be able to acquire equal strength.' But although not a pacifist, MacDonald hated war and the suffering it inevitably brought. He voted against granting the Liberal government war credits to finance the conflict. It was a stance supported by only four other Labour MPs. He therefore resigned the chairmanship of the Party that August.

At times of crisis, MacDonald's views were invariably clouded by fine phrases and verbose rhetoric. Take this passage from a letter of September 1914:

> We cannot go back, nor can we turn to the right or to the left. We must go straight through. History will, in due time, apportion the praise and blame, but the young men of the country must, for the moment, settle the immediate issues of victory. Let them do it in the spirit of the brave men who have crowned our country with honour in the times that are gone. Whoever may be in the wrong, men so inspired will be in the right.

On the one hand, MacDonald seems to have felt that now the war was in progress then it must be fought to a finish. He was also worried – as were his German Social Democrat colleagues – that if the Labour Party came out against the war it might be outlawed, split apart and therefore undo much of his previous hard work. On the other hand, he himself opposed what he considered to be, at least in its origins, an unnecessary conflagration. In the overheated and jingoist circumstances of the time, MacDonald's criticisms led many to brand him as a traitor.

The abuse and hostility that MacDonald endured stoically over the next four years contradict the view that he was essentially an opportunistic and unprincipled man. The press smeared him as pro-German. Fellow socialists like H.G. Wells, a bellicose supporter of the war, described MacDonald and Hardie's views as 'the spiteful, lying chatter of the shabbiest scum of Socialism.' Horatio Bottomley published the evidence of MacDonald's illegitimacy on the front page of his journal *John Bull*. MacDonald was duly thrown out of his local golf club in Scotland.

Yet despite this frenzied hatred, MacDonald still addressed meetings even though violence was likely; once, at Plumstead Common, South London in August 1918, his opponents issued ex-servicemen with nailed sticks and bottles in order to disrupt a meeting. Finally, when the war was over, the press helped make sure that MacDonald lost his seat at Leicester by over 14,000 votes in the 'Khaki' election. MacDonald faced these tribulations alone, without Margaret's support and advice.

But, and this was perhaps MacDonald's greatest achievement, he had held the Labour Party together. Although only fifty-seven Labour MPs were elected at the 1918 election it was clear that, putting to one side the jingoist fervour whipped up by Lloyd George, the Labour Party was poised to replace the Liberals as the opposition to the Conservatives. Labour's position was helped by the Representation of the People Act 1918 giving the vote to all men over the age of twenty-one and most women over the age of thirty (note the chauvinistic difference).

As a result, the electorate nearly tripled from 7.5 million voters in 1910 to over 21 million in 1918. While many working-class people did not necessarily vote Labour the majority did – as first-time voters they had no previous allegiances to overturn – and in a 'first past the post' system the Liberals faced the perennial difficulty of being squeezed out.

The Labour Party was in fact transforming itself from a loosely federated alliance into a capable, centralised and national organisation. The constitution of December 1918 had for the first time allowed both the formation of local branch parties and individual membership. The hard work needed to establish the new machinery was largely undertaken by Arthur

Henderson, secretary between 1911 and 1934. Despite reverses in the future, the Labour Party was now a permanent part of the political landscape.

Kenneth Morgan once noted that '. . . it was Henderson who ensured that the unions dominated the machinery of the party at every stage', embodying Keir Hardie's conviction that they should form the backbone of any viable working-class party. Like Hardie, MacDonald and many other Labour leaders, Henderson himself had originally been a Liberal.

Union dominance reflected the maxim that the piper calls the tune. Labour Party finance was mostly provided via the Trade Union Act of 1913 which permitted unions to establish political funds, automatically levied on members. Individual trade unionists could contract out of the payment if they wished, but apathy meant that by 1924 only 2 per cent of trade union members did so. Michael Pinto-Duschinsky, the expert on political finance, once estimated that this political levy raised approximately £2.5 million between 1914 and 1927, or around £35 million at 1980 prices.

In return the unions controlled the Labour Party machinery: all twenty-three members of the National Executive were elected by the annual Party Conference. As the trade union block vote swamped that of the constituency parties, only individuals favoured by the unions could therefore be successful. In addition, forty-nine of the fifty-seven Labour MPs returned in 1918 were trade union nominees.

The Labour Party's improved efficiency was matched by that of the trade union movement itself. In 1914 Britain had no fewer than 1,100 unions – Germany in 1911 had only fifty-one – but after the war they reorganised. The General Council of the TUC was set up in 1921, as was the Amalgamated Society of Engineers. Next year the massive Transport and General Workers' Union emerged from twenty-three different unions. 1924 saw the formation of the General and Municipal Workers' Union.

As the trade unions grew, so did the Labour Party. It was

never a straightforward success story. Trade union membership peaked in 1920 at eight million and then dropped away to five million, but the size of such figures only underlined how important an institution the trade unions had become. The Liberals, devoid of any institutional link, were increasingly marginalised.

An imposing symbol of the British labour movement's newly acquired permanence was the eight-storey Transport House specially built for the Transport and General Workers' Union in Smith Square, close to the Houses of Parliament. One of the first steel and concrete frame buildings erected in London, it was opened on 15 May 1928 by Ramsay MacDonald and Ernest Bevin, General Secretary of the Transport and General Workers' Union. The Labour Party moved its headquarters here, graphically demonstrating the umbilical link between itself and the trade union movement. The TUC was also based at Transport House. The political and industrial wings of the British labour movement could hardly have been in closer proximity.

In many ways the Labour Party was a thoroughly progressive force. The 1918 Constitution, for instance, sanctioned the setting up of Women's Sections, of which there were 2,000 by 1932. Although the inspirational Mary Macarthur had tragically died of cancer in 1921 aged forty-one, her example lived on in the work of three women in particular. Susan Lawrence and Margaret Bondfield both became MPs in 1923 and then parliamentary secretaries in the short-lived Labour government of 1924. Five years later Bondfield was appointed the first ever woman Cabinet minister. Marion Phillips was elected the first women's secretary of the Labour Party in 1925 and also edited *Labour Woman*.

But the Labour Party's creation of an electoral machine based on the might of trade union finance and its block vote at the annual conference entailed losses too – particularly the dissipation of the pioneering ardour exhibited by various socialist groups over the previous forty years. The prospect of paid jobs and careers within the movement meant that the committee room began to edge out the unpaid amateur and the street-corner meeting. A disciplined party machine was bound to place the block vote and the mandate before socialist education or any search for 'the New Life'. The Independent Labour Party, vanguard of the old evangelical spirit, went into irreversible decline.

Some old-style revivalism undoubtedly surfaced in the love and affection which Labour Party members displayed towards inspirational figures such as the miners' leader A. J. Cook, the Clydeside MP James Maxton and the East End MP George Lansbury. It should also be remembered that the character of the labour movement often varied from city to city – between Glasgow and Liverpool, for instance – and that middle-class 'converts' sometimes grated on working-class recruits. As Fiona MacCarthy has written of William Morris, 'Like so many British middle-class converts to the left, he found fellowship much easier in the abstract than the imminent.' Nonconformists did not always see eye to eye with libertarians.

The reverence with which many in the labour movement treated Ramsay MacDonald owed much to the way in which he embodied popular hopes and aspirations. Take this description of a MacDonald visit to the mining valleys of South Wales in 1924:

> When the time arrived for the meeting to begin, the hall was packed to suffocation and the street outside was crowded with people, many with tickets, who had failed to get in. When Ramsay arrived the vast audience inside – and outside – joined in the singing of one of their favourite hymns – the bard Watcyn Wyn's vision of the day when every continent 'neath the firmament would hail the Nazarene. The address was in tune with the hymn – with peace on the horizon if only we had the courage to reach out. The crowd was thrilled and after the Prime Minister had gone on his triumphant way to Aberavon the streets rang with shouts and songs till the early hours of Sunday.

Yet MacDonald and a handful of other 'old-style' revivalists comprised a dwindling exception. The quest for the New Jerusalem remained but now it was a far-off and probably unattainable hope, secondary to the administrative detail of running a practical, down-to-earth organisation worried about the payment of subscriptions. The ethical dimension explored in the last chapter on 'Socialism and the New Life' was shunted off to one side. Moral considerations were dismissed as 'airy-fairy' stuff.

Organisational efficiency was rarely matched by any precision in policy. Both the Constitution of 1918 and the statement *Labour and the New Social Order* which accompanied it were largely the work of Sidney Webb. However, his main concern focused on what David Howell has called the 'maximisation of support' and Webb gave few if any hostages to political fortune. Take the famous Clause Four of the Constitution that proposes:

> To secure for the producers by hand or by brain the full fruits of their industry and the most equitable distribution thereof that may be possible, upon the basis of the Common Ownership of the Means of Production and the best obtainable system of popular administration and control of each industry and service.

Every phrase and almost each word in this clause was open to widely differing interpretations – an argument against it much used by Tony Blair and his supporters when the clause was replaced in 1995.

The British labour movement was clearly committed to change within the system. A few 'hotheads' might still talk of revolution, of emulating the Bolsheviks, but their rhetoric was a million miles from the centre of power. Instead, Ramsay MacDonald and his senior colleagues stressed the need for caution and compromise: 'Change must proceed from the bottom upwards, otherwise it has no foundation.

That means patience, work, trouble.' One event demonstrated the fundamentally constitutional and non-revolutionary nature of this mainstream British Left.

In 1919 a rash of strikes was launched by the 'Triple Alliance' of miners, railwaymen and transport workers, hoping to turn the political agitation of that year into wage increases and better working conditions. Sections of the Establishment feared that Britain might be going the way of Czarist Russia. Prime Minister Lloyd George was rather more shrewd. He called together the union leaders. As the miner Robert Smillie recalled, they were determined not to be talked over by this 'seductive and eloquent Welshman':

'He was quite frank with us from the outset,' Bob went on. 'He said to us: "Gentlemen, you have fashioned, in the Triple Alliance of the unions represented by you, a most powerful instrument. I feel bound to tell you that in our opinion we are at your mercy. The Army is disaffected and cannot be relied upon. Trouble has occurred already in a number of camps. We have just emerged from a great war and the people are eager for the reward of their sacrifices, and we are in no position to satisfy them. In the circumstances, if you carry out your threat and strike, then you will defeat us.

'"But if you do so," went on Mr Lloyd George, "have you weighed the consequences? The strike will be in defiance of the government of the country and by its very success will precipitate a constitutional crisis of the first importance. For, if a force arises in the state which is stronger than the state itself, then it must be ready to take on the functions of the state, or withdraw and accept the authority of the state. Gentlemen," asked the Prime Minister quietly, "have you considered, and if you have, are you ready?" From that moment on,' said Robert Smillie, 'we were beaten and we knew we were.'

It is doubtful if Lenin would have reacted in quite the same way.

\*     \*     \*

The parliamentary road to socialism did seem realisable, particularly when Ramsay MacDonald and the first Labour government took office in January 1924. MacDonald himself had been returned to Parliament in 1922 as MP for Aberavon and in the first ever party leadership contest he narrowly defeated J.R. Clynes by sixty-one votes to fifty-six. He won mainly because of the support of the left-wing Clydeside MPs – one of them wore a label which read 'High explosive, handle carefully' – who were swayed by MacDonald's brave stand during the war and by the fact that he was a fellow Scot.

At the 1923 election, despite press smears that the Labour Party would introduce 'compulsory free love' (surely a con-tradiction in terms!), the Party increased its representation to 191 seats. The Conservatives remained the largest party with 255 seats while the Liberals held 158 seats. Tory leader Stanley Baldwin decided to give the Labour Party the taste of office without power, knowing full well that as a minority government Labour would be unable to introduce radical measures.

As MacDonald began forming his minority administration, parts of the Establishment absurdly over-dramatised the poten-tial threat of this socialist party. They would have been much less anxious had they known the reverential thoughts of J.R. Clynes, one of the Party's leading figures, as he and his colleagues went to Buckingham Palace to receive their seals of office:

> As we stood waiting for His Majesty, amid the gold and crim-son magnificence of the Palace, I could not help marvelling at the strange turn of Fortune's wheel, which had brought MacDonald the starveling clerk, Thomas the engine-driver, Henderson the foundry labourer and Clynes the mill-hand, to this pinnacle beside the man whose forebears had been kings for so many splendid generations. We were making history! We were, perhaps, somewhat embarrassed, but the little, quiet man whom we addressed as 'Your Majesty' swiftly put us at our ease.

Presumably this sense of history was not marred by the spectacle of Stephen Walsh, the diminutive Minister for War, continually getting his ceremonial sword jammed between his legs.

Some Labour MPs in the House of Commons felt sufficiently excited to sing 'The Red Flag'. MacDonald solemnly promised George V that he would try to break this unfortunate habit. And when it came to the question of the correct court garb for the meeting with His Majesty – would they or wouldn't they dress up? – of course they did. It is interesting to speculate what Keir Hardie might have done: his Scottish Labour Party had recently demanded the abolition of monarchy.

In her diary Beatrice Webb describes 'laughing over Wheatley [a Clydeside militant] – the revolutionary – going down on both knees and actually kissing the King's hand.' Not that Mrs Webb advocated anything different. She thoughtfully founded a club for the new Cabinet members' wives so that they too could be schooled in the proper etiquette. Left-wing commentators always flay MacDonald and his colleagues for this 'flunkeyism', but Philip Snowden realistically pointed out that 'the constituents of the Labour members who appeared in the full uniform were rather pleased to see the photographs in the newspapers of their representatives in all this glory.'

This first Labour government contained an extraordinary mix of individuals. There was of course MacDonald himself, now applauded for his moderation by sections of the press which only a few years before had labelled him a traitor. He also took the post of Foreign Secretary, forcing him to work horrendous sixteen-hour days. Philip Snowden at the Exchequer directed his venomous speeches less at the official Opposition but rather at his own left-wingers. Arthur Henderson was at the Home Office, Sidney Webb at the Board of Trade. Jimmy Thomas was put in charge of the Colonial Office, determined to prove that the Empire was safe in his hands.

The maverick George Bernard Shaw turned down the offer

of a peerage and the post of government spokesman in the House of Lords, arguing that he preferred his own name and that it was a waste of time anyway. The one left-winger in the administration, John Wheatley, Minister of Housing, proved to be the most successful, passing legislation which led to the construction of half a million new homes.

Apart from Wheatley's Act, the administration did little other than demonstrate its caution. Admittedly, it was very much a minority government – fewer than one in three MPs belonged to Labour – but the ten-month experience revealed several major weaknesses. Crucially, this first generation of Labour MPs, most of them veterans of the early pioneering days, were essentially propagandists, full of evangelical enthusiasm and passion but short of practical ideas. Their timidity was neatly summed up by Cabinet member Josiah Wedgwood, who thought the slogan of the 1924 government was 'We must not annoy the Civil Service.'

Without a programme or much sense of direction the government was content to drift, waiting for the Conservatives sooner or later to remove them from office. They achieved this by first of all fomenting a row over a supposedly seditious article published in a Communist journal, causing the Liberals to withdraw their support, and then in the subsequent election by the so-called 'Zinoviev Letter', which whipped up fears of the Bolshevik menace to Britain. As I have argued in *We, The Nation*, the authenticity of the letter was and is a secondary issue to the skilful use made of it by the right-wing press, aided and abetted by Conservative Central Office. The Conservatives duly returned to power in November 1924.

One area in which MacDonald's Labour Party completely lost out to the Conservatives was in the sphere of political propaganda. On the face of it this was surprising in view of the early socialists' success in building support by means of rallies, marches, pamphlets and open-air meetings. But in many ways the Left had become fixated – and still is, to some extent – on these methods, failing to get to grips with modern communications.

As early as 1910 Conservative Central Office had been over-hauled, the role of its party agents upgraded and 'Literature' and 'Speakers' departments created. The Conservatives also churned out huge quantities of propaganda material: in 1927 alone over 18 million anti-union leaflets were issued. During the 1920s they were financing fleets of mobile vans which criss-crossed the country, as well as running residential colleges where speakers were trained to put over suitably anti-socialist arguments.

One telling episode from the October 1924 general election demonstrates how, in this respect at least, the socialist MacDonald was the hidebound reactionary and the Conservative leader Stanley Baldwin the innovator. For the first time ever, the British Broadcasting Company (later Corporation or BBC) allowed the leaders of the three main political parties to broadcast on the radio, reaching an estimated audience of some 3–4 million listeners – a figure infinitely larger than any reached in a lifetime of street-corner oratory.

Despite the repeated warnings of the Company's head John Reith, Ramsay MacDonald spoke live from the City Hall in Glasgow and made no attempt to adapt his platform style to the intimacy of radio listening. At times he even turned his face away from the microphone. One observer commented tactfully:

> He [MacDonald] raised his voice to its highest pitch and he dropped it to a whisper. He turned to the right and to the left, and even behind him, and spoke to all parts of the hall. He strode up and down the platform and was at varying distances from the microphone all the time. This is extremely effective for those who are present in the hall, but very detrimental for broadcasting.

Herbert Asquith, the Liberal leader, also relayed his speech from a live meeting. Stanley Baldwin, however, broadcast from the BBC's headquarters in London, making sure that he arrived early and was thoroughly briefed on how best to alter his delivery in order to communicate effectively.

MacDonald's 1924 government was also bedevilled by the fact that few if any of its ministers had devoted much time or energy to drawing up realistic policies which could be implemented. In one respect, of course, this was understandable because only a handful of the Cabinet, usually ex-Liberals, had experienced office before. But after the failures of 1924 it might have been expected that the Labour Party would sit down and methodically hammer out effective measures for the future. They didn't. The German journalist Egon Wertheimer noted this vacuum on the eve of the 1929 general election; he thought that the Party was placing its hopes in 'the right improvisation at the right moment.'

Very different from this rather lackadaisical attitude were four young Conservative MPs, among them Harold Macmillan, who in 1927 published a book called *Industry and the State* that argued for 'economic democracy', National Wages Boards and a great expansion in welfare work. And it was the Liberal Party which in March 1929 issued a manifesto called *We Can Conquer Unemployment* demanding much greater government intervention in the economy. Both these plans contained ambiguities and evasions but at least they grappled with the problems of a new era, notably the widespread unemployment – 10 per cent of the workforce had no jobs – which persisted during the 1920s.

The Labour Party's lack of preparation was tragically echoed too by the events leading up to the General Strike of May 1926 in which the unions showed themselves to be poor strategists when faced by an antagonistic government. British mine owners were trying to enforce cuts in the already meagre wages of their men. On 31 July 1925 the Conservative government agreed to step in and avert a possible strike by means of a nine-months' subsidy – a temporary union victory prematurely dubbed 'Red Friday'. It was clear, however, that when the subsidy ran out a conflict would be inevitable.

The government made full use of the breathing space to organise and make detailed plans, beefing up its Organisation for the Maintenance of Supplies (OMS) while the trade unions did nothing. When the strike began on 3 May 1926, trade union leaders were amazed at the spontaneous upsurge of grassroots support shown by workers all over the country for the miners. For example, more railwaymen came out on strike in 1926 than in support of their own dispute in 1919 – even the Ministry of Labour called the strike 'an extraordinarily impressive demonstration of working class solidarity.'

But it was obvious that the trade union leaders were appalled at the tiger which they had unwittingly unleashed. In the words of historian Julian Symons, they 'feared the consequences of complete victory more than those of a negotiated defeat' – just as they had in 1919. They made little attempt to give a lead to their side, turning down the offer of the Independent Labour Party to help put across to the public their case. As another commentator has written, 'This machine, easily the most efficient and widespread socialist organisation in Great Britain, could organise more than 700 public meetings a week, yet the offer was never taken up.' It was with acute relief that the General Council of the TUC found a way of calling off the General Strike after nine days, leaving the miners to fight on alone and be defeated.

One notable feature of the strike has been stressed by Symons, whose account of the conflict was first published in 1957. The 1987 edition had a new preface by the author in which he contrasted the absence of bitterness or sabotage shown in 1926 with the much more acrimonious atmosphere surrounding the miners' strike of 1984–85: 'The strikers of 1926 were a war-weary generation, almost all of whom remembered the horrors of trench warfare and poison gas. They shrank from violence because they had suffered it.'

★　　★　　★

Throughout the 1920s the ailing Liberal Party, already split between the followers of Asquith and of Lloyd George, found themselves pushed towards the political fringe by the British electoral system which helped the Labour Party establish itself as the major rival to the Conservatives. This marginalisation was duly confirmed by the results of the general election held in May 1929 when the Labour Party won 287 seats, the Conservatives 260 and the Liberals just 59.

MacDonald's second administration was therefore a minority government like his first, but this time at least the minority was much less pronounced than in 1924. Moreover, sections of the Liberal Party were apparently in favour of a radical strategy – just as Labour had supported the Liberals between 1906 and 1914.

The story of the 1929–31 Labour government is quickly and sadly told. The New York stock exchange crash of October 1929 led to economic depression in Britain and world-wide. Business confidence collapsed, men and women lost their jobs. Unemployment rose inexorably above the 10 per cent figure. In 1930 alone the figure doubled to over two and a half million people out of work.

Philip Snowden, yet again Chancellor of the Exchequer and wedded to the traditional orthodoxy of free trade, the gold standard and *laissez-faire*, pinned his hopes on world economic recovery. When this didn't happen, he was lost. The Prime Minister relied on a cheery but totally false optimism; the newly elected Labour MP Aneurin Bevan once discussed the crisis and was breezily told by MacDonald that 'Recovery is just around the corner' – just as a later Conservative Chancellor of the 1990s, Norman Lamont, spent much time whistling in the dark.

There was an alternative to hand. Sir Oswald Mosley, a junior minister in the government, presented a memorandum in January 1930 calling for the public control of imports and banking as well as an increase in pensions in order to boost purchasing power. When the memorandum was rather perfunctorily turned down, Mosley promptly resigned.

By the summer of 1931 the crisis had worsened. Snowden's only policy was to cut back government spending and he demanded a 10 per cent reduction in unemployment pay. The Cabinet split. Outside the government the General Council of the TUC refused to accept this cut, which meant that the trade union or industrial wing of the labour movement was at odds with the Labour Party or political leadership. The alliance which sustained the British labour movement was now under threat.

For the first but not the last time, matters were complicated by uncertainty as to where ultimate power was to be located. Did it lie with the Labour Prime Minister, the Cabinet, the Parliamentary Labour Party, the Party Conference, the trade unions, the constituency Labour Parties or some combination of them all? The conundrum dogged future Labour leaders and governments.

At the end of August 1931 Ramsay MacDonald, frustrated by his Cabinet's refusal to authorise cuts, suddenly jettisoned his administration. Instead he formed a National Government made up of himself, Snowden and Jimmy Thomas together with assorted Conservatives and Liberals. MacDonald justified his actions by arguing that only a National Government could solve the country's economic problems.

The Labour Party suddenly found itself without its leader and out of power. Much worse was to follow. At the October 1931 general election the National Government, in reality the Conservatives, scored an emphatic victory by returning 554 MPs to the Labour Party's meagre 46. Virtually overnight it seemed that the gains and achievements that MacDonald and the Labour Party had won over the course of twenty-five years had been wiped out. The Party had shrunk to little more than its 1906 level of parliamentary representation.

The economic crisis had overshadowed the entire period in office of MacDonald's second Labour government. At first MacDonald himself concentrated on foreign affairs before growing domestic difficulties claimed his attention. It made little difference. MacDonald lacked the ability to deal with the crisis; as his successors Clement Attlee, Harold Wilson and James Callaghan also discovered, Britain's economic problems seemed insurmountable. In MacDonald's case, economic illiteracy was compounded by an incapacity to ask for, let alone accept, colleagues' advice.

In February 1885 William Morris' Socialist League had published a manifesto claiming that 'we shall look to it that there shall be no distinctions of rank or dignity amongst us to give opportunities for the selfish ambition of leadership which has so often injured the cause of the workers.'

By 1931 Ramsay MacDonald had long since happily embraced 'the selfish ambition of leadership'. Even the Prime Minister's supporters habitually remarked on his aloofness. Egon Wertheimer observed that 'One can perhaps more readily picture him sitting and dreaming by his fireside or wandering with a knapsack on the moors alone with Nature . . .' than cajoling his administration into wide-ranging socialist change. When backbenchers went to see their party leader he invariably read his correspondence as they talked to him. His social circle contained rather more Duchesses than trade unionists.

MacDonald's colleague Philip Snowden had lived off his reputation as the Labour Party's economic expert for years and his views were rarely challenged within the Party. He was a fine emotional speaker, typical of the first generation of speakers. One famous Snowden peroration ended:

> But the only way to regain the earthly paradise is by the old, hard road to Calvary – through persecution, through poverty, through temptation, by the agony and bloody sweat, by the crown of thorns, by the agonising death. And then the resurrection to the New Humanity – purified by suffering, triumphant through Sacrifice.

After such rhetoric it must have been difficult for Snowden

to return to earth and flesh out the Labour Party's economic approach – and he didn't. Instead he instinctively relied on the orthodoxies of Victorian Liberalism, as his biographer noted: 'He was raised in an atmosphere which regarded borrowing as an evil and free trade as an essential ingredient of prosperity.' The Treasury thought likewise and, as Winston Churchill put it in one of his vivid phrases, 'The Treasury mind and the Snowden mind embraced each other with the fervour of two long-separated kindred lizards.'

Throughout the crisis of 1929–31 Snowden relentlessly maintained that the only answer to a recession lay in wage cuts. In his autobiography he claimed never to prepare his speeches, preferring instead to draw from 'the stock of accumulated material.' Likewise, as Chancellor he depended on accumulated economic wisdom perhaps suitable for the past but inadequate for the present crisis. Professor Robert Skidelsky, who has analysed these events in detail, concluded scathingly that 'With him at the Exchequer, no Government stood much chance in the circumstances of 1929.'

Certainly nothing could be expected of the other member of the Labour troika, Jimmy Thomas, who was charged with finding a solution to mass unemployment. Not even his most fervent supporters ever claimed that fresh thinking was Thomas' forte. He also had a drink problem and spent much of the time in tears, vainly trying to understand the mountain of documents which his advisers loaded on him. Others who might have helped the administration were unavailable. John Wheatley had blotted his copybook with a botched libel case and Ernest Bevin was not even in Parliament, preferring to wield much greater power outside.

But the disaster that destroyed the government was obviously due to rather more than personal failings. The Labour Party had completely failed to prepare for the economic situation, unlike some other social democratic parties such as the administration in Sweden which, by judicious use of government intervention, coped with precisely the same sort of difficulties.

The whole nature of MacDonald's Labour Party shied away from hard and detailed thinking about policy: Snowden and MacDonald's cloudy exhortations were all too symptomatic of the Party's approach. To quote Skidelsky again: 'Socialism explained the past and promised the future; it had nothing constructive to offer the present.' A party dominated by trade unions preoccupied with 'bread and butter issues' was not, in the 1920s at least, best placed to be innovative. Few of the Labour ministers had ever run anything in their lives, other than a trade union; their scanty economic and financial expertise proved no match for Treasury and business interests.

It is unfair to heap all the blame on MacDonald himself. Throughout the unfolding crisis, as his biographer David Marquand has shown, he received contradictory and ambiguous advice from the Treasury, the rest of the civil service, his Cabinet and Labour MPs. No clearcut radical course of action was open to him. But, even if there had been, one doubts that the MacDonald of 1931, tired and isolated, would have taken it.

His last few years were tragic. Pledged to defend the Gold Standard and the old economic order, instead he took Britain off it – with no discernible result. He was genuinely upset to see the Labour Party so badly defeated at the October 1931 election; Philip Snowden preferred to round on his former colleagues with a vengeance, accusing their programme of being 'Bolshevism run mad'. A young Harold Wilson witnessed the bewilderment that Snowden's behaviour caused in his own constituency of Colne Valley: '. . . I saw the Valley almost flooded with the tears of those who a month earlier would almost have died for Snowden, and I saw those tears gain a new bitterness as Snowden attacked his colleagues in those acid election speeches and broadcasts.'

MacDonald always hoped to return to the Labour Party, regarding the formation of the National Government as a temporary measure. But it was not to happen. He completely under-estimated the loathing his former Party now felt for him; in their view the traitor had brought down an elected government and then nearly destroyed it as a parliamentary force. He was therefore surprised and deeply upset to receive a letter from the Labour Party's national organiser expelling him: 'It began "Dear Sir", and it ended not with a signature, but with a rubber stamp and initials underneath. They wanted to insult me.'

He even lost his seat at the 1935 general election, ironically enough beaten by a former Clydeside supporter, Manny Shinwell, although he later regained a place in Parliament at a by-election. Ramsay MacDonald died in November 1937. His ashes lie beside those of Margaret in Spynie churchyard, near Lossiemouth.

The sad fate of Ramsay MacDonald, the man who had done so much to build up the British Labour Party but then brought it crashing down, is often dismissed as the inevitable outcome of his essentially vain and opportunist character. This 'betrayal complex' always appeals to sections of the British Left who have applied it to several other figures in decline or disgrace. Conveniently it means that they don't have to examine their own ideas or ways of trying to bring about political change and can simply blame individuals for the failures of the movement.

This 'betrayal' interpretation ignores the fact that for many years MacDonald was the undisputed and enormously popular leader of the Labour Party. His basic strategy of gradually ousting the Liberals by Labour as the main opposition to the Conservatives in a two-party system barely altered over three decades. This could not be accomplished by wild revolutionary antics because it was imperative to win over the middle ground of the electorate who had for years happily voted Liberal.

Few within the labour movement had quarrelled with MacDonald's approach at the time and it seems unfair to accuse him of inconsistency. His career vividly reveals both the merits and flaws of 'labourism' in that he was prepared to work within the system as he understood it and yet still to cling to that same system when it was threatened, as in 1931.

Essentially, Ramsay MacDonald was the pioneer who had to govern, but didn't know how. And yet the permanence of his achievement was, paradoxically enough, shown even at the October 1931 election. Despite all the forces ranged against it, the Labour Party still managed to attract six million votes. The unity of the British labour movement was one important reason why fascism did not gain ground here as it did in much of Europe between the wars and MacDonald deserves some of the credit for this.

But labourism is not a single and coherent set of ideas. The challenge facing the Labour Party was how to try and create a different form of labourism which, unlike that associated with MacDonald, could win power in a parliamentary democracy and then use it. How best, in other words, to progress from the initial pioneering phase towards the next administrative phase?

MacDonald's labourism was not, however, unchallenged in the 1920s. Lenin had once attacked MacDonald for his 'inability and lack of desire to really prepare the party and the class in a revolutionary manner for the dictatorship of the proletariat.' That MacDonald would probably have had no idea what Lenin was talking about shows how deep was the schism between the reformist and revolutionary strands within the British Left. How successful, then, were Britain's revolutionaries, banded together in the new Communist Party, in their attempt to introduce 'the dictatorship of the proletariat'?

# British Revolutionaries in the 1920s

'A Red football team was recently formed in South Shields.'
NEWS ITEM IN THE *WORKERS' WEEKLY*, 10 FEBRUARY 1923

'Lenin's name rang like magic in my ears . . . That day on which I met Comrade Lenin was the greatest of my life.'
HARRY POLLITT, GENERAL SECRETARY OF THE COMMUNIST PARTY OF GREAT BRITAIN

'The one outstanding and – by contemporary standards – highly original quality of the English is their habit of *not killing one another.*'
GEORGE ORWELL

Which British revolutionary was sometimes called 'Britain's Lenin', was imprisoned five times for his political beliefs, had a Moscow street named after him, and whose centenary in 1979 was marked in the then Soviet Union by the issue of a special commemorative stamp? The answer is John Maclean. Until recently, almost everyone hearing this name would justifiably have responded 'Who?', so completely has his name been omitted from the history books.

In the last few years, however, there has been renewed interest in Maclean and, just as happened with William Morris, various factions are busy fighting over his legacy. He has been claimed as a Scottish nationalist, an anarchist and a Communist, as well as being dismissed as mentally unbalanced.

It does not seem to matter that for all his personal bravery Maclean never came anywhere near leading a revolution. In fact, when the British authorities did with some reason fear that a rising was about to take place – in Glasgow on 31 January 1919 when thousands of people demonstrated in favour of a forty-hour week – he was a hundred miles away lecturing in Manchester. It is difficult to imagine Lenin missing the October Revolution in Russia. That Maclean managed to be in the wrong place at the right time somehow sums up the lack of success experienced by British would-be revolutionaries.

Leon Trotsky once tried to identify, in characteristically leaden prose, an important British political phenomenon:

> . . . the most radical elements of the contemporary British Labour Movement are mostly of Scotch or Irish race. The union in Ireland of social with national oppression, in face of the sharp conflict of an agrarian with a capitalist country, gives the conditions for sharp changes in consciousness. Scotland set out upon the road of capitalism later than England; a sharper break in the life of the masses of the people causes a sharper break in political reaction.

In more comprehensible English, why is 'the Celtic fringe' so important to the history of British Left? Invariably the Welsh, Irish or Scots have played significant roles out of all proportion to their numbers. In part this reflects a political interest and consciousness often more aware and informed than in England.

These national groups have had much to complain about. The Irish famine in the 1840s, for instance, led to mass migration to Scotland, where the nineteenth-century 'clearances' of the Highlands later forced thousands of people out of their homes and generated a lasting sense of outrage. Irish famine victim and Scottish clearance refugee alike were often sucked into Glasgow, which by 1914 was disfigured by several of the worst slums in Europe with over a thousand people to an acre in particularly squalid areas.

John Maclean was born in Pollokshaw near Glasgow in 1879. Both his parents had witnessed the clearances at first hand as children and Maclean's grandmother never let the small boy forget what anguish had been inflicted. He was brought up under a strict Calvinist regime and, although he became a Marxist early on his life and joined left-wing friends in playing cricket on Sundays in order to scandalise the elders of the kirk, some of this Calvinism clung to him until his death. A non-smoker, teetotal and heartily opposed to gambling as 'counter-revolutionary', even his best friend James MacDougall made no great claims for Maclean's levity: 'He had little sense of humour, and when . . . he introduced a joke . . . it was clumsily done.'

Maclean trained as a teacher and, by studying at nights, obtained a part-time MA at Glasgow University in 1904. By this time, however, his complete and absorbing passion was left-wing politics. Influenced by Robert Blatchford's writings and then by Karl Marx – he once declared '*Merrie England* is the primary school of socialism, but *Das Kapital* is the University' – he joined Hyndman's Social Democratic Federation (SDF) in late 1902 despite the fact that the SDF, weak in England, was even weaker in Scotland.

Maclean threw himself into political agitation, holding hundreds of open-air meetings and expounding Marx's ideas tirelessly. Calling himself 'a dispeller of ignorance', even his summer holidays were devoted to propaganda tours in Scotland and the north of England. He attracted extraordinarily large numbers of students for classes which, as his lecture notes show, called for hard, abstract thinking. At one point his regular weekly attendance in Glasgow was 493, a figure inconceivable today. There is no doubt that Maclean was helped by his considerable powers of oratory, hinted at by MacDougall. Here is his description of Maclean in 1914 as he fiercely opposed the war:

Who that ever saw can forget the tense, drawn face of the orator, his broad features, high prominent cheekbones, his heavy, bushy eyebrows, firm, cleanshaven mouth, his glowing eyes, and the stream of natural eloquence that fell from his lips? As he drove on, his prematurely grey hair shone in the reflected light of the street-lamps, and his forehead became covered with sweat. The soul of the man leapt out of his eyes and took possession of that vast audience. Not a man, woman or child but knew that they saw a David before them casting defiance against the capitalist Goliath. They knew that all the organised power of the British state was against him, ready to crush him whenever the ruling parties in London might say that it would further their cause. His hearers knew that for these precious words of exhortation and of hope the man would have to pay, and pay dearly.

It is surprising that Maclean found the time to get married, but his wife Agnes must soon have realised that both she and their two daughters, Jean and Nan, would come second to his political work. Eventually, Agnes made her husband choose between her and politics: he chose politics. Maclean regretted their separation, imploring Agnes to return – but not if that meant giving up his propaganda.

The outbreak of war in August 1914 brought Maclean to prominence. As we have already seen, some left-wing leaders such as Hyndman and Blatchford welcomed the chance to fight 'the German menace'. They were patriots first, socialists second. Maclean opposed the war. Still based in Glasgow, an important munitions and shipbuilding centre, he led the campaign against the raising of rents, against conscription and against 'dilution' under which trade unions agreed to accept the temporary suspension of certain labour customs and practices for the duration of the war.

After a dispute with the headmaster, Maclean lost his teaching job and in 1915 became a full-time revolutionary, supporting himself from the fees received for his classes and by the sale of political pamphlets. In 1916 he was sentenced to three years' imprisonment after a typically inflammatory speech. His spirits were lifted by the October 1917 Revolution in Russia which seemed to confirm his diagnosis of impending capitalist collapse and gave revolutionaries a sense that history was indeed on their side. One of Maclean's colleagues, Harry McShane, was to write of this revolution's impact: 'We had only known working-class revolt; now we could talk about working-class power.' Maclean's growing international reputation was demonstrated by his appointment in February 1918 as the Bolshevik Consul in Glasgow.

Released from gaol, Maclean was soon back there again in 1918 after further 'seditious' speeches brought a harsh sentence of five years' imprisonment. Maclean accused the prison authorities of poisoning his food. According to the evidence available, this seems unlikely. More probable is that Maclean's unending labours had brought about a nervous breakdown. To mark the end of the war in late 1918 he was released early. Most men would have convalesced for a few months, but not Maclean. Like Keir Hardie before him, he never for a moment doubted the righteousness of his beliefs, whatever the personal costs.

In the aftermath of the war the authorities worried about possible threats to political stability from a number of sources. The suffragettes planned to continue their often violent campaign for the vote, whilst the troops soon realised they were not returning to 'homes fit for heroes'. Many soldiers were disgusted at the slowness of demobilisation or by the prospect of being sent to Russia to fight in the war launched by fourteen Western European countries to crush the new Bolshevik regime.

Various mutinies broke out in Britain, details of which are still being uncovered, but Winston Churchill wrote that 'in several cases considerable bodies of men were for some days entirely out of control.' Police forces in parts of the country went on strike, as did the workforce in many industries. In Glasgow, or 'Red Clydeside' as it was dubbed by journalists, the strike was led by the engineers who demanded a forty-hour week. By the end of January 1919 things were coming to a head, although, as already mentioned, Maclean himself was away lecturing in the north of England.

On 31 January 1919 the strikers planned a march to the Council Chambers in George Square, Glasgow. The authorities, fearing an uprising, were desperately worried that many of the marchers had recently been well-trained soldiers. As Scotland Yard's Director of Intelligence anxiously noted, 'It must be remembered that in the event of rioting, for the first time in history, the rioters will be better trained than the troops.'

Between 30,000 and 40,000 marchers gathered and then set off in an orderly fashion for George Square where they were greeted by police who seem to have lost their heads and lashed out indiscriminately with their batons. One newspaper described the scene: 'The square soon assumed the appearance of a miniature battlefield. Figures prone and sitting strewed the ground.' Scores of arrests were made and the wounded taken inside the Chambers where the ground floor resembled, in the words of another journalist, 'a field hospital during the war. Dozens of the victims were laid out on the floor . . .' The strikers hurriedly dispersed. One of their leaders, Manny Shinwell, thirty years later a Cabinet minister under Attlee, reached home only by disguising himself with a false beard made from a broom.

Next day the government ostentatiously sent six tanks to Glasgow which were displayed in the streets. Armed troops were given explicit instructions that their fire should be 'effectual': 'it is undesirable that firing should take place over the heads of rioters or that blank cartridges should be used.' There was indeed no further talk of revolution – not that there had been much among the strikers in the first place. In fact the Cabinet Papers reveal that government ministers talked more about 'the revolutionary nature of the present agitation' than the 'agitators' themselves. Within a few days the strike was over. Why had this potential British revolution come to nothing?

There were several reasons. For one thing, only sections of the Glasgow workforce, mainly the skilled craftsmen, were in fact out on strike. The national leaderships of other unions had wanted no part in the forty-hour week agitation and therefore the strikes failed to spread outside Glasgow. Nor was any strike pay available, so that it was always doubtful just how long the strikers could stay out. The unarmed strikers had never really contemplated the use of force.

Finally, the leaders of the strike were themselves confused, as one of their leaders, Willie Gallacher, later admitted: we had 'no plan, no unity of purpose, watching one another and waiting for and wondering what was going to happen. We were simply playing with the masses who were behind us, although we didn't stop long enough or think deeply enough to understand it.' When the strikers were attacked by the police, the first reaction of Gallacher and the other leaders was, laudably, to get them away to safety. Lenin would not have responded so humanely, prepared as he was to accept the bloodshed accompanying revolution.

Would Maclean's presence in Glasgow on 31 January have made any difference? Almost certainly not. No single individual, not even Maclean, could have overcome the formidable obstacles in the way of a successful rising. Journalists and participants later dwelt lovingly on 'Red Clydeside' and Britain's 'near' revolution (in Britain revolution always seems to be 'near'), but in hindsight the discontent barely seems 'pinkish'. At the general election in December 1918, just a month before, ten out of Glasgow's fifteen constituencies had been won by Conservative candidates.

The authorities moved quickly to ensure that such events would not happen again and they adopted a carrot and stick approach. The carrot was the Insurance Act of 1920 entitling some unemployed men to financial benefit; the stick was the Emergency Powers Act of 1920 that strengthened the hands of the authorities in times of crisis – as was later demonstrated during the General Strike of 1926.

The previous chapter explored the relentless growth of the British Labour Party in the first decades of this century, based as it was on trade union money and personnel. But not everyone approved of these developments and many socialists tried to shift the labour movement onto a different path. Could things have been different?

One weakness of the non-Labour Party Left was its fragmentation. A list of some of the associations brings this out. There was the SLP, SPGB, NSP, SLF, BSP, WSF, the South Wales Socialist Society (SWSS), the National Shop Stewards' Committee and the National Guilds League – a veritable alphabet soup. All had very small memberships, which didn't stop any of them from being convinced of their own rectitude. More energy was expended in attacking the errors of their comrades than was spent assailing the Conservatives. They differed widely in their beliefs; some, as we have seen, had opposed the recent war, while others had revelled in it – H.M. Hyndman, for instance, happily wrote to Whitehall offering to investigate the activities of 'German spy waiters' in London.

Lenin and his Bolshevik party, disgusted at the way in which the international labour movement had collapsed into its national divisions on the outbreak of war in 1914, were determined to found a new International. This, the Third or Comintern (Communist International), was formed in Moscow in March 1919 to direct the activities of the various national Communist Parties. Bolstered by the unique prestige of having successfully carried through a revolution, the Soviet Communist Party inevitably called the Comintern tune.

Hoping to fuse the various left-wing factions, Lenin was prepared to finance just such an amalgamation. Theodore Rothstein, a distinguished journalist and historian of Russian birth who had lived in England for over twenty years, was responsible for dispensing 'Moscow gold'.

How much money did Rothstein have available to spend? His son Andrew estimated the figure at £15,000 over two years. Jim Braddock, who was on the committee which handled the Communist Party's finances, put it at £85,000 over an eighteen-month period, a massive sum when compared with the income from individual contributions which totalled just £7,500 over that same period. More recently, Francis Beckett alleges that in 1922 the party was asking Moscow for the equivalent of what would be well over £1 million in today's terms.

This 'Moscow gold' sometimes reached Britain via unusual cloak-and-dagger routes. In his memoirs Francis Meynell tells an exciting story of bringing back some jewels which had been hidden in jars of Danish butter. The jewels were not exclusively for the Communist Party; £75,000 worth went towards the newspaper the *Daily Herald*.

Much ink has been spilt on the question whether, without this financial lubrication, a Communist Party would still have been formed in this country. The answer is 'yes'; most British revolutionaries could see that the sectarianism of the many factions was only helping their opponents. The biggest stumbling block was the bickering among the groups about the 'correct' attitude to be taken towards the Labour Party. What the financial assistance did ensure was that any new organisation would be run on Bolshevik lines.

The 'Circular of Invitation' sent out to interested groups by the committee setting up the new body stipulated three 'fundamental bases' – already a certain kind of dehumanised jargon was becoming familiar. They were acceptance of 'the dictatorship of the proletariat', that is of working-class power and the need for forcible suppression of opponents if required; recognition of the Soviet system as the best available; and obeisance to the authority of the Comintern itself, based in Moscow.

This last condition was attacked by several British revolutionaries who argued that the Russians, at a distance of several thousand miles, were hardly best placed to pronounce on the tactics and strategy to be adopted in Britain. As John Maclean put it, 'The less the Russians interfere in the internal affairs of other countries at this juncture, the better for the cause of revolution in those countries.'

The counter-argument was put by Theodore Rothstein who claimed that although 'every country is "peculiar",' the same social factors – modern industry, capitalism, the proletariat and now the world war – influenced them all and 'are bound to produce the same effects.' In other words, communism, or at least the Bolshevik version of it, had universal validity which outweighed the specific circumstances, whether it be its history or culture, of individual countries.

This dispute between nationalist and internationalist views might seem a dull irrelevancy. In fact, it was a conflict crucial to the development of British socialism and hence of British politics. Was the non-Labour Party Left to go its own way, adapting to British circumstances and events? Or was it rather to cede authority to the Comintern, a body devoted to the short-term interests of the Soviet Union and ignorant of Britain? Lenin, for instance, always referred to 'John Maclean of England' – a stupid mistake in view of Maclean's pronounced Scottishness.

In effect, Lenin and the Comintern wanted the European Left to be split into two rigid and opposing camps. In one corner was to be labourism or the social democrats whom Lenin despised as weak and vacillating. In the other were the various Communist Parties, disciplined and resolute in their pursuit of 'the class struggle'. Divisions within the international labour movement resulted in the formation of the German Communist Party in December 1918, the French Communist Party in December 1920 and the Italian Communist Party in January 1921.

Britain, however, was different. Here the labour movement had not split apart over the war, mainly due to Ramsay MacDonald's sterling efforts. Neither was Marxism an influential tradition. The British Communist Party was therefore almost certain to be a small minority grouping and yet they were subject to the same rules as everyone else. The 16th thesis of the Comintern read: 'All the decisions of the Congresses of the Communist International, as well as the decisions of the Executive Committee, are binding on all parties belonging to the Communist International.' No room for doubt or equivocation there.

The Communist Party of Great Britain (CPGB) was formally set up in July 1920 – at a time when the radical political tide of 1919 was ebbing fast. The party claimed a membership of only 3,000, much less than the combined total of the various groupings such as the BSP and the SLP which were absorbed into the new body. John Maclean was one person who did not join.

Sylvia Pankhurst also fell foul of the new organisation. For eight years she had run a newspaper called *Workers' Dreadnought*. The new Communist Party wanted to take it over, dictating policy and appointing a different editor without even consulting Pankhurst. She argued that this was all too typical of the authoritarian behaviour of the new party: '. . . in the weak, young, little-evolved Communist movement of this country discussion is a paramount need, and to stifle it is disastrous.' Pankhurst was expelled from the Party and the newspaper closed down.

From the outset the Communist Party showed that Moscow's wishes were imperative, no matter what was actually happening in Britain. One of its founder members, J.T. Murphy, attended a Comintern session at which the Soviet tried to hammer the 'correct' ideas into their obstinate British comrades: 'We had *got* to learn that a Communist Party was the general staff of a class marching to civil war, that it had to be disciplined, a party organised on military lines, ready for every emergency, an election, a strike, an insurrection.'

British Communists were even prepared to jettison hard-won gains which had been painstakingly acquired over decades, including the right to vote. The 1920 Circular of Invitation, for example, laid down that an essential principle of the new party would be 'the Soviet idea as against Parliamentary democracy i.e. a structure making provision for the participation in social administration only of those who render useful service to the community.'

These are chilling words indeed. Who was to decide what was or was not 'useful service'? The British Communist Party also applauded the Bolshevik suppression of minority groups whose views were conveniently labelled 'counter-revolutionary'. They made no protest when Trotsky brutally put down the rising of the Kronstadt sailors in 1922 and two years later the leadership actually wrote to *Pravda* categorically stating that a British revolutionary government would ban groups whose policies were deemed to be against the revolution.

However, there was little likelihood of a British revolutionary government. Britain simply was not, much though Moscow might have wanted it otherwise, in a militant mood. Instead of trying to adapt itself to the difficult situation, the British Communist Party found itself lumbered with a set of policies and ideas repugnant to the majority of the population.

Pleas from the Party's own supporters that this was a suicidal approach made no difference. Apart from the warnings of Maclean and Sylvia Pankhurst, even Communists such as John S. Clarke, a delegate at the 1920 meeting of the Comintern, argued that 'Ideas imported from Russia must be modified to suit the changing conditions'; 'To copy their [Soviet] tactics under our conditions, and without their backbone, will be the acme of folly.' A Soviet Bolshevik party, fighting desperately for its life in a civil war, understandably adopted a highly disciplined and centralised system. In Britain it was, or should have been, different.

Many early members of the Communist Party had enjoyed varied careers. John S. Clarke had been first a sailor and then at seventeen a lion tamer. He even started his own zoo in Newcastle as well as working as a journalist. There was the fiery trade union organiser Ellen Wilkinson; the historian and journalist Raymond Postgate who had been gaoled for his anti-war activities and who was later to found *The Good Food Guide*; the distinguished typographer Francis Meynell; and the oddball J. Walton Newbold who dressed as scruffily as possible because he hoped this made him more proletarian. When elected MP for Motherwell in 1922, he sent Lenin a telegram which boasted 'Have won Motherwell in Scotland for Communism'.

The growing centralisation of the British Communist Party meant that individuals such as Clarke and Wilkinson soon left. Their departure exacerbated the prejudice that intellectuals were 'objectively' allies of the ruling class and also helped to give the party an exclusive class-based approach typical of no other British left-wing organisation. John Maclean gave his reason for not joining as 'The Communist Party has sold itself to Moscow, with disastrous results both to Russia and to the British revolutionary movement.'

The tragedy for Maclean and others like him was that no space remained on the British Left for any organisations other than the huge and dominant Labour Party and a small Communist Party. Individuals who refused to submit to either were doomed to impotence. From the 1920s until today, many socialists have agonised over whether to join either organisation and try to change them from within, or else set up a new and miniscule body. In 1996, for instance, Arthur Scargill and a small group of sympathisers broke away from Labour and formed the Socialist Labour Party. A principled stand, maybe; but also politically futile.

John Maclean's experiences offer an ominous portent for Mr Scargill. The Scot's isolation exacerbated his physical and mental ill-health. He was left very much alone; even his former colleague, Harry McShane, felt there was no alternative to joining the Communist Party. Instead, Maclean set up the small Scottish Workers' Republican Party, but it lacked both members and influence. He continued his exhausting round of propaganda, even though friends such as Dora Montefiore noticed that two further gaol sentences had left him 'a mental wreck'.

In November 1923, aged just forty-four, Maclean caught pneumonia after he had given away his overcoat to a destitute West Indian, and he died. The Jamaican wrote to Maclean's widow Agnes: 'He was the greatest Man in Scotland one great lump of kindness and sincerity.' It was a moving epitaph to a life which had promised much but in fact achieved little.

By 1922 the fledgeling British Communist Party was in trouble. Lenin had predicted that when Britain lost much of its overseas empire then its living standards would drop and the working-class would become more receptive to Marxist ideas – but this forecast showed no signs of coming true. The stiff and formal Marxism – or Marxism-Leninism as it was increasingly called – propagated by the party duplicated many of the flaws of H.M. Hyndman's ideas.

The party was stuck in a ghetto largely of its own making. Its dull and linguistically-impoverished Marxism rejected the pluralism and tolerance which had characterised the British Left up to 1914. Members were expected to read and then learn off by heart passages from the works of Lenin, Marx and Stalin. Talking of this era, the Communist historian A.L. Morton once remarked that 'there had to be a Marxist view of everything from biology to postage stamps':

> . . . we still had, in the Marxist education of those very early days, a form of catechism – you asked: what is a class? – and you had an answer; what is a commodity, and you had the answer. What is value? What is surplus value? And when you had grasped the answers to all the questions you were Marxists!

Such learning by rote has uncanny parallels with aspects of the Catholic church.

One critic has pointed out that Lenin's writings are full of aggressive words and metaphors such as camps, offensives, guerrilla warfare, firing squads, shooting, attack, seize, exterminate. The Communist Party imitated this 'militarisation' of language, turning its back on the old radical traditions of accessibility and tolerance. Party publications abounded with talk of 'rank and file', 'cadres', 'vanguards', 'comrades' and so on – all terms which, like a masonic handshake, identified the faithful but excluded everyone else. Any party which called for a 'dictatorship', as in the dictatorship of the proletariat, completely misread British public opinion.

The Comintern bought the party its headquarters at 16 King Street, Covent Garden in 1921, but not even Moscow's subsidies could disguise the British Communists' desperate plight. Instead of examining the situation on its merits, the Comintern held to a 'line' which applied in each and every country. In Germany, France and Italy the respective Communist Parties did not have a large Labour Party to contend with; in Britain it did. No matter: Moscow's solution to the crisis was to insist that the British party was not 'Bolshevik' enough, a fault that should be rectified immediately.

A Commission of Inquiry was set up, headed by two young men very different from each other and yet who between them ran the British Communist Party for the next thirty-five years. One was Harry Pollitt, an outgoing Lancashire boilermaker and inspiring public speaker. Pollitt's personal charm was acknowledged by even his fiercest political opponents. The other was Rajani Palme Dutt, a forbidding and very serious intellectual who tolerated no criticism of the Soviet Union because, as one of his colleagues put it, 'that would be for him like a sin against the Holy Ghost'.

Sent down from Balliol College, Oxford, in 1916 because of his anti-war views and then imprisoned in Aldershot Detention Barracks for six gruelling months, Dutt returned to Oxford the next year and still obtained a First. His father was an Indian doctor, his mother was Swedish. When Harry Pollitt was in Wandsworth Prison during the General Strike of 1926 he learnt to fart the *Internationale*. It is difficult to imagine Palme Dutt having bodily functions.

Pollitt's autobiography *Serving My Time* is, at least to begin with, a lively picture of the life of a political agitator in the early years of this century. He provides a moving portrait of his mother, a millworker who brought up her family on very little money. The young Pollitt knew Robert Blatchford's writings by heart and loved the friendly atmosphere of the local Clarion Fellowship Cycling Club.

He showed much courage in 1914 by holding open-air meetings attacking the war and was frequently manhandled and assaulted. Once he returned home to find a gauntlet of maimed and jeering soldiers. He was involved in virtually every left-wing campaign between 1914 and 1920 and then joined the Communist Party. Harry Pollitt was most certainly not the foreigner or opportunist that Fleet Street loved to believe made up the party's membership.

Subsequently, however, *Serving My Time* becomes very dull as Pollitt dutifully parrots the party line, printing huge chunks of his speeches and articles. This mind-numbing exercise is a feature of most Communist autobiographies and starkly reflects the deadening effect of Comintern Marxism. On one occasion, in 1939, Pollitt did oppose Moscow's directives and was briefly sacked from the post of General Secretary which he had held for ten years.

Palme Dutt never once, despite all the vagaries and inconsistencies, expressed any doubts. He edited *Labour Monthly* magazine for over fifty years, writing its 'Notes of the Month' which exercised an international influence. It is remarkable to read them today and see how Dutt could argue something one month and completely contradict himself the next. For this 'British Pope', God was indeed in Moscow.

The Commission of Inquiry recommended a new conception of what the Communist Party was and should be − in effect a thorough 'Bolshevisation' which meant instituting 'democratic centralism'. This powerful doctrine, enshrined in yet another horrible 'masonic' phrase, laid down that orders should flow from above down to party members – centralism, yes, democratic no. Once a 'line' had been announced from on high, each party member had to act on it unreservedly, no matter what he or she really thought. It was a concept that left no room for individual conscience let alone discussion or debate. Left-wingers like George Lansbury hated it: 'I told Lenin that the Bolshevik doctrine of discipline was abhorrent to me, that I could never put my mind into someone else's keeping.'

The Bolshevik approach – which Lenin had largely formulated during his residence in London in the early years of this century – introduced an authoritarianism all the more damaging because the Comintern was exclusively concerned with what Joseph Stalin in 1925 called 'Socialism in one country', that is, the Soviet Union. If Moscow knew it all, disagreement was heresy and heretics must be reviled and then expelled.

The British Communist Party operated a 'panel' system under which only people nominated by the old Executive were eligible for election to the new Executive. The Congress of the Party had to vote for the recommended list in its entirety – and it always did. This ensured a stable and quiescent leadership: only twenty-seven men and one woman served on the Politburo (another unattractive term) between 1922 and 1952. Unswerving loyalty to Moscow was displayed by the other European Communist Parties: Palmiro Togliatti effectively ran the Italian Communists between 1926 and 1964 and Maurice Thorez the French Communists between 1930 and 1964.

Such practices and beliefs explain why the national Labour Party repeatedly turned down the Communist Party's requests for affiliation and in 1924 decreed that individual Communists could no longer be members of the Labour Party as well. Two years later, nearly a quarter of the Communist Party were still individual members of the Labour Party but were then systematically expelled. The British Left was now irrevocably split between the Labour Party and the Communist Party, as Lenin had wanted, but without the sort of results he had anticipated.

Both sides used each and every dirty trick in order to infiltrate 'the other side'. Communist techniques were highly publicised – but prominent Labour politicians proved no less conniving. Herbert Morrison, for instance, was the chief 'Witchfinder General'. As his biographers noted: 'Morrison was himself not above using the techniques of the communists. He planted his own reliable members inside their organizations and whenever someone offered to defect to the Labour Party he asked him to remain and supply information. In this way he could acquire their documents.' The actions of Morrison and also of Ernest Bevin who fought an unceasing war against Communists inside the trade union movement made a nonsense of Tory claims that Labour was 'soft' on Bolshevism.

The British Communist Party was in a Catch-22 situation. Being so small it relied on the Soviet Union, but being dependent on the Soviet Union meant that it could not grow. The ideological hold of Moscow was confirmed when, from the middle of the 1920s, party branches set up 'Lenin Corners'. Members were expected to stand reverentially in front of these shrines for a few moments in silence.

It was, of course, a deification of Lenin totally contrary to anything taught by Marx and so similar to rites within the Catholic church as to be perverse. Moscow's hold was strengthened from 1926 when promising young party recruits were sent to the Lenin School in Moscow where they were trained as revolutionaries in the Bolshevik mould. One indication of the closeness of the links was that Harry Pollitt claimed to have visited Moscow no fewer than twenty-seven times between 1921 and 1930.

In such circumstances few British Communists showed much dissent – Trotsky's expulsion from the Soviet Union in 1928 caused barely a ripple. One who did was Shapurji

Saklatvala. An Indian born in Bombay to a wealthy Parsee family, he came to Britain in 1905. 'Sak' had political friends of all persuasions but his hatred of imperialism prompted him to join the Communist Party. In the early 1920s some parliamentary candidates stood simultaneously as both Labour and Communist Party candidates because, as we have seen, it was possible until 1924 to belong to both organisations.

In 1922 Saklatvala was elected Labour MP for Battersea North in London. He lost his seat in 1923 but won again in 1924. Even though a Labour government was in office, Prime Minister Ramsay MacDonald permitted Special Branch to tap Saklatvala's telephone, open his letters and raid his home. In 1926 the MP was actually gaoled for two months for sedition after a speech he delivered in Hyde Park; on the face of it, therefore, a model revolutionary.

But, in fact, 'Sak' had not completely discarded his background and upbringing. In 1927 he initiated his five children into the Parsee religion at a huge meeting at Caxton Hall and was promptly censured by the Party. Saklatvala lost his seat in 1929 and died in London in 1936. His ashes were laid to rest at the Parsee burial ground in Brookwood, Surrey.

Saklatvala's defiance was virtually unique. On a whole range of issues the 'line' as laid down from above was absolute. The multitude of ideas put forward by William Morris, Edward Carpenter, Robert Blatchford and others was sacrificed at the altar of 'scientific socialism'. Moral questions were unimportant as was any discussion of, say, women's issues; as David Marquand has commented, '. . . scruples are presumably as out of place in the class war as in any other war.' There was more debate whether the new newspaper, the *Daily Worker*, should carry racing tips than on more substantial political issues.

Nationalism was another issue rarely tackled, as John Maclean found out, and largely forgotten too was the artistic and cultural side of the movement – this was best dealt with 'after the Revolution'. Socialism was no longer about human beings but about power. In some places an alternative 'red' culture did sprout, such as Lumphinnans in Scotland, Mardy in Wales and Chopwell in Durham. Here, in or near to the 'Celtic fringe', activities included 'Red funerals' and the provision of reading rooms and bookshops. Hywel Francis and David Smith have described a few of the activities that took place in Mardy:

> ... there were the Young Pioneers and the 'Redlets' for the children removed from the Scouts and Wolf Clubs, competitions for boxers in Russia, and to raise a soccer team to visit the Soviet Union. 'Lenin weeks' in the coalfield and secular funerals that replaced one form of pomp with another – red ribbons in place of black ties, with wreaths in the shape of the hammer and sickle not the cross, rendition of the 'Red Flag' or the 'Internationale' instead of Welsh hymnology ...

But these Red Moscows were exceptional. Elsewhere the overwhelmingly working-class members of the Communist Party, many of whom were unemployed or had been victimised because of their political opinions, were isolated.

The opportunity had existed for the creation of a left-wing party which was outside of and alternative to Ramsay MacDonald's Labour Party. The remarkably high proportion of votes received by Communist Party candidates in the general elections of 1922 and 1923 – their (admittedly few) candidates averaged 25 per cent of the poll – confirmed this.

But the chance was thrown away by the leadership's subordination to Moscow. Instead of trying to come to terms with all the problems of being revolutionaries in a non-revolutionary situation, they abdicated independence of both thought and action. No 'good' socialism can be built on the foundations of servility.

The nadir of this attitude came in 1928 when the Comintern decided that, owing to internal Soviet demands, Communist Parties all over the world must switch to a 'Class versus Class' stance. Again, note the jargon. Communists now drew no distinctions between the vast majority of people who did not think as they did. Labour Party voters and members alike were considered as 'bad' as Conservatives. Because the mainstream of the labour movement had deceived the workers into the illusion of gains, they too should be condemned as 'social fascists'. Social democracy was, in fact, the same as fascism.

This approach could only increase the party's isolation and unpopularity. In 1929 party members were advised to spoil their ballot papers at the general election, a thoroughly negative action which summed up the depths to which the party had sunk. Over the next four years, as membership dropped to below 3,000, the party virtually ceased to exist.

What made this so tragic were the admirable qualities of numerous individual Communists. Many went to prison for their views, and during the General Strike of May 1926 most of the leadership were in Wandsworth gaol where they conducted heated political discussion on bits of lavatory paper passed from cell to cell.

One of the prisoners, Tommy Jackson, a voracious reader, discovered the novels of Jane Austen and read them pressed against the bars in order to make as much use of the daylight as he could. Another remarkable founder member of the party was Tom Mann, a veteran socialist who had been heavily involved in the Dock Strike of 1889 and whose sincerity was never doubted even by his political opponents such as Philip Snowden.

Quite apart from the leadership, over a thousand other British Communists were arrested during the General Strike, which is a remarkable tribute to their energy and courage. To join the Communist Party offered no prospect (except for the party functionaries) of material gain, but instead victimisation and the disruption of one's personal life. Tragically, these sacrifices were made in the name of a cause and a party which was unworthy of them. Because the New Jerusalem had become identified with the Soviet Union, important sections of the British Left set off down a road which proved a dead end.

In the 1920s the Labour Party, rooted as it was in the trade unions, ousted the Liberals as the main opposition to the Conservatives. The failure of the British Communist Party ensured that Labour monopolised the Centre-Left of British politics from then until now.

# Part Two

*From Clement Attlee to James Callaghan*

'THE GOAL I ASK US TO AIM AT IS NO NEW JERUSALEM, SIMPLY
A COUNTRY WITH STABLE PRICES, JOBS FOR THOSE WHO WANT
THEM AND HELP FOR THOSE WHO NEED IT.'
    Denis Healey interviewed in the *Guardian*, 17 March 1980

# 6

# The Thirties

## A New Beginning

'Marxism, in the hands of Marx and Engels, is the most fruitful conception both for the study of society and for action in it which we have yet achieved.'

A. L. ROWSE, 1933

'. . . most English people [in the 1930s] were enjoying a richer life than any previously known in the history of the world: longer holidays, shorter hours, higher real wages.'

A.J.P. TAYLOR, *ENGLISH HISTORY 1914–1945* (1970)

'. . . if our concern is with practical politics, we do better to decide the direction of advance than to debate the detail of Utopia. We must see clearly the next stretch of the journey. But we need not spend time now in arguing whether, beyond the horizon, the road swerves left or right.'

HUGH DALTON, 1935

After failing to cope with an economic crisis, the Labour government was soundly defeated at the subsequent general election. Several leading figures split off to form a new political party, while the Labour Party itself swung to the Left. The militant wing within the Party was led by the MP for Bristol South East who was the son of a peer. After a bitter internecine struggle the Left was defeated and a more moderate political programme was produced. Despite further election defeats, these policies eventually brought the Labour Party, after a decade and a half out of office, to a stunning victory at a general election.

What period does this synopsis refer to? It may sound like a summary of the 1980s and 1990s, but in fact it describes the 1930s and 1940s, a period which in uncanny ways foreshadowed recent events. For the election defeat of 1979, read 1931; for the Social Democrats, read MacDonald's National Labour Party; for Tony Benn, MP for Bristol South East and the son of Lord Stansgate, read Sir Stafford Cripps, MP for Bristol South East and the son of Lord Parmoor; for the 1983, 1987 and 1992 defeats, read 1935.

Of course the next question is: will there be a contemporary parallel to Labour's triumph at the 1945 election?

'The Thirties' have been much fought over by both politicians and historians. Was it a 'Red Decade' in which a generation of gullible young men threw in their lot with Stalin's Russia? Or a decade of hunger marches, dole queues and the means test? An era dominated by a so-called National Government which appeased fascism on the continent – W.H. Auden's 'low, dishonest decade'? Or a time of rising living standards for the majority; not of dole queues but of cinema queues – 20 million British people went to the cinema each week.

Some 2,000 Britons may have fought for the International Brigade in Spain, 45 million didn't. There were indeed hunger marches, but just as significant were George V's Jubilee celebrations of 1935 which proved so popular that they were extended. Was the success of Victor Gollancz's Left Book Club a more accurate barometer of the new period than the political apathy noted by such observers as George Orwell and J.B. Priestley?

The year 1931 marked the end of the first phase in the history of the British Labour Party. The Party had established itself as the main opposition to the Conservative Party by squeezing out the Liberals. Keir Hardie and his successors had created a modern political party rooted in the trade union movement which was pragmatic, moderate and constitutional. The Far Left, in the shape of the Communist Party, remained weak and unpopular.

But the major problem with this first phase was that Hardie and the other pioneers had never been clear what the Labour Party should actually do now that it was here to stay. It was a formidable electoral machine certainly, but to what end? Left-wing propaganda was always better at stressing wrongs than proposing remedies, but in order to bring about lasting social and political change the labour movement, particularly the Labour Party, had to come up with viable programmes and policies. How best should the New Jerusalem be achieved? Was it to be 'talk, talk' or – 'plan, plan'?

The most pressing problem after MacDonald's unexpected departure in 1931 was to find a new leader from the handful of forty-six Labour MPs, one-half of whom had been miners, who survived the October 1931 general election. The only Cabinet minister to retain his seat, and perhaps the last of the great pioneering generation of Keir Hardie socialists, was George Lansbury. He was duly elected to the post by his fellow MPs.

Lansbury was only three years younger than Keir Hardie and more than seven years older than Ramsay MacDonald. Although born in Suffolk in 1859 where his father worked as a navvy on the new East Anglian railways, Lansbury was always identified with the East End of London. Here he was brought up and lived for the rest of his life, apart from a brief spell in Australia. Several of the individuals mentioned so far in this book have been Scots, embodying Scotland's fertile contribution to British socialism. Lansbury represented the East End's significant role.

His political career was typical of many other socialists. Beginning as a Liberal, he then joined the Marxist SDF and went through the gamut of speaking at ill-attended meetings, often arriving to find no audience at all 'except for a dog or two and, perhaps, a stray child.' Lansbury then threw in his lot with the new Labour Party.

He was certainly one of the most attractive and appealing personalities that the British Left has ever produced. Photographs of him invariably show a happy smiling man whose obvious sense of humour contrasts with the severity of, say, Keir Hardie or John Maclean. The novelist Naomi Mitchison has described what often happened at the end of a meeting where Lansbury had just spoken: 'Afterwards men and women in the audience crowded round just to touch his coat sleeve and to feel comfort and refreshment.'

Lansbury was a devoted family man and a convivial friend whose home at 39 Bow Road in the East End remained open to all-comers at almost any hour. He once explained that he would rather live among his constituents and receive complaints from them in person, even if this meant a brick through the window, than just get a letter. Most MPs both before and since Lansbury's day would not agree. His son-in-law, Raymond Postgate, detailed Lansbury's day-to-day work in the East End:

> He was, in Bow itself, a sort of universal consultant – doing by himself work which 'Citizens' Advice Bureaux' try to do to-day. Almost daily the house in Bow was called at by men and women who were in legal, personal or financial difficulties and wanted 'G.L.' (the initials were by now commonly used) to advise and help.

His unostentatious style of living was rather different, for example, from the splendour of Ramsay MacDonald's later career. Lansbury was unusual too in combining his ethical socialism – he always regarded the Bible as a revolutionary document – with a wealth of practical and administrative experience. Not only did he run his own sawmill and timber business, for many years he led the Poplar Council, probably the poorest council in Britain. Lansbury's efforts on behalf of his local constitutents earned him the nickname 'the John Bull of Poplar'.

Lansbury was always prepared to make a stand for his beliefs. In 1912 he had resigned his seat as an MP in order to publicise his support for the suffragettes, not regaining it until 1922. In 1921 he led the movement known as 'Poplarism'. No matter how poor Poplar was, it still had to pay the same sums to central government as did much wealthier boroughs like Westminster and Kensington. In 1921, for example, West London with a rateable value of £15 million had just 4,800 people out of work. Poplar, with a rateable value of £4 million supported 86,500 people who were unemployed. In Lansbury's words, 'the poor had to keep the poor'.

Poplar Council decided, illegally, to stop collecting the rates for outside bodies such as the police. On 29 July 1921 the councillors headed by Lansbury marched five miles to the Law Courts in the Strand to put their case. He put the Council's case succinctly: 'If we have to choose between contempt of the poor and contempt of Court, it will be contempt of Court.'

In September 1921 the Poplar councillors were found guilty and sentenced to prison; the men in Brixton, the women in Holloway. Over the following weeks daily processions were held outside both gaols and Lansbury often addressed the crowds through the bars of his cell. He carried on handling council business in the governor's office. After six weeks the councillors were released and a measure of 'rates equalisation' enacted. Lansbury was also a renowned journalist, editing the *Daily Herald* and then his own weekly. Like almost all the first generation of British socialists, he was a fine speaker. A firm patriot, his programme for reform was revealingly titled *My England*. He steadfastly resisted MacDonald and Snowden's demands for economic cuts during the second Labour government.

In view of these qualities, why wasn't this seeming paragon of a socialist a brilliant success as Labour Party leader? Lansbury was not a failure, for he certainly helped restore party morale, especially when it is remembered that the National Government had more than ten times the number of Labour MPs. Yet essentially the Party under his leadership marked time. Sadly, Lansbury had become leader too late. By 1931 he was a man of seventy-two with years of unceasing activity behind him. For the rest of his life he was dogged by ill-health, spending six months in hospital in 1934 after breaking his thigh in a fall. His adored wife Bessie had died the year before. One of the big 'ifs' is what might have happened if Lansbury had led the Labour Party in the 1920s in place of MacDonald. But he didn't.

There was another reason for Lansbury's comparative ineffectiveness. He remained a convinced pacifist, reflecting, along with Keir Hardie, one important and honourable strand within the British Left; in his own words, '. . . are we not taught that, because Christ Himself became flesh, therefore all life is sacred?' The difficulty with this belief in the 1930s was that it was virtually suicidal to turn the other cheek to Hitler and the Nazis. Pacifism might claim a moral victory, but in human terms it entailed much suffering.

Lansbury resigned as leader at the 1935 Labour Party Conference over this very issue, his exit hastened by a brutally realistic and hard-hitting speech from Ernest Bevin who argued that might must be met by might. Lansbury spent much of the late 1930s visiting Hitler and Mussolini, hoping to persuade them to change their views and actions. Like Neville Chamberlain, he had little success.

The failure of Lansbury's missions abroad should not obliterate his many achievements. His death in 1940 marked the passing of the last of the old guard, those socialist activists of the late nineteenth century who had presided over the decisive growth of the British Labour Party. He left only a small sum in his will, having been generous with his resources to the end. It is very moving to sit in the Tower Hamlets Local History Library and read the scores of letters sent to his family by people of every class, background and opinion who fervently admired and revered Lansbury.

His political ideas and beliefs sprang from a deep-rooted love and affection for his own country and its people. A.J.P. Taylor called him 'the most lovable figure in modern politics'. George Lansbury has left behind an example of personal and moral integrity which offers a benchmark for future generations. He was the last Labour leader to view politics primarily in Christian and ethical terms until the arrival of Tony Blair. The subject of two excellent biographies already in the 1990s, Lansbury looks set to become increasingly more of a contemporary than an historical figure.

Before 1931 Marxism had been a negligible force in British life. But, after the collapse of the MacDonald administration in 1931, it became almost fashionable. The writer and poet Kathleen Raine once recalled: 'Not to be a Marxist then was held to be a mark either of incorrigible selfishness or lack of seriousness.' Conservative historian Robert Blake agrees: 'In the 1930s it was intellectually disreputable to be a Tory – anyway if you were a young man.'

At both Oxford and Cambridge two parallel actions revealed the shift in attitudes. Undergraduates were no longer such automatic members of the Establishment as they had been in May 1926 when the majority cheerfully blacklegged during the General Strike. In February 1933 the Oxford Union passed a resolution that 'in no circumstances' would they fight for King and country. The outrage was predictable: the *Daily Express* claimed that the resolution had been supported by 'woozy-minded Communists and sexual indeterminates'.

On Armistice Day in Cambridge, 11 November 1933, students laid an anti-war wreath on the memorial and were attacked by their colleagues. The Communist October Club was founded as too was a branch of the Party itself. The prominence of the October Club was largely due to a handful of talented students, as the careers of three of them testify. David Haden Guest was a star pupil of the philosopher Wittgenstein before teaching in Moscow, starting a 'People's Bookshop' in

Battersea, London and then lecturing at University College, Southampton.

His successor as Communist Party organiser was Charles Madge who left the university because of a relationship with Kathleen Raine. Madge subsequently founded the path-breaking organisation Mass Observation which, from the late 1930s, pioneered the study of popular beliefs and opinions. He was in turn succeeded by John Cornford, a poet and political activist whose charismatic personality galvanised everyone he met. These undergraduates were not just armchair theorists; both Guest and Cornford were later killed fighting for the Republicans in the Spanish Civil War.

At Oxford, student radicalism was less spectacular – although even here the future novelist Barbara Pym, surely an unlikely revolutionary, marched behind the October Club banner. The movement was guided by the economics don G.D.H. Cole, a prolific writer and lecturer who constituted a one-man think-tank. He also found the time to write a detective novel each year with his wife Margaret, herself a fine historian. At the London School of Economics the animating force was Professor Harold Laski, a journalist and academic much loved for his inspiring lectures and personal generosity – there were always queues outside his door as people waited for advice. Also a councillor in Fulham, Laski's writings explored the relationships between liberty, democracy and socialism.

Some students, especially in Cambridge – particularly the much studied circle of Philby, Blunt, Burgess, Maclean and now John Cairncross – threw in their lot with the Soviet Union. Most, however, did not. But how could they make their political voice heard? Which parties or groups could they join on leaving university? One important body was the Socialist League led by Sir Stafford Cripps.

Today Cripps is best remembered for the 'austerity' measures he took to promote economic growth when Chancellor of the Exchequer in Attlee's post-war government. His hairshirt asceticism was a prominent feature of his own life. A lifelong teetotaller but chainsmoker, service in the Red Cross during the First World War had destroyed his digestive system so that he was necessarily a vegetarian. Cripps' two meals a day consisted of raw fruit or vegetables, soured milk, and brown bread and butter with the occasional baked potato thrown in as a luxury. As if this wasn't punishing enough, he invariably got up at four each morning and plunged into a cold bath. His sense of self-righteousness could be overpowering; Churchill once remarked that 'there, but for the grace of God, goes God.'

Cripps, who was born in 1889, came from what had originally been a Conservative background. His father, for many years a Tory MP, was duly ennobled but then shifted his political allegiance over to Labour, serving in both Ramsay MacDonald administrations of 1924 and 1929–31. His son Stafford went to Winchester and then won a scholarship to Oxford, although he actually ended up at London University because the science facilities were so much better.

In the 1920s he built up a formidable reputation at the Bar and became the youngest KC in 1927. But whereas most barristers were happy to take the money and run, Cripps often represented trade unions at little or no charge. For example, he argued the miners' case at the inquiry into the Gresford colliery disaster in September 1934 in which 265 men were killed. Cripps' fourteen-hour summing-up lasted over three days.

His undoubted talents marked him out for political office and he was elected MP for Bristol East at a by-election in January 1931. Serving as MacDonald's Solicitor-General he proved a moderate member of the administration, and when in August 1931 MacDonald asked him to join the National Government Cripps agonised for twelve days before turning down the offer. But then Cripps, like many other people who remained in the Labour Party, swung sharply leftwards in response to the collapse of MacDonald's government and the election debacle.

In October 1932 he set up the Socialist League which as a ginger group endeavoured to provide ideas and research for the use of the Labour Party. Its membership ranged from J.T. Murphy, a gifted writer and organiser once a founder member of the Communist Party but since expelled, to the young Michael Foot and Barbara Betts (later Castle), to the outstanding journalist H.N. Brailsford. Another recruit was Sir Charles Trevelyan, the park gates of whose mansion in Northumberland were decorated with the hammer and sickle. But it was Cripps who soon dominated the League, both intellectually and also financially, subsidising a body which never had more than 3,000 members.

In a series of pamphlets and lectures Cripps argued that any future Labour administration must be willing to take drastic emergency action if it was serious about introducing radical change in Britain. In *Can Socialism Come by Constitutional Methods?* he suggested that a socialist government might have 'to make itself temporarily into a dictatorship'. It should abolish the House of Lords and if necessary prolong the life of Parliament for a further term 'without an election'. He hinted too at electoral reforms 'to eliminate the power of money.'

Cripps also advocated passing a statute giving the government powers to control all financial dealings in the City of London; this legislation would not be subject to judicial review. He then went on to demand that 'the whole financial machinery' of Britain, and not just the City, should be taken over by the state.

It was a startlingly bold series of proposals, much more drastic than anything later put forward by Tony Benn in the 1980s. And in January 1934 Cripps aimed his fire at an even more controversial target. In what became known as his Buckingham Palace speech, he suggested there might be royal opposition to any radical government. The subsequent outcry caused Cripps to back down smartly. Opponents began to question his sanity, exactly as they did with Tony Benn; Cripps was becoming 'a dangerous political lunatic', as Hugh Dalton had already written in his diary the year before.

If you read Cripps' writings today, several points emerge. Like his aunt, Beatrice Webb, he placed inordinate faith in 'experts'. At one point he claimed that the working of several measures 'is not a matter for submission to the electorate, [it] is a matter for the experts' – no doubt Cripps and the Webbs among them. He was often inconsistent, one moment calling for 'a temporary dictatorship', the next attacking the right wing for associating socialism with dictatorship. Michael Foot put it neatly: 'His [Cripps] Marxist slogans were undigested; he declared the class war without ever having studied the contours of the battlefield.'

There was, however, little chance that Cripps would be able to implement his plans – and he gave no indication as to how popular electoral support might be obtained. For a start, the League had virtually no contact with the trade unions who acted as the power brokers in the labour movement. The General Secretary of the TUC, Walter Citrine, did attend one League meeting and his account summed up the yawning gulf between power and posture.

> It was altogether an interesting meeting and in response to an invitation to meet the group again I wound up by saying that I thought we had come to discuss practical politics. What I had found, however, was that we were discussing ultimate Socialist objectives of a theoretical character. I did not propose to waste my time further in doing so.

Cripps' aggressive rhetoric often obscured the valuable work done by other members of the League. Its first chairman was an able civil servant, E.F. Wise, who died tragically young in November 1933. The list of League publications show the fruits of much more detailed thinking than anything produced by Cripps. G.D.H. Cole, for instance, published study guides which dealt with the gold standard, the Bank of England, banking generally and credit control. Harold Laski was another regular contributor.

But the research side of the League's activities was often

overlooked because of Cripps' confrontational stance. Ben Pimlott once noted that the League 'merely grouped together the party intellectuals in an inward-looking huddle which enabled them to reinforce their own convictions without the distasteful need for compromise.' He continued, in words which are relevant well beyond the 1930s, 'the more the League kept its own company the more it became convinced of its own rightness.'

In early 1937 the League embarked on a suicidal joint campaign with the Independent Labour Party and the Communist Party, calling for a Popular Front. This led to its inevitable disaffiliation from the Labour Party and closure. The impotence of the Labour Left was brought home in 1939 when both Cripps and Aneurin Bevan were expelled from the Labour Party. One permanent legacy of Cripps' efforts in the 1930s was the weekly newspaper *Tribune* which in years to come offered a rallying point for the Labour Left.

The Socialist League must be judged a failure. How successful was the political organisation further to its Left, the Communist Party of Great Britain? Still mired in the 'Third Period' and calling for the vilification of all non-Communists, it proved unable to take advantage of the collapse of MacDonald's government. Instead of offering a constructive alternative to the Labour Party it dissipated its time initiating breakaway unions such as the United Clothing Workers' Union and the United Mineworkers of Scotland, both of which challenged the idea of solidarity, which was a touchstone of labour sentiment.

Internationally the Comintern in Moscow completely misjudged events, claiming that Hitler's accession to power in January 1933 was devoid of political significance. It also ordered that no Communist Party should discuss this decision. None did. Belatedly, the Comintern realised that it was better to build alliances than destroy them and gradually by 1935 it moved to a 'Popular Front' policy. Non-Communists were now acceptable.

The British party had been slow to adopt the 'Third Period' line and as late as 1935 its programme was called simply *For A Soviet Britain*, as if the public was ever likely to welcome a 'foreign' government. The necessity for a Popular Front was in any case less immediately obvious in Britain than in France or Spain where working-class organisations were split into a variety of often antagonistic factions. Here, as trade union leaders like Citrine argued, Britain already possessed a Popular Front made up of trade unions, the Labour Party and the Co-operative movement.

Many members of the Labour Party and the trade unions also remembered that just a few years before they had been abused as 'social fascists'. The publisher Victor Gollancz became a stalwart of the Popular Front but apparently never knew that the Communists had ever had any other policy (Orwell commented in his usual acerbic way that 'It's frightful that people who are so ignorant should have so much influence'). Others proved less politically illiterate, recalling that Communist candidates stood against Labour Party candidates at elections and that the party had also promoted breakaway unions.

The Popular Front campaign represented an attempt to heal the post-1917 split in the British labour movement between the moderates and the militants. It proved a failure − it was eighteen years too late. When the Communist Party applied for affiliation to the Labour Party in 1935 the request was turned down on two grounds. First of all the Communist Party's call for 'the dictatorship of the proletariat' was deemed to be in conflict with the Labour Party's 'defence of political democracy'. Secondly, the request stemmed from the Comintern's change of tactics and not from any principled stand.

The Communist Party challenged the National Council of Labour to scrutinise its accounts in order to disprove 'Moscow gold' accusations − the offer was never taken up − and it does indeed appear that the subsidies had been stopped in the mid-1930s. In 1937 the party dropped the idea of the dictatorship of the proletariat. The *Daily Worker* omitted the Hammer and Sickle emblem and slogan 'Workers of the World, Unite!' from its front page. But still the Labour Party refused affiliation.

As it turned out, the Labour Party was correct in its assessment. If the Communist Party really had changed its spots it would have candidly confronted its own past. It didn't. In 1937 the veteran Communist Tom Bell, another Scot, published a short history of the Party which dealt with the sectarian 'Third Period' in some detail. This was heresy. As the party was now in favour of a Popular Front, then it must always have been in favour of a Popular Front.

Bell's book was vitriolically reviewed in *Labour Monthly* by the journalist and typographer, Allen Hutt. The Communist Party leadership quickly 'withdrew' Bell's book, writing to all individual members demanding that copies be returned immediately to party headquarters – hardly an example of the tolerance and freedom of debate which should have characterised the Popular Front.

The myth of party infallibility ensured that fresh party recruits frequently failed to understand the zig-zags in policy and soon left. The turnover of members in Brighton, for instance, changed every two years. Even internal party publications admitted that members sometimes proved unable to answer criticisms when the 'line' was altered: '. . . it must be confessed that too often our Party comrades are baffled in their attempts to answer such questions and need to have recourse to others to help them out of their difficulties.' In the summer of 1939 the party line was to change once more – its third major reversal in less than a decade – and then again two years later in 1941.

Between 1935 and 1939 the party went to almost any lengths to curry favour. The Young Communist League announced that it would welcome recruits from members of religious groups, boy scouts and girl guides, while on May Day 1938 leading Scottish Communists paraded in tartan bearing pictures of such unlikely early Communists as Robert Bruce,

William Wallace, Robbie Burns and Robert Louis Stevenson. Membership did grow, reaching over 17,000 in 1939. Freed from the Comintern's shackles – during the Popular Front period Moscow recognised the validity of 'national roads to socialism' – Marxism for the first time established a significant presence in Britain.

Most historians prefer to concentrate on the much-tilled and academically respectable soil of the Auden, Spender, Day Lewis, MacNeice coterie, overlooking the many individuals whose commitment to the Left proved more lasting and fruitful. The late 1930s saw a flowering of radical intellectual work. Apart from Marxist scientists like J.D.Bernal, J.B.S.Haldane, Hyman Levy and Joseph Needham, Marxist musician Alan Bush founded the Workers' Musical Association in 1936 whilst Francis Klingender and others set up the Artists' International Association. Many theatre people, including Paul Robeson, were involved in Unity Theatre in London and its branches outside the capital.

Of the historians and critics, outstanding figures included Montagu Slater, Randall Swingler, Edgell Rickword, Jack Lindsay, Gordon Childe, A.L. Lloyd, Rex Warner, A.L. Morton, Christopher Caudwell, Ralph Fox, Alick West, T.A. Jackson, Dona Torr, James Boswell and Professor George Thomson. There were new magazines such as *Left Review* and *Modern Quarterly*, the Marx Memorial Library and Workers' School was founded, and the Communist Party publishers Lawrence and Wishart brought out English–language versions of Marx's works.

Every single one of these individuals remained 'on the Left' for the remainder of their lives, displaying a resilience which reminded E.P.Thompson of the tenacity of eighteenth-century dissenters. Several lived close to each other in north Essex and formed a kind of alternative left–wing community.

This Marxism of the mid-1930s was not, unlike in the 1960s and 1970s, primarily of an academic bent. For one thing it was not always advisable for left–wing dons to publicise their opinions: historian Christopher Hill published his early work under the pseudonym C.E. Gore, Joseph Needham was also 'Henry Holorenshaw' and Cambridge economics don Maurice Dobb was the anonymous editor of the volume *Britain Without Capitalists*. This Marxist tradition was deliberately populist, aiming at a largely non-university educated readership.

No matter how eminent their official positions, university socialists such as G.D.H. Cole and R.H. Tawney happily immersed themselves in the adult education movement. They had to explain their ideas before very varied audiences. In the preface to one of his books, R.H. Tawney paid tribute to his adult education classes: 'The friendly smitings of weavers, potters, miners, and engineers, have taught me much about the problems of political and economic science which cannot easily be learned from books.'

One splendid example of how best to write for a general readership without being patronising was provided by Professor J.B.S.Haldane, a scientist from a distinguished family (his sister was the novelist Naomi Mitchison). He was renowned for his courage in trying out experiments with himself as the guinea pig. Professor of Genetics and then of Biochemistry at London University, Haldane's academic credentials were impeccable but he was not afraid of popularising his ideas, writing a book for children and from 1937 a weekly column in the *Daily Worker*. All 345 articles offered a lucid and concise summary of an often abstruse topic. The *Daily Worker* itself, even if unable to see the Soviet Union as anything other than a workers' paradise, was a splendid and vigorous read. Claud Cockburn was one of its regular contributors. The newspaper reached a circulation of over 100,000 on Saturdays.

The Left Book Club, run by the publisher Victor Gollancz, turned out to be a particularly influential creation of the late 1930s. The idea of a membership club had first been floated in the United States: members received the monthly choice but could then choose other titles at reduced prices. The Left Book Club was formally established in the summer of 1936.

The three people who chose and commissioned the books were Gollancz, Harold Laski and the writer John Strachey. Neither Gollancz nor Laski were members of the Communist Party; nor was Strachey, who was regarded as a more valuable asset if he didn't join.

Strachey, whose uncle was the writer Lytton Strachey, had once been a Labour MP and initially flirted with the New Party set up by Sir Oswald Mosley after he had resigned from MacDonald's government. Strachey then swung sharply to the left, rather like Sir Stafford Cripps. In the 1930s he published three lengthy books which were Marxist in tone and produced under the supervision of the Communist Party's chief ideologist, Palme Dutt. Even more successful was his shorter work *Why You Should Be A Socialist*, a phenomenon which sold over 300,000 copies.

Dutt and the Communist Party leadership naturally saw the Left Book Club as a valuable recruiting ground. Dutt once wrote to Strachey claiming that the Club's success was 'probably the greater because it is recognised by the general public as an independent commercial enterprise on its own feet, and not the propaganda of a particular political organisation.' Perhaps, but others proved more discerning, as Gollancz's biographer Ruth Dudley Edwards has pointed out: '. . . his propaganda alienated from the outset all Tories and most Liberals and anti-communist Labour. Bereft of other friends, Victor was thrown into the arms of the Communist Party.' Of the Club's first twenty-seven books, fifteen were written by Communists. But in the context of the Popular Front, this was not necessarily a handicap. Membership climbed to a remarkable 60,000, organised into 1,300 groups and kept informed by the monthly *Left News*.

Digesting the Left Book Club publications today is something of a slog. A.J.P. Taylor thought that the Club acted as a safety valve in which reading became 'a substitute for action, not a prelude to it'; Club members 'worked off their rebelliousness by plodding through yet another orange-covered publication.' The most accessible titles were generally the less political volumes such as George Orwell's *The Road to Wigan Pier* and Wilf Macartney's *Walls Have Mouths* about British prison conditions.

The official historian of the Left Book Club presented the project as one of sweetness and light. It wasn't. The Labour Party in the shape of one of its leading figures, Hugh Dalton, began to manoeuvre for space in *Left News* as well as places on the editoral board. The Communist Party also demanded official representation and local readers' groups campaigned for a measure of internal democracy.

Gollancz vacillated between the various vested interests. He turned down Orwell's book about the Spanish Civil War, *Homage to Catalonia*, before a word had been written because he knew Orwell would offend the Communists by his views. At the same time Gollancz planned to include two prominent Liberals on the selection committee and rename the Club the Anti-Fascist Association in order to widen its appeal. Gollancz's energy helped make the Club a success, but he was wildly over-optimistic in his aims: 'I believe, as I have always believed, that we shall eventually reach a quarter of a million [members].'

In fact any future plans for the Club were dashed by the signing of the Nazi-Soviet Pact in August 1939 which shattered Gollancz's faith in the Communist Party. The Left Book Club declined rapidly, although it was not officially wound up until 1945. It is always difficult to assess the power and influence of ideas; A.J.P. Taylor might have been rude about the Club, but it undoubtedly played a part in liberalising the British middle classes – with results that became evident both during and after the war. Conservatives bemoaning Labour's electoral triumph in 1945 often pointed an accusing finger at the Left Book Club, with some justification.

Within the mainstream labour movement fresh thinking was hampered, as it often still is, by the cumbersome institutional machinery set up by the Labour Party in 1918. Resolutions to conferences were cobbled together into 'composite' resolutions and then briefly and superficially debated at Conference – the 'debate' being among delegates who had either made up their minds already or were mandated to vote in a certain way regardless of the arguments voiced.

The resolutions lived or died by the trade union block vote, which was adept at stopping new ideas or initiatives but feeble at promoting them. With so many interest groups at work inside the Labour Party and the larger trade unions – and Britain was renowned for its huge number of unions – then 'logrolling' made it easy for one group to scotch a proposal which was potentially threatening: 'I'll stop this resolution for you if you help stop that one for me.' Such practices persist to this day.

As G.D.H. Cole and others pointed out, the Labour Party had no proper research facilities available to formulate and discuss ideas or policies. In any case the labour movement traditionally distrusted what it thought of as 'cleverness'. By contrast the Conservative Party, often dismissed as 'the stupid party', had established a research department in 1929. The bureaucratic shambles was all the more obstructive because in response to '1931' the unions tightened their grip on the Labour Party. Never again would a Ramsay MacDonald dazzle and dominate the movement over the heads of union bosses.

A National Joint Council of trade unions and Labour Party leaders set up in 1932 met the day before the Labour Party's own body, thus pre-empting and vetting contentious issues. Historian Henry Pelling has even called the Labour Party at this time 'the General Council's party'. The trade unions rarely welcomed rigorous analysis of the current situation. They swiftly stamped on a plan to rename the Labour Party 'the Socialist Party'. Instead they put their weight behind professional and competent party leaders whom they could trust, such as Clement Attlee and Herbert Morrison.

This weight was of course derived from the unions' financial clout. Although the Conservative government had taken advantage of the defeat of the General Strike to pass legislation stipulating that union members now had to 'contract in' to contribute to the political levy, the measure had only limited effect. In fact, as Michael Pinto-Duschinsky has noted:

> By the 1930s there was no real shortage of money for the Labour party from the trade unions. The party's main difficulty stemmed from the fact that long years of reliance on union political levies meant that additional sources of funds had not been developed. In particular, the availability of easy union money had hindered the growth of Labour's constituency organizations.

Not only did trade union finance discourage local grassroots activity, many of the MPs who reached Parliament because of union support were of distinctly second-rate quality: solid, dependable, unadventurous. In effect the trade unions had not advanced beyond the first phase of the British labour movement, namely that of foundation and consolidation. Understandably, they were concerned above all to protect their members' interests, mainly levels of pay and working conditions. These essentially sectional and industrial concerns discouraged the unions from developing broader political and national strategies. One telling demonstration of this conservatism: few if any of the trade unions in the 1930s possessed research departments.

Take the issue of unemployment which was at the heart of domestic politics in this decade. If the National Government had few suggestions about what might be done, then the trade unions had even less. What did the TUC do in the 1930s? What programmes did it hammer out, what publications did it issue? Nothing. Instead the TUC came up with the idea of creating unemployed clubs and issuing their members with chess sets and footballs! The only controversial TUC action this decade came when Walter Citrine accepted a knighthood in 1935, to the disgust of some in the labour movement.

The TUC's paralysis of nerve inevitably spread to the cautious and timid Parliamentary Labour Party. The only political success came in 1934 when the energetic Herbert Morrison led Labour to its first ever victory at the London County Council elections. Otherwise the National Government under Ramsay MacDonald and then Stanley Baldwin was able to coast along undisturbed by its opponents. Looking back at this period, John Saville has delivered a bleak but accurate assessment:

> . . . the most striking political characteristic of the 1930s was the way in which successive Conservative governments were able to ignore, on all fundamental matters, the Labour Party inside Westminster and the political and industrial movements outside.

For some on the Left, subscribers to the 'betrayal thesis' which claims that trade union and Labour leaders are always traitors and cowards, this caution was yet further evidence of personal weakness. It was not as simple as this. Weak leadership reflected a weak membership – or perhaps non-membership as the trade unions lost nearly half their total number between 1920 and 1933.

Apathy and political demoralisation were widespread. Turnouts at elections dropped. Mass Observation's 1939 study *Britain* revealed a politically ignorant population. In Scotland everybody was so passive that the authorities encouraged the playing of football not as an antidote to revolution but in an attempt to wake people up a bit. With his usual bluntness, George Orwell pointed out that although a great deal of money was raised for the Republican side during the Spanish Civil War it probably represented less than 5 per cent of the sum spent on the football pools each week. He lamented that 'there is no turbulence left in England.'

Is that it then? The 1930s as a total write-off for the British Left? In terms of immediate and practical results, yes. But, with hindsight, the groundwork was clearly being laid for the political transformation of the 1940s and the creation of a powerful consensus which dominated both Labour and Conservative thinking until the late 1970s.

Crucial to this burgeoning 'middle-way' opinion during the 1930s was its largely non-party political character. Contributors to this mood – it was too vague to categorise as a movement – ranged from the Conservative Harold Macmillan to Liberal John Maynard Keynes, and to socialists Hugh Dalton and Evan Durbin. All recognised the value of patience, appreciating that the National Government's huge majority ruled out the 'quick fix' in favour of the 'long haul'.

The ending of free trade in 1932 meant that the intellectual justification for the Liberal Party with its abhorrence of tariff barriers and import restrictions had dissolved. The vacuum was filled by the vogue for planning and state intervention pioneered by the Soviet government which embarked on its Five Year Plan in 1928 and apparently completed it within four years. The Soviet experience provided a fruitful example and not a rigid and doctrinaire blueprint to be followed down to the last detail. No one could accuse, say, Harold Macmillan or Hugh Dalton of being 'fellow travellers' and, in any case, the Soviet lesson was reinforced by the success of President Roosevelt's 'New Deal' in the United States.

The genesis of the British approach can be traced back to Macmillan's joint authorship of *Industry and State* in 1927 and the Liberal manifesto *We Can Conquer Unemployment* of 1929. The pace quickened in the 1930s when it became clear that neither orthodox Conservatism nor traditional ethical socialism could deliver the economic growth needed to reduce unemployment. In 1931, for example, *Weekend Review* published a National Plan for Britain, advocating state intervention, a series of Five Year Plans, a 'Business University', 'economic democracy' and equality of sacrifice. The overwhelmingly favourable reponse led to the foundation of PEP (Political and Economic Planning) in October 1931. Both this body's name and the title of its journal, *Planning*, testified to the 'big idea' of the 1930s progressives. Similarly another new body, the Federation of Progressive Societies and Individuals, published a journal from April 1934 which was called *Plan*.

The Next Five Years Group also issued several policy documents and its wide membership formed what was effectively a British Popular Front. Harold Macmillan published *The Middle Way* in 1938, calling for a Minimum Wage Act, a National Investment Board and planning for full employment. Outside, non-partisan bodies like the Pilgrim Trust explored the issue of *Men Without Work*. John Boyd Orr studied working-class diet. The Women's Health Inquiry Committee researched into *Working-Class Wives*, journalists such as George Orwell and Fenner Brockway helped to publicise how the other half – or more – lived. On and on it went.

Naturally there could be no uniformity or party line in this maelstrom of ideas, apart from recognising that the former economic orthodoxy of free trade, the gold standard and balanced budgets were now the discarded relics of the Victorian age. Always stimulating and provocative, none of these publications could be dismissed as the work of 'party hacks'. Taken as a whole, they amounted to a body of material far more impressive than anything produced by the Labour Party or the trade unions, as well as being more constructive than most Left Book Club publications.

Important contributions were certainly made by individual members of the Labour Party, often sponsored by the domineering and noisy character of Hugh Dalton, possibly the most important left-wing figure of the 1930s. Not only did Dalton help shift the Labour Party's foreign policy away from a quasi-pacifism towards outright opposition to Hitler and Mussolini and the consequent need to accept rearmament, he also helped make these 'Big Ideas' acceptable to the timorous Labour Party.

On the face of it, Dalton was an unlikely recruit to the Labour Party, although, as Kenneth Morgan justifiably pointed out, the Labour Party has always been a 'remarkably generous refuge for social eccentrics'. Born in 1887, Dalton's father had been the personal tutor to the future King George V and then a Canon at Windsor Chapel. Hugh was sent to Eton and King's College, Cambridge, where he fell under the spell of the poet and Fabian Rupert Brooke. Another important influence was Keir Hardie who had visited the university in February 1907. His endurance in the face of undergraduate hostility so impressed Dalton that he always regarded 'Keir Hardie Night' as 'his own, personal, Damascus Road': 'I admired his total lack of fear or anger, his dignified bearing, his simplicity of speech and thought and faith . . .'

After service in Italy during the First World War, Dalton was appointed a lecturer at the London School of Economics. An unhappy marriage and the tragic death of his young daughter allowed Dalton to channel his formidable energies into politics. That he should have thrown in his lot with the Labour Party – and experienced no prejudice despite his privileged background – illustrates once again how the Party was quietly expanding away from the predominantly working-class character of its early days.

Always gossiping and intriguing, Dalton was never an easy man to get on with and his personal antipathy towards his old tutor J.M. Keynes perhaps delayed the acceptance of 'Keynesianism' within the Labour Party. Keynes claimed that 'The outstanding faults of the economic society in which we live are its failure to provide full employment and its arbitrary and inequitable distribution of wealth and income.' Government intervention, if selective and planned, could boost the economy by means of the multiplier and therefore increase consumption if necessary. It was a mistake to try and balance the budget year by year. Instead of being a passive 'nightwatchman' adjudicating between rival claims, the government should adopt an energetic and active role – behave as a player rather than a referee or umpire.

Although his *General Theory* was not published in book form until 1936, the direction of Keynes' ideas had been known for several years before then. Dalton and others realised that, in Stuart Holland's words, Keynes '. . . seemed to offer a middle way between over-centralised Soviet planning and an anarchic unplanned capitalist market.' Fascism and communism were no longer the only political choices on offer. Keynes had provided the economic justification for European social democracy, offering a framework for piecemeal but important progress rather than revolutionary upheaval.

What distinguished Dalton and his circle from Harold Macmillan's 'non-Labour' group was the greater emphasis that they as left-wingers placed on the need for equality. But they shared a preference for detail rather than wild assertion and for the practical over the theoretical – which is why Dalton called his most important book *Practical Socialism for Britain*. The detail was not necessarily very exciting. Just look at the titles of three of Evan Durbin's 1930s books: *Purchasing Power and Trade Depression*, *The Problem of Credit Policy* and *Socialist Credit Policy* – hardly bedside reading.

Nevertheless it was significant that Durbin and his colleagues in the New Fabian Research Bureau, set up by the indefatigable Cole, together with the XYZ Club of Labour sympathisers in the City of London, were prepared to go into such topics in this depth. A founder of the XYZ Club, Nicholas Davenport, explained that he was worried by the vague and woolly thinking of the Left Book Club: 'I was alarmed by this Marxist programme because the Labour Party was so ignorant of the workings of the financial system that it was bound to create havoc if it attempted to put it all under government control.'

Not all their thinking was the product of library work. Although the Labour Party in Britain was out of office from 1931 onwards, it could still watch and learn from social democratic parties elsewhere. In 1938 Hugh Gaitskell admitted that left-wing governments in the past had not always been very good at handling financial and monetary problems but now they could point to the successful administrations in Sweden, in New Zealand and also to the 'New Deal' in America which had all achieved power via the ballot box.

The Swedish example was especially encouraging. After winning power in 1932, the Swedish Social Democrats had launched an ambitious economic programme of government intervention and public works. Despite the vociferous hostility of several vested interests which came under attack, they won a further election in 1939.

Dalton and his group started to win the intellectual arguments on the Left. Their thinking can be clearly seen in *Labour's Immediate Programme*, adopted by the Party in 1937, which remarkably sold over 400,000 copies in a pictorial version. The change in John Strachey's views is also notable. Strachey's three books published in the 1930s breathe Marxist fire and brimstone; in 1940 his *A Programme for Progress* is full of New Deal sweetness and light.

The small acorns of 1930s middle-way beliefs did, in fact, generate the post-war oak trees of British economics and politics. The Labour Party now possessed a proper economic blueprint. Without a suitable programme, Dalton knew that the Party would never succeed in winning the electoral support of the middle ground of voters whose allegiance was vital if Labour was ever to win a majority of seats in a parliamentary system.

These arguments uncannily reflect those deployed by Tony Blair in the 1990s. Arguably, the facts seem to speak for themselves. Just as membership of the Party today under his leadership has increased rapidly so too did membership of the Labour Party then; according to historian John Saville, it almost doubled between 1929 and 1937, rising from 230,000 to 447,000.

The Labour Party's new economic 'realism' was matched by the gradual change in its foreign policy. The 1934 Peace Ballot organised by the Peace Pledge Union had shown a high level of support for the League of Nations. The difficulty was that the League of Nations proved powerless in the face of dictators bent on aggression such as Hitler and Mussolini.

For much of the 1930s the official Labour Party attitude was to oppose rearmament under the National Government. Not until 1937 did Hugh Dalton, Ernest Bevin and others within the Party persuade the majority that, regrettably, the idealistic hopes of George Lansbury and his followers were not sufficient weapons with which to fight fascism and that Prime Minister Neville Chamberlain's policy of appeasement must be opposed. It represented a distinctive break from the 'brotherhood of man' internationalism characteristic of the first phase of the British Labour Party – the sincere beliefs of the Keir Hardie generation.

In effect, a New Labour Party was being born. The older 'first phase' pioneers had either died out or, in a handful of cases, left the Party in 1931. On the Left, the Independent Labour Party (ILP) disaffiliated in 1932 and wandered off into the political wilderness. The trade union link still remained as the bedrock of labourism but it was noticeable that several important figures were starting to emerge who came from a privileged rather than a manual working-class background: Clement Attlee, Hugh Dalton, Evan Durbin, Hugh Gaitskell. These new-style politicians were much less interested in pious hopes and windy aspirations than in facing up to the opportunities and challenges of office. They wanted to grapple with power, not just talk about it.

Socialism and the British Left are not, however, just about cerebral and intellectual commitment, an affair of footnotes and research references. One essential part – the heart – must concern human feelings and loyalty to one's family, friends and community. Despite the wasteland that the 1930s represented for the British Left, several campaigns such as the Hunger Marches kept alive the spirit of hope and resistance.

The Hunger Marches were led by Wal Hannington's National Unemployed Workers' Movement (NUWM). Although initially founded in 1922, it was only in the early 1930s that a series of marches ending in mass rallies in London attracted public attention. The NUWM's agitation was all the more important in view of the Labour Party's failure to mount a single campaign on this issue. Hannington himself was an engineer and a founder-member of the Communist Party but he never got caught up in party disputes, concentrating instead on his trade union activities and on building up the NUWM. The NUWM was firmly rooted in each community, handling the cases of people of all political persuasions and none as they appeared before the Public Assistance Committees which decided on levels of dole money.

By 1932 the NUWM had a national membership of more than 50,000, over ten times that of the Communist Party. It was a thoroughly legal body, sometimes to the despair of the Comintern in Moscow which occasionally, depending on which 'line' was in operation at any one time, demanded more militant action. The Hunger Marches had a galvanising effect on the towns through which they passed, particularly in the south of England where residents suddenly found the human consequences of widespread unemployment passing by their front doors. The Lancashire contingent of the 1932 march had a memorably radicalising effect on Oxford University students, as too did their counterparts in Cambridge.

The NUWM gave the unemployed themselves a feeling of human worth. As one contemporary remembers, 'the constant agitation preserved above all else the sense of dignity of the unemployed man and woman. They really felt that here was a struggle they could take part in, that they weren't just on the scrap heap.' In his memoirs Hannington noted the NUWM's value in preventing the growth of fascism here in Britain – in Germany, for example, the Nazis had come to power on the backs of the jobless. On one occasion an NUWM campaign did force the government to withdraw the meagre new rates of benefit introduced at the end of 1934.

The most famous march of the 1930s was not, however, organised by the NUWM. In 1936 the Labour MP for

Jarrow likewise led a protest ending up in London. Ellen Wilkinson was a remarkable individual, not just because of her indomitable spirit but because she was a woman. Looking back over previous chapters of this book, one can see that the history of the British Left had been largely a masculine preserve. There were of course exceptions – Eleanor Marx, Annie Besant, Beatrice Webb, Sylvia Pankhurst, Mary Macarthur – but generally Mrs Marx, Mrs Hardie, Mrs Morris, Mrs Maclean and so on were background figures. 'Feminism' did not appear on the male agenda.

In fact, one disappointing aspect of the Communist Party in the 1920s and 1930s was that instead of exploring such issues it had reproduced a male hierarchical form of organisation. Reading the biographies and autobiographies of male socialists, invariably one comes across a throwaway paragraph where tribute is paid to the wife on whom the domestic burden fell. The wives of prominent trade unionists were commonly referred to as 'trade union widows'.

Margaret Bondfield had achieved Cabinet status in MacDonald's 1929–31 government, the first woman of any party to do so. But Ellen Wilkinson was perhaps unique in the fire and zeal which she brought to her political activities. Raised in a Methodist household in Manchester, she won a scholarship to Manchester University in 1910, joining both the Fabians and the Independent Labour Party – again demonstrating the flexibility and tolerance of these early socialist bodies.

Women's organiser for the shopworkers' union, Wilkinson was also a founder member of the Communist Party but left in 1924, the same year she was elected Labour MP for Middlesbrough East. Conditions here were so bad that she claimed 'Middlesbrough is a book of illustrations to Karl Marx.' She lost her seat in the 1931 debacle but returned to Parliament in 1935 as MP for Jarrow. If Middlesbrough was run down and deprived then Jarrow proved to be even worse. J.B. Priestley had visited the town in the autumn of 1933 and was appalled at what he found:

One out of every two shops appeared to be permanently closed. Wherever we went there were men hanging about, not scores of them but hundreds and thousands of them. The whole town looked as if it had entered a perpetual penniless bleak Sabbath. The men wore the drawn masks of prisoners of war. A stranger from a distant civilisation, observing the condition of the place and its people would have arrived at once at the conclusion that Jarrow had deeply offended some celestial emperor of the island and was now being punished. He would never believe us if we told him that in theory this town was as good as any other and that its inhabitants were not criminals but citizens with votes.

A tiny woman – only four feet ten inches tall – and with striking red hair, Ellen Wilkinson's energy and cockiness led sections of the press to dub her 'Little Miss Perky' and she was determined that Jarrow would not suffer in silence. She always remained on the Left: her flat in London even had a portrait of Lenin over the bed.

Knowing that parliamentary action would bring no result because of the National Government's huge majority and, as a former journalist, well aware of the value of publicity, Wilkinson set out on 5 October 1936 with two hundred Jarrow men (ironically enough, women were discouraged) to march to London. Again, as with the Hunger Marches of the NUWM, the official labour movement disapproved and told local Labour Party branches not to offer aid or assistance. Most disobeyed.

The impact of the Jarrow March was heightened by the book that Wilkinson later published under the striking title *The Town That Was Murdered*, issued by the Left Book Club. Once again such initiatives were instrumental in shifting middle-class opinion towards the Left – even if the electoral benefits of this change were not apparent until nearly a decade later.

The day before Wilkinson had set out on the Jarrow March, an event took place in the East End of London that possessed both a symbolic and a practical value. In the autumn of 1932 Sir

Oswald Mosley had set up his British Union of Fascists (BUF), modelling it on the counterparts in Italy and Germany. Mosley insisted on being called 'Leader' and coached his followers to give the fascist salute. He deliberately fostered anti-Semitism with the aim of attracting more members, particularly in the East End where Jewish people acted as convenient scapegoats for the poor living conditions which were none of their making.

In the summer of 1936 Mosley announced that he would lead a BUF march through the East End. The Labour Party, erring on the side of timidity as was usually the case in the 1930s, advised its members to stay indoors on 4 October 1936. The *Daily Herald*'s advice was 'Keep Away'. Thousands of people of all creeds and beliefs ignored this suggestion and instead formed a massive human barrier which Mosley's fascists, despite vigorous police efforts, could not penetrate. The march had to be re-routed along the empty and deserted City of London. The Battle of Cable Street showed that fascism would not take root in Britain as easily as it had done on the Continent.

The Communist Party was in the forefront of resistance to Mosley at both Cable Street and at Bermondsey in October 1937 when another BUF march was aborted. The party could be effective when, as had also been the case with the Hunger Marches, it started from grass-roots activity and organised from the bottom up, rather than obeying orders from above. The British Left needed an organisation distinct from the trade-union dominated Labour Party.

One of the shouts at Cable Street was 'They Shall Not Pass', a slogan publicised by the Republican government in Spain which in the summer of 1936 had been attacked by General Franco's fascists. The vigorous campaign on behalf of the Republicans was one of the great causes of the 1930s, if only because the issues seemed so clear: an elected government had been assaulted by a force demonstrably from the same stable as those in power in Berlin and Rome.

Not only were enormous rallies and demonstrations held in Britain – again in opposition to the wishes of the trade union and Labour leadership which called for a policy of non-intervention – but some 2,000 Britons went to Spain to fight for the Republic. One of them, the future leader of the Transport and General Workers' Union, Jack Jones, wrote of the volunteers' conviction that 'international solidarity required something more than reading about it at home.' Most recruits came from working-class homes.

That the Republicans were defeated in Spain and Chamberlain's National Government recognised the new Franco regime with indecent haste, somehow sums up the frustration of the 1930s for the British Left. Despite the huge commitment of activists – for example, scientist J.D. Bernal was involved in no fewer than thirty-five different committees in addition to his own research and a complicated personal life, whilst memoirs and autobiographies depict a similar pace of activity led by many others – the complacency of the National Government could not be dented.

But, at the very least, the groundwork was laid for a new and different Britain that was to emerge from the crucible of the Second World War – and campaigns such as the Hunger Marches and the 'Aid Spain' movement had kept alive the spirit of protest.

There was, however, one other reason why the Left made little headway in the 1930s. On many issues it was socialists who apparently held the moral trump cards. But on one they didn't and they sometimes found themselves defending the indefensible, with terrible consequences from then up to today.

# Grand Illusions

## British Socialists and Stalin in the 1930s

'What matters it whom we kill . . .'
HUGH MACDIARMID, *FIRST HYMN TO LENIN*, 1931

'Shoot the Reptiles!'
EDITORIAL HEADLINE IN THE *DAILY WORKER*, 24 AUGUST 1936

'There is no crime of Stalinism that cannot be more than matched in this century's annals of Western behaviour, in or out of Europe.'
PROFESSOR V.G. KIERNAN, *THE TIMES*, 28 OCTOBER 1987

Even his political opponents liked and respected Willie Gallacher, Communist MP for West Fife from 1935 to 1950. Born into a poverty-stricken working-class family in Scotland, Gallacher's fierce independence first showed itself as a boy when he played truant from the local Catholic school in protest at the regular beatings he received for not attending Mass. At twelve he began work as a grocer's delivery boy before training as an engineer. In his spare time he worked loyally as John Maclean's lieutenant, trying to spread his Marxist beliefs.

In 1920 Gallacher was yet another founder-member of the Communist Party of Great Britain. Imprisoned four times during his career for uttering seditious and revolutionary views, in September 1939 he was the only Member of Parliament brave enough to oppose Chamberlain's 'Munich' trip to meet Hitler. He remained devoted to his wife Jean through their tragic married life. Their two sons died at birth and both the boys they subsequently adopted were killed fighting in the Second World War. The widespread love and devotion that Gallacher inspired was demonstrated when thousands of people took to the Fife streets for his funeral in August 1965.

Was Gallacher then a paragon of left-wing virtue? In some ways, yes. But in one crucial respect, no. Gallacher visited the Soviet Union in 1937 at the height of Stalin's purges, but saw nothing and said nothing even though the scale of the slaughter taking place around him was immense. He published one of several volumes of autobiography after the Khrushchev revelations of 1956 had shown how devastating the purges were. Yet once again he simply ignored the unwelcome facts. For Gallacher, Stalin's 'excesses' had not happened.

Ivor Montagu practised a similar kind of self-deception. A man of extraordinarily wide interests and great charm who made films with Alfred Hitchcock, he founded the International Chess Federation and was for many years non-playing captain of the British table tennis team as well as the first chairman of the International Table Tennis Federation because he turned out to be the only delegate who spoke all the necessary languages. Such was his love for his wife Hell that on her death he simply lost the will to live and died a few weeks later. Yet Montagu spent much of the late 1930s defending the Moscow Trials and the purges, reviling Stalin's victims and abusing those who defended them.

Finally, consider the case of Sidney and Beatrice Webb. Sidney was ennobled as Lord Passfield after serving in MacDonald's two Labour governments, but still worked with Beatrice on writing several thoroughly researched historical volumes. During the 1930s the couple suddenly discovered the wonders of Stalin's Russia, and in 1936 they published a 1,257-page book called *Soviet Communism: A New Civilisation?*

By the next year the Webbs knew the answer to their rhetorical question – subsequent editions of the book dropped the question mark from the title. They were open about their love affair with the Soviet Union. Beatrice herself once commented: 'Old people often fall in love in extraordinary and ridiculous ways – with their chauffeurs for example: we feel it dignified to have fallen in love with Soviet Communism.'

How on earth could individuals as humane, personally benevolent and gifted as Gallacher, Montagu and the Webbs support and condone mass murder? Scrupulously outraged by a single breach of civil liberties in Britain – Victor Gollancz's firm published several apologia for Stalin and yet Gollancz was at the same time Vice President of the National Committee for the Abolition of the Death Penalty [in Britain] – they turned a blind eye to killing, torture and imprisonment on a huge scale in the Soviet Union. How can political commitment cause sane people to throw their senses to the winds and argue that black is red and tomorrow may well be white?

This is certainly the most tragic chapter in the book. It shows how quickly idealism and naivety can slip into brutal complicity. The results of this 'grand illusion' were to damage enormously the British Left. First of all, it tarred socialism in Britain and elsewhere with the 'Moscow Trials' brush and allowed the political Right then and since to make much capital out of the episode. Secondly, the growing realisation as to how much special pleading had gone on explains to some extent why the British labour movement has traditionally been suspicious of left-wing intellectuals. Not all the defenders of the purges were intellectuals, certainly, but a disproportionate and vocal number were.

Finally, 'grand illusions' reveals much about a state of mind to which political activists seem peculiarly prone: that understandable allegiance to a cause can easily become 'My Cause Right or Wrong', no matter how blatant the wrong. This is certainly *not* a state of mind confined to the Left. Also in the 1930s, for instance, a variety of British people threw in their lot with Hitler, travelling to Nazi Germany and expressing fulsome admiration for the new regime's achievements, discreetly overlooking or excusing the treatment of Jews, trade unionists and minorities.

Some criticised Hitler's methods, but contented themselves with the omelette and eggs argument. Winston Churchill, for example, is usually portrayed as an almost lone voice in the 1930s wilderness, ceaselessly warning of the Hitler menace. And yet in an article of 1935, which he republished in October 1937, Churchill wrote that:

> Although no subsequent political action can condone wrong deeds or remove the guilt of blood, history is replete with examples of men who have risen to power by employing stern, grim, wicked and even frightful methods, but who, nevertheless, when their life is revealed as a whole, have been regarded as great figures whose lives have enriched the story of mankind. So may it be with Hitler.

Many of the individuals discussed in this chapter advanced similar arguments, but for them it was Joseph Stalin and not Adolf Hitler whose life enriched mankind.

Perhaps this chapter holds lessons for the British Left today and in the future. It is vital to discriminate between different issues and to maintain a sense of proportion. There are degrees of injustice. Those who used to chant that Mrs Thatcher was a fascist, or who criticised the IRA after the Brighton bombing in October 1984 for not having done the job properly, only undermine the very cause which they seek to promote.

Why was there such an emotional commitment to the cause of the Soviet Union in the 1930s? There had, of course, been supporters of the regime ever since 1917, and the Communist Party of Great Britain had championed the Bolsheviks since its foundation in 1920. But a conjunction of events at the end of the 1920s and the beginning of the 1930s led to a much greater identification with the Soviet Union. The first Five Year Plan, launched in 1928, seemingly offered a planned system of economic progress as well as full employment very different from the anarchy and chaos of Western capitalism, particularly after the 'Great Depression' began in the autumn of 1929.

Secondly, the ignominious collapse of MacDonald's Labour government in August 1931 apparently revealed the perils for socialists of relying on parliamentary progress. As one member of the 'intellectual Left' commented: 'The discredit of Labour made even staunch supporters of the Party in Bloomsbury mutter that perhaps far more radical measures of Marxism were necessary to defeat reaction and stop the drift towards a new war.'

In his memoir, *My Silent War*, Kim Philby claimed that the events of August 1931 decisively prompted him to throw in his lot with the Soviet Union.

Professor Paul Hollander has shown in exhaustive detail how political pilgrims of the Left hostile towards the system in their own country generally gravitated towards a compensatory and uncritical love of another. George Bernard Shaw visited Russia in the summer of 1931. On his last evening he wrote in the visitors' book of his Moscow hotel: 'Tomorrow I leave this land of hope and return to our Western countries of despair.' In his manuscript about this journey, Shaw blithely called the Soviet Union 'this earthly paradise for professional men'.

For many socialists deeply critical of Britain and the National Government, the Soviet Union became the repository of their hopes and optimism; in one famous phrase, 'I have seen the future and it works!' Many scientists such as J.D. Bernal admired the USSR as an exemplar of rational and ordered progress: 'science is communism', he argued. There, it seemed, long-term planning prevailed over short-term considerations and Soviet scientists were treated with the respect and admiration that Bernal thought was lacking in Britain.

Writers and artists also found the Soviet Union a model society to be emulated and praised. In 1937 the Communist Cecil Day Lewis, later to be Poet Laureate between 1968 and his death in 1972, edited a volume of essays called *The Mind in Chains*. Naturally, the mind was in chains only in this country and not in Stalin's Russia. Anthony Blunt thought that 'In the present state of capitalism the position of the artist is hopeless' whereas in the USSR a thriving workers' culture was being built. Musician Alan Bush lauded Soviet music at the expense of British music. Critic Edgell Rickword applauded the new Soviet constitution – of course, Britain didn't even have a written one which he could criticise. Novelist Rex Warner saw everything clearly: 'There is no longer any hope in capitalism . . .'

The conviction that everything 'over there' was rather better than it was 'over here' reached absurd and chilling depths. Bernard Shaw claimed that it was difficult to get Soviet prisoners to leave gaol because conditions inside were so pleasant and relaxing. And in his book *Soviet Democracy*, published in 1937 by Victor Gollancz's Left Book Club, Pat Sloan noted: 'Compared with the significance of that term in Britain, Soviet imprisonment stands out as an almost enjoyable experience.' It is doubtful whether the millions of people who passed through Stalin's Gulags or 'holiday camps' would have agreed.

Approval of the Soviet Union was reinforced by sycophantic praise of Stalin – enthusiasts could even purchase their own Stalin Calendars – and by what has been called 'the techniques of hospitality' by which gullible visitors were gulled even more. The travel agency Intourist was set up in 1929 and its Soviet staff of hundreds specialised in arranging suitably impressive itineraries. Tourists were naturally shown only the best and most modern sights on their carefully planned routes. Schedules were so hectic that little time was left for doubt or speculation. When visitors were allowed to choose where to go, it was only from a vetted list.

Few of these tourists could speak Russian in order to ask awkward questions, and in any case they were carefully kept away from ordinary Russians. In 1924 when a TUC delegation visited an electricity factory, secret police members actually replaced the real workforce. When Bernard Shaw went into a restaurant he found to his immense surprise and gratification that both the waitresses were experts on his plays. Predictably enough he then announced the superiority of Russian waitresses over their British counterparts.

Anything primitive or inefficient was blamed on the disastrous legacy of the Czars. Visitors were swamped by handbooks and pamphlets containing masses of statistics that proved things were indeed getting better all the time. Dutifully, many British observers transcribed these dollops of information in their own works. Sir Walter Citrine, General Secretary of the TUC, visited Russia in 1935. Though often sceptical about what he saw, even he could not resist reproducing 'Rates of Wages of the Workers in the First National Kagonovitch Ball–Bearing Works in Moscow' and even 'Earnings at Underwear Factory, No 6, Moscow'!

Copious supplies of alcohol and quantities of food greeted the visitors. Above all, they were fêted and flattered. When Shaw went to the theatre, proceedings were suddenly interrupted by the unfurling of a banner which read in English 'To the brilliant master, Bernard Shaw – a warm welcome to Soviet soil'. When Sidney and Beatrice Webb came the next year, they were delighted to be treated, in Sidney's words, like 'a new type of royalty'. The Webbs were, in fact, regarded as a joke among even Soviet officials because of their habit of uncritically writing down in notebooks everything they were told.

If anything untoward did happen during a visit, it was easy enough to fob off visitors until they went home. During Shaw's trip, he and Tory MP Nancy Astor attended a function at the British Embassy. A telegram was unexpectedly handed to Lady Astor sent by a Professor Krynin, a political exile then based at Yale University. He begged Shaw and Astor to persuade their Soviet hosts to let his family leave the country. Astor badgered the authorities but they simply stalled for time. After her departure, Western journalists who tried to visit the Krynin family found they had 'disappeared'.

The Moscow Trials of August 1936, January 1937 and March 1938 were the climax of the purges unleashed by Stalin as he systematically imposed his dictatorship by exterminating any possible rivals or threats to his rule. Even today the scale of the slaughter is unknown. Robert Conquest in *The Great Terror* estimated that one million people died in 1937–38 alone. His book was serialised in post-glasnost Russia and it is accepted that Conquest's figures are too low.

Such figures are mind-boggling. To try and bring out what these massacres meant in personal terms: on just one day in 1937, Stalin and his lieutenant Molotov signed 3,167 death warrants before going off to the cinema for the rest of the evening. Of the 139 members of the Central Committee of 1934, 98 were eventually shot. Old revered Bolsheviks were suddenly unmasked as longstanding traitors. Of the seven members of the 1924 Politburo, six were executed or murdered; the seventh was Joseph Stalin. In September 1989 the *Independent* newspaper carried a letter from Colonel-General Dimitri Volkgonov, Chief of the Institute of Military History in Moscow. He wrote of the effect of the purges on the Red Army: 'The situation in the Soviet armed forces was dire: in 1937–38 the army was "purged" of over 40,000 men: out of the 108 members of the old military council only 10 retained their posts.'

Did this carnage cause misgivings among British admirers, both Communist and Labour? Far from it. Here was a country, they argued, whose leader really knew how to deal with opposition to socialism – remember that, as we saw in the previous chapter, barrister Sir Stafford Cripps was blithely calling for a 'temporary dictatorship' and the suspension of elections. No doubt they would have been less pleased if the Opposition had been treated like this in Britain. Bernard Shaw justified Soviet actions thus: 'The plain truth is that all civilised governments exact minimum standards of conduct which they enforce by killing the people who do not attain them. Our question is not to kill or not to kill, but how to select the right people to kill.'

This cold-blooded attitude is all too reminiscent of one strand in Fabian thought, which was always rather impatient with fallible human beings and their regrettable tendency not to behave exactly as the Fabians desired. David Caute once observed: 'The Webbs were excellent examples of the type which prefers mankind to people; which originally intends to sacrifice a few to save everyone and ends by sacrificing everyone to save a few.'

Several distinguished British lawyers supported the conduct of the Moscow Trials. The eminent barrister D.N. Pritt KC, Labour MP for North Hammersmith and a member of the Party's National Executive, defended the proceedings and helped allay the qualms of people around the world. During the first Trial of August 1936 he does seem to have felt that the evidence against the accused was a little shaky, but then quickly recovered himself and assured the readers of his pamphlet that 'over nearly the whole of the case the available proof did not require to be brought forward.' Pritt would not have accepted this argument if he had been a defending counsel in Britain – and even Pritt regretted the absence of a jury in the Moscow Trials.

Another barrister, Dudley Collard, watched the 1937 Trial. In a widely circulated pamphlet he informed his readers that 'in the result the court was more merciful than I would have been!' As fourteen of the seventeen defendants at this particular Trial were shot and the other three were imprisoned for long sentences, it is difficult to know quite how the court could have been less merciful.

A number of explanations have been put forward to exonerate those who defended the Trials and the purges. The first is 'we didn't know what was going on'. The problem with this defence is that numerous writers *at the time* argued that the proceedings were faked and that widespread abuse of civil liberties was endemic in the Soviet Union. Moreover, many of those critics were longstanding socialists and so could not be dismissed as typical anti-Soviet reactionaries.

For example, take Fenner Brockway, throughout his life an independent socialist of honesty and integrity. As early as 1927 he was writing in unequivocal terms to the Russian Council of People's Commissars:

> . . . Not even my admiration for your wonderful achievements, my realisation of the immense significance of the maintenance of the Workers' Republic for 10 years, can close my ears to the cry of the Socialists in prison and exile in Russia. I know what imprisonment means, and I cannot do other than associate myself with those who, for their convictions, are undergoing imprisonment now.

Critics of the Trials at the time included Dr Friedrich Adler, Secretary of the Labour and Socialist International. His influential pamphlet of 1936, *The Witchcraft Trial in Moscow*, systematically analysed the judicial proceedings. He commented that the defendants were always convicted on 'voluntary' confessions and never on written documents; that there was no right of appeal; that supposedly crucial meetings of the conspirators had taken place at the Hotel Bristol in Copenhagen in 1932, even though this hotel had in fact been demolished in 1917; and that the indictment of the defendants, their trial, sentence and execution had all taken place in just eleven days. Adler also emphasised the bizarre and hysterical language of prosecutor Vyshinsky whose concluding words were 'I demand that dogs gone mad should be shot, every one of them!'

Another critic was F.A. Voigt, a respected journalist on the *Manchester Guardian*, which was itself critical of the proceedings. He published his articles in book form in 1938 under the title *Unto Caesar*. Condemning the 'massacres' taking place, he explained exactly how and why the defendants confessed:

If there is any recalcitrance it is broken by a threat, often no more than hinted at, to wife or husband, child or friend. And who in the world will *not* 'confess' if the penalty for refusal be the liberty, or even the life, of a mother or child?

Voigt also gave clear evidence of the effects of sleep deprivation on the defendants.

The labour movement's own newspaper, the *Daily Herald*, with a circulation of over two million copies each day, attacked the proceedings from the start. A typical editorial of 30 January 1937 said that 'Truly the Revolution is devouring its own children'; and 'There remains horror at the deed [of execution], pity for the victims, and dismay at the condition of the Soviet Union after 20 years of Soviet rule.'

Also hostile was the veteran socialist Emrys Hughes, Keir Hardie's son-in-law, who used his small circulation but prestigious *Forward* to campaign against the Trials. Walter Citrine in his account *I Search For Truth in Russia* was outspoken about the dictatorship of Stalin and the complete uniformity of opinion: 'To argue with a Russian Communist is to argue with a gramophone record of Stalin.' Some of Kingsley Martin's editorials in the *New Statesman* magazine were ambiguous on the Trials, but many well-respected contributors such as Leonard Woolf condemned them.

Extraordinary in their wealth of detail about conditions in the Soviet Union were two books by Vladimir and Tatiana Tchernavin whose *Escape from the Soviets* (1933) and *I Speak for the Silent* (1935) were issued in Britain by the reputable publisher Hamish Hamilton. Both books still retain a power to shock comparable with Solzhenitsyn's *One Day in the Life of Ivan Denisovich*, published over twenty-five years later.

The Tchernavins apparently aroused the special ire of the Soviet authorities because of their professional qualifications: she had been a senior assistant at the Hermitage, he was a lecturer at the Agronomical Institute. Their books tell of the sudden motiveless arrests, the forced labour, the harsh

penal camps, the shootings without trial, the atmosphere of
suspicion and mistrust. Huge letter boxes were installed on
street corners into which people could drop denunciations of
each other. Those who 'confessed' were called, in prison slang,
'novelists' and their confessions 'novels'. The Tchernavins
detailed exactly how and why people confessed in order to
spare family and friends.

The point has been made: such evidence was produced
and publicised at the time by sympathetic observers. Certainly
more details became available after the 'revelations' of 1956,
but much information existed before then. How could Pritt,
Collard, the Webbs and others see things so wrongly? Malcolm
Muggeridge, a journalist who visited Russia in the early 1930s
as a sympathiser but had the integrity to see what was going
on and change his mind, provides an effective summary: 'The
people who came to the Soviet Union wanted so passionately
to see certain things in being that they could not see anything
different. They were not liars. You could just not change their
minds with facts.'

Muggeridge's words apply just as well to those 'believers'
who never visited the Soviet Union but who read about
it safely at home. His argument is implicitly endorsed by
the recent Communist Party history of the period. Noreen
Branson writes of the party leadership that:

Fundamental to their approach was the belief – held by all
Communists – that all persecution, tyranny and injustice
had their roots in the capitalist system, and in capitalist
property relations. It followed that, where the capitalist
system was abolished, tyranny and persecution would wither
away; insofar as they still manifested themselves in Russia, this
was a hangover from Tsarist days, soon to disappear.

Clearly such a belief could, and did, excuse anything.

A second defence was that to have spoken out would only
have helped the Soviet Union's enemies without necessarily
helping the victims. The Welsh miners' leader Arthur Horner

was aware of illegalities taking place but argued: 'I knew . . .
that if I publicly spread my doubts about some of the things
that were going on I would not assist my friends, but would
give a weapon to those who would stop at nothing to destroy
the Soviet Union.'

Some private representations were indeed made to the
Soviet authorities, but with little evidence of success. And, in
any case, by not speaking out in public much more damage was
in the end inflicted on the Soviet Union. Most importantly,
injustice and cruelty is injustice and cruelty wherever and
under whoever it happens. Selective moral outrage destroys
any case for socialism as a fairer and more just way of
organising society.

A third possible defence is that in the circumstances of the
1930s, most notably the rise of fascism on the Continent,
people simply had to choose between two rival camps: fascism
or communism. This is a more understandable argument.
Wherever one looked, fascism seemed to be gaining power:
Italy, Portugal, Germany, Poland, Hungary, Romania, Austria
. . . Denis Healey was a Communist at Oxford in the late 1930s.
His autobiography puts the choice starkly:

> For the young in those days, politics was a world of simple
> choices. The enemy was Hitler with his concentration camps.
> The objective was to prevent a war by standing up to
> Hitler. Only the Communist Party seemed unambiguously
> against Hitler.

At the same time historian Eric Hobsbawm was a Communist
at Cambridge and he has argued that:

> . . . modern political choice is not a constant process of
> selecting men or measures, but a single or infrequent choice
> between packages, in which we buy the disagreeble part of
> the contents because there is no other way of getting the rest,
> and in any case because there is no other way to be politically
> effective.

But at what point can the package be returned to the retailer as defective: after a thousand deaths, ten thousand, a million? Should one really condone the 'disagreeable part' – torture, murder – in order to savour the rest of the menu? It was difficult in the 1930s to be against fascism without thereby falling into the Soviet camp, but millions of people managed it. Neither were Nazi Germany and the Soviet Union the only choices on the menu. This was also the time of Roosevelt's New Deal government in the United States and of social democratic administrations in Sweden and New Zealand.

Anthony Blunt once claimed that almost all the intelligent Cambridge undergraduates became Marxists in the mid-1930s because of the rise of Hitler. He was magisterially rebuked by Noel Annan:

> This is arrogant rubbish. It is characteristic of communists and the extreme left to move solely within the tiny circle to which they belong, only extending from time to time a tentacle like an octopus to ensnare some potential comrade who swims past their lair. Their numbers were really very small and by no means all of them were brilliant. True, they made up for this by making a lot of noise, suffering martyrdom by selling the *Daily Worker* outside the Mill Lane lecture-rooms and hissing when 'God Save the King' was played at the flicks. But such myopia on the part of Professor Blunt is barely credible. There were plenty of bright and intelligent undergraduates at other colleges who were not attracted by communism . . .

The deep-rooted problem was that many on the British Left failed to distinguish between fascism, liberal democracy and Communism. For some, Chamberlain was as 'bad' as Hitler. It took a world war for people who thought like this to see the crucial difference. As Louis MacNeice wrote in 1939 in his *Autumn Journal*:

> Our top-heavy tedious parliamentary system
> Is our only ready weapon to defeat

The legions' eagles and the lictors' axes.

Looking back at this 'grand illusion', it is striking how many acute individuals allowed themselves to be deceived, especially when they were often intellectuals trained to be critical and thorough. Utopian aspirations led many sincere socialists to worship a system and a society at the expense of their fellow human beings.

Harry Ferns was a young Canadian who studied at Cambridge in the 1930s and joined the Communist Party. Later, after the war, he became Professor of Politics at Birmingham University. His excellent memoir *Reading from Right to Left* (1983) explores the passions of the time. In the 1930s, Communists like him 'did not regard the spilling of blood in a good cause as wicked and forbidden'; '. . . we prided ourselves on the realism which enabled us not to shrink from the stern dictates of history.' In other words, back to the familiar 'You can't make an omelette without breaking eggs.' But as Colin Welch once pointed out in his review of a book about Walter Durranty, an influential American journalist who defended the purges, 'you could break every egg in the world without making an omelette.'

Ferns also commented on the arrogance of Marxism, which flatters men and women by making them the centre of everything. Stalin played up to this feeling when he remarked that Bolsheviks were 'engineers of the soul'. Cecil Day Lewis provided a good summary of this feeling:

> Inoculated against Roman Catholicism by the religion of my youth, I dimly felt the need for a faith which had the authority, the logic, the cut-and-driedness of the Roman church – a faith which would fill the void left by the leaking away of traditional religion, would make some sense of our troubled times and make real demands on me. Marxism appeared to fill the bill.

This faith developed the rigidities of many other religious faiths, even down to instigating its own Inquisition which sought out and punished heretics whose views differed from the current orthodoxy. The possibility of dissent, of contradicting Stalin's infallibility, was not allowed. But just to make sure, the meetings of renegades were disrupted and broken up as one Communist of the time, Joe Jacobs, admitted in his autobiography when he says that his colleagues systematically pursued a vendetta against J.T. Murphy, a former Communist leader who had been expelled from the party.

Even to talk to 'heretics' was unwise. Edward Upward, a friend of Isherwood and Auden and a longstanding supporter of the Left, has provided a frightening picture of one party member being ostracised for suspected Trotskyist leanings. The main protagonist of Upward's novel, Alan Sebrill, exhibits extraordinary self-deception when justifying the treatment meted out:

> His sense that their behaviour towards Bainton had been defi-
> cient in ordinary human kindness gave place to a recognition
> that if the [Communist] Party were to disappear from the
> world there would be no hope for humanity. The showing
> of kindness to a few deviationist human individuals could lead
> to disaster for human beings in general.

Such an attitude excuses any personal inhumanity. And lest it be thought that such a scene was just a novelist's imaginings, Margaret McCarthy in her autobiography depicts an almost identical situation at a local Communist Party meeting:

> I sat among them, sensitive to the atmosphere of the meeting,
> furtive, shifty, thick with moronic bigotry, and it seemed to
> me that I could not breathe, that I was choked and blinded
> by the fog of imbecile, foul and unnecessary conspiracy, the
> conspiracy of comrade against comrade.

McCarthy defended the accused, although she knew what it would mean for her: 'I was destroying myself, going out into the darkness and the blankness alone, an outcast, an untouchable, with neither hope, nor belief, nor comradeship, nor understanding.' She was so upset that she even considered suicide.

That such things could happen among people who genuinely believed themselves to be working for 'the greater good' shows how some ideologies and beliefs can end up destroying what they hope to create. A sense of individual human worth, of tolerance, understanding and humour – all these qualities must surely be at the heart of any concept of 'socialism', if only to prevent any more 'grand illusions'.

# New Worlds for Old?

## Labour's Brave New World

On the first day of the 1945 Parliament, Labour's new MPs celebrated their election triumph by singing 'The Red Flag'. Here are two very different reactions:

'My complacency melted in a minute. I began to fear for my country.'

CONSERVATIVE MP OLIVER LYTTELTON

'. . . mildly disturbed . . . These youngsters still had to absorb the atmosphere of the House. But I recognised that it was largely first-day high spirits.'

HERBERT MORRISON, LABOUR LEADER OF
THE HOUSE OF COMMONS

King George VI met President Truman on 2 August 1945 just after Labour's triumph at the July general election:

Truman: 'I hear you've had a revolution.'
George VI: 'Oh no, we don't have those here.'

'This Colliery Is Managed By The National Coal Board On Behalf Of The People'

SIGNS ERECTED IN 1947 WHEN THE MINES WERE BROUGHT INTO
PUBLIC OWNERSHIP

Clement Attlee was one of the most unlikely individuals ever to lead a British political party. Quiet, unassuming and with the appearance of a suburban bank manager, he seemed to be, in Churchill's famous phrase, 'a sheep in sheep's clothing'. His great interests in life were cricket, his old public school, detective stories and doing *The Times* crossword. From the moment he was elected leader of the Labour Party in 1935 his position came under attack from rivals, but twenty years later he was still there. It was Attlee's Party that trounced Churchill's in the 1945 general election, and Attlee's government which shaped post-war Britain.

Like Keir Hardie, Attlee left behind few clues as to what made him tick. His memoirs are unrevealing, and a series of television interviews given just before his death in 1967 are bland and uninformative. A former colleague wrote of Attlee that he 'would never use one syllable where none would do.' Television interviews and the whole paraphernalia of the modern media were anathema to him.

One illuminating piece of film captures Attlee being greeted at an airport by a battery of cameras. Asked whether he would like to comment on some political controversy, he snaps 'No' and stalks off. A friend of Denis Healey once remarked that a conversation with most people was like a game of tennis; with Attlee it was like feeding biscuits to a dog: all you got out of him was yup, yup, yup.

Attlee was born in middle-class and respectable Putney in 1883. His father, a successful solicitor, sent his son to Haileybury public school and then to Oxford after which he read for the Bar at the Inner Temple. But Attlee's life was to change in October 1905 when he visited Haileybury House, the settlement established in the East End of London by his public school. As Attlee recalled in his memoirs many years later, this visit proved to be 'a decisive step in my life'.

Institutions such as Haileybury House introduced privileged public schoolboys to social work in the poorer parts of London. They sometimes had a patronising air about them, a sense of missionaries penetrating the wilds to impart a little learning and culture to the natives before scampering back to civilisation. In his autobiography George Lansbury was critical of the men and women:

> who went to East London full of enthusiasm and zeal for the welfare of the masses, and discovered the advancement of their own interests and the interests of the poor were best secured by leaving East London to stew in its own juice while they became members of parliament, cabinet ministers, civil servants . . .

Lansbury's resentment of 'outsiders' who came, saw and left was understandable. But Attlee was different. Horrified by the poverty and deprivation he saw around him, he decided to live in the East End, not for a few weeks but for years in order to campaign for political change. He soon joined the Stepney branch of the Independent Labour Party. In 1908 his father died, leaving him a comfortable private income of £400 a year; again, he resisted the temptation to depart for middle-class suburbia.

Instead Attlee joined the Fabians and worked as a lecture secretary for the Webbs, explaining and arguing in support of Beatrice Webb's Minority Report on the Poor Law. He subsequently had a short spell as secretary of Toynbee Hall and then in 1911 was appointed one of the official 'explainers' of Lloyd George's National Insurance Act. He also lectured at Ruskin College in Oxford and at the new London School of Economics. In the light of these posts it might be assumed that Attlee had a gift for oratory or public speaking – then the surest way to progress within the labour movement. In fact he hadn't, relying instead on hard work and thorough attention to detail to carry him through.

When war broke out in 1914 Attlee had no qualms about where his duty lay. A convinced patriot, he fought throughout the conflict, being twice wounded and finally reaching the rank of Major. On his return to the East End, he was elected Mayor of Stepney and then, in 1922, MP for Limehouse. That same year he married Violet Millar, the start of a happy and long-lived relationship even though Violet herself was not at all interested in politics (gossips whispered that she was at heart a Tory).

In the 1920s Attlee was a dedicated backbench MP, briefly tasting office in 1924 as Under Secretary of State for War in the first Labour government. In Ramsay MacDonald's second administration he was once again at the War Office. When this government collapsed in 1931 Attlee had no doubts about where he stood, regarding MacDonald's actions as 'the greatest betrayal in the political history of the country.'

So far Attlee's career had been steady but hardly spectacular; no one could have foreseen the momentous events ahead. At the October 1931 election the Labour Party was almost destroyed as an effective parliamentary force when only forty-six MPs were returned. Attlee was one of them – which not only confirmed the value of representing a solid working-class constituency, but was surely the reward for the dedicated and selfless efforts of his younger days. For want of anyone better and because more obviously suitable candidates, such as Herbert Morrison, had lost their seats he was elected deputy to George Lansbury, standing in when the elderly Party leader was ill.

Even more surprisingly, when Lansbury resigned in 1935 it was Attlee, with the support of most MPs who had seen his dedicated efforts over the previous four years, who defeated Herbert Morrison and Arthur Greenwood in the leadership contest that November. Most observers still felt that this was merely a stopgap appointment until someone more appropriate and certainly more charismatic should take over. But once at the summit, Attlee was not to be budged.

That Attlee did become leader of the Labour Party was not of course due to good luck alone. His election could be said to symbolise the changes taking place within the labour movement. Broadly, the committee room was ousting the street-corner meeting; effective political administration was becoming more important than cloudy idealism or rhetoric. In short, the Attlees were displacing the Hardies.

Between 1935 and 1940 Attlee proved to be a largely anonymous figure, publishing two exceedingly dull books called *The Will and the Way to Socialism* and *The Labour Party in Perspective*. He also made a few left-wing gestures such as welcoming the 1936 Hunger Marchers to Hyde Park and visiting the International Brigade in Spain. He took little interest in the intellectual work of men like Dalton, G.D.H. Cole and Evan Durbin which was slowly transforming his own party.

In fact, throughout his career Attlee was always suspicious of the 'thinkers', dismissing them in his memoirs as 'the intelligentsia who can be trusted to take the wrong view on any subject.' They in turn did not have a high opinion of Attlee; at the beginning of the war Hugh Dalton privately referred to him as 'the Rabbit' and thought Attlee 'at no time . . . big enough or strong enough to carry the burden.'

Attlee's chance to prove Dalton and his many other critics wrong came in 1940 when the Labour Party joined Churchill's coalition government. His post as deputy Prime Minister from February 1942, during which he concentrated on the domestic front, brought to the fore his undoubted administrative talents. And the conflict itself prompted a groundswell of opinion from Right to Left. This anti-fascist war brought the Labour Party and the trade unions back to the centre of the political stage after nearly a decade in the wings.

'Total War', as the conduct of the war effort was called because it required the mobilisation of the entire population, brought massive social, economic and political upheaval. The old order – or the *Guilty Men* as a contemporary diatribe co-authored by Michael Foot put it – proved incapable of building and sustaining a war effort which could combat the Germans on equal terms.

Whether it was evacuation, or the Blitz, or rationing, or conscription, everything shook up the traditional way of doing things. Suddenly the three main ideas which had underpinned the Labour Party's approach in the second half of the 1930s – government intervention, the need for planning, and welfare provision – became politically respectable. They were now deployed by the Churchill administration with barely a murmur of dissent. The *Daily Express* might have termed food rationing 'a dreadful and terrible iniquity' but everyone else knew that equality of sacrifice demanded nothing less. Market forces were clearly irrelevant when it came to, say, medical treatment after an air raid: human need was rather more important than the size of a victim's bank account.

With hindsight, after their massive defeat at the 1945 election, Conservatives inevitably looked back and tried to find scapegoats for their loss. They developed a 'demonology' that included CEMA, the government-sponsored arts agency which later grew into the Arts Council as well as ABCA, the army education service. One backbench Tory MP wrote anxiously to Churchill's Parliamentary Private Secretary in 1942, '. . . for the love of Mike do something about it [army education] unless you want to have the creatures coming back all pansy-pink.'

Others blamed publisher Allen Lane and his Penguin Books or else Sir William Beveridge for his Report, issued in December 1942, advocating decent welfare and employment insurance and which marked a new acceptance by the state that it had a responsibility for the well-being of its citizens. A shortened version of the Report sold over 600,000 copies. Reactionaries like Evelyn Waugh dated 'the fall' from the German attack on the Soviet Union in June 1941 which led to an Anglo-Soviet alliance and widespread admiration for the successes of the Red Army. All these factors reinforced what Asa Briggs once called the links between warfare and welfare, confirming that 'in many respects the character of the war effort provided the most important propaganda of all.'

It would be wrong to categorise this wartime mood as revolutionary or even socialist. Looking now at, say, J.B.

Priestley's short radio talks *Postscripts* or the 'Plan for Britain' published in the influential magazine *Picture Post,* or the ideas of the new Common Wealth party which ran candidates in protest at the war's electoral truce and which by 1944 had two MPs and 15,000 members, one is struck by their call for solid, decent human values – values which were as much humanitarian as they were political. After suitable adjustment they could easily be accommodated within the established system. Fortunately, there had been no invasion of Britain, no defeat, and as a result no collapse of traditional institutions such as Parliament, the monarchy or the civil service.

Contemporary surveys by Mass Observation as well as the eyewitness accounts of writers who worked in factories, showed that many people continued in their largely apolitical way, untouched by and uninterested in the visions of a New Jerusalem that some socialists were trying to conjure up. Mass Observation's study *War Factory* (1943) noted 'the dangerous decline in positive citizenship, especially among the young' before continuing that 'the majority of them [factory workers] are so little interested in the war that they do not care whether their work is important to it or not . . . This negative attitude to the war is to a large extent characteristic of all country districts.'

Nevertheless the embryonic opinion polls did show that the war was transforming popular opinion; a survey conducted in the middle of 1943 found that 25 per cent of the sample had moved to the Left since the war had begun, but only 4 per cent to the Right. In particular, the views of the 'élite' were changing. Lord Annan's autobiography *Our Age* charts how and why his generation moved into positions of power and influence in the 1940s. Reacting against the horrors of, say, Jarrow revealed by J.B. Priestley or Ellen Wilkinson, these opinion-formers were much more progressive, humane and idealistic than their predecessors. Socialists had traditionally favoured state intervention and now, too, many Conservatives joined them, keen to show they had taken to heart Disraeli's aphorism of the 'Two Nations'. Both agreed that:

> ... palpable injustices and differences in the life chances of the well-to-do and of the poor could be diminished by public expenditure and redistributive taxation; and the agents to bring about change were the bureaucrats of central and local government under the control of their elected ministers and councillors.

This collectivist determination to create a better society went hand in hand with the new post-war consensus, which lasted from the 1940s to the 1970s. It was heralded by the publication in the summer of 1944 of the White Paper *Employment Policy*, which recognised that post-war governments should have '... as one of their primary responsibilities the maintenance of a high and stable level of employment.'

Again, it should be emphasised that this was not a socialist consensus; two of the key individuals who contributed to it, J.M. Keynes and Sir William Beveridge, were both Liberals, while it was the Conservative R.A. Butler who introduced the Education Act of 1944. During the 1945 election campaign, Westminster Conservative Association actually reprinted Harold Macmillan's book *The Middle Way* in order to prove that Labour's nationalisation proposals had been stolen from the Tories.

Several Labour politicians held vital posts in the war coalition. Apart from Attlee, Herbert Morrison was an able and energetic Home Secretary, Ernest Bevin a formidable Minister of Labour and Hugh Dalton headed the Ministry of Economic Warfare. The Labour Party had indeed 'come in from the political cold'. But much would depend on the outcome of the general election to be held at the end of the war, the first for ten years. Could the Labour Party, led by a comparatively little-known individual, possibly defeat a

Conservative Party led by a world-famous statesman who in the eyes of many had won the war for Britain?

Few professional politicians on the British Left, or the Right for that matter, fully realised the seismic changes wrought in the political climate by the war. Although its membership had leapt to nearly 60,000, the Communist Party still thought that Winston Churchill was bound to win an election and therefore argued for the coalition government to continue. Attlee and his colleagues were also apprehensive, fearing that Churchill's status would prove to be the Conservative Party's trump card just as the victorious Lloyd George had triumphed at the end of the First World War.

The Conservatives certainly made the most of 'the Churchill factor', simply calling their manifesto *Mr Churchill's Declaration of Policy to the Electors*, even though he himself admitted privately: 'I have no message.' One perceptive commentator wrote that Conservative candidates were sent into the electoral fray armed with little more than a photograph of Churchill.

The Labour Party manifesto *Let Us Face the Future* encapsulated the policies produced by Hugh Dalton and his circle in the 1930s, subsequently tempered by wartime events. These included nationalisation of the basic industries; development of a welfare state and in particular a national health service; the expansion of education and a commitment to full employment. The Labour Party stressed that it put 'the nation above any sectional interest', unlike the Conservatives who favoured the better off. Neutral observers thought that not only did Labour seem to be a unified party, but their candidates were generally younger and more vigorous than their opponents.

The two major parties fought very different campaigns. Churchill toured the country in semi-regal style, attracting huge crowds. Attlee, by contrast, was driven around by his wife Violet in the family's battered old car. In later years behaviour like this – akin to Michael Foot's amateurish style as leader during the 1983 campaign – would have had party managers tearing out their hair, but in 1945 it chimed in with the mood of a thoughtful, eager electorate.

Possibly for the first time since the Civil War in the 1640s, Britain displayed a widespread political consciousness which was reflected in the large meetings and the huge amount of literature bought and read. Blackburn, for example, differed little from other constituencies in the popular excitement aroused – after all this was the first time since 1935 that millions of people who had come of electoral age could cast a vote. The agent for the young Labour candidate, Barbara Castle, remembered it being 'an election campaign with an evangelical flavour'. The final rally concluded with a crowd of 10,000 to 12,000 crammed into the Market Square, Blackburn, singing 'Jerusalem'.

In this politically alert atmosphere crude ploys such as Churchill's suggestion that a victorious Labour government would eventually introduce 'some form of Gestapo' in order to implement their policies backfired badly; both *The Times* and *The Economist*, for instance, condemned this broadcast as 'artificial' and 'lamentable'. The London *Evening Standard* tried a similar stunt, printing pictures of Labour's National Executive beneath the caption 'These People Want to be Dictators. Study Their Faces!' But in 1945, for the first and so far last time, the national press was evenly divided in its support for the two major parties. In many ways the 1945 general election was like the old-style hustings contests, and Labour seemed to have the better arguments.

As the votes were counted, it quickly became clear that certain groups had been radicalised by the war. Leah Manning, the Labour candidate in Epping, Essex, has described what happened:

The count took place in the Drill Hall at Epping, and when the constituency boxes were opened, I was well down – radiant smiles from the Tory candidate's wife. But when the soldiers' vote came to be counted, my pile crept up and up. I was well in, by a majority of over a thousand.

Due to difficulties of communication, only 60 per cent of servicemen actually voted, but they proved to be solidly Labour. The Tory MP of 1942 was proved right: the troops had indeed returned 'pansy-pink'. In addition, two-thirds of the new voters reaching their majority since 1935 also supported Attlee's party.

The result was announced on 26 July 1945 to a mixture of public shock, disbelief and joy. The Labour Party led by Clement Attlee had won 393 seats to the Conservatives' 213, a huge majority. Some people lit bonfires and danced happily in the streets but for others it was a disaster, a first step on the way to what novelist Angela Thirkell dubbed 'A Brave New Revolting World'. Evelyn Waugh recalled that, for people like him, it was as if Britain was under occupation. Even now, in the 1990s, one still hears bitterness in many Conservatives' voices as they recall how an ungrateful nation stabbed Churchill in the back.

However, a Gallup poll showed that 56 per cent of the sample had voted for sweeping change and – for all his undoubted prowess as a wartime leader – Winston Churchill was not seen as the politician who, in peacetime, would preside over such changes. Gratitude for the past, but no confidence that he could introduce a New Jerusalem.

The Labour Party won seats all over the country, even in previously barren areas such as the south-east and the west Midlands, as well as most rural districts. Broadening its appeal well beyond the working classes, Labour attracted enough of the middle-class vote to win a majority. In the past, the Conservative Party had made much of its claim to be a national party, but now Labour could echo this assertion. For the only time in its history, the Labour Party had won a majority of seats in England alone.

Labour's strength was confirmed at a local level by its big

gains in the municipal elections of November 1945, the county council elections of March 1946, and the urban and rural district elections in April 1946. As E.P. Thompson once noted:

> Labour, which had advanced its position on a multitude of wartime committees, now emphatically consolidated its local and regional positions: on boards of school governors, hospital management boards, on the magistrates' bench, on Watch Committees, in the intricate networking of local authority and on the workshop floor and in industrial committees.

Labour Party membership doubled to almost half a million individual members in 1945 and then rose again to 645,345 the next year, attracting into its ranks teachers, technicians, health care workers, social workers – professional people who in previous years might have voted Labour but rarely considered joining the Party. A quarter of Labour's MPs were university graduates, in striking contrast with their predecessors of 1906.

Devastating for the Conservatives, the election result was no better for the Liberal Party which had hoped to benefit from their links with Beveridge. They put up over three hundred candidates but were almost wiped out, returning just twelve MPs. Scores of lost deposits added to the humiliation. The fate of the Foot family was telling. Father Isaac and two sons stood as Liberal candidates and all three were defeated. Another son Michael, a Labour candidate, was elected.

For most political leaders, such a triumph would have been a heady experience and indeed for some of Attlee's colleagues it certainly was. Hugh Dalton wrote in his diary: 'That first sensation, tingling and triumphant, was of a new society to be built, and we had the power to build it. There was exhilaration among us, joy and hope, determination and confidence. We felt exalted, dedicated, walking on air, walking with destiny.'

Attlee, in contrast, just seemed mildly baffled at the electorate's verdict. His family had not bothered to discuss what might happen if he became Prime Minister, breakfasting together at their north London home on 26 July in ignorant bliss of what was to come. Likewise King George VI noted in his diary that the new Prime Minister seemed 'very surprised that his Party had won . . .'

His leadership was still under attack. Almost as Attlee was on his way to Buckingham Palace to see the King, Herbert Morrison proposed that the Parliamentary Labour Party should be allowed a vote on the leadership issue. Morrison was aided in his manoeuvrings by his lover Ellen Wilkinson and by the chairman of the Party, Harold Laski, who had written a blunt letter to Attlee at the start of the election claiming that his leadership lacked '. . . a sense of the dramatic, the power to give a lead, the ability to reach out to the masses . . .' But Morrison and his co-conspirators came up against Attlee's most powerful supporter, Ernest Bevin, who swiftly threw his considerable political weight behind Attlee and the attempted coup came to nothing. Even Morrison's generally sympathetic biographers have problems explaining away his conduct.

Attlee returned to 10 Downing Street at the head of the first Labour government to have a clear majority. Here was the chance to build a New Jerusalem in England's green and pleasant land.

Despite the singing of 'The Red Flag' in the House of Commons – exactly as MacDonald's government of 1924 had been serenaded into office – and the fears of Conservative MPs like Oliver Lyttelton, the keynote of Attlee's early days in office was continuity. Parliament met for two weeks but then broke up for six weeks' holiday, hardly the act of an administration planning drastic changes. The Cabinet had an average age of over sixty, though of course age is not everything: the vigorous Lord Addison, appointed Leader of the House of Lords at seventy-six, was still going strong five years later.

Unlike the MacDonald government of 1924, this was a thoroughly experienced Cabinet – only Manny Shinwell and Aneurin Bevan of its senior figures had not served in the War Cabinet. The administration certainly contained some remarkable individuals. Attlee himself, for example, retained his down-to-earth way of doing things. When the Prime Minister went to open a new cinema in the East End in 1947, he arrived and left by bus. Herbert Morrison, a bouncy and energetic Cockney had run the London County Council and for all his intriguing was a brilliant administrator. His obsession with politics rendered him oblivious to his appearance: 'On one occasion he came to a meeting of the [London County] Council's most important committee – the General Purposes Committee – without his dentures, persisted in speaking at the meeting and seemed quite unaware of what other members may have thought.'

There was the High Anglican Sir Stafford Cripps, nicknamed 'The Red Squire' because he owned a mansion house near Lechlade in Gloucestershire; the pugnacious Ernest Bevin, almost as broad as he was tall; the Old Etonian Hugh Dalton; and the fiery Welsh orator Nye Bevan. Among the junior ministers were the former Clydesider Shinwell who had once laid out an abusive Tory in the House of Commons with a single punch; the ex-Welsh miner Jim Griffiths; the Marxist guru of the 1930s John Strachey; and Ellen Wilkinson. Twelve of the twenty Cabinet ministers were of working-class origin.

It was a formidable array of talents, which did not of course guarantee that they got on well. Morrison and Dalton were plotters; Bevin detested Morrison as 'a scheming little bastard' whom he wouldn't trust further than he could throw him while Bevan liked Cripps, who in turn was suspected by the others. On and on it went. Probably the greatest of Attlee's achievements was to keep the Cabinet pulling in roughly the same direction over the next six years; as Bevin put it, 'By God, he's the only man who could have kept us together.' When Attlee failed to do so in 1951, there were acrimonious resignations from the Cabinet and the Labour Party was soon out of office.

Nobody has ever quite explained either Attlee's success or his contradictions. This was, after all, a man who told his junior ministers that 'If I pass you in the corridor and don't acknowledge you, remember it's because I'm shy'; on the other hand, his scathing comments once reduced a Cabinet minister to tears. A.P. Herbert had a good go at explaining this enigma in a poem, one verse of which reads:

> Yet by some shy mysterious art
> He rules the roost, if not the heart.
> It may be 'character' – it may
> Be just his clever, cunning way.

Despite the militant backgrounds of some Cabinet members – both Morrison and Bevin had once belonged to the old Marxist Social Democratic Federation – the Fabian influence proved strongest, itself a reflection of the administrative and bureaucratic demands of 'Phase Two' of the British labour movement. Fabian detail was now more important than ethical assertion. More than half the Party's MPs were Fabians, forty-five were in the government and ten in the Cabinet. The new administration concentrated on the three major issues of nationalisation, planning and the introduction of a welfare state.

The overriding difficulty was that although it might not have suffered as badly as some countries, Britain was still in a parlous state. A quarter of its national wealth had been wiped out, as had two-thirds of its export trade. No fewer than four million houses had been destroyed or damaged by German bombing, while essential services had deteriorated. Watching films of the period, one always notices the bleak and derelict locations glimpsed in the background.

This dire wartime legacy was made much worse by the ending of Lend–Lease, the system of American financial aid that had sustained the British war effort. Within days of the general election, the Democratic administration led by

Truman cancelled assistance because it was worried by the socialistic tendencies of its supposed colleagues in Britain. The government was therefore always teetering on the edge of financial crisis.

Perhaps just as worryingly, the key figures within the Labour administration were economic virgins. Although Hugh Dalton was the most financially literate of Labour politicians, his friend Nicholas Davenport has described the new Chancellor visiting his home a few days after the election: 'I had also to explain the difference between jobbers and brokers on the Stock Exchange about which he knew nothing . . . Here was one of the big men in the Labour Party taking up high office who seemed to be utterly ignorant of the workings of the monetary system.'

The Attlee government's economic policy, as elsewhere in Europe, centred on the extension of public ownership. The mines and railways were two basic utilities which by 1945 proved to be thoroughly dilapidated, and not just because of the war. Britain's mines had operated at a loss for years, run by many different companies paying low wages and with a horrific accident record. By 1945 even the coal owners recognised the need for some form of centralised body; *The Economist* commented soon after the Labour administration took office: 'Support for the principle of public ownership of the mines is very wide, extending probably to two and a half of the three parties.'

As for the railways, the amalgamation of numerous companies into the 'Big Four' in 1921 had led to little modernisation – for instance, the use of diesel engines was virtually unknown before the war. During the conflict itself, the four independent companies had proved unable to cope with the increased flow of freight and a system of centralisation was introduced from 1941. Here too, as with the mines, the desirability of public ownership had practically been settled already and there was little opposition to the idea.

In fact, as Attlee later recalled in his memoirs, 'Of all our nationalisation proposals, only Iron and Steel aroused much feeling, perhaps because hopes of profit were greater here than elsewhere.' The consensus in favour of the virtues of public ownership therefore embraced Labour, Liberal and most Conservatives alike. Only a handful of seemingly maverick Tories maintained that market forces should once again be given their head.

But how exactly was nationalisation to be carried out? The famous Clause Four of 1918 called for 'the common ownership of the means of production, distribution, and exchange, and the best obtainable system of popular administration and control of each industry or service.' Like so many manifestos and policy statements, this was admirable in intention but lacking in detail.

In the past, some Labour politicians had welcomed the idea of workers' control. Attlee himself had claimed in 1935 that 'workers' control is an essential part of the new order', but ten years on such ideas had been quietly shelved, mainly due to the influence of Herbert Morrison who favoured the public corporation approach – indeed his London Passenger Transport Board led by Lord Ashfield and Frank Pick had given the capital perhaps the world's finest underground system. Morrison, who was responsible for overseeing government legislation in this area, justified nationalisation on the grounds of economic efficiency, not as a step towards socialism.

Ministers went to the policy cupboard and found it empty of solid fare. Shinwell, the new Minister of Fuel, asked the Labour Party's headquarters at Transport House for its documents on coal nationalisation and discovered that though it had been party policy for years only two papers existed and one of these was in Welsh. Similarly, when George Strauss, the Minister of Supply, began to handle steel nationalisation in the summer of 1947 he too found that no detailed planning had been carried out by the Labour Party or its sympathisers. Certainly no draft legislation had been drawn up.

The Labour government therefore had little idea how much compensation should be paid to former owners for their assets.

The sums turned out to be extremely generous: £164 million for the mines, nearly £1,000 million for the railways, and later on £540 million for electricity and £265 million for the gas industry, all paid for out of general taxation. Most owners were delighted to be rid of their loss-making ventures on these terms.

The 1946 Act nationalising the coal industry also set up the National Coal Board (NCB). Its composition showed the continuing influence of the old coal owners – the new chairman Lord Hyndley had formerly been chairman of the largest private group of collieries – and there was no provision for direct miner representation on any of the NCB's committees above pit level.

The Transport Act of 1946 transferred into state ownership the railways, canals and most long-distance road haulage, setting up the Transport Commission. Despite the protracted efforts of the National Union of Railwaymen to introduce some measure of industrial democracy, relations between management and workforce remained as it had been under private ownership. Nor did the government obtain a unified transport policy, primarily because separate boards administered the rail and road systems under a directive to compete against each other.

Other measures of nationalisation covered the Bank of England in 1946, electricity in 1947 and gas in 1948. Continuity of personnel seemed imperative here too. At the Bank the governor, the deputy governor and all the other leading officials were reappointed to their posts: eight of the heads of the gas boards had been former executives of private gas companies.

The Attlee government's nationalisation programme suffered from a number of defects: all the industries taken over were bankrupt and backward: the unprofitable 20 per cent of British industry. Extravagant compensation was paid to companies; and the old management structures and relationships were transferred unchanged from the private to the public sector. The editor of *The Economist*, Geoffrey Crowther, speaking to an American audience in 1949, summed up the whole experience: 'The ordinary resident in England, unless he happens to have been a shareholder in any of the expropriated companies, is unable to detect any difference whatever as a result of nationalisation.'

The workforce in the various industries seem to have been disappointed too. Surveys in *Railway Review* showed that less than 15 per cent of the sample thought that as railwaymen they had any share in the running of their industry. Similarly, in the mines the National Coal Board was as distant as, and acted no differently from, the old coal owners. Dissatisfaction flared up at the 1948 TUC Conference, and both managers and trade union leaders confessed themselves puzzled by the frequent number of unofficial strikes: over 8,000 between 1947 and 1951. A series of studies on the nationalised industries by the Acton Society, undertaken between 1950 and 1952, reported a widespread feeling among the rank and file that public ownership had merely provided 'jobs for the boys'. The 'same old gang' was still in charge.

The long-term consequences of the Attlee nationalisation measures proved important. Because the industries nationalised had all been on the verge of bankruptcy a strong association was naturally established in the public mind between socialism and bureaucratic inefficiency. It did not matter one iota that these public utilities provided a cheap infrastructure of services for the benefit of private industry. Company profits soared from £643 million in 1938 to £1,586 million in 1948 and then £1,830 million in 1949.

As for the rest of the government's economic policy, much had been made at the 1945 election of Labour's claim that it was the natural 'planning' party in contrast to the Conservative reliance on 'market forces'. The war had made planning respectable and *Let Us Face the Future* dwelt on the prospects of a future national plan for Britain. If this was to be executed with any degree of success then an efficient economic staff was vital. But with only fifteen economists in the economic section of the Cabinet and the same number of statisticians in the Central Statistical Office, government planning could be little more than a rather desperate whistling in the dark.

Not surprisingly – and this prefigured events under Harold Wilson's premiership in the 1960s – when the Attlee government faced a convertibility crisis for the pound in 1947, Washington turned out to know rather more about what was happening than Whitehall itself. The pound also had to be hurriedly devalued by 30 per cent in September 1949.

No national plan was ever produced and when an *Economic Survey* was finally published in 1947 it revealed that 'planning' now amounted to little more than piecemeal exhortation to private industry as was evident in the tentative and ineffective National Investment Board, though the Distribution of Industry Act certainly helped bring industry to previously run-down areas.

Exchange controls were never introduced, so that £645 million flooded out of the country between 1947 and 1949. The advisers and consultants appointed by the government often came from important private firms and were thus at least implicitly hostile to Labour's reliance on planning and controls. Unilever, for example, filled ninety posts in the Ministry of Food, twelve of them senior positions.

This problem of personnel was again one which the Labour Party had never really thought through. In 1920 Beatrice Webb had declared that a socialist order would require '. . . a dedicated Order, something resembling the Society of Jesus, which should exact a high standard of training, discipline and self-control among its members, and which would furnish, therefore, a leadership of the élite to guide the mass of citizens to a Socialist State.' Webb's proposal, with its typically Fabian enthusiasm for 'experts', was never implemented. Instead Attlee's then Minister of Fuel, Hugh Gaitskell, wrote despairingly in his diary of how difficult it was to find suitable people for high managerial positions in the newly nationalised coal industry.

The nadir of this disorganised style of government came with the fuel crisis in early 1947 when harsh weather brought a 25 per cent drop in coal supplies. February proved to be the coldest month in Britain so far this century. Manny Shinwell – of whom Kenneth Morgan has scathingly commented that 'Shinwell's amazing longevity and colourful personality over eight decades of political activity have masked his almost consistently disastrous record in office' – was unable to cope, although such a shortfall had long been forecast. Britain's exports were hit and her economic recovery was dented. Even though Mass Observation reported that most people thought the government had muddled through reasonably successfully, there need not have been a crisis in the first place.

The Labour government's social reforms centred on the development of a welfare state. Although the Liberals had introduced old-age pensions in 1908 and a national unemployment insurance system in 1911, these measures offered little more than a patchwork provision of services.

During the 1920s and 1930s no administration displayed more than a passing concern in social welfare and only the impact of 'total war' generated basic welfare services. The family means test was replaced, social security benefits were raised and family allowances were introduced. A sequence of White Papers on health, insurance and employment was published by the coalition government towards the end of the war, demonstrating official acceptance of the philosophy of the welfare state. The Labour government was active in the fields of social security, health, education, housing and jobs.

There were three major pieces of legislation on social security: the Industrial Injuries Act 1946, which incorporated much of the Beveridge Report; the National Insurance Act 1946; and the National Assistance Act 1948 that established a safety-net for all those who did not fall within the scope of the two 1946 Acts.

All three measures were an immense improvement on the

situation in the 1930s, introducing 'the idea of a national minimum' which no less a person than Sir William Beveridge regarded as 'a peculiarly British idea'. It wiped away almost the last vestiges of the Poor Law mentality, which had deemed it a crime to be poor. No matter what the individual flaws of the legislation, it was a marked step forward from the era of the means test and lengthy dole queue which had tainted pre-war Britain. As Peter Hennessy has put it, 'pre-1940 what little existed was for the poor; post-1940 the principle of selection gave way to universality, to the notion of flat-rate contributions and an equality of benefit for all as a bonding of a common citizenship.'

However, a number of shortcomings were apparent. For instance, the National Insurance Act followed in the path of the Liberal legislation in being founded on the contributory principle of insurance. Unlike a non-contributory scheme funded out of general taxation, the labour force was therefore already paying for their benefits out of deductions from their wages. Levied at a flat rate, the contributions in fact operated as a regressive form of taxation. Nor were benefits tied to the cost of living.

The provisions of the National Assistance Act were soon being used by thousands of people because the meagreness of national insurance benefits – reflecting a lingering bias against anyone getting 'something for nothing' – forced many to resort to means-tested national assistance. Two writers estimated that: '. . . the National Insurance benefits are so inadequate both in scale and scope that already by 1951 no less than two-and-a-half million people were being submitted to a means test. This is no less than one in every twenty of the population.'

During the war, improvements in health care had been brought about by centralisation under the Emergency Medical Service, and the principle was securely established that medical provision should be supplied on the grounds solely of need. Building on this consensus, Aneurin Bevan, the new Minister of Health, pushed through the National Health Service Act of 1946 which came into force in July 1948.

The great virtue of the National Health Service (NHS) was that it removed this vital area of life from the untender mercies of market forces, although some pay beds were still retained within the state system. Bevan found himself unable to create a full-time salaried service and sadly the new health centres – intended to emphasise the value of preventive medicine within the community – largely fell a victim to government cuts in the later 1940s. Nevertheless, these defects should not obscure the central achievement of the NHS and fittingly the service has retained massive popular support ever since its introduction.

The Education Act of 1944 introduced by the Conservative MP R.A. Butler had provided the framework within which Ellen Wilkinson, the Minister of Education, was to work. She raised the school-leaving age to fifteen but never sixteen as promised, and made no attempt to discourage private education. Little support was given to those local education authorities not producing plans on a tripartite system of grammar, technical and secondary modern schools. Instead Wilkinson and her successor George Tomlinson emphasised the virtues of the élitist grammar schools, thus ensuring that the secondary moderns would suffer from inferior resources and prestige. Much to its credit, however, the Labour government increased expenditure on education.

Opinion polls showed that housing was regarded by the electorate as the most important issue of the 1945 election. Attlee immediately broke one promise by not setting up a separate Ministry of Housing, and Aneurin Bevan naturally struggled to handle both this department and that of health. Hugh Dalton noted in his diary Bevan's supposed remark: 'I never spend more than an hour a week on housing. Housing runs itself.'

The relative failure of the government's housing programme is shown by considering how many houses were, in fact, built. Some 230,000 houses were completed in 1948 compared with

350,000 in 1938 – the administration therefore fell a long way short of its own target of 400,000 houses a year. Cuts in the housing budget in 1948 and 1949 further reduced the numbers, and a survey of 1951 concluded that there were 750,000 fewer houses than households – a far cry from the fulfilment of Labour's election pledge that every family should enjoy a good standard of accommodation. Shortages of material and manpower meant that this promise was always wildly optimistic. But, despite all the economic problems, one million permanent houses were built during the years of the Attlee governments.

Bevan was also responsible for section 132 of the Local Government Act of 1948 which allowed local authorities to spend up to the product of a 6d rate for the provision of entertainment, drama, music and so on. In Janet Minihan's words, 'Section 132 at last eliminated the need for special enabling legislation and gave local authorities uniform opportunities to encourage cultural activities throughout their districts.'

As for the pledge to introduce full employment, from 1945 to 1951 a high level of employment was indeed maintained. The number of jobless was restricted to about 3 per cent of the labour force. This was a significant improvement on the situation in the 1930s; in fact, the Labour government's main complaint related to the shortage of labour available. That virtually full employment was achieved under the Attlee governments today seems wellnigh miraculous. It undoubtedly helped foster a more civilised and contented society. From the perspective of the 1980s and 1990s when having three million people out of work seems to be the norm – and widespread joblessness has generated crime, drug-taking and social breakdown in some parts of the country – this surely constitutes one of the Labour administration's major feats.

No one could doubt the energy with which Attlee and his colleagues tried to tackle the many problems facing the country. In 1946 alone, eight major pieces of legislation were placed on the statute book. Herbert Morrison in his book *The Peaceful Revolution* claimed that between 1945 and 1948 over two hundred public Acts of Parliament were passed. By the end of 1946 the India Secretary Lord Pethick Lawrence was so exhausted by his efforts to secure a peaceful British withdrawal from India that only during Cabinet meetings did he find the time to sleep. No one could bear to wake him up.

Peter Hennessy in his excellent evocation of this period, *Never Again*, provides a dramatic example of this 'political overload' by summarising the flow of business in the Cabinet during the first fortnight of 1947. The range of issues discussed is mind-boggling, from Persia and Palestine, atomic weapons, withdrawal from India and the electricity bill to the banning of mid-week football matches. Such a pace brought problems in its wake, notably those of ill-health – and it should be remembered that the key, not especially youthful, figures in the administration had been continuously in office since 1940. All of the government's 'Big Four' (Attlee, Bevin, Morrison and Cripps) had lengthy spells in hospital. Bevin was to die in 1951, Cripps in 1952.

Naturally tempers frayed and sometimes ambitious politicians exhibited the worst sides of their profession. The best example of this concerns Sir Stafford Cripps, apparently so upright and pure. During the fuel crisis of 1947 he was blithely writing to the beleaguered Manny Shinwell that 'all your colleagues are anxious to help in every way they can and to share both the responsibility and the kicks.' At the very same time, Cripps was urging Attlee to sack Shinwell.

Nor were matters helped by a hostile press. Writing of these Attlee years, the veteran *Sunday Times* journalist James Margach concluded: 'I have never known the Press so consistently and irresponsibly political, slanted and prejudiced.' The government was eventually goaded into appointing a Royal Commission to investigate Fleet Street – whose recommendations led to the setting up of the Press Council in 1953 – but by then the damage had been done. The Ross Commission's report in general proved so feeble that, in Peter Hennessy's words, it 'scarcely scratched the paintwork of a Press Lord's Rolls Royce.'

Ill health and a prejudiced press were compounded by the sheer bad luck of unfortunate events beyond any government's control. The world wheat shortage in 1946 meant that bread rationing had to be introduced, a hardship avoided during the war. One unfortunate mistake was Hugh Dalton's unintended Budget leak in 1947. He spoke to a journalist on his way to the chamber and by chance parts of his speech appeared in the papers before he had finished speaking in the House. Dalton was obliged to resign.

The government was also harried by an energetic right-wing group called the British Housewives' League. Nor was it helped by the way in which Lord Woolton and R.A. Butler shifted the Conservative Party away from what now seemed to be untenable attitudes towards a critical acceptance of the new consensus. Their *Industrial Charter* of 1947 insisted that they too were committed to a welfare state and to full employment. Under the chairmanship of Lord Woolton, Conservative Central Office was overhauled and modernised.

In 1955, John Strachey was to claim that 'if a man were asked to name the greatest single achievement of the British Labour Party over the past 25 years, he might well answer, the transformation of the British Conservative Party.' In the 1980s the boot was securely on the other foot and it was Mrs Thatcher boasting how the Labour Party had been transformed by being pulled towards the Conservative stance.

Although popular support for Labour generally remained high – the government did not lose a single seat at sixty-eight by-elections during its time in office, a record that more recent administrations have almost succeeding in reversing – by 1948 the Labour government was clearly running out of steam. Important figures like Morrison were calling for 'consolidation' rather than further reforms. Chancellor Cripps' White Paper of February 1948 demanded wage restraint, whilst his budget of that year shifted the emphasis from direct to indirect taxation which always bears more heavily on the lower paid. Widescale distribution of wealth was postponed, as economist Dudley Seers noted in his book *The Levelling of Incomes since 1938*, published in 1951: '. . . there has been no continuation after 1944 of the previous trend towards equality of distribution.'

The government proceeded cautiously with iron and steel nationalisation, proposing to set up an Iron and Steel Corporation that would own the assets and liabilities of the steel companies but would otherwise undertake no change at all in their organisational and administrative structures. The existing management and even the identities and names of the companies were to be retained intact. It was in fact little more than a cosmetic exercise, but by 1948 business interests and industrialists felt confident enough to go on the offensive against the government – public relations firms like Aims of Industry were active, particularly in the 'Mr Cube' campaign opposing government plans for Tate & Lyle's sugar empire. TATE NOT STATE was the clever slogan adopted.

The Steel Bill fell foul of the Tory majority in the House of Lords and thus the Attlee government found itself embroiled in a constitutional battle as well. The result was the Parliament Act of 1949, which did not abolish either hereditary peers or introduce an elected second chamber but instead cut to one year the House of Lords' power to delay bills passed by the House of Commons. The Iron and Steel Act did not come into operation until February 1951 because the government had agreed that the result of the 1950 election should be regarded as a mandate.

The Labour government won the 1950 election but with a majority of only six seats. The administration limped on until another general election held in October 1951. The Labour Party received just under 14 million votes, the highest received by any party in Britain until the Conservatives' 14.1 million in 1992, but the vagaries of the electoral system and the collapse of the Liberal Party vote (they put up just 109 candidates compared with 475 the year before) ushered the Conservatives back to power. After six years Attlee and the Labour Party left office. It was to be thirteen years before a Labour Prime Minister returned to Downing Street.

How should one rate the Attlee government? Mrs Thatcher's administrations in the 1980s saw the attempted dismantling of, and hostility towards, the three main post-war assumptions: government intervention, planning and state welfare. But it is a testimony to the strength and appeal of this social-democratic consensus that so much has remained intact – and Mrs Thatcher herself had to announce that the National Health Service was safe in Conservative hands (even if several of the reforms radically altered its workings).

Post-war Britain has seen not only a remarkable rise in living standards but also the creation of a society in which people are better fed, better housed, better cared for, better educated and more fully employed than in the 1930s. Much of this success was due to Attlee's 1945–51 governments and to the dedicated and practical work of the Prime Minister himself and his colleagues. To criticise aspects of this record is not to call into question its outstanding overall achievement.

The administration's main omission was to shy away from implementing major institutional changes. Attlee always prided himself on his empirical and pragmatic approach: 'We were not afraid of compromise and practical solutions. We knew that mistakes would be made and that advance would be often by trial and error.' He remained something of an Establishment man, albeit a more progressive and humane Establishment. Attlee once described himself as 'basically a Victorian' and he took enormous pride in the success of 'My young Haileyburyians in the House . . .' It is also true that the war had not brought the collapse or dis-credit of long-established institutions, as happened throughout much of Europe. As the great European administrator Jean Monnet once noted, 'It was the price of victory – the illusion that you could maintain what you had, without change.'

There was something symbolic and revealing about Attlee's decision to rebuild the bombed House of Commons exactly as it had been before the war, even though this meant that all the people's representatives could not attend at the same time as there was not room for them. Similarly, the Labour government had no truck with the idea of Scottish Home Rule as expressed in 'the Covenant': 'By 1950, the Covenant had attracted well over a million signatures. The government, however, brushed it aside. It offered no new initiatives other than increasing the already large numbers of civil servants in the Scottish Office.'

The good things which the Attlee administration did, such as the introduction of legal aid and family allowances, were too often marred by unimaginative failures elsewhere – for instance, not introducing the principle of equal pay for women civil servants or schoolteachers. It was also telling that the Labour government provoked less constitutional conflict than either the 1906 Liberal government or the New Deal administration in the United States in the 1930s.

The government steered clear of far-reaching reform of, say, the voting system, the secret services, the civil service, the monarchy, the armed forces, public schools, the judiciary, the press, the rating system, local government (such as correcting the rampant gerrymandering in Northern Ireland) and indeed from any grand gestures other than the Festival of Britain held in 1951. In 1947 Mass Observation suggested that people were 'ready for radical action' but had been disappointed by the lack of 'spectacular appeals' and 'wider explanation' from the government.

Attlee and his colleagues also completely failed to understand the economic moves towards European integration taking place on the Continent, as we will see more fully in the next chapter.

It was inevitable that the government, heavily influenced

by the trade union connection, would tend to favour a system of corporatism involving government, employers and unions. This approach encapsulated the invariably top heavy approach at the heart of Fabian philosophy. The civil servant or 'the man in Whitehall' was always thought to know best. The resentment displayed by ordinary people explains in part the success of the Ealing comedy films of the period which often portrayed 'a little man' fighting back against inflexible bureaucracy.

Attlee once claimed that William Morris was the patron saint of his government, but Morris would surely have brought some much needed flair and imagination to the administration. The Prime Minister's personal puritanism imparted a rather grey feel. According to Peter Hennessy, Cabinet ministers and their wives 'lived in fear of invitations to Chequers because of the freezing bedrooms and the thimblefuls of sherry the Attlees served.'

Looking back on the Attlee years Aneurin Bevan, decidedly not a Puritan, observed that: 'Our name became identified with greyness and dullness, frugalities, shortages.' In France the Monnet Planning Commission effectively restructured French industry after the war. In Britain, by contrast, nationalisation and planning became indelibly associated with incompetence and waste. The Conservative Party slogan for the 1951 election was 'Set the People Free'.

But the Attlee governments were also handicapped by what would become a permanent feature of the post-war world, one which brought with it debilitating consequences both political and economical: the Cold War.

—— ——

# With Us or Against Us?

## The Cold War Years in Britain

'Either with Christ or against Christ; either with His Church or against His Church.'

POPE PIUS XII, DECEMBER 1946

'The opinion of the Trade Unions is that the Bevanite activities are a deliberate attempt to undermine the leadership in the same way as Hitler and the communists did. There is no difference whatever between them.'

WILL LAWTHER, LEADER OF THE MINERS, WRITING IN THE
*DAILY TELEGRAPH*, 29 JANUARY 1953

'How can you support a public schoolboy from Winchester [Hugh Gaitskell] against a man born in the back streets of Tredegar?'

ANEURIN BEVAN'S QUESTION TO MINERS' LEADER
SAM WATSON, 1954

On the afternoon of 8 January 1947, six Cabinet ministers met at 10 Downing Street to decide whether Britain should build its own nuclear weapon. The most powerful member of this committee, whose very existence had been kept secret from the rest of the Labour Cabinet, was the Foreign Secretary Ernest Bevin. His thick, bulky appearance embodied the pugnacity and strength with which he steamrollered friends, colleagues and enemies alike.

That Bevin was Foreign Secretary at all was a tribute to his personal determination. Born in Somerset in March 1881, he was the illegitimate son of a farmworker, Mercy Bevin, and never knew who his father was. His mother died when he was eight and he was brought up by a half-sister. Bevin left school at eleven to work on a local farm scaring away the birds. This was still his job in 1894, the very year that Thomas Hardy published his last novel which begins with a small boy scaring away the birds. But if Hardy's Jude was to remain obscure, Bevin became an international statesman who shaped the post-war world.

At thirteen Bevin moved to Bristol where he worked as a drayman and joined the Bristol Socialist Society, just as Ramsay MacDonald had done ten years before. A lay preacher and a union activist, Bevin made a local name for himself by forming the unemployed into a 'Right to Work' committee. One protest that he organised is still remembered in Bristol. His friend and biographer Francis Williams described what happened:

> One Sunday shortly before morning service in Bristol Cathedral a great crowd of unemployed assembled in Horsefair. There they formed in orderly procession and, with Bevin at their head, marched to the Cathedral. As the service began they entered, and, with Bevin leading them, silently took up places along every aisle of the great church. They remained there without stirring throughout the service, many of them clearly in great distress from hunger, all of them poorly clad; a mute challenge to the Christian conscience of every worshipper. When the service ended they filed slowly and quietly out of the Cathedral and, without speaking a word, reformed into procession and marched back to the Horsefair. There after a few words from Bevin who told them to go back to their homes without disturbance they dispersed.

In 1914 Bevin was appointed a full-time trade union organiser. He made his name after the war as 'the Dockers' KC' when, during the official inquiry into dockers' wages, he brought into court plates of meagre food demonstrating what a docker's wage meant in terms of privation. Producing the exact amount of bacon allowed for by the Cambridge university 'expert', A.L. Bowley, Bevin asked him whether this was nutritionally sufficient for a man 'to discharge ships and carry heavy grain'. He remorselessly continued: 'I want to ask any employer, or you, or the Court, whether a Cambridge professor is a competent judge of a docker's breakfast . . .'

Bevin proved to be the driving force behind the formation of the Transport and General Workers' Union in 1922, the largest in Britain. He was elected its General Secretary, a pivotal position which meant that for the next thirty years he was a dominant figure in the labour movement. Brooking no internal opposition within the union, he earned the nickname 'Boss Bevin'. His approach to both life and politics was simple: 'There is nobody in the world who submits to anything but force.'

In 1935 Bevin's fierce speech at the Labour Party Conference calling for British rearmament prompted the pacifist George Lansbury to resign as Labour Party leader. When friends told Bevin that he had dealt unnecessarily harshly with the venerable Lansbury, he replied even more brutally: 'Lansbury has been going about dressed in saint's clothes for years, waiting for martyrdom. I set fire to the faggots.'

During the Second World War Bevin moved from the trade union world onto the national stage. Elected MP for Wandsworth in 1940 and appointed Minister of Labour in the Churchill government, he was responsible for mobilising all available man- and woman-power. When Labour won the general election in 1945 Bevin had expected to be Chancellor of the Exchequer, but to his surprise found himself appointed Foreign Secretary.

Bevin brought to this post a hearty dislike of communism, perhaps because much of his time in the 1920s and 1930s had been spent combating what he regarded as communist infiltration of his union. He urged the West to stand up to the Soviet Union and in 1948 authorised American B-52 bombers

stationed in Britain to carry atomic bombs, thereby surrendering an important slice of national sovereignty. Ironically,
the Conservatives who in years to come complained most
about losing power to Europe never seemed to mind about
this client status.

The Foreign Secretary's squat, Sumo-like physique and force
of character often intimidated and scared Labour opponents.
As the future Prime Minister Jim Callaghan, then a critic of
Bevin, wrote in 1946, 'We must stop letting Ernie hypnotise
us. The curious thing is that most of us are half afraid of him
– he is so massive, immovable and apparently impenetrable to
any influence he does not wish to acknowledge.'

Bevin's unyielding stance proved crucial in the formation
of the North Atlantic Treaty Organisation (NATO) in April
1949. He also pushed through the decision that Britain needed
its own bomb, making sure that the huge £100 million cost
of the project was concealed in the 'secret budget'. The Cold
War became several degrees colder.

'Defence' has often been a problem for the British labour
movement because of the conflicting strands of thought
that co-exist within it. Pacifism, internationalism, 'Little
Englandism', 'John Bull-ism', Christian socialism, Quakerism
– these traditions give different answers to the question of how
Britain should defend itself. Labour leaders who agreed with
each other on much else had sometimes taken opposing views
on this topic: Attlee and Dalton, for instance, both fought in
the First World War; Lansbury and Morrison were anti-war
protesters.

During the Second World War the United States, the Soviet
Union and Britain formed an anti-fascist alliance even though
the Soviet Union had traditionally been regarded as an enemy.
As the hostilities came to an end, previously suppressed tensions
started to surface. The United States and the Soviet Union in
particular began to jockey for position in the post-war world.
Always the realist, Stalin coldly observed: 'This war is not as

in the past; whoever occupies a territory also imposes on it his own social system. Everyone imposes his own systems as far as his army can reach. It cannot be otherwise.' Already communism and capitalism were carving up the world between them.

Generally, Labour and the Conservatives had operated a bipartisan policy under which both parties agreed on the objectives to be pursued. But there were sometimes differences in emphasis, and during the 1945 election campaign the Labour Party stressed that it alone could handle the Soviet Union. Its manifesto *Let Us Face The Future* had reminded the electorate: 'Let it not be forgotten that in the years leading up to the war the Tories were so scared of Russia that they missed the chance to establish a partnership which might well have prevented the war.'

Within months of this statement, however, Attlee's Labour government had changed its mind on the possibility of partnership. Instead it became sucked into a new 'war', the Cold War. 'We' were in the right, 'They' were, of course, in the wrong.

The very existence of the Cold War demonstrated the internationalism of the modern twentieth-century world: no country could now be an island. A series of events – the failure to hold free and fair elections in Eastern Europe, Marshall Aid, the coup in Czechoslovakia, the Berlin Airlift, the formation of NATO and the Warsaw Pact – led to bitter hostility. It was a tragedy of misunderstanding; in Denis Healey's words, 'We took too seriously some of the Leninist rhetoric pouring out from Moscow, as the Russians took too seriously some of the anti-Communist rhetoric favoured by American politicians.'

Much of this chapter deals with the effects of American interference in Britain and Western Europe, involvement which was sometimes secret, furtive and anti-democratic. But it must be stressed that Soviet interference in the new Eastern European regimes was much more overt and far-reaching. It is absolutely vital to keep a sense of proportion. Arthur Koestler correctly pointed out how foolish it was to equate an 'imperfect democracy' (USA) with an 'imperfect totalitarian regime' (USSR).

The extent of American involvement in Western Europe after 1945 is still little known. Why? The Americans themselves were understandably reluctant to publicise their activities whilst British historians have shied away from such a controversial topic – one journalist commissioned to write an article on just this subject had his material rejected by the *Sunday Times* on flimsy grounds. Many on the Left have not raised the matter because the Soviet Union did not exactly have clean hands. Revelations about one side would inevitably lead to revelations about the other.

The foundations of American involvement were laid during the latter part of the war when several US union leaders set up committees in order to help influence post-war labour affairs. Several of those involved such as Jay Lovestone had once been Communists but were now zealous anti-Communists. Lovestone remained a bachelor because, as he put it, he was 'married to the idea of preventing the Kremlin from dominating the world.' Another key figure, Irving Brown, was nicknamed 'Scarface' which somehow epitomises the sleazy, underhand tactics often deployed at the time.

Lovestone, Brown and their circle paid most attention to Italy and France. Both countries possessed a formidable Communist Party that had benefited from the discrediting of indigenous right-wing organisations which, with a few notable exceptions, had been either fascist during the war or had collaborated with the Germans. Elections held in 1945 and 1946 gave the Communist Parties in Italy and France scores of seats and also a share in government. American concern at Communist electoral success turned to alarm in the winter of 1946–47 when impending European economic and political collapse seemed likely. Chaos would benefit the Communists, allowing them to claim that the only viable system was the Soviet one.

The Americans responded in two ways. First of all President

Truman announced the so-called 'Truman doctrine' in March 1947, declaring that his government was prepared to play an active role outside the United States: 'I believe that we must assist free peoples to work out their destinies in their own way.' This interventionist stance was backed up by material support. Following a plan drawn up by General George Marshall, the United States pumped economic aid into Western Europe in an attempt to stave off disaster: between 1948 and 1951 a massive $13,000 million of assistance was made over to European governments.

Secondly, the Americans undermined the Communist challenge by setting up rival left-wing but distinctly non-Communist parties and by splitting Communist-controlled unions; they also financed various right-wing organisations. In Italy, the Christian Democrats received $1 million; in France it was General de Gaulle who was funded. The right-wing union Force Ouvriére in France was encouraged to break away from the Communist-dominated CGT. In Italy a split within the General Confederation of Labour was fomented by American money, whilst right-wing Catholic unions were also assisted.

The Communist-organised World Federation of Trade Unions was likewise torn in two when Western trade unions were persuaded to withdraw and to form instead the new International Congress of Free Trade Unions (ICFTU) in December 1949. Much of this was done to a chorus of anti-Communist frenzy: 'Reds' were seemingly here, there and everywhere. At the time, of course, the frenzy seemed justified: after all, the Soviet Union had tested its own atomic bomb in August 1949, years before the West had expected, and China had been seized by the Communists under Mao Tse-Tung.

The mood was less overheated in Britain but even here the usually restrained Harold Macmillan called for a 'Christian crusade against Communism', whilst George Orwell, admittedly a sick man, kept lists of suspected Communist conspirators. But these were relatively isolated phenomena. The Labour

Party of Attlee and Bevin had never been seriously threatened by the small British Communist Party and the government's response to industrial unrest would have been robust enough for a hard-line Conservative administration. Troops were used in eleven disputes between 1945 and 1951; strike-breaking became almost a reflex action for this Labour government. The police were often asked to find evidence that strikes were Communist initiated, but invariably had to report that no such evidence existed.

Much of the running was made by the Foreign Office, still smarting from its disastrous policies of the decade before; as Anne Deighton has put it: 'The appeasement analogy became the worst form of abuse within the Foreign Office, and to stand up to the Russians an expiation for not standing up to Hitler.' In January 1948 the Labour government set up an organisation under Foreign Office auspices which was called, innocuously enough, the Information Research Department (IRD).

Paid for out of the secret fund maintained by all governments, the IRD had its own publication called *Freedom First* which it distributed together with newsletters and other briefings to several hundred key British trade union organisers. It also 'placed' articles favourable to the United States and British view of international affairs in the domestic and foreign press. By 1951, more than a thousand 'items' a year were being placed here and abroad. Influential figures such as Bertrand Russell, Stephen Spender, Denis Healey and historian Hugh Trevor-Roper all had information 'planted' on them, mostly unwittingly.

The IRD also moved into publishing, producing over a hundred anti-Communist 'background' books in the 1950s and 1960s. Between 1960 and 1971 these were published in conjunction with the respected firm of Bodley Head. Regular anti-Communist briefings were supplied to senior BBC staff, and the Corporation obligingly agreed to 'temper its broadcasts to accord with the national interest.' By the mid-1950s the

IRD's staff of three hundred occupied the massive Riverwalk House in Vauxhall, London.

Occasionally the IRD worked alongside other agencies such as MI5. In his biography of Sir Dick White, a former head of both MI5 and MI6, Tom Bower describes one particularly bizarre operation when agents 'were encouraged to disrupt subversive organisations, even impregnating lavatory paper with an itching substance at halls used by communist organisations.' Smoke-filled rooms full of uncomfortable bottoms. But then spies often inhabit different worlds from the rest of us: in 1918 Sidney Reilly, so-called 'Ace of Spies', had concocted a plan to debag Lenin and Trotsky and then parade them trouserless through the streets of Moscow to general ridicule. Later, of course, the CIA experimented with exploding cigars in order to bring down General Castro.

Such antics makes the use of the term 'intelligence services' even more of a laughable misnomer. But careers were blighted and lives wrecked in Cold War Britain, if only by the dollops of inaccurate information stored on file and recycled by organisations like Economic League who supplied blacklisting services for employers. Everything was done without parliamentary knowledge or scrutiny.

The IRD remained active until the second half of the 1970s – it even assisted the pro-Europe campaign during the 1975 EEC referendum – but was closed down in 1977 by the new Foreign Secretary, Dr David Owen. Information about the IRD is difficult to find; many of its files have been destroyed by government weeders on the patently untrue grounds that the material was not 'of sufficient historical importance to be selected for permanent preservation'. However, 165 files of documents were released in August 1995.

At times the Attlee administration did flirt with widescale anti-Communist measures, formulating plans to penalise 'subversive or misleading propaganda' with up to fourteen years' imprisonment and to outlaw 'attempts to disrupt the nation's economy.' In the event, traditional British respect for civil liberties saved the day and the proposals were dropped by the Cabinet.

The trade union movement, reflecting the small role that communism had always played in Britain as well as the botched zigzagging policies of the British Party, was also predominantly anti-Communist. The TUC issued two pamphlets, *Defend Democracy* and *The Tactics of Disruption*, both of which attacked Communist activities. In 1949 the Transport and General Workers' Union began to dismiss its Communist officials in a series of actions reminiscent of the blacklisting operating in the United States.

What did this international polarisation of the late 1940s mean in individual, personal terms? To place the British experience in perspective, one should glance at events in the United States. In 1947 President Truman, leader of the Democrats, enacted a Loyalty Order which failed to make any distinction between being a socialist and working as a spy or traitor. Worse still, it established the notion of 'guilt by association' under which previous contact with a 'subversive', even if only on personal and non-political grounds, was sufficient in itself to make one 'a potential subversive'. There were no rules of evidence.

A recent book by the journalist Carl Bernstein, *Loyalties*, revealed the scale and scope of the surveillance of suspects. His parents, once members of the American Communist Party, were the subject of more than two-hundred separate surveillances over a four-year period. When researching his book, Bernstein found that the intelligence procedures had been so exhaustive that even the names of the guests at his own Bar Mitzvah in 1957 were meticulously recorded. His parents remained under FBI surveillance for no less than thirty-five years. Historian David Caute's book on the subject is aptly titled *The Great Fear*.

Were similar actions taken in Britain? The government introduced civil service 'vetting' under which none of the formalities or safeguards of a usual administrative hearing were observed: no witnesses could be identified, no evidence was given and no legal representation allowed. On the other hand, 'suspects' were transferred to different posts rather than being dismissed outright; the attitude was 'we should not make any martyrs.' Above all, compare the scale of this vetting with that in the United States: in 1952, 134,000 civil servants were subject to checks; in America, by 1955 the figure had reached nine million. In Britain 25 civil servants were dismissed, 25 resigned and 88 were transferred; in America, 9,500 government employees were sacked and 15,000 resigned.

Some prominent Communists in Britain did suffer checks to their careers. Andrew Rothstein, a founder member of the Party, was dismissed from his post at London University on the grounds of 'inadequate scholarship'. J.D. Bernal lost his place on several government committees; lists of his supporters were sent to the authorities. Similar events happened to Professor J.B.S. Haldane. Historian A.J.P. Taylor was banned from the Third Programme because his talks were considered too pro-Soviet. Within the universities, as Eric Hobsbawm has recalled, it was difficult for a left-winger to find a post after the Berlin Airlift in the summer of 1948, but those in place were not sacked. Some left-wing actors found that their work at the BBC dried up, whilst the Corporation had its special vetting department.

Nevertheless, of the forty-five Communists I spoke to specifically about this period very few had experienced any direct harrassment or even unpleasantness. Traditional British a-politicism and the feeling that people's opinions were their private affair guaranteed a reasonably tolerant atmosphere. David Caute has likewise pointed out that there was no Un-British Activities Committee, Parliament did not go witchhunting and no loyalty oaths were instituted. Nor were there more than a handful of 'Communist' election smears directed at left-wing candidates.

In fact, in rather typically English fashion, at the height of the Cold War the Labour Party's Transport House still played its annual cricket match against the staff of the Communist *Daily Worker*. British respect for civil liberties creaked and groaned during the Cold War but survived largely intact – unlike in Eastern Europe where political trials, purges, imprisonment, torture and sometimes murder were rife.

However, this subject remains shrouded in secrecy – the purges within the civil service, the Labour Party and the unions were conducted internally by the organisations themselves – and pieces of information are still emerging which might well alter this relatively rosy picture. For example, it now appears that in 1951 the Attlee government was informed by MI5 that a quarter of a million files were held on British Communists or suspected Communists – evidence of an enormous operation. Mark Hollingsworth and Richard Norton-Taylor have noted that without a written constitution, individuals were and are devoid of statutory rights protecting their civil liberties.

As one Conservative expert in this area, Lord Bethell, has noted, the entire episode offered convincing proof of 'the anti-Soviet credentials of the British Labour Party', which never of course stopped unscrupulous Tory politicians from trying to tar the Party with the Red brush.

Where the Cold War did prove devastating in Britain was in the broader political and economic spheres. The decision to create Britain's own nuclear weapon and then, in April 1949, to become a founder member of NATO meant that the country's shaky economy was committed to a financial burden it could not afford. By 1949 the Labour government was spending £750 million – 10 per cent of its national income – on defence. The British army was still three times its 1939 size, even though the economy was suffering from a shortage of manpower. Indeed, between 1945 and 1950 Britain spent a higher proportion of its national income on defence than the United States.

The Korean War, which broke out in 1950, only exacerbated the problem. Money that could have been spent on improving living standards at home was instead poured into an unpleasant and unnecessary war abroad. As Peter Hennessy has put it:

> The dramatic turnaround, from a payments surplus of £307 million in 1950 to a deficit of £369 million in 1951 was especially tragic as this was *the* golden opportunity in the entire postwar period for a sustained export-led boom which, with luck, might have put the British economy on to a higher and sustainable trajectory before Germany, in particular, recovered to the point where our export markets were once more highly vulnerable.

The either/or choice set up by the Cold War ensured that Britain acquired some particularly unsavoury allies such as Syngman Rhee, the leader of South Korea. After the Czechoslovakian coup in February 1948, Hugh Dalton thought this might well be what the future held in store. He wrote in his diary: 'We should have to drag ourselves back behind the USA . . . we should have to line up with all the worst reactionaries and the Catholic Church! Ugh!'

Another damaging consequence of the Cold War was that Britain's 'special relationship' with the United States precluded any search for more fruitful relationships. As early as the 1920s Ernest Bevin had wanted 'to inculcate the spirit of a United States of Europe at least on an economic base. . . .' He called for an economic United States of Europe 'spreading from the borders of Russia to the borders of France . . .' At the 1945 Labour Party Conference, Bevin had happily talked of the possibility of a 'Third Way' between the United States and the Soviet Union.

In the Cold War climate such aspirations went by the board as too did much of the internationalism dear to the hearts of earlier leaders like Keir Hardie and Ramsay MacDonald. Instead a rather belligerent insularity came to the fore; as Denis Healey pungently expressed it, 'The Labour Party has never been prepared to learn anything from the experience of foreigners.' Bevin's Parliamentary Private Secretary, Pierson Dixon, remarked on the Foreign Secretary's assumption that, in 1945, Britain was still more important than the United States and the Soviet Union.

So-called special relationships with both the United States and the Commonwealth meant that the Labour government displayed little interest in developments in mainland Europe – even though the Americans themselves were in favour of an integrated Europe. The Attlee administration opposed both the European Defence Community and the Coal and Steel Community set up in April 1951. The Party's two leading foreign policy experts, Bevin and Dalton, were both hostile to any European idea. Herbert Morrison's reason for opposing the Coal and Steel Community was a classic demonstration of Labour Party insularity: 'It's no good, we cannot do it, the Durham miners won't wear it.'

With the benefit of hindsight it is easy to claim that here was the moment when post-war Britain took a wrong turn, but there was at the time a substantial section within the Labour Party calling for the creation of a 'United Socialist States of Europe' (USSE) – meetings of the 'Europe Group' from December 1947 regularly attracted more than eighty Labour MPs. On behalf of the Labour Party's ruling National Executive Committee, Hugh Dalton did indeed endorse the philosophy of the USSE but nothing further was ever done. In the Cold War atmosphere, any middle way was inevitably destined to be squeezed out.

'Humanity, not only in the USSR but in all countries, will always be deeply in his [Stalin's] debt.' This eulogy by the eminent historian Christopher Hill in 1953 showed that British Communists still had not shaken off their 'Russia Complex'. But whereas between 1941 and 1945 association with the victorious Red Army had brought benefits, now, with the onset of the Cold War, the Soviet link was disastrous.

The Communist Party had emerged from the war with its

highest ever membership of nearly 60,000 and high hopes
for the 1945 election. In the event the British electorate
drew a sharp distinction between admiration for the Soviet
role in winning the war, and voting Communist. Only two
Communists were actually elected; Willie Gallacher retained
his seat in West Fife and Phil Piratin won in Mile End, East
London. These victories neatly encapsulated the Scottish and
Jewish contributions to British communism. But the election
of just two MPs contrasts poorly with the 104 Communists
elected in France in 1946, and shows the tenuousness of the
party's position in Britain.

Party membership did continue to rise, reaching a high
in 1946 – although the French Communist Party numbered
800,000 and the Italians a gigantic 1.7 million. The leadership
tried to make the party more friendly and less 'alien': for
instance, the 'Politburo' was now renamed the Political
Committee. New offices for the *Daily Worker* were built
on Farringdon Road, London, in 1948 – a bleak 'Stalinist'
structure designed by Erno Goldfinger, the man responsible
for the nasty DHSS building at the Elephant and Castle. (Ian
Fleming is supposed to have taken his name for the villain in
*Goldfinger*.) Saturday sales of the *Daily Worker* reached 120,000
and a Scottish edition of the paper was started.

But the impact of the Cold War meant that the peak of
Communist expansion had been reached. Before the Cold
War it had been to the party's advantage to be linked with
the Soviet Union; after the Berlin Airlift of 1948 it definitely
was not. The Comintern had been killed off by Stalin during
the war, but in October 1947 the Communist Information
Bureau (Cominform) was established. The British party was
too small to be invited to join but it unhesitatingly obeyed the
new orders which signalled a return to the sectarian rigidities
of the 'Third Period' between 1928 and 1935.

Dissent was once again heresy, as Tito and the Yugoslav
Communists found out when they refused to nationalise their
industries and collectivise their agriculture on Soviet lines.

The trauma of breaking with Moscow comes through in the memoirs of one of Tito's senior associates, Milovan Djilas, who had to persuade himself that 'In any event – life is possible without Stalin's love', almost the words of an excommunicated Catholic talking about the Pope.

Throughout Eastern Europe, one-party states were established and purge trials weeded out potential troublemakers. By 1951 there were 350 labour camps in Czechoslovakia alone, holding 100,000 prisoners. No fewer than 278 senior party officials had been killed for holding 'incorrect' political views. Just as they had done in the 1930s, leading British Communists welcomed these measures. Willie Gallacher wrote *The Case for Communism* which was published by Penguin Books in 1949:

> . . . But what about the opposition [in Eastern Europe]? What opposition? The parties in the Government bloc represent the people, and carry forward a policy in the interests of, and for the welfare of, the people. Those who want to put the clock back are enemies of the people. There can be no toleration for such.

As Pope Pius XII put it, those who are not with us are most certainly against us. In a grim imitation of the Cominform the Church set up its own six-country Catholic International to stimulate anti-communism.

Within the British party, disagreement was met by denunciation and expulsion rather than debate. To dissent from 'the line' handed down from above was often to ensure not just political ostracism but personal isolation too, because most members' best friends also belonged to the party. Investigation of a suspect's views bore all the hallmarks of a medieval inquisition. The young E.P. Thompson, later a distinguished historian, was a party member in the 1940s and early 1950s and has recalled what took place:

> That time produced one of the sharpest mental frosts I can

remember on the Left. Vitalities shrivelled up and books lost their leaves. It was about this time that the Party blocked the publication of Hamish Henderson's translation of Gramsci's prison letters – it had been discovered (we were told) that Gramsci was guilty of some nameless 'deviation'.

Thompson remembers attending party meetings at which hacks publicly scolded and 'unmasked' various unreliable individuals, and notes too how the accused found it almost impossible to defy this God-like party:

> It was a shameful episode and I shared in the shame, for, however 'youthful' I was, I had allowed myself to be made use of as a part of the team of uncultured yobboes and musclemen under the command of the elderly Burns. But I was sad and puzzled also that my heroes had not allowed me to fight on their side. They had at once lost all their customary confidence, wit and vitality when placed in the formal posture of receiving criticism from one of the Party's senior officers.

Excruciating was the widespread 'Stalin worship'. Future Labour MP Eric Heffer was then a Communist: 'We accepted all Stalin's actions . . . I remember Party meetings where speeches were littered with phrases like "As Comrade Stalin has said . . ."' Professor Hyman Levy also noted the cult of personality – as the Soviet leaders later called it – was in fact the cult of just one personality: 'During the later years of Stalin's life, if his name was mentioned at a party meeting, the members stood up in silent reverence.' Alan Sebrill, the protagonist in Edward Upward's novel *The Rotten Elements*, suffers a nervous breakdown but found 'he could stop his trembling by thinking of Stalin and by speaking the name of Stalin, repeatedly but not quite aloud, much as a religious believer might have called on the name of God.'

In such an unpromising climate the last vestiges of electoral support for the British Communist Party soon faded away. In

1950, 97 of its 100 election candidates lost their deposits (and Gallacher and Piratin their seats); in 1951, all ten candidates lost their deposits. That same year the party launched a silly and negative crusade called 'I Hate America'. But British Communists were consoled by the fact that, no matter how torrid the domestic situation, at least communism seemed to be strengthening world wide. As Harry Pollitt once blithely remarked: 'We may have lost St Pancras but we've won in China.'

Who were the party 'minders' or 'musclemen' responsible for carrying out the line? The man E. P. Thompson refers to above was Emile Burns, a former Cambridge student who was in charge of the party's intellectuals. Another apparatchik was James Klugmann, yet one more Cambridge Communist of the 1930s whose name periodically surfaces in 'Third Man' spy books. To his credit, however, Klugmann was openly Communist and made no secret of his views. His personal life shows the closeness of the British Communist Party 'family'. He married Kitty Cornforth, sister of yet another Cambridge Communist Maurice Cornforth who for twenty-five years was managing director of Lawrence and Wishart, the party's publishing house.

Klugmann was a man of great erudition and charm who over the years amassed a magnificent collection of material on the history of the British radical movement. During the Second World War he worked for SOE (Special Operations Executive) in Cairo, helping to parachute British soldiers into Yugoslavia to fight alongside Tito's Partisans. He was in his element and there is an evocative portrait of Klugmann in historian Basil Davidson's account of his experiences, *Special Operations Europe*.

But in 1948 Tito was dramatically expelled from the Soviet camp. Stalin now argued that the Yugoslav Communists had all along been an agent of Trotsky, of the Nazis, in fact of anyone opposed to the Soviet Union. Tito's past in particular must therefore be exposed. European Communist Parties were expected to mount campaigns vilifying him, and who better in the British party to denounce Tito than James Klugmann? He duly produced a book called *From Trotsky to Tito*, even though he must have known he was writing fiction and not fact.

But those who live by the party line can sometimes die by it too. When the line changed a few years later and Tito returned to favour, Klugmann was left with egg on his face. His book was withdrawn: he had perjured himself for nothing. Most people would have resigned from an organisation that pressured its members into doing such things. He didn't. Commissioned by the party to write its history, he duly produced two unreadable volumes distinguished more for what is left out than what is put in. Klugmann regretted writing both the Tito book as well as his two histories and promised that the next volume would be an honest account. He died in 1977 before he was put to the test.

If the Cold War severely damaged the Communists, then it proved almost as disastrous for the non-Communist Left. Whereas the Communist Party had not challenged the either/or choice between 'Washington' and 'Moscow', the Labour Left did at least try. But if you did not unequivocally choose one side or another then political opponents could easily smear you as a 'fellow traveller'.

Early evidence of this technique in action was provided by the fate of the 'Keep Left' group, a body of Labour MPs which during the late 1940s tried to formulate a Third Way (similar to what Ernest Bevin had proposed in 1945) between the two superpowers. But under the unrelenting pressure of the Cold War to choose one side or another, the group was soon whittled down to just a handful of members. It was a foretaste of what would happen in the 1950s to the Bevanites.

Like George Lansbury, Aneurin Bevan possessed a charismatic personality, making him one of the British Left's most attractive figures. He is rightly looked upon as the architect of the Labour Party's 'jewel in the crown', namely the National Health

Service. Today, more than thirty years after his death, his name is invoked as frequently and as reverentially as that of Keir Hardie himself. Which only goes to show how reputations and opinions change: in his lifetime Bevan was hated not just by his political opponents – the memoirs of Conservatives such as Lord Kilmuir fizz with rage when his name is mentioned – but even by supposed colleagues for, as they saw it, stirring up trouble and harming Labour's electoral chances. On one occasion Hugh Gaitskell even claimed to see 'extraordinary parallels between Nye and Adolf Hitler. . . .' In the last few years of his life, Bevan was by contrast bitterly attacked by former friends and supporters when he changed his mind over nuclear disarmament and opposed CND (Campaign for Nuclear Disarmament).

So far this book has sketched out the major contributions that both Scotland and the East End have made to the British Left. Bevan epitomised the Welsh connection, drawing as it did on a radical heritage centred on the working man's club, the library and adult education classes. Although Bevan received little formal education, the absence was more than made up for by this network of militant culture which produced outstanding miners' leaders such as A.J. Cook, Arthur Horner and Will Paynter. Much of this was due to the creative influence of 'the Fed': the South Wales Miners' Federation. Will Paynter has explained what made this body so special:

> The Fed was a lot more than a trade union; it was a social institution providing through its leaders an allround service of advice and assistance to the mining community on most of the problems that could arise between the cradle and the grave. Its function became a combination of economic, social and political leadership in these single industry communities . . . The leaders of the local miners' lodges were very much more than representatives dealing with problems of wages and conditions of employment in the mines. They were acknowledged social leaders called upon to help and advise

in all kinds of domestic and social problems; they were indeed the village elders to whom the people went when in any kind of trouble.

The Fed instilled in Bevan a love of discussion and of debate with friends and opponents; one of his favourite sayings was 'This is my truth; now tell me yours.' He was never afraid to admit that he might be wrong. Perhaps it should be emphasised that this sense of community was also rooted in mutual hardship and loss. Arthur Horner's grandfather was brought home in bits in a sack after an underground explosion; Aneurin Bevan's father died in his son's arms, choked to death by pneumoconiosis.

Bevan began work down the mines when he had just turned fourteen – the age when many of his future political opponents were in their first year at private school – but he left the pits after a series of accidents. With his energy and gift for public speaking, despite a pronounced stammer, he made a name for himself as a town and county councillor. In 1929, at the age of only thirty-three, Bevan was elected Labour MP for the safe seat of Ebbw Vale. He held it at the 1931 landslide.

Although himself a fine parliamentary orator, Bevan was always critical of the way in which the House of Commons muffled debate and conflict. His only book *In Place of Fear* provides a graphic description of a new Labour MP arriving at the Commons for the first time:

His first impression is that he is in church. The vaulted roofs and stained-glass windows, the rows of statues of great states-men of the past, the echoing halls, the soft-footed attendants and the whispered conversation, contrast depressingly with the crowded meetings and the clang and clash of hot opinions he has left behind in his election campaign. Here he is, a tribune of the people, coming to make his voice heard in the seats of power. Instead, it seems he is expected to worship: and the most conservative of all religions – ancestor worship.

Frustrated by the huge majority of the National Government in the 1930s, Bevan and his wife Jennie Lee, herself an MP at twenty-four, supported several extra-parliamentary campaigns. His agitation for a Popular Front even resulted in his expulsion from the Labour Party in 1939. But although keenly aware of the deadening effects of Parliament, Bevan was sure that only by means of this institution could power be won and exercised.

He always scorned left-wing zealots who were afraid of the compromises of power. When Jennie Lee had voluntarily left the Labour Party some years before, Bevan was scathing: '. . . why don't you get into a nunnery and have done with it? Lock yourself up in a separate cell away from the world and its wickedness? . . . it is the Labour Party or nothing.' He himself was soon readmitted to the Labour Party after his expulsion. During the war Bevan sniped at Churchill's policies, particularly his caution in launching a 'Second Front' against the Germans, and earned himself the Prime Ministerial rebuke that he was 'a squalid nuisance'.

Perhaps the first sign that Bevan was going to be something more than 'a beloved rebel' like the Clydeside MP Jimmy Maxton, a man loved by all but essentially an impotent force in British politics, came in late 1941 when Bevan was appointed editor of the weekly *Tribune*. His iconoclastic manifesto published in early 1942 robustly claimed that 'Even the parties of the "Left" seem to be mentally muscle-bound and repeat old phrases with less and less conviction.' It was highly appropriate that George Orwell, another socialist who delighted in pointing out that the emperor sometimes wore no clothes, should have been *Tribune*'s literary editor at this time.

Bevan's opportunity to create rather than to criticise came, as we saw in the last chapter, after the Second World War. Although Bevan's record in charge of housing was patchy, his work at the Department of Health drew on his earlier experiences with the Tredegar Medical Aid Society. Started by a group of miners and steelworkers in 1890, the Society offered a form of communal medical aid and was a fine example of working-class self-help. As Hywel Francis and Dai Smith have commented, 'His riveting, passionate championing of the new Health Service was but an extension of the collective and accumulated concerns of the South Wales miners, their communities and their own, often sophisticated, local medical schemes.'

But Bevan also needed other and very different skills to pilot the Act through Parliament – Field Marshall Montgomery once declared that Bevan's handling of the doctors deserved the attention of all students of strategy. The months of thorough and careful work which Bevan devoted to the legislation demonstrated that he was in a class apart from many British left-wingers for whom assertion was all and the detail nothing.

Although Bevan had a tendency to let his mouth run away with him – as in 1948 when he called Tories 'lower than vermin' – he was a loyal and successful member of the Cabinet; he refused to join the manoeuvrings against Attlee in 1947, dismissing what he called 'palace revolutions'. He was therefore understandably put out when Hugh Gaitskell was promoted over him to be Chancellor of the Exchequer in October 1950. The underlying friction between Gaitskell and Bevan came to a head over the 'teeth and spectacles' issue in April 1951. Gaitskell presided over an economy burdened by a huge £4,700 million defence programme deemed necessary in view of the Korean War. He began to look for economies and advocated levying a modest charge for National Health Service patients acquiring teeth and spectacles.

The sum involved was small, just £23 million, but for Bevan this charge struck at the heart of the sacrosanct principle of free treatment. The bulk of the Cabinet was worried about the rising cost of the welfare state but confident that the savings could be found elsewhere. At the end of the debate, the majority decided to follow convention and support the

Prime Minister and Chancellor rather than Bevan and he, together with Harold Wilson and John Freeman, resigned from the government. The Labour Party lost the subsequent election, primarily because the electorate was suspicious of a divided party.

> The trade unions' influence upon the Party is due to two reasons: 1) money, lots of it, and 2) votes, many of them. This money will be spent and these votes cast in the direction which will further trade union policy . . .

Trade union leader Sir Charles Geddes' blunt remarks epitomised the hold that the unions maintained over the Labour Party. After all, the unions had created the Party in the first place, and it was the unions who provided five-sixths of its income.

The ready availability of trade union money had hindered the Party's efforts to raise small-scale funds at the constituency level, unlike the Conservative Party who excelled at this. Indeed, as Michael Pinto-Duschinsky puts it, 'The combination of strong union funding and weak voluntary efforts has made it impossible for Labour to escape from its dependence upon the trade unions, which was already becoming burdensome in the 1930s.'

In addition, the trade unions sponsored between a third and a half of all Labour MPs, usually sending their 'low flyers' to Parliament and keeping the most talented behind in the union. Nomination was often a reward for loyal service rather than ability and not suprisingly the Parliamentary Labour Party often had a rather stolid and unimaginative feel to it. The Labour Party put the interests of the producer (union members) well before those of the consumer (the general public). At the annual conference, the right-wing stance of the major unions in the 1950s ensured that the Bevanites would be defeated in any internal civil war.

Bevan had wanted to examine the record of the Attlee

government with a view to finding a way forward in the
future. Writing in 1951 Richard Crossman warned that '. . .
the Labour Party is in danger of becoming not the party of
change, but the defender of the post-war status quo.' Such
a post-mortem was, however, anathema to several powerful
trade union leaders who, in the context of the Cold War,
were only too ready to categorise unwelcome questions as
being 'Communist inspired'.

E.P. Thompson and many others have noted that anti-
communism always provided a good excuse for inertia. Arthur
Deakin succeeded Ernest Bevin as leader of the mammoth
Transport and General Workers' Union and his quarterly
reports have been referred to as 'a sustained commentary'
on the dangers of Communist activity. Deakin's description
of the, to him, troublesome dockers' leaders captured his
blunderbuss style; he called them '. . . a moronic crowd of
irresponsible adventurers who do not know how much they
are being exploited by foreign elements for purposes they do
not see or understand.'

Apart from the autocratic way in which Deakin ran his own
union, he and his right-wing colleagues – Tom Williamson
of the General and Municipal Workers, Will Lawther of the
miners and William Carron of the engineers – wielded the
block vote which, under the Labour Party constitution of
1918, was integral to the running of the Party. They not
only controlled the voting at each Party Conference but also
in effect nominated eighteen members (the twelve trade union
seats, the five places kept for women, and the Treasurer) of
the twenty-five seat Labour Party National Executive. This
left only seven remaining seats, which were voted for and
occupied by the constituency parties' representatives. Barbara
Castle claimed at the 1953 Conference that 'The Labour
Movement is in danger of dying a death of three million
cuts – the block votes of four men.'

The heavy-handed methods of Deakin and his colleagues
were replicated by the behaviour of some right-wing Labour

councils, particularly in London, Liverpool and Newcastle. They offered an uncanny mirror image of the 'democratic centralism' used by their hated Communist opponents and in effect refought the Cold War inside the ranks of the British labour movement. William Carron of the engineers, for instance, deployed a series of underhand techniques to ensure that his union's vote was cast in favour of the leadership. When Will Lawther was interrupted while speaking at a Labour Party Conference, he replied clearly if inelegantly: 'Shut your gob.'

The control of the union bosses was reinforced by Transport House under the Labour Party's general secretary, Morgan Phillips. This was labourism at its worst: bureaucratic and unimaginative, reliant on frequent calls for 'loyalty' and downgrading such activities as socialist education for fear that individuals might think for themselves. Personal animosities seemed all consuming; Herbert Morrison once muttered to a woman as his erstwhile colleague Bevan walked past, 'Don't ever trust that man, he is wicked.'

Bevan was in no respect a Communist sympathiser. One has only to read his introduction to Denis Healey's book about Communist takeover techniques in Eastern Europe, *The Curtain Falls* (1951), to see how virulently he hated these oppressive regimes. Another prominent Bevanite, Richard Crossman, edited a famous series of essays called *The God That Failed* in which six former Communists or Communist sympathisers berated the USSR and its satellites, whilst Michael Foot's *Tribune* regularly denounced the systematic abuse of civil liberties in the Soviet bloc.

Bevan was not, in fact, seeking to overturn Labour Party policy or to denigrate the record of the Attlee government in which he had served for nearly six years as a loyal and hard-working member. Instead the Bevanites simply wanted to hold the Party to its commitments. But how best to group themselves in the face of the party machine? As 'Keep Left' had found, if the dissidents organised then they were accused of being a party within a party; if they didn't, they were picked off one by one.

One further ingredient in the tragedy is that the Bevanites were not some crackpot sect. They included forty-seven MPs and two peers. Ian Mikardo has listed their achievements:

> Those forty-nine people included five ex-Ministers, two future Leaders of the Party, fourteen future Ministers, nine current or future members of the Party Executive and nine who were to become peers out of merit, not patronage. We had among us six distinguished writers, and nine members who were in the front rank of parliamentary orators and debaters.

Bevan himself was not a conspirator nor even much of an organiser, building up few important trade union contacts, and in 1952 the Bevanite group, such as it was, was disbanded. But instead of this decision leading to a frank and fraternal exchange of views, the atmosphere worsened. The Bevanites were popular at grassroots level and won six out of the seven constituency seats on the National Executive in 1952.

The Labour establishment was horrified. The party machine then embarked on a policy of expulsions, loyalty pledges – a grotesque parody of McCarthyism – and smears. Morgan Phillips even kept dossiers on the Bevanites and other Labour rebels which he filed under the heading 'Lost Sheep'. The Party's equally formidable national organiser, Sara Barker, specialised in closing down troublesome constituency parties, which meant that individuals automatically lost their membership and then had to reapply individually, a strategy for purging the Bevanite left.

To their credit the Bevanites opposed all expulsions from the Labour Party, unlike the unprincipled Communists and their supporters who actually ganged up with the Labour Right to expel Trotskyists.

Bevan's book *In Place of Fear*, published in 1952, exemplified all the virtues and flaws of the British Labour Left. Warm, generous and humane, it was a moral call to arms illuminated by several striking phrases: '. . . no society can legitimately call itself civilised if a sick person is denied medical aid because of lack of means.' He insisted too, that democratic socialism 'accepts the obligation to choose among different kinds of social action and in so doing to bear the pains of rejecting what is not practicable or less desirable.'

But *Fear* completely fails to specify what this 'social action' might involve, and the book is by turns vague and verbose. The most feeble chapter, 'The Transition to Socialism', should have been the strongest. 'Planning' is advanced as a virtue but is never discussed in any detail. Typically, there is nothing about economic growth. These absences reflect not just Bevan's own comparative lack of interest in the nuts and bolts of socialism, but are also a perennial weakness of the Labour Left – Hugh Dalton, for instance, always called the *New Statesman* 'The Belly-Achers Bulletin'. Essentially a product of, and reaction to, the Cold War, the Bevanites lacked the resources or ability to rise above it.

The publications of Bevan's followers were rarely more illuminating in sketching out any future New Jerusalem and sometimes startlingly wrong. Writing in 1959 after a decade of unparalleled economic growth in the West, Richard Crossman claimed that '. . . the planned Socialist economy, as exemplified in the Communist States, is proving its capacity to outpace and overtake the wealthy and comfortable Western economies.' The next year Crossman went on to attack the Labour Right's theorist Anthony Crosland for his '. . . failure to observe the terrifying contrast between the drive and missionary energy displayed by the Communist bloc and the lethargic, comfortable indolence of the Western democracies.'

For all his undoubted qualities, Bevan was a difficult man to work with. Ian Mikardo suggested that 'The trouble with Nye was that he wasn't a team player . . .' and often avoided or postponed difficult decisions. Richard Crossman voiced a similar complaint: 'He dominates its [Bevanite] discussions simply because he is fertile in ideas, but leadership and organisation are things he instinctively shrinks away from.' In an assessment written after Bevan's death Crossman was even more critical:

> . . . his trouble was precisely he did not grow up and remained a man of immense promise which rarely bore fruit. . . . His real weaknesses were, first and foremost, his indolence . . . his second defect was a streak of cowardice. To put it bluntly, at critical moments he was inclined not to be there – an attack of bronchitis, perhaps, or just a sheer disappearance to his house in the country to avoid an unpleasant meeting or postpone a decision.

Such candid criticism makes one glad not to have been a friend of Crossman! Attlee once pointed out that Bevan wanted to be both rebel and leader but, in fact, it was not possible to combine the two. But whatever criticisms anyone can make about Aneurin Bevan, nothing can take away from him the fact that he was the prime instigator of the National Health Service.

The failure of the Bevanites was due to much more than the personal characteristics of Nye Bevan himself. The Cold War ensured that many of the democratic and libertarian impulses of the anti-fascist Second World War were lost. Anything unorthodox or radical could so easily be tarred with the Communist or 'fellow traveller' brush, and the Labour Left proved unable to break this ideological and administrative stranglehold.

This defeat guaranteed that the Labour Left was unable to put forward any constructive rethinking. Instead it was the Labour Right, untainted by any possible 'pro-Communist' slur, which filled the vacuum. The tragedy was that over several important issues, such as the need to extinguish Britain's imperial role, the Labour Left proved to be correct.

Above all, perhaps, the 1950s exhibited a distinctly unattractive image of the British Left, squabbling, expelling, criticising.

It showed only too clearly how the Cold War poisoned the political atmosphere. Herbert Marcuse, one of the intellectual influences behind the rise of the New Left in the 1950s and 1960s, once claimed that: '. . . our goals, our values, our old and new morality must be visible already in our actions. The new human beings whom we want to help to create – we must already strive to be these human beings right here and now.'

No matter what the validity of the 'Bevanite' or 'Gaitskellite' camps, both failed Marcuse's injunction. The 1950s teach the British Left one negative lesson: how not to conduct a political party or a political debate. During the 1940s the Labour Party had painstakingly established its image as a truly national political body – the British electorate traditionally punishes a divided party. The antics of the 1950s did much to fragment the united image.

# 10

——  ——

# Expanding Horizons
## New Lefts 1956–63

'I get impatient with those who think that everybody must continually be taking an active part in politics or community affairs! The vast majority find their happiness in their family or personal relations, and why on earth shouldn't they!'

HUGH GAITSKELL, OCTOBER 1955

'Take an aspirin, comrade.'

COMMUNIST PARTY LEADER HARRY POLLITT'S REPORTED ADVICE TO A COLLEAGUE WORRIED ABOUT THE SOVIET INVASION OF HUNGARY IN 1956

'Total abstinence and a good filing-system are not now the right sign-posts to the socialist's Utopia: or at least, if they are, some of us will fall by the wayside.'

ANTHONY CROSLAND, *THE FUTURE OF SOCIALISM*, 1956

Aneurin Bevan and Tony Crosland disagreed about many things. They were on opposite sides during the Labour Party's internal civil war in the 1950s and never seem to have struck up much of a personal relationship. But they did agree on one crucial point: any concept of socialism had to be about the quality of life, about enhancing people's ability to enjoy themselves. This 'pleasure principle' was at the root of both men's socialist beliefs.

Bevan and Crosland alike were sometimes accused of frivolity and a lack of seriousness. Bevan was called a 'Bollinger

Bolshevik' and a 'lounge-lizard Lenin' because of his liking for champagne and the high life, but he was also a man whose private pleasures included writing poetry. The handsome Crosland was never short of girlfriends and these relationships, in the balanced judgement of his future wife Susan, brought much enjoyment to both parties. His holidays were spent alone exploring architecture all over the world.

In his influential book *The Future of Socialism* (1956), Crosland criticised Sidney and Beatrice Webb for 'their lack of temptation towards any of the emotional or physical pleasures of life' and continued: '. . . it is not only dark Satanic things and people that now bar the road to the new Jerusalem, but also, if not mainly, hygienic, respectable, virtuous things and people, lacking only in grace and vitality.'

Bevan and Crosland were both 'Cavaliers', sometimes to their detriment in terms of political advancement. Until the 1950s the Roundhead tradition largely dominated the British labour movement, reflecting the Nonconformist strand which had contributed much to the early days and provided a bedrock of support for the new Labour Party. Although individual Fabians enjoyed drama and music, the Fabian leadership itself was largely indifferent to the arts or to more personal issues. For instance, George Bernard Shaw found it impossible to persuade his fellow Fabians to publish either Oscar Wilde's *The Soul of Man under Socialism* or to do justice to William Morris' *News from Nowhere*.

The Communist Party, too, had also frowned upon culture as a diversion. It was something to be 'dealt with' after the Revolution. Instead, comrade, why aren't you out selling the *Daily Worker*? Following Lenin's example, the party called for asceticism and orthodoxy in members' private lives. Morality was subservient to the dictates of the party: as the Communist Benjamin Farrington, Professor of Classics at University College, Swansea, once put it: '. . . where there is a Communist Party and where there is Marxist guidance, there is a clear moral principle to guide our actions in the violent times in which we live.'

The Communist Party even warned members that 'moral and personal weaknesses' could be 'seized upon by the enemy'. It tried to discourage one of its star recruits, Professor J.B.S. Haldane, from being divorced by his first wife. To be fair, many Communist leaders in Britain such as Pollitt, Gallacher, Dutt and Campbell enjoyed happy and monogamous marriages and there was no doubt that some early Cavaliers, most notably Victor Grayson, came to unhappy ends.

Drink in particular was a recurring temptation which damaged the political careers of, for example, J.H. Thomas, Arthur Greenwood and, later, George Brown. In private, trade union leaders might well have enjoyed their 'beer and sandwiches'; in public they embodied the virtues of working-class respectability.

If it was sometimes difficult for men like Bevan and Crosland to live their lives as they wished, then it was much harder for women. In her autobiography *The Tamarisk Tree*, Dora Russell has shown how repressive both labourism and communism were on libertarian issues and how they kept clear of such subjects as birth control and abortion. When Russell tried to get a resolution on birth control debated at a Labour Party meeting in 1924, she was told by Marion Phillips, the Woman's Officer of the National Party, that 'Sex should not be dragged into politics, you will split the Party from top to bottom.'

Dora Russell rejected this advice and helped set up the Workers' Birth Control Group in 1924. The Abortion Law Reform Association was founded in 1936 but, on the whole, the Labour Party shied away from such campaigns in case they antagonised potential Catholic voters – the support which often guaranteed the return of their candidates in parts of Lancashire and Scotland.

Of course, much depended on which class a woman belonged to. Novelist Naomi Mitchison's memoirs of the inter-war years show how the availability of effective contraception enabled her circle to live active lives which included husbands – in her case the Labour lawyer Dick Mitchison – lovers, families and a full working life. One of Mitchison's friends was Margery Spring Rice who in 1939 published a book called *Working-Class Wives, Their Health and Conditions* and here a very different story is told.

Based on information collected from 1,250 women, the picture as presented by Spring Rice is one of unending toil and anxiety. Half the women spent twelve hours or more a day standing up while 65 per cent said that their daily two hours of 'leisure' included shopping, mending, sewing and doing household jobs:

> . . . the women whose poverty and consequent hard work demand the greatest measure of consideration and carefully planned reform [were not able to join outside organisations]. The poorest women have no time to spare for such immediately irrelevant considerations as the establishment of a different system, a better education, a more comprehensive medical service, of some sort of organised co-operation.

It should also be remembered that until the 1960s both abortion and homosexuality were still illegal, divorce was difficult, birth control was often primitive and a lack of money or anything resembling 'youth culture' severely curtailed any libertarian impulses. In addition, the Cold War reinforced notions of caution and conformity; as Robert Hewison neatly put it, 'The Cold War tended to freeze public attitudes, and counselled silence about private ones.'

From the mid–1950s, however, the taken–for–granted orthodoxies started to seem less immutable. Living standards began to rise in the post-Second World War boom and affluence offered people greater opportunities and wider horizons. The arrival of 'the consumer society' was heralded by the ending of the rationing of most foodstuffs in 1954 and of meat in 1956. Commercial television, which was on the air from 1955, confirmed and stimulated the growth of the advertising industry.

New consumer durables such as telephones, cars and household appliances like fridges and ovens brought more leisure and increased mobility. The two and a half million cars and one million television sets in Britain in 1951 had expanded to over eight million cars and fourteen million television sets by 1964. The first supermarkets were built and in 1955 Mary Quant opened Bazaar on the King's Road, Chelsea, a boutique aimed directly at the young. Quant's husband and partner Alexander Plunket Greene hoped that it would change 'the depressing and stultifying life young Londoners then led.' Bill Haley toured England in 1957 with his new rock and roll music. And there were few more potent signs of expanding horizons than the four million British people taking holidays abroad by 1961.

These trends and transitions inevitably generated political stirrings. The stark and simplistic choice thrown up by the Cold War – either for Washington or for Moscow – and the division between Labour and Communist began to seem less categoric.

The first signs that Eastern Europe, or 'the People's Democracies' as Communists called them, were no such thing emerged in Berlin in June 1953 when a workers' rebellion caught the authorities off guard. The rising was put down, but only after the regime was shown to be dependent on coercion and not on consent. Yet this was a minor storm when compared with the convulsions to come in 1956. Eric Hobsbawm has remarked of that year: 'As far as I know most Communists in most countries lived for several months in the political equivalent of a nervous breakdown.'

After Stalin's death in 1953 the tension slackened in the Soviet Union and therefore in Eastern Europe too. The Great Dictator had gone; the purges and mass executions, if not the gulags, stopped – although the East Germans had found how limited this tolerance was. But the new Soviet leadership under Khrushchev did edge away from the Stalinist era. 'As Stalin said' was no longer an argument clincher. However, no one who went to Moscow for the 20th Congress of the Communist Party of the Soviet Union in February 1956 had any idea what revelations awaited them.

Fortunately, we have a non-Soviet eyewitness account of events. The Italian Vittorio Vidali was a longstanding Communist who had endured imprisonment, torture and exile under Mussolini's regime but remained a loyal party man even though thirty-eight friends and comrades had perished in Stalin's purges. Most people would surely have asked themselves whether any cause demanding human sacrifice on so massive a scale deserved support. Such a question never seems to have occurred to Vidali, demonstrating yet again how Communists identified completely with anything the Soviet Union, or at least Stalin, did.

Vidali's account of the Congress tells of the hurried meetings, the surveillance of foreign delegates by the KGB and the snatched conversations with survivors of the purges, one of whom bitterly told Vidali: 'It is terrible to die as a traitor after having faithfully served the cause; there is no greater sorrow!'

As he sat through the Congress proceedings, Vidali gradually realised that none of the Soviet leaders could bring themselves to mention Stalin's name. Something momentous was happening but, typically, the Khrushchev revelations were delivered at a 'secret session' from which non-Soviet delegates were excluded. Although leading non-Russian Communists soon found out what Khrushchev had said, the speech was only published in full in the summer of 1956 by the American State Department. Suddenly it was clear that the purges, trials and prison camps had not been figments of overheated Western reactionary imagination. Stalin's critics had, in fact, been right all along.

Within the British Communist Party responses to the speech varied. For hard-line Stalinists such as Rajani Palme Dutt nothing had altered. He wrote airily that even the sun – presumably Stalin – has spots, which was a strange way to dismiss the deaths of millions. Apologists for the Moscow Trials, such as the lawyer D.N. Pritt, later expressed a few grudging words in a single sentence in three volumes of autobiography and then passed speedily on to other matters.

Others couldn't manage even that. In the official biography of Harry Pollitt published in 1976, page after page is devoted to political trials in South Africa and the United States yet there is not a single word about the Moscow Trials. But if his biographer twenty years later proved unable to write about the Trials, Harry Pollitt himself never really recovered from the revelations of the 20th Congress.

The party was already in severe difficulties because of Soviet impatience at its meagre size. In fact, Moscow was seriously considering its extinction, calling instead for some form of alliance with the Bevanites. The British response to the revelations was mealy-mouthed. Apparently some 'mistakes' had been committed – at first they could not bring themselves to use the word 'crimes' – but these miscalculations should not detract from outstanding Soviet economic success and the construction of socialism. How hollowly this reads in view of the economic crisis in Russia today.

Scores of party members complained to party headquarters in King Street that this was surely an inadequate response to mass slaughter. Slowly, the party leadership steeled itself to talk about 'grave injustices' in the Soviet Union. But enough was enough. Party members were then ordered to get on with the task of bringing Bolshevism to Britain. The doctrine of democratic centralism, or of obedience to orders from above, meant that such a decision could be duly enforced.

But, of course, once a hole had appeared in the dyke wall, it rapidly grew bigger. Some Communists began to argue that these 'grave injustices' had arisen in part because of the authoritarian nature of each individual Communist Party and of the Communist movement in its entirety. They claimed that the party's massive bureaucracy – and the Communist Party had more full-time officials to its membership than the Conservative or Labour Parties – led to an ossified and top-heavy organisation.

In July 1956 the two Communist historians, E.P. Thompson and John Saville, produced the first number of an unofficial journal which they called *The Reasoner*. On its title page was a quotation from Karl Marx himself: 'To leave error unrefuted is to encourage intellectual immorality.'

Alarm bells sounded in King Street. Thompson and Saville were told to cease publication. In the past they might well have done. But now, in 1956, no. The Emperor had been seen to have no clothes. They published two more issues and were suspended from the party, whereupon both resigned. Other members were also resigning in the wake of Khrushchev's secret speech. The miners' official Lawrence Daly complained that the fact that the leadership had once been unanimously pro-Stalin and was now unanimously anti-Stalin showed that fundamentally nothing had changed. Further shocks were still to come.

In October 1956 the Hungarian people rose against their own Communist regime. The *Daily Worker* sent one of its journalists, Peter Fryer, to Hungary to report on events. Fryer was deemed 'reliable': a Communist for fourteen years and on the staff of the *Daily Worker* for the last nine. But when he arrived in Hungary, Fryer realised what was happening: 'I saw for myself that the uprising was neither organised nor controlled by fascists or reactionaries . . .'

Fryer's reports to the paper back in London conveyed this message. He also analysed what this repressive Communist regime had meant for the Hungarian people: 'To speak one's mind, to ask an awkward question, even to speak about political questions in language not signposted with the safe, familiar monolithic jargon, was to run the risk of falling foul of the ubiquitous secret police.'

Fryer went on to condemn both himself and others for

their tacit acquiescence in what had been going on: 'It is a tragedy that we British Communists who visited Hungary did not admit, even to ourselves, the truth about what was taking place there, that we defended tyranny with all our heart and soul.' Fryer had smashed his own 'grand illusions'.

His reports to the *Daily Worker* back in London were censored by the acting editor George Matthews because they contradicted the official Communist 'line' on Hungary, which was that this was a fascist rising. The official line was never wrong; Fryer was therefore unreliable and – despite Communist commitment to the freedom of the press – his reports were not be to be printed. The Soviet tanks duly rolled into Budapest and the rising was put down at the cost of 20,000 Hungarian lives.

Peter Fryer promptly resigned from the *Daily Worker* as did one in four of its entire staff and 7,000 individual Communists, representing about 20 per cent of the entire party. The enmity within the British Communist Party was so bitter that when Unity Theatre in London staged a dramatisation of the Hungarian events fist fights broke out in the audience. The Communist Party leadership did what it always had done in a crisis; in the words of journalist Llew Gardner, who resigned, 'The party survived on its constant appeal to loyalty.' John Gollan, who had succeeded Harry Pollitt as general secretary of the party when the latter retired because of ill health, was complacent about people leaving the party: 'They are not our best comrades, otherwise they would not have left.'

*Hungarian Tragedy*, the title of Peter Fryer's book about what had happened, destroyed any moral claims the Communist Party might still possess to represent the oppressed and downtrodden. But if anyone in the West believed that the events of 1956 proved 'We' were the angels and 'They' were devils, they were wrong. The West itself had not emerged unblemished from the events of that year. The 'either' of Communism had been tarnished, but then the Suez crisis during which Eden's Conservative government mustered a last imperial twitch had hardly demonstrated the virtues of the 'or' of Western capitalism.

Disturbing, too, was the degree of complicity between East and West; 'we won't interfere in your crisis (Budapest/Suez) if you don't interfere in ours (Suez/Budapest).' Eden's Suez venture destroyed any chance, admittedly small, of Western intervention to help the Hungarians, which explains the appearance of placards reading 'Eden, Murderer of Budapest'. Complicity between the two superpowers has been confirmed by the publication of the diary kept by the Yugoslav Ambassador in Moscow in 1956, Veljko Micunovic:

> Khrushchev said that British and French aggressive pressure on Egypt provided a favourable moment for a further intervention by Soviet troops. It would help the Russians. There would be confusion and uproar in the West and the United Nations, but it would be less at a time when Britain, France and Israel were waging a war against Egypt. 'They are bogged down there, and we are stuck in Hungary,' Khrushchev said.

What did this upheaval mean to socialists in Britain? Paradoxically the Cold War had given individual Communists a sense of identity in what seemed to be a distinctly hostile world. The novelist Mervyn Jones has put it well:

> In a real sense, the Party was held together by the ferocity of the cold war, the pressure of enemies on every side, the incessant onslaughts on the Soviet Union and Communism in the press and in speeches by both Tory and Labour politicians – onslaughts which included some home truths, but also a torrent of distortion and slanders. It seemed cowardly, and even indecent, to withdraw from the battle.

The events of 1956 broke up this Cold War mentality: Suez and Hungary awoke people 'from a kind of political trance . . .' It also destroyed the traditional identification between the Marxist Left and the Communist Party. Before 1956, to be a Marxist in Britain meant that you were almost certainly a member of the Communist Party. After 1956 the spell of the Communist Party was broken.

Out of 1956 came what commentators, always eager to find a new label (fresh from discovering 'Angry Young Men'), called 'the New Left'. In fact, the name was only suggestive and not a dogmatic straitjacket; it lumped together many different individuals and ideas but it was clear, however, that the New Left varied in several important ways from the 'Old Left'. In one typology, the Old Left was authoritarian, centralised, philistine and puritan while the New Left was libertarian, decentralised, open and experimental; the New Left offered '. . . more the style of an encounter group than a vanguard cadre.'

In the 1930s the Communist Party had voiced, in the words of member Philip Toynbee, very definite views on everything: 'There was a "line" for love; there was almost a line for friendship.' The New Left discarded this approach and emphasised instead the qualities of generosity, tolerance and humanity. Above all, there was a rediscovery of the moral basis of political activity, a recognition that individuals and their feelings were not worth sacrificing for 'the Party' or any other body. Stuart Hall has recalled:

> From the beginning we said that politics, seen as having to do principally with formal political parties, elections, getting the vote out, parliamentarianism, was ideological, confining. We raised issues of personal life, the way people live, culture, which weren't considered the topics of politics on the left.

This New Left therefore represented a return to the ideas explored in Chapter 3, 'Socialism and the New Life', which had characterised much of the British Left up to 1917 before the labour movement split into the two camps of labourism and communism. It was no coincidence that one of the New Left's leading figures, E.P.Thompson, had written a massive study of William Morris. Although originally published in 1953 during the Cold War when Thompson was still a Communist and therefore, as some critics pointed out, accepted the idea of the dictatorship of the proletariat, enough of Morris' insights remained in the book to emphasise the moral dimension of politics.

Official Communist Party reaction to the New Left was revealing. One of its few remaining intellectuals, English lecturer Arnold Kettle, dismissed 'middle-class people . . . spouting a lot of pious generalisations about socialist humanism.' To party believers, 'socialist humanism' was heresy because it turned its back on the rigid 'class warfare' approach. In practice it offered a welcome and long overdue enlargement of what 'politics' was and might be. The New Left's energy spawned a host of activities that ranged from single issue campaigns such as CND and Shelter to the idea of community politics.

To recognise some weaknesses of the New Left is not to denigrate its largely positive contribution. For almost the first time since the days of Morris, Carpenter and Blatchford, the moral dimension had been restored to political activity. But in rebelling against Communist Party rigidity, the New Left often went too far the other way and decried the need for any kind of formal organisation. Hostile to the Parliamentarianism of Hugh Gaitskell's Labour Party, which in the 1950s sometimes seemed to think electoral campaigning every five years or so was the be-all and end-all of politics, the New Left failed to turn a mood into a movement.

The New Left was also singularly unable to create any coherent vision of the future, unlike Anthony Crosland's *The Future of Socialism* which had become the Bible of the Labour Right. As always, the Left poured forth books, pamphlets and magazines but invariably these publications preferred easy posturing or vague rhetoric to mapping out a possible way forward. At a conference held in Oxford in 1987, several individuals active in the 1950s looked back on the movement with characteristic honesty. Raphael Samuel noted that they had stood for 'comprehensive redevelopment' in housing (eg. tower blocks) and that the New Left had said nothing about the family, women's rights or homosexuality.

One good example of the New Left's gap between rhetoric and reality, and wonderfully ironic in view of the author's later pronounced change in opinions, was Paul Johnson's essay 'A Sense of Outrage' published in 1958. Johnson called for the abolition of the monarchy and of the House of Lords, the dispossession of the public schools and Oxbridge, the disestablishment of the Church and the end of the Honours List. What is more, all these changes had to take place simultaneously. The author omitted to provide any inkling as to how this might be done.

The New Left also displayed a tendency, seen too in the 1930s, to focus heavily on international affairs. In one sense such internationalism is admirable; but it is less so if pursued at the expense of domestic or 'bread and butter' issues. This tendency was apparent, too, in its most successful offshoot, CND.

> Gaitskell and Nye Bevan are preparing for a sell,
> They want to get the votes and keep the atom bomb as well,
> But NATO's going to send us all to shovel coal in hell,
> If we don't ban the H-bomb now.

This song was composed by some London medical students for use on CND marches to Aldermaston in Berkshire. The surprise, perhaps, is the coupling of Aneurin Bevan's name with that of Hugh Gaitskell. As bitter political rivals they had disagreed on almost every political issue. But from the mid-1950s Bevan began to shift his stance – his close colleague Barbara Castle feels that 'he was tired of martyrdom' – and in 1957 he shocked friends and colleagues at the Labour Party Conference by delivering a speech attacking unilateral disarmament, pleading with delegates not to send any Foreign Secretary 'naked into the conference chamber'.

More woundingly still, he remarked that his opponents were guilty of an 'emotional spasm'.

Bevan came under virulent attack for his apparent volte-face – his wife Jennie even claimed that the hostility led directly to Bevan's early death – and was accused of opportunism. In fact, his decision had been thought through. Bevan's international contacts with Soviet leaders like Khrushchev had convinced him that if Britain did unilaterally renounce the bomb then it would make no difference whatsoever to the behaviour of the two superpowers. He also felt that the Labour Party would never win a general election with a unilateralist defence policy – an argument often voiced in the 1980s.

Bevan's speech heightened the sense of public anxiety felt about the proliferation of nuclear weapons. Although British governments both Labour and Conservative had drawn a veil of secrecy over the subject, by the mid-1950s Britain's defence rested largely on the nuclear deterrent and was locked in with that of the Americans, as was shown by the number of US bases located in the country.

In 1957 the Conservative Defence Minister Duncan Sandys published a White Paper detailing the modernisation of Britain's nuclear capabilities. The following year's Defence White Paper was candid about the dangers: 'It must be recognised that, however carefully the balance of armaments is held, or thought to be held, there always remains a possibility that some unforeseen circumstance or miscalculation might spark off a world-wide catastrophe.'

As the careers of Keir Hardie and George Lansbury showed, the British Left has always contained a strong tradition of pacifism and anti-militarism. CND also attracted everyone who detested nuclear weapons in the wake of Hiroshima and Nagasaki as well as drawing upon the vein of idealism which had been submerged in the 'realpolitik' of the Cold War.

But it was Bevan's speech of 1957 that gave the movement its impetus. Outraged by his remarks, the novelist J.B. Priestley wrote a vitriolic article in the *New Statesman* scorning the 'VIP-Highest-Priority-Top-Secret-Top-People Class, men now so conditioned by this atmosphere of power politics, intrigue, secrecy, insane invention, that they are more than half-barmy.'

Reaction to Priestley's article turned out to be so massive that, ironically enough, a 'Top People' pressure group was formed. Philosopher Bertrand Russell was its president, Canon Collins of St Paul's was chairman. Of the nineteen names on the first year's executive, no fewer than thirteen had entries in *Who's Who*. CND's sponsors included John Arlott, Peggy Ashcroft, Benjamin Britten, Edith Evans and Henry Moore. CND also maintained good contacts with the media: both Kingsley Martin, the editor of the *New Statesman*, and Michael Foot, editor of *Tribune*, were leading figures in the campaign.

CND possessed no formal membership nor was it intended to be a permanent organisation, but its leaders soon found that widespread public support almost hijacked the campaign and they had to condone such activities as the annual Easter march to Aldermaston, first held in 1958. By March 1959 CND had over 270 local groups and 12 regional committees. Particularly noticeable was the attraction CND held for the young. Previously 'youth' had been regarded as a stage of life to be got through as fast as possible on the way to maturity. Now the social changes transforming Britain in the 1950s prompted young people to be more vocal and expressive, and political involvement in CND was one manifestation of this mood.

Although CND was sometimes dismissed as the 'duffle-coat brigade' it is interesting that twenty years before Saatchi and Saatchi marketed Mrs Thatcher, CND was fully aware of the importance of 'image'. Its *Advice to Marchers* was explicit: 'Don't do anything or wear anything that will distract the attention of the world from the great issues with which we are concerned.' The Executive even recommended that a delegation to Moscow should include 'a young and photogenic mother'. The CND symbol itself, which Peggy Duff noted was ideal for graffiti, became an international sign.

CND undoubtedly proved to be '. . . essentially a middle-class movement, and had relatively little working-class and trade union backing.' Or, as A.J.P.Taylor pithily expressed it, CND was 'a movement of eggheads for eggheads . . .' Its overwhelmingly middle-class membership showed that from this point onwards most radical political campaigns were not exclusively aimed at the manual working class – a recognition of changing social trends. It also suggests why the campaign was generally peaceful and orderly with little shouting on the annual march.

However, CND did get the backing of the prominent trade union leader Frank Cousins, General Secretary of the huge Transport and General Workers' Union. With his support and the acquiescence of other unions, the Labour Party Conference in 1960 narrowly passed a unilateralist motion.

CND astutely gave prominence to the 'stars' backing the movement, but, as always, the hard graft was done by 'the poor bloody infantry' who remained out of the spotlight. Mervyn Jones has noted the important role that women played in the campaign, and CND's secretary was the formidable Peggy Duff. Her career symbolised much of the dedication and selfless commitment at the root of the British Left over the last century.

Duff's husband, a journalist, was killed at the end of the war when reporting on a bombing raid over Germany, leaving her with three small children to bring up alone. This tragedy did not prevent Peggy Duff from being involved in several campaigns, seeking the kind of idealism that had drawn her to the Common Wealth party during the war. She worked first for 'Save Europe Now' run by Victor Gollancz to alleviate starvation among the victims of the war and soon learnt to stand up to Gollancz. His socialism never prevented him from displaying autocratic tendencies. 'He used to make up for his extreme pacifism by extreme aggressiveness. His daughter used to say, "You should hear him if the bath water is cold."'

Peggy Duff was business manager of *Tribune* newspaper

from 1949 to 1955 and a firm supporter of Nye Bevan as well as being a councillor in St Pancras, London, for fifteen years. After CND she worked for a number of organisations, including the campaign to abolish capital punishment ('the only one we won') and against the Vietnam War. She died in London in 1981. Her autobiography *Left, Left, Left* is a record of a woman without personal ambition determined to live up to William Morris' phrase: 'To grumble and not to act, that is throwing away one's life.'

It is wrong to dismiss CND as of little importance because of its failure to rid Britain of nuclear weapons. Cabinet papers of the time, for instance, show the extent of Prime Minister Harold Macmillan's alarm at its success. But one problem which CND never resolved had likewise dogged the Left Book Club. Moral indignation is not sufficient in itself to generate political change and CND, like the New Left generally, was apolitical. Political power in Britain did not lie in the roads of Berkshire or even at Aldermaston itself, and no one quite knew what to do after the March was over.

The Committee of 100 organised 'sit-downs' outside the Ministry of Defence in Whitehall, but the authorities cracked down hard on its leaders and some received prison sentences. There was also growing friction between CND's 'top people' and the ordinary membership. As Adam Sisman has noted in his biography of A.J.P. Taylor: 'He was unwilling to hand over control to the teachers and social workers who made up the foot-soldiers of the Campaign; while for their part, many of the younger radicals thought Alan (and some of the other members of the Executive Committee) slightly fogeyish, his talk of the Anti-Corn Law League antiquarianism.'

Mervyn Jones often warned CND groups that 'You're up against professional politicians. They're in this business for a lifetime. They don't intend to argue with you – they're waiting for you to get tired.' Jones was absolutely right. CND may have won the day at the 1960 Labour Party Conference, but there was always next year, and the year after that . . . In fact, it needed only twelve months for the Labour Right to organise the trade-union block vote and reject unilateralism. The moral fervour of CND was ultimately no match for professional politicians.

External events also conspired against CND. The peaceful outcome of the Cuban Missile Crisis in October 1962 apparently showed that the superpowers could draw back from the edge. The signing of the Partial Test Ban Treaty in July 1963 reassured many people that the nuclear deterrent, for all its awfulness, might never have to be used. With hindsight, however, the forthright opposition to unilateralism of Hugh Gaitskell and his associates in the Labour Party had clearly doomed CND to defeat on the British political stage.

Assessments of Hugh Gaitskell differed wildly. For his opponents he was, in Bevan's jibe, 'a dessicated calculating machine', a lofty and arrogant Hampstead intellectual who knew little and understood even less of the rank and file. His friends and colleagues, on the other hand, idolised him, complaining that his cold public image bore no relation to the warm individual whose passion for dancing into the late hours left his circle exhausted.

One thing which everyone did agree on was Gaitskell's intellectual honesty, his scrupulous refusal to fudge or muddy issues. As Richard Marsh, a young politician then on the fringes of the Gaitskellites, later wrote in his autobiography, 'He [Gaitskell] was a man whose integrity was absolute, who saw everything in black and white. If he thought it was even slightly grey, he went out of his way to make it black and white, so that everybody could see the difference.'

In some ways his integrity is strangely reminiscent of that of Keir Hardie. The difference was that Hardie created and led what was initially a very small organisation. By the 1950s, when Gaitskell became leader of the Labour Party, both its size and that of the trade unions meant that compromise, ambiguity and equivocation were often essential weapons in the leader's armoury. Clement Attlee, for instance, knew the value of saying nothing, as Gaitskell once noted in his diary: '. . . one of Clem's peculiarities is that of out-silencing people. It is a useful weapon. Nothing can be more embarrassing if you cannot get a man to talk.' Gaitskell, however, was always direct and uncompromising.

Educated at Winchester and Oxford, Gaitskell worked as an adult education tutor in the Midlands for the Workers' Educational Association before spending the 1930s as an economics lecturer at London University. He was one of Hugh Dalton's group which drew up detailed Labour Party policies for the future. During the war Gaitskell worked as a civil servant at the Ministry of Economic Warfare, an experience that taught him how to negotiate the corridors of power. Elected MP for South Leeds in 1945, within little more than two years he was Minister of Fuel and Power. Three years later Gaitskell was appointed Chancellor of the Exchequer.

His meteoric rise owed much to the support of Hugh Dalton who, ever since his own resignation as Chancellor over a budget leak, had channelled his formidable energies into promoting his protégés. As we have already seen, Gaitskell's promotion upset rivals like Aneurin Bevan who felt that this 'johnny come lately' had leapfrogged over him. Bevan had spent sixteen years on the backbenches waiting for power, Gaitskell less than a year.

Gaitskell's short spell as Chancellor was dominated by the need to finance Britain's part in the Korean War, a struggle which led to the dispute with Bevan and the latter's resignation from the Cabinet. Although ostensibly over 'teeth and spectacles', the fight between the two men was in reality about more than this; as Gaitskell himself put it, 'It was a battle between us for power – he knew it and so did I.'

Gaitskell won in 1951, just as he did in 1954 when he defeated Bevan for the post of Labour Party Treasurer and, most importantly of all, in December 1955 when Gaitskell was elected leader of the Party after Attlee's resignation. The problem for Gaitskell was that he led a political organisation torn apart by internal feuding and faced by a Conservative Party that had won the last two elections and was benignly in charge of a Britain where living standards were increasing.

Critical of the Bevanites for failing to recognise the social and political changes that were transforming the country, Hugh Gaitskell was determined that the Labour Party should become a party of government rather than just a party of protest. The two theorists who did analyse Britain in the 1950s, John Strachey and Anthony Crosland, were neither of them on the Left of the Labour Party. Both Strachey and Crosland published their most important books in 1956.

John Strachey was the former Marxist of the 1930s who had been a Minister in Attlee's governments. His *Contemporary Capitalism* was a dense book that grappled with the legacy of Karl Marx. He argued that Marxists were wrong to claim that the State was nothing but an instrument of the ruling class: 'The fact is that in the conditions of contemporary democracy the State and its vast powers are rather prizes for which all sorts of interests are struggling and competing.' Strachey also maintained that economic instability might well provoke a harsher Conservatism than Eden's and Macmillan's in the 1950s; as his latest biographer has put it, 'Few could have predicted the nature of "Thatcherism" with such deadly accuracy.'

But it was Anthony Crosland's *The Future of Socialism* which proved the more significant of the two works, partly because despite its 529 pages it was surprisingly well written for a complex book of political theory. Today the book is sometimes dismissed because of its seeming complacency that British economic growth could be taken for granted. This is a little unfair: in a new edition published only eight years later, in 1964, Crosland did note the comparatively poor performance of 'the Anglo-Saxon economies'.

In any case *The Future of Socialism* was always intended to be more than just an economic forecast. First of all, Crosland grappled with the realities of day-to-day power in Britain with a detail and knowledge absent from, say, the publications of the Left Book Club, Bevan's *In Place of Fear* or the future writings of the New Left.

Secondly, Crosland also stressed the libertarian strand of socialism, claiming the mantle of William Morris and anticipating future developments on the Left. He attacked the divorce laws, the licensing laws, the illegality of homosexuality, the abortion laws, censorship of books and plays and so on: 'Most of these are intolerable, and should be highly offensive to socialists, in whose blood there should always run a trace of the anarchist and libertarian, and not too much of the prig and prude.'

Finally, Crosland recognised that British society was changing enormously – and the Labour Party simply had to face up to this future. What was called 'revisionism' constituted '. . . an explicit admission that many of the old dreams are either dead or realised . . . now the certainty and simplicity are gone; and everything has become complicated and ambiguous.' In particular the British working class no longer formed so clear-cut and definite a grouping as had been the case in Keir Hardie's day.

This working-class culture was, as we have seen, primarily defensive rather than offensive, moderate and not revolutionary. Between the late nineteenth century and the 1940s it had been relatively homogeneous and fixed but now, paradoxically, the very reforms which the Labour Party had introduced after the war were undermining this uniformity. To take just one indicator, in 1900 three-quarters of Britain's workforce had been manual labourers; the figure in the 1950s was below two-thirds and still dropping.

The changes introduced by the Attlee governments seemed to suggest that gentle reformism rather than any energetic prosecution of the 'class war' offered the best way forward; as Elizabeth Durbin has succinctly put it, 'The essence of the revisionist case for socialism is that the capitalist market system can be transformed into a collectivist state without recourse to violent class struggle.' Redistribution rather than confiscation.

Crosland and his fellow sympathisers were trying to redirect the rod which the Labour Party had partly made for its own back. In the 1930s a progressive coalition was formed which, between 1945 and 1951, did much to alleviate the distress of the 'have nots' by introducing welfare benefits, supervising full employment and so on. But by the 1950s, many former 'have nots' had become 'haves' and were therefore more inclined to identify with the system in the shape of the Conservative Party, particularly when it was the Tories who were presiding over sustained economic growth. Labour was in danger of representing the now much smaller number of 'still have nots', unlikely ever to form an electoral majority.

To some on the Left, such rethinking was anathema. Harry Pollitt, for instance, was blunt: 'The Labour Party type of "new thinking" is peddled with such a patronising, pompous, "You were never at Haileybury, Winchester, Oxford or Cambridge" air on the part of alleged Labour leaders who have never been in a strike or lock-out, hunger march or dole queue . . .'

The Labour Left likewise luxuriated in moral condemnation of this New Britain. 'Our people have achieved material prosperity in excess of their moral stature,' claimed Aneurin Bevan at the Labour Party Conference in 1949. Ten years later he returned to the same theme: '. . . it is a vulgar society of which no decent person could be proud.' At the same Conference Michael Foot echoed Bevan's remarks: '. . . we have to change the mood of the people in this country, to open their eyes to what an evil and disgraceful and rotten society it is.' Richard Crossman was yet another socialist who speculated that 'The luxuries, gadgets, entertainments and packaged foodstuffs which so many workers enjoy in our Affluent Societies may strike him [an outside observer] as irrelevant and even vulgar and immoral . . .'

Bevan and Crossman both owned farms as well as additional residences in London while Michael Foot lived in a pleasant part of Hampstead. Evidently, material prosperity with all its luxuries and gadgets had not blunted their own moral stature.

Gaitskell's circle, on the other hand, was emphatic about the virtues of this prosperity: 'We are glad to see people better-off, and have no patience with those who are comfortably off themselves yet seem to resent the prosperity of others.' Consumption of consumer goods per head in Britain in the 1950s rose by over 20 per cent. The revisionists argued that to win power in a parliamentary democracy the Labour Party had to broaden its appeal, just as it had done in 1945. The Labour Party had to be a national party rather than an amalgam of sectional interests.

Gaitskell's arguments were apparently confirmed by the behaviour of other European socialists. In West Germany, for instance, the Social Democrats dropped their old Marxist ideological baggage at the 1959 Bad Godesberg Conference. By accepting the need for private ownership and membership of NATO, they demonstrated that for them progress would come about by building a social–democratic post-war Germany and not by its overthrow. Piecemeal and moderate change was preferable to revolutionary upheaval, equality more important than wholesale public ownership. If the West German Social Democrats were the forerunners of this important shift in political approach, colleagues in other countries followed suit. The French socialists in effect also started again in 1959.

Valuing integrity and clarity above anything else, Gaitskell was dismayed by the manifestos of his own Party which had wanted to nationalise one group of industries in 1950, none in 1951, and a completely different group in 1955 – just the kind of inconsistency which he thought weakened the Labour Party. Sometimes, however, his lack of political cunning damaged Labour. During the Suez crisis in 1956 he broadcast an appeal to dissident Tory MPs to overthrow their own Prime Minister, Sir Anthony Eden – a blatant appeal which prompted the Conservative ranks to regroup and unite.

His determination to update and modernise the Labour

Party was strengthened by the result of the 1959 general election when, despite a lacklustre and inefficient campaign, Harold Macmillan's Conservatives still increased their majority. However, they had helped by engineering a pre-election boom. A Conservative Party poster read, 'Life's better under the Conservatives: don't let Labour ruin it.' Gaitskell himself made an election campaign blunder by promising that his Party would not raise taxes if they won, even though the proposed programme was expensive. Not surprisingly the electorate was doubtful that he had done his sums.

This defeat meant that in the fifty-three years of its existence the Labour Party had enjoyed a parliamentary majority for just six of them. Gaitskell's response to the election defeat of 1959 split the Labour Party almost as much as did the dispute over unilateralism and defence.

> Has the very name 'Labour' become a vote loser on balance? . . . It would be unthinkable to give up the name 'Labour', which holds the loyalty of millions. But might there be a case for amending it to 'Labour and Radical', or 'Labour and Reform'?

Douglas Jay's article in the small-circulation magazine *Forward* opened a contentious can of worms. Published just a few days after the October 1959 defeat, Jay, a minister in the Attlee governments after the war and one of Gaitskell's closest friends, speculated on how and why Labour had lost. He pointed to two handicaps, namely the Labour Party's 'class image' and the fear that it wanted to nationalise everything in sight. One thing Jay did not mention was Clause Four.

Hugh Gaitskell, however, seized on Jay's musings and pointed to Clause Four as an issue that needed to be settled urgently. This clause, as we have seen, was vague and uncertain. It appeared on members' cards, but it is doubtful if more than a handful of non-Party members had ever heard of it. Few expected the Labour Party ever to force through the sweeping 'common ownership of the means of production, distribution and exchange', in other words 100 per cent nationalisation. In which case, said Gaitskell, it was a symbol of an outdated Party and should be scrapped. The public would never accept confiscatory legislation or penal taxation.

But however convincing the intellectual arguments were for the revisionists, what the supremely rational Gaitskell overlooked was that the Labour Party, like most other political bodies, is made up of both irrationality and rationality in equal proportions. Emotion is as important as intellect, borne out by the ease with which antagonists in the drama reached for religious imagery.

Harold Wilson, for instance, opposed Gaitskell and claimed that tampering with Clause Four was like denying the authority of Genesis: 'We were being asked to take Genesis out of the Bible. You don't have to be a fundamentalist to say that Genesis is part of the Bible.' Trade union leader Frank Cousins maintained that: 'We can have nationalisation without socialism – we cannot have socialism without nationalisation.'

Gaitskell found that many of his usually loyal supporters in the labour movement distrusted this campaign as unnecessarily rocking the boat. Denis Healey, for example, later looked back with surprise and used arguments very similar to those which Tony Blair heard in 1994 and 1995:

> I never understood why Hugh Gaitskell made that tremendous fuss about Clause 4. If only he'd kept quiet about it no one would have noticed it, or even remembered it was there. I mean, can *you* remember the ten commandments?

Even the wielders of the trade union block vote turned against Gaitskell and eventually he had to back down. The leaders of the German Social Democrats at Bad Godesberg had had no block vote to contend with. Gaitskell shied away from reforming voting procedures in the Labour Party – primarily because the block vote was usually his surest support.

In addition, Gaitskell's arguments were dismissed by some within the labour movement as being all too typical of the 'Hampstead set' of intellectuals. This attitude towards the Party's thinkers formed an indelible strand within labourism. It held that intellectuals were fine in their place but from time to time they needed bringing down to earth. Revisionism was suspect because of its members' addresses.

Gaitskell had always felt a little uneasy inside the labour movement, rarely participating in the curious rituals and behaviour which bound members together. As Peter Shore has pointed out, he did not come from the traditional Labour Right of the trade unions or local government and was the only Labour leader between Attlee and Kinnock who had never been elected onto the National Executive by the grassroots constituency parties. In fact, Gaitskell continually lambasted what he saw as the gaping chasm between the Party activists and the electorate; in his diary, for instance, he bemoaned the poor quality of the speeches at the 1956 Conference, '. . . in the sense that most of them are remote from reality, miles and miles from the electorate.'

The way in which Gaitskell tortured himself on this issue is vividly demonstrated in the following passage:

> We, as middle-class socialists, have got to have a profound humility. Though it is a funny way of putting it, we have got to know that we lead them because they can't do it without us, without our abilities, and yet we must feel humble to working people. Now that's all right for us in the upper-middle class, but Tony [Crosland] and Roy [Jenkins] are not Upper and I sometimes feel they don't have a proper humility to ordinary working people.

Nor were the Gaitskellites helped by some rather wishful and half-baked enthusiasms; Anthony Crosland was a great football fan, prompting him to write a long article in 1961 suggesting that the emergence of Tottenham Hotspur as the first really professional team demonstrated 'a shift in the national mood from complacency to dynamism.' If only the answer to national economic decline did lie on the playing fields of England.

Gaitskell was soon embroiled in yet another dispute that struck at the heart of the new image he was trying to project. In 1960 the Campaign for Nuclear Disarmament (CND) pushed through a resolution at the 1960 Scarborough Labour Party Conference calling for nuclear disarmament. Gaitskell responded with a famous speech containing the much-quoted passage that, 'We will fight and fight and fight again to bring back sanity and honesty and dignity, so that our Party with its great past may retain its glory and its greatness.'

Over the next twelve months the Campaign for Democratic Socialism (CDS), set up by the Labour Right, agitated to overturn this motion. Carefully cultivating the press, and with no membership or subscriptions so as not to break Party rules – some suspect that funds, at least in part, were derived from CIA sources – CDS targeted groups and individuals with great success and at the 1961 Conference unilateralism was defeated. Ironically, CDS set the pattern for the various internal left-wing groups that were organised to change the Labour Party in the 1980s.

Clause Four, CND – but this was not the end of Gaitskell's battles. In the early 1960s Macmillan's Conservative government began to explore the possibility of entering the Common Market. Although Gaitskell had forcefully attacked CND for its narrow national concerns in believing that Britain could stop the world because it wanted to get off, he came out against a closer relationship with Europe, even though the majority of CDS members were convinced 'Europeans'.

One continuing characteristic of the British labour movement, at least until recently, has been its insularity. Gaitskell shared this view. His friend Michael Postan once observed that 'He [Gaitskell] had reasoned himself into international socialism, but his vision of the future was one of England's

Jerusalem.' Gaitskell's speech at the 1962 Labour Party Conference in Brighton rejected the application for membership in almost embarrassingly 'Little Englander' language, decrying 'the end of a thousand years of history'. Perhaps the most telling criticism of Gaitskell's stance as the leader of a supposedly radical body was voiced by R.A. Butler, a leading figure within the Conservative Party: 'For them a thousand years of history books. For us the future.'

Looking back at Gaitskell's political career it reads like one fight after another: with Aneurin Bevan, with the Bevanites, over Clause Four, with CND, over Europe. Aneurin Bevan died in July 1960, Hugh Gaitskell in January 1963, and somehow their premature deaths before either had a further chance to display their undoubted talents in office summed up the barrenness of the 1950s and early 1960s for the British Left.

The parallels between Hugh Gaitskell's attempts to create a 'New Labour' Party shorn of Clause Four and Tony Blair's similar efforts in the 1990s are of course striking – except for the earlier leader's anti-European stance. Both politicians aimed their message at the public rather than party members, both were distrusted by some because of their privileged backgrounds. But whereas Gaitskell had only limited success in his reforms, Tony Blair's party management has proved triumphant.

Back in 1963 the Labour Party still looked like an election loser. It took a series of blunders by the Conservatives and the appearance of a seemingly new and dazzling Labour leader to revive the Party's fortunes.

# Harold Wilson's New Britain

## Britain in the 1960s

'We need men with fire in their bellies and humanity in their hearts. The choice we offer . . . is between standing still, clinging to the tired philosophy of a day that is gone, or moving forward in partnership and unity to a just society, to a dynamic, expanding, confident and above all purposive New Britain.'

HAROLD WILSON LAUNCHING THE LABOUR PARTY'S 1964
GENERAL ELECTION CAMPAIGN

'Callaghan recalls that in 1964 he was glooming over the statistics in his new study at Number 11, on his first day in office [as Chancellor of the Exchequer]. Suddenly Reggie Maudling [the outgoing Conservative Chancellor], carrying a number of suits over his arm, put his head round the door and said: "Good luck, old cock. Sorry to leave things in such a mess."'

JOHN COLE, *AS IT SEEMED TO ME* (1995)

'. . . the insufferable, smug, sanctimonious, naive, guilt-ridden, wet, pink orthodoxy of that sunset home of the third-rate minds of that third-rate decade, the 1960s.'

NORMAN TEBBIT, QUOTED IN THE *INDEPENDENT*,
22 FEBRUARY 1990

Few political reputations have plummeted so swiftly as that of Harold Wilson after his resignation as Prime Minister in March 1976. Even though he won four out of five general elections as the leader of his party and transformed Labour from the no-hopers of the 1950s to the seeming natural party of government in the 1970s, few people could find much good to say about the Wilson years.

Conservatives argued that he accelerated Britain's economic decline by caving in to every interest group, particularly the trade unions, and presiding over a general decline in moral standards. Socialists looked back in disappointment at the high hopes raised by Wilson and then seemingly dashed. The Wilson of 1963 and 1964 who had promised 'to build a new Jerusalem' was, by 1970, a cynical fixer and opportunist. Adherents of neither party noted that, despite extravagant promises, Britain's economic problems had certainly not been solved.

More recently, however, two sympathetic but critical biographies of Wilson by Ben Pimlott and Philip Ziegler have started to redress the balance, whilst Lord Wilson's own death in May 1995 also called forth tributes to a man whose personal kindness and sense of humour were never in doubt. Some Labour supporters also argued that, if Harold Wilson the astute party manager had still been at the helm in the early 1980s then the SDP would never have been formed and, so the argument went, 'Thatcherism' would surely have been nipped in the bud.

Differing interpretations of the Wilson era, both its successes and failures – even the disagreements as to which was which – will shape the future of the Labour Party over the next few decades.

Born in Yorkshire in March 1916, Harold Wilson came from a Liberal background, although any interest in politics was subordinate to his intense desire for academic success. After winning an outstanding First at Oxford he stayed on as a junior don before working as a civil servant during the Second World War. He rather belatedly joined the Labour Party in 1940. Elected a Labour MP just five years later in the 1945 election landslide, Wilson's abilities ensured spectacular advancement. In 1947, at the age of thirty-one, he joined the Cabinet as President of the Board of Trade. It was a meteoric rise known only by Pitt the Younger and William Gladstone.

Wilson made a name for himself with a catchy phrase which alerted him to the influence of the media, a power he subsequently deployed to great effect. In November 1948 he launched what he called 'a bonfire of controls' by scrapping various restrictions which had required the issuing of over one million licences on certain commodities. Already some left-wingers voiced doubts about this enthusiastic embrace of market forces.

Nevertheless in April 1951 Wilson surprised most people by resigning alongside Aneurin Bevan over the 'teeth and spectacles' issue. But Wilson was too shrewd to throw in his hand completely with a group that, because of the right-wing trade union block vote, was doomed to defeat. He happily took Bevan's place in the Shadow Cabinet when the latter resigned in 1954, much to the disgust of several Bevanites.

Keeping his head well below the parapet when Hugh Gaitskell tried to ditch Clause Four of the Constitution, Wilson's views on nuclear disarmament were also ambiguous. He actually stood against Gaitskell in 1960 in a leadership contest, not expecting to win but in order to put down a marker for the future.

After Gaitskell's unexpected death early in January 1963, Wilson was elected leader of the Parliamentary Labour Party, defeating George Brown and James Callaghan who between them split the natural right-wing majority. He was enormously helped by Brown's tempestuous but unreliable reputation. Many MPs had not in fact been happy with the quality of the two main candidates; in Tony Crosland's famous phrase, they were forced to choose between a crook (Harold Wilson) and a drunk (George Brown).

Just as damaging as the alienation of the Leader from powerful sections of the Parliamentary Party was the poor condition of Labour generally. In 1955 Wilson himself had described the Labour Party machine as 'still at the penny-farthing stage in a jet-propelled era', but little reorganisation followed his scathing report.

In other words, Harold Wilson was the new leader of a dispirited organisation which had lost three general elections in a row and still bore the scars of a recent and bitter internal civil war. How was Wilson – never a socialist virgin who preferred the purity of impotence to the constructive compromise of office – to secure electoral victory in such unpromising circumstances?

Harold Wilson was the first Labour leader to feel comfortable with the medium of television. Normally it was the Conservatives who excelled in the media field, pioneering new techniques of campaigning as well as being the first party to draw systematically on opinion polls, the first to use mass advertising and the first to commission market research.

The Labour Party's hidebound approach to communication had been memorably demonstrated by Clement Attlee's only visit to the BBC studios. One observer remarked that Attlee 'sat obstinately silent and disapproving and departed as coldly as he had come.' Tony Benn, himself a former television producer, could be found lamenting in his diaries in May 1958 that:

> . . . it made me despair that none of our Party leaders have television sets. They are totally unaware of these great developments that are going on which are influencing the minds and thought of the voters. How can one lead a great Party unless one keeps in touch with the people?

Aneurin Bevan had ignored the cameras, lyrically complaining that the paraphernalia of polls and advertising would '. . . take all the poetry out of politics'. Hugh Gaitskell had painstakingly endured the new techniques of modern political life. Harold Wilson, in contrast, welcomed them. During the 1950s, with the help of Tony Benn, he trained himself to be an excellent studio performer, learning the value of talking in natural tones, of speaking in short and memorable phrases – an early master of 'the soundbite' – and of holding a pipe to stop him waving his arms about. Wilson also made sure he was never photographed wearing his glasses, an example imitated in later years by both the Queen and Mrs Thatcher.

Still only in his mid-forties, Wilson's energy was con-clusively demonstrated by the thirty-two major speeches and innumerable broadcasts he delivered in just three months following his election as Labour Party leader – the provincial bounce noted many years later by one obituarist. But Wilson knew full well that more was needed, some message or theme to grab the electorate's attention yet not expose the cracks in his own party. And what better appeal to modern Britain could there be than the idea of modernity itself?

Under this banner Wilson could present both himself and Labour as vigorous and go-ahead when compared to the lofty grandeur of Harold Macmillan's administration, which was being torn apart by the Profumo scandal. In particular, this modern image was calculated to appeal to sections of the middle class or 'the middle ground' whose support had been won in 1945 and needed to be regained in the 1960s if the Labour Party was to have any realistic chance of winning an election.

Such a stance almost made a virtue of Labour's 'wilderness years', leaving the Party untainted by recent economic anxieties yet promising a fresh start. 'Thirteen Wasted Years' was the Labour Party slogan. Wilson also embraced the idea of scientific change and progress with enthusiasm – which, to be fair, was more than a convenient figleaf. This subject had always interested him. His father had been an industrial chemist and at Oxford Wilson had specialised in the study of technological advance. In his preface to the Labour Party document *Science and the Future of Britain* he wrote: 'the central feature of our post-war capitalist society is the scientific revolution.'

Needless to say, this revolution was infinitely more attractive to Wilson than any revolution entailing barricades and bloodshed. It also had the merit of distracting the voters' attention away from the unpopular subject of nationalisation.

Even more encouragingly, Wilson had only to glance across the Atlantic to see how John F. Kennedy had taken America by storm in 1960. Kennedy's youth and energy contrasted so vividly with the solid but dull Republican years of the 1950s; and in the rest of Europe 'old-timers' such as de Gaulle and Adenauer were being ousted from power. It did not matter that Wilson himself was fudging several issues – an expediency which Hugh Gaitskell, for example, would have rejected. Nor was it thought disturbing that Wilson's speeches sometimes displayed a flatulence reminscent of Ramsay MacDonald at his worst. Take this passage from a speech about 'Science and Society':

> Whoever could make two ears of corn or two blades of grass to grow upon a spot ground where only one grew before would deserve better of mankind and do more essential service to his country than the whole race of politicians put together.

No matter: the crucial thing was to catch a mood and here Wilson succeeded. For him, this was much more significant than details in manifestos or policy documents, which few people read anyway. The enthusiasm which Wilson generated clearly comes across in Tony Benn's diaries. In May 1963, for instance, more than a year before the election took place, Benn was writing happily: 'There is all the excitement of a revolutionary movement, with plans for this and that already afoot – just as if we were partisans poised for a victorious assault upon the capital.'

Faced by the new, low-key Conservative leader Sir Alec Douglas-Home who had replaced Macmillan, Wilson's vigour was instrumental in helping the Labour Party in October 1964 to win 317 seats to the Conservatives' 304 and the Liberals' 9. After thirteen years out of office Harold

Wilson had managed to take his party back to power – but only just.

On the face of it, Harold Wilson's 1960s Cabinets could claim to be the most academically brilliant of all time; that of 1966 contained no fewer than eight Oxford Firsts. But, of course, a high IQ is no guarantee of political success nor does it bestow the ability to get on well with one's colleagues. The Wilson governments from 1964 to 1970 were riven with extraordinary personal rivalry and dissension, the most internecine since – well, the last Labour government under Attlee.

Conservative Cabinets don't seem so prone to this internal bickering, or at least until the Margret Thatcher years their members did not feel compelled to publish diaries and memoirs which told us the full sordid details. Hugh Gaitskell was right when he wrote in his diary that 'Ambition certainly does seem to kill the pleasanter aspects of human nature.'

Unlike Attlee's Cabinets, Wilson's contained few members of working-class origin. It was a transformation epitomised by the experiences of the Jenkins, father and son. At the age of eighteen, Arthur, an able member of the Attlee administrations, had been toiling away as a miner. His son Roy, at precisely the same age, was an undergraduate at Balliol College, Oxford, and cutting a self-confident swathe through intellectual circles. Here was Labour penetrating the Establishment and taking its rightful place at the seats of the mighty.

Like Attlee's Cabinet, however, Wilson's also contained several powerful and conflicting personalities. Apart from the Prime Minister himself, there was George Brown, belligerent and forceful; the politically shrewd James Callaghan; two well-known peers in Lord Gardiner and Lord Longford; trade union leader Frank Cousins; and Richard Crossman, known from his schooldays as 'Double Crossman'.

Also present were Douglas Jay who had been one of Hugh Gaitskell's circle, pugnacious Denis Healey and the dry, schoolmasterly Michael Stewart. Another former Oxford don, Patrick Gordon-Walker, lost his seat in the 1964 election when his Conservative opponent fought an unpleasant racist campaign. He failed to be elected at a Leyton by-election in 1965 and had to resign as Foreign Secretary. The formidable Barbara Castle was also in the first Cabinet and later recruits included Tony Crosland, Roy Jenkins and Tony Benn.

Wilson emphasised his government's commitment to economic growth and technological advance. In *The Future of Socialism*, less than ten years before, Crosland had claimed that '. . . the contemporary mixed economy is characterised by high levels both of employment and productivity and by a reasonable degree of stability . . .' By the early 1960s, however, neither high employment nor productivity could be taken for granted any longer. For one thing, competition from the Third World was increasing, the EEC was becoming a formidable rival and Japan was forging ahead. The British economy was burdened by the legacy of its imperial past which necessitated the financing of a military presence 'east of Suez' that could not be afforded. The Wilson government also inherited a huge balance of payments deficit of over £500 million from the Conservatives – Reggie Maudling's 'mess'.

Clearly there was much to be done and a neutral observer might have anticipated that with thirteen years in which to prepare, the new administration would have been armed with a mass of blueprints and plans. In fact, just as in 1945, few detailed strategies were to hand, even for reforms as crucial as the shift towards comprehensive education, the abolition of the eleven-plus exam or the raising of the school-leaving age to sixteen.

This characteristic lack of preparation was not a new failing. In his memoirs George Brown was blunt about how the Party ran its 'administrative and research departments on the most ridiculous shoestring':

> In those vital days I, as Deputy Leader of the Party, Chairman of the Home Policy Committee and heaven knows what else,

had to work in a tiny office in the House of Commons with just one secretary for all attempts at co-ordinating policy, plus my constituency work, plus my parliamentary work.

The omission was all the more ominous because Harold Wilson had encouraged people to believe that a time of peace and plenty was assured under his administration. The Labour manifesto had highlighted such issues as increased pensions and better education, health and housing because these represented the commitments that everyone in the Labour Party could agree about.

The new government acted swiftly to remove prescription charges and also promised to raise the level of pensions in the immediate future. The 'money men', whose confidence or otherwise in the British economy was vital, regarded these actions as being all too typical of profligate socialism and within a few weeks of the election a damaging run on the pound put both sterling and the government under pressure. In his own account of these years, Wilson noted how undemocratic these pressures were:

> We had now reached the situation where a newly-elected Government with a mandate from the people was being told, not so much by the Governor of the Bank of England but by international speculators, that the policies on which we had fought the election could not be implemented; that the Government was to be forced into the adoption of Tory policies to which it was fundamentally opposed. The Governor confirmed that this was, in fact, the case.

Moreover, Wilson and his Chancellor of the Exchequer, James Callaghan, had already drastically reduced their options by deciding on day one not to devalue the pound. Wilson knew full well that Attlee's Labour administration had been the last to devalue in 1949 and he was determined not to begin his time in office with a similar admission of economic weakness. The Prime Minister was understandably concerned too that

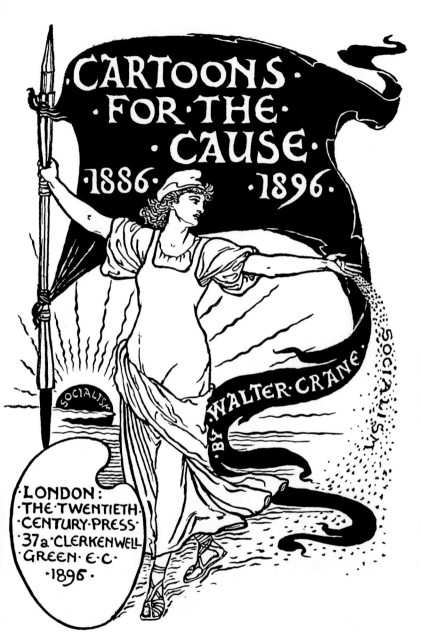

Walter Crane, a friend of William
Morris, was an effective radical
propagandist. The Twentieth
Century Press now houses the
Marx Memorial Library.

The Independent Labour Party, founded by Keir Hardie in 1893, later spawned the Labour Party.

The first Labour Party Conference, held in 1906. Keir Hardie and Ramsay MacDonald flank the chairman.

Keir Hardie (1856–1915). 'He will stand out for ever as the Moses who led the children of labour in this country out of bondage' – J. Ramsay MacDonald.

*Above* Robert Blatchford (1851–1943), the ex-Army man who created the Clarion movement and wrote the bestseller *Merrie England*.

*Left* H.M. Hyndman (1842–1921): lawyer, journalist, county cricketer and the founder in 1884 of Britain's first Marxist Party.

'Labour inside the gate' of Parliament in 1906, confronting the three evils of sweating, landlordism and monopoly.

Sidney Webb (1859–1947): indefatigable politician, writer and co-founder of the London School of Economics and the *New Statesman*.

*Opposite* Dockers gather on Tower Hill during the strike of 1912 – an example of the 'mass action' in which the labour movement had its roots.

Two effective Labour Party posters: 'Use Your Head!' (1922) and 'Men & Women Workers Your Chance At Last' (1929).

A fine cartoon by artist and politician J.F. Horrabin, used in the 1929 general election campaign.

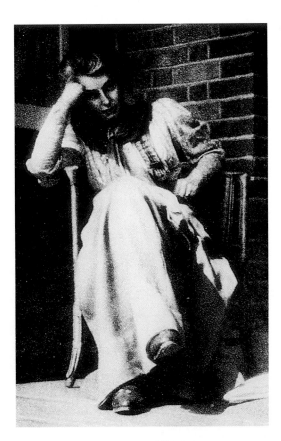

George Bernard Shaw's photograph of a young, beautiful and wistful Beatrice Webb (1858–1943).

MacDonald and a minority Labour government enter office for the first time, in January 1924.

Philip Snowden, a socialist pioneer who was reviled as a 'traitor' to the cause after 1931.

August 1931: the ignominious end of the second Labour government. Note how MacDonald had aged.

*Above* A very moving photograph: a group of unemployed blind people marching to London in October 1936 pause briefly at Slough.

Labour's Big Three: Clement Attlee flanked by the stolid Ernest Bevin and the equally pugnacious Herbert Morrison.

*Right* One of the most famous election posters of them all: 'And Now – Win The Peace' (1945).

Aneurin Bevan, creator of the National Health Service, and his wife Jennie Lee, creator of the Open University.

A very serious-looking platform at the Party Conference of 1945: Hugh Dalton and Ellen Wilkinson on one side of Jim Crawford; Harold Laski and Clem Attlee on the other.

Two former Bevanites deep in thought: Barbara Castle and Harold Wilson, plus trademark pipe.

George Brown, in charge of the 'National Plan', and Jim Callaghan, in charge of the Exchequer, discuss Britain's mounting economic problems in October 1964, but rule out devaluation of the pound.

Michael Foot addresses the Labour Party Conference in October 1973. Jim Callaghan looks bemused, Ian Mikardo lights his pipe and Tony Benn looks pleased with himself.

The avuncular Jim Callaghan spearheads Labour's election campaign in April 1979, but the electorate preferred to go Mrs Thatcher's way.

Michael Foot and his deputy Denis Healey in particularly belligerent mood.

Neil Kinnock and his deputy Roy Hattersley search the horizon for electoral victory in 1987 – and were still searching in 1992.

In the 1980s the Red Rose ousted 'The Red Flag'.

Leaders present and leaders future: John Smith confers with his deputy, Margaret Beckett, and the then shadow Home Secretary, Tony Blair.

the higher cost of imports after any devaluation, particularly of food, would hit working-class families disproportionately hard and that devaluation would 'featherbed' British industry by artificially boosting the export trade. On the other hand, the pound was clearly over-valued and devaluation would have given the economy a welcome boost.

The government troika – Wilson, Callaghan and deputy leader George Brown – decided not to devalue and also to forbid debate about the matter. As a result, this issue was and remains shrouded in secrecy. The fog is unlikely to lift because, in typically British style, the papers of the devaluation lobby have been 'lost'. Clearly the decision not to devalue was taken by three men drained by the strenuous election campaign. Douglas Jay, for one, has regretted that, 'It is characteristic of our system that a senior minister takes on the job of running a great department and trying to govern the country when he is twenty-four hours away from utter physical exhaustion.'

Wilson's continuing hostility to devaluation was also influenced by the secret deal he concluded in July 1965 with Lyndon B. Johnson's administration in the United States. Clive Ponting's research has shown how the Americans, worried that devaluation of the pound would in turn increase pressure on the dollar, were prepared to shore up the Wilson government as long as the pound was not devalued.

This deal seems to have been known only to Wilson and Chancellor Callaghan – a man who, as Wilson himself had confessed in March 1963, '. . . knew no economics and listened to the last advisers.' But why should Wilson have needed American support so badly? The explanation for this apparent British servility is to be found in the delusions of grandeur which influenced this new Labour government just as much as it had previous Conservative ones.

In the summer of 1947 George Orwell had put his finger on the nub of the question: 'Britain can only get free of America by dropping the attempt to be an extra-European power.' Harold Wilson clearly did not agree, declaring as he did in

November 1964 that 'We are a world power, and a world influence, or we are nothing.' It was immensely revealing of the 'Rule Britannia' streak within some circles of the Labour Party that Wilson regarded this problem as an either/or: either a top dog or oblivion. Most other countries' leaders accepted that political life was more complicated and less 'macho' than this simple binary division.

Wilson was clearly not alone in his sentiments; government spending on foreign aid and overseas commitments rose from just over £50 million in 1952 to more than £400 million by 1964. Yet, as Leslie Stone observed:

> . . . Britain's economic power in relation to its chief trading competition had been steadily waning. By the late sixties, its Gross National Product was estimated at $109 billion – well behind West Germany ($150 billion), France ($140 billion) and Japan ($167 billion). However, Japan devoted less than one per cent (0.9 per cent) of its GNP to expenditure on defence, while West Germany spent only 4.3 per cent. The figure for Britain was a whopping 5.7 per cent – a proportion exceeded among West European nations only by Portugal, which had serious colonial problems in Angola and Mozambique on its plate.

The imperial past struck back by giving Britain's leaders an attachment to overseas commitments that could not be met without drastically weakening the economy. Harold Wilson only began to shed his 'East of Suez' illusions after 1967 when it was already too late to alter his government's economic plans.

The tragedy of the Labour government's – or at least its leadership's – determination not to devalue and to regard the level of the pound as some kind of national virility symbol meant that it was inevitably pushed into policies of deflation and harsh measures in an attempt to defend the pound.

The swingeing cuts of July 1965 and July 1966 made a mockery of the so-called 'National Plan' which Wilson had originally proposed as the centrepiece of his modernising

Britain strategy. The Plan was put together by George Brown and a new creation, the Department of Economic Affairs (DEA). By switching the emphasis from consumption to investment the Plan was to establish targets for industry and, by constructive planning, to ensure that they were met.

The Labour Party had always been identified as the 'natural' party of planning, in contrast to the Conservatives who were thought to prefer reliance on free enterprise and the operation of the market. In fact, both parties, reflecting the mood of the post-war consensus, had paid lip-service to the virtues of planning; in June 1947 Herbert Morrison could even claim that '. . . the idea of planning is by now above and beyond party politics.'

It was rather less clear what this meant in practice. The Attlee government had introduced a new body called the National Investment Council which, as a purely advisory group, gently chided private industry to be more efficient, but to very little effect. Only four 'Development Councils' were set up and it is ironic that Harold Wilson himself, as we saw earlier, initiated a bonfire of the controls usually associated with planning.

In the 1950s the statements of thinkers such as Anthony Crosland echoed Morrison's remarks: 'The issue now is not whether but how much and to what purpose to plan.' France, in particular, seemed to exemplify exactly how governments could activate the economy. Immediately after the war Jean Monnet introduced his 'Commissariat au Plan':

> Each of its 'modernisation committees' brought together thirty, forty, or fifty people from business, industry, the trade unions, and the administration, to discuss production targets, supplies, shortages, productivity bottlenecks, and future investment plans – not just as representatives of this interest or that, but as members of a team. In a typical year, 3,000 people from all over France might gather in the Plan's headquarters at 18 rue de Martignac, while a single official there might handle the files of 500 separate firms.

Throughout the 1950s France's growth rate was significantly higher than Britain's, and the Labour Party under Harold Wilson pledged itself to escape from what were seen as the 'stop-go' policies of previous Conservative governments. These had led to a predictable series of events neatly summarised by Professor David Marquand: whenever there was full employment, demand rose and imports were sucked in. The balance of payments then came under pressure and sterling weakened. The government refused to devalue, which left only the option of reducing demand by means of deflationary cuts in spending. These measures produced rising unemployment which in turn prompted the government to boost demand in an attempt to deal with it, whereupon the whole circle started again: stop-go, stop-go.

The Labour Party's resolution to plan its way out of the stop-go cycle did not extend to planning the planning while in opposition. The idea for the expansionary DEA, intended to counter the influence of the parsimonious Treasury, is thought to have been hastily concocted by Wilson and George Brown on the back of an envelope during the course of a taxi journey. In his autobiography Brown confirmed the story: 'Harold Wilson and I travelled together in a taxi, and it was on that ride to the House that we decided firmly to set up a Department of Economic Affairs and that I should head it.'

When the DEA began work immediately after the election it possessed one desk and one chair – Frank Cousins had a similar experience at the new Ministry of Technology: 'No headquarters, no staff, not even funds.' It also became clear that in part the creation of the DEA enabled Harold Wilson to play off his two rivals for the 1963 leadership contest against each other. With George Brown at the DEA and James Callaghan at the Treasury, both departments were soon engaged in fratricidal 'turf wars' over their respective roles and influence.

Callaghan's Exchequer moved quickly to isolate the upstart DEA. Despite George Brown's energy and love of a fight, his department was continually producing plans and figures that forecast high rates of economic growth of around 4 per cent, which were then transformed into optimistic daydreams because of Chancellor Callaghan's deflationary cuts. The National Plan itself, published to noisy fanfares in 1965, turned out to consist of 'little more than the printed replies to a questionnaire sent to industries about their estimates of inputs and outputs on the assumptions of 25 per cent real growth by 1970.'

The DEA was also hampered by the difficult personality of George Brown himself. Something of a 'raging bull', he had lost the leadership contest with Wilson in 1963 precisely because of doubts about personality. Talking to one of his supporters at the time, Woodrow Wyatt, he asked where it had all gone wrong. 'You must face it,' said Wyatt, 'it's because you're so dreadfully rude to people when you're drunk.' 'What makes them think I'm rude to them just because I'm drunk?' was Brown's truculent response. The diaries of Crossman, Castle and Benn show that Brown's behaviour did not improve as a Cabinet minister and his demonic energy often deteriorated into drunken rantings and ravings.

Not surprisingly, the DEA proved little more than an irrelevance and after Brown moved to another post successive ministers exerted even less influence on the British economy. The Department was quietly allowed to expire in 1969. As for Brown himself, after no fewer than seventeen attempted resignations he finally threatened once too often and found his offer taken up. As Harold Wilson generously put it, 'His [Brown's] strengths far exceeded his weaknesses, but it was his weaknesses which ended his ministerial career.'

One vital flaw in the Wilson strategy was that, although the Cabinet was bursting with dons and journalists, none of them possessed any managerial experience. As Tam Dalyell has written of his friend Richard Crossman, 'He had never actually run anything.' Few Cabinet ministers had much practical experience of wealth creation. An economics don might well boast tons of theoretical expertise, but this was rarely of much help when dealing with the pragmatism of an ICI or Unilever chariman. In May 1968 Crossman himself referred to '. . . the lack of success of the interventionist policies of Peter Shore and Tony Wedgwood Benn, young men who with carefree arrogance think they can enter the business world and help it to be more efficient.'

Some of these well-meaning but ineffectual chickens would come home to roost only in the future. In the first flush of his administration Harold Wilson's dynamism and seeming competence impressed many. Any difficulties could be explained away by blaming the Conservatives for leaving behind such a mess. Alternatively, Wilson could complain that his government was hamstrung by its tiny majority, and his Chief Whip, Ted Short, has described the perilous actions needed to sustain the government. Unconscious backbench MPs were regularly wheeled into the House, and on one occasion Short refused to let thirteen Scottish Labour MPs travel down together by road: 'Our majority could have been extinguished in an accident on the motorway.'

The Prime Minister called for a fresh election in March 1966 and throughout the campaign carefully portrayed the Labour Party in national and patriotic terms in order to maximise support. In his two television broadcasts Wilson apparently used the word 'Britain' forty-two times, 'government' thirty-nine times and 'Labour' not once.

Helped by the fact that the Conservatives had a new and largely unknown leader in Edward Heath, Wilson's strategy seemed to pay off when the electorate returned Labour to power with a gain of forty-eight seats. As in 1945, the Labour Party had won a thumping majority. Attlee's governments had introduced much of social democratic Britain. What could Wilson's achieve?

After the election, Wilson could no longer rely on the 'small majority' excuse. Moreover it was now two years since the Conservatives had governed. Nor could he claim that his

Cabinet was inexperienced in office. Yet, armed as they were with the full panoply of civil service resources, it was difficult to understand why the new Labour administration should once again lack detailed and thought-through policies. One reason for this omission lay in the personality of the Prime Minister himself.

When Harold Wilson was elected leader of the Labour Party in 1963 he knew full well that, like Margaret Thatcher in the following decade, the vast majority of his senior colleagues had voted against him – in fact only a single member of the Shadow Cabinet, Fred Lee, supported Wilson. The advantage was that he was beholden to no grouping in particular; the disadvantage, as David Howell has pointed out, was that 'In office Wilson paid for his earlier independent strategy; his earlier isolation from any faction meant that he lacked a dependable basis of support. The result was a tendency to surround himself with advisers who acted as a necessary reassurance, but also as an insulator against disturbances from outside.'

The most controversial member of this 'kitchen Cabinet' was Wilson's secretary, Marcia Williams, later Lady Falkender, who acted as an informal cheer-leader. Opponents of Wilson sometimes tried to make mischief out of their relationship. According to Andrew Roth, unscrupulous Gaitskellites launched a whispering campaign in 1960 during the leadership contest, forcing Wilson, his wife Mary and Marcia Williams to hold a semi-public tea-party to try and refute the rumours.

Always worried about his own position, Wilson continually moved ministers from department to department so that they could not build up a permanent power base from which to challenge him. What one commentator called his 'Artful Dodger' style of government meant that the civil service benefited from this high-powered game of musical chairs because no minister was really able to get on top of his job, apart from Denis Healey who remained as Minister of Defence from 1964 to 1970. Anthony Crosland once claimed of ministers that: 'It takes you six months to get your head properly above water, a year to get the general drift of most of the field, and two years really to master the whole of a department.'

Wilson rarely allowed anyone two years in the same post. The Wilson government also lacked a 'fixer' like Herbert Morrison who as Leader of the House of Commons in the Attlee administration had eased through legislation with a minimum of fuss.

By elevating tactics above principle, Wilson's personalised approach to politics undermined any consistent strategy. National problems were elbowed aside by the requirements of party management. Virtually every member of the government seems to have spent much of their time either 'leaking' to the press or thinking about it, emulating Wilson's own conduct. Douglas Jay was a minister in both the Attlee and Wilson governments and claimed that the latter was a much less happy affair than the former, while Tony Benn once recorded that 'Cabinets used to spend sometimes as long on discussing the leak after the last Cabinet as they did on the business of the agenda for that day.' Ministers such as Richard Marsh used to hide things from their putative colleagues.

In this poisonous atmosphere even Wilson's closest supporters began to doubt his qualities. Richard Crossman was, in his own words, 'an absolutely solid Harold man' yet his diaries reveal the Prime Minister's drift and inconsistency. As early as December 1964 Crossman notes: '. . . the Cabinet isn't very firm or very stable because the central leadership isn't there, the sense of priorities, the sense of grip that you need.' By June 1965 he is lamenting, 'Here we are, drifting along, with our momentum halted and the Civil Service taking over more each day.'

In December 1966, after the second election, Crossman observes of Wilson that 'His main aim is to stay in office. That's the real thing and for that purpose he will use almost any trick or gimmick if he can only do it.' By April 1969 Crossman is berating 'the muddle-headed incompetence of the central direction of the party . . . He is just a figure posturing there in the middle without any drive except to stay as Prime Minister as long as he can.'

On and on it goes. Tony Benn, then one of Wilson's kitchen Cabinet, thought the Prime Minister was 'a manipulator who thinks he can get out of everything by fixing somebody or something.' Perhaps Tony Crosland, a former Gaitskellite, put it more succinctly: 'The trouble with Harold is that one hasn't the faintest idea whether the bastard means what he says even at the moment he speaks it.' No one doubted Wilson's drive and resilience, and other hard-working members of the Cabinet sometimes found it difficult to keep up with him. Nevertheless, this energy so often failed to produce results.

July 1966 saw yet another run on the pound, but devaluation was once again ruled out in favour of a further bout of deflation. The modernising 'white heat' image of only two years before now seemed a very distant memory. Eventually, despite a protracted struggle, the pound was devalued by 14 per cent in November 1967. Wilson himself delivered a disastrous broadcast about the 'pound in the pocket' which, according to himself, almost seemed to exult in the decision.

The Wilson governments proved more successful with their taxation policies. Previous Labour governments had generally preferred to administer the existing system, and when they did introduce new taxes they were often swiftly replaced by incoming Conservative governments. Attlee, for instance, had introduced a 100 per cent development tax levied on unearned land value, but this was discarded by the Churchill administration in 1953.

The Wilson government introduced three new taxes, Selective Employment Tax, Capital Gains Tax and Corporation Tax. Additionally, in the absence of substantial economic growth, Labour had to raise taxes in order to pay for increased welfare spending. Between 1964 and 1970, taxes on personal income rose from an average of 10 to 14 per cent. However, one academic commentator has calculated that the net effect of Labour's financial policies did indeed make the rich poorer and the poor richer.

But if the Wilson governments failed to tackle Britain's longstanding economic weaknesses, they were responsible for a series of libertarian measures, associated above all with the Home Secretary Roy Jenkins, which helped to humanise the country. In many ways the High Politics of Cabinet reshuffles and departmental comings and goings pass most people by. These social changes affected everyone – by 1970, for instance, for the first time, the government was spending more on education than on defence.

The Labour administration initiated, or at least did not obstruct, homosexual reform, abortion reform, divorce reform, the end of theatre censorship, the abolition of capital punishment and the banning of corporal punishment in prisons. It supervised the introduction of equal pay legislation, redundancy payments, the Law Commission, the Ombudsman, legislation outlawing racial discrimination, the expansion of higher education and the publication of state papers after thirty years and not fifty.

The Lord Chancellor, Lord Gardiner, oversaw criminal law reforms, the establishment of the Family Division of the High Court and changes in property and matrimonial law. He also appointed the first ever woman High Court judge. The select committees introduced in 1969 provided much-needed scrutiny of the executive. The age of majority was lowered from twenty-one to eighteen and the Civic Amenities Act 1967 introduced conservation areas in order to protect Britain's heritage. The Open University was set up through the efforts of Bevan's widow Jennie Lee, the first Minister of the Arts, who ensured that arts spending doubled. Likewise Jim Griffiths was appointed the first Secretary of State for Wales.

In many ways this avalanche of reform represented yet another area of the post-war consensus forged in the 1930s and 1940s: it can be seen as the social equivalent of the welfare state and full employment. The measures marked a welcome return to some of the libertarian themes discussed in Chapter 3, 'Socialism and the New Life', and which can be traced from Edward Carpenter through to E.M. Forster, Bloomsbury and Noel Annan's *Our Age*. Personal relationships and friendships were paramount and anything that obstructed them, especially legal constraints, was suspect. Not every member of the Cabinet supported these reforms; George Brown, for one, opposed the legalisation of homosexuality, muttering to Barbara Castle that 'This is how Rome came down.'

One Marxist critic of the Labour Party, David Coates, called the Wilson governments' record in the field of social reform 'appalling', yet he failed to mention a single one of the above changes. Although the 1964–70 administrations did not solve Britain's economic problems (which government can claim it has?), its social reforms were a remarkable achievement.

There were two drawbacks to this legislation and the behaviour it condoned. First of all, it is wrong to exaggerate just how widespread these changes were outside London. Roy Hattersley has recently put it well:

> The sixties – which no doubt swung in London – barely moved out of the vertical in Sheffield. All I can remember of those rebellious times is an angry demonstration outside a dress shop which was exhibiting a topless evening gown, and a visit to Chesterfield Repertory Theatre to see the local company's production of John Osborne's *Look Back in Anger*. There was not an angry young man in the house.

Secondly, the notion of rights and privileges also carry with them the corresponding burden of obligations and duties. Previous libertarians such as George Lansbury had always been preoccupied with the aim of helping others, rather than oneself, to be free: of selflessness rather than selfishness. As Robert Blatchford once expressed it: 'The aim of socialism is to substitute the word "ours" for the words "mine" and "thine".'

Too many people indulging in the new social climate started from the other way around.

Today some right-wing commentators and politicians like Norman Tebbit vigorously castigate this supposedly permissive society, and undoubtedly some people did use their freedoms in selfish ways. But to claim that, say, consenting male adults behaving as they wished in private, or theatre-goers seeing *Oh! Calcutta!* live on stage, represented the start of some twentieth-century Sodom and Gomorrah is ridiculous and comes ill from people who usually make much of the philosophy that people should have as much freedom to choose as possible.

Although the social reforms of the Wilson administration certainly matched the changes introduced by Gladstone's one hundred years before, it did not imitate the earlier government's attack on institutional inertia. Needless to say, the monarchy was an issue that Wilson decided to tiptoe around; in his diaries, Richard Crossman describes with some disgust the time that a Cabinet minister had to spend rehearsing the ceremony of becoming a Privy Councillor:

> I don't suppose anything more dull, pretentious, or plain silly has ever been invented. There we were, sixteen grown men. For over an hour we were taught how to stand up, how to kneel on one knee on a cushion, how to raise the right hand with the Bible in it, how to advance three paces towards the Queen, how to take the hand and kiss it, how to move back ten paces without falling over the stools – which had been carefully arranged so that you did fall over them.

Crossman himself botched up reform of the House of Lords. What had seemed to be all-party support for a measure abolishing the right of hereditary peers to vote in the Lords was torpedoed by the unlikely combination of Michael Foot and Enoch Powell. Powell felt the reforms went too far while Foot considered they did not go far enough. When Crossman did attempt something innovative, such as the introduction of experimental closed-circuit televising of the Commons, he discovered that he alone of the Cabinet ministers had voted for the proposal.

The Fulton Committee found that the civil service was prejudiced against professional and technical experts and proposed some important changes. As Clive Ponting has put it:

> The crucial recommendation was the abolition of classes within the Civil Service. If this had been implemented then the generalist administrators (the public school-Oxbridge-educated arts graduates) would lose their key roles as amateur advisers to ministers to professionally qualified accountants, economists and statisticians.

This reform should have been close to the heart of Harold Wilson's desire to create 'a dynamic, expanding, confident and above all purposive new Britain.' Anyone who watched the series *Yes, Minister* can imagine Sir Humphrey Appleby's reaction to these proposals. By leaving the implementation of the Fulton Report to the Applebys of the civil service, the Wilson government guaranteed that nothing would be done, and it wasn't. In both Germany and France at exactly the same time, ministries were being reorganised and modernised – but then Harold Wilson himself had been a civil servant for a number of years.

The Official Secrets Act remained intact. Prescription charges, abolished with a flourish in 1964, were reimposed in 1968. Despite promises, the government – or at least three ministers, namely Wilson, Healey and Gordon-Walker who failed to inform their Cabinet colleagues of the decision – did not cancel the Polaris nuclear project. Again, despite promises, a wealth tax was never implemented.

Surrounded by his loyal kitchen Cabinet, Harold Wilson became increasingly isolated and paranoid, hankering after an American Presidential-style form of leadership. Time and again, whether it was over arms sales to South Africa, or support for American involvement in Vietnam, or the introduction of the Commonwealth Immigration Act in 1968 which denied Kenyan Asians who held British passports the right to enter the country, the actions of the Wilson government seemed shabby and opportunist, lacking any political, let alone ethical, principles.

One telling illustration of this moral vacuum occurred after the declaration of unilateral independence by Ian Smith's Rhodesian regime in November 1965. Sanctions directed at the rebel government were thwarted by the major oil companies, determined to maintain the flow of oil into Rhodesia. The oil companies introduced 'swap' arrangements with a French company which allowed them to evade the letter of the law. It is unclear how much the government knew about these underhand dealings. At best they were guilty of carelessness and of not asking relevant questions; at worst, they were accomplices to the oil companies' behaviour.

An underlying weakness of the Wilson governments was that they never attracted good policy ideas whether it be from members of the Cabinet or from extra-parliamentary sources. The diaries of Crossman, Castle and Benn show ministers desperately coping with short-term departmental crises and therefore never able to stand back from the fray. Colleagues often urged Tony Crosland to produce an updated version of his book *The Future of Socialism*. His response? 'I'm too bloody busy running a major government department; let them do the new thinking.'

The disappointment that many Labour Party members felt at their own government caused thousands to cancel their membership. It was in the 1960s that many constituency parties began to disintegrate. The four inner London constituencies of Bermondsey, Peckham, Dulwich and Southwark, for example, had boasted a membership of 12,500 in 1952; by the end of the 1960s, the figure was barely 2,000. By 1970 the Party had fewer than 300,000 members and no more than 141 professional agents – approximately a half of Conservative resources.

Similarly, the Communist Party was declining inexorably in terms of both numbers and influence. It may have opposed the Soviet invasion of Czechoslovakia in 1968, but its protests would hardly have caused Moscow to lose any sleep. Individual Communists, however, were typically active in a variety of local activities such as squatters' movements, tenants' associations, neighbourhood law centres and a range of cultural activities stretching from community theatre to folk music. Other socialists disillusioned with both the Labour Party and the Communist Party continued the trend, first established by CND, of no longer basing themselves exclusively on the manual working class. The most important of these movements was composed of students.

In the 1960s student numbers doubled at universities, polytechnics and colleges of further education. Unlike the previous decade when students had been docile and accepting, the new generation voiced their complaints as noisily as possible. Dissatisfaction with the teaching and conditions spilled over into protest against American military involvement in Vietnam. Like CND members, the students were firmly anti-political, dismissing elections as charades and, similarly, they usually had no idea what to do after a demonstration was over. For want of anything better, the demo became an end in itself, full of sound and fury but signifying not a lot. E.P. Thompson once scathingly dismissed the events of 1968 as 'a rich kid's revolutionary farce'.

Perhaps one reason for Thompson's dismissive remark was that many of the students in the West had little sense of perspective. Tariq Ali organised several VSC (Vietnam Solidarity Campaign) marches. In his own words, 'We wished to transform Western civilisation because we regarded it as politically, morally and culturally bankrupt.' But in Czechoslovakia, where a real uprising took place in 1968, David Caute has rightly observed that 'The Czechoslovak reform movement, students included, was working for precisely the freedoms which Western radicals were rejecting as bogus and manipulative . . .'

The Revolutionary Students Socialist Federation (RSSF) – the longer the name, the further away from reality – was brutally frank in its manifesto of November 1968, committing itself to '. . . the revolutionary overthrow of capitalism and imperialism and its replacement by workers' power, and bases itself on the recognition that the only social class in industrial countries capable of making the revolution is the working class.' The only problem with this ringing declaration was that the RSSF had few contacts with, or influence among, the British working class.

In fact, the one working-class demonstration which did take place in 1968 showed how misguided some students were in romanticising the revolutionary potential of the British working class. In April 1968 Conservative MP Enoch Powell delivered his notorious 'rivers of blood' speech deploring immigration. A few days later he was sacked from the Shadow Cabinet by Edward Heath, whereupon 4,000 London dockers went on strike in support of Powell's views. The dockers and the Smithfield meat porters also marched to the Houses of Parliament to voice their racist opinions. Some of the more thoughtful students were horrified by these actions. As David Widgery expressed it:

> Here were workers doing what we International Socialists were recommending: rank-and-file activity, political struggle on an industrial basis – only they were doing it the other way round. So it was all blowing up in our faces . . .

Some students retreated into sectarian isolation, setting up tiny little groups which then divided into even tinier groups. Widgery provided a thirty-eight-page classification giving a split-by-split taxonomy of these left-wing bodies, among which were to be found the 'Microfaction' and the snappily titled 'Committee to Defeat Revisionism, for Communist Unity'.

One important section of this counter-culture turned away in despair from Britain towards European and Third World Marxism. The New Left dismissed the socialist tradition that the Left should speak to everyone and not just to a few. The 'Old Left' had not always been successful in this, but it had at least tried. The Communist Party, for instance, had often insisted that intellectuals joining the party should first undertake menial tasks, while adult education, which included men as gifted as G.D.H. Cole and R.H. Tawney, had always been an effective influence. In a striking phrase, Cole once said that WEA tutors were the true missionaries of the day, doing the kind of work which at one time the churches used to carry out.

This 'missionary' tradition was now discarded because the 'New New Left' contended that British socialism lacked a good healthy dose of 'theory', which could only be imported from abroad. The British Left had indeed often exhibited a dull and insular pragmatism, but to condemn it in its entirety was to throw out the baby with the bathwater. In fact, *New Left Review* knew little and cared a lot less about Britain's own radical heritage. In one essay, for instance, its editor Perry Anderson claimed that, 'The vast majority of those intellectuals who had briefly been on the Left [in the 1930s] swung to the right . . .' A glance at Chapter 6 shows how wrong Anderson's assertion was.

No matter, a series of 'rave' notices introduced the readers of *New Left Review* to the work of several European thinkers. The latest theory was invariably couched in an arcane and inaccessible language understood only by those few in the know and which generally displayed what Perry Anderson himself, in suitably arcane language, later complained was 'its very surplus above the necessary minimum quotient of verbal complexity'. 'It is possible to be learned and a fool,' as R.H. Tawney once noted.

Such obfuscation sometimes camouflaged the more generous impulses of the 1960s agitation which, at its best, represented a disgust with organised electoral politics in favour of a libertarian 'do-it-yourself' approach. Even Michael Stewart, Foreign Secretary in the Wilson government, remarked on the greater tendency towards 'group action' in the 1960s. Referring to his Fulham constituency he wrote:

> In 1945 I would receive letters which said, in effect, 'Conditions in this street are awful; please do something about it.' The 1970 version would be, 'We have formed a residents' association to deal with some problems in this neighbourhood; will you please come to the inaugural meeting.'

In later years these impulses resurfaced as a new concern for feminism, for the environment and for 'single issue' campaigns which activists, unimpressed by the Labour Party, pursued in their own way.

With hindsight, the traditional Labour world – cities, factories, manufacturing industries, council estates, the *Daily Herald* – was disintegrating. The old collective certainties on which Keir Hardie had based his new political organisation were being challenged by a more individualistic, high-spending, irreverent and less deferential *Sun*-reading culture: the computer terminal rather than the cloth cap. The implications for the British Labour Party were immense.

As Harold Wilson surveyed the political scene from his bunker at No. 10 Downing Street, increasingly at odds with the electorate who delivered crushing blows in the local elections of 1968 and 1969, with the Labour Party Conference (between 1964 and 1970 the Conference voted against government measures on no fewer than thirteen occasions), the Parliamentary Labour Party and even his own Cabinet, inevitably he began to look for explanations for the delayed appearance of his 'New Britain'.

The large Labour majority meant that the party whips found it difficult to dragoon backbenchers into voting for measures they did not support. In March 1967 a number of MPs abstained in protest at the White Paper on Defence. A furious Wilson responded at the next meeting of the Parliamentary Labour Party:

> All I say is watch it. Every dog is allowed one bite, but a different view is taken of a dog that goes on biting all the time. If there are doubts that the dog is biting not because of dictates of conscience but because he is considered vicious, then things happen to that dog. He may not get his licence renewed when it falls due.

Not only was this an extraordinarily arrogant and tactless attitude to adopt towards MPs of his own party, it was bound to be counter-productive. Two months later, thirty-six Labour MPs voted against the government's proposal to apply for Britain to join the Common Market and a further fifty-one abstained. As it turned out, the application was in any case vetoed by General de Gaulle.

At odds with much of his own party, Wilson started to turn his attention towards what he thought was trade union obstructiveness. During the seamen's strike in 1966, for instance, he had tried to play the 'Communist bogey' card, blaming a handful of supposedly Communist agitators on the union executive and thereby hoping to put pressure on the union to call off the action. Conservative leader Edward Heath was unimpressed when Wilson showed him the evidence for this assertion. A damaging dock strike the following year was led by the Communist Jack Dash, nicknamed 'the Red Napoleon', whose men had benefited from the de-casualisation of dock work but whose militancy was beginning to drive employers to find other, cheaper and more reliable docks at which to unload.

The obvious difficulty facing any Labour government was

that ever since Keir Hardie, the link with the trade unions had been central to the very existence of the Labour Party and had ensured that it successfully ousted the Liberal Party as the major rival to the Conservatives. It was the trade unions that provided the bulk of party funds and therefore any attempt to interfere with the paymasters was bound to be provocative.

In addition, post-war corporatism — the cosy alliance between government, employers and trade unions — had strengthened the hand of the unions, as too had full employment. One symbol of the unions' permanence and power was the opening in March 1958 of its new headquarters, Congress House in Bloomsbury, decorated by sculpture by Jacob Epstein. The state trumpeters of the Royal Horse Guards sounded a special fanfare for the event. Throughout the 1950s successive Conservative governments had proved only too eager to discuss anything and everything with prominent trade unionists: 'beer and sandwiches' at the Ministry of Labour.

One story brings out this burgeoning self-confidence. In 1959 a new young Labour MP, Richard Marsh, won first place in the ballot for Private Members' bills. As a former trade union organiser, he wanted to introduce a Factory Bill for white-collar workers. Marsh telephoned the TUC's assistant general secretary, Vic Feather, for help. Feather barely gave him the time of day: 'Well, we're not interested, lad, in back-bench MPs. If we want legislation, we deal with the Ministers.'

The trade unions had always been sectional bodies, concerned above all with the welfare of their own members rather than national issues. Their understandable concentration on wage bargaining ensured that their actions were usually seen or experienced negatively. The unions' only power was to withdraw their labour, which almost always inconvenienced the public. There were few single industry unions. The motor car industry, for instance, contained men from twenty-two different unions. Between 1964 and 1966 there were thirty unofficial strikes for every one official strike sanctioned by a union.

The trade unions' narrow and defensive stance was illustrated by the fact that, with the notable exception of Ernest Bevin, the record of leading trade unionists drafted into Labour governments was often disappointing. For instance, Frank Cousins, the leader of the Transport and General Workers' Union, was brought in as Minister of Science and Technology in 1964 but was uncomfortable dealing with civil servants and the minutiae of administration. In July 1966 he resigned in protest at the Prices and Incomes Bill, which in effect banned all prices and wage increases for the next six months.

However, there had been few instances of union corruption, certainly when compared with the regular cases of business and company fraud. One bad example had occurred in the 1950s when the Electrical Trades Union (ETU) was run by a handful of Communists who illegally fixed ballots in order to retain power. They were helped by the fact that less than 20 per cent of the membership had bothered to vote in the 1955 and 1959 elections. It took a court case to break their hold.

The problems plaguing the Wilson government included the rash of unofficial strikes and the new ploy of 'working to rule', a technique pioneered by shop stewards who were the militant arm of the unions. For many people the image of the shop steward was synonymous with the rigid character of Brother Fred Kite, played by Peter Sellers in the film *I'm All Right Jack*. In the film the company's management is shown to be unscrupulous and incompetent, but it the Sellers' part which people tend to remember.

Although now very much a part of the Establishment – its centenary in 1968 was marked by the issue of a commemorative stamp – the TUC frequently disapproved of 'wildcat' actions but found itself unable or unwilling to do anything about it. The prominence given to trade union behaviour by the right-wing press meant that matters were rarely kept in proportion; the academic expert H.A. Turner recorded: 'An effective anti-influenza serum would probably be of more measurable benefit to the economy than an effective anti-strike law – and perhaps be less difficult and costly to produce.'

Crossman noted in his diaries the Prime Minister's musings on the effectiveness of the American Democratic Party, which had no formal links with the unions. Wilson waited for the report of the Donovan Commission, which had been set up to inquire into trade unions, hoping that it would recommend drastic measures. In fact, its modest advice was that pay bargaining should be operated on a more centralised basis but that otherwise, for want of a better alternative, labour relations should remain as they were. This was not good enough for Wilson. He asked Barbara Castle to tackle the union problem.

The daughter of a tax inspector and active member of the Independent Labour Party, Barbara Betts was educated at Bradford Girls' Grammar School and Oxford where she was an active member of the Labour Club. In the 1930s she worked for the left-wing weekly *Tribune*. She married the journalist Ted Castle and in 1945 was elected MP for Blackburn. Sir Stafford Cripps appointed her his Parliamentary Private Secretary.

In the 1950s Castle had been a Bevanite but found opposition frustrating. Like Bevan, she always preferred the challenge of government to the purity of impotence: 'This is the real morality: having to choose, having not to choose. Anybody can be on the side of the angels when there's never a devil around.'

Harold Wilson appointed her Minister for Overseas Development in 1964 and then moved her to the Ministry of Transport. In the face of much opposition, it was Barbara Castle who in October 1966 introduced the breathalyser in order to curb drunken driving. Her energy and determination is fully evident in her diaries – at least four members of the Wilson Cabinets, Gordon Walker, Crossman, Benn and Castle kept accounts – which are a memorable mix of the personal and the public. Politics was important to her but not exclusively so.

Just read her account of the family dog dying from a terminal illness: 'I do not remember ever having spent a more wretched evening. I tried to work and wept into my typewriter. Of course, it *would* be the night Ted [her journalist husband] was kept late at the office with the monetary crisis – as if I cared about that.'

The opposition that Barbara Castle faced over the breath-alyser was negligible when compared with the storm raised by her White Paper *In Place of Strife* of January 1969 when she was Minister of Employment and Productivity. As a Bevanite who had spent much of the 1950s fighting right-wing union leaders, she had no great illusions about organised labour. She therefore decided to recognise the trade union position by introducing what in her view was a charter giving the unions statutory rights:

> So, first and foremost, *In Place of Strife* was a charter of trade union right: the right to belong to a trade union, safeguards against unfair dismissal, the right to disclosure of information for bargaining purposes, the 'check-off' system of collecting trade union dues, protection for sympathetic strikes and steps towards industrial democracy: long-standing trade union demands, many of which have since been met.

Conversely Mrs Castle thought that if trade union members had rights, then they also owed duties: 'If power is to be shared so must responsibility.' *In Place of Strife* called for penal clauses to be levied against strikers taking part in unofficial action, a twenty-eight-day pause before a strike could begin and, in notable anticipation of the future, secret ballots of union members before industrial action could be called.

In effect, Barbara Castle was trying to reform the unions before someone else did it for them. But, unlike any post-war administration whether it had been Conservative or Labour, Castle and Wilson were proposing to introduce legal restraints on their own colleagues, allies and financial backers. Like

Hugh Gaitskell before them, they under-estimated both the entrenched interests that dominated the unions and their collective ethos of labourism, which valued solidarity above everything else – even economic efficiency.

There did seem to be popular support for *Strife*, but this was no help in passing the proposals through the Cabinet and then Parliament where one in three Labour MPs were sponsored by the trade unions. What made it worse was that Wilson's highly personalised style of management over the previous five years returned to haunt him. Few of his own Cabinet now trusted him. The politician who led the opposition was Jim Callaghan whose attitude was simple; when told by one backbencher that union reform was inevitable, he replied, 'OK, if it's so inevitable, let the *Tories* pass it. All I'm saying is that it's not *our* issue.'

Wilson also miscalculated in introducing such an important measure towards the end of his term in office when his incomes policies had already exhausted the fund of political goodwill which the unions originally had towards a Labour government. In addition, several major unions had recently elected left-wing leaders. Hugh Scanlon was now President of the Engineers, Lawrence Daly General Secretary of the Mineworkers and Jack Jones of the Transport and General Workers' Union. In his autobiography Jones claims that 'Wilson and Castle were basically academics and it was difficult to persuade them to see things from a shop-floor angle.' Mrs Castle in particular seems to have rubbed male chauvinist union leaders like Frank Chapple up the wrong way: 'She carried her own irritation powder . . .'

Wilson and Castle found themselves increasingly isolated as everyone else in the Cabinet gradually withdrew their support for the bill. Tony Benn recorded their defeat:

> Harold and Barbara then became extremely bitter. Harold threatened to resign several times and said he wouldn't do what the Cabinet wanted him to do and they would have to

look for a new Leader, and so on; people were completely unmoved by it. His bluff was called and he just looked weak and petty, he spoke too much, he interrupted, he was angry. Barbara was frantic in the usual Barbara sort of way.

The TUC came up with a face-saving device for Wilson and Castle, namely a 'solemn and binding' agreement that in cases of unofficial strikes the union would do their best to get their members to return to work. 'Mr Solomon Binding' became a joke with which political opponents flayed Labour. Everyone knew that the unions had won. The paymasters had established that the tune to be played was theirs and theirs alone.

The *In Place of Strife* debacle showed that the Labour Party – 'Old Labour' – was still essentially a trade union party. The fortunes of the two remained inextricably linked. This was bound to cause problems if and when the trade unions, still growing, failed to move with the times and became unpopular with the public at large. As Barbara Castle warned, their failure to adapt under their own steam meant that, in the 1980s, this job would be done for them in a much harsher way.

The episode revealed much, too, about Harold Wilson. As his biographer Philip Ziegler has pointed out, 'The story of *In Place of Strife* is of peculiar importance in Wilson's life as being almost the only occasion in a career devoted to the pursuit of consensus in which he flung compromise and party unity to the winds and fought his battle to the verge of the last ditch.'

The mishandling of *In Place of Strife* somehow symbolised the cul-de-sac down which the Wilson government had manoeuvred itself. The hopes of a 'New Britain' had long gone. In June 1970 the Conservatives under Heath won the general election, to the surprise of many leading Labour figures. Perceptive observers such as Barbara Castle had noted their misgivings during the campaign: '. . . I have a haunting feeling there is a silent majority sitting behind its lace curtains, waiting to come out and vote Tory.' Tony Benn noted his reaction when the first result came in, showing an enormous swing to the Conservatives: 'In a fraction of a second, one went from a pretty confident belief in victory to absolute certainty of defeat.' Somehow it signified the way in which the hopes of just six years before had been dashed.

Looking back at Harold Wilson's two governments of 1964–1966 and 1966–1970, the verdict must be that despite successes, especially in the social sphere, there was an inability to translate rhetoric into action, particularly when it came to core economic issues. Wilson was superb both in opposition and at winning elections, but rather less certain when talk of Britain's economic decline had to be turned into action aimed at reversing this slide.

As Kenneth Morgan has put it, 'In the end, public relations superseded public planning, tactics swamped strategy, and cosmetics dominated economics.' Two years of 'hard slog' between 1968 and 1970 did produce a balance of payments surplus, but this achievement was hardly the one that those enthusiasts for Wilson's New Britain would have expected after six years of a Labour government. Average economic growth between 1966 and 1970 was no more than 1.8 per cent a year whilst inflation doubled to over 6 per cent and unemployment had begun to edge up.

Was there more to what Clive Ponting called a 'breach of promise' than the personal failings of the Prime Minister? After all, if the immensely subtle and pliable Harold Wilson – a politician who had at various times been identified with every faction in his party – could not pull the rabbit of economic growth out of the hat, then it is highly unlikely anyone else could have done better.

Clearly the problem was more deep-rooted than mere personal failings. The Attlee governments after the Second World War had marked an end as well as a beginning. A social democratic society had been created and in its wake both Conservatives and Labour had done little more than administer it. This consensus was sometimes dubbed

'Butskellism', a recognition that R.A. Butler's Conservative approach was very similar to that of Hugh Gaitskell's.

It was as if a sturdy and comfortable family car which had given excellent service over the years had now begun to develop a series of faults. Instead of scrapping the car and buying a new one, the Wilson administration had instead confined itself to tinkering, with patching up here and there and hoping this would suffice. Worse still, Wilson had promised but failed to convert the saloon into a jazzy new sports model.

The Labour government had very briefly sketched out a blueprint for a new model, but this was soon scrapped. Wilson was therefore restricted to ad hoc repair work and 'crisis management'. If this failing undermined the Wilson years of the 1960s when the car was still in relatively good shape, how much worse would the problems be in the late 1970s, after yet further disrepair and bad treatment?

# Endings

## The British Left in the 1970s

'In all my dealings with the NUT [National Union of Teachers] at that time, I never once heard mention of education or children.'

BERNARD DONOUGHUE, SENIOR POLICY ADVISER AT
NO. 10 DOWNING STREET BETWEEN 1974 AND 1979

'You know there are times, perhaps once every 30 years, when there is a sea-change in politics. It then does not matter what you say or what you do. There is a shift in what the public wants and what it approves of. I suspect there is now such a sea-change – and it is for Mrs Thatcher.'

JAMES CALLAGHAN, LABOUR PRIME MINISTER, SPEAKING IN
MAY 1979 JUST BEFORE THE CONSERVATIVE ELECTION
VICTORY WAS KNOWN

'I have never been ashamed of being a [Labour] Party man, despite the media, because in my generation we owed a great debt to the Party. When education was a privilege and not a right, the movement was our education. We joined it out of our experience. We didn't express that in class terms, we joined the Party because of inequality – the theory came later.'

JAMES CALLAGHAN, OCTOBER 1980

The Cabinet Minister who had led the opposition to Barbara Castle's *In Place of Strife* proposals was James Callaghan, sometimes described by his colleagues as 'the Keeper of the Cloth Cap'; in other words, he was considered to be the individual

who would fight hardest to maintain the trade union–Labour
Party link.

Beginning work in the 1930s as a clerk in the Inland
Revenue and then being elected an MP in the landslide of
1945, Callaghan's subsequent political career was the familiar
story of a man once on the Left – in 1945 he had voted
against Britain's financial arrangements with the Americans
and resigned his junior ministerial post – who shifted gradually
towards the Right of the Labour Party. In the 1950s he was
a staunch Gaitskellite. He stood against Harold Wilson in the
1963 leadership contest, coming third behind Wilson and
George Brown but gaining enough votes to ensure himself
a senior post in any future Labour government.

Jim Callaghan owned a farm in Sussex and often claimed
to embody what he called his 'God-given common sense.'
His speeches were full of expressions like 'Bless my soul'
and he clearly fancied himself as Labour's belated answer to
Stanley Baldwin, though Harold Wilson also coveted this role.
Callaghan certainly emulated Baldwin in his keen sense of
political power, and he remains the only man to have occupied
the four major offices of Chancellor of the Exchequer, Home
Secretary, Foreign Secretary and Prime Minister.

It was rather less clear what if any political ideas motivated
him. Back in 1956 Hugh Gaitskell had commented in his
diary: 'He [Callaghan] is a most talented Parliamentarian and
a man of very considerable charm, but he seems to me to have
absolutely no philosophical basis. You never know what he is
going to say.' Jim Callaghan's most lasting achievements have,
in fact, nothing directly to do with politics; as Parliamentary
Secretary at the Ministry of Transport at the end of the Attlee
governments, he resurrected two forgotten projects that led to
the introduction of zebra crossings and cat's eyes.

Callaghan was appointed Chancellor of the Exchequer in
1964. His most important and fateful decision proved to be
his first: not to devalue the pound. The next three years were
spent defending this position. The devaluation of November

1967 was clearly an admission of defeat and Callaghan was moved to the post of Home Secretary. In August 1969 he sent British troops into Ulster. Working on the recipe for political success which he had supposedly outlined to George Wigg back in the 1940s – namely waiting for the trade unions to decide their line and then following them – Jim Callaghan successfully defeated Barbara Castle's proposals for trade union reform. Ten years later his actions would return to haunt him.

In March 1974 Callaghan became Foreign Secretary in Harold Wilson's minority government, a post he continued to hold after the October election had given Labour a small majority. He spent most of the next two years renegotiating Britain's place in the EEC and therefore missed the domestic drama as the Wilson administration struggled to cope with rampant inflation, rising unemployment and zero economic growth.

Unlike the Labour governments of 1945 and 1964, Wilson's 1974 administration came to office armed with a formidable batch of programmes and plans. After 1970 the Labour Party had devoted much time to drawing up suitable blueprints for any future Labour government; at one point over fifty committees and nearly a thousand people were hard at work on behalf of the National Executive Committee (NEC), the Party's ruling body when out of office. The only problem was that Harold Wilson and most of his Cabinet strongly opposed the NEC's proposals – Wilson deliberately failed to turn up at meetings.

The Labour Party Constitution drawn up in 1918 by Sidney Webb and Arthur Henderson had reflected the variety of opinions and organisations that made up the British Labour Party. In particular, Webb and Henderson ensured that the federal Party had no single source of authority. Instead a tripartite balance was envisaged between the Parliamentary Labour Party, the constituency Labour Parties and the Party's annual Conference, which was in turn dominated by the trade union block vote.

Such an arrangement, admirable in theory and often in practice, nevertheless meant that the Party was prone to factionalism because different groups could wield influence in one or other of the three bodies. By contrast the Conservative Party's lines of authority were rather more flexible and informal and discouraged internal pressure groups.

The situation was even more complex whenever a Labour government took office. Labour Prime Ministers and Cabinets argued that national concerns had to take priority over party matters and thereby felt justified in ignoring unwelcome Conference decisions. A Labour Prime Minister can supplement his party powers with that of national patronage. When the Labour Party is out of office, the National Executive Committee elected by the annual Conference regains its influence.

An early example of the friction between the NEC and the leader of the Parliamentary Labour Party came in 1945 when Chairman Harold Laski tried to prevent Clement Attlee becoming Prime Minister. It was in the 1970s, however, that tempers frayed when the NEC, partly in response to the seeming disappointments of the Wilson governments between 1964 and 1970, moved leftwards.

The rank and file was also becoming much less deferential to the leadership. As Patrick Seyd and other commentators noted, the 1970s witnessed a growing radicalisation of three groups in particular within the Labour Party: local councillors, activists, and a number of prominent trade union leaders. In addition, women members and, to a lesser extent, black people also argued that radical internal reforms were needed. In effect, the various shades of opinion within the Labour Party were turning into factions or 'tendencies'.

The advantage of this diversity was and is that the Labour Party often encompasses a vigour and excitement superior to its political rivals. The drawback is the image of disunity this turmoil conveys to the electorate – as much time can be spent fighting internal battles as external ones. Harold Wilson once claimed that:

> This party is a bit like an old stagecoach. If you drive it rapidly, everyone aboard is either so exhilarated or so seasick that you don't have a lot of difficulty. If you keep stopping, however, then everyone gets out and starts arguing about which way to go.

Wilson's own governments of 1964–70 had brought the stagecoach to a grinding halt, and now everyone was only too keen to discuss future directions.

In the Labour past most of its successful pressure groups had been created by its right wing, notably the Campaign for Democratic Socialism which helped Hugh Gaitskell reverse the 1960 Conference resolution in favour of unilateralism. Now, however, left-wing groups such as the Campaign for Labour Party Democracy (CLPD), formed in 1973, brought disciplined pressure to bear on local constituency parties and then on the annual Conference by putting forward suggested resolutions and working hard to get them accepted.

This leftwards shift was reinforced by the changing political complexion of unions such as the Transport and General Workers' Union and the Engineers. Back in the 1950s the Labour Party leadership could rely on the stolid and unquestioning support of leaders such as Arthur Deakin and William Carron in order to defeat the Bevanites by means of the block vote. But now, in the 1970s, the 'Big Two' were more left-wing and less inclined to offer unthinking support for Harold Wilson and his Cabinet colleagues. Left-wing unions naturally put left-wing nominees on the NEC.

In 1973 the old 'proscribed list', which had banned members of certain groups and bodies – usually Communist or Trotskyist – from joining the Labour Party was scrapped. From now on the Labour Party was such a broad church that anyone, even 'atheists', were welcome. With 'no enemies to the Left', there was a place for everyone. The Trotskyist Militant Tendency would later make the most of this opportunity.

These organisational changes were reinforced by the determination of many never again to have a government like Harold Wilson's between 1966 and 1970, which had clearly run out of steam and ideas on how best to create a new and fairer Britain. Industrial events in the early 1970s also seemed to confirm that militancy could sometimes pay off.

The Heath government took office in 1970 with a 'no lame ducks' policy under which industrial failures would no longer be bailed out by the state. In the summer of 1971 the men in the yards of the Upper Clyde Shipbuilders organised a 'work in' to protest at forthcoming redundancies. Well led by their shop stewards who included Jimmy Reid and Jimmy Airlie, the men won the support of the labour movement and the Scottish public. In February 1972 the Heath administration backed down, writing off £17 million in old losses and providing a further £18 million for capital development.

This volte-face repudiating Heath's original intention to unshackle market forces was confirmed by the Industry Act of 1972 which supported intervention. Trade union action also defeated Heath's Industrial Relations Act intended to reform the industrial movement, and the two miners' strikes of 1973 and 1974 patently demonstrated that the nominal government under Heath was no longer in charge.

Revived interest in Marxism since the 1960s also prompted the Labour Left to scorn piecemeal political reform in favour of a much grander and wide-ranging approach. The failures of British capitalism were attributed to low productivity and an inefficient private sector. In particular, for decades British investment in the public sector had lagged behind that of its rivals. Influential figures on the NEC working committees urged Britain to emulate the Italian public corporation IRI (Instituto di Riconstuzione Industriale), which controlled not just ailing industries but also supervised thriving sectors of the economy.

The Attlee governments had nationalised run-down and bankrupt industries, giving state enterprise a bad name because it was identified with apparent failure. On the other hand, for economists like Stuart Holland, IRI's record in '. . . promoting investment, countering recession caused by investment hesitation in the private sector, locating all employment from entirely new plant in the problem region of the Italian South, and directly or indirectly countering the challenge to national sovereignty from multinational companies . . .' offered a refreshing contrast. Any future Labour government should create a body with much more clout than Wilson's Industrial Reorganisation Corporation which had patently lacked the resources to restructure British industry.

The NEC's plans included the creation of a National Enterprise Board which would take a stake in up to twenty-five of the country's leading manufacturing firms. The leading banks and insurance companies were to be nationalised. Planning agreements would ensure the fulfilment of economic targets. Measures of industrial democracy would give the workforce a greater say in the running of each business and import controls would protect Britain's balance of payments. As they conflicted with EEC rules, it was therefore essential that Britain should leave the Common Market. Finally, a wealth tax levied on the rich would siphon off money for redistribution to the poor.

Overall these ideas represented a return to the fundamentalist Clause Four tradition of the Labour Party in abeyance since the days of Gaitskell and which Wilson's 'New Britain' had not revived. They entailed a massive increase in the role of government, marking a break from the mixed economy which had been at the heart of the post-war consensus administered by both Labour and Conservative governments since 1945.

It is hardly surprising that the 'old guard' in the form of Tony Crosland, who himself had always argued that the issue of public ownership was largely irrelevant, fiercely opposed these new policies. In 1971 he had claimed that: 'No one can say the party is in sight of formulating a better set of policies than we had in June 1970, when we were dismissed from office.' Not surprisingly, he described the new NEC proposals as 'idiotic' and 'half-baked', but they still appeared in the Labour Party's programme of 1973 and in both the 1974 election manifestos.

Crosland's invective is mild when compared with the strictures of another Cabinet minister, Edmund Dell, who has since published a scathing account of his own government's incompetence between 1974 and 1976. Here is Dell's assessment of Labour's position on entering government in 1974: 'There is no comparable example of such intellectual and political incoherence in a party coming into office in the twentieth century history of the United Kingdom.'

Dell's comments are given additional weight because his previous career with ICI had taught him something about the wider industrial and business world. In general, however, when looking back on these heated debates the most striking feature is how inexperienced in economic matters most of the participants were. Take Denis Healey, for instance, who was appointed Shadow Chancellor of the Exchequer in 1972 and luridly warned the rich that he would make their pips squeak. In his memoirs Healey himself candidly admitted his own lack of expertise:

> . . . I had no ministerial experience in the field. Moreover, I had no more knowledge of economics than the average newspaper reader – and I had never bothered to look at the City pages. Now I had to engage the Government over every aspect of finance, taxation, industrial and economic policy.

Tony Benn, a leading advocate of the new approach, was hardly more economically literate. An MP since the age of twenty-five, he had only ever worked for the BBC and therefore possessed no direct experience of industry. Bernard Donoughue, senior adviser at No. 10 between 1974 and 1979, commented on meeting Benn and his advisers that: '. . . none of them conveyed the impression that they had any direct experience of working life or had the least idea of what made a factory or a service industry succeed or fail.' Similarly Joel Barnett, a trained accountant who for five years was Chief Secretary at the Treasury, has pointed out that several Cabinet colleagues could not even read a simple balance sheet.

But if Harold Wilson and his Cabinet faced unsettling internal pressures, the external position proved even worse. In the long term, the share of British manufactured goods in the world export market had declined from over 20 per cent in the 1950s to under 10 per cent in the 1970s. Competition from the Third World and fellow EEC countries was intensifying. The pound was overvalued and sterling crises always likely. Inflation was rising steadily and, in fact, averaged 16 per cent a year between 1974 and 1978. Unemployment climbed inexorably past the one million figure. Finally, the oil crisis of 1973–74 saw a quadrupling in prices and plunged the world economy into prolonged recession.

If that was not enough, Wilson led a minority government between March 1974 and October 1974 and even the second general election of 1974 gave it only a tenuous majority. As David Coates has observed, 'A majority of three for a party in which two of its members were under police investigation [for alleged involvement in local government corruption] was not the strongest base from which to launch a busy legislative programme, and even that slender majority did not last long.'

Lumbered with Labour Party policies which he heartily disapproved of, facing a world recession and in charge of a country which had just been through the turmoil of strikes and three-day weeks, Wilson's approach as Prime Minister seemed to be one of 'do as little as possible'. He himself admitted to one close adviser soon after taking office in 1974 that 'I have been around this racetrack so often that I cannot generate any more enthusiasm for jumping any more hurdles.' Even when the government attempted to do something positive, such as the introduction of the Northern Ireland Assembly, its policies were destroyed by the Ulster Workers' Council strike of May 1974 and direct rule had to be re-established.

Wilson's 'do-nothing' stance was also behind his decision to hold a referendum in 1975 over Britain's membership of the EEC. This was taken not on the grounds that the people should have a say in the matter, but because it would best hold the Labour Party together in the face of the 1973 Conference decision – with which he disagreed – that any future Labour government should withdraw from Brussels. This resolution had been reaffirmed by a margin of two to one at a special Conference held in April 1975. As was so often the case during the Wilson years, the Conference and the party leadership disagreed.

The question of Europe was not simply a Labour Right versus Labour Left issue nor one of 'nationalism versus internationalism'. Hugh Gaitskell, for instance, had been opposed to membership, as was his prominent supporter Douglas Jay. On the other hand, Gaitskellites Roy Jenkins and Bill Rodgers were strongly in favour whilst both Denis Healey and Tony Benn changed their minds on this issue. Some Labour leaders argued that the important links with the Commonwealth and the United States would be jeopardised by membership of the Common Market, others maintained that Britain's economic decline meant that any other policy would be suicidal.

As it turned out, the referendum result of June 1975 was decisive. The public voted two to one to stay within the EEC. In the aftermath of the result, Harold Wilson demoted Tony Benn from his crucial post at the Department of Trade and Industry to a less important job at the Department of Energy, confirming how the Labour government was diluting and undermining the National Executive's proposals of the early 1970s. Remaining within the EEC was a massive reversal of policy.

Just as crucially, the unprincipled and cynical way in which the Labour leadership – particularly Harold Wilson

– had handled this European issue fuelled growing public dissatisfaction with politics in general and the Labour Party in particular. Roy Jenkins later came to the conclusion that 'the handling of the European question by the leadership throughout the 1970s did more to cause the party's disasters of the 1980s than did any other issue.'

Other opportunist somersaults followed. The National Enterprise Board (NEB), for example, when it was eventually set up, was given funds of only £1,000 million over four years – not nearly enough for the state to establish a significant role within the private sector let alone occupy 'the commanding heights of the economy'. Instead the NEB found itself propping up uneconomic businesses like British Leyland and British Steel. It was left to deal with 'the walking wounded of the industrial collapse', reinforcing once again the link between public control and inefficiency first established by the Attlee governments.

The Wilson administration backed away from nationalising the banks and the insurance companies, whilst planning agreements turned out to be a farce. Not a single agreement was signed with any company other than Chrysler and with the National Coal Board, in any case a part of the government; nor did companies have to disclose relevant information to the unions.

Another letdown was in the field of industrial democracy: co-opting members of the workforce onto the board and giving them a greater say in the running of the business. This issue had been explored in an inquiry headed by Professor Alan Bullock. Even his watered-down proposals aroused conflicting opinions within the trade union movement because some argued they would dilute and confuse the function of trade unions. The proposals were quietly shelved.

The government proved even less successful when dealing with the private sector because of its inability to bargain with multinational companies on equal terms. The companies knew full well that the Labour administration was desperate not to increase unemployment and so in the last resort they could always threaten to close down their factories and move to another country. Chrysler, for example, was one organisation that shamelessly took the government for a ride, obtaining a large subsidy of over £160 million but eventually selling out to another company which promptly closed down its factories, despite the earlier state support.

To left-wing accusations that he was 'betraying' party policy, Wilson could always claim that the Parliamentary Labour Party (PLP) was free to go its own way. The constitutional position was, in fact, confused. The 1907 Labour Party Conference had established that Conference resolutions were binding on the PLP, but added this important proviso: 'on the understanding that the time and methods of giving effect to these instructions be left to the Party in the House [of Commons], in conjunction with the National Executive.'

Harold Wilson was therefore perfectly entitled to argue, and frequently did so, that in his opinion 'the time and methods' were not right for the implementation of the NEC's policies. His attitude was bound to result in a campaign for a new relationship between the various sections of the movement.

It was only to be expected that Harold Wilson should tire of politics, subject as he was to a persistent 'dirty tricks' campaign which had lasted for years and included libels in the *Daily Mail* – always the Conservative Party's best Fleet Street friend – burglaries of his friends and rumours of disaffection among the intelligence services and the army which turned out to be well-justified. Peter Wright's book *Spycatcher* details the anti-Wilson hysteria which infected parts of the British establishment. In any case, Wilson had always intended to resign in 1976 on reaching the age of sixty.

In April 1976, six contenders entered the ballot to elect not just a party leader but also a Prime Minister. Five of the contestants had been educated at Oxford University – Tony Benn, Denis Healey, Roy Jenkins, Anthony Crosland and Michael Foot – which was testimony to the changing character and background of the Parliamentary Labour Party. Compare their educational attainments with those of Keir Hardie, Ramsay MacDonald, J.R. Clynes and Ernest Bevin, whose schooling had been virtually non-existent.

But it was the sixth contender, James Callaghan, who had left school at sixteen, who eventually won. The contest went to a third ballot in which Callaghan defeated Foot by a margin of 176 votes to 137. Voting was still confined to members of the Parliamentary Labour Party, a procedure that some MPs had begun to criticise. Rather touchingly, when the chairman of the Parliamentary Labour Party told him he had won, Callaghan cried. 'Prime Minister,' he said to himself. 'And I never even went to university.'

Callaghan had indeed made it to the top of the greasy pole, but this was the politician who, back in 1969, had sabotaged Barbara Castle's *In Place of Strife* proposals. Yet he now faced both a severe economic crisis and the might of the trade union movement on whose support his political career had rested.

The diaries of Richard Crossman, Barbara Castle and Tony Benn, which cover the Wilson governments of 1964 to 1970, all tell a story of hopes dashed and expectations frustrated. The 'inside' stories so far published of the 1974 to 1979 Labour governments – namely from Benn and Castle again, but also from Wilson's press secretary Joe Haines, from Bernard Donoughue, Joel Barnett and Edmund Dell – make even gloomier reading. Each week seems to have brought a fresh crisis that was promptly mishandled just in time for the government to lurch into the next pitfall. In Donoughue's pungent words, 'It was like being on the sinking Titanic, but without the music.'

Joel Barnett's account, for instance, is dominated by the long search for cuts that repeatedly had to be made in the health, housing, education and social security budgets. Denis Healey delivered no fewer than fourteen budgets between March 1974 and June 1978. Ministers developed all kinds of ploys in order to resist cuts to their own departments. During one session Peter Shore, the Minister for the Environment, thumped the table with such vigour that fellow members of the Cabinet began to fear for his health:

> . . . the moral for spending Ministers must be to behave in as prickly a manner as possible. Better still, leave the impression that if you lose, you might not only resign, but become so convulsed with the strength of your case as to push your blood pressure right up and collapse on the Cabinet table.

The major problem for the government was that the orthodox techniques propounded by Keynesianism for use in economic recession no longer seemed to work. Denis Healey pulled the familiar levers in order to increase demand. He therefore cut the rate of VAT, froze rents, increased food subsidies and raised pensions, a policy which one historian has since called 'Father Christmas economics'.

Unfortunately, Healey's policies resulted in raging inflation which was in turn fuelled by the indexed pay increases granted to certain employees by the Heath government. Unemployment rose whilst economic growth stagnated. One explanation was that, because governments of all persuasions were nominally committed to full employment, public money was often diverted to propping up uneconomic businesses in deprived areas which the government could not allow to go bust for political reasons.

Such considerations explained the Chrysler debacle. Harold Wilson had not dared let the firm fold with the loss of nearly 40,000 jobs. Martin Holmes scathingly concluded that: 'The artificial preservation of jobs in fossilised industries was the central feature, in practice, of the government's industrial strategy.'

The Labour government's interventionist hopes were undermined too by the lack of practical expertise to be found inside the Department of Industry. One of the Party's leading financial experts, Harold Lever, has complained that: '. . . the civil servants in the Department of Industry were ill-equipped to make investment decisions. They had no background in industry and no experience.' According to Joe Haines, the Treasury proved even less helpful, being completely devoid of new ideas and desperately favouring either a statutory incomes policy or huge expenditure cuts. But that was not the end of it, as Denis Healey has written:

> For my first budget, three weeks after I took office, the Treasury gave me an estimate of the PSBR [Public Sector Borrowing Requirement] in 1974–5 which – leaving aside all the fiscal changes later in the year – turned out to be £4,000 million too low. This was the equivalent of 5.4 per cent of that year's GDP. The magnitude of that one forecasting error was greater than that of any fiscal change made by any Chancellor in British history. Two years later, in 1976, the Budget estimate of the PSBR was £2,000 million too high; and in November of that year I handed an estimate to the IMF [International Monetary Fund] which turned out to be twice as high as it should have been . . . If I had been give accurate forecasts in 1976, I would never have needed to go to the IMF at all.

In view of such startling ineptitude – even though the best civil service brains are supposed to end up at the Treasury – it is perhaps remarkable that Britain did not go bust years ago.

One further problem was that the financial markets, capitalist to the nth degree, have always distrusted socialist governments and often therefore panic, moving funds away from sterling. Harold Wilson, of course, knew all about this; in his history of the 1964–70 governments he wrote of the events leading up to devaluation in November 1967: '. . . what strikes me now as then was the suddenness with which we had been overwhelmed by the operations of a speculative market.' Writing of his time as Prime Minister, Jim Callaghan was more descriptive: 'The markets behaved with all the restraint of a screaming crowd of schoolgirls at a rock concert.'

In such circumstances the pound was always under pressure and within weeks of his election as Prime Minister, Callaghan faced a major sterling crisis. It must have been horribly reminiscent of events twelve years before when he had been Harold Wilson's Chancellor of the Exchequer. Pressure on the pound coincided with a bungled attempt by the Bank of England – running the Treasury a close second in the incompetency stakes – to bring down the value of sterling when they committed the schoolboy error of selling on an already falling market. Suddenly the pound was plummeting fast. Denis Healey was forced to increase interest rates yet again and draw up plans for the further cuts necessary if a loan from the IMF was to be obtained.

On 28 September 1976 the situation deteriorated so rapidly that Healey, on his way to an international conference, was forced to turn back at Heathrow. He travelled instead to the Labour Party Conference to demonstrate that the government had things in hand, opening his speech with the dramatic words, 'I come from the battlefront.' The discrepancy between a government struggling with day-to-day events and the Conference was vividly revealed by a motion passed only the day before calling for the nationalisation of the banks.

At this same Conference of 1976, Jim Callaghan's speech hammered the final nails into the coffin of Keynesianism:

> We used to think you could spend your way out of a recession and increase employment by cutting taxes and boosting spending. I tell you in all candour that this option no longer exists, and that insofar as it ever did exist, it only worked by injecting a bigger dose of inflation into the system.

But if Keynesianism was dead, then this Labour government was apparently left with only one other option: go to the IMF for aid. This was entirely in line with the thinking of the forceful Denis Healey. Educated at Bradford Grammer School and then Oxford, Healey headed the Labour Party's

International Department after the war. He had moved a long way from his student Communist days at university and was an aggressive Gaitskellite during the Labour Party's civil wars in the 1950s.

Healey had been Minister of Defence from 1964–70 and – although a formidable politician – never bothered to build up a following in the Party, largely because of his bluntness towards his colleagues. Ian Mikardo described Healey as 'a political bully wielding the language of sarcasm and contempt like a caveman's cudgel.' Another reason becomes evident from Healey's autobiography *The Time of My Life* which shows that for him the important things in life are not necessarily political: family, books, travel, the arts, good food and drink. From the summer of 1976 he had little time for any of these passions as he and Callaghan struggled to save the British economy from collapse.

The events of the next few months have been told in detail by two journalists, Stephen Fay and Hugo Young, whose pacy account of the negotiations with the IMF reads like a high-powered thriller. Bankers check into hotels under assumed names. Telephones are bugged. The 'hot line' between Callaghan and President Ford in Washington gets hotter. Callaghan secretly tries to enlist the help of Chancellor Schmidt of West Germany. Meetings are held, at the end of which no one is quite sure who has said, or agreed to, what. The upshot was that in early December 1976 the Cabinet met to decide whether to support the strategy of Chancellor Healey who demanded immediate government spending cuts of £1 billion with a further £1 billion to come the following year if an IMF loan was to be secured.

Different options were available. Tony Benn, for instance, argued that the IMF terms should be rejected in favour of a retreat into a siege economy behind a wall of import controls; in effect a policy of 'socialism in one country'. Denis Healey ridiculed this argument: 'He [Tony Benn] wants us to withdraw into the citadel, but only so long as we can slip out occasionally to borrow the money to buy the bows and arrows we'll need to shoot at the besieging armies.'

Tony Crosland, the Foreign Secretary but also a trained economist, was equally unhappy with the prospect of further cuts in welfare yet failed to come up with a viable alternative. One Cabinet colleague recalled what happened:

> That was the day Croslandism died. He [Crosland] said to me: 'This is nonsense, but we must do it.' He knew it meant the abandonment of his position as a revisionist theorist. He knew he was going up a cul-de-sac. It was a tormenting time for him. I watched him, torturing himself.

Edmund Dell describes Crosland's proposals as having 'something in common with King Lear's helpless outcry against the cruelty of his daughters.'

'Croslandism' had maintained that a greater measure of equality could be achieved by means of economic growth, planning and state intervention. But now, in the mid-1970s, almost every variable in that equation no longer held true. The world recession had also underlined the fact that Britain's national sovereignty over her own economic affairs had been sharply reduced.

But if Croslandism was rejected then so too was the fundamentalist Clause Four approach of Tony Benn, though even his political opponents such as Joel Barnett have stressed how cogently he argued his case. One important reason was his lack of success in funding three workers' co-operatives which had grown out of 'sit-ins' held after management announced plans to close down the Meriden motorbike works, Kirkby Manufacturing and the *Scottish Daily News*. Always the realist, Joel Barnett has written that: 'The three co-operatives had one thing in common: they all began life with just about the worst possible prospects for success.' Despite £10 million of investment, they all collapsed.

Benn's opponents made much of these failures and although

£10 million was indeed a paltry sum when compared with the £800 million distributed to industry in 1974–75 alone, the episode demonstrated yet again the Left's patchy record when it comes to wealth creation rather than distribution. This valid criticism has often been levelled at the trade union movement, not that British management always proved very successful at the same task.

By the mid-1970s mounting wage costs clearly lay at the heart of Britain's increasing uncompetitiveness. But in view of the historic and continuing links between the trade unions and the Labour Party, it was very difficult for the political arm of the movement to reform its industrial and financial arm, as Harold Wilson and Barbara Castle knew only too well. David Owen, a junior minister at the time, feels that if the Labour government had stood up to the unions over *Strife* and won, then in turn the general election of 1970 would have been won.

But of course the government had backed down. Why? The figures spoke for themselves. By 1979, for instance, 151 out of 269 Labour MPs were sponsored either by a trade union or by the co-operative movement. The union block vote comprised no less than 89 per cent of the entire vote at each annual Conference, whilst union donations provided virtually the only source of money for the Party's general election fund. The division between the industrial and political wings of the movement was evident at NEC meetings where the politicians sat on one side of the table, the trade unionists on the other.

Full employment had greatly increased trade union power because managers now had no 'reserve army of the unemployed' to call upon. It was often easier, and less costly, for employers to buy off union demands, thus stoking up wage inflation. The leaders of the largest unions, such as the Engineers and the Transport and General Workers', were very powerful figures and ever since the Conservatives had introduced the National Economic Development Council in 1962 they had become accustomed to dealing with government and employers on equal terms.

Between 1968 and 1978 Jack Jones was General Secretary of the two-million-strong Transport and General Workers' Union. Jones' autobiography *Union Man* testifies to his wide-ranging influence. Dubbed 'Emperor Jones' by his critics, he found that not only did his suggestions end up as government legislation – as with the arbitration and conciliation service ACAS and the employment protection statutes – but he was also courted by Prime Ministers from Heath to Wilson and Callaghan; asked to be a minister and a peer; invited to address five hundred top international businessmen in Switzerland and shared jokes with the Queen and Prince Philip. Never self-conscious or nervous, Jones was always supremely confident that he, as leader of the country's biggest union, deserved nothing less.

It was, and is, true that the only way most workers can defend their interests is through collective bodies such as trade unions. As Will Hutton has put it, 'British trade unions, founded and defined in corporate opposition to capital, were never organised to do other than champion a very narrow conception of working-class interest.' This confrontation was institutionalised in an annual wage round: the Bosses in one corner took on the Workers in the other.

But the only sanctions the unions can impose are to withdraw their labour, work to rule or 'go slow', which normally affects public opinion negatively. By the 1970s the unions were becoming ever more unpopular. Even a sympathetic observer such as journalist Robert Taylor criticised their ramshackle organisation, their anti-intellectualism and the 'insular outlook of many union leaders'.

The unions did little to combat this unappealing image; for instance, they rarely sponsored arts projects or other 'good will' initiatives. In 1956 Tony Crosland had advised them to widen their agenda of collective bargaining towards fringe benefits, and four years later the TUC did pass a resolution noting that 'the trade union movement has participated to only a small extent in the direct promotion of plays, films, music and literature and other forms of expression . . .'

Out of this resolution grew the short-lived Centre 42 project, spurred on by the playwright Arnold Wesker. Festivals and concerts were held, but the labour movement failed to provide either finance or audiences; as Wesker himself admitted, the general public found the association between trade unions and the arts rather offputting. The Roundhouse in Camden was acquired in the summer of 1964, but the whole initiative simply fizzled out. In addition, few trade union leaders were ever associated with non-union issues – unlike Jack Jones who did much to try and raise the level of pensions.

The unions' concentration on wage levels was sometimes dubbed 'economism'. Cabinet minister Barbara Castle's reaction to Mrs Thatcher's election as leader of the Conservative Party in February 1975 was revealing:

> . . . men have been running the show as long as anyone can remember and they don't seem to have made much of a job of it. The excitement of switching to a woman might stir a lot of people out of their lethargy. I think it will be a good thing for the Labour Party too. There's a male-dominated party for you – not least because the trade unions are male-dominated, even the ones that cater for women. I remember just before the February election last year pleading on the NEC for us not to have a completely producer-oriented policy, because women lose out in the producer-run society. The battle for cash wage increases is a masculine obsession. Women are not sold on it, particularly when it leads to strikes, because the men often don't pass their cash increases on to their wives.

Mrs Castle went on:

> What matters to women is the social wage. Of course, no one listened to me: even to suggest that the battle for cash wage increases might be a mirage is to show disloyalty to

trade unionism! I believe Margaret Thatcher's election will force our party to think again: and a jolly good thing too. To me, socialism isn't just militant trade unionism. It is the gentle society, in which every producer remembers he is a consumer too.

Most people's memories of the 1974–79 Labour governments are dominated by images of trade union unrest, secondary picketing and civil disorder that culminated in 'the Winter of Discontent' of 1978–79. This is misleading because, in fact, for the first three and a half years of this government the so-called 'Social Contract' brought prolonged and peaceful wage restraint which helped to bring inflation down from a peak of nearly 30 per cent in the summer of 1975.

The difficulty with any incomes policy was that not only did it fetter the bargaining powers of the strongest trade unions, but it also required union leaders to 'do the government's dirty work' for them by imposing restraint on their own members. This could only be a short-term policy because, in the end, trade union leaders' loyalty was to their members rather than to a government, even a Labour one. If they lost contact with their members then the shop stewards, who were much closer to the workforce on the shop floor, stepped into the vacuum.

The Attlee government had introduced formal wage restraint, a measure duly rejected within just two years by trade union leaders otherwise impeccably loyal to the administration. In the 1960s Harold Wilson relied on a Prices and Incomes Board. His legislation had provoked the resignation of the most important trade union Cabinet member, Frank Cousins. Both experiences bore out only too well the truth of Cabinet minister Michael Stewart's remark:

Throughout the whole history of incomes policies, now stretching over a generation, the trouble has been that governments do not consciously embark on such policies until acute economic difficulty obliges them to do so. In consequence, the policy always takes the form of telling people that their standard of life must either remain stationary or go down; and this makes the whole idea unpopular.

At the beginning of the 1974 Labour government the trade union leadership acted thoroughly responsibly in its attitude towards pay increases, especially when senior management displayed no such restraint and the government's price controls turned out to be ineffective. They also tried to make a go of the Social Contract initiated by Jack Jones which went some way towards meeting Barbara Castle's 'social wage' arguments. Speaking at the 1975 TUC Conference, General Secretary Len Murray could hardly have been more explicit:

> Some people, for a time, are going to have some reduction in their living standards. We are a low wage country. That is because our country's industrial performance has been low, below that of our competitors; because investment has been too low and too often in the wrong places and because in turn productivity has been too low. We cannot put that right in real terms merely by paying ourselves more money.

This stance could not survive for long. The Labour government did pass legislation strengthening the union movement and the rights of its members, such as the Trade and Union Labour Relations Acts of 1974 and 1976, a Health and Safety at Work Act, a Sex Discrimination Act and an Equal Pay Act. But even these measures were of secondary importance behind the issue of wage claims.

The perceived failure of Harold Wilson's 1964–70 governments had led to a general demoralisation within the Party as a whole. Ben Pimlott has recalled his experiences when joining an inner-city party in the late 1960s:

> The memory is scarcely golden. It was not just the evidence of membership decline, or the lack of youth. It was the weary cynicism, the lack of collective ambition, the indifference to political issues. Each new recruit had a different story: the difficulty of joining, ward parties which never met, the corruption of local councillors, agents exclusively concerned with raising their own salaries, GMCs which could not raise a quorum, and, above all, keenness treated as evidence of subversion.

It was hardly to be wondered at that many young socialists left the Labour Party in disgust. Some channelled their energies into single-issue campaigns such as Shelter, Child Poverty Action Group, the Anti-Apartheid Movement or even the Young Liberals.

Others joined the 'Far Left' groups like International Socialism (who later became the Socialist Workers' Party), the International Marxist Group or the Workers' Revolutionary Party. Members of most of these groups were numbered in dozens rather than hundreds, although their energy and vociferousness often disguised this fact. As had been the case with Hyndman's Social Democratic Federation or the Communist Party, the number of ex-members always outnumbered present recruits.

One interesting sidelight shows that although the British Communist Party had never been very successful in its own right, it was not a negligible force. Three of the four key individuals discussing wage policy at this time – Denis Healey, Len Murray of the TUC and Hugh Scanlon of the Engineers – were all former members of the Communist Party, whilst the fourth, Jack Jones, had fought for the Communist-dominated International Brigade during the Spanish Civil War in the 1930s. Two other important union leaders, Clive Jenkins and Frank Chapple, had also once been party members.

The 1970s witnessed a marked expansion in radical culture – there were at least twenty-five left-wing publishers together with a network of bookshops and dozens of journals and magazines. The ten radical bookshops open in 1970 had grown to 150 by 1980 and the use of the small photo-offset printing press and the IBM composer for typesetting ensured that these shops were always bursting with pamphlets and newspapers.

Today, much of this material is faintly comical because of the revolutionary posturing which seems to have been de rigeur, wonderfully epitomised by one incident: students gathering in the rooms of left-wing Cambridge don Raymond Williams, lolling on the floor and fervently discussing how best to dispose of the monarchy whilst deferential college servants brought in tea and cakes. It irresistibly reminds one of the scene at the end of George Orwell's *Animal Farm* when the pigs take over.

In particular, the fight against Edward Heath's Industrial Relations Act led some radicals to believe that the millennium was now at hand. For instance, Tariq Ali of the International Marxist Group published a book in 1972 called *The Coming British Revolution* predicting that: '. . . the coming decade will see the beginning of social upheavals and explosions which will totally shatter the complacency of the British bourgeoisie as it tries to adjust to the changed situation.' A Postscript added confidently that 'we shall once again see soviets in Europe in the 'seventies.' In view of Tariq Ali's distinguished later career as a television producer it was probably just as well that his forecast proved inaccurate.

Few within the British labour movement paid even lip-service to women's issues. Robert Taylor observed that when 'female' matters came up for debate on Tuesday mornings at the annual TUC Conference, the male delegates always stampeded towards the bars. The offputting 'male' language of both trade unions and Labour Conferences – 'Brother this' and 'Brother that' – subtly excluded women. The Communist tradition of referring to fellow party members as 'Comrades' was hardly more inviting.

It was little different elsewhere on the Left, as Lynne Segal has recalled in terms reminiscent of the complaints voiced throughout this book:

> . . . while women were active in all the campaigns that were going on, they were active in a subordinate way. So they were the ones licking the envelopes and making the cups of tea. They were the ones doing the background work while the men were in the foreground.

One important feature of the women's movement was that it valued those personal feelings and experiences which both labourism and communism had usually ignored as irrelevant. What you said and did was certainly important, but so too was *how* you said and did things. Why shouldn't people say 'I don't know' or even – horror of horrors – 'I was wrong'? All this was very different from the dogmatism characteristic of several parts of the British Left.

Many on the Left failed to recognise that, in Beatrix Campbell's words, '. . . protest has only a limited life – it has to ferment into the politics of the possible.' At the same time the British Right was showing how this could be done. The 1970s saw the establishment of institutions such as the Centre for Policy Studies, or the rejuvenation of older bodies like the Institute of Economic Affairs.

Unlike the left-wing groups, however, these 'think-tanks' made it their business to know the way around 'the corridors of power' and were fully aware of how best to present proposals in a clear and concise way. Their publications became required reading for ambitious Conservative MPs. It is difficult to imagine that Labour MPs found much of use in the pages of *New Left Review* or *Socialist Worker*.

This renaissance in right-wing thinking was particularly adept at homing in on the expansion of personal choice. 'Labourism' was especially vulnerable to the onslaught because it had traditionally been associated with controls, size and faceless bureaucracy. Collective action had so often been impersonal and the anti-government mood played on this dissatisfaction.

Take the question of council house sales. There was no intrinsic reason why people should not own their homes, except that it went against the Labour Party's instinctive preference for 'mass' over individual choice. Labour governments, just like Labour councils, implicitly agreed with Douglas Jay (a minister under both Attlee and Wilson), when he had claimed that 'the Gentleman in Whitehall is usually right' – christened the 'We Know Best' tendency. Roy Hattersley once described the rules and regulations laid down by the Labour council in Sheffield:

> There was a time when pigeon-keeping was prohibited on Sheffield council estates and when, in the same city, it was an offence (punishable with eviction) to paint a front door in anything except the stipulated colour, to fence in pieces of garden which were adjacent to individual houses but designated collective property, or to make structural changes inside or outside which, in private property, would have been unhesitatingly designated as improvements.

This bossy and prohibitive uniformity always represented one powerful strand within Fabian thinking. Just as tower blocks were originally considered a beneficial exercise in social engineering – and if people didn't like being storeys up in the sky without a garden but with vandalised lifts, that was their problem, not 'ours' – so council house sales were ruled out. Tenants' rights were potentially subversive and therefore frowned upon.

It would be both wrong and unfair to denigrate the generous spirit which originally lay behind this approach. In Plymouth, for instance, more buildings were demolished in order to meet the requirements of a grand post-war plan than had been destroyed by massive German bombing – but few people then demurred. Similarly in October 1958 Tony Benn visited a brand new fourteen-storey skyscraper of modern flats in his Bristol constituency:

To see the bright airy rooms with the superb view and to contrast them with the poky slum dwellings of Barton Hill below was to get all the reward one wants from politics. For this grand conception of planning is what it is all about. The people were happy, despite the grumbles about detail.

If only such optimism could have been maintained, but it wasn't. The defects of this broad brush approach soon became all too clear – even if few Labour MPs themselves lived in tower blocks: good enough for other people but not for themselves. The preoccupation with 'mass' this or 'mass' that was where the two traditions of labourism and communism once again converged. Both exemplifed what Colin Ward has called 'the ideological stranglehold of state worship on the left.'

The Labour government did not tackle the problem of Britain's increasingly shabby and run-down public services, particularly that of transport, starved as they were of resources. This guaranteed that the concept of nationalisation remained an unpopular albatross around Labour's neck.

Socialist thinkers like Tony Crosland had always regarded high public expenditure as morally praiseworthy and so the standard left-wing response was naturally to call for more public money. This reaction completely ignored the objection that the rise in public expenditure – from 46 per cent of the gross domestic product in 1965 to 60 per cent in 1976 – was seen as threatening by many. As Robert Skidelsky once put it:

> Big Brother has crept up on us, not in the shape of a mad, bloodthirsty dictator, but in the far more insidious form of the Caring Expert, who claims knowledge of what a better future would look like, and uses taxpayers' money as well as regulations to bring it about.

It was also an inadequate response in the harsh economic climate of the 1970s because sufficient public money was never likely to be available. In an article in the *Guardian* Joel Barnett, a former Treasury minister, outlined the dilemma:

> All in all then, there are no miracles left. We have to face the unpalatable fact that with, at best, low rates of economic growth, and at worst, nil or even negative growth, public expenditure cuts will be necessary – not to create room for Conservative-style tax cuts, but to ensure that socialists' priorities in public expenditure are safeguarded and that vital public services are not deprived of essential additional funds. This seems self-evident, yet even to whisper that a future Labour Government will have to cut public expenditure brings forth serious charges and dire threats of expulsion, as I know to my cost.

Problems could not always be solved by throwing money at them. The ethos of the nationalised industries insisted that they should be run in favour of the producers themselves, primarily the trade unions, rather than the consumers – an attitude rather different from that of large private companies like Marks and Spencer which recognised that innovation and change were the keys to continuing success.

Take the Co-operative movement for example, once a pillar of the collectivist society on which the British labour movement had been built. By the 1970s it seemed like a relic of the past and certainly less attractive than its supermarket rivals. As a *Guardian* editorial shrewdly asked after the May 1979 election: 'How many consumers today find it more liberating to do business with North Thames Gas than to shop at Sainsbury's or Marks and Spencer?'

By the 1970s labourism was clearly in crisis. Keir Hardie had been right to base his new political party on the trade union movement, putting down roots which allowed it to oust the Liberal Party as the main opposition to the Conservatives and also to allow Labour governments irregular spells in office. But, of course, society had moved on since Hardie's day: labourism and the trade unions hadn't. 'Old Labour' was past its sell-by date. The kind of party which had provided young James Callaghans with their education was no more.

Labour's strengths had been derived from a sense of class solidity – although not in the aggressive sense of class conflict that Karl Marx had supposedly identified – which generated a clearcut identity. Economic and social changes, notably the decline in the number of manual workers and the shift to service industries, was gradually undermining this identity whilst the destabilising effects of Mrs Thatcher's governments of the 1980s were still to come. The 'private' was increasingly seen as preferable to the 'public'.

With no fresh ideas either of its own or coming from outside, the Callaghan government devoted its energies to remaining in office. By-elections whittled down the fragile majority and in March 1977 a deal was struck with David Steel's Liberal Party. This 'Lib-Lab Pact' allowed the Liberals, eager to come inside after decades in the political wilderness, the illusion of power and won Labour the benefit of more time in office.

The Callaghan government fought desperately to maintain its pay norms which established a ceiling for wage increases. In November 1977 a firemen's strike called in support of a 30 per cent pay claim was defeated only by sending in troops. But by the summer of 1978 the pay dam was beginning to burst. After three years of wage restraint, union members were understandably restive, particularly more skilled workers who had seen the erosion of pay differentials. The atmosphere was in any case made more acrimonious by the effects of deflation and of cuts in public expenditure. Unemployment was still rising, as too was the number of people below the official poverty line which nudged up from 1.4 million to 2.2 million.

Both Jack Jones and Hugh Scanlon, personally committed to the present Labour administration, had retired and union conferences began to pass resolutions attacking continued wage restraint. Negotiations between the government and the unions came up with a suggested figure of 5 per cent for future wage increases; a figure which today Denis Healey and others consider was much too low. Most of those involved in the discussions felt sure that Callaghan would call an election for the autumn of 1978 and that the target would be revised if Labour won.

In fact the Prime Minister, to the surprise of most of his colleagues, postponed an election and so the 5 per cent figure stood. From this point onwards, everything went wrong. The Labour Party Conference itself voted by a margin of two to one against any form of wage restraint. An avalanche of pay claims in the 20 to 30 per cent range came surging in, and the government was even defeated by its own backbenchers in December 1978 when it attempted to continue sanctions against private firms that awarded employees in excess of 5 per cent.

'Free collective bargaining' was fine for members of strong unions with negotiating muscle but less so for anyone else, especially for those in no union at all. The pay claims put in by railwaymen, road haulage drivers, hospital workers and oil-tanker drivers were pursued aggressively by the employees involved, using secondary picketing if necessary. Callaghan himself dubbed it 'free collective vandalism' and the government's special Cabinet Committee devoted to pay seemed, in Joel Barnett's words, 'to meet almost round the clock'.

Even the weather conspired against the government – the winter of 1978–79 was foul and cold. Jim Callaghan attended an international conference in sunny Guadeloupe and returned to find the country manifestly falling apart, and an ever more vociferous right-wing press prepared to make up remarks or stories if need be. The unpopularity of the industrial wing of the labour movement inevitably rubbed off on its political arm.

The government seemed powerless in the face of the actions of its own erstwhile supporters, the unions, and drifted hopelessly – handicapped too by its tenuous parliamentary majority. In the 1960s the then General Secretary of the TUC, George Woodcock, boasted that the trade union movement had moved out of Trafalgar Square and into the committee rooms of power. In the winter of 1978–79 it looked as if it was going back to Trafalgar Square. At one point ministers even considered sending tanks into ICI's medical headquarters, which was being blockaded by strikers, in order to retrieve drugs and other essential equipment. A State of Emergency was nearly declared on several occasions. The Conservative Party's advertising agency, Saatchi and Saatchi, produced posters under the title 'Labour Isn't Working'.

One particularly horrifying episode occurred when grave-diggers working on Merseyside refused to bury the dead. Seen widely on television, such incidents did enormous damage to the trade union movement. In his memoirs Jim Callaghan, a robust defender of union interests, remarked sadly that, 'Even with the passage of time I find it painful to write about some of the excesses that took place.'

At the time, the Labour government simply threw in the towel. The TUC General Council met Callaghan and his advisers to try and salvage something from the wreckage; according to Frank Chapple, the Prime Minister said simply: 'We are prostrate before you, but don't ask us to put it in writing.'

The Liberals pulled out of the pact with the government in July 1978 and Callaghan had to search around for alternative political allies. Devolution of power to Wales and Scotland raised its head and so once again the government began to curry favour, not on any principled grounds but simply in order to cling to office. Roy Jenkins' plea – 'You cannot break up the United Kingdom in order to win a few seats in an election' – went unheeded. The Ulster Unionists were promised more seats if they stuck with the government. Wheeling and dealing behind closed doors, here was labourism at its most unattractive.

James Callaghan finally called an election for May 1979. The run-up was marked by a bitter row over the contents of the manifesto. Although the 1974–79 governments had not introduced its drastic proposals calling for massive political change, the NEC remained some way to the Left of the Prime Minister and most of his Cabinet colleagues. The NEC's working committees had produced a series of radical plans including the outright abolition of the House of Lords. Overwhelmingly passed at the 1977 Labour Party Conference, the NEC naturally expected to see the proposal included in the election manifesto.

In fact, Callaghan and his advisers at No. 10 rewrote the manifesto at the last moment, excluding the more left-wing schemes. The NEC proved powerless in the face of this reversal. The dispute proved to be a portent of the internal rows which were to shake the Labour Party in the 1980s.

The Labour campaign centred almost exclusively on Jim Callaghan, but despite his own personal popularity and the achievements of the previous five years, such as higher real pensions and the introduction of the child benefit scheme, the Conservatives won a clear forty-three-seat majority. Ironically, only one in two trade unionists actually voted for their 'own' party.

This election defeat of May 1979 marked the end of the second phase in the history of the British Labour Party. With hindsight, the Attlee governments between 1945 and 1951 had clearly represented an end and not a beginning. Phase one – the pioneering or 'hearts' phase associated, above all, with Keir Hardie – had finished in 1931 with the collapse of Ramsay MacDonald's administration.

Phase two – consolidation and administration – had seen the creation of a modern social democratic state based around the three principles of government intervention, public ownership and a welfare state. This, the 'minds' phase, was largely accomplished by 1951. Subsequent governments, both Conservative and Labour, had basically just administered this machine.

But the makers of British social democracy had not entirely solved one important problem, namely the provision of steady and sustained economic growth. As this flaw increasingly raised its head, governments resorted to more drastic measures, such as Wilson and Castle's *In Place of Strife* plans, Edward Heath's free market policies of 1970–72 and his Industrial Relations Act, and the Callaghan government's 5 per cent pay policy. When economic growth faltered and the number out of work rose to one and quarter million, the relationship between government, employers and trade unions was bound to break down. A similar crisis faced social democratic parties all over Europe.

What remains remarkable and worth emphasising is the overall success of this post-war consensus in raising living standards, in providing welfare and generally in creating a better and more humane Britain. One reason for these achievements was the width of the consensus that had grown out of the 1930s and 1940s. Compare, for instance, the autobiographies of two individuals from very different backgrounds, Will Paynter's *My Generation* and Noel Annan's *Our Age*.

Paynter began work on a farm at age thirteen, was sent down the mines the next year and took part in the Hunger Marches in the 1930s. Imprisoned several times for his views, he was a member of the International Brigade in the Spanish Civil War and sat on the executive of the South Wales Miners' Federation between 1936 and 1968. Noel Annan, on the other hand, went to public school and Cambridge. At the age of only forty he was appointed Provost of King's College, Cambridge, and his career since has been full of glittering prizes and awards. Yet despite the obvious contrast in their careers, both Paynter and Annan heartily agreed that modern Britain was an immeasurably more humane and civilised society when compared with inter-war Britain.

By the late 1970s, however, commentators such as Jeremy Seabrook began to publish books with titles like *What Went Wrong?*, bemoaning the way in which the British labour movement had lost its moral dimension. It had certainly failed to rise to the intellectual challenge of constructing a post-Keynesian order. Noel Annan has concluded that the greatest error of 'our age' was '. . . to neglect – and some even to despise – the need for their country to become more efficient and more productive in business and industry; and their greatest failure to persuade organised labour to join in that enterprise.'

Could the British labour movement move on and create a new programme and new ideas which built on the best of the two earlier phases – a synthesis of both 'hearts' and 'minds' – and secure its place in a post-industrial Britain unsure of its role or its future?

# Part Three

## *Into the Twenty-First Century?*

'I ... PONDERED HOW MEN FIGHT AND LOSE THE BATTLE, AND THE THING THAT THEY FOUGHT FOR COMES ABOUT IN SPITE OF THEIR DEFEAT, AND WHEN IT COMES TURNS OUT NOT TO BE WHAT THEY MEANT, AND OTHER MEN HAVE TO FIGHT FOR WHAT THEY MEANT UNDER ANOTHER NAME.'

William Morris, *A Dream of John Ball* (1886)

# 13

## Towards the Precipice

### Michael Foot and the Labour Party in the Early 1980s

'Like Germany after 1945, Britain after Thatcher will be a scene of destruction.'

PROFESSOR ERIC HOBSBAWM, 1988

'. . . I always felt like a passenger in an aeroplane which was being flown by an unqualified pilot.'

ROY HATTERSLEY ON MICHAEL FOOT AS LEADER OF THE LABOUR PARTY

'The truth about Michael Foot's place in history is that he was the man who saved the Labour Party.'

MERVYN JONES, *MICHAEL FOOT* (1994)

In May 1979, James Callaghan's Labour government was comprehensively defeated by Mrs Thatcher's Conservative Party. Previous Tory administrations had displayed the pragmatism and moderation thought to be characteristically British, but, despite quoting St Francis of Assisi's prayer of understanding as she stood on the threshold of 10 Downing Street, here was a Prime Minister prepared to dispense with niceties.

She came to power armed with a radical agenda and – unlike Edward Heath's brief and unsuccessful 'free market' approach in the early 1970s – the political will to carry it through. Her primary targets included the three post-war assumptions previously accepted by both Labour and Conservative governments: full employment, government intervention to boost the economy where necessary and the necessity for a welfare state. The trade unions, too, were seen as an over-mighty force requiring subjugation.

Many Conservative policies of the 1980s undermined important vested interests which had traditionally sustained the Labour Party: the unions lost members, council houses were sold off, manufacturing industries went to the wall. Both labourism and the Labour Party were put on the rack.

Much of the policy had been worked out in opposition between 1974 and 1979; the Conservatives were well briefed, unlike the unprepared Labour governments of 1945 and 1964. As one of Mrs Thatcher's then colleagues, John Biffen, noted:

> What was distinctive about the Thatcher government was its determination to pursue relentlessly these objectives. There were to be no U-turns. Futhermore, the Thatcher Tories had undertaken massive and detailed work in opposition. From the outset, the government could present its objectives to the civil service aware of the difficulties and having the political will to discount them.

Mrs Thatcher's victory undoubtedly represented, as Jim Callaghan had observed in May 1979, part of a wider sea-change in world politics which was not restricted to Britain. In both the United States and West Germany, right-wing governments were elected to office and then retained power at subsequent elections. But socialists did not face inevitable electoral defeat: the French Socialists gained power in May 1981, the Spanish in October 1982.

Could the British Left emulate their French and Spanish colleagues? How should supposed radicals react to a distinctively radical administration that sold off council houses and public companies such as British Telecom, that favoured service industry over its manufacturing counterpart and fettered the powers of the trade unions – policies undermining the powerful vested interests which for decades had sustained the British Labour Party? The four responses centred on the intellectual and the political, the local and the industrial.

In *The Lion and the Unicorn*, George Orwell criticised one particular aspect of the British Left:

> The mentality of the English left-wing intelligentsia can be studied in half a dozen weekly and monthly papers. The immediately striking thing is their generally negative, querulous attitude, their complete lack at all times of any constructive suggestion. There is little in them except the irresponsible carping of people who have never been and never expect to be in a position of power.

Orwell's essay was first published in 1940, but he could well have been writing fifty years later.

For some, the Thatcher 'nightmare' could only possibly be brief. Oxford don R.W. Johnson, for instance, commented that '. . . the [Thatcher] ship is heading due North for the Pole and will, ere long, encounter vast and fearsome icebergs; and that nothing is more certain than that the crew will ultimately, and not altogether unreasonably, mutiny.' A brilliant prediction if only Johnson's article had been published on 30 August 1989; in fact, it had appeared ten years earlier on 30 August 1979.

Others, whistling noisily in the dark, contented themselves with the thought that Mrs Thatcher's success was merely a temporary aberration and that she would be soundly defeated at the next election. Then, as the German Communists had said when the Nazis came to power in 1933, it will be 'our turn'. After the 1983 and 1987 and 1992 elections, these optimists were still twiddling their thumbs and awaiting their delayed turn.

Some thought political opposition meant chanting a single slogan – 'Thatcher Out' – but nothing more. Others, unable to wound Mrs Thatcher politically, resorted to personal sneers. In a notorious article published in the *Sunday Telegraph* on 10 January 1988, several critics of the Prime Minister were invited to give their considered opinions of her. Academic Mary Warnock criticised Mrs Thatcher's appearance: she was 'packaged together in a way that's not exactly vulgar, just *low*.' Poet Peter Porter thought she was 'bullying, stupid and brutal'. Artist David Gentleman found her 'arrogant, tasteless and vain'. Jonathan Miller called her 'loathsome, repulsive in every way'. Alan Bennett declared that Mrs Thatcher was a paid-up philistine, 'typical of the people who go to the Chichester Festival'. On and on it went. With friends like this, it was unclear if the British Left actually needed enemies.

Even more negative was the picture of 'Thatcher's Britain' conveyed in books, films and plays. The heroine of Margaret Drabble's novel *A Natural Curiosity* compains that 'England's not a bad country – it's just a mean, cold, ugly, divided, tired, clapped-out, post-imperial, post-industrial slag-heap covered in polystyrene hamburger cartons.' Playwright Hanif Kureishi disagreed with Miss Drabble's heroine; England was not a 'slag-heap' but, rather, a 'rat-hole':

> England seems to have become a squalid, ugly and uncomfortable place. For some reason I am starting to feel that it is an intolerant, racist, homophobic, narrow-minded, authoritarian rat-hole run by vicious, suburban-minded materialistic philistines who think democracy is constituted by the selling of a few council houses and shares.

A few intellectuals completely lost their heads when faced with a political philosophy they did not like. For the usually acute Eric Hobsbawn to compare 1980s Britain, when living standards in real terms actually rose by a third, to the state of Germany in 1945 – cities razed to the ground, millions dead, no essential services – is paranoia. Like the little boy who cried 'wolf' once too often, what words would Professor Hobsbawm use if fascism really came to Britain?

This damaging inability to discriminate was all too reminiscent of the 'grand illusions' explored in Chapter 7. Professor Ben Pimlott, for instance, started a magazine which he called *Samizdat* after the name given to the illegal literature produced by dissidents in Communist countries. Both its title and that of the campaigning Charter 88 clung to the coat-tails of dissent in Eastern Europe. An editorial in the *Independent* commented that the magazine's title was 'making an extreme and unconvincing statement about the nature of the society in which we live.'

*Samizdat* claimed that opinion in Britain 'is controlled not by fear of the gulag but more subtly through the persuasive powers of the deferential media.' The majority of the press in Britain is right-wing, often squalidly and xenophobically so. It is also true that seven out of eleven daily newspapers vociferously supported Mrs Thatcher at, say, the 1987 election and delighted in trashing Labour leaders, policies, MPs and activists.

But look at *Samizdat*'s editorial board and its contributors: Ben Pimlott, Eric Hobsbawm, Margaret Drabble, Peter Kellner, Jonathan Porritt, Roy Hattersley: no one could ever claim that they are denied access to the media. Their views appear regularly in the *Sunday Times*, the *Guardian*, on television and radio and so on – as indeed they should. But then to turn around and talk of the deferential media's control of opinion is surely misplaced. Reading Timothy Garton Ash's description of the purges and restrictions common in Czechoslovakia in 1984 puts these complaints into some kind of perspective.

Orwell's point has surely been made. There were many good reasons to take issue with Conservative policies in the 1980s: the squandering of North Sea oil, the emphasis on consumption at the expense of investment, the dismantling of parts of the welfare state, the human consequences of mass unemployment, the cavalier attitude towards research, development and training, the chronic underfunding of scientific research . . . But so often the Left, consumed by a personal hatred of Mrs Thatcher, failed to make the arguments, and the contest was allowed to go by default.

British labourism has often been uncomfortable with 'intellectuals'. In an earlier chapter we saw that the hostility towards Gaitskell and his 'Hampstead set' arose in part because of their seeming isolation from the working-class rank and file. Even a Gaitskellite like George Brown detested anyone who had been to university and he once resorted to fisticuffs in a House of Commons' corridor with Richard Crossman. Similarly, trade union leaders like Ernest Bevin were suspicious of people sitting around 'thinking', which explains the patchy educational facilities of most trade unions. Jack Jones stood for the post of Chancellor of the University of London in order to help 'bring the University down from the clouds and nearer to the people.'

This pragmatic and hard-headed attitude is fine as far as it goes, which is not far. Sometimes it barely extends beyond the 'We're here because we're here' stage. Does this matter? Yes, because ideas and general moods of opinion do play a crucial part in how people vote. In the 1930s and 1940s the intellectual climate gradually shifted Labour's way; in the 1970s it moved towards the Conservatives. Richard Crossman, himself a tutor for the Workers' Educational Association (WEA) in the 1930s, was clear about the significance of this 'battle of ideas':

> The first essential for the election of a Left-Wing government in Britain is the creation of a favourable climate of opinion among non-political voters. And, although the practical politicians hate to admit it, the truth is that this favourable climate can never be created by the Labour Party itself, but only by the 'disloyal intelligentsia' – the journalists, writers, playwrights and critics who are able to discredit the Establishment and to air Left-Wing ideas when they are still too novel for the practical politicians to adopt . . . The psychological landslide to the Left [in the 1930s and early 1940s] was set in motion not by party organisation or party propaganda, but by those

who contributed to the *New Statesman*, joined the Left Book Club, taught evening classes for the WEA and, during the war, lectured for the Army Bureau of Current Affairs.

Not even the most partisan British socialist could claim that the 1980s saw the creation of Crossman's 'favourable climate of opinion among non-political voters'. But if the intellectual response to 'Thatcherism' was negligible, how about the political challenge spearheaded by Tony Benn?

Tony Benn has been subjected to much shameful personal abuse. Some right-wing papers have been obsessed by his wish to be called Tony Benn rather than Anthony Wedgwood Benn, whilst cartoonists regularly depicted him as a 'Fuhrer' or 'Dictator'. The *Sun* on 22 May 1981 headed an article 'Mr Benn – Is He Mad or a Killer?' whilst the *News of the World* in September 1981 referred to 'Citizen Benn who shouts from the rooftops the debt we owe to a man called Joseph Stalin.' In fact, he stands firmly in one tradition of English radicalism which wants, as he sees it, to take power away from the élite and restore it to the people themselves.

Benn was born in April 1925, next door to the London home of Sidney and Beatrice Webb. His father had served in Attlee's post-war governments and was duly ennobled as Viscount Stansgate. Educated at Westminster and Oxford before working in television and then securing the seat of Bristol South East, Sir Stafford Cripps' old constituency, Benn was heavily involved during the 1950s in the Movement for Colonial Freedom.

After his father's death in 1960, Tony Benn fought a long and eventually successful three-year battle to renounce his peerage because of his determination to continue in the House of Commons. The struggle was carefully chronicled in his diaries which have now been published in six hefty volumes and give the reader a grandstand view of the British Labour Party both in government and opposition from the 1940s up to 1990. Benn received little support from the Labour leadership during this campaign, confirming yet again the Party's timidity when it came to institutional change.

With his abundant ability and enthusiasm, Benn was soon a leading figure in the Labour Party and served in the Wilson governments in the 1960s. As Postmaster-General he began the issue of commemorative stamps. In July 1966 he was promoted to the Cabinet as Minister of Technology and brought to the post his typical energy and thoroughness: after changing his mind over the Common Market he promptly bought all forty-four volumes containing the EEC's rules and regulations. In view of his comparative youthfulness, if he had just kept his head down he might well have become leader of the Labour Party in due course.

But he didn't. Instead his own experiences in office had convinced him that sweeping changes were required if a fair and just society was to be established. In March 1973 he remarked that '. . . the Party without Karl Marx really lacks a basic analytical core' – even though three years later a first reading of *The Communist Manifesto* prompted him to write in his diary: '. . . I found that, without having read any Communist text, I had come to Marx's view.'

As Hugh Dalton had already discovered, hell hath no fury like the British Establishment who sees 'one of us' defect to 'the other side' and Benn came under virulent attack. Unlike most socialists, his ideas became more and not less left-wing. The reaction of sceptical colleagues was summed up by Harold Wilson's aside that 'He immatures with age.'

In the early 1970s Benn played a crucial part in shifting the National Executive Committee (NEC) towards the left and in 1974 he was appointed Secretary of State for Industry. He led the campaign to take Britain out of the Common Market and after the referendum Wilson promptly demoted Benn to the Energy Department. In Neil Kinnock's words, 'Benn bought the move to Energy. All he could do was to visit oil-rigs. It was a walk-over for the Prime Minister.' Tony Benn ruminated sadly in his diary:

> . . . the Referendum campaign and the defeat on 5 June was a far bigger defeat for the Left – and for me in particular – than I had realised. Like bereavement, it hits you but at first you don't really take it on board . . . the Department of Energy is really a side Department.

Inside the Cabinet he argued in vain for traditional left-wing measures of massive nationalisation and increased public spending, but no matter how many the defeats he always came back off the ropes – reminding one critic of a particularly resilient squash ball. Despite his disagreements, however, he did not resign from the government as Aneurin Bevan and Harold Wilson had done in 1951, or as Messrs Heseltine, Lawson and Howe did in later years. It was an omission which Tony Benn later regretted. Fellow left-wingers like Barbara Castle were also in two minds about Benn: 'I suddenly saw why I mistrust Wedgie. What is so wrong about him is that he never spells out that responsibility involves choice and the choices facing this country are by definition grim for everybody.'

After the 1979 election defeat, several leading Labour figures were complacent. John Silkin, for example, thought that 'The Party does not need to do anything very much except to update itself', whilst Peter Shore happily claimed that 'History is on our side.' Tony Benn, however, was more acute in recognising that this defeat must lead to something quantitatively and qualitatively different. The Labour Party was entering a drastic new phase in its development.

His strategy for the Labour Party was based on the premise that the British post-war consensus had come to an end. If Mrs Thatcher's government represented the right-wing response to this breakdown, then the labour movement in turn should produce a tough left-wing programme. At the heart of Benn's programme was the quest for 'accountability'. The following remarks come from an interview of July 1977:

I watch everybody else with power like a hawk and I say to myself, when I see other people with power, who are they accountable to? When I see the head of an oil company, who is he accountable to? When I see the editor of *The Times*, who is he accountable to? When I see anyone with power, a banker, who is he accountable to? . . . I think the most terrible thing is when people give up their critical examination of those who exercise power and say, 'let us leave it all to the wise men at the top, they know.'

By these rigorous standards the Labour leadership was barely accountable to anybody at all and Benn argued it was high time the party activists, of use during elections but then cynically discarded for the next five years, should be more involved in party affairs. His feelings were reinforced by the resentment many party members felt at the highhandedness of both Harold Wilson and Jim Callaghan in ignoring the wishes of the NEC.

Party leaders got away with this casual attitude because the structure of the Labour Party Constitution had created a tripartite division of power between the constituency parties, the Parliamentary Labour Party and the annual Conference. In effect the Conference was dominated by the trade unions because of their block vote. The constituency activists received the worst of this deal because they exerted little influence on sitting MPs and could always be swamped by the block vote at Conference. When drawing up the Constitution, Sidney Webb had complained that constituency parties 'were frequently unrepresentative groups of nonentities dominated by fanatics, cranks, and extremists.' In private, many other Labour leaders would have wholeheartedly agreed with Webb.

Constituency activists had and have always been suspicious of their leaders who enjoy luxurious life styles. In his definition of what Labour is for and against, quoted in 'Beginnings', Ben Pimlott cites 'personal wealth' as something which Labour opposes. Wealthy socialists have often come in for criticism. After his death in 1896, for instance, William Morris was attacked for leaving a will worth the then huge sum of £55,000, Ramsay MacDonald was excoriated for mixing in 'High Society' and, more recently, Aneurin Bevan, Richard Crossman and Jim Callaghan have owned large farms which critics have sometimes tried to use in political arguments. Similarly, Tony Blair's expensive residence has aroused the ire of party opponents.

Few socialists have been so candid as Lord Shawcross, a Labour MP after the war, who admits in his memoirs that 'I was not living in a particularly modest way: a flat in Dolphin Square, London; a country home; a yacht; two cars; two or more horses; a nanny and cook.' His socialist friends urged him to live in South London and send his children to state schools. At least Shawcross was honest: 'It would have meant a complete change in my whole philosophy and mode of life which I was too selfish to contemplate.' Most wealthy socialists are not so frank.

Wealth per se was perhaps less the complaint than the isolation which both it and, sometimes, parliamentary or ministerial office brought. Richard Crossman typified this unreality when he left the Cabinet in 1970 and became the editor of the *New Statesman*. Mervyn Jones was an observer:

> The trouble wasn't so much his age (he was sixty-two) as the fact that he had spent most of the intervening period in the rarefied atmosphere of the corridors of power. It was phenomenal to see how insulated he had been from life in the real world; he seemed to peer about, vainly seeking to pick up the threads, like Dr Manette after his release from the Bastille. There were many anecdotes about his ignorance of what anything cost – a round of drinks, the train fare to Brighton, the stamp on a letter.

When the magazine's deputy editor pointed out that plummeting sales were caused in part by having too many MPs' by-lines over boring copy, Crossman's response was elephantine: 'Delete "MP" from their by-lines.'

Even Tony Benn confided to his diary that, after losing office in 1979, he had experienced a novel experience when catching the London tube to Heathrow: 'It is the first time for many years that I have travelled non-VIP, entirely on my own: being a Minister with chauffeur-driven cars and helicopters and police escorts makes you out of touch.'

Benn's analysis was therefore in many ways correct. The Parliamentary Labour Party in the 1970s was on the whole dull, stodgy, middle-aged, male and, of course, white. New ideas, whether they were to do with feminism or the environment, workers' co-operatives or libertarian issues, simply passed them by.

He was right too in noting the familiar pattern whereby left-wing Labour MPs succumbed to the charms of parliamentary life and shed their radicalism. Looking back through this book, time and again 'militants' determined to resist the blandishments of the Establishment have settled down to a comfortable backbench existence and rapidly lost any contact with the Party outside Westminster. The autobiography of the former fiery Clydeside MP David Kirkwood, *My Life of Revolt*, depicts just such a process. Victor Grayson's refusal to let this happen makes him such a fascinating figure and, of course, Dennis Skinner follows in the same tradition.

In effect, Tony Benn was calling for a 'New Model Labour Party' in which MPs were no longer to be the representatives at Parliament of all their constituents, including those who had not voted for them. Instead they would act as delegates answerable to the constituency activists at local Labour Party meetings. Benn's critics naturally branded his scheme 'revolutionary' and 'harebrained'.

They were wrong. It was not a novel demand; as long ago as 1902 this proposal surfaced inside the Labour Representation Committee but Keir Hardie, using his considerable political weight, had ensured its defeat. Similarly, Tony Benn's plan to reduce future Labour Prime Minister's powers of patronage had been foreshadowed by Stafford Cripps' call – in his Socialist

League days in the 1930s – for the Cabinet to be elected by the Parliamentary Party as a whole.

Tony Benn's campaign was sustained by well-organised groups such as the Campaign for Labour Party Democracy (CLPD), which targeted carefully chosen MPs and their constituencies as well as proposing 'model resolutions' for local endorsement which ended up at the annual conference. The CLPD was, above all, a grouping of activists and for all Tony Benn's talk in his two books *Arguments for Socialism* and *Arguments for Democracy* about giving power to the people, the unrepresentative activists still called the tune – 'unrepresentative' because only a very small proportion of people in Britain take part in political activity. Much was made of the 'silent majority', although left-winger Ian Mikardo had a good riposte: 'The Good Samaritan was an activist: those who passed by on the other side were members of the Silent Majority.'

Even so, there was something a little offputting for most people about Tony Benn's furious energy – 200 meetings a year for ten years, writing 320 letters in a day by hand – and the assertion by Ken Livingstone (the then leader of the Greater London Council) who claimed that 'There is no such thing as a non-political part of life.' As we saw in an earlier chapter, Hugh Gaitskell for one would not have agreed.

Helped by the defection of former Cabinet minister Reg Prentice – the victim of alleged left-wing infiltration, he joined not the Liberals but the Conservatives in October 1977 – Benn and CLPD made out a convincing case, assisted by the 'stay-away' behaviour of certain prominent MPs. Tom Driberg, a former Bevanite, was a moot case in point. Although he lived in the Barbican, just a few miles from his constituency in Barking, East London, Driberg hated visiting his parliamentary seat. His biographer is candid:

He often gave the impression that every moment spent in the constituency was an excruciating ordeal for him. On the rare occasions when he did go to a knees-up in Barking he

stood about with a forbidding scowl on his face, complaining
furiously if he was brought any drink other than Bell's whisky
with ice; after half-an-hour he would then say 'I've had
enough' and demand to be driven back to London.

Labour members could surely be forgiven for voicing dissatisfaction with Driberg's behaviour. The lofty attitude taken
by some opponents towards the activists – summed up in
Roy Hattersley's dismissal of '. . . the army of political riff-raff
who infiltrated the Labour Party in the late sixties and early
seventies . . .' – certainly did not help.

This 'army' proved to be a remarkably successful campaigning force and it was soon widely accepted that not only must
MPs be more accountable, but some form of electoral college
should elect the party leader. But although CLPD stressed how
much more democratic this system would be, in practice it was
the trade union vote which yet again decided the end result.

Traditionally the Labour Right had dominated the Party
but their power was on the wane. One symbolic defeat had
occurred over Barbara Castle's proposals, *In Place of Strife*, to
reform the unions in 1969; in David Owen's words, 'It was
we, the supposedly hard men on the Right, who had lost our
nerve.' The Labour Left was in good organisational shape by
1980, the Labour Right less so – suffering from what John
Cole has called 'that prima donnaism which is the affliction of
political organisations where too many members have recently
held, and lost, senior office.'

The Labour Right got drawn into a quagmire of percentages:
should the unions have 50 per cent of the electoral college for
choosing a leader, or 40 per cent or 33.33 per cent? What
about the PLP? Or the CLPs? This unattractive wheeling
and dealing culminated during a special conference held
at Wembley in February 1981. Shenanigans such as these
prompted the breakaway of some senior Labour Party figures,
namely Dr David Owen, Shirley Williams, Bill Rodgers and
Roy Jenkins, who formed the Social Democratic Party (SDP)

in March 1981. They planned to make the SDP the kind of party Labour would have been if only it too had experienced a 'Bad Godesberg' conversion like their German colleagues.

From the vantage point of today, knowing as we do the eventual fate of the SDP, it is easy to minimise the threat the new party then posed to Labour. But as the SDP's historians, Ivor Crewe and Anthony King, have pointed out: 'By historical standards the building of the SDP was a considerable success. Within fifteen months of its launch it possessed a skilfully constructed constitution, an elected leader, a comprehensive programme of policies and a professionally staffed headquarters. The SDP leaders achieved their objectives of establishing a centralized and professional national organization largely free from faction fighting. Its election funds were sufficient in 1983 for the best-financed third-party campaign for sixty years.'

From this point on – and of crucial importance for the 1980s as a whole – the anti-Conservative opposition was now fragmented between the SDP, the Liberals and Labour. In a first-past-the-post electoral system, this division helped Mrs Thatcher and the Conservatives to dominate the decade. Many socialists had said harsh things about Harold Wilson, but it is interesting to speculate whether the SDP would have split away if he had still led the Labour Party.

The Benn campaign was strengthened by the enhanced fortunes of the Campaign for Nuclear Disarmament (CND) which was now attracting support again after a period of decline between the mid-1960s and the late-1970s. Once again, as in the aftermath of Hungary and Suez, international actions on both sides of the 'iron curtain' provided the catalyst.

On the one hand the Americans introduced Cruise missiles into Britain, while the Soviet Union installed their own SS-20s and also invaded Afghanistan. The Labour Party went unilateralist and, unlike in 1960, remained so. Well led by Monsignor Bruce Kent and Joan Ruddock, at its peak in 1984 CND could claim 90,000 national members with a further quarter of a million people enrolled in local groups.

Unilateralism was, of course, a policy irrevocably associated with the Labour Party's new leader, Michael Foot, who had been a leading figure in the earlier movement.

Although Michael Foot comes from a distinguished West Country Liberal family, he has been a socialist since the 1930s and first made his name as a journalist and author. Colleagues always contrasted the savagery of Foot's writings with the private gentleness of the man himself. Jim Callaghan has written of Michael Foot that: 'His absence of self-seeking is matched only by his optimistic belief that even the most unworthy colleague has some redeeming trait . . .' Like George Lansbury, Foot aroused genuine affection in even his bitterest political opponents.

In 1945 he was elected an MP for Plymouth and became a committed Bevanite, editing the weekly paper *Tribune*. Foot was certainly no 'fellow traveller' where the Soviet Union was concerned. The ferocity of his attacks on this supposedly socialist regime made a nonsense of *Sunday Times* allegations in 1995 that he had been a Soviet dupe.

Foot's commitment to international peace meant he was heavily involved in the 1950s with CND, which caused a falling out with Aneurin Bevan after Bevan's speech at the Labour Party Conference in 1957 when he had renounced unilateralism. The two men were eventually reconciled and after Bevan's death in 1960 Foot inherited his parliamentary seat at Ebbw Vale as well as writing a two-volume biography of his mentor.

Michael Foot's passionate tub-thumping oratory with its call for traditional socialist policies earned him the label 'the darling of the Left' and he seemed little interested in the day-to-day practicalities of political power. In 1966, for instance, he was asked to take his friend Frank Cousins' post in the Cabinet as Minister of Employment but on grounds of principle he refused.

In 1974, however, Foot unexpectedly joined the Cabinet as Minister of Employment and over the next five years proved to be a loyal member of the Wilson and then the Callaghan governments. Like Aneurin Bevan and Barbara Castle, Foot had come in from the backbench cold, even though old habits sometimes died hard. Cabinet colleague Edmund Dell complained that Foot always spoke as if he was addressing a public meeting.

When James Callaghan resigned as leader in November 1980, Foot defeated Denis Healey in the leadership contest by 139 votes to 129. That Foot won in a straight Left versus Right contest, whereas he had been decisively beaten by Callaghan just four years before, showed how the Parliamentary Labour Party was changing its complexion.

But, as is generally the case with the Labour Party, things were never as straightforward as they seemed. Several MPs on the right of the Party, alarmed by the leftwards drift and convinced that their political future lay elsewhere, apparently voted for left-winger Michael Foot in order to justify their future actions in leaving Labour for the SDP.

Michael Foot's long-held unilateralist views chimed in with the revitalised CND which maintained that Britain should dismantle its nuclear weapons, whatever was happening elsewhere in the world. Since these weapons were immoral per se, it would be intrinsically wrong to use them as bargaining counters. The moral force of this renunciation would supposedly be enough for other countries to follow Britain's lead.

However admirable in theory, in practice this was an example of the Labour Left's often unrealistic attitude towards foreign affairs. National groups inevitably generate international tensions and antagonisms, the task is therefore to contain and deal with these tensions. A policy of 'stop the world, I want to get off' is not the best nor most practical way of doing this. As historian James Hinton, himself a CND activist, has put it, 'Peace activists have been as prone to delusions of imperial grandeur as have Britain's rulers. The Pax Britannica bequeathed a legacy of "imperialist pacifism".'

Foot and Benn concurred on unilateralism, as they did on another crucial issue, namely withdrawal from the EEC – a policy which amazed Labour's fellow European socialists. When asked how the subsequent 'siege economy' would affect the living standards of the British people, let alone exactly who Britain would trade with, Labour's anti-EECers had no convincing answer. Neither could Tony Benn explain why he, one of those most responsible for Harold Wilson's decision to hold a referendum on this issue in 1975, did not accept and abide by the vote of the people.

But Michael Foot and Tony Benn, on the face of it brothers-in-arms, soon fell out dramatically. Foot complained that Tony Benn's campaign was producing levels of internal bitterness not experienced since the civil war days of the 1950s; to the public, the Labour Party was once again behaving like a sectional body rather than a national party. The faction fighting inevitably muted the Labour Party's response to Mrs Thatcher's government which, by 1981, was wracked by industrial recession, rising unemployment and outbreaks of rioting in London, Liverpool and Bristol.

Foot's annoyance with what he regarded as unnecessary diversions came to a head in 1981 when Tony Benn announced his intention to challenge Denis Healey for the post of deputy leader of the Labour Party under the new electoral college system. The antagonism caused by this contest was evident at the 1981 Labour Party Conference in Brighton when hostilities were so bitter it was difficult to believe that this was the annual meeting of one single fraternal body and not that of several ferociously hostile groups. At one fringe meeting, an MP who had not voted for Tony Benn was greeted by shouts of 'Judas'.

In April 1987 Benn himself looked back and noted in his diary that 'the trouble with the 1981 deputy leadership campaign was that it was directed at members of the Party, whereas it should have been directed at the public . . .' It was a problem that few on the Labour Left ever addressed:

preaching to the converted is always easier than challenging non-believers. For the Labour Right, Healey's success saved the Labour Party. If Benn had won, substantial numbers of MPs would certainly have deserted to the SDP in a possibly fatal exodus.

Although Tony Benn had narrowly lost in 1981 to Denis Healey, his influence and that of his supporters was evident in the so-called 'Alternative Economic Strategy' (AES) which sought withdrawal from Europe and a massive programme of nationalisation. At times the sophistication of the analysis echoed Roy Hattersley's dismissal of Tony Benn '. . . who thought that it was possible to get the economy back on its feet by repeating a series of cliches concerning greed not need, the inherent weakness of capitalism and the innate wisdom of the workers.'

The influence of the AES was evident during the 1983 general election, which the Labour Party fought on the basis of its most radical manifesto ever, promising 'irreversible change' – a phrase that, in a political democracy, seemed alarmingly authoritarian. It certainly contained some startling inanities, such as the contradictory assertion that 'Unilateralism and multilateralism must go hand in hand if either is to succeed.'

One leading Labour MP, Gerald Kaufman, called it 'the longest suicide note in history' and the Conservatives, under the chairmanship of Cecil Parkinson, bought up copies of the manifesto so that they could publicise it themselves, knowing that this would only help their cause. They were also bolstered by the successful Falklands campaign of 1982.

It was blindingly obvious, too, that for all his personal qualities the electorate simply did not see Michael Foot as a potential Prime Minister. The Conservatives, devoted as they are to the pursuit of power, would have clinically despatched such a 'no hope' leader: after all, they later ditched Margaret Thatcher because Tory MPs felt they could not win another election under her leadership.

The Labour Party, by contrast, has always been more

soft-hearted towards its leaders. They depart when they want
to. Polls showed that a massive 49 per cent of the electorate
would be more likely to vote Labour if Denis Healey was the
leader. One or two MPs privately suggested that Foot should
stand down, but he decided against the idea and staggered on.
The Conservatives would not have been so tender.

Another marked difference in how the Conservatives and
Labour fought this 1983 election revealed how ossified and
antiquated much of the British labour movement had now
become. The Labour Party conducted a campaign that would
have done Keir Hardie proud. Their campaign committee was
'a rag, tag and bobtail affair'; 'people I had never seen before
seemed to wander in and out giving advice and then vanishing'
– in the words of Sam McCluskie, chairman of the campaign
committee.

The special computer installed at Walworth Road headquarters broke down, the Party's own pollster Robert Worcester
was only given the funds to start research in early 1983,
and the advertising agency hired to present Labour's case
– the first time Labour had used such an organisation –
began work only five weeks before the general election
and even then was excluded from the actual running of
the campaign. As the head of the agency Johnny Wright
complained:

> We wouldn't think of launching a new brand of washing-up
> liquid or a can of soup in anything under nine months to a
> year and that's rather more trivial than advertising a major
> political party.

Jim Mortimer, the Party's General Secretary, detested the
use of private polls in any case, claiming to know what
working people were thinking merely by looking at trade
union conference agendas. That he should equate the two
testified to just how detached sections of the British Labour
Party had become from the general public.

Inevitably, Michael Foot's own campaign focused predominantly on his supporters rather than those undecided voters who needed to be won over. For example, no special facilities were provided for journalists accompanying his entourage nor were his speeches co-ordinated with those of other leading members of the Party. At one point the running of Foot's national tour proved so inadequate that the police themselves requested more formal planning. One journalist travelling with the Labour leader concluded:

> In the end, the Labour leader was beaten by an unwieldy schedule, a speaking style that was too discursive for the television age, a manifesto that took an academic semester to explain and, finally, a too personalised and too personable approach to his own politics – one worthy of his heroes of the eighteenth century.

In his own account of the 1983 election, published as *Another Heart and Other Pulses*, Michael Foot replied to the abuse and misrepresentations which he had patiently suffered throughout. But he also noted the puzzling contrast between 'the fighting spirit in our rank-and-file and the mood of the general electorate.' Although Foot agreed that this was an election fought out on television he complained that because of his 'inordinate list of public meetings' he actually saw less of it than anyone else, which surely sums up the inadequacies of his campaign. For Michael Foot, as for many then on the Left, the message was all and the medium nothing.

Mrs Thatcher's Conservative Party won a sweeping 144-seat majority. Labour secured a miserly 28 per cent share of the poll – its worst result since 1918 – while its 8.4 million votes was only just ahead of the 7.8 million cast for Alliance candidates. That a month before the Labour Party had held its own in the local elections clearly showed there had been nothing 'inevitable' about the result. As Crewe and King have pointed out, in large parts of suburban, small-town and rural Britain the Liberal–SDP Alliance replaced Labour as the main opposition to the Conservatives. Under a system of proportional representation the Alliance would have won not 23 seats but 161, and would probably have formed part of a coalition government.

By 1983, the political wing of the British labour movement had clearly failed even to dent a triumphant and self-confident Conservative government and faced a dangerous new rival which had secured almost as many votes.

The poor campaign run by the national Labour Party contrasted unfavourably with the populist if controversial flair shown by the Greater London Council (GLC) and its young leader Ken Livingstone who was quite prepared to use the GLC's resources to campaign against Mrs Thatcher's government. Both the GLC and various other left-wing councils were keen to show that what the Labour Party had failed to do at national level, they could surely achieve at local level. This represented the third challenge to the Conservative administrations led by Mrs Thatcher

Ken Livingstone was a good example of the radicalisation that had swept across the Labour Party in the late-1960s following the disillusion felt with Harold Wilson's governments. He was elected a Lambeth councillor in 1971 and two years later won a seat on the GLC. Supported by his wife Christine who was a schoolteacher, Livingstone devoted himself full-time to local London politics. The Labour Party won a majority at the May 1981 GLC elections and the day after the result the thirty-five-year-old Livingstone ousted the previous Labour leader, Andrew McIntosh. The *Sun* newspaper greeted his victory with the banner headline RED KEN CROWNED KING OF LONDON.

The GLC's former headquarters, County Hall, stands just across the river from the Houses of Parliament and Livingstone and his colleagues delighted in adopting policies diametrically opposed to Mrs Thatcher's. The Council introduced cheap fares on public transport in a 'fares fair' programme until it was banned by the House of Lords. Livingstone himself turned down an invitation to attend the royal wedding in 1981 and, more controversially, he called for the withdrawal of British troops from Ireland. The GLC was also heavily criticised by sections of the press for funding several minority groups; by the end of 1983 the GLC had given grants to more than a thousand voluntary organisations.

Throughout the 1980s the Labour Party generally polled much better in local elections than it did nationally. In part this regional resistance offered an alternative to the Conservatives' Westminster dominance. The GLC, Liverpool, Sheffield, Glasgow and smaller London councils such as Islington, Camden and Lambeth challenged the government's insistence on privatisation and budgetary cuts. Conservative ministers no doubt bridled in their chauffeur-driven cars as they passed through 'nuclear free zones'.

The relentless 'witch-hunting' tendencies of the press were zealously paraded during the Peter Tatchell affair. Bermondsey, a declining inner-city part of London, had been represented between the wars by the charismatic doctor Alfred Salter who, supported by his wife Ada, had successfully introduced the ideals of the 'garden city' movement. The thriving local party boasted some 3,000 members. After the Second World War, however, Bermondsey was run by the Labour Right in the form of MP Bob Mellish and council leader John O'Grady; by 1978 local membership had declined to less than four hundred.

An influx of energetic activists led by Peter Tatchell revitalised the Party but quickly came into conflict with the old guard who preferred to let sleeping dogs die. In 1981 Tatchell was selected as the parliamentary candidate, to the disgust of his opponents who played up his Australian origins and his homosexuality. Under pressure, Michael Foot seemingly refused to accept Tatchell's selection, thus generating an open season led by the *Sun* and some other papers. It is deeply depressing to read Tatchell's account of events – the smears, the death threats, obscene letters and forgeries – and he duly went down to a crushing defeat at a by-election in February 1983.

The council that grabbed most of the headlines was in Liverpool and the activities there of the Militant Tendency caused as many headaches for Michael Foot as for Mrs Thatcher. The Far Left in Britain has always been unsure on the 'ideologically correct' attitude to be taken towards the Labour Party. An activist such as Gerry Healy dismissed it as irrevocably reformist and therefore set up the Workers' Revolutionary Party (WRP); overwhelming self-confidence in his beliefs was expected to make up for the tiny membership. Most of these 'Far Left' groups managed to attract at least one star name: Vanessa Redgrave joined the WRP, journalist Paul Foot belonged to International Socialism, later the Social-ist Workers' Party, and Tariq Ali fronted the International Marxist Group.

Militant, however, argued that the Labour Party was, like it or not, the largest working-class organisation in Britain and therefore members should pursue what was called 'entryism'. Their brand of Marxism was fundamentalist to the nth degree, wanting to nationalise the whole of British industry, which would then presumably be run by the editorial board of the *Militant* newspaper. But it was Militant's energy and powers of organisation rather than their ideas that allowed them to take over run-down and apathetic Labour Party branches.

The GLC and several other councils tried to promote local economic recovery by setting up a network of enterprise boards and agencies. The Greater London Enterprise Board (GLEB), for instance, analysed the London economy in great detail, but simply did not have the resources to buck the trend of world economic recession.

Another flaw was hardly novel. Many Conservatives have been closely involved in the business of wealth creation, whether in industry or the City. Rather fewer socialists possess such a background, which explains why the Confederation of British Industry (CBI) and the Institute of Directors have traditionally been wary of Labour governments. Looking back in 1987 at the New Left of the 1950s, economist Michael Barratt Brown noted that:

> . . . we often appeared, except in the practice of writing and the arts, like a bunch of amateurs. We could not even run a coffee bar without losing money – how much less could we be trusted to manage the country's foreign trade. This lack of managerial skills became more obvious than ever when the Greater London Council and some other Labour authorities set up enterprise boards to manage business enterprises. The lessons have still not been learned. As yet there is still no Labour management college, nor even courses in management at the trade-union colleges.

Sadly, many of the new enterprises went bankrupt, just as the three co-operatives at Kirkby, Meriden and the *Scottish Daily News* had collapsed during the previous Labour government.

Finally, however powerful these local councils were on their own patch, they simply could not defeat the national government which had introduced rate-capping and surcharged individual councillors for overspending. In Liverpool, well-known individual members of Militant such as Derek Hatton were expelled from the Labour Party.

Mrs Thatcher decided to get rid of the GLC and the other metropolitan councils. Elections scheduled for May 1985 were perfunctorily scrapped and the GLC and its counterparts abolished, to be replaced instead by Conservative-appointed bodies. It was an affront to democracy but the powerlessness of the Labour Party, the GLC and the other councils in the face of the Conservative government's actions demonstrated just how centralised power had become in Britain. The muted protest showed how, in part, the 'Loony Left' succeeded in alienating public support. Local socialism had been roundly defeated by national conservatism. Ken Livingstone himself ended up on the other side of the Thames when he was elected an MP in 1987.

Although Tony Benn was vociferous in his calls for greater democracy throughout British society, one institution noticeably exempt from his strictures was the trade union movement. Paradoxically, Benn's attitude was echoed by the Labour Right which also preferred to let sleeping dogs lie because the block vote had traditionally supported the leadership of the Party.

Likewise the Labour Left were happy with the status quo, but in their case they were gambling on the prospect that in the near future the block vote might well become left-wing in character. Anyone who argued that this obsession with arithmetic – are we going to get the USDAW vote, and what about the firemen? – was distinctly undemocratic and unsocialist was given short shrift.

Evidence of this disdain for what most people would regard as democracy is copiously provided by the autobiography of Clive Jenkins. A shrewd and highly capable negotiator, Jenkins had carefully built up what was originally a small union with a membership of just 11,000 in 1947 into the giant Manufacturing, Science and Finance (MSF) which by 1988 had more than 650,000 members plus an income of £18 million a year and real estate assets worth over £40 million. An empire had indeed been born.

Clive Jenkins was also happy to wield his influence inside the Labour Party like some feudal baron of centuries past. There is a memorable episode in his autobiography *All Against the Collar* in which Jenkins and a handful of union and Labour Party cronies meet for dinner in 1980 and decide among themselves that Michael Foot rather than Denis Healey should succeed Jim Callaghan as leader – and blow the rest of the Party. Three years later, he and fellow trade union leader Moss Evans settle on Kinnock as Foot's successor.

The industrial response to Mrs Thatcher was no more successful than the ideological, the political or that of local government. By outlawing secondary picketing, curbing the closed shop, sequestrating union assets if necessary and calling for pre-strike ballots, the Conservative Party's step-by-step policies had reformed the unions in a much more drastic fashion than Barbara Castle's original *Strife* proposals had ever envisaged.

The unions were also under pressure from a falling membership that dropped from over 50 per cent of the workforce in 1979 to less than 40 per cent by 1989. But instead of offering potential members compelling reasons why they should join a trade union in the first place, most union leaders condemned the 'Tory laws' outright and called for their complete repeal, even though several of them had proved popular with their own membership. In one case, however, Mrs Thatcher's government was directly challenged. This was during the miners' strike of 1984–85.

Sometimes likened to the Brigade of Guards in terms of its prestige, the National Union of Mineworkers (NUM) was regarded in a special light by the rest of the labour movement because of the unique dangers its members faced daily in their jobs. In the 1960s the Wilson governments were in favour of nuclear power and the pits began to be run down at the rate of one closure each week. The NUM initially offered little resistance.

In the 1970s the NUM's backbone stiffened and in both 1972 and 1974 the NUM went on strike in defiance of Edward Heath's Conservative government, winning each time. The 1972 dispute witnessed what was dubbed 'the Battle of Saltley Gate' when the picketing miners and their supporters managed by sheer weight of numbers to close down the Saltley coke works in the Midlands. The miners' official who had supervised this operation was Arthur Scargill of the Yorkshire NUM.

Arthur Scargill left school at fifteen and went down the mines. His father was a Communist and he himself joined the Young Communist League. He quickly moved up through the ranks of the Yorkshire NUM, earning the nickname of 'the miners' QC' when he worked as the compensation agent arguing his members' cases. He fully realised the importance of television and at the age of only thirty-five was elected President of the Yorkshire Miners in 1973. In December 1981 Arthur Scargill was elected President of the NUM nationally, succeeding Joe Gormley. He won 70 per cent of the votes cast.

If no one doubted Scargill's devotion to his members, then few questioned either his hostility towards the Conservative government or his hope that a national strike might bring down Mrs Thatcher, just as ten years before it had brought down Edward Heath. The difficulty facing Scargill was that the NUM's long tradition of pit-head democracy stipulated that strike action had to be approved by a substantial majority. Three times Scargill called for a ballot in favour of industrial action and each time he lost. In addition, the government chose a new head of the Coal Board, Ian McGregor, who had almost halved the workforce in the British steel industry.

In March 1984 the Coal Board announced the sudden closure of Cortonwood pit in Yorkshire. The Yorkshire miners came out on strike but Scargill refused to call a national ballot of his members, even though surveys suggested that this time he might well have won a majority for industrial action. Instead, Scargill and his supporters adopted a policy of 'picketing out' other areas, notably in Nottinghamshire where many miners refused to strike. This was bound to lead to scenes of violence as miner fought against miner. The NUM pickets tried but failed to close the coking works at Orgrave in the Midlands.

The government had prepared carefully for just such a strike by keeping coal stocks deliberately high – at enormous cost to the taxpayer whose pockets they were normally so solicitous about. The then Chancellor of the Exchequer, Nigel Lawson, has recalled in his memoirs that Conservative preparation for the strike was 'just like re-arming to face the threat of Hitler in the late 1930s' – a stance confirmed by Mrs Thatcher's lurid talk of 'the enemy within'.

At its 1984 Conference the TUC promised the miners 'total support' but union leaders discovered their members were unwilling to risk their own jobs when not all the miners were out on strike anyway. Despite the heroic sacrifices of individual miners and their families, more and more began to trickle back to work. Finally, after no less than a year, the NUM had to abandon the strike. Arthur Scargill's tactics contrasted unfavourably with the disciplined behaviour of the dockers in the 1889 strike when their leaders realised that public support for their action was imperative.

Since the end of the strike, however, fresh details have emerged showing the lengths to which the Conservative administration went in its resolution to win at all costs. The full resources of the 'secret state' – phone tapping, the use of agents provocateurs, the carte blanche given to the police – were deployed, assisted by contacts in the press and television. At one point, the multitude of phone taps placed on miners' officials caused the continuously running tape-recorders to come to a grinding halt as the tapes ran out.

Labour governments have always been targeted by the Establishment. We have seen how Harold Wilson was the subject of a thirty-year campaign, whilst his Lord Chancellor, Lord Gardiner, thought his phone was bugged and when he had to hold confidential conversations with his colleague, Attorney-General Sir Elwyn Jones, the two of them were driven around Green Park. Gardiner once approached the Home Secretary, Frank Soskice, in order to check the accuracy of the files kept on him. Soskice was naturally embarrassed – he wasn't allowed to see the files either. In this 'Alice In Wonderland' situation, perhaps one should reiterate that it is the elected politicians who are supposed to exercise power.

More covert bodies are often used. The Information Research Department has already been discussed, as well as such underhand operations as the blacklisting Economic

League, but sometimes prominent Labour politicians and trade unions leaders such as George Brown and Frank Chapple have proved only too happy to pass on information about potentially 'subversive' colleagues (needless to say, their respective memoirs are strangely silent on this topic). In the early 1960s, for instance, the Macmillan government set up a trade union group called *IRIS* with a secret payment of £40,000 – nearly half a million pounds at today's values – which fed information back to the intelligence services.

In view of such activities, it is not surprising that, as Seumas Milne has shown in disturbing detail, the campaign against Arthur Scargill continued for several years after the end of the strike in 1985, assisted by the crooked financier and newspaper proprietor Robert Maxwell. The *Daily Mirror* printed numerous allegations about Scargill, subsequently shown to be false, to try and destroy any lingering influence the miners' leader possessed. The editor of the *Mirror* at the time, Roy Greenslade, is refreshingly candid about how the intelligence services operate: 'Most tabloid newspapers – or even newspapers in general – are the playthings of MI5. You're the recipients of the sting.' Scores of journalists and broadcasters were signed up by the intelligence services in the 1970s

The failure of the strike accelerated the rate of pit closures. Deprived of the men who had joined the breakaway Union of Democratic Mineworkers (UDM), the NUM's membership fell below the 100,000 mark and then dropped like a stone. The UDM was clearly a government ploy and it was only later that its leaders realised that they had been duped. By then, of course, it was too late.

Symbolic of the NUM's demise was the closure in December 1990 of Mardy Colliery, the last deep mine in the Rhondda Valley. The shaft had been sunk in 1875 at a time when Keir Hardie was still a miner and the Labour Party was not to be formed for another thirty years. At its peak, no fewer than 100,000 miners worked in the Rhondda Valley alone (including my great-grandfather). But, in a dispiriting sign of the times, the pit at Mardy was closed down and has been grassed over, returning the valley to its original state of 1875. The Rhondda Heritage Park opened in May 1991.

By the middle of the 1980s, the British Left was therefore in a sorry mess. The election result of 1983 showed that substantial sections of the middle classes who were not unilateralist or in favour of Britain leaving Europe were happy to vote for the Liberal–SDP Alliance, whilst huge chunks of the working–class vote was now 'Thatcherite'. Tony Benn's campaign might have brought changes within the Labour Party, but had certainly not attracted popular support.

In fact, Labour Party membership had dropped to just 276,692 by 1982 – the lowest recorded since 1929. Since 1979 alone membership had almost halved as individuals disillusioned by the internal faction fighting decided that they could spend their lives more happily elsewhere. A national appeal for funds had met with a poor response; the situation was so dire that mantelpiece collection boxes were being made available.

The unions had no idea what strategy to adopt in the face of a hostile government and the defeat of the miners showed that an industrial challenge was unlikely to be effective. Ken Livingstone's GLC and the other metropolitan councils were about to be abolished. Far Left groups such as the Socialist Workers' Party and the International Marxist Group were miniscule. CND had failed to win over a majority of the public. The intellectual Left was winning few arguments as the ideological tide flowed ever more strongly towards the Right. The future for the British Left looked bleak indeed.

# 14

---

# Towards the Middle Ground
## Neil Kinnock's Labour Party

'I got to be Leader of the Labour Party by being good on
television.'
NEIL KINNOCK QUOTED IN MICHAEL COCKERELL,
*LIVE FROM NUMBER 10* (1988)

'Ramsay MacKinnock'
PLACARDS SEEN DURING THE MINERS' STRIKE OF 1984–85

'The Labour Party's major problem is psychological. We have not
got our opponents' arrogant belief in the right to rule.'
BARBARA CASTLE, *FIGHTING ALL THE WAY* (1993)

At both first and subsequent glances Neil Kinnock was very
much a man of the Labour Left. A politician whose oratorical
skills helped him win a safe parliamentary seat at the age of just
twenty-nine, he was a passionate admirer of Nye Bevan and
contributed a preface to Bevan's book *In Place of Fear* when
it was republished in 1978. He was also Welsh, a former adult
education tutor and a passionate supporter of CND.

Associated with the emotional rather than the intellectual
wing of British socialism, Kinnock was educated at Cardiff
University. Some Oxbridge socialists apparently never forgave
him for this, although after the mess that Harold Wilson's
many Oxford Firsts had got themselves into this was surely
a recommendation rather than a stigma. For four years he

worked as a tutor for the Workers' Educational Association (Hugh Gaitskell, Roy Hattersley and Robin Cook have also been full-time WEA tutors, which testifies to the admirable breadth of that organisation) in East Glamorgan before being elected MP for the safe seat of Bedwellty in 1970.

Throughout the 1970s Kinnock was on what would later be called the 'Hard Left' of the Parliamentary Labour Party. In 1975, for instance, he called for the total confiscation of all incomes over £10,000 a year (£46,000 at 1992 prices). With such views he was unsurprisingly little interested in serving in the Callaghan government of 1976–79, spending an unmemorable year as the Parliamentary Private Secretary to Michael Foot.

However Kinnock's popularity with the Party at large duly paid off in 1978 when he was elected to the National Executive Committee, the constituency 'top of the pops' charts. He did courageously campaign against the devolution proposals for Wales even though he knew that he would suffer personal vilification for his efforts. In 1980 Kinnock helped organise Foot's successful leadership bid but the next year, disturbed by what he saw as the fanaticism and intolerance of Tony Benn's supporters, controversially abstained in the deputy leadership contest. Ironically enough, Benn's campaign was spearheaded by the Campaign for Labour Party Democracy (CLPD); when CLPD had been set up in 1973, Kinnock was one of its first signatories.

Like Bevan, Kinnock always had a tendency to let his mouth run away with him. For example, his remark about Mrs Thatcher glorying in other people's guts during the Falklands War almost matched Bevan's 'lower than vermin' jibe. But a more important similarity was that Kinnock possessed a strong streak of pragmatism, just as Bevan had. When the Independent Labour Party (ILP) broke away from the Labour Party in 1932, Bevan had sneered that they were political virgins going off into the wilderness. Kinnock felt the same way about the antics of some of Tony Benn's supporters. For both Bevan and Kinnock, principles counted for little without the political power to implement them – and in modern Britain, even though Parliament itself has lost much of its authority, political power still depends on victory at a general election.

Neil Kinnock was undeniably ambitious and, according to his defeated opponent Roy Hattersley, spent a year positioning himself to take over from Michael Foot after the defeat at the election of 1983. Certainly he was helped by the machinations of trade union leaders Clive Jenkins and Moss Evans who, shamelessly wielding the cudgel of the block vote, seem to have sewn up Kinnock's election within twenty-four hours of the election result. He won on the first ballot, securing 71 per cent of the votes. At the age of forty-one Kinnock was the leader of the Labour Party even though he, unlike several members of his Shadow Cabinet, had never experienced ministerial office.

But Kinnock led a party in parlous condition which faced a Conservative government with a massive 144-seat majority dominated by a confident leader and the Liberal-SDP Alliance that had polled only half a million votes fewer than Labour in 1983. The electorate had clearly shown what they thought of the Party's election policies – unilateralism, withdrawal from Europe, opposition to the sale of council houses and demands for a massive increase in state intervention – and the prolonged internal squabbling of the previous three years.

In June 1983 *The Economist* compared Labour's policies with those of its European counterparts, concluding that the British party possessed by far the most left-wing programme – and this in a country that had elected Mrs Thatcher. As Neil Kinnock himself later wrote of the 1979–83 years, 'It was almost as if sections of the party measured the purity of their socialism by the distance which they could put between it and the minds of the British people.'

Trade union membership was plummeting as fast as individual Labour Party membership, which had in turn collapsed from a total of 702,000 in 1972 to well below the 300,000 mark. That no one knew for certain what the figures were simply confirmed the inadequacy of the Party's antiquated machinery. The trade unions showed little sign of adapting to the demands of the 1980s, particularly the legislation requiring pre-strike ballots and the election of officers, and their only consistent strategy seemed to be one of 'we are against'. Arthur Scargill and the NUM were poised to embark on a bitter and protracted strike without balloting their membership.

On a personal level, Neil Kinnock knew full well that two-thirds of the Shadow Cabinet had in fact voted for his opponent Roy Hattersley and, moreover, that he himself favoured the policies of unilateralism and retreat from the EEC which the electorate had decisively rejected.

Clearly the British labour movement needed to spend some time analysing what had happened and where it was going. Extraordinarily enough, much of this analysis was provided under the stimulus of the Communist Party.

'The CP [Communist Party] in the eighties acted like the Labour revisionists of the fifties . . .' Hugh Gaitskell and his circle would have had an apoplectic fit if they had read this remark in *The Times* by Martin Jacques, Communist and editor of the party's monthly *Marxism Today*, but Jacques was right.

In this book I have often been critical of the British Communist Party. Apart from its flagrant disregard for human violations in the 'Soviet bloc' – abuses which tarnished the name of communism let alone socialism – the party failed to create a useful, viable and provocative left-wing body outside the Labour Party. Instead, by surrendering autonomy to an organisation based thousands of miles away in Moscow whose knowledge of and interest in socialism in Britain was sketchy, the Communist Party rarely assisted the British Left.

The only years in which British Communists had enjoyed relative freedom to go their own way – between 1935 and 1939 and then 1941 to 1948 – proved, not surprisingly, the years in which the party grew both in size and influence. In fact the further away from the leadership diktat in King Street, Covent

Garden, the more valuable the party's efforts proved, namely its role in the Hunger Marches and the 'Aid Spain' movement during the 1930s. Many individual Communists had played an admirable and selfless role in local bodies tackling the problems of tenants, squatters and pensioners.

Nationally, however, the Communist Party seemed to be an anachronism in an age of New Lefts and other trendy left-wing organisations. The party desperately tried to shed some of its traditional associations: the *Daily Worker* adopted the apparently more friendly title of the *Morning Star*, whilst the leadership opposed the Soviet invasion of Czechoslovakia in 1968. The party's programme *The British Road to Socialism* now accepted that parliamentary success offered the best way forward, even though sceptics pointed out that an organisation without a single MP since 1950 was hardly an expert in this field. In any case the Communist Party was bound to lose out to the Labour Party as the electoral representative of the Left in a 'first past the post' system discouraging minority parties.

The Communist Party's industrial influence, traditionally its strength, had inevitably declined along with manual trades such as engineering and mining and overall it was in a perilous financial state. Disaster was staved off by selling its Covent Garden headquarters for a useful sum and moving to a cheaper building in Smithfield which had once been a pub called the Crossed Keys. The pub's Catholic sign depicting the keys of St Peter continued to adorn the front of the building. Shamefully, subsidies from the Soviet Union were reintroduced.

Confusion among British Communists was matched by that of their European counterparts. The Italian Communists had always boasted a tradition of limited pluralism, mainly because as an underground body under Mussolini it had missed out on the full rigours of the 'Third Period', whilst the Spanish party was developing what it called 'Eurocommunism'. In other words, arguing that individual parties should work out their own programmes and policies free from Moscow's tutelage. Obvious surely, but it was sixty years before European Communists felt able to face up to this responsibility.

British Communists began to think for themselves rather than parrot some party line. Their successful series of study schools called 'Communist Universities of London' firmly emphasised the values of pluralism and tolerance. Even more inconoclastic was the transformation of the party's theoretical monthly *Marxism Today*. Founded back in October 1957, it had been edited by James Klugmann and was stuffed full of long and dense articles read only by the very enthusiastic or the deeply committed.

But when Klugmann died in 1977 his young assistant Martin Jacques took over and turned the magazine away from the party faithful towards the less committed. The logo stridently declaring that *Marxism Today* was the monthly journal of the Communist Party was discreetly removed from the front cover, a distribution deal was concluded with W.H.Smith, and its range of contributors was widened to include Liberals, Conservatives, pop stars and actors. The design was radically improved and updated.

In March 1978 Eric Hobsbawm gave the annual Marx Memorial Lecture which was later published under the title *The Forward March of Labour Halted?* Hobsbawm challenged the 'magnificent journey' approach to the labour movement which, like some left-wing version of the Whig Theory of History, maintained that Labour's progress was inevitable. Far from it: after all, look at how quickly and brutally Hitler and the Nazis had destroyed the powerful German labour movement in the 1930s.

Hobsbawm himself had once remarked that 'My own instinct has always been to say that the place for Marxist historians to publish is right where the people that are not Marxists can read them' and he drew attention to changes long noted by non-socialist commentators but which now, because the eminent Hobsbawm had mentioned them, could be freely discussed on the Left. In particular, the 'world of labour' which had spawned the modern British labour movement – a world of collectives, class, cities, factories – was dissolving. After all, barely one trade unionist in three had actually voted Labour – their 'own' party – at the 1983 general election.

Instead Hobsbawm pointed to certain social and economic trends which in fact gathered pace during the 1980s. There was the shift away from jobs in manufacturing industry – from 7.2 million in 1979 to 5.2 million in 1989 – to service industries which in 1989 employed more than 15 million people. The number of home owners had risen from 40 per cent in 1959 to 66 per cent in 1987. The growth of share-ownership had been stimulated by the Conservative government's 'privatisation' programme: 11 million share owners outnumbered the country's 8.5 million trade union-ists. Many more women were working, whilst geographical mobility had increased significantly.

The trade unions had proved impotent in the face of this maelstrom of change. For one thing, the movement – sometimes humorously referred to as 'TIGMOO' ('this great movement of ours') – had always been based on something of a sleight of hand. As Lewis Minkin, the expert on the Labour and trade union link, has noted:

> A lot of committed activity and much changing of hats by delegates creates the image of a mass movement. And always concealing the reality was the last of national affiliated membership and card votes cast in the names of millions – many of whom had not positively chosen to be included and some of whom had no idea that they were participating.

It was striking how many of these points had originally been made by Tony Crosland, Hugh Gaitskell and their fellow Labour Party 'revisionists' back in the 1950s. A publication called *Must Labour Lose?*, issued in 1960 after Labour's crushing election defeat the previous year, had presciently debated many issues that Professor Hobsbawm and others finally noticed twenty years later. Rita Hinden, for example, noted that Gaitskell's Labour was seen as too sectional, too identified with nationalisation and too divided. The success of Harold Wilson as a campaigner in winning elections meant that this analysis had been put in moth-balls.

But, of course, the social changes had not gone away. Nor could some commentators like R.W. Johnson resist pointing out that it was a member of the dwindling Communist Party, Eric Hobsbawm, who was providing intellectual sustenance for the Labour Party:

> It was strange indeed to think that Labour needed to take instruction in such areas from someone who was a lifelong member of quite another political party, one whose regular and vertiginous decline had in no way been stemmed by the wise counsel Professor Hobsbawm had been able to offer its leadership on such matters.

These social and economic trends did not automatically mean that socialism was outdated, but they did suggest that much rethinking was needed. Perhaps the most depressing aspect of the debate was the paucity of the response which greeted Hobsbawm; many of his critics, such as Communist trade union leader Ken Gill and the editor of the *New Left Review*, Robin Blackburn, blithely maintained that, in fact, the British Left was advancing or was just about to – and this in 1981 as a decade of Thatcherism got under way.

Nor was this process of rethinking likely to be carried out by traditional Communists, nicknamed 'tankies' because they had supported the sending in of Soviet tanks to Hungary in 1956 and Czechoslovakia in 1968. For them, 'Marxism' was writ in stone and remained true and 'scientific' now and for ever. Martin Jacques and his circle, however, brushed aside such prejudices and instead tried to identify the British Left with the future rather than the past. Rejecting completely the orthodox notion of 'party infallibility', *Marxism Today* began to play the kind of gadfly role that the Communist Party should always have adopted but because of the Moscow connection had shunned.

However, the magazine did shy away from several issues. For instance, although it certainly had an impact within the British Left, *Marxism Today* proved unable to reach large numbers of readers. Perhaps in recognition of this failure, it never discussed the lack of political interest in Britain, an apathy which could be seen in its own circulation figures. According to *Willings Press Guide 1989*, *Marxism Today*'s circulation was a miniscule 13,153 copies. This meant it lagged behind *Lancashire Today* (15,000), *Scottish Farmer* (25,050) and a long way behind *Flower Arranger* (57,000). Politics in Britain has always been a distinctly minority interest and when Tony Benn called for annual Parliaments, the hearts of most people dropped.

*Marxism Today* tried to insist that its contributors write in more accessible language; although often successful in this, certainly when compared with many other left-wing publications, the tone and substance of its contents still showed how the socialist tradition had become isolated from ordinary English. Its *New Times* collection, for example, repeatedly used language reminiscent of the worst of the old days, containing such obscurantist gems as 'the most advanced flexible specialisation strategies', 'universal human-life realisation', 'the Brazilianisation of advanced capitalism' and even 'Japanisation'.

In their introduction to this book, Stuart Hall and Martin Jacques claimed that 'The very proliferation of new sites of social antagonism makes the prospect of constructing a unified counter-hegemonic force as the agency of progressive change, if anything, harder rather than easier.' It is interesting to speculate what the human beings who might presumably constitute this 'unified counter-hegemonic force' would make of this nonsense.

Moreover Martin Jacques, unable to run *Marxism Today* without financial assistance from the Communist Party, could do nothing about the magazine's biggest albatross: its own title. It was stuck with the word 'Marxism' at a time when 'Marxism' either meant nothing at all or else suggested the repressive and crumbling regimes of Eastern Europe and was therefore to be condemned.

Nevertheless, *Marxism Today* did represent a more thoughtful and less knee-jerk response to the Conservative administration than some of the responses noted in the previous chapter – George Orwell could well have written for the magazine. It exemplified Martin Jacques' own attitude: 'I hate living in the ghetto. I like getting on with everyone. I like mixing with the right because they keep you on your toes and you learn things.'

And the magazine did have some influence on Neil Kinnock, even though Eric Hobsbawm became understandably tetchy at repeated suggestions that he was the Labour leader's 'guru'.

Whatever the validity of the intellectual arguments debated in *Marxism Today*, Neil Kinnock knew full well that he had to cope with rather more urgent short-term problems – particularly the divided and incompetent image the Labour Party presented to the public. Although Kinnock was much better known for his evangelistic qualities, it was the sinuous skills of the party manager that were urgently required. The Labour Party both nationally and locally needed sorting out.

First of all, he kept his distance from miners' leader Arthur Scargill, even cutting his hair shorter in order to play down any physical resemblance between the two men. He also followed the advice of his media advisers and began wearing more formal and darker suits for television interviews as they gave a more statesmanlike impression.

Secondly, trusted advisers were placed in charge of the party machinery. Larry Whitty succeeded Jim Mortimer as General Secretary in 1985 in order to tackle the chronic financial crisis as well as reorganise the Party's headquarters in Walworth Road, in South London. The move from Labour's traditional home alongside the Transport and General Workers' Union in Transport House suggested a decline in union influence. The Party's dozen separate departments were streamlined into just three: Publicity, Organisation and Research.

Thirdly, Kinnock built up a large personal office, appointing advisers such as Patricia Hewitt, Charles Clarke and John Eatwell with whom he felt comfortable. Critics like Tony Benn accused him of 'pioneering a presidential style which is quite foreign to our own traditions' but from Benn's point of view much worse was to come. Peter Mandelson had been appointed head of communications and campaigns in September 1985 and he made it crystal clear that the Party would adopt many of the media skills familiar to the Conservatives. The left-wing Campaign Group of Labour MPs was still denouncing the use of opinion polls.

This transformation is best demonstrated by the different approaches of Jim Mortimer and Peter Mandelson himself. Mortimer had hated the Saatchi & Saatchi techniques deployed by the Tories during the 1983 campaign:

> I can assure you that the Labour Party will never follow such a line of presentation in politics. The welfare of human beings, the care of people and the fact that we want to overcome unemployment – these are the tasks before us, not presenting people (politicians) as if they were breakfast food or baked beans.

Mortimer was wrong; Mandelson condemned Labour's 'blatant failure to communicate with the voters' at the 1983 election and was determined it would never happen again.

The over-inflated importance of the National Executive Committee itself, which expected to rule the party roost when Labour was out of office, was pruned back. The power base of the Left since the 1970s, the NEC's ninety sub-committees had specialised in spewing forth innumerable policy documents. Kinnock and his allies cut them back to just twenty. He also began taking on his party opponents in public, most famously at the Labour Party Conference in 1985 when he lambasted the Militant council in Liverpool for its grossly irresponsible behaviour. Militant supporters began to be expelled – a course of action which implicitly revived the proscribed list abolished in 1973.

Traditionally it had been the Labour Right that had dominated councils – Herbert Morrison's Greater London Council, the Braddocks in Liverpool, T.Dan Smith in Newcastle – but the rise of the so-called 'Loony Left' and their actions in Lambeth, Islington and elsewhere gave the right-wing press any number of convenient and damaging targets.

However, Kinnock did not publicly condemn Arthur Scargill for bringing the miners out on strike without a ballot. In later years, he looked back and claimed that this was the biggest mistake of his leadership. In private, he was scathing, describing Scargill as 'the labour movement's nearest equivalent to a First World War general.' This was Labour's 'lost year', even though Arthur Scargill claimed with typical bravado in July 1985 that the strike had changed the course of British history. Sadly, it did no such thing. Scargill's intransigent leadership proved unable to halt the decline of the industry: the 250,000 miners of 1982 have shrunk to fewer than 10,000 today.

Neil Kinnock's critics were furious. Tony Benn, for instance, confided this entry to his diary on 20 May 1984: 'Heard Neil Kinnock on the one o'clock news. His interviews are like processed cheese coming out of a mincing machine – nothing meaty, just one mass of meaningless rhetoric that defuses and anaesthetises the listener.'

Nevertheless the Labour leader also began to look for ways of increasing democracy within the Party and in particular of reducing both the power of the trade union block vote and of local activists. Somewhat belatedly, he edged towards the policy of 'one member, one vote' or OMOV as it became known. But Kinnock had to tread carefully – in fact he was defeated on this very issue at the 1984 Conference – because of a central dilemma: under party rules only the trade union block vote could reform the trade union block vote and the trade unions accounted for 89 per cent of the votes cast at Conferences. Farcically, this block vote amounted to no less than six million votes – yet only three and a half million unionists had actually voted Labour at the 1987 election.

But, of course, trade union money underpinned the Labour Party whose financial needs were only likely to grow: the Party was to spend £4,200,000 during its 1987 election campaign alone. The cost of new campaigning techniques – from direct mail shots to computer-aided telephone interviews – required large sums of money. Over a half of Labour MPs were sponsored by the unions.

The unions themselves were of course under pressure from a declining membership, and their steadfast opposition to Conservative legislation calling for ballots and elections had reinforced the public impression that they were unrepresentative bodies. As Bryan Gould tactfully put it, 'It was clearly a serious political mistake, and a denial of socialist principle, to allow others to espouse the cause of democratising the trade unions.'

And yet this same union tie continued to give the Labour Party an important link with a substantial chunk of the electorate, namely the organised working class. For many commentators, this association provided Labour with the backbone to see off the breakaway Social Democrats whose defectors had singularly failed to consult their potential union allies before their departure. As the historian Lewis Minkin commented, 'Their style and tone of addressing the unions was often derogatory and just as often deeply resented.' Unlike both their Conservative and Labour rivals, the Alliance did not represent any particular special-interest group.

As the SDP's historians have noted, the party was spread very thinly across Britain with often no more than eighty to eighty-five members in each constituency. In some places, the

Social Democrats never really existed: '. . . there was no SDP to speak of in the heavily industrial and solidly working-class belts of south Wales, central Scotland and the Black Country.' When political times became hard, SDP activists simply melted away whilst Labour's, reinforced by their trade union allegiances, kept trudging on.

The value of the Labour – trade union link was, much to the government's surprise and displeasure, confirmed by a series of ballots held between April 1985 and March 1986. Hoping to pierce the Labour jugular by cutting off its traditional source of finance, the Conservative government – at the prompting of Employment Secretary Norman Tebbit – passed the Trade Union Act of 1984 stipulating that unions must conduct a ballot of their members if they wished to maintain a political fund. All thirty-seven ballots went in favour of a fund. Of nearly seven million ballot papers issued, almost one-half were returned and of that number no less than 83 per cent voted 'yes'.

It proved to be a striking affirmation of the link between the industrial and political wings of the movement. One could imagine Keir Hardie puffing out his chest in pride and saying 'told you so.' As the *Guardian* could not resist pointing out: 'In giving the unions back to their members, Mr Tebbit may have offered the unions a lifeline of survival for which they in the long run may be profoundly grateful.'

Rather like a snake shedding its skin, the Labour Party began to abandon key longstanding policies. Withdrawal from the EEC was quietly dropped. Nationalisation and massive public intervention were put on the back burner and the sale of council houses was accepted. Not all the new union laws would be repealed. Penal rates of taxation would not be levied. The House of Lords would not be abolished outright. Much of the 1970s and 1980s Labour programme as embodied in the Alternative Economic Strategy (AES) whether it was import controls or planning agreements, was discarded.

But Labour did not ditch all its spending aspirations. Nicholas Timmins has remarked that 'Labour went into the

1987 election with a welfare state shopping list that can be summed up by the one word "more" – a programme whose priority jobs and welfare element was alone costed by the party at £6 billion and by the Tories at several times more.'

Ironically, Kinnock's transformation of Labour was greatly helped by his own left-wing background, just as both Ramsay MacDonald and Harold Wilson's initial radical leanings had allayed the fears of some. The spectacular own goals of his critics helped too. In early 1987, at a crucial by-election in Greenwich, the local Party fielded an identikit left-wing activist who duly lost the seat to the Social Democrat candidate. This failure allowed Kinnock to tighten the NEC's control of election candidates.

In fact Kinnock's success as a party manager contrasted revealingly with Hugh Gaitskell's comparative failure to get his way thirty years before. Left-wing critics argued that he was returning the Party to the bad old authoritarian days of General Secretary Morgan Phillips who had kept a strict hold over the party, but Kinnock and his supporters knew that the images of extremism and disunity associated with Labour were electorally debilitating.

However no one knew what the Labour Party actually stood for. Most people recognised what it was not, essentially 'Not Michael Foot's Labour Party' – and in this absence the Party played its 'Neil and Glenys' card during the 1987 election campaign for all it was worth, just as Harold Wilson more than twenty years earlier had dealt the 'modern party for a modern world' card. Music from Brahms introduced the glossy political broadcast, directed by Hugh Hudson, which focused exclusively on the leader, his wife and their family. Kinnock's personal rating in the polls shot up 19 per cent overnight. The Conservatives were rattled and although Labour lost, the government's majority was reduced.

But most worrying for Neil Kinnock and his advisers was that although commentators agreed that the Labour Party had run a better campaign than its opponents, the Conservatives still secured a huge 102-seat majority. The Labour Party's share of the vote only inched up from 28 per cent in 1983 to 31 per cent in 1987, a long way behind the 37 per cent achieved as recently as 1979 and an irrefutable sign of the Left's inadequate response to Mrs Thatcher in the 1980s. In 1959 Hugh Gaitskell's Labour Party had run a superior campaign to the Conservatives and lost, but still won just under 44 per cent of the vote. Despite all the blood, sweat and tears of the previous four years, Labour's vote had risen by barely 3.5 percent, even though Michael Foot was no longer leader.

One partial consolation was that the electoral system finally killed off the SDP's hopes of replacing Labour. As Crewe and King pointed out, under a system of proportional representation the Alliance would have won 143 seats in 1987 and almost certainly formed part of a coalition government. Instead they won a measly total of twenty-two seats.

But why had Labour performed so disappointingly? In part, the Tory-supporting tabloids had done their usual bit: 73 per cent of the *Sun*'s election coverage, 54 per cent of the *Daily Mail*'s and 46 per cent of the *Daily Star's* was 'Labour-knocking' copy. But there was more to it than that. Research after the defeat suggested that Labour's extremist and divided image, its lack of economic credibility and its unilateralist defence policy had cost a crucial 7 per cent in public support since 1964. The Conservatives had made much of Labour's non-nuclear defence policy, issuing a poster which showed a soldier with his hands up, surrendering.

The Labour Party continued its search to present a much softer image to the electorate; the Red Rose rather than the Red Flag. Unilateralism was promptly ditched and the closed shop was no longer regarded as sacrosanct. Here was the Labour Party being turned into a moderate middle of the road body by a politician whom Hugh Gaitskell would have distrusted as an extremist, and yet the changes amounted to no less than the Labour Party's own 'Bad Godesberg':

> The colour of Party membership books was changed from red to blue and Party members were expected to stop addressing each other as Comrade and to use the term 'party friend'. The flag of the Federal Republic was now flown alongside the traditional red flag above the party headquarters . . . The overriding aim of the Party leadership in the years after Bad Godesberg was to participate in Government.

This description in fact refers to the changes which took place within the German Social Democrats in the 1950s, but obvious parallels can be drawn with the Labour Party in the 1980s and 1990s. Certainly the transformation seemed to be taking place with the support of the Party at large. In 1988 Tony Benn challenged Neil Kinnock for the leadership. Of the 586 constituencies that voted, only 112 – much less than a quarter – backed Benn. It was a crushing blow for the Labour Left.

But despite the slaughter of sacred cows, it was still unclear what the Labour Party actually stood for: what were its values and motivations, its ideals and programmes? After the 1987 election Peter Mandelson called for further changes if Labour was ever to win another election: 'I think this requires switching from a policy committee based process to a communications-based exercise.' Yet however good the communications might be, people still wanted to know where Labour stood on taxes, labour laws, the EEC and federalism, health, housing, education and so on.

The NEC initiated a series of seven 'Policy Reviews' which proved to be, in commentator Martin Jacques' words, 'an exercise in exorcism' and were disappointingly vague as to how Labour proposed creating 'Socialism with a Human Face'. Members of the committees, determined not to accumulate the £34 billion bill in pledges totted up by the 1987 election proposals, reacted rather like rabbits caught in the car headlights.

Labour clearly possessed no distinctive economic approach. In the 1930s the Party had drawn upon the work of J.M. Keynes; in the 1970s all it had to offer was the gloomy and unpopular Alternative Economic Strategy (AES) calling for a massive extension of the state. The AES had now been junked but replaced by – what?

Some critics argued that the Labour Party needed to find, as Mrs Thatcher had done, a 'Big Idea', but it seemed desperately short of even good little ideas. One possibility put forward was 'market socialism'. As Bryan Gould, a linchpin in the 1987 election campaign, explained in his book *A Future for Socialism*: 'Our basic stance should therefore be that there is nothing inherently unsocialist about the market mechanism, if used for well-defined and properly understood purposes, and if properly regulated and monitored.'

The admission that market forces would play an important part in the Labour Party's economic strategy showed how far Neil Kinnock's Labour Party had adjusted itself to the new political climate under Mrs Thatcher – just as in the 1940s it had been the Conservative Party that adjusted to the Labour Party. But market socialism proved elusive when explaining what it would actually mean in practice.

One perceptive critic, Ferdinand Mount, homed in on Labour's dilemma: 'if you keep common ownership in the script, then it must still be the state which is directing the play. "Socialism without the state" is a pleasant but vacuous thought. Hamlet without the Prince would make a more satisfying night out.'

Throughout 1989, 1990 and 1991 the Labour Party steadily published a range of position papers outlining its views and policies on any number of issues. The Party even started to address itself to the issue of wealth creation itself. In the not so distant past socialists, whether they be Tony Crosland or Aneurin Bevan, had lived in times when economic growth could almost be taken for granted. The question of the distribution of the cake was therefore paramount.

But now the cake was obstinately refusing to grow at all – and it was unlikely that persuasion alone would prevail upon the haves to surrender their wealth to the have-nots. If they were to be electorally credible, socialists had to show that they too knew how to stimulate economic growth.

In general, socialists had been uncomfortable when it came to wealth creation. Marxists and others had endlessly condemned 'materialism' – other people's if not always their own – and traditionally the electorate associated the Labour Party with 'hard times' or with disaster: the mishandling of the Great Depression by MacDonald's government; Cripps' austerity measures after the Second World War; devaluation and the collapse of the National Plan under Harold Wilson; the bailing out of the Callaghan administration in 1976 by the International Monetary Fund. At local level, too, the actions of some Labour-controlled councils meant that the Party was often associated with 'big public spending' and the mismanagement of resources.

Likewise opinion polls usually showed that the Conservatives scored much higher than Labour on the question of economic competence, and there was a widespread feeling that socialists were often more concerned with the distribution of wealth than its creation. But it was and is economic prosperity that gives people the opportunity for choice and the ability to exercise more control over their own lives; as Beatrix Campbell once put it, 'All this anti-consumerist talk is so anti-mass pleasure . . .'

Only future economic growth can provide the resources to destroy the inequalities which still disfigure our society. The Labour Party must either deliver a better quality of life or become irrelevant because, as Bryan Gould once pointed out, the early leaders of the labour movement did not say 'Join us and accept a lower standard of living.'

Labour was quick to attack the apparent Conservative disinterest in the manufacturing industry – there was no net investment throughout the 1980s (it would be interesting to speculate what the Japanese thought of this) and no fewer than twelve different Conservative Ministers passed through the Department of Trade and Industry between 1979 and 1990. But somehow this new-found solicitude for industry came rather oddly from a party whose leading figures had never had anything whatsoever to do with industry or finance.

Labour proposals included technology trusts, a National Investment Bank, regional development agencies, tax allowances for research and training, a Ministry for Women, and a Freedom of Information Act guaranteeing access to information. Some proposals such as the National Economic Assessment with its annual publication sounded ominously like Harold Wilson and George Brown's National Plan, which of course went horribly wrong.

Yet somehow this outpouring did not add up to the 'favourable climate of opinion' which Richard Crossman and others had talked about. Admittedly, it is never easy for the opposition to generate shifts in opinion but there was little sign of overwhelming public support for, or even interest in, the Labour Party's programme. After all the Conservative government was buttressed by the benefits of North Sea oil and did not shy away from using the full resources of the government machine to publicise its privatisation measures, most notably in the 'Tell Sid' adverts in 1986, which heralded the sale of British Gas.

Labour also faced a rabidly articulate right-wing press exemplified by the *Sun*. As William Shawcross, biographer of Rupert Murdoch, has expressed it: 'The *Sun*'s political skill lay in its ability to attack Labour politicians with a vigour well outside the competence of the Tory machine and even the plain-speaking Mrs Thatcher.' In January 1994 the *Sunday Times*, another of Murdoch's newspapers, admitted that 'Too many newspapers during the Thatcher years were in the pockets of the government . . .' Kinnock himself was under sustained attack by television interviewers such as David Frost who allowed himself to be briefed beforehand by right-wing commentators such as Brian Crozier.

One continuing problem was that the language and style of the socialist intelligentsia remained turgid and unmemorable. Whereas the broadly right-wing *Spectator* magazine took on a new lease of life during the 1980s because of its sparkling literary qualities, the left-wing *New Statesman* continued to decline, shedding both readers and influence. That the language of Labour had become so stilted reflected the Left's loss of self-confidence.

Certainly the Policy Reviews set no one's imagination racing. The possibility of dissent was minimised by presenting them to the Party Conferences of 1989 and 1990 as a package, to be rejected or accepted in their entirety. Somehow this authoritarian and safety-first approach summed up the whole exercise. Throughout the 1980s Mrs Thatcher's Conservative government proved to be the true radical, whilst the Labour Party was hidebound and stately.

Why this sense of disappointment? The basic reason lay in the old and stultifying legacy of labourism – admirable in its day, but its day had long since gone. Whereas the Conservatives had needed only three years in the latter half of the 1940s to adapt to the new post-war mood, Labour was still struggling after ten. Take the composition of the Parliamentary Labour Party in 1990: of 229 MPs, less than one in ten were women, and only four were black or coloured. Looking at these proportions, an outside observer would have thought that Britain was an all-white, 90 per cent male society.

When Karl Marx wrote in 1852 that 'The tradition of all the dead generations weighs like a nightmare on the brain of the living', he could have been describing the weight of labourism which inhibited the Party in the 1980s. In general, the unions' influence tended to inhibit; as one critic put it, 'their influence in policy-making has been generally negative; "closing-off" certain options.' As late as 1989 the TUC was still calling for the repeal of all the Conservative legislation of the 1980s.

After the 1987 election a sample of people was asked to draw pictures of the Conservative and Labour Parties: 'The Tories were associated with success, smiling families, high tech – all painted in bright colours. With Labour we are plunged into a grim and Dickensian world of decay and failure: cloth caps, smoke-stack industries, poverty and failure – all portrayed in plain black and white.' It was a long time since the Harold Wilson era in the early 1960s when Labour had tried to identify itself with technological progress.

Three things in particular were wrong. First, typically, there was what Eric Hobsbawm called 'the terrible insularity' of the Policy Reviews. Anyone would think that it had been the British Labour Party that had been electorally triumphant rather than some, but not all, of its continental counterparts.

Secondly, the usual institutional timidity was to the fore, a feeling that labourism was happy to work the system in which it grew up. Take proportional representation (PR), which Labour's leadership was opposed to and which would surely be embraced by any radical party. In his lengthy restatement of modern democratic socialism, *Choose Freedom*, Roy Hattersley proved unable to spare a single sentence in his 254 pages for this subject nor to a proposed Bill of Rights.

Thirdly, surveys and opinion polls had told the Labour leadership what the electorate was against, but had failed to tell them what it was for. Instead the Labour Party became 'safe' to the point of dullness, not normally the characteristic one would associate with an organisation which, after all, was intended to challenge the status quo.

One sympathetic critic, David Marquand, was indeed right to point out that 'The object of the 1989 Policy Review was not to mobilise a constituency behind a set of principles; it was to tailor a programme for a set of constituencies. Opinion research told the party managers what themes would "play" with the voter. The review groups then did their best to weave the themes concerned into a plausible whole.'

Labour's loss of identity was reflected in its continuing and precipitous decline as a national organisation. More than 60,000 people left the Party between 1984 and 1988; in many areas of Britain Labour had almost ceased to function as an important agency. For example in Wales, traditionally a part of the Celtic fringe vital to the Party and boasting twenty-five MPs in 1990, only 20,000 people were paid-up members. In the northern region, the figure was just 18,000. Observers commented on the 'de-energized feeling' of proceedings and the lack of activism.

Where were these departees going to? Certainly not to the fringe groupings of the Far Left, despite their posturing and noise. The dwindling Communist Party was torn apart by the defection of the *Morning Star* newspaper into the 'hardline' camp and as usual battles between the comrades were conducted with a bitterness and vehemence characteristic of much 'fraternal' debate. As is so typical of the fissiparous Left, the Communist Party went out of existence but spawned instead two new bodies, the Communist Party of Britain and the Democratic Left.

Other groupings fared equally badly. The Workers' Revolutionary Party, which boasted the allegiance of Vanessa and Corin Redgrave, was led by the small, rotund and bespectacled figure of Gerry Healy who, it was revealed at his death, had over many years exercised a kind of Marxist *droit de seigneur* on young female comrades – confirming how even the most dedicated of revolutionaries found it difficult to reconcile the rhetoric of female emancipation with its reality.

The Socialist Workers' Party (SWP) was undoubtedly the most visible of groups: no demonstration was complete without its horde of ubiquitous banners urging people to buy the *Socialist Worker* newspaper. Its litany that Labour and trade union leaders always betrayed or 'sold out' the workforce meant that the party championed grassroots struggles. At a time when union representation was under persistent challenge from employers emboldened by the initiatives of the Thatcher government, this was often admirable.

But the SWP's facile claims that revolution was just around

the corner – never mind the fact that the workers continually gave Mrs Thatcher thumping electoral victories – and the party's authoritarian methods of democratic centralism which mirrored the old Communist Party at its worst, ensured that membership never even reached the 10,000 mark.

At least the SWP did possess a sense of purpose, however misguided. The Labour Party on the other hand, supposedly an iconoclastic body dedicated to changing British society, was now drifting. Labour's approach seemed to boil down to the claim that 'We Are Not The Conservative Party', lying low, saying little and hoping that a tide of anti-Thatcherism plus a dash of Europeanism and some help from a failing economy would bring the Labour ship into a safe electoral port.

This negative stance personalised the issues and was always likely to be scuppered if Mrs Thatcher left office. This duly happened in November 1990 when Conservative MPs – with an unerring eye for their own electoral prospects – decided that the Prime Minister, despite her three successive victories (but also creating the Poll Tax), was unlikely to win a fourth victory and should therefore be replaced.

Labour's policy cupboard was now left looking distinctly bare. Not only was some foolish abuse hurled at the departing Mrs Thatcher – Jack Straw, the Shadow Minister of Education, called her 'an evil woman', which made one wonder what adjective he would have applied to a Stalin or Hitler – but the Party's short-termism had left it patently devoid of either Keir Hardie-like ideals or Clement Attlee-like administrative plans.

Neil Kinnock for example, despite his previous belief expressed as recently as 1983 that 'It is inconceivable that we could transform this society without a major extension of public ownership and control' was now happy to tell the right-wing Institute of Directors that Clause Four of the Party's constitution was irrelevant and meaningless: 'They were the tunes of glory coming out. Well, we've stopped that nonsense.' But Labour had singularly failed to come up with any other tunes.

In their study of the 1987 election, experienced observers David Butler and Dennis Kavanagh claimed that:

> Since 1979 the Conservatives had located a large constituency of 'winners', people who have an interest in the return of a Conservative government. It includes much of the affluent South, home-owners, share-owners, and most of those in work, whose standard of living, measured in post-tax incomes, has improved appreciably since 1979.

But they did add a sting in the tail: 'The rub is that continued economic prosperity may be the necessary lubricant to maintain the coalition.'

When the Lawson boom – which had indeed lubricated the Conservative Party election victory at 1987 – came crashing down, the Tory coalition would surely collapse. But although it may have been the Conservatives who had been largely responsible for the slump – despite the energetic way they blamed the world recession – the Tories were still most trusted to right the ship, notwithstanding their public disagreements over Britain's membership of the European Exchange Rate Mechanism (ERM). For example, a poll of April 1992 showed that 52 per cent of the sample thought the Conservatives were best suited to tackle Britain's economic problems; only 31 per cent preferred to trust Labour.

One continuing problem for Labour was simple: its lack of money. The Party decided to target its resources on the forthcoming general election: although the Conservatives spent £11.1 million in 1992, Labour was not far behind with its £10.6 million. But of course such rough equality was achieved at a cost. Labour had spent far less in the run up to the election. Between 1987 and 1992 the Conservatives devoted £73 million to their campaigning efforts, Labour just £47 million. Equally telling, by 1992 the Tories could afford more than 350 full-time agents whilst Labour employed fewer than 50. As Martin Linton has said of the 1992 campaign, 'The gap was only closed by opening up another gap elsewhere.'

This is of course one of the great unmentionables of British politics. Although stringent regulations apply at constituency level, nationally anything goes. Individual donations, no matter what the source, do not have to be declared by political parties. In 1992 alone, for instance, the Conservatives received £19 million in gifts – of which £15 million came from undisclosed and anonymous sources. On 19 June 1993 *The Times* wrote of Lord McAlpine, the party's treasurer between 1975 and 1990, that 'he raised more than £100 million for the cause, money that went a long way to ensuring that the 1980s were a decade of one-party rule.'

Where did the money come from? We will never know. Between 1979 and 1984, for instance, the Conservative Party issued no accounts whatsoever – and this at a time when it was energetically forcing the trade unions 'to clean up their act'. Lord McAlpine shamelessly tries to throw a smokescreen over this crucial episode either by claiming that most of the money came from the sale of jam at party bazaars – a nation less of shopkeepers than ardent jam-eaters – or maintaining that because he sometimes invited journalists from the *Guardian* into his office for a drink then somehow the whole question of accountability was instantly solved. In no other European country would such behaviour be tolerated, and it was a massive factor in ensuring Labour was always outgunned financially by its opponents.

More information is coming to light but, of course, after the event when it is too late. For instance, it was revealed in March 1996 that a group of Hong Kong businessmen donated no less than £3.8 million to the Conservative Party in the run up to the 1992 election. Here is one area of British politics that any future Labour government should surely clean up without delay.

Labour's lack of a coherent philosophy and programme was most cruelly summed up by the restraints placed on Neil Kinnock himself. His natural exuberance and spontaneity was reined in and replaced by an artificial seriousness.

In her autobiography Barbara Castle describes going to see Kinnock just before the 1992 election:

> I could talk to him freely because he knew I believed in him. 'Neil,' I pleaded, 'your speeches are too statistical. Why don't you talk more about values?' 'I know,' he replied, 'but they won't let me,' and he looked at the door as though his minders might break in.

David Hare's semi-documentary play *The Absence of War* depicts this process at work.

The replacement of Margaret Thatcher by John Major somehow gave the electorate the impression that, despite the previous uninterrupted years in office since 1979, the Conservatives had started again. The Conservatives also made the most of what it called 'Labour's tax bombshell', namely the admission by the Shadow Chancellor that anyone earning over £22,000 could expect to pay more tax. One in six taxpayers would have been hit, but Tory propaganda managed to portray it as yet another example of Old Labour's tax, spend and borrow inclinations.

On the question of law and order, too, the Conservatives were preferred to Labour. Just before the 1992 election Gallup found that 46 per cent of the sample thought the Tories were best placed on this issue; just 25 per cent thought that Labour would do a better job. During the actual campaign, Labour mistakenly raised the question of Proportional Representation in the final few days – Kinnock refused to state publicly his own position – and also organised the notorious rally in Sheffield which helped move the earth or at least Middle England.

The election on 9 April 1992 proved yet another disappointment. Labour's vote had edged up just 2 per cent to a grand total of 34.5 per cent – still someway behind its 38 per cent mark in 1979. In other words, after thirteen long years Labour had still not matched the level of support it had enjoyed when the era of Conservative government had actually begun.

An editorial in the *Sunday Times* three days later, headed simply 'Socialism, RIP', was brutal:

> In the end, the Tories could not even give it away, though there were times during the campaign when they looked intent on doing just that. But even the worst Tory campaign in living memory coupled with the best Labour one, the longest recession since the war, an election fought largely on Labour issues, lingering resentment about the poll tax and a bungled Tory budget could not secure a Labour victory. With so much working to Labour's advantage, yet the result a fourth Tory term, it is hard to imagine what it would take to give Labour power. The most significant lesson of the general election of 1992 is that, in its present form, Labour is unelectable.

But then Labour had clearly been unelectable in both 1983 and 1987, forcing the Party, at Neil Kinnock's urging, to change itself drastically – but with what result? Yet another defeat.

One major problem was Kinnock himself. For all his many virtues and achievements as a party manager, the electorate simply did not see him occupying 10 Downing Street. Paradoxically, as Roy Hattersley and others noted, he had been chosen back in 1983 because of his left-wing views on Europe and nuclear defence, but it was these same views which alienated public support. And when he began to ditch these same views, he was perceived as opportunist and unprincipled. Kinnock simply could not win. In David Owen's words: 'I am genuinely pleased by the changes that Neil Kinnock has made in Labour Party policy since 1988 and it cannot have been easy for him to reverse his own position. But I ask myself, as I suspect do many others, does he truly believe the policies he now espouses?'

Even if there was no need to dwell on Kinnock's supposed personal flaws – his baldness, red hair, freckles and 'a certain brand of Welshness' – as one newspaper editorial did, there was no doubt that he was perceived as falling between two stools: lacking the principles of Hugh Gaitskell or the ability to win elections of Harold Wilson. Margaret Thatcher was typically scathing: 'Mr Kinnock, in all his years as Opposition leader, never let me down. Right to the end, he struck every wrong note.'

But Kinnock had ensured that the Labour Party survived as a viable political force. Even in 1987, commentator John Cole noted, the Alliance took second place in 228 of the Conservatives' 375 seats and in many places had a better chance of winning than did Labour. In 1992, however, the Liberal Democrats were second to the Tories in less than half their seats: 'The next election was clearly going to be more of a Conservative – Labour battle than any since 1979.' Kinnock deserves much of the praise for this.

And, touchingly, he received a staggering 30,000 messages and letters of support from members of the public after the defeat on 9 April 1992. Few, if any, politicians in recent times could have matched such a figure.

Yet the Conservatives' fourth election victory in a row meant that since 1918, when Labour began to edge out the Liberals as the main opposition party, Labour had only twice secured working majorities at a general election.

Clearly, much still remained to be done.

# 15

# New Worlds, New Labour?
## Tony Blair and the Labour Party in the 1990s

'It was not Keir Hardie who formed it [the Labour Party], it grew out of the bowels of the Trades Union Congress.'
ERNEST BEVIN, 1931

'Politics is a moral activity. Values should shine through at all times. You could either call it evangelism or salesmanship. I want the spirit of the evangel but the success of the good salesman.'
JOHN SMITH, JULY 1992

'Labour is a party of government or it is nothing.'
TONY BLAIR, JUNE 1995

The unexpected defeat on 9 April 1992 pitched many socialists into a mire of gloom and despondency. It was difficult to see how Labour could ever win a general election again. After all, the Party had systematically shed both the extremist policies and image that had supposedly contributed to its defeats in the 1980s, whilst the Shadow Cabinet was at least as able and energetic as its Conservative counterpart and came across better on television.

But still, despite this transformation, Labour's share of the popular vote was lower in 1992 than it had been in 1979. Thirteen years of 'Hard Labour' and the Party seemed to be going nowhere.

The depression was deepened by the crowing of the hated *Sun* newspaper which proudly claimed on its front page that IT WAS THE SUN WOT WON IT. The headline was quickly withdrawn but, ironically, here was one tabloid headline that indeed proved to be accurate. Research carried out by Martin Linton at Nuffield College, Oxford, suggests the paper helped swing half a million votes to the Conservatives: 'sufficient, if the swing had been the same in every marginal, to give Labour and the Lib-Dems one more seat than the Conservatives.'

The combination of press hostility and the Conservative ability to garner massive and undeclared funds from all over the world was too much for many in the shrunken Labour Party, which now numbered barely a quarter of a million members. There was a collective deflation and loss of interest in politics.

Matters were not helped by the actions of the Major administration. It had effectively bought the election with extra spending on health, social security and education, allowing the public sector borrowing requirement to double from £26 million in 1992 to £50 billion in 1993. Then, with the election safely won, the Tories embarked on the very tax increases for which they had condemned Labour in the election campaign the year before. The bungled departure from the ERM was almost the final straw.

The scale of demoralisation meant that few people had the inclination to indulge in retrospective recrimination, although a few mutterings were directed at John Smith for his alternative budget which was blamed for giving Conservative Central Office the opportunity to portray Labour as the same old 'tax and spend' party. But if Labour was doomed to lose every election at which it proposed higher taxes to pay for its interventionist programme, then why have a Labour Party in the first place?

Notwithstanding this *sotto voce* criticism, which John Smith later accepted, he was clearly Neil Kinnock's probable successor. One of the handful of Labour MPs with Cabinet experience – he had served as Secretary of State for Trade under Jim Callaghan between 1978 and 1979 – Smith had earned respect throughout the Party for his conspicuous loyalty to Kinnock, even though a succession of polls had suggested that Labour under Smith was more likely to win an election.

In such circumstances, Conservative MPs would almost certainly have deposed their leader, as had been done in 1990 with Mrs Thatcher, but Kinnock was saved by the unwieldy rules governing the election of Labour leaders. This cumbersome but more democratic process called for the participation not just of MPs at Westminster but also of the unions and the constituencies. A Tory-style coup was therefore out of the question; in fact, throughout Neil Kinnock's eight and a half years as leader there was no serious plotting against him. Apart from his hardcore enemies on the Labour Left, most people recognised that he alone could generate the much-needed internal changes.

Kinnock quickly resigned after the election defeat, departing with a farewell blast against the press, and John Smith was duly seen as the anointed successor.

John Smith embodied all the considerable virtues of 'Old Labour': the moderation, the solid roots in the community, the link with the working class in the form of the trade union movement. Not even as a youngster had Smith flirted with the Labour Left and he had been happy to call himself a Gaitskellite. Like Hugh Gaitskell, Smith had no truck with unilateralism; unlike Gaitskell, he was a convinced European, breaking the party whip in 1971 in order to vote for British entry.

But Smith was pragmatic enough not to elevate this disagreement into a festering dissatisfaction with, and eventual departure from, the Party, unlike Roy Jenkins or David Owen. In the early 1980s when Labour was committed to unilateralism and withdrawal from Europe, Smith simply kept his head below the barricades. His high reputation at Westminster was not matched by constituency support, so that he was never remotely likely to be elected onto the National Executive Committee.

That Smith's competence and dedication were widely admired is borne out in the unlikely source of Tony Benn's diaries. Although ideological poles apart, Benn never lambasts Smith with the vehemence which he regularly metes out to Kinnock. Smith's strong Scottish and family roots gave him an important non-political base, whilst his bank manager-like appearance contradicted the tabloid portrayal of Labour as a collection of wild-haired and eye-rolling maniacs: the balding and bespectacled Smith could not have been more different.

By the end of the 1980s the Labour Party had roughly divided into two camps, namely the modernisers who wanted to tear the Party up by its roots and start again, and the traditionalists happy to ride out the Thatcherite storm in the confident expectation that, sooner rather than later, it would be Labour's turn again.

These two camps were never clearcut, as the case of John Smith himself shows. Although accepting that the Party must change and adapt to new circumstances, he understood too the value of its foundations, particularly the trade union connection. He was therefore never terribly interested in debating either the merits of 'one member one vote' (OMOV) or of Clause Four. For Smith, such divisive exercises distracted from the real business of opposing the Tories root and branch.

Smith's stance was rather different from the conspicuous iconoclasm of his main challenger for the leadership, Bryan Gould. Whereas Smith was the solid Scottish Establishment man, Gould was the outsider from New Zealand who appeared more sympathetic to radical change. It was Gould who at the 1987 election had helped mastermind Labour's whizzkid election campaign. He followed this up with a book called *A Future for Socialism* which happily embraced the need for competition and markets. By contrast, Smith was much too pragmatic to devote time to writing treatises.

For all his chirpiness Gould possessed no solid base within

the Party and he was handicapped, too, by his decision to run for the posts of both leader and deputy leader. He went down to defeat in each contest. It proved to be the end of his active political career in Britain. Hostile to Europe and Britain's membership of the Exchange Rate Mechanism (ERM) – which Smith and his colleagues supported – Gould sulked in his tent before departing to New Zealand. He was virtually the only politician of talent whom Labour lost in its wilderness years: a tribute to the management of Neil Kinnock and John Smith, or perhaps testimony to Labour's incurable optimism that the next election was theirs.

Old Labour had never been entirely happy with the so-called 'beautiful people' surrounding Neil Kinnock, particularly the media pundits and advisers gathered in the Shadow Communications Agency who, according to some, bypassed the central apparatus of the Party and boasted too much influence for unappointed and unelected advisers. The Shadow Communications Agency was therefore shunted into the sidings. Only a grudging exponent of OMOV, Smith positively condemned suggestions that Clause Four, which committed Labour to sweeping nationalisation, should be tampered with. When Jack Straw, a modernising member of the Shadow Cabinet, published a pamphlet calling for its revision, a furious Smith marched into Straw's office and bawled him out.

Smith was also content with the Party's stance on the necessity for a national minimum wage and for retaining universal benefits. Nor did Smith show much interest in the alleged misbehaviour of the Labour council in his own constituency of Monklands. Smith's biographer thought this story 'refused to take legs and walk'; he was wrong. An independent report chaired by Professor Robert Black later found that nepotism on the council was rife: sixteen of the twenty-one members of the council had sixty-eight relatives who worked for it, whilst sectarian discrimination was flagrant. As the *Guardian* put it, 'The situation in Monklands is an abuse of power.'

Generally, Smith seemed to favour a 'one more heave' approach. Labour was in fundamentally good shape, particularly when compared to a seemingly incompetent Conservative administration dogged by uncertainty and internal bickering. If the Party kept to the straight and narrow then electoral victory was inevitable. However, Labour had heaved mightily at both the 1987 and 1992 elections with very little effect and, no matter how unpopular the Conservatives might be between times, they were highly skilled at winning general elections.

Some critics did begin to murmur that Smith's strategy was inadequate. Two youthful leading members of his Shadow Cabinet, Gordon Brown and Tony Blair, were also thought to be anxious that Labour was relapsing into its semi-comatose shape – and apparently Smith was preparing to crank up once more for the fray. Sadly, of course, we will never know what might have been because John Smith died unexpectedly of a heart attack in May 1994.

The sense of national loss felt at Smith's death showed that here indeed had been a profoundly decent and honourable politician at a time when politicians were not held in high esteem. The huge number of visitors to his grave at Iona Abbey bear this out: by June 1995 a reported one thousand visitors were arriving at the churchyard each day.

The Labour Party observed a respectful period of mourning after Smith's death but, of course, politics goes on and inevitably minds soon turned to the question of the succession. One obvious contender was Gordon Brown, a fellow Scot and ally of John Smith's who had stepped into his shoes as Shadow Chancellor. Politics was and always had been at the core of Brown's life, whether as an historian, pamphleteer or MP. He was handicapped by his Scottishness – the Party was unlikely to welcome two Scots in a row as leader – and by his rather grim demeanour. Brown spent much time on television responding to bad news like a particularly gloomy undertaker.

Brown's main rival was the Shadow Home Secretary Tony

Blair, who, by contrast, seemed to brim over with high spirits. If Brown never smiled, then Blair never stopped. In an age where appearance was deemed crucial, this was a vital asset for Blair. Robin Cook, for instance, a talented and articulate senior Labour figure was ruled out of the race because his looks were thought to resemble those of a garden gnome.

Whereas Brown came from the trusty Scottish Labour culture, Blair was an Englishman who, although educated at Fettes, the leading Scottish public school, had gone on to Oxford, been a London barrister, lived in London and now represented a constituency in the north of England. If Brown was the archetypal insider, fully conversant with arcane Labour rituals, Blair possessed a rather more complicated inheritance.

On the one hand he, too, was an insider who had enjoyed an effortless rise through the Party. In 1982, fighting a hopeless by-election in the safe seat of Beaconsfield during the Falklands war, he had espoused the then Party orthodoxy of unilateralism and withdrawal from Europe. The next year he landed a safe seat – there were not many of these during Labour's calamitous election of 1983. Promotion to the Shadow Cabinet and a place on the National Executive Committee soon followed and in 1992, at the age of just thirty-nine, he was appointed Shadow Home Secretary.

On the other hand, Tony Blair was also a Labour outsider. Many years ago the veteran left-wing agitator Tom Mann declared that 'Unless a Socialist leader has been in prison his education has been neglected.' On this score alone, Blair was indeed uneducated. Or, to use the more modern imagery of biographer Jon Sopel:

> He doesn't talk wistfully of bygone days, conjuring up folklore memories of comrades on winter mornings huddling together around a brazier outside the factory gates or the historic battles on the picket lines as organised labour fought against the power

of capital to bring that socialist dream one step closer. Blair wears none of the Labour movement's campaign medals, nor bears its battle-scars.

The very notion of this smart Islingtonian barrister stationed on a picket line is incongruous to say the least – ritual talk of 'This Great Movement Of Ours' scarcely less so.

This distance from labourism, which perhaps Hugh Gaitskell alone of previous Labour leaders had shared to any extent, meant that Blair felt no great affection for the movement's sacred cows. As the Shadow Employment Secretary he moved swiftly to ditch the Party's previous and longstanding commitment to the pre-entry closed shop, earning the plaudits of *The Times*: 'It was a very smooth performance indeed.'

As Shadow Home Secretary after 1992, Blair was happy to talk about crime, punishment, values and much else – language often used by earlier socialists but studiously avoided for at least half a century. In particular, he articulated the deep sense of outrage felt throughout Britain over the Jamie Bulger case when a young child was murdered, a revulsion propelled no doubt by Blair being a parent of three young children himself. As he wrote in March 1993 – in the *Sun* newspaper – 'It's a bargain – we give opportunity, we demand responsibility. There is no excuse for crime. None.'

Although Blair was understandably loathe to talk in public about his own deeply held personal views, his Christian Socialism meant that, for him, political activity was an extension of morality. He was happy to talk about right and wrong, good and bad.

Unlike John Smith, Tony Blair was a moderniser through and through, happy to use the media to get his views across. In fact his campaign cost around £80,000 – full colour leaflets were printed in Gujarati and Urdu in order to appeal to Asian members of the Labour Party – and his ability to attract wealthy and well-connected backers was crucial. The momentum was going all one way, as Gordon Brown tactfully recognised by withdrawing from the fray. The bankruptcy of the Labour Left was demonstrated by its inability to put up a candidate: Tony Benn, for instance, was now a respected veteran confined to shouting advice from the sidelines. Blair was finally opposed by John Prescott and Margaret Beckett, who had been deputy leader under John Smith.

Tony Blair was duly elected the new leader on 21 July 1994 – with Prescott as his deputy – and he started with the inestimable advantage of knowing that the great majority of the Shadow Cabinet (thirteen out of seventeen members) had voted for him, unlike Harold Wilson and Neil Kinnock who were faced by potentially hostile Shadow Cabinets. Secondly, all three sections of the Party had voted overwhelmingly for him.

Blair had apparently been granted carte blanche to do as he wished.

The new leader's analysis of the position facing the Party was relatively uncomplicated. Labour had been penalised for failing to respond to the social and economic changes which had transformed Britain in the 1970s and 1980s. Changes in class barriers and the expansion of the managerial and professional classes alone had naturally reduced the size of the Labour vote by a crucial 5 per cent.

Such shifts did not automatically make the Labour Party unelectable, but did suggest that the Party must change in order to keep up. To stand still was, in fact, to go backwards. For Blair, therefore, the changes initiated by Neil Kinnock were important but remained substantially incomplete. The 'Permanent Revolution' must continue and not lose momentum, as apparently happened under John Smith's brief stewardship.

Although for most Labour members Margaret Thatcher was still the devil incarnate, Blair was publicly prepared to praise parts of the Thatcherite era. In many ways this bravely recognised the attributes which made industry and commerce successful – as Sir John Harvey-Jones put it, 'Management is about change, and maintaining a high rate of change'. It also acknowledged the success of the Conservative Party itself which, despite its reactionary and hidebound image, has persistently renewed and adapted itself to the future.

The contrast between the electoral success of the Conservative Party and the patchy record of Labour was startlingly obvious. Since Labour had become the main anti-Conservative Party as long ago as the 1920s, it had won only two decisive victories at general elections, whilst the governments produced by those victories held office for a grand total of nine years.

Blair and his circle therefore initiated a series of important changes. First of all, there was the subtle change of name. Just as Bill Clinton in the United States had secured his presidential nomination by appealing to the 'New Democrats', so did Blair begin calling his Party 'New Labour' in order to signal a fresh start. In an earlier chapter, we saw how Douglas Jay, a prominent follower of Hugh Gaitskell, had suggested a new name in the aftermath of the 1959 election defeat – and been promptly shot down in flames.

In 1991, when researching the first edition of this book, I invited scores of Labour members to consider changing the Party's name if it seemed to be an electoral handicap. The outrage at my suggestion was palpable. Five years later, these same activists do have the grace to look a little sheepish as they happily talk about New Labour.

Secondly, Blair needed some major internal change to signal to the electorate that here indeed was a new Party. His eye settled on the famous Clause Four of the Labour Party constitution, printed on every membership card, that called for the wholesale nationalisation of, apparently, everything. Gaitskell's attempts to ditch Clause Four had been rebuffed.

For Blair and others, the Clause was uncomfortably reminiscent of Labour's blunderbuss Alternative Economic Strategy of the early 1970s, which demanded the virtual abolition of the private sector. Large businesses and small, multinationals and family affairs – from now on, it seemed, we must all work for the state. This was Labour at its most bureaucratic and totalitarian, all too redolent of Soviet Communism. Although never a viable policy, it seemed even less so after the Conservative government's privatisation programme had proved popular in the 1980s.

Clause Four was not important in itself: not many people putting a cross against the Conservative candidate in the polling booth thought to themselves 'I am not voting Labour because of Clause Four'. Fewer than a handful of Labour Party members knew, let alone cared, what the clause said – only academics and Tony Benn could recite the actual wording. This was precisely the argument of those doubters more than thirty years ago who had urged Gaitskell not to make this an issue: 'who cares?' Here was a storm in a teacup best avoided.

But for Blair, Clause Four represented an opportune scapegoat. If the Labour Party was to mean what it said and say what it meant – it was hard not to lapse into the kind of soundbite politics thought obligatory by some of his entourage – then Clause Four had to be changed.

In retrospect, after his victory, it was easy to look back and say that the clause represented a soft target. In fact Blair had been defeated on this very issue at the Party Conference in 1994 and at times grassroots opposition did seem to endanger his position, aided by the unscrupulous use of phoney polls published in such publications as *Tribune*. As it turned out, of the 441 constituency parties which held a ballot on this question, just three voted in favour of the retention of the old clause. Some 85 per cent of the Labour members taking part supported Blair's revised version of the clause. Where Gaitskell had conspicuously failed, Blair had triumphantly succeeded.

Blair combined his assault on the clause with a commitment to rebuilding a new mass party. Throughout the 1970s and 1980s Labour Party membership had fallen sharply as the young in particular, disillusioned by the seemingly shabby behaviour of some Labour politicians, preferred to join single-issue campaigns which were more friendly and flexible. Tony

Blair's determination was bolstered by the experience of his own constituency party in Sedgefield, County Durham which boasted a membership of over 2,000 rather than the 470 of the average constituency.

Labour Party membership began to edge towards and then crept over the 300,000 mark, many of whom had joined since Tony Blair's election as leader. Blair himself travelled around Britain to campaign on the Clause Four issue and spoke to some 30,000 members, often arousing an enthusiasm rarely generated by political activity for many years. He insisted on talking the same language to party members as he did to the country at large.

This was an important breakthrough. As we have seen in the latter chapters of *To Build A New Jerusalem*, the socialist tradition of plain speech had gradually been buried under an avalanche of academia, jargon and obfuscation. Social-ists seemed able to communicate only in obscure language and terminology which, to the rest of the public, was as comprehensible as Swahili. The insights of people such as Robert Blatchford were denigrated in favour of a fashionable and debilitating trendiness.

In the past, too, Labour members had often practised a form of political schizophrenia, employing two totally different languages depending on whom they were address-ing. As Brian Walden, a Labour MP before becoming a television pundit, put it: 'I used to be told that . . . the clever thing to do was to call policies "socialist" when talking to party members and something else when talking to the electorate. That begs the question: who is being fooled?'

For Blair, everyone and anyone was a potential Labour supporter and voter. One big laugh he got at many meetings was to mention as a throwaway aside that even Tories were now thinking of voting Labour. Observers noted the shock of the unexpected as Blair said this but, of course, unless many of the people who had voted Tory at the 1979, 1983, 1987 and

1992 elections did switch their allegiance then Labour would once again remain out of office.

The dramatic growth in party membership automatically triggered internal changes within the Labour Party voting system. In the 1970s the trade union block vote had amounted to no less than 90 per cent of the votes cast at the annual Conference. Any one of the big three unions possessed a vote larger than the constituency parties put together, as Conservative Central Office never ceased to delight in pointing out.

Now, however, the trade union block vote was reduced to 70 per cent and the upsurge in membership meant that this would automatically be slimmed down to 50 per cent. In February 1996 it was also agreed that unions would discontinue their sponsorship of individual MPs in favour of advancing money to various constituencies.

Blair and his supporters devoted much time to internal party matters, just as Neil Kinnock had been forced to do. If it was unclear how important such issues were to the general public, at least their firm handling deliberately gave the impression of a politician in control. In many ways Blair had no other option, primarily because the so-called 'modernisers' within the Labour Party had few roots. As John Rentoul, another of Tony Blair's biographers acutely pointed out:

> The idea of 'modernisation' was a conscious attempt to fill the ideological vacuum on the Left. As such it was rather narrowly based. It did not arise from a social movement outside the party, or from the grass roots or the unions within it. It was synthesised by the parliamentary leadership, drawing on such intellectual forces as the Left could muster.

Modernisation naturally extended to Labour's policies as well. Labour had once seemed in hock to every single interest group able to raise a petition or put through a phone call. In other words, less a national party than a sectional body representing an assorted amalgam of vested interests – a rainbow coalition as insubstantial and temporary as a rainbow itself.

For Blair, acting as a pushover was the easy but impotent option. As he once put it, 'Being brave is being able to say no to people. Being brave is standing up for what you believe in, even if it makes enemies or brings you into conflict with other parts of the Party.'

Labour had once possessed so many policies – on everything from 'stray cats to world disarmament' – that it seemed beholden to all. The shopping list of commitments was promptly slimmed down, whilst several key Conservative policies such as internal competition, league tables and selection were grudgingly accepted.

Take the field of welfare. As Nicholas Timmins comments, Blair turned around previous Labour thinking by arguing that a big social security bill was a sign of failure, not success, and that the system in turn should foster success and not dependency: 'Blair stole more Tory-sounding language, declaring the state should offer "a hand up" not "a hand out" and that Labour was "not about bigger benefits but moving people from benefit to work".'

But even more revelatory was the new Clause Four which referred to a dynamic economy and 'the enterprise of the market and the rigour of competition'. Capitalism, however modified or smoothed, was here to stay. Socialism, however nebulous or undefined, was redundant. No longer was there a yawning gap between lip service and practice.

Blair was also keen to play down high expectations. His advisers continually stressed that the economy was almost certainly in a worse shape than expected – remembering perhaps the mess that Reggie Maudling had left for Jim Callaghan in 1964 – and that any future Labour government would enter office with at least one hand tied behind its back. Compare this caution with the almost reckless optimism stoked up by Harold Wilson's 'white heat' in 1964.

★   ★   ★

In keeping with the sense of urgency which Blair insistently conveyed, it was just as well that, in the words of a friend and commentator Martin Jacques, he 'travels light', unencumbered by Labourist baggage. Previous leaders had spent much time stroking the socialist traditions, gladhanding the old and venerable, paying obeisance to the Red Flag. For Blair, New Jerusalem was so far off as not to be worth thinking about.

In his comparatively exposed position, it was understandable that, like Neil Kinnock before him, Blair should create a loyal and dedicated office of helpers. In a media-driven age, the position of press officer was vital. Alastair Campbell was a gamekeeper turned poacher (or perhaps the other way around), a journalist who clearly knew how to play the game, as had Bernard Ingham under Mrs Thatcher. And, like Ingham, Campbell seems to enjoy cultivating an image of unsmiling bluntness.

Policy advisers included David Miliband, the son of Marxist Professor Ralph who had, in a delicious irony, spent a lifetime arguing that Labour was irredeemably reformist and weak. There was also Anji Hunter, a long-time friend, and Blair's wife Cherie, a successful barrister. Another confidant was Peter Mandelson, the media adviser and legendary 'spin doctor'. Interestingly enough, several important figures had Communist backgrounds, showing that this Party always punched above its numerical weight: Peter Mandelson had once been in the Young Communist League, Martin Jacques was for many years a prominent Communist, and Martin Kettle, a *Guardian* journalist who helped redraft some of Blair's speeches, also came from a well-known Communist family.

Blair's presidential style followed on from his analysis of the Party's relative lack of success. Hindered by the image of disunity, Blair determined that from now on leaders would clearly lead and, remembering the difficulties of Wilson and Callaghan, he had a point. As noted earlier, Kenneth Morgan has stressed the traditional Labour cult of the leader, but the difference now is that the full range of the mass media can be utilised. One shudders to think what the vain Ramsay MacDonald would have got up to today.

Blair and his entourage were also impatient at the inadequacies of the Party's policy-making machinery. In the past, resolutions submitted to Conference were spatchcocked into an unholy mess and then perfunctorily debated before having their fate decided by the trade union block vote. As Barbara Castle had tellingly pointed out, Conference was useless when it came to selecting policy priorities:

> Faced with the choices governments have to make, delegates refused to choose. Instead they passed every resolution embodying the party's long-term aspirations with overwhelming majorities and the demand for action now. In 1975, when I was still Secretary of State for Social Services, acutely aware of the choices that had to be made, I watched almost with despair as conference passed resolution after resolution demanding the socialist millennium overnight, regardless of the cost. Geoff Bish, the party's head of research, remarked to me that we ought to have a tote at the back of the platform on which the cost of every decision was clocked up, so that conference could see to what it was committing itself.

This reckless irresponsibility was precisely the sort of behaviour that Blair planned to ditch. Kinnock's Policy Reviews had also bypassed the traditional procedure. Conference became less of a bear-garden as delegates were repeatedly reminded that the television cameras were on them. That no full Conference report has been issued since 1990 demonstrates its diminished status. Critics like Tony Benn complained that it was being turned into an American-style rally at which members were expected to bring not resolutions but balloons and funny hats.

But opponents could always point back to the era of 'Bennery' and its conspicuous lack of success. Anyone can pass the most impeccable socialist resolutions in opposition or discuss them theoretically – but so what? If it was accepted that good intentions were hopeless without power or office, then, according to the Blair analysis, the rest followed naturally.

Blair's overriding aim was to reconnect Labour to the mainstream: to be a member or supporter of the Labour Party would no longer place one in the fringe or marginal category. This also meant, like any general, Blair tried to neutralise potential enemies and maximise support.

The former strategy was exemplified by the Labour leadership's more accommodating attitude towards sections of the press. Throughout this book we have seen the unrelenting hostility towards Labour displayed by such papers as the *Daily Mail* and the *Sun*. But Blair launched a charm offensive aimed at their proprietors, Viscount Rothermere and Rupert Murdoch. He was happy to write columns in the *Sun*, to speak at Murdoch's 'News Corp Leadership Conference' in Australia in July 1995, and even to urge Labour MPs to work harder at getting 'more positive coverage' in the tabloids. In the recent past, the word 'tabloid' had been second only to 'Thatcherite' as a term of abuse. In 1983, for instance, the Party had vetoed the idea of placing advertisements in the *Sun* on ideological grounds.

As for the second, Blair seemed to believe Labour should have 'no enemies to the Right', in other words any potential supporter – no matter what their previous convictions or behaviour – was welcome. Interviewed in the *Daily Telegraph* (or 'Torygraph' as most Labour people had always called it) in July 1994, Blair claimed that 'Positions I have been setting out in the course of the leadership campaign on the economy, education, welfare and crime are the positions I believe many *Telegraph* readers entirely agree with.'

Former members of the Social Democrats were welcomed back into the New Labour fold as if they were prodigal sons and daughters, even though many on the Left wanted to spurn these 'traitors'. Some of Blair's advisers, such as Peter Mandelson, were thought at least privately to favour much closer links with the Liberal Democrats.

It was all part of the Blair circle's plan to maximise possible support, if only because Blair did not want to experience the same problem that had bedevilled Harold Wilson and Jim Callaghan in government: vocal sections of the Party publicly criticising and condemning the Labour administrations' conduct. A possible pact with the Liberal Democrats would allow a Blair government safely to ignore and isolate the Labour Left.

And, looking a little further into the future, electoral reform and the introduction of some form of proportional representation might well lead to political realignment, but with Tony Blair and his supporters in the driving seat. In recent decades, whenever this issue was discussed, commentators normally assumed that the realignment would take place after Labour had been crushed at a general election and dissolved into bitter faction fighting.

But Blair is playing for high stakes: might this nightmare scenario still take place if New Labour, despite its transformation, loses the next election, its fifth defeat in a row? Instead, by throwing down the gauntlet and doing everything possible to win the election, Blair hopes to ensure that radical change will be at his behest – that the defeated Conservatives, split by their disagreements over Europe, will themselves fall apart.

In which case Blair will have brought about the very realignment in British politics ardently wished for but never achieved by 'the Gang of Four' – Roy Jenkins, David Owen, Bill Rodgers, Shirley Williams – and the Social Democrats in conjunction with the Liberals.

Blair was fortunate to be facing a tired Conservative government with a dwindling Commons majority and wracked by arguments over Europe. The so-called 'sleaze factor' was exacerbated by the shabby behaviour of several backbench Tories and by the less than straightforward government actions probed in the Scott inquiry. But Blair's relentless style did not, of course, mean that the long-term problems which had dogged the Party for so many years had simply vanished.

First of all, some critics never failed to point out that Blair was not exactly 'one of us'. Euro MP Ken Coates, a veteran left-winger who had been snapping at the heels of Labour leaders when Blair was still in short trousers, was scathing about this young man's lack of socialist credentials. A leading member of the Socialist Workers' Party was even more personal: 'It's not simply an unpleasant thing about his personality, or an unfortunate fact that he comes from a horrendous middle-class background.'

No doubt Blair can live quite happily with such opponents; and also with Arthur Scargill who finally decided that the Labour Party had now sold out for good and formed a breakaway grouping called the Socialist Labour Party. With typical grandiosity, Scargill claimed that the SLP would put up a candidate in every seat at the forthcoming election. If so, the SLP was likely to join the long list of fringe parties who clutter the ballot paper and receive a derisory handful of votes.

The loud cries of 'betrayal' voiced by Scargill and others allowed the Blair entourage to claim that here indeed was proof positive the Labour Party had changed and that the 'Hard Left' was now marginalised.

A more wounding criticism sometimes made – and which once spurred Blair to threaten legal action – was the allegation that New Labour was in reality no more than the 'SDP Mark 2'. Although happy to welcome back former SDP-ers into the Labour fold, he knew that most members who had stuck by the Party even in the dark days of 1981–83 when Labour under Michael Foot nearly perished, would not countenance such talk: this was indeed a change too far. Anyone favouring a pact with the Liberal Democrats tended to keep their heresies to themselves.

Secondly, although New Labour boasted proudly about the influx of recruits, it was unclear just how active these newcomers were. Was this just the credit card set signing up to garner political cred and nothing more? A recent study in *Labour Party News* showed that nearly one half of the newcomers joined the Labour Party precisely because of the Blair leadership, but that less than half had actually attended a branch meeting since signing up.

The fanfares welcoming the new members helped disguise the fact that in 1994 the Party also lost 40,000 members. One commentator who has studied both major parties suggested that 'As the Labour Party moves to become a party of mass membership we may well see a similar pattern as in the Conservative Party where members join the Party – realise they have no say or influence – and then leave.'

It was uncertain how much leeway New Labour was making among younger people, a particularly important constituency if only because 43–45 per cent of under-25s did not bother to vote in 1992. The British Youth Council discovered that a fifth of eighteen to twenty-five year-olds are not registered to vote, four times as many as in any other age group. However membership of Young Labour has now reached 25,000 – more than three times the combined total of the Young Conservatives and Young Liberals – and the average age of a Labour MP is forty-eight, rather than the Tory sixty-two.

Women too were apparently not joining New Labour in the same proportion as men: just 35 per cent of the total. Here is a potentially vital blow to Blair's hopes of electoral success. At the 1992 general election, '48% of women's votes went to the Conservatives and 34% to Labour. The similar figures for men were 46% and 37%, a gender gap of six points.' This outcome was the more worrying because the Conservatives had fielded just 63 women candidates as opposed to Labour's 138.

Labour introduced a number of 'women only' shortlists for selected parliamentary seats, a policy that has now been declared illegal. Many felt that the leadership was not entirely unhappy with this decision, fearing that it had raised the spectre of Labour being run by 'special interest' groups. But of course women, forming more than half the population, are rather more than a special interest. Beatrix Campbell put it most succinctly:

> Labour's obsession is electability, but it still does not seem to see the connection between women and winning. The party used to think it could win with working-class men. Now it seems to think it can win with the men of the middle class. What it doesn't know is how to win with the women of all classes.

One intriguing sign of change in the Labour-union relationship slipped through almost unnoticed at the 1995 Party Conference. In the past, a rule stipulated that all Labour Party members, 'if eligible', must belong to a trade union. The new rulebook has changed the phrase to 'if applicable' which, according to party officials, leaves the matter up to the individual concerned.

The problem of money can never be entirely resolved. Although the increase in individual membership reduced the proportion of funds that the Party received from the unions, the dilemma was most blatantly summed up by Tom Sawyer, once a leading unionist but now Labour's General Secretary, when he had declared 'No say, no pay.' As we have seen, Labour has never excelled at raising money, if only because the trade union connection discouraged other initiatives. For instance the German Social Democrats, who do not receive financial backing from their unions, still manage to raise four times the income of the British Labour Party even before state funding is taken into account.

However New Labour seemed to be more successful and more innovative in raising money than Old Labour. Its so-called 1,000 Club of businessmen who had contributed at least £1,000 proved successful, telephone canvassing was stepped up and the Co-op Visa card giving the Party £5 for each new application certainly helped. In fact, Labour has been able to earmark a total of £12.3 million for the next election campaign, 30 per cent more than in 1992.

One pathbreaking new scheme, which came to light in February 1996, was the plan to spend £240,000 on setting up Labour's own lottery. The finance subcommittee was also considering the idea of scratchcards. An unnamed left-winger plaintively asked what capitalist fund-raising tool would be used next: 'We should rely on the goodwill of members and the trade union movement, not on some people's urge to get a fast buck for doing nothing.'

Another obstacle in New Labour's path remained the crucial question of policies and programmes. The Party was in a cleft stick: if it announced future commitments then public expectations would be raised and the Conservatives given a target at which to shoot. If, on the other hand, Labour stayed mum and said that their policies would be unveiled only when in office, then they were justifiably accused of vagueness.

The long-term problem was that the collapse of the social democratic consensus at the end of the 1970s – based on government intervention and the provision of a welfare state funded by general taxation – had left social democratic parties all over the world helpless in the face of the New Right's emphasis on privatisation and markets. Blair was happy to acknowledge this change: 'I believe Mrs Thatcher's emphasis on enterprise was right.'

If, as a radical party, Labour wanted to challenge and change the status quo then this could only be done with public money. But the sums required were unlikely to be available simply through economic growth, implying therefore redistribution through higher taxation on the 'haves'. But the 1980s and early 1990s seemed to show that any party promising higher taxes was doomed to electoral defeat. Even though polls might well suggest that people would selflessly pay higher taxes in order to fund education and health programmes, when closeted inside the polling booth it usually turned out to be a different story.

Take the famous example of President Bush who asked people to read his lips and then pledged no new taxes. In 1990 he reneged on his promise and raised taxes – although the only tax in the controversial 1990 budget which hit the middle classes was a gas tax of precisely 5 cents. But it did not matter, the perception remained that Bush had broken his promise and increased taxes enormously.

The Bush experience seared itself into the consciousness of politicians everywhere and doubtless lay behind the Conservative assault on 'Labour's tax bombshell' in the 1992 election. At a lecture delivered in the City of London in May 1995, Tony Blair warned of a 'long and gruelling slog' ahead of any future Labour government which would put the task of curbing inflation before any promises to increase public spending. As the *Daily Telegraph* commented: 'Deploying words that could have come from any Conservative minister, and delight any Tory backbencher, the Labour leader said Britain could only sustain a tax structure that would attract inward enterprise from overseas.'

But if New Labour was not going to raise extra revenue, then what was it here for? Unlike John Smith who was wedded to a national minimum wage and the goal of full employment, Tony Blair was less specific. At one point New Labour seemed to be trying to steal the Tory clothes on this issue and claiming that it was the party standing for low tax and low inflation. Shadow Chancellor Gordon Brown even proclaimed his aspiration of levying income tax at ten pence in the pound, a proposal swiftly denounced as a gimmick by professional economists.

In private, John Smith had once said that 'If we can't get the growth, we can't have the programme. That is a truism about government.' It would be near electoral suicide to be quite so blunt in public. But if Smith was right, and minimal economic growth is likely, then why bother to change governments at all? It was hardly a compelling reason for voting Labour, let alone joining the Party.

Studies of the Labour Party membership suggested that the majority remained loyal to more traditional socialist methods of public ownership. In December 1994 Patrick Seyd and Paul Whiteley concluded that 'public ownership remains a touchstone issue for two-thirds of the grassroots membership.' They continued with a set of figures guaranteed to give nightmares to the instigators of New Labour:

> Between 10 and 25 per cent want the entire financial service, chemical, engineering, motor, electronic, computer, plastic and textile sectors of the economy to be publicly owned. A further 25 per cent would like some public ownership of the pharmaceutical, aircraft construction, electronic, ship-building, engineering, petrochemical, computer and financial service sector.

Certainly the Parliamentary Labour Party had their roots in the public sector, as Byron Criddle outlined:

> For decades now, Labour has been the party of the public sector, the more so as the proportion of MPs from manual working backgrounds has shrunk, to just 22 per cent of the parliamentary party in 1992. The public sector prevails, whether in the guise of the traditional teachers, lecturers and social workers, or officials in the public sector unions, or that of leading municipal figures such as the Sheffield MPs David Blunkett and Clive Betts, who built parliamentary careers straight up out of the local council.

Criddle went on to analyse the Labour candidates selected in sixty key seats and concludes that they 'appear to fit the stereotype of Labour as a "tax and spend" party which helped it to lose in 1992.' But how was this public sector to be financed and, if the influential lobby on its behalf did get its way, expanded?

New Labour's dilemma was exposed by the publication of

Peter Mandelson's book *The Blair Revolution*. Mandelson has been the Party's leading fixer since the days of Neil Kinnock, although suffering an eclipse during the John Smith regime. Astute at making full use of the media to put across Labour's case to best advantage – something that Conservatives had been doing for years – Mandelson was also a close aide of Tony Blair and his book, co-written with Roger Liddle, a former SDP-er, offers a convenient snapshot of New Labour.

Predictably enough, apart from its sharp portrait of a Britain in the 1990s beset by job insecurity, negative equity and long-term unemployment, *The Blair Revolution* also details very clearly the differences between 'Old' and 'New' Labour. For example, much is made of the transition from delegate democracy to direct democracy and the failures of policy making in the past: 'The 1980 decision to withdraw from Europe was taken after a debate [at the annual Conference] of only thirty minutes.'

But when turning to the world outside Labour, the book becomes very unclear in describing one of the most passionless and anodyne 'revolutions' of all time. No hostages are given to the Conservatives. Trust us, vote for us at the next election, and then we will show you what we can really do. The authors are not interested in traditional socialist shibboleths such as *Equality*, the title of one of R.H. Tawney's finest books: 'Differences in income and personal spending power are the inevitable consequences of the existence of markets.'

*The Blair Revolution* is particularly feeble when it discusses Labour in government, unsurprisingly perhaps because it has been so long since Labour has inhabited the corridors of power. Bob Woodward's account of the early days inside the Clinton White House, *The Agenda*, shows in alarming detail how a supposedly reforming administration can get bogged down. The book should be obligatory reading for the Shadow Cabinet. As Woodward concludes, 'Clinton also did not project a sense of command. Only in isolated moments was he able to dispel the feeling of unease and directionless that seemed to have taken hold early in his presidency.'

Turn to Mandelson and Liddle and note the banality of their advice: 'The quicker ministers settle down and establish a rapport and confidence with their staff the better. A checklist for incoming ministers should include, first, take the time to meet as many of the department's staff as possible.' And on and on the checklist remorselessly continues. If future Labour ministers really do need such simplistic guidance then they should not be ministers in the first place.

As regards the issues of wealth creation, redistribution and the relationship between the private and public sectors, they are buried beneath platitudes. Take taxation: 'The real issue is not high versus low tax, as the right tries to claim, but fair rather than unfair tax.' One specific proposal is the grant of a £5,000 dowry to newly married couples, a suggestion with marginal relevance to the creation of any New Britain.

The *Guardian* once analysed Tony Blair's speech at the Party Conference in October 1994 and came up with a table of 'Blairspeak' in-words and out-words. In a speech of 6,639 words which was rated by the newspaper as suitable for children aged nine to ten upwards, the word 'new' was used thirty-three times, 'change' twenty-nine times, 'responsibility' fourteen times, 'community' eleven times; also scoring well were 'market', 'social' and 'trust'.

As for the out-words, 'struggle', 'comrade' and 'Clause Four' did not appear; 'strike' and 'bosses' were mentioned once, 'class' twice, 'revolution' three times and 'social(ism)' four times. It is not just Old Labour who worry about the apparent lack of substance of New Labour. One journalist who recently spent some time with Peter Mandelson asked him what all his energetic politicking was for:

The moral purpose of this is less clear: 'It's difficult for me to describe it to you. I know what's right. I know what I should be doing . . .' Earlier, in the car from Wellingborough, he had said that 'hopelessness' angered him; otherwise, the two days had passed without reference to injustice, socialism, or conflict of any kind.

One important New Labour argument is that firms and businesses should be less geared to short-term profit and more alert to their wider, social responsiblities. In the late 1980s, for example, Bryan Gould wrote glowingly of the ESOPs (Employee Share Ownership Plans) in America and the wage-earner funds in Sweden. By the middle of 1991 fifty ESOPs were up and running in Britain. More recently, Will Hutton has developed the 'stakeholder' concept in his bestseller *The State We're In*.

Hutton's analysis is clear: 'The British economy is organised around a stock-market-based financial system and clearing banks averse to risk.' With managers concerned above all with the short-term interests of their shareholders, companies devote far fewer resources to investment in research and development than many of our competitors. His prescriptions are also clear:

> The triple requirement is to broaden the area of stake-holding in companies and institutions, so creating a greater bias to longterm commitment from owners; to extend the supply of cheap, longterm debt; and to decentralise decision-making. The financial system, in short, needs to be comprehensively republicanised.

Companies should work in partnership with 'stakeholders', such as their workforce, customers and the wider community. A less confrontational system of industrial relations would entail a constructive role for the unions. Hutton writes approvingly of the 'social market' economies prevalent in Germany and Japan, praising the interventionist activities of MITI (Ministry of International Trade and Industry) in Japan as a suitable role model. Britain should be building a high-skill, high-investment economy rather than the cut-throat flexible labour markets, job insecurity and underinvestment which seem to be the goal of successive Conservative governments.

Naturally Hutton's ideas came under attack from the Right. But, just as Blair's circle could point to the conspicuous lack of success of 'Bennery' a few years before, since 1979 Britain has slipped down the world economic table from thirteenth to eighteenth position. In other words, Conservative policies – despite having the enormous benefits of North Sea oil – had not been a raging success.

A more important objection was that, as Hutton himself noted, such a drastic recasting has never been carried out in any country before without the experience of defeat in war, economic collapse or revolution, all of which, fortunately, are not on the cards. In any case the proposals would seemingly entail government intervention in the industrial and financial sectors – Professor John Kay, for example, has spoken of a Stakeholding Act forcing directors to recognise wider responsibilities.

This would seem impractical in a highly competitive world as well as being virtually impossible to police. Also, Labour's track record in this respect – the National Plan of the 1960s, the failed National Enterprise Board of the 1970s or the shelved Bullock report on industrial democracy – is not promising. Few Labour politicians have direct experience of wealth creation. Take the professions of the last three leaders: barrister, barrister, adult education tutor.

It was also pointed out by *The Economist* in February 1996 that the 'social market' economies held up as exemplary by Hutton were themselves in difficulties: 'The oddity of such talk now is that, after two decades of relative underperformance, the American and British economies have for the past decade performed as well as or better than those of Japan and continental Europe. Moreover, the stakeholder version of capitalism that these evangelists seek so fervently to propagate has itself come under unprecedented strain.'

Even if the above difficulties are solved by a Labour

government's satisfactory development of 'stakeholding', the global economy severely restricts any national government's scope. The international mobility of capital today means that the markets can outpower virtually any government – as was made painfully clear to the Conservative administration in September 1992 when Britain was forced out of the Exchange Rate Mechanism. The figures are mindboggling. As Martin Walker has pointed out, 'cross-borders securities transactions were seven times larger than the entire British GDP in 1990.' Walker goes on:

> Like the nature of superpower war, the global economy has grown beyond the capacity of nation states to control it. It is increasingly difficult even to talk coherently of national economies, when so much of the world's growth potential is now locked in offshore and multinational structures that are designed to avoid any single state's direction. Just as the coming of total war created the need for superpowers with the capacity both to wage and to control it, so the coming of the global economy is creating the need for economic superpowers.

Peter Mandelson and Roger Liddle note this development but point out that governments can still influence the supply side of the economy in order 'to enhance skills, promote investment, and enlarge our economic capacity . . .' This is all commendable but such improvements will take some years to feed through, and with Labour's record the Party is unlikely to be in office when they do.

In reality, the ideological tide is still flowing in the Right's direction. Vincent Cable has expressed it best: 'the central economic ideas for the foreseeable future will be those of the right: markets, competition, private ownership, entrepreneurship . . . The argument is about different types of capitalism and competition between them.'

New Labour's talk of 'One Nation Socialism' is both a tacit recognition of this trend and an attempt to occupy the middle ground supposedly vacated by the Hard Right Tories. New

Labour is seemingly everyone's friend: house owners, victims of crime, small businessmen, parents, consumers, citizens. Almost no one seems to be left out, except perhaps for the members of the present Conservative Cabinet. Just as One Nation Toryism was supremely inclusive, so too is One Nation Socialism, even at the price of blandness.

The one area in which the Labour leadership has been more specific is institutional reform. Blair has advocated such reforms as elected mayors, a Freedom of Information Act, the incorporation of the European Covention of Human Rights into British law, a referendum on the voting system and the abolition of the voting rights of hereditary peers. These proposals would certainly shake up the system, escaping from the lethargy once beautifully described by E.P.Thompson: 'we lie upon our heritage like a Dunlopillo mattress and hope that, in our slumbers, those good, dead men of history will move us forward.'

The impetus behind these plans came from the campaigning group Charter 88, which has long called for constitutional reform. However, not only do successive Labour governments have a poor record in this field – for example, their failure to reform the House of Lords in the 1960s or set up devolved assemblies in the 1970s – but a Labour administration could easily get bogged down in this area.

This may not prove to be a problem after all. New Labour is already dragging its feet, even before those same feet are behind the desks in Whitehall. Peter Mandelson, the Party's Civil Service spokesman, was quoted in *The Times* of 6 March 1996 as saying that the passing of a Freedom of Information Act – one of Labour's few commitments to legislation – might have to wait. The government's code on openness should be 'bolstered and more liberally interpreted', with legislation following 'in time'. Here is New Labour sounding very much like timid Old Labour.

The final problem among many facing Tony Blair centres on his authoritarian style of leadership. Each and any disagreement is seen as an act of disloyalty and swiftly jumped on: for example, the rows over the choice of school for his own son and Harriet Harman's, or the lack of discussion on the future of the monarchy.

Understandably, Blair and his advisers are fully aware that disunity has always cost Labour dear. The British electorate mistrusts a squabbling party. The obverse of this is that any democratic organisation needs healthy debate and argument unless it desires 'the unity of the graveyard'. Herbert Morrison once said that socialism was what a Labour government did; nowadays, socialism is what Tony Blair says it is.

Margaret Thatcher worked along similar lines. In her memoirs, Lady Thatcher was honest: 'as I often did in government, I was using public statements to advance the arguments and to push reluctant colleagues further than they would otherwise have gone.' The pressures brought to bear on Shadow Education Minister David Blunkett in particular seem remarkably similar.

The cult of the leader is cringingly apparent in the second chapter of Peter Mandelson and Roger Liddle's book *The Blair Revolution*. Devoted to Blair himself, it vies with the 'Our Great Leader' biographies once churned out in praise of dictators in Eastern Europe and North Korea.

If Tony Blair does become Prime Minister, then he will almost certainly begin by breaking party rules which stipulate that an incoming leader must include all the members of the Shadow Cabinet in the real Cabinet itself. As the Shadow Cabinet now comprises nineteen members, he will theoretically have little room for manoeuvre. Just as Blair unilaterally decided to appoint the Chief Whip and the members of the Whip's office, he is likely to follow Neil Kinnock's example who robustly declared in January 1987, 'I shall decide who is in the Cabinet . . .'

Similarly, Tony Blair and his advisers are happy now to talk about 'membership power' and to advocate the balloting of Labour Party members on key issues. But what if, some months into a new Labour administration taking unpopular decisions, the membership proves less supportive? Ironically, there will be no trade union block vote for the leadership to fall back on. Party democracy might well turn out to be a double-edged sword.

Despite these criticisms and difficulties, the Labour Party continues to ride high in the opinion polls and Blair himself persists in pushing forward and keeping the Party on the move. In many ways this is inevitable: paradoxically, Tony Blair is a radical who leads a defensive and reactionary body. If the momentum stalls, then he will be in trouble.

The 'permanent revolution' goes on, whether it be in policy – in February 1996 Labour's education spokesman David Blunkett said that comprehensive education had failed successive generations of children over the last thirty years – or in continued refinements to the Party's communications offensive. For instance, the 'Rapid Response and Rebuttal Unit' set up to answer bad publicity was joined in 1996 by a new £2 million 'soundbite factory' opened close to the Houses of Parliament. In the 1940s the Conservative Party regularly briefed hecklers with questions who were then despatched to cause trouble at Labour Party meetings. Today their methods are more sophisticated, but Labour looks set to match anything they can come up with.

Destabilised by the impact of Thatcherism, the Conservative Party often veers uncertainly between the free market and One Nation traditions. Europe was pushed on to a backburner as the Cabinet seemed unsure whether to promise a referendum on a single European currency. The response to Blair's proposals regarding the House of Lords was extraordinary; chairman Brian Mawhinney resorted to a semi-mystical extolment of the peers whilst the *Sunday Times*, normally a voice urging Britain to embrace Hong-Kong style meritocracy and classlessness, printed a piece by historian Andrew Roberts which lovingly detailed the peers' eccentricities, depicting the Upper Chamber as some kind of upper-class care in the community.

In fact, as Roy Jenkins pointed out in a magisterial letter to *The Times*, on at least six other occasions this century governments have tried to reform the upper chamber. He castigated 'the farce of the modern Conservative Party treating the invasion of the hereditary principle as a dastardly depredation.'

Early in 1996 the electoral fortunes of British Labour's counterparts around the world took a tumble, notably in Australia and Spain where longstanding left-of-centre parties were ejected from office. However the primary cause of their defeat seems to have been the desire for a change, and no country in the Western world has been dominated for so long by a single party as Conservative Britain.

The task for Tony Blair, his colleagues and the Labour Party will be to combine the tasks of principle and electability; to answer with a resounding affirmative the pertinent question posed by Ben Pimlott: 'is it possible for a progressive government in the modern world to link the fate of those who are seriously deprived to that of ordinary citizens, without committing electoral suicide?'

In the run-up to every election, serious commentators mutter that if Labour don't win this time then the Party will surely split and fall apart. It was said in 1987 and again in 1992. Each time the Party managed to regroup, reorganise, reform and return. But if the Conservatives do win the next election, which will make it five in a row, then it is difficult to imagine what more Labour can do.

If, despite having clambered laboriously and painfully back towards the mainstream, the Party remains unelectable, then it is difficult to see that Labour – whether it be 'Old' or 'New' – has a future.

# Conclusions

'Where there is no vision the people perish.'
  KEIR HARDIE, QUOTED IN CAROLINE BENN, *KEIR HARDIE* (1992)

'The will to Socialism is based on a lively sense of wrongs crying for redress.'
  G.D.H. COLE, *THE SIMPLE CASE FOR SOCIALISM* (1935)

'. . . I don't actually believe that people vote for programmes. They vote for perspectives, they vote for hopes and fears. I don't believe that most of the people who voted overwhelmingly for Labour in 1945 knew exactly what their programme was.'
  PROFESSOR ERIC HOBSBAWM, 1985

'Most people couldn't care less about the future of socialism, but almost everyone cares about the future of Britain.'
  PAUL HIRST, 1989

The British Labour Party is and always has been an invigorating coalition of people, ideas and interests. Trade unionists rub shoulders with politicians, factory workers sit next to Oxbridge intellectuals, Puritans jostle with Roundheads, Nonconformists collaborate with atheists, Marxists (sometimes) exchange jokes with social democrats.

Looking at this jumbled, unpredictable development of the Labour Party, a number of themes clearly run through its history. The tension between idealism and realism, for instance, or the difficult relationship between Party and government.

The grassroots have generally urged Labour administrations to move faster and further; the leadership talks of the realities of power and hints at economic problems so perilous they cannot be disclosed in public.

Also apparent is the contrast between Labour as an outside force, determined to reform the status quo in drastic ways and to take on the Establishment. But there is also Labour the insider, the scrupulously constitutional and monarchical body happily welcomed into the corridors of power.

And what about the conflict between principle and power? Should Labour stand for what it believes in or believe in what is likely to win elections? Or is there no necessary division between the two camps in any case?

The rich and vigorous history of the British Labour Party can best be broken down into three phases. First of all, the pioneering and evangelical stage as this new body sponsored by the trade unions slowly detached itself from the Liberal Party. The driving force were the orators and the zealots, the men such as Keir Hardie or Philip Snowden, who often felt moved to tell his audiences that 'The Sun of Righteousness is rising with healing in its wings. The Christ that is to be appears. A new and brighter order will arise. It is the promised New Jerusalem.'

That Snowden went on to be a bad Chancellor of the Exchequer revealed the yawning gap between rhetoric and reality which characterised this period that lasted from the 1880s to the 1930s, culminating in the downfall of the Labour government in the summer of 1931. To have one's heart in the right place was not enough.

The second phase – the mind – grew up and developed during the 1930s and the war years as a new generation of Labour leaders – capable administrators such as Clement Attlee, Hugh Dalton, Herbert Morrison and Ernest Bevin – came to the fore. Based on government intervention, the mixed economy and the provision of welfare for all, this phase was typified by the Attlee governments of

1945–51 which introduced the post-war consensus administered by both Tory and Labour alike until the end of
the 1970s.

By then, of course, this framework was under attack and in
1979 Mrs Thatcher and the Conservatives returned to power.
Not only was the old social democratic tradition now at an
end but the revolutionary tendency too – never particularly
strong in Britain – had been discredited by association with
the Soviet Union. In November 1989 it disintegrated along
with the Berlin Wall.

Why should both traditions, the labourist and the militant,
have collapsed in the last decades of the twentieth century?
Because they were created by and in a world that essentially
no longer exists. The 'world of labour' known to Keir Hardie
and H.M. Hyndman was one of manual labour, steam power,
factories, a limited franchise, friendly societies, widespread
poverty, virtually non-existent social services and comparatively primitive communications. Large numbers of people
concentrated together sharing many of the same experiences
naturally developed a collective identity which, in its turn, led
to the emergence of mass political parties claiming to speak for
the working class.

Despite much huffing and puffing, the Labour Party has
remained out of office for the best part of two decades. As
for the trade union movement, which had after all spawned
Labour as its political voice, matters continued to deteriorate.
In 1979, for instance, unions affiliated to the Trade Union
Congress boasted a grand total of twelve million members;
today the figure is fewer than seven million. The mighty
Transport and General Workers' Union, the child of Ernie
Bevin, has shrunk from two million members to less than a
million.

In a plural society with a myriad of beliefs, cultures and
expectations, the old collective orthodoxy seemed unwieldly
and inflexible. Trade unionists increasingly thought of themselves as also being parents, consumers, tax payers, property

owners, shareholders, citizens, the victims of crime and much else besides.

And, of course, it is impossible to write about the Labour Party and ignore the Conservative Party. As I have argued elsewhere, in terms of power, influence and longevity, the British Conservative Party can claim to be the world's most successful political organisation. For Labour to be faced by such a formidable body is hard indeed – rather as if a fairly ordinary football team had to play Manchester United or Liverpool every Saturday.

The task of British Labour today is and has been ever since the 1970s to create a fusion of the two previous stages, to offer people a programme which possesses both a vision of a better tomorrow and practical steps as to how it will be built – to join together hearts and minds.

The moral dimension is vital, as early socialists knew full well, namely the search for a better life for all. Any number of studies published recently demonstrate the massive inequalities which still disfigure our society. No one can fail to be aware of the homeless who increasingly huddle in doorways or the mentally disturbed who roam the streets.

The commitment should be clear, expressed most eloquently by an Archbishop of Canterbury, William Temple, during the Second World War:

> Why should some of God's children have full opportunity to develop their capacities in freely-chosen occupations, while others are confined to a stunted form of existence, enslaved to types of labour which represent no personal choice but the sole opportunity offered? The Christian cannot ignore a challenge in the name of justice. He must either refuse it or, accepting it, devote himself to the removal of the stigma.

Note the clarity of Temple's language, the passion and excitement which is often conspicuously lacking from both New and Old Labour verbiage alike. Without these qualities then Roy Hattersley's warning will become ever more pertinent: 'If politics is deteriorating in the public mind it is because it has become less of a moral crusade and more a marketing exercise.'

But of course an ethical approach is not in itself enough. Lord (Nigel) Lawson recently lauded the practical success of market capitalism: 'Socialism, by contrast, has been forced by practical failure onto the high ground of morality.' The public will expect any government to be competent and capable, to deliver economic growth and rising living standards.

The Labour Party needs to show that it can benefit from the skills and experience of a wide range of individuals from different backgrounds – business people, civil servants, professional people, women, ethnic groups, young people – and, in effect, create a reform coalition of all the talents as broadly happened between 1935 and 1945.

The Labour Party may have modernised and reformed itself, but can it do the same for Britain? There is a nice story about Aneurin Bevan taking up his post at the Ministry of Health in 1945. His first act was to sink into the well-upholstered chair in his new ministry – and then banish it. 'This won't do,' he declared, 'it drains all the blood from the head and explains a lot about my predecessors.'

Labour always needs to fight the urge to settle into the comfortable chair and remain there. Instead, any future Labour administration needs to fuse together hearts and minds, just as Bevan himself managed to do during his years in office.

It is a formidable task indeed as Britain edges uncertainly towards the next century. But despite the undoubted trials and tribulations ahead, the need 'to build a New Jerusalem' remains with us. And I still believe that our better and more generous impulses can and will defeat our worst, which is a good reason for ending with the closing lines from Shelley's *Prometheus Unbound*:

To suffer woes which Hope thinks infinite;
To forgive wrongs darker than death or night;
To defy Power, which seems omnipotent:
To love and bear; to hope till Hope creates
From its own wreck the thing it contemplates;
Neither to change, nor falter, nor repent;
This, like thy glory, Titan! is to be
Good, great and joyous, beautiful and free;
This is alone Life, Joy, Empire and Victory.

# BRITISH LABOUR MOVEMENT:

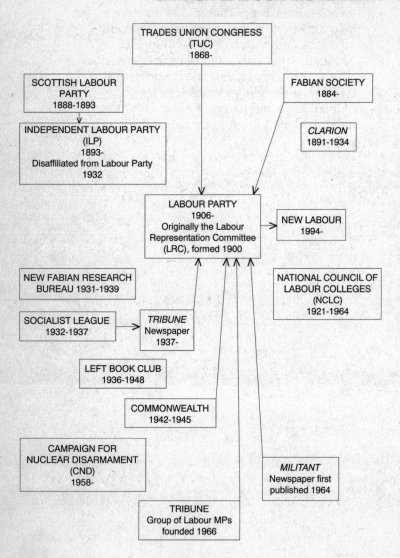

TRADES UNION CONGRESS
(TUC)
1868-

SCOTTISH LABOUR
PARTY
1888-1893

FABIAN SOCIETY
1884-

INDEPENDENT LABOUR PARTY
(ILP)
1893-
Disaffiliated from Labour Party
1932

*CLARION*
1891-1934

LABOUR PARTY
1906-
Originally the Labour
Representation Committee
(LRC), formed 1900

NEW LABOUR
1994-

NEW FABIAN RESEARCH
BUREAU 1931-1939

NATIONAL COUNCIL OF
LABOUR COLLEGES
(NCLC)
1921-1964

SOCIALIST LEAGUE
1932-1937

*TRIBUNE*
Newspaper
1937-

LEFT BOOK CLUB
1936-1948

COMMONWEALTH
1942-1945

CAMPAIGN FOR
NUCLEAR DISARMAMENT
(CND)
1958-

*MILITANT*
Newspaper first
published 1964

TRIBUNE
Group of Labour MPs
founded 1966

# Organisations and Parties

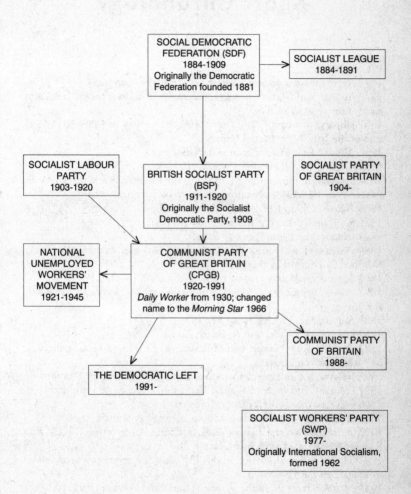

SOCIAL DEMOCRATIC
FEDERATION (SDF)
1884-1909
Originally the Democratic
Federation founded 1881

SOCIALIST LEAGUE
1884-1891

SOCIALIST LABOUR
PARTY
1903-1920

BRITISH SOCIALIST PARTY
(BSP)
1911-1920
Originally the Socialist
Democratic Party, 1909

SOCIALIST PARTY
OF GREAT BRITAIN
1904-

NATIONAL
UNEMPLOYED
WORKERS'
MOVEMENT
1921-1945

COMMUNIST PARTY
OF GREAT BRITAIN
(CPGB)
1920-1991
*Daily Worker* from 1930; changed
name to the *Morning Star* 1966

COMMUNIST PARTY
OF BRITAIN
1988-

THE DEMOCRATIC LEFT
1991-

SOCIALIST WORKERS' PARTY
(SWP)
1977-
Originally International Socialism,
formed 1962

# Short Chronology

PART ONE

1848 April: Chartist demonstration at Kennington Common.

1849 August: Karl Marx arrives in London where he lives for the remaining thirty-four years of his life.

1851 January: formation of the Amalgamated Society of Engineers (ASE), one of the first 'New Model Unions'.

1856 August: Keir Hardie born in Lanarkshire.

1858 January: Beatrice Potter (later Webb) born.

1864 September: formation in London of the International Working Men's Association (IWMA), later known as the First International.

1868: Trades Union Congress (TUC) established.

1871: legal recognition of trade unions.

1884 January: the Fabian Society formed.

1884 August: The Democratic Federation becomes the Marxist Social Democratic Federation (SDF).

1888 April: Keir Hardie stands in the Mid–Lanark by-election.

1888 June: Bryant and May's matchgirls' strike, initiated by Annie Besant.

1889 August: the dockers' strike begins.

1889 December: publication of *Fabian Essays*.

1892 August: Keir Hardie takes his seat in the House of Commons as MP for West Ham South.

1893 January: the Independent Labour Party (ILP) formed in Bradford.

1891 October: first issue of Robert Blatchford's *Clarion* newspaper.

1896 October: death of William Morris.

1898: West Ham elects the first Labour-controlled council.

1900: formation of the Labour Representation Committee (LRC) with Ramsay MacDonald as its first secretary.

1901: House of Lords decision in the Taff Vale case prompts several unions to affiliate to the LRC.

1903: Mrs Pankhurst forms the Women's Social and Political Union (WSPU).

1906 January: the LRC becomes the Labour Party, with twenty-nine Labour MPs; Keir Hardie is elected chairman.

1907 May: Lenin's RSDLP holds its 5th Congress in London.

1907 July: Victor Grayson is elected MP for Colne Valley.

1911 January: first appearance of the *Daily Herald*.

1914: publication of Robert Tressell's novel *The Ragged Trousered Philanthropists*.

1914 August: outbreak of the First World War, a conflict welcomed by Mrs Pankhurst, Hyndman and Blatchford but not by Keir Hardie.

1915 September: death of Keir Hardie.

1918 January: Labour Party Constitution accepted.

1918 February: John Maclean appointed Bolshevik Consul in Glasgow.

1919 January: the Battle of George Square in Glasgow.

1919 March: formation of the Communist International (COMINTERN), the Third International, in Moscow.

1920 July: the Communist Party of Great Britain (CPGB) formed in London.

1921 July: George Lansbury leads the Poplar councillors to the Law Courts.

1922: the Transport and General Workers' Union (TGWU) established with Ernest Bevin as General Secretary.

1924 January: the first Labour Government, with Ramsay MacDonald as Prime Minister; loses office at the October general election.

1926 May: the General Strike lasts nine days.

1928 May: Transport House opened in London, headquarters of the Transport and General Workers' Union and the Labour Party.

1929 May: formation of second Labour Government.

1930 January: first issue of the *Daily Worker* newspaper.

1931 August: collapse of MacDonald's government; the Labour Party is heavily defeated at the October general election.


PART TWO

1932 October: Sir Stafford Cripps helps establish the Socialist League.

1935 November: Clement Attlee elected leader of the Labour Party to replace George Lansbury.

1936 May: the Left Book Club initiated by Victor Gollancz.

1936 July: outbreak of the Spanish Civil War.

1936 August: the first Moscow Trial.

1936 October: the Battle of Cable Street in the East End of London.

1936 October: the Jarrow March led by the town's MP Ellen Wilkinson.

1937 January: first issue of the weekly *Tribune*.

1937 November: the death of Ramsay MacDonald.

1940 May: the Labour Party joins the coalition government.

1942 December: publication of the Beveridge Report.

1945 July: the Labour Party wins the general election with 393 MPs to the Conservatives' 213.

1947 January: a secret Cabinet committee decides that Britain should make its own nuclear weapons.

1948 July: the National Health Service comes into operation.

1949 April: the North Atlantic Treaty Organisation (NATO) is established.

1949 September: the pound is devalued.

1950 February: the general election cuts Labour's majority to six.

1950 June: start of the Korean War.

1951 April: Aneurin Bevan, Harold Wilson and John Freeman resign from the government.

1951 October: the Conservatives win the general election.

1955 December: Hugh Gaitskell succeeds Clement Attlee as the leader of the Labour Party.

1956 October: Anthony Crosland publishes *The Future of Socialism*.

1956 October: the Hungarian uprising is crushed by the Red Army.

1958 January: the Campaign for Nuclear Disarmament (CND) is formed; the first of what become annual marches to Aldermaston takes place that Easter.

1959 October: the Labour Party loses its third general election in a row.

1960 July: death of Aneurin Bevan.

1960 October: the Labour Party Conference passes a unilateralist defence motion, prompting Hugh Gaitskell to make his 'fight' speech.

1963 January: death of Hugh Gaitskell; succeeded by Harold Wilson.

1964 October: Labour just win the general election.

1965 July: Harold Wilson makes a secret deal with the American government not to devalue the pound.

1966 March: the Labour government increases its majority.

1967 November: the pound is devalued by Chancellor of the Exchequer James Callaghan.

1969 January: Barbara Castle publishes her *In Place Of Strife* proposals for trade union reform; they are withdrawn in June.

1969 August: Home Secretary James Callaghan sends the troops into Ulster.

1970 June: the Conservatives under Edward Heath unexpectedly win the general election.

1973 January: Britain enters the European Economic Community (EEC).

1974 February: a Labour government under Wilson returns to office and wins a small majority at the October 1974 general election.

1975 June: referendum on the EEC produces a 2–1 result in favour of staying in.

1976 April: James Callaghan succeeds Harold Wilson as leader of the Labour Party and Prime Minister.

1976 December: the Cabinet agrees to the cuts demanded by the International Monetary Fund (IMF).

1977 March: the 'Lib–Lab' Pact signed.

1979 May: the Conservatives under Mrs Thatcher win the general election with a forty–three–seat majority.

PART THREE

1980 November: Michael Foot succeeds James Callaghan as leader of the Labour Party.

1981 February: a special conference held at Wembley to introduce constitutional changes within the Labour Party prompts the breakaway of the Social Democratic Party (SDP).

1981 May: Labour wins the Greater London Council (GLC) elections; Ken Livingstone is elected leader of the GLC.

1983 June: the Conservatives easily win the general election with a 146–seat majority.

1983 October: Neil Kinnock is elected leader of the Labour Party.

1984 March: the miners' strike begins.

1987 June: the Conservatives win the general election with a 102–seat majority.

1990 November: Mrs Thatcher resigns as Prime Minister.

1992 April: the Conservatives led by John Major unexpectedly win the general election. Neil Kinnock resigns as Labour leader a few days later.

1992 July: John Smith is elected leader of the Labour Party.

1994 May: John Smith dies after a heart attack.

1994 July: Tony Blair is elected Labour leader with John Prescott as deputy.

1995 April: a special conference of the Labour Party authorises the replacement of the traditional Clause Four.

# Notes

Full publication details of the titles cited in the notes are given in the Select Guide to Further Reading. The dates refer to the edition I used.

## Beginnings

p.1    *Politics about power*: James Margach *The Anatomy of Power* (1979) vii

p.1    *Workers of world*: Raymond Plant 'Servant or Master?' in *The Times*, 2 October 1990

p.1    *A third not knowing party*: *Daily Telegraph*, 14 May 1987

p.1    *Institute of Directors study*: *Daily Telegraph*, 3 September 1986

p.1    *Election holiday boom*: for example, *Evening Standard*, 26 May 1983

p.1    *Less than one-twentieth*: Stephen Harding, David Phillips, Michael Fogarty *Contrasting Values in Western Europe* (1986) p.77

p.2    *RSPB figures*: *The Economist*, 13 August 1994

p.2    *37 Clerkenwell Green*: see Andrew Rothstein *The House on Clerkenwell Green* (1983)

p.6    *Jargon*: George Orwell *The English People* (1947) p.34

p.6    *State monopoly capitalism*: Ralph Miliband *Marxism and Politics* (1977) p.96

p.7    *Reverse snobbery*: Anthony Barnett in Channel Four's tribute to Raymond Williams, *A Journey of Hope*, 19 June 1990

p.10    *Cult of personality*: Kenneth O. Morgan *Labour People* (1987) p.1

p.11    *Explorer of the past*: Lytton Strachey *Eminent Victorians* (1928) vii

p.12    *1,600 files*: David Marquand *Ramsay MacDonald* (1977) p.797

p.12    *Dalton's diaries*: see the article by his editor, Ben Pimlott, in the

*Listener*, 17 July 1980. By piling together the diaries of Dalton, Crossman and Benn you don't prop up a table so much as make one.

p.12    *Benn's letters*: *Daily Telegraph*, 16 November 1990

p.13    *Labour is known*: Ben Pimlott, 'The Future of the Left' in Robert Skidelsky (ed) *Thatcherism* (1988) p.83

p.13    *Pleasures of the past*: David Cannadine *The Pleasures of the Past* (1989)


CHAPTER ONE
## Who Cares About Keir Hardie?

p.17    *Right thing*: G.D.H.Cole *James Keir Hardie* (1941) p.8

p.17    *Abstraction*: David Lowe *From Pit to Parliament* (1923) p.36

p.18    *Hardie's 'garb'*: Frank Smith *From Pit to Parliament* (undated) p.7

p.18    *Gardiner*: A.G.Gardiner *Prophets, Priests and Kings* (1908) p.217

p.19    *Alone*: J.Bruce Glasier *James Keir Hardie: A Memorial* (undated) p.65

p.20    *Unfortunate class*: Caroline Benn *Keir Hardie* (1992) p.150

p.20    *Hardie's illegitimacy*: Fred Reid *Keir Hardie: The Making of a Socialist* (1978) pp.185–192

p.21    *Shorthand*: Frank Smith, p.4

p.21    *Daylight*: G.D.H.Cole, p.8

p.22    *Men with no property*: Henry Pelling *A History of British Trade Unionism* (1976) p.32

p.23    *Applegarth*: Asa Briggs *Victorian People* (1965) p.186

p.24    *Man made*: James Maxton *Keir Hardie: Prophet and Pioneer* (undated) p.9

p.24    *Not democrats*: John Vincent *The Formation of the British Liberal Party 1857–1868* (1972) p.35

p.25    *Damn charity*: William Temple *Christianity and Social Order* (1942) p.14

p.25    *Good pits guide*: Caroline Benn, p.27

p.26    *Trevelyan meeting*: William Stewart *J.Keir Hardie* (1925) p.44

p.28    *Country of workers*: E.J.Hobsbawm *Industry and Empire* (1969) p.154

p.28    *Without violence*: Henry Pelling (ed) *The Challenge of Socialism (1968) p.9* p.28     *Human sentiment*: Hamilton Fyfe *Keir Hardie* (1915) p.71

p.29     *Labourism*: John Saville 'The Ideology of Labourism' in R. Benewick, R.N.Berki and B.Parekh *Knowledge and Belief in Politics* (1973) pp.213–226

p.29     *Ethics*: J.Keir Hardie *From Serfdom to Socialism* (1907) p.35

p.30     *Toynbee Hall report*: Reg Beer *Matchgirls Strike 1888* (undated) p.41

p.31     *Sexual favours*: Jonathan Schneer *Ben Tillett* (1982) p.14

p.31     *Order and calm*: H.H.Champion *The Great Dock Strike* (1988) p.6

p.32     *Needles in Burns*: Leonard Cottrell *Madame Tussaud* (1951) p.174

p.32     *European parties*: Norman Stone *Europe Transformed 1878–1919* (1983) pp.48–49

p.32     *Word masses*: see the sparkling essay by Asa Briggs 'The Language of "Mass" and "Masses" in Nineteenth-Century England' in D.Martin and D.Rubinstein (eds) *Ideology and the Labour Movement* (1979) pp.62–63

p.32     *Personal influence*: Asa Briggs *Victorian Cities* (1969) p.65

p.33     *Eight hours*: Rowland Kenney *Westering* (1939) p.24

p.33     *Nation yours*: Hamilton Fyfe, p.119

p.34     *Major and miner*: Kenneth O. Morgan *Keir Hardie: Radical and Socialist* (1975) p.51

p.35     *Wings clipped*: J.Bruce Glasier *Keir Hardie: The Man and the Message* (1919) p.10

p.35     *Howling*: William Stewart, pp.93–94

p.37     *Rueful countenance*: A.G.Gardiner, p.216

p.37     *Few friends*: David Lowe, p.36

p.37     *Laughter at discount*: S.G.Hobson *Pilgrim to the Left* (1938) p.46

p.37     *Vicious tastes*: J.Keir Hardie, p.100

p.37     *Dress shirt*: A.G.Gardiner, p.214

p.37     *Mrs Glasier*: Kenneth O.Morgan, p.11

p.38     *Annie Hines*: Fred Reid, pp.170–171

p.38     *Sylvia Pankhurst*: Kenneth O.Morgan, pp.164–166; Caroline Benn, p.266–267

p.38     *Agitator*: Hamilton Fyfe, p.61

p.39     *Tillett's stammer*: Jonathan Schneer, p.24

p.39     *Shipping Federation*: John Saville 'Trade Unions And Free Labour: The Background To The Taff Vale Decision' in Asa

Briggs and John Saville (eds) *Essays in Labour History* (1967) p.324; *Eye-Ball Buster*, p.335

p.40    *Mann's head*: F.C.Ball *One Of The Damned* (1973) p.111

p.40    *Nose broken*: Jonathan Schneer, p.31

p.40    *Old romance*: J.R.Clynes *Memoirs: Volume One 1869–1924* (1937) p.34

p.40    *Twenty-three unionists*: see David Martin 'The Instruments of the People?' in D.Martin and D.Rubinstein (eds) *Ideology and the Labour Movement* pp.125–146

p.41    *Deferential*: Hyndman quoted in Lord Elton *Ramsay MacDonald* (1939) p.133

p.41    *Survey of MPs*: *Review of Reviews*, June 1906, vol XXXIII, pp.568–582; *secular*, p.582

p.41    *No manual labourers*: W.H.Mallock 'The Political Power of Labour' in *The Nineteenth Century*, vol 60, August 1906, p.211

p.42    *Child dies*: Jack London *The People of the Abyss* (1978) pp.121–122; also see Robert Barltrop *Jack London* (1977) pp.80–82

p.42    *Race of seers*: Emrys Hughes *Keir Hardie*, pp.3–4

p.43    *Sale of honours*: G.R.Searle *Corruption in British Politics 1895–1930* (1987), passim; for specific instances, see A.J.Davies *We, The Nation: The Conservative Party and the Pursuit of Power* (1995) pp.168–171

p.43    *Du Cros*: F.C.Ball *One Of The Damned* pp.73–74

p.44    *Cadbury and Carnegie*: Caroline Benn, pp.79, 162

p.44    *de la Warr*: George Lansbury *The Miracle of Fleet Street* (1925) pp.13–14

p.44    *Tory gold*: see e.g. S.G.Hobson, p.52

p.44    *Relied on unions*: Michael Pinto-Duschinsky *British Political Finance 1830–1980* (1981) p.65

p.44    *Adult organisation*: Margaret Cole *Beatrice Webb* (1945) p.136

p.45    *Webbs' loo*: Kingsley Martin *Father Figures* (1966) p.136

p.45    *The Potters*: Margaret Cole, p.13

p.46    *Absorbed*: Norman and Jeanne MacKenzie *The First Fabians* (1977) p.127

p.46    *Only one view*: Caroline Benn, p.291

p.46    *Death*: MacKenzies, pp.129, 134

p.48    *Fabian journalists*: E.J.Hobsbawm essay 'The Fabians Reconsidered' in his collection *Labouring Men* (1964) p.250

p.48    *Head only*: MacKenzies, p.155

p.48    *One and one*: Margaret Cole, p.43

p.48    *Babies*: quoted in Ruth Brandon *The New Women and the Old Men* (1990) p.109

p.49    *Community: Our Partnership* (1948) p.222

p.50    *Moses*: MacDonald's introduction to William Stewart, xxi

CHAPTER TWO
## The Mild-Mannered Desperadoes

p.51    *'Marxists'*: Wilhelm Liebknecht *Karl Marx: Biographical Memoirs (1975) p.71*

p.51    *Against wall*: Lenin quoted in Paul Johnson *A History of the Modern World* (1983) p.67

p.52    *Fight to knife*: Charles Poulsen *The English Rebels* (1984) p.179

p.52    *Government preparations*: Reg Groves *But We Shall Rise Again* (1938) pp.180–181

p.52    *Gunsmiths and telegraph system*: John Saville *1848: The Briish State and the Chartist Movement* (1987) p.112

p.52    *Gagging Act*: Theodore Rothstein *From Chartism to Labourism* (1983) p.143

p.53    *Vault of heaven and Feargus Rex*: R.G.Gammage *History of the Chartist Movement 1837–1854* (1969) pp.45, 292

p.53    *Loss of nerve*: Donald Read and Eric Glasgow *Feargus O'Connor* (1961) p.131

p.55    *Chelsea mob*: Andrew Davies *Literary London* (1987) p.30

p.56    *Railway clerk*: Asa Briggs *Marx in London* (1982) p.53

p.56    *Kinkel*: Rosemary Ashton *Little Germany* (1986) p.153; see also S.S.Prawer *Karl Marx and World Literature* (1976) pp.186–196

p.56    *One hundred organisations*: Jacques Freymond and Miklos Molnar 'The Rise and Fall of the First International' in M.M.Drachkovitch *The Revolutionary Internationals, 1864–1943* (1966) p.14

p.57    *Pistol*: reminiscences of Theodore Cuno in *Reminiscences of Marx and Engels* (undated) p.211

p.57    *Lack of money*: Yvonne Kapp *Eleanor Marx: Volume One* (1972) p.36

p.58    *Prussian spy*: Yvonne Kapp, p.290

p.58    *Marxes' humour*: Eleanor Marx-Aveling in *Reminiscences*, p.254

p.58    *Pub crawl*: Wilhelm Liebknecht, pp.150–151

p.59    *Rule Britannia*: James Hinton *Labour and Socialism* (1983) p.55

p.60    *Non-participatory*: eg. Arthur Marwick *British Society Since 1945* (1982) pp.164, 276

p.61    *Marx and melodrama*: Wylie Sypher 'Aesthetic of Revolution: the Marxist Melodrama' in *The Kenyon Review*, summer 1948, pp.431–444

p.61    *Start a business*: Yvonne Kapp, p.45

p.61    *Marx and importance of clarity*: S.S.Prawer, pp.159,357

p.61    *Brainless*: Wilhelm Liebknecht, p.82

p.61    *Lack of translation*: Kirk Willis 'The Introduction and Critical Reception of Marxist Thought in Britain, 1850–1900' in *The Historical Journal*, 20, 2, (1977) pp.423,442

p.62    *Cricket blue*: H.M.Hyndman *Record of an Adventurous Life* (1911) p.20

p.63    *Workers' universities*: John Taylor *From Self-Help to Glamour: the Workingman's Club, 1860–1972* (1972) p.93

p.64    *Millenium*: Edward Carpenter *My Days and Dreams* (1916) p.246

p.64    *Revolutionary cabinet*: Francis Williams *Ernest Bevin* (1952) p.23

p.64    *Monday morning*: Barbara W. Tuchman *The Proud Tower* (1980) p.360

p.64    *Hyndman's business activities*: Chushichi Tzusuki *H.M. Hyndman and British Socialism* (1961) pp.140–144

p.64    *Desperadoes*: Beatrice Webb, diary entry for 6 March 1924, quoted in Neal Wood *Communism and British Intellectuals* (1959) p.75

p.65    *SDF membership*: P.A.Watmough 'The Membership of the Social Democratic Federation, 1885–1902' in *Bulletin of the Society for the Study of Labour History*, no 34, spring 1977, pp.35–40

p.65    *Marxism and unions*: see the excellent essay by E.J. Hobsbawm 'Karl Marx and the British Labour Movement' in his collection *Revolutionaries* (1977) pp.95–108

p.65    *Pedantic tone*: William Morris letter to J.Bruce Glasier, 9 March 1892, in William Morris Gallery, Walthamstow

p.65    *Sectarianism*: H.M.Hyndman, p.444

p.66    *Support for institutions*: Ross McKibbin 'Why was there no Marxism in Great Britain?' in *English Historical Review*, vol XCIX, no 391, April 1984, p.329

p.66   *The election*: Robert Tressell *The Ragged Trousered Philanthropists* (1965) pp.526ff

p.67   *New SDF methods*: T.A.Jackson *Trials of British Freedom* (1940) p.180

p.67   *Charles Booth*: H.M.Hyndman, pp.331–332; for a spirited defence of the SDF and its influence, see John Foster, 'The Merits of the SDF' in *Bulletin of the Marx Memorial Library*, no 105, autumn 1985, pp.25–37

p.68   *100,000*: Bernstein quoted in Walter Kendall *The Revolutionary Movement in Britain, 1900–21* (1969) p.323

p.68   *Connell's appearance*: Viscount Snowden *An Autobiography: Volume One 1864–1919* (1934) p.72

p.68   *Poachers' union*: J.R.Clynes *Memoirs: Volume One 1863–1924* (1937) p.87

p.68   *Spirit of revolt*: Mike Pentelow 'Early fighter in a tough game' in *Land Worker*, May 1990

p.68   *Two-hour introduction*: Viscount Snowden, p.72

p.69   *100 guinea dress*: Frances, Countess of Warwick *Afterthoughts* (1931) p.161

p.69   *Meeting with Blatchford*: Frances, Countess of Warwick *Life's Ebb and Flow* (1929) p.91

p.69   *Warwick's train*: E.J.Hobsbawm 'Hyndman and the SDF' in his collection *Labouring Men* (1964) p.233

p.70   *Coronation*: Gareth Stedman Jones *Languages of Class* (1983) p.211

p.70   *Election address*: Reg Groves *The Strange Case of Victor Grayson* (1975) p.31

p.70   *Wedding rings*: Rowland Kenney *Westering* (1939) p.141

p.70   *House of murderers*: Reg Groves, p.69

p.70   *Comments on Grayson*: Edward Carpenter, p.260; and Laurence Thompson *Robert Blatchford* (1951) p.202

p.71   *Grayson's disappearance*: David Clark *Victor Grayson: Labour's Lost Leader* (1975) pp.125ff

p.71   *Lenin on Grayson*: David Clark, p.3

p.72   *Union jack*: Prince Peter Kropotkin *Memoirs of a Revolutionist* (1899) p.377

p.72   *British tolerance*: Colin Holmes 'Immigrants, Refugees and Revolutionaries' in the special issue of *Immigrants and Minorities*, 'From the Other Shore', vol 2, no 3, November 1983, pp.8–14 p.72    *Chatterers*: Jonathan Schneer *Ben Tillett* (1982) p.3

p.73    *Lenin and Nadia*: see Nadezhda Krupskaya *Memoirs of Lenin* (1970)

p.73    *Lenin and morality*: quoted in Anthony Wright *Socialisms* (1986) pp.53–54

p.73    *Iskra*: Andrew Rothstein *Lenin in Britain* (1970) pp.12–13

p.74    *Communist Club*: see Ivan Maisky *Journey into the Past* (1962) passim

p.74    *Mental dynamite*: Chushichi Tsuzuki, p.56

p.74    *Brotherhood church*: *Bulletin of the Marx Memorial Library*, July/September 1957, no 3, p.4

p.74    *The 5th Congress*: Arthur P.Dudden and Theodore H. von Laue 'The RSDLP and Joseph Fels' in the *American Historical Review*, vol LXI, no 1, October 1955, pp.26ff

p.75    *Long speeches*: Angelica Balabanoff quoted in Isaac Deutscher *The Prophet Armed: Trotsky 1879–1921* (1970) p.140

p.75    *Daily Mail*: Dudden and von Laue, p.27

p.76    *Webbs on Fels*: Beatrice Webb *Our Partnership* (1948) p.291

p.76    *Fels loan*: Mary Fels *Joseph Fels* (1920) p.237

p.76    *Loan paid back*: Dudden and von Laue, p.47

CHAPTER THREE
## Socialism and the New Life

p.77    *1883 letter*: Philip Henderson (ed) *The Letters of William Morris to his Family and Friends* (1950) p.176

p.77    *Ours*: Reg Groves *The Strange Case of Victor Grayson* (1975) p.111

p.77    *Hyndman*: Stephen Winsten *Salt and his Circle* (1951) p.64

p.77    *Marjorie Davidson*: Norman and Jeanne MacKenzie *The First Fabians* (1977) p.95

p.77    *Oliviers*: Ruth Brandon *The New Women and the Old Men* (1990) p.99

p.78    *Give money away*: Fiona MacCarthy *William Morris* (1994) p.542

p.78    *Uncomfortable*: John Trevor *My Quest for God* (1897) p.223

p.79    *Victorian age*: A.H.Moncur Sime *Edward Carpenter: His Ideas and Ideals* (1916) p.140

p.79    *Socialism as religion*: MacKenzies, p.159; also see Stephen Yeo 'A

New Life: The Religion of Socialism in Britain, 1883–1896' in *History Workshop*, issue 4, autumn 1977, pp.5–56

p.80    *Shining eyes*: Laurence Thompson *Robert Blatchford* (1951) p.101

p.80    *Christ and communism*: J.Keir Hardie *From Serfdom to Socialism* (1907) p.217

p.81    *Other-worldliness*: F.G.Bettany *Stewart Headlam: A Biography* (1926) p.217

p.81    *First socialist organisation*: Kenneth Leech 'Stewart Headlam, 1847–1924, and the Guild of St Matthew' in M.B.Reckitt (ed) *For Christ and the People* (1968) p.64

p.82    *Guild numbers*: Peter d'A. Jones *The Christian Socialist Revival 1877–1914* (1969) p.129

p.82    *Socialist Salvation Army*: John Trevor, p.242

p.82    *Socialist Ten Commandments*: Fred Reid 'Socialist Sunday Schools in Britain 1892–1939' in *International Review of Social History*, vol XI, 1966, pp.18–47. There was also a Proletarian School Movement with its 'Ten Proletarian Maxims', a Proletarian Flute Band etc.: see the monthly *Proletcult* published between March 1922 and July 1924 (copies in the British Library)

p.82    *Singing*: Francis Meynell *My Lives* (1971) p.111

p.83    *Labour Party hymns*: David Clark *Victor Grayson* (1975) p.35

p.83    *Religious movement*: Philip M.Williams *Hugh Gaitskell* (1982) p.333

p.83    *Genesis*: report in *The Times*, 16 December 1989

p.84    *Releases imagination*: Fiona MacCarthy *William Morris* (emphasis in original) p.587

p.85    *Great change*: see chapter 'How The Change Came' in G.D.H.Cole *William Morris* (1946) pp.96–121

p.86    *Angry*: Asa Briggs (ed) *William Morris: News from Nowhere and Selected Writings and Designs* (1984) p.13

p.86    *University education*: J.Bruce Glasier *William Morris and the Early Days of the Socialist Movement* (1921) p.38

p.86    *Three Musketeers*: Jack Lindsay *William Morris: His Life and Work* (1975) p.269

p.86    *Epilepsy*: Penelope Fitzgerald's introduction to William Morris *The Novel on Blue Paper* (1982) x

p.87    *Frightful ignorance*: 'William Morris's Socialist Diary' in *History Workshop*, issue 13, spring 1982, p.23

p.87    *My good luck*: Fiona MacCarthy, p.400

p.88     *Dreading quarrels*: Morris letter to J.Bruce Glasier, 5 December 1890, at William Morris Gallery, Walthamstow

p.88     *Poet Laureate*: E.P.Thompson *William Morris: Romantic to Revolutionary* (1977) p.603

p.89     *£50 guarantee*: Andrew Rothstein 'William Morris at Clerkenwell' in *The Times*, 11 April 1966

p.89     *May Morris*: Edward Carpenter *My Days and Dreams* (1916) p.218

p.89     *Engels on Morris*: R.Page Arnot *William Morris, The Man and the Myth* (1964) p.57

p.89     *Fascist Weekly*: R.Page Arnot, p.120

p.89     *Morris at SPAB*: Nikolaus Boulting 'The law's delays: conservationist legislation in the British Isles' in Jane Fawcett (ed) *The Future of the Past* (1977) p.16

p.90     *Snowing paper*: William Morris *The Beauty of Life* (1974) p.17

p.90     *Dream of London*: William Morris *The Earthly Paradise* (1868–1870)

p.90     *Buying my wall-papers*: quoted in J.R.Clynes *Memoirs: Volume Two 1924–1937* (1937) p.263

p.91     *Most effective*: entry on Blatchford by Judith Fincher Laird and John Saville in Joyce Bellamy and John Saville (eds) *Dictionary of Labour Biography* (1976) volume 4, p.37

p.91     *Manchester slums*: Robert Blatchford *My Eighty Years* (1931) pp.186–187

p.92     *Pint of bitter*: Margaret Cole *Makers of the Labour Movement* (1948) p.195

p.92     *Everything else*: Laurence Thompson p.114

p.92     *'Clarionese'*: Judith A. Fincher *The Clarion Movement: A Study of a Socialist Attempt to Implement the Co-operative Commonwealth in England 1891–1914* (Manchester: MA Thesis, 1971) p.178

p.93     *Reader's comfort*: Robert Blatchford *English Prose And How To Write It* (1925) p.18

p.93     *Least attention*: Robert Blatchford *Merrie England* (1895) pp.104, 109

p.94     *Grayson quote*: Reg Groves, p.80

p.94     *Hardie quote*: Laurence Thompson, p.117

p.95     *Chartist women*: R.G.Gammage *History of the Chartist Movement 1837–1854* (1969) p.77

p.95     *Male bonding*: Raphael Samuel in the *Guardian*, 4 October 1984

p.95    *Male trade unionists*: Iris Minor 'Working-Class Women and Mat-
        rimonial Law Reform 1890–1914' in D.Martin and D.Rubin-
        stein *Ideology and the Labour Movement* (1979) p.103

p.95    *Six sisters*: Edward Carpenter, p.32

p.96    *Paddington Station*: Ruth Brandon, p.178

p.96    *Aveling*: H.M.Hyndman *Further Reminiscences* (1912) p.142

p.97    *Besant's enthusiasms*: Yvonne Kapp *Eleanor Marx: Volume One*
        (1972) p.268

p.97    *Fifty-one books*: MacKenzies, p.53

p.97    *A priest*: Annie Besant *Autobiographical Sketches* (1885) p.177

p.97    *High ideas*: Annie Besant *An Autobiography* (1939) p.177

p.98    *Prevent conception*: *Autobiographical Sketches*, p.122

p.99    *Bradlaugh photographs*: 'Introduction' by Dr George Arundel to
        *An Autobiography*, p.14

p.100   *Belfort Bax*: Sheila Rowbotham *Hidden from History* (1973) p.95

p.100   *Island*: Caroline Benn *Keir Hardie* (1992) p.200

p.100   *Absolute equality*: William Morris letter to J.Bruce Glasier, 24
        April 1886, at William Morris Gallery, Walthamstow

p.100   *Average wages*: Sheila Rowbotham, p.108

p.101   *Six obstacles*: Barbara Drake *Women in Trade Unions* (1921)
        pp.198–202

p.101   *Men not single-minded*: Hannah Mitchell *The Hard Way Up*
        (1968) p.149

p.101   *Broken pane*: Mrs Pankhurst quoted in George Dangerfield *The
        Strange Death of Liberal England* (1961) p.170

p.102   *Shaw and Headlam*: Andrew Davies *The East End Nobody Knows*
        (1990) p.82

p.102   *Ideas of authority*: Oscar Wilde *De Profundis and other writings*
        (1973) p.24

p.102   *Gross vices*: Sheila Rowbotham and Jeffrey Weeks *Socialism and
        the New Life* (1977) p.21

p.102   *Shaw's letters*: Edward Carpenter *Edward Carpenter 1844–1929:
        A Restatement and Reappraisal* (1970) p.23

p.102   *Cambridge*: Edward Carpenter *My Days and Dreams* p.72

p.103   *Rigid vegetarians*: Gilbert Beith (ed) *Edward Carpenter: In Appreci-
        ation* (1931) p.220

p.104   *Forster*: Gilbert Beith, p.76

p.104   *Brown Dog*: see Colin Hughes 'Memorial to vivisection riots' in
        *The Times*, 13 December 1985

p.105  *Crusaders*: Clement Attlee *As It Happened* (1954) p.35

p.105  *Rank and file*: W.Stephen Sanders *Early Socialist Days* (1927) p.98

p.106  *Magnetic force*: George Orwell *The Road to Wigan Pier* (1962) p.152

p.106  *Redefinition of socialism*: John Rentoul *Tony Blair* (1995) p.303

CHAPTER FOUR
## Tho' Cowards Flinch and Traitors Sneer

p.108  Feel proud: Howard Spring *Fame is the Spur* (1940) p.262. Film and novel have different endings. Spring is more sympathetic towards Shawcross than Nigel Balchin, the writer of the screenplay. There is an excellent discussion of the film by Raphael Samuel in David Lusted (ed) *Raymond Williams: Film TV Culture* (1989) pp.57–66; also see J.Richards and A.Aldgate *Cinema and Society 1930–1970* (1983) pp.75–86

p.108  *Mass meeting*: James Hinton *Labour and Socialism* (1983) p.113

p.109  *The god*: J.Ramsay MacDonald – Centenary Commemoration, held at the House of Lords, 12 October 1966 p.3

p.109  *Legendary being*: Egon Wertheimer *Portrait of the Labour Party* (1929) p.176

p.109  *Eyes plucked*: Gwyn Williams in John Gorman *Banner Bright* (1976) p.16

p.110  *Watchmaker*: Lord Elton *The Life of James Ramsay MacDonald* (1939) p.28

p.110  *Bristol SDF*: Lord Elton, pp.45, 47

p.110  *Cyclists' Club*: M.A.Hamilton *J.Ramsay MacDonald* (1929) p.25

p.110  *Work on DNB*: M.A.Hamilton, p.29

p.111  *Fellowship*: David Marquand *Ramsay MacDonald* (1977) p.24

p.111  *Wanting to be Prime Minister*: Ruth Brandon *The New Women and the Old Men* (1990) p.97

p.111  *Election address*: Lord Elton, p.74

p.112  *Lincoln's Inn Fields*: Herbert Tracey *From Doughty Street to Downing Street* (1924) p.58

p.113  *Churchill's remark*: J.R.Clynes *Memoirs: Volume Two 1924–1937* (1937) p.200

p.113  *Economic creeds*: Ramsay MacDonald's foreword to Joe Corrie *The Road the Fiddler Went* (undated) p.114   *Any interpretation*: Viscount Snowden *An Autobiography: Volume One* (1934) p.216

p.114   *Leave economics to Snowden*: Kenneth O.Morgan *Labour People* (1987) p.23

p.114   *Socialism not economics*: David Lowe *From Pit to Parliament* (1923) p.104

p.115   *Rail strike violence*: Bob Holton *British Syndicalism 1900–1914* (1970) pp.104–105

p.116   *Blue Book*: J.Ramsay MacDonald *Margaret Ethel MacDonald* (1912) p.136

p.116   *Heart in grave*: David Marquand, p.135

p.116   *Difficult task*: J.Keir Hardie *From Serfdom to Socialism* (1907) p.95

p.116   *ILP Manifesto*: Henry Pelling (ed) *The Challenge of Socialism* (1968) p.207

p.116   *Hardie's daughter*: Hamilton Fyfe *Keir Hardie* (1935) p.136

p.117   *Race, patriotism*: John Cockburn *The Hungry Heart* (1956) p.274

p.118   *Cannot go back*: Ralph Miliband *Parliamentary Socialism* (1972) p.44

p.118   *Danger of being outlawed*: W.Abendroth *A Short History of the European Working Class* (1971) p.59

p.118   *Wells' remark*: Lord Elton, p.248

p.118   *Plumstead Common*: M.A.Hamilton, p.72

p.118   *Held party together*: Ross McKibbin *The Evolution of the Labour Party 1910–1924* (1974) p.243

p.118   *1918 Act*: Ross McKibbin, xv

p.119   *Henderson influence*: Kenneth O.Morgan, p.80

p.119   *Political levy*: Michael Pinto-Duschinsky *British Political Finance 1830–1980* (1981) pp.69–71

p.119   *Number of unions*: David Caute *The Left in Europe* (1966) p.139

p.120   *Building of Transport House*: information from Regan Scott, Librarian, 6 March 1991

p.120   *Trade union influence*: David Coates *The Labour Party and the Struggle for Socialism* (1975) p.13

p.121   *Middle-class*: Fiona MacCarthy *William Morris* (1994) p.450

p.121   *MacDonald's Welsh meeting*: description by Jim Griffiths quoted in David Coates, ix

p.122   *Maximisation*: David Howell *British Social Democracy* (1980) p.32

p.122   *Change from bottom*: J.Ramsay MacDonald *Wanderings and Excursions* (1925) p.285

p.123   *1919 strike*: quoted in Aneurin Bevan *In Place of Fear* (1978) pp.40–41

p.124   *Label on coat*: Charles Loch Mowat *Britain Between the Wars* (1956) p.147

p.124   *Free love*: Charles Loch Mowat, p.169

p.124   *At Buckingham Palace*: J.R.Clynes, volume one, pp.343–344

p.125   *Walsh's sword*: Peter Slowe *Manny Shinwell* (1993) p.130

p.125   *The Red Flag*: David Marquand, p.304

p.125   *Webb's club*: Margaret Cole *Beatrice Webb* (1945) p.141

p.125   *Constituents*: Viscount Snowden, volume two, pp.662–663

p.126   *Shaw's peerage*: J.R.Clynes, volume two, p.46

p.126   *1924 slogan*: Keith Jeffery and Peter Hennessy *States of Emergency* (1983) pp.77–78

p.126   *Zinoviev Letter*: A.J.Davies *We, The Nation: The Conservative Party and the Pursuit of Power* (1995) pp.222–224

p.127   *18 million leaflets*: Keith Middlemas *Politics in Industrial Society* (1979) p.202

p.127   *1924 broadcasts*: John Antcliffe 'Politics of the Airwaves' in *History Today*, March 1984, pp.4–10

p.128   *Right improvisation*: Egon Wertheimer, p.195

p.128   *Economic democracy*: Robert Boothby, John Loder, Harold Macmillan and Oliver Stanley *Industry and the State* (1927) p.143

p.129   *OMS*: Jeffery and Hennessy, p.111

p.129   *Striking railwaymen*: Noreen Branson *Britain in the Nineteen Twenties* (1975) p.181

p.129   *Consequences of victory*: Julian Symons *The General Strike* (1987) p.143

p.129   *700 meetings*: R.E.Dowse *Left in the Centre* (1966) p.128

p.129   *War-weary*: Julian Symons, x

p.130   *Recovery around corner*: Aneurin Bevan, p.47

p.132   *Selfish ambition*: quoted in Henry Pelling (ed) *The Challenge of Socialism* (1968) p.147

p.132   *Knapsack*: Egon Wertheimer, p.175

p.132   *Backbenchers*: Robert Skidelsky *Politicians and the Slump* (1967) p.392

p.132   *Earthy paradise*: Keith Laybourn *Philip Snowden: A Biography* (1988) p.167

p.133   *Raised in atmosphere*: Keith Laybourn, p.97; Churchill, p.97

p.133   *Accumulated material*: Viscount Snowden, volume one, p.103

p.133   *Not much chance*: Robert Skidelsky, p.393

p.133   *Thomas in tears*: Kingsley Martin *Editor* (1969) p.57

p.134   *No clear advice*: David Marquand, p.792

p.134   *Snowden's broadcast*: Ralph Miliband, p.191

p.134   *Colne Valley*: J.Ramsay MacDonald – *A Centenary Commemoration*, p.11

p.135   *Rubber stamp*: Lord Citrine *Men and Work* (1964) p.288

p.136   *Lenin's comment*: *Lenin on Ramsay MacDonald* (1934) p.19

CHAPTER FIVE
## British Revolutionaries in the 1920s

p.137   *Lenin's name*: Harry Pollitt *Serving My Time* (1940) pp.123, 129

p.137   *Not killing*: George Orwell *The English People* (1947) p.40

p.137   *Maclean stamp*: see Robert Chesshyre 'The Man Who Brought Britain To The Brink of Revolution' in *Observer Magazine*, 13 July 1980, p.24

p.138   *Scots and Irish*: Leon Trotsky *Where Is Britain Going?* (1926) p.44

p.139   *1,000 an acre*: Iain McLean *The Legend of Red Clydeside* (1983) p.18

p.139   *Cricket on Sunday*: William Joss in P.M.Kemp-Ashraf and Jack Mitchell (eds) *Essays in Honour of William Gallacher* (1966) p.44

p.139   *Gambling*: Guy Aldred *John Maclean* (1932) p.33

p.139   *Little humour*: B.J.Ripley and J.McHugh *John Maclean* (1989) p.2

p.139   *Blatchford and Marx*: Tom Bell *John Maclean* (1944) p.8

p.139   *Lecture notes*: Tom Bell, pp.128–130

p.139   *Weekly attendance*: Nan Milton (ed) *In the Rapids of Revolution* (1978) p.11

p.139   *Maclean's oratory*: Nan Milton *John Maclean* (1973) pp.83–84

p.141   *Impact of October 1917*: Harry McShane and Joan Smith *No Mean Fighter* (1978) p.94

p.141   *Poison and breakdown*: Ripley and McHugh, pp.96, 102

p.141   *Churchill and mutinies*: Walter Kendall *The Revolutionary Movement in Britain 1900–21* (1969) p.189

p.142   *Director of Intelligence*: James Hinton *Labour and Socialism* (1983) p.134

p.142    *Newspaper reports*: Walter Kendall, p.138; *troops firing*, p.139

p.142    *Shinwell's beard*: Peter Slowe *Manny Shinwell* (1993) p.86

p.142    *Cabinet*: Cabinet Papers, PRO CAB 23/9 WC 529; also see Chanie Rosenberg *1919* (1987) pp.78–79

p.143    *No plan*: William Gallacher *Revolt on the Clyde* (1978) p.226

p.143    *1918 election*: Christopher Harvie *No Gods and Precious Few Heroes* (1981) p.22

p.144    *German waiters*: Chushichi Tsuzuki *H.M.Hyndman and British Socialism* (1961) p.243

p.144    *Role of Theodore Rothstein*: hostile accounts in Raymond Challinor *The Origins of British Bolshevism*, Nan Milton and Walter Kendall; favourable in David Burke 'Theodore Rothstein, Russian Emigré and British Socialist' in *Immigrants and Minorities*, vol 2, no 3, November 1983 and John Saville's introduction to Theodore Rothstein *From Chartism to Labourism*

p.145    *£15,000*: Andrew Rothstein in *Labour Monthly*, vol 51, no 12, December 1967, p.567

p.145    *£85,000*: Jack and Bessie Braddock *The Braddocks* (1963) p.44

p.145    *Over £1 million*: Francis Beckett *Enemy Within* (1995) p.21

p.145    *Jewels*: Francis Meynell *My Lives* (1971) pp.120–122

p.145    *Bickering delayed formation*: L.J.Macfarlane *The British Communist Party* (1966) pp.47–56, 279

p.146    *Less interference*: Nan Milton *Rapids*, p.225

p.146    *Rothstein argument*: David Howell *A Lost Left* (1986) p.200

p.146    *Maclean of England*: Nan Milton *John Maclean*, p.243

p.147    *Pankhurst episode*: Henry Pelling *The British Communist Party* (1975) pp.19–20

p.147    *Got to learn*: Walter Kendall, p.228

p.147    *Desire for peace*: Fernando Claudin *The Communist Movement: From Comintern to Cominform* (1975) p.60

p.148    *Soviet idea*: Monty Johnstone 'Early Communist Strategy for Britain: An Assessment' in *Marxism Today*, September 1978, p.287

p.148    *Letter to Pravda*: Martin Durham 'British Revolutionaries and the Suppression of the Left in Lenin's Russia, 1918–1924' in *Journal of Contemporary History*, vol 20, no 2, April 1985, p.214

p.148    *Imported ideas*: John S.Clarke *Pen Pictures of Russia Under the 'Red Terror'* (1921) pp.188, 194

p.148    *Lion tamer*: Raymond Challinor *John S.Clarke* (1977) p.14

p.149    *Telegram*: Betty Vernon *Ellen Wilkinson* (1982) p.36

p.149    *Intellectuals and Communist Party*: Gary Werskey *The Visible College* (1988) p.150; also Neal Wood *Communism and British Intellectuals* (1959) p.24

p.150    *Mental wreck*: Dora B.Montefiore *From a Victorian to a Modern* (1927) p.201

p.150    *Jamaican's letter*: Iain Maclean, p.244

p.150    *Learning off by heart*: Stuart Macintyre *A Proletarian Science: Marxism in Britain 1917–1933* (1980) p.87

p.150    *Postage stamps and catechisms*: A.L.Morton in *Bulletin of the Marx Memorial Library*, no 106, spring 1985, p.21

p.151    *Lenin's language*: Paul Johnson *A History of the Modern World* (1983) p.55

p.151    *King Street*: Walter Kendall, p.436 note 13; also on financial assistance, see Roderick Martin *Communism and the British Trade Unions 1924–1933* (1969) p.44 and Hugo Dewar *Communist Politics in Britain* (1975) pp.43, 87

p.151    *Pollitt's charm*: Kevin Morgan *Harry Pollitt* (1993) pp.42, 48

p.151    *Holy Ghost*: John Callaghan *Rajani Palme Dutt* (1993) p.38

p.152    *Pollitt and Internationale*: William Campbell *Villi the Clown* (1981) p.21

p.153    *Bolshevik discipline*: George Lansbury *The Miracle of Fleet Street* (1925) p.41

p.153    *Panel*: Francis Beckett, p.41

p.153    *Politburo*: Henry Pelling, p.189 – almost half were Scots. However Pelling's figures do not square with the lists of Central Committee members provided in Noreen Branson *History of the Communist Party of Great Britain 1927–1941* (1985) pp.339–341

p.153    *Quarter in Labour Party*: Noreen Branson, p.5

p.154    *Morrison's methods*: Bernard Donoughue and G.W.Jones *Herbert Morrison* (1973) p.102

p.154    *Lenin Corners*: Harry McShane and Joan Smith, p.213

p.154    *Recruits to Moscow*: for example, twenty Welsh miners were sent between 1928 and 1933, see Hywel Francis in *Journal of Contemporary History*, vol 5, no 3, 1970

p.154    *Pollitt to Moscow*: Henry Pelling, pp.54–55

p.155    *Phone tapped*: Mike Squires *Saklatvala* (1990) pp.49–50

p.155    *Sak censure*: *Workers' Life*, 5th August 1927; and *Dictionary of National Biography* (1931–1940) p.779

p.155    *Sak's ashes*: Mike Squires, p.206

p.155    *Scruples*: David Marquand *Ramsay MacDonald* (1977) p.19

p.155    *Racing tips*: see for example the *Daily Worker* 3 January 1930, 16
         January 1930, 10th February 1930. The *Daily Herald* had faced
         the same problem ten years before: Raymond Postgate *The Life
         of George Lansbury* (1951) pp.142–143

p.155    *Culture after revolution*: Andrew Rothstein 'The Workers' Cul-
         ture' in *The Plebs*, February 1922, p.41

p.156    *Young Pioneers*: Hywel Francis and David Smith *The Fed* (1980)
         p.161; also see Stuart Macintyre *Little Moscows* (1980) passim

p.156    *High votes*: Stuart Macintyre *A Proletarian Science* p.32

p.157    *Spoiling ballot papers*: Michael Woodhouse and Brian Pearce
         *Essays on the History of Communism in Britain* (1975) p.188

p.157    *Toilet paper*: Wal Hannington in Kemp-Ashraf and Mitchell,
         p.32

p.157    *Jane Austen*: Vivien Morton and Stuart Macintyre *T.A.Jackson:
         A Centenary Celebration* (undated) p.23

p.157    *Snowden on Mann*: Viscount Snowden *An Autobiography: Volume
         One 1864–1919* (1934) pp.75–76

p.157    *1,000 arrests*: James Hinton and Richard Hyman *Trade Unions
         and Revolution* (1975) p.47

p.157    *Communist Party's devotion to Moscow*: confirmed by John Saville
         *The Labour Movement in Britain* (1988) p.53

CHAPTER SIX
## The Thirties

p.161    *Fruitful conception*: A.L.Rowse 'The Significance of Marx' in *The
         Plebs*, March 1933, vol XXXV, no 3, p.61

p.161    *Enjoying a richer life*: A.J.P.Taylor *English History 1914–1945*
         (1970) p.396

p.161    *Practical politics*: Hugh Dalton *Practical Socialism for Britain* (1935)
         p.27

p.162    *20 million cinema-goers*: John Stevenson *Social Conditions in Britain
         Between the Wars* (1977) p.43

p.162    *Jubilee celebrations*: George Orwell 'Patriots and Revolution-
         aries' in Victor Gollancz (ed) *The Betrayal of the Left* (1941)
         p.244; *fatalism of 1930s*: A.H.Halsey *Change in British Society*
         (1981) p.156

p.163   *Wrongs and remedies*: James Jupp *The Radical Left in Britain 1931–1941* (1982) p.125

p.163   *Dog or two*: Jonathan Schneer *George Lansbury* (1990) p.38

p.164   *Touching coat*: Naomi Mitchison *You May Well Ask* (1986) p.185

p.164   *Brick through window*: St John B.Groser *Politics and Persons* (1949) pp.22–23

p.164   *Lansbury's home*: Raymond Postgate *The Life of George Lansbury* (1951) p.104; also Edgar Lansbury *George Lansbury* (1934) pp.50, 67

p.165   *'John Bull of Poplar'*: entry by M.A.Hamilton in *The Dictionary of National Biography*, 1931–1940 (1949) p.525

p.165   *Rating value*: St John B.Groser, p.25

p.165   *Contempt of court*: Noreen Branson *Poplarism 1919–1925* (1979) p.46

p.165   *Lansbury in Brixton*: Edgar Lansbury, pp.73–75

p.166   *Lansbury's health*: Raymond Postgate, p.291

p.166   *Christ himself*: quoted in Bob Holman *Good Old George* (1990) p.76

p.167   *Lovable figure*: A.J.P.Taylor, p.191 fn.3

p.167   *Not to be a Marxist*: Kathleen Raine *The Land Unknown* (1975) p.92

p.167   *Intellectually disreputable*: Robert Blake *The Conservative Party from Peel to Thatcher* (1985) p.255

p.167   *Daily Express*: Alan Jenkins *The Thirties* (1975) p.62

p.167   *Guest*: Carmel Haden Guest (ed) *David Guest: A Memoir* (1939); for Madge, see his excellent article in *The Times Literary Supplement*, 14 December 1979; for Cornford, Pat Sloan (ed) *John Cornford: A Memoir* (1936)

p.168   *Pym*: Hazel Holt and Hilary Pym (eds) *A Very Private Eye* (1984) p.35

p.168   *October Club*: Stuart Samuels 'English Intellectuals and Politics in the 1930s' in Philip Reiff (ed) *On Intellectuals* (1969) pp.213–214

p.168   *Queues for Laski*: Kingsley Martin *Father Figures* (1966) p.157

p.169   *Cripps' diet*: Froom Tyler *Cripps* (1942) p.12; *cold bath*: Kenneth O.Morgan *Labour People* (1987) p.163

p.169   *Gresford*: From Tyler, p.23

p.169   *Twelve days' agonising*: Ben Pimlott 'The Socialist League:

Intellectuals and the Labour Left in the 1930s' in *Journal of Contemporary History*, vol 6, no 3, 1971, p.17

p.170  *Trevelyan's gates*: Philip M.Williams (ed) *The Diary of Hugh Gaitskell 1945–1956* (1983) fn.69 p.76

p.170  *Cripps' financial aid*: Ben Pimlott *Labour and the Left in the 1930s* (1986) pp.34–35

p.170  *Dictatorship*: Sir Stafford Cripps *Can Socialism Come by Constitutional Methods?* (1933) p.5

p.170  *Financial controls*: Sir Stafford Cripps 'Democracy and Dictatorship' in *Political Quarterly*, October – December 1933, p.478; and Sir Stafford Cripps *The Choice for Britain* (1934) p.7

p.170  *Buckingham Palace*: Eric Estorick *Stafford Cripps* (1949) pp.124–125

p.170  *Lunatic*: Hugh Dalton *The Fateful Years* (1957) p.107

p.171  *Experts*: Sir Stafford Cripps *The Choice for Britain*, p.8

p.171  *Marxist slogans*: Michael Foot *Aneurin Bevan 1897–1945* (1975) p.158

p.171  *Interesting meeting*: Lord Citrine *Men and Work* (1964) p.300

p.172  *Huddle*: Ben Pimlott 'The Socialist League', pp.37–38

p.172  *United Clothing Workers' Union*: S.W.Lerner *Breakaway Unions and the Small Trade Union* (1961) pp.85–143

p.172  *Idea of solidarity*: Roderick Martin *Communism and the British Trade Unions 1924–1933* (1969) p.189

p.172  *Comintern and Hitler*: Isaac Deutscher *The Prophet Outcast: Trotsky 1929–1940* (1970) p.201

p.173  *European Popular Fronts*: D.E.McHenry *The Labour Party in Transition 1931–1938* (1938) p.256

p.173  *United front*: Sir Walter Citrine *I Search for Truth in Russia* (1936) p.286

p.173  *Orwell on Gollancz*: Ian Angus and Sonia Orwell (eds) *An Age Like This* (1970) p.580

p.173  *Labour Party affiliation*: *Daily Worker*, 30 January 1936; *Labour Party Conference Report* 1936, 'British Labour and Communism' pp.296–300

p.173  *Dropped dictatorship*: Hugo Dewar *Communist Politics in Britain* (1976) pp.123–124

p.173  *Scrutinise books*: Noreen Branson *History of the Communist Party of Great Britain 1927–1941* (1985) p.154

p.173  *Subsidies stopped*: Fancis Beckett *Enemy Within* (1995) p.61

p.174  *Hammer and sickle*: see *Daily Worker*, 1 January 1937 p.174   *Hutt's review*: Labour Monthly, July 1937, pp.382–386

p.174   *Withdraw book*: private information from two Communist Party members of the 1930s, both of whom wish to remain anonymous

p.174   *Brighton turnover*: Ernie Trory *Between the Wars: Reflections of a Communist Organiser* (1974) p.107

p.174   *Baffled*: Tom Campbell on 'Party Education' in *Party Organiser*, no 1, July 1938, p.22

p.174   *Girl guides*: see 'Who can be a Member of the League?' in *Our Youth*, June 1938, no 3

p.174   *Scottish May Day*: Christopher Harvie *No Gods and Precious Few Heroes* (1981) p.102

p.175   *Dissenters*: see the splendid article by E.P.Thompson 'Organising the Left' in *The Times Literary Supplement*, 19 February 1971

p.175   *Rickword*: for information on Rickword, Slater, Swingler etc. see John Lucas (ed) *The 1930s: A Challenge to Orthodoxy* (1978)

p.176   *Hill as Gore*: Rodney Hilton in D.Pennington and K.Thomas (eds) *Puritans and Revolutionaries: Essays Presented to Christopher Hill* (1978) p.43

p.176   *'Holorenshaw'*: Gary Wersky *The Visible College* (1988) p.169

p.176   *Tawney's weavers*: quoted in *R.H.Tawney: A Portrait By Several Hands* (undated) p.7

p.176   *Haldane popularising*: Charlotte Haldane *Truth Will Out* (1949) p.21

p.176   *100,000 sales*: James Jupp, p.93

p.177   *Dutt and Strachey*: see letters inside Dutt's personal copies held at the Marx Memorial Library, London

p.177   *Independent enterprise*: Hugh Thomas *John Strachey* (1972) p.155

p.177   *Propaganda alienating*: Ruth Dudley Edwards *Victor Gollancz* (1987) p.232

p.178   *Official history*: Dr John Lewis *The Left Book Club* (1970)

p.178   *Internal friction*: Stuart Samuels 'The Left Book Club' in *Journal of Contemporary History*, vol 1, no 2, 1966, pp.71–72

p.178   *Anti-Fascist Association*: Hugh Thomas, p.179

p.178   *250,000*: Victor Gollancz editorial in *Left News*, no 31, November 1938

p.179   *Lack of research*: G.D.H.Cole *History of the Labour Party from 1914* (1948) pp.123–124

p.179   *Against intellectuals*: David Howell *British Social Democracy* (1980) p.56; for the Conservatives, see John Ramsden *The Making of Conservative Party Policy* (1980)

p.179    *National Joint Council*: Roger Eatwell and Anthony Wright 'Labour and the Lessons of 1931' in *History*, February 1978

p.179    *Name change*: Roger Eatwell *The 1945–1951 Labour Governments* (1979) p.26

p.180    *No shortage*: Michael Pinto-Duschinsky *British Political Finance 1830–1980* (1981) p.77

p.180    *Chess sets*: Henry Pelling *A History of British Trade Unionism* (1976) p.207

p.181    *Bleak assessment*: John Saville 'May Day 1937' in Asa Briggs and John Saville (eds) *Essays in Labour History 1918–1939* (1977) p.239, a judgement repeated in John Saville *The Labour Movement in Britain* (1988) pp.72–73

p.181    *Loss of membership*: Tony Lane *The Union Makes Us Strong* (1974) p.131

p.181    *Scottish football*: Christopher Harvie, p.120

p.181    *Pools*: George Orwell *The Lion and the Unicorn* (1982) fn. p.48

p.182    *Middle way*: see Arthur Marwick 'Middle Opinion in the Thirties: Planning, Progress and Political "Agreement"' in *English Historical Review*, April 1964, pp.285–298; and more recently, Elizabeth Durbin *New Jerusalems* (1985) passim

p.182    *Soviet influence*: L.P.Carpenter 'Corporatism in Britain, 1930–1945' in *Journal of Contemporary History*, 11, 1976, p.10

p.182    *National Plan*: *Week-End Review*, 14 February 1931

p.182    *PEP*: Kenneth Lindsay 'Early Days of PEP' in *Contemporary Review*, February 1973, pp.57–61

p.183    *Plan*: see R.A.Wilford 'The Federation of Progressive Societies and Individuals' in *Journal of Contemporary History*, 11, 1976, pp.49–82

p.183    *For these publications generally*: John Stevenson, pp.227ff

p.183    *Better than Labour Party*: Arthur Marwick 'The Labour Party and the Welfare State in Britain 1900–1948' in *American Historical Review*, vol LXXIII, no 2, 1967, p.395

p.184    *Generous refuge*: Kenneth O.Morgan, p.121

p.184    *Keir Hardie Night*: Ben Pimlott *Hugh Dalton* (1985) pp.44–45

p.184    *Dalton and Keynes*: Ben Pimlott *Hugh Dalton*, p.160

p.185    *Keynes and middle way*: Stuart Holland 'Keynes and the Socialists' in Robert Skidelsky (ed) *The End of the Keynesian Era* (1977) p.68; also see the fine article in the same collection by Robert Skidelsky 'The Political Meaning of the Keynesian Revolution'

p.185  *I was alarmed*: Nicholas Davenport *Memoirs of a City Radical* (1974) p.75

p.185  *Left-wing governments*: Hugh Gaitskell in Margaret Cole and Charles Smith (eds) *Democratic Sweden* (1938) p.96

p.186  *400,000 copies*: Ben Pimlott *Hugh Dalton* p.238

p.186  *Membership doubled*: John Saville 'May Day 1937', p.277, fn.9

p.186  *1934 ballot*: James Jupp, p.5

p.188  *Labour Party not campaigning*: John Saville 'May Day 1937', p.241

p.188  *NUWM 50,000*: John Callaghan *The Far Left in British Politics* (1987) p.40

p.188  *Constitutional NUWM*: Chris Cook and John Stevenson 'Historical Hide and Seek' in the *Guardian*, 25 August 1978; Henry Pelling, pp.64–65

p.188  *NUWM in Oxford*: Marion Slingova *Truth Will Prevail* (1968) p.19; *in Cambridge*: Gary Werskey, p.21

p.188  *Constant agitation*: A.L.Morton 'The 1930s' in *Bulletin of the Marx Memorial Library*, no 106, spring 1985, p.23

p.188  *Barrier against fascism*: Wal Hannington *Never On Our Knees* (1967) pp.330–331

p.188  *Withdrawal of regulations*: Ralph Miliband *Parliamentary Socialism* (1972) p.215

p.189  *Book of illustrations*: Betty D.Vernon *Ellen Wilkinson* (1982) p.76

p.190  *Jarrow*: J.B.Priestley *English Journey* (1977) p.298

p.190  *Women discouraged*: Betty D.Vernon, p.141

p.191  *BUF and Bermondsey*: Noreen Branson, pp.168–171

p.192  *International solidarity*: Jack Jones foreword to Judith Cook *Apprentices of Freedom* (1977) viii

p.192  *Thirty-five committees*: Kingsley Martin, p.111; for similar frenetic activity, see for example Joe Jacobs *Out of the Ghetto* (1978) p.214 and Douglas Hyde *I Believed* (1950) p.58

CHAPTER SEVEN
**Grand Illusions**

p.193  *Opposing Chamberlain*: *Dictionary of National Biography, 1961–1970* p.416

p.194    *Gallacher's memoirs*: in the USSR, 1937, William Gallacher *The Rolling of the Thunder* (1947) pp.190–191; post-1956 *The Last Memoirs of William Gallacher* (1966)

p.194    *Spoke languages*: Ivor Montagu *The Youngest Son* (1970) p.357

p.194    *Defending Trials*: see for example *Left Book Club News*, October 1936 and *Left News*, April 1937

p.195    *Chauffeur*: Margaret Cole *Beatrice Webb* (1945) p.173

p.195    *Capital punishment*: Ruth Dudley Edwards *Victor Gollancz* (1987) p.244

p.195    *Those who supported Stalin*: 'Nearly all moneyed people who enter the left-wing movement follow the "Stalinist" line as a matter of course.' George Orwell writing in July 1938, *An Age Like This* (1970) p.381

p.195    *Admirers of Nazis*: Richard Griffiths *Fellow Travellers of the Right* (1980) passim

p.196    *Churchill's article*: Robert Rhodes James *Churchill: A Study in Failure* (1973) pp.291–292

p.197    *Discredit of Labour*: John Lehmann *The Whispering Gallery* (1955) p.178

p.197    *Philby*: Kim Philby *My Silent War* (1969) p.15

p.197    *Rejecting own society*: Paul Hollander *Political Pilgrims* (1981) p.231

p.197    *Land of hope*: introduction by Harry M.Geduld to Bernard Shaw *The Rationalization of Russia* (1964) p.31; *earthly paradise*, p.82

p.197    *Future that works*: David Caute *The Fellow Travellers* (1973) p.24

p.197    *Science is communism*: Gary Werskey *The Visible College* (1988) p.176

p.198    *Blunt*: C.Day Lewis (ed) *The Mind in Chains* (1937) p.108; Rickword, p.245; Warner p.30

p.198    *Prisoners not leaving*: Bernard Shaw, p.91

p.198    *Enjoyable experience*: Pat Sloan *Soviet Democracy* (1937) p.111

p.198    *Intourist*: Sylvia R.Margulies *The Pilgrimage to Russia* (1968) p.63

p.199    *Waitresses*: Bernard Shaw, p.16

p.199    *Statistics*: Sir Walter Citrine *I Search for Truth in Russia* (1936) pp.92–93, 100

p.199    *Banner*: Bernard Shaw, p.19

p.199    *Royalty*: Norman and Jeanne MacKenzie *The First Fabians* (1977) p.407

p.199  *Krynin affair*: Harry M.Geduld introduction to Bernard Shaw, pp.21–23; also see Christopher Sykes *Nancy* (1979) pp.387, 398

p.200  *Stalin at cinema*: Robert Conquest *The Great Terror* (1990) p.235

p.200  *98 of 139*: Ian Grey *Stalin* (1982) p.276

p.200  *Military purges*: Volkogonov letter in the *Independent*, 19 September 1989

p.201  *Who to kill*: Bernard Shaw, p.112

p.201  *The Webbs*: David Caute, p.69

p.201  *Pritt's influence*: Joe Jacobs *Out of the Ghetto* (1978) p.226

p.201  *Available proof*: D.N.Pritt *The Zinoviev Trial* (1937) p.9

p.201  *More merciful*: Dudley Collard *Soviet Justice and the Trial of Radek and Others* (1937) p.79

p.202  *Brockway's letter*: quoted in obituary of Brockway by Raphael Samuel in the *Independent*, 2 May 1988

p.202  *Hotel Bristol*: Dr Friedrich Adler *The Witchcraft Trial in Moscow* (1936) p.14

p.202  *Manchester Guardian*: Hugo Dewar 'The Moscow Trials' in *Survey*, no 41, April 1961, p.93

p.203  *Recalcitrance*: F.A.Voigt *Unto Caesar* (1938) p.344

p.203  *Daily Herald/New Statesman*: see Peter Deli 'The Image of the Russian Purges in the *Daily Herald* and the *New Statesman*' in *Journal of Contemporary History*, vol 20, no 2, 1985, pp.261–282

p.203  *Emrys Hughes*: Hugo Dewar, p.94

p.203  *Gramophone record*: Sir Walter Citrine, p.256

p.204  *Street corners*: Tatiana Tchernavin *Escape from the Soviets* (1933) p.65

p.204  *Novelists*: Vladimir Tchernavin *I Speak for the Silent* (1937) pp.178–185

p.204  *Muggeridge*: quoted in Sylvia R.Margulies, p.187

p.204  *All persecution capitalist*: Noreen Branson *History of the Communist Party of Great Britain 1927–1941* (1985) p.247

p.205  *Not spreading doubts*: Arthur Horner *Incorrigible Rebel* (1960) pp.214–215

p.205  *Private representations*: for example by J.D.Bernal, see Gary Werskey, pp.209–210

p.205  *Simple choice*: Denis Healey *The Time of My Life* (1989) p.34

p.205    *Modern political choice*: E.J.Hobsbawm 'Intellectuals and Com-
         munism' in his collection *Revolutionaries* (1977) p.27

p.206    *Arrogant rubbish*: Noel Annan writing in the *Times Literary
         Supplement*, 7 December 1979, quoted in Laurence and Helen
         Fowler *Cambridge Commemorated* (1984) p.323

p.207    *Spilling blood*: H.S.Ferns *Reading from Right to Left* (1983)
         p.129

p.207    *Breaking eggs*: Colin Welch 'Or the greatest liar?' in the *Spectator*,
         22 September 1990

p.207    *A faith*: Cecil Day Lewis *The Buried Day* (1969) p.209

p.208    *Breaking up meetings*: Joe Jacobs, p.87

p.208    *Alan Sebrill*: Edward Upward *In the Thirties*, 1962, published as
         part of the trilogy *The Spiral Ascent* (1977) pp.176–177

p.208    *Bigotry*: Margaret McCarthy *Generation in Revolt* (1953) p.253;
         *suicide*, pp.254–255

CHAPTER EIGHT
## New Worlds for Old?

p.210    *Complacency*: quoted in Henry Pelling 'The 1945 General
         Election Reconsidered' in *Historical Journal*, 23, 2, 1980, p.414

p.210    *Mildly disturbed*: Herbert Morrison *An Autobiography* (1960)
         p.251

p.210    *George VI*: William Harrington and Peter Young *The 1945
         Revolution* (1978) p.207

p.211    *One syllable*: Douglas Jay quoted in Peter Hennessy 'The man
         who built the welfare state' in *The Economist*, 11 November
         1989, p.26

p.211    *Biscuits to dog*: Wilfred Fienburgh in Denis Healey *The Time of
         My Life* (1989) p.153

p.211    *Haileybury*: Clement Attlee *As It Happened* (1954) p.19

p.212    *East London visitors*: George Lansbury *My Life* (1928) p.130

p.213    *Violet Millar*: Trevor Burridge *Clement Attlee: A Political Biogra-
         phy* (1985) p.55

p.213    *Greatest betrayal*: Clement Attlee, p.74

p.214    *Intelligentsia*: Clement Attlee, p.86

p.214    *'The Rabbit'*: Dalton quoted in T.D.Burridge *British Labour and
         Hitler's War* p.42

p.214    *Wartime shift*: massively chronicled in Angus Calder *The People's*

*War* (1971), more briefly in Andrew Davies *Where Did The Forties Go?* (1984)

p.215　*Iniquity*: Susan Briggs *Keep Smiling Through* (1975) p.153

p.215　*Pansy-pink*: quoted in Bill Schwarz 'The tide of history' in Nick Tiratsoo (ed) *The Attlee Years* (1991) p.151

p.215　*Warfare, welfare*: Asa Briggs 'The Welfare State in Historical Perspective' in *Archives Européennes de Sociologie*, 1961, no 2, p.227

p.215　*Character of war*: Paul Addison *The Road to 1945* (1975) p.129

p.216　*Factory feeling*: J.T.Murphy *Victory Production* (1942) pp.33, 82; Mass Observation *War Factory* (1943) pp.9, 45; R.P.Lynton 'Factory Psychology in the Transition' in *Pilot Papers*, vol 1, no 1, January 1946, p.68

p.216　*1943 poll*: Tom Harrisson 'Who'll Win?' in *Political Quarterly*, vol XV, no 1, January – March 1944, p.27

p.217　*Palpable injustices*: Noel Annan *Our Age* (1990) p.12

p.217　*Westminster Conservatives*: Paul Foot *The Politics of Harold Wilson* (1968) p.341

p.218　*No message*: Lord Moran *Churchill* (1966) p.183

p.218　*Only a photograph*: Virginia Cowles *No Cause for Alarm* (1949) p.72

p.218　*United Labour Party*: Charles Madge (ed) *Pilot Guide to the General Election* (1945) pp.91–92

p.218　*Age of candidates*: Mark Abrams 'The Labour Vote in the General Election' in *Pilot Papers*, vol 1, no 1, January 1946, pp.17–18

p.219　*Blackburn*: Wilfred De'Ath *Barbara Castle* (1970) p.65

p.219　*versus broadcast*: Mark Abrams, pp.16–17

p.219　*Dictators*: Granville Eastwood *Harold Laski* (1977) p.130

p.219　*Hustings*: William Harrington and Peter Young, p.157

p.219　*Press equal*: Roger Eatwell *The 1945–1951 Labour Governments* (1979) pp.41–42

p.219　*Epping count*: Leah Manning *A Life for Education* (1970) p.164

p.220　*Servicemen's vote*: Penny Summerfield 'Education and Politics in the British armed forces in the Second World War' in *International Review of Social History*, vol XXVI, 1981, part two, p.133

p.220　*Two-thirds*: Mark Abrams, p.7

p.220    *Sweeping change*: Roger Eatwell, p.50

p.221    *Labour's position*: E.P.Thompson 'Mr Attlee and the Gadarene Swine' in the *Guardian*, 3 March 1984

p.221    *¼ graduates*: Mervyn Jones *Michael Foot* (1994) p.136

p.221    *First sensation*: Hugh Dalton *High Tide and After* (1962) p.3

p.221    *Attlee's surprise*: Henry Pelling, p.408

p.222    *Ignorant bliss*: Peter Hennessy *Never Again* (1992) p.86

p.222    *Sense of dramatic*: Kenneth O.Morgan *Labour in Power 1945–1951* (1984) p.37

p.222    *Morrison's attempted coup*: Bernard Donoughue and G.W.Jones *Herbert Morrison* (1973) pp.339–340

p.222    *Average age*: Anthony Howard 'We Are the Masters Now' in Michael Sissons and Philip French (eds) *The Age of Austerity 1945–1951* (1963) p.20

p.223    *Attlee on bus*: Andrew Davies *The East End Nobody Knows* (1990) p.98

p.223    *Morrison's dentures*: Bernard Donoughue and G.W.Jones, p.175

p.223    *Shinwell's punch*: Peter Slowe *Manny Shinwell* (1993) p.182

p.223    *12/20*: Kenneth O.Morgan *Labour People* (1987) pp.79–80

p.223    *Scheming*: Bevin quoted in Donoughue and Jones, p.346

p.223    *Kept us together*: quoted in Maurice Shock's entry on Attlee, *Dictionary of National Biography 1961–1970* (1981) p.55

p.224    *Shy/tears*: Kenneth Harris 'The man in the empty taxi' in the *Daily Telegraph*, 22 July 1995

p.224    *Herbert's poem*: quoted in Trevor Burridge, p.3

p.224    *Number of Fabians*: Norman and Jeanne MacKenzie *The First Fabians* (1977) p.409

p.224    *Films*: for example, Ealing's *Hue and Cry* (1946) and *Passport to Pimlico* (1948)

p.225    *Utterly ignorant*: Nicholas Davenport *Memoirs of a City Radical* (1974) p.149

p.225    *Nationalisation proposals*: Clement Attlee, p.165

p.226    *Workers' control*: Robert S.Dahl 'Workers' Control of Industry and the British Labour Party' in *American Political Science Review*, vol XLI, October 1947, pp.875–900

p.226    *Two papers*: Alan Sked and Chris Cook, *Post-war Britain* (1979) p.31; also Emmanuel Shinwell *Lead with the Left* (1981) p.131. However Shinwell's biographer, Peter Slowe, calls Shinwell's claims a 'lie' in *Manny Shinwell* (1993) p.208

p.226    *Iron*: Godfrey Hodgson 'The Steel Debates' in Michael Sissons and Philip French, p.305

p.226    *No draft legislation*: Roger Eatwell, p.49. Also see Richard Crossman's complaint that the Attlee government failed '. . . to do its homework in the years before it achieved power' in his essay 'The Lessons of 1945' in P.Anderson and R.Blackburn (eds) *Towards Socialism* (1965) p.153

p.227    *Compensation figures*: Robert A.Brady *Crisis in Britain* (1950) pp.110–114, 147–147, 162–163, 245–251

p.228    *Ordinary resident*: Geoffrey Crowther 'British socialism on trial' in *Atlantic Monthly*, May 1949, p.27

p.228    *Railway Review*: David Rubinstein *Socialism and the Labour Party: the Labour Left and Domestic Policy, 1945–1950* (undated) p.6

p.228    *Jobs for boys*: for example, Action Society Trust *The Men on the Boards* (1951) p.12 and Acton Society Trust *The Worker's Point of View* (1952) pp.7–8

p.228    *Company profits*: Dudley Seers *The Levelling of Incomes Since 1938* (1951) p.72

p.229    *Unilever figures*: A.A.Rogow with Peter Shore *The Labour Government and British Industry 1945–51* (1955) p.62

p.229    *Dedicated Order*: Rodney Barker 'The Fabian State' in Ben Pimlott (ed) *Fabian Essays in Socialist Thought* (1984) p.34

p.229    *Lack of suitable people*: Philip M.Williams (ed) *The Diary of Hugh Gaitskell 1945–1956* (1983) p.89

p.230    *Shinwell's longevity*: Kenneth O.Morgan 'Britain in the Dark' in the *Guardian*, 24 April 1987

p.230    *Fuel crisis*: Tom Harrisson 'British Opinion Moves Towards a New Synthesis' in *Public Opinion Quarterly*, vol 11, no 3, Fall 1947, p.336

p.231    *British idea*: Sir William Beveridge *The Pillars of Security* (1943) p.143

p.231    *Pre-war*: Peter Hennessy, p.128

p.231    *National Insurance Benefits*: James Harvey and Katherine Hood *The British State* (1958) p.237

p.232    *Salaried service*: D.Stark Murray *Why A National Health Service?* (1971) p.80

p.232    *Health centres*: Arthur Marwick 'The Labour Party and the Welfare State in Britain' in *American Historical Review*, December 1967, p.402

p.232 *Debate on education*: see conflicting views of David Rubinstein and Billy Hughes in *History Workshop Journal*, no 7, spring 1979, pp.156–169

p.232 *One hour*: Hugh Dalton, p.352

p.233 *Section 132*: Janet Minihan *The Nationalization of Culture* (1977) p.242

p.234 *200 Acts*: Herbert Morrison *The Peaceful Revolution* (1949) p.90

p.234 *Pethick Lawrence*: William Golant 'Clem and Ernie' in *The Times*, 29 November 1980

p.234 *Two-faced Cripps*: Peter Slowe, p.224

p.234 *Hostile press*: James Margach *The Abuse of Power* (1978) p.86

p.235 *Rolls-Royce*: Peter Hennessy, p.329

p.235 *Housewives' League*: Elizabeth Wilson *Only Halfway to Paradise* (1980) p.167

p.235 *Woolton/Butler*: A.J.Davies *We, The Nation: The Conservative Party and the Pursuit of Power* (1995) pp.150–151, 284

p.235 *Strachey*: his foreword to A.A.Rogow with Peter Shore, x

p.236 *Mr Cube*: Rogow with Shore, pp.142–145; also Henry Pelling *The Labour Governments, 1945–1951* (1984) pp.217, 233

p.237 *Compromise*: Clement Attlee, p.163

p.237 *Basically Victorian*: Trevor Burridge, p.10

p.237 *Young Haileyburians*: Kenneth Harris *Attlee* p.406

p.237 *Price of victory*: Monnet quoted in Peter Hennessy, p.392

p.238 *Covenant*: Kenneth O.Morgan *Labour in Power*, p.308

p.238 *Equal pay*: Morgan, p.56

p.238 *Lack of constitutional conflict*: David Marquand *The Politics of Nostalgia*, University of Salford inaugural lecture, 25 October 1979, no pagination

p.238 *Ready for radical action*: Mass Observation *Peace and the Public* (1947) p.13

p.239 *Ealing and bureaucracy*: films include *Passport to Pimlico* (1948), *Whisky Galore* (1949) and *The Lavender Hill Mob* (1951)

p.239 *William Morris*: E.J.Hobsbawm 'Morris on Art and Socialism' in *Our Time*, April 1948, p.176

p.239 *Attlee and sherry*: Peter Hennessy, p.275; Nicholas Davenport also thought that many members of the Attlee government 'were ostentatiously Puritan in their mode of living and dressing'. *Memoirs of a City Radical*, p.88

p.239    *Greyness*: John Campbell *Nye Bevan and the Mirage of British Socialism* (1987) p.365


CHAPTER NINE
**With Us or Against Us?**

p.240    *Pope Pius*: quoted in Donald Sassoon *The Strategy of the Italian Communist Party* (1981) p.59

p.240    *Lawther*: Mark Jenkins *Bevanism: Labour's High Tide* (1979) p.180

p.240    *Backstreets of Tredegar*: quoted in Michael Foot *Aneurin Bevan 1945–1960* (1975) p.435; however Foot then goes on to question the authenticity of this remark

p.241    *Bristol Cathedral*: Francis Williams *Ernest Bevin* (1952) p.20

p.242    *Bacon episode*: Peter Weiler *Ernest Bevin* (1993) p.28

p.242    *'Boss Bevin'*: Francis Williams, p.116

p.242    *Force*: Peter Weiler, p.18

p.242    *B-52s*: Peter Weiler, p.179

p.243    *Callaghan on Bevin*: Jonathan Schneer *Labour's Conscience* (1988) p.55

p.244    *Stalin and imposing regimes*: Roger Pethybridge 'The Soviet Union' in *History Today*, vol 33, October 1983, p.30

p.244    *Taking too seriously*: Denis Healey *The Time of My Life* (1989) p.101

p.244    *Koestler*: Bill Jones *The Russia Complex* (1977) p.185

p.245    *Sunday Times*: Richard Fletcher *The CIA and the Labour Movement* (1977) p.5

p.245    *Lovestone unmarried*: see his obituary in the *Guardian*, 12 March 1990

p.245    *'Scarface'*: obituary of Brown in the *Daily Telegraph*, 17 February 1989

p.246    *Details of US finance*: Trevor Barnes 'The Secret Cold War' in the *Historical Journal*, vol 24, no 2, 1981 and vol 25, no 3, 1982; Don Thomson and Rodney Larson *Where Were You, Brother?* (1978); Roy Godson *American Labor and European Politics* (1976) passim

p.246    *Crusade*: Anthony Sampson *Macmillan* (1968) pp.88–89

p.246    *Orwell's lists*: Bernard Crick *George Orwell: A Life* (1980) p.388

p.247    *Strike-breaking*: Peter Hennessy and Keith Jeffrey 'How Attlee stood up to striker' in *The Times*, 20 November 1979 p.247   *Appeasement analogy*: Anne Deighton 'Introduction' in Anne Deighton (ed) *Britain and the First Cold War* (1990) p.5

p.247   *IRD generally*: David Leigh in the *Guardian*, 27 January 1978, and *Frontiers of Secrecy* (1980) pp.218–224; 'The Ministry of Truth' in *The Leveller*, March 1978, no 13, pp.11–13; Richard Fletcher in the *Observer*, 29 January 1978

p.247   *Background books*: Richard J.Fletcher 'British propaganda since World War II – a case study' in *Media, Culture and Society*, vol 4, no 2, April 1982, p.105; Lyn Smith 'Covert British Propaganda: The Information Research Department, 1943–1977' in *Millennium*, vol 9, no 1, spring 1980, pp.75–77; Paul Lashmar 'Covert in glory', *New Statesman*, 3 March 1995, pp.14–15

p.247   *Briefing BBC*: Nigel Williamson 'Propaganda unit run secretly 'to foil Labour Left', *The Times*, 18 August 1995

p.247   *Tempering broadcasts*: W.Scott Lucas and C.J.Morris 'A very British Crusade: the Information Research Department and the beginning of the Cold War' in Richard J.Aldrich (ed) *British Intelligence, Strategy and the Cold War, 1945–51* (1992) p.98

p.248   *Debagging Lenin*: Christopher Andrew *Secret Service* (1986) p.318

p.248   *IRD and 1975 referendum*: Nicholas Bethell 'Celebrity team used in secret anti-Soviet campaign', *The Times*, 17 August 1995

p.248   *Outlawing CP*: Peter Wilby '"Conspiracy" obsessed the Attlee Cabinet' in *the Sunday Times*, 4 January 1981

p.249   *200 surveillances*: Carl Bernstein *Loyalties* (1989) p.151

p.249   *Great Fear*: David Caute *The Great Fear* (1978)

p.249   *Civil service vetting*: Eleanor Bontecou 'The English Policy' in *The Federal Loyalty-Security Program* (1953) pp.251–273

p.250   *Martyrs*: Peter Hennessy 'Successful cold war purge without hysteria' in *The Times*, 6 January 1981

p.250   *Comparison UK/USA*: Herbert H.Hyman 'England and America: Climates of Tolerance and Intolerance' in D.Bell (ed) *The Radical Right* (1964) pp.269–306

p.250   *Bernal*: Gary Werskey *The Visible College* (1988) p.278 and Maurice Goldsmith *Sage* (1980) p.189

p.250   *Taylor*: A.J.P.Taylor *A Personal History* (1982) p.234

p.250   *Summer 1948*: interview with E.J.Hobsbawm in *Radical History Review*, no 19, winter 1978–79, pp.111–131

p.250   *Actors*: see, for example, the obituary of Alex McCrindle in the *Independent*, 10 May 1990 p.250   *BBC vetting*: Mark Hollingsworth and Richard Norton-Taylor *Blacklist!* (1988) pp.97–121

p.251   *Purged themselves*: Karen Potter 'British McCarthyism' in Rhodri Jefferys-Jones and Andrew Lownie (eds) *North American Spies* (1991) p.148

p.251   *Cricket match*: Ivor Montagu *The Youngest Son* (1970) p.60

p.251   ¼ *million files*: Stephen Ward 'MI5 held Cold War files on 250,000 British "Communists"', the *Independent*, 1 December 1994

p.251   *Anti-Soviet credentials*: Nicholas Bethell 'How Labour kept Stalin at bay', *The Times*, 18 August 1995

p.251   *Defence figures*: P.S.Gupta *Imperialism and the British Labour Movement, 1914–1964* (1975) p.284

p.252   *Dramatic turnaround*: Peter Hennessy *Never Again* (1992) p.415

p.252   *Ugh*: Bill Jones, p.176

p.252   *United States of Europe*: Francis Williams, pp.152, 153

p.252   *Foreigners*: Denis Healey, p.353

p.253   *Pierson Dixon*: Peter Weiler, p.147

p.253   *Bevin v Europe*: Lord Gladwyn *The European Idea* (1966) pp.45, 50; also Richard Mayne *Postwar* (1983) p.304

p.253   *Durham miners*: Bernard Donoughue and G.W.Jones *Herbert Morrison* (1973) p.481

p.253   *Europe Group*: Jonathan Schneer, p.66

p.253   *Humanity*: Christopher Hill 'Stalin and the Science of History' in *Modern Quarterly*, vol 8, no 4, autumn 1953, p.212

p.254   *Drawing distinction*: Iain MacLaine *Ministry of Morale* (1979) pp.208–209

p.255   *Stalin's love*: Milovan Djilas *Conversations with Stalin* (1963) p.82

p.255   *Czechoslovakia*: see Karel Kaplan *The Short March* (1987) pp.133–147

p.255   *Opposition*: William Gallacher *The Case for Communism* (1949) pp.134–135

p.255   *Catholic International*: Roy Godson *American Labor and European Politics* (1976) p.103

p.256   *Party meeting*: E.P.Thompson 'Edgell Rickword' in *PN Review*, vol 6, no 1, supplement, XXVI–XXVII

p.256   *Comrade Stalin*: Eric Heffer 'Joseph Stalin' in the *Independent Magazine*, 30 December 1989 p.256   *Standing up*: Gary Werskey, p.311

p.256   *Sebrill and trembling*: Edward Upward *The Spiral Ascent* (1977) p.470

p.257   *Hate America*: Neal Wood *Communism and British Intellectuals* (1959) p.181

p.257   *Lost St Pancras*: Francis Beckett *Enemy Within* (1995) p.141

p.257   *Klugmann in Cairo*: Basil Davidson *Special Operations Europe* (1980) pp.83–87

p.258   *Cold War pressure*: David Rubinstein *Socialism and the Labour Party: The Labour Left and Domestic Policy, 1945–1950* (undated) p.14

p.259   *Nye and Hitler*: Janet Morgan (ed) *The Backbench Diaries of Richard Crossman* (1981) p.410

p.259   *The Fed*: Will Paynter *My Generation* (1972) p.110

p.260   *My truth*: Jennie Lee *My Life with Nye* (1988) p.211

p.260   *Grandfather in sack*: Arthur Horner *Incorrigible Rebel* (1966) p.11; *Bevan's father*: Aneurin Bevan *In Place of Fear* (1978) p.45

p.260   *First impression*: Aneurin Bevan, p.26

p.261   *Nunnery*: Jennie Lee *Tomorrow is a New Day* (1939) p.151

p.261   *Bevan's manifesto*: Douglas Hill (ed) *Tribune 40* (1977) p.27

p.261   *Tredegar*: Michael Foot *Aneurin Bevan 1897–1945* p.66

p.262   *Riveting championing*: Hywel Francis and David Smith *The Fed* (1980) p.434

p.262   *Montgomery*: Michael Stewart *Life and Labour* (1980) p.71

p.262   *Palace revolutions*: Michael Foot *Aneurin Bevan 1945–1960* (1975) p.92

p.263   *Trade unions' influence*: Geddes quoted in Martin Harrison *Trade Unions and the Labour Party Since 1945* (1960) p.195

p.263   *Trade union money*: Michael Pinto-Duschinsky *British Political Finance 1830–1980* (1981) p.155

p.264   *Labour Party and change*: Richard Crossman *Planning for Freedom* (1964) p.40

p.264   *Anti-communism*: E.P.Thompson 'The Peculiarites of the English' in *The Poverty of Theory* (1978) p.75

p.264   *Deakin's sustained commentary*: Kenneth O.Morgan *Labour in Power, 1945–1951* (1984) p.76

p.264   *Moronic crowd*: Leslie Hunter *The Road to Brighton Pier* (1959) p.85

p.264  *Death of cuts*: Castle quoted in Christopher Driver *The Disarmers* (1964) p.84

p.265  *Carron's technique*: see Lewis Minkin *The Labour Party Conference* (1980) pp.185–187 for a hilarious description

p.265  *Shut your gob*: Michael Foot, p.377; to be fair to Lawther, he then went on to say, 'If your wisdom were commensurate with your clamour, you would be wise' – Leslie Hunter, p.54

p.265  *Evil*: Bernard Donoughue and G.W.Jones *Herbert Morrison* p.518

p.266  *Forty-seven Bevanites*: Ian Mikardo *Back-bencher* (1988) p.120

p.266  *Bad atmosphere*: see, for example, Jack and Bessie Braddock *The Braddocks* (1963) p.203

p.266  *Lost sheep*: Kenneth O.Morgan p.67

p.266  *Sara Barker*: Andy McSmith *John Smith* (1994) p.23

p.266  *Versus expulsions*: Mark Jenkins *Bevanism* p.182

p.267  *No society*: Aneurin Bevan, p.100; *obligation*, pp.201–202

p.267  *Not interested in policy*: Barbara Castle 'Crossman's last diaries' in *The Listener*, 5 March 1981

p.267  *Belly-achers*: Nicholas Davenport *Memoirs of a City Radical* (1974) p.109

p.267  *Planned economy*: R.H.S.Crossman 'The Affluent Society' in *Planning for Freedom* p.96; *terrifying contrast*, p.120

p.267  *Not a team player*: Ian Mikardo, p.151; *avoided discussions*, p.109

p.267  *Dominates discussions*: Janet Morgan (ed) p.53

p.268  *Didn't grow up*: Anthony Howard *Crossman* (1990) pp.162–163

p.268  *Rebel and leader*: Janet Morgan (ed) p.406

p.268  *Labour Left squeezed*: David Howell *The Rise and Fall of Bevanism* (undated) p.35

p.268  *Labour Right*: Bill Jones, p.213

p.268  *Labour Left and Empire*: Jonathan Schneer, p.215

p.269  *Our goals*: Marcuse quoted in Nigel Young *An Infantile Disorder?* (1977) p.40

CHAPTER TEN
## Expanding Horizons

p.270  *Get impatient*: Philip M. Williams *Hugh Gaitskell* (1979) p.391

p.270  *Aspirin*: Frank Chapple, *Sparks Fly!* (1984) p.54

p.270  *Abstinence*: C.A.R.Crosland *The Future of Socialism* (1956) p.524

p.271　*Lounge lizard*: John Campbell *Nye Bevan and the Mirage of British Socialism* (1987) pp.64ff

p.271　*Bevan's poetry*: Jennie Lee *My Life with Nye* (1980) p.309

p.271　*Crosland's girlfriends*: Susan Crosland *Tony Crosland* (1982) p.64

p.271　*Dark satanic things*: C.A.R.Crosland, p.522

p.271　*Fabians and arts*: I.M.Brittain *Fabianism and Culture* (1982) pp.177–180, 209, 210, 212

p.271　*Shaw's complaint*: D.D.Egbert *Social Radicalism and the Arts* (1970) p.44

p.272　*Moral principle*: B.Farrington in *The Communist Answer to the Challenge of Our Time* (1947) p.47

p.272　*Warning members*: Mark Jenkins *Bevanism: Labour's High Tide* (1979) p.210

p.272　*Haldane divorce*: Charlotte Haldane *Truth Will Out* (1949) p.176

p.272　*Not dragging in sex*: Dora Russell *The Tamarisk Tree* (1975) p.172

p.273　*Effective contraception*: Naomi Mitchison *You May Well Ask* (1986) p.69; see the whole chapter 'Patterns of Loving', pp.69–81

p.273　*Twelve hours*: Margery Spring Rice *Working-Class Wives, Their Health and Conditions* (1939) passim

p.273　*Freezing attitudes*: Robert Hewison *In Anger: Culture in the Cold War 1945–60* (1981) p.122. It should also be noted that a homosexual such as the Labour MP Tom Driberg never gained even junior ministerial office; in his memoirs Driberg claimed that this was due to Clement Attlee and Harold Wilson being 'deeply prejudiced puritans': Tom Driberg *Ruling Passions* (1978) p.198

p.274　*Cars and television*: Michael Pinto-Duschinsky 'Bread and Circuses? The Conservatives in Office, 1951–1964' in Vernon Bodganor and Robert Skidelsky (eds) *The Age of Affluence 1951–1964* (1970) p.56; also see Arthur Marwick *British Society Since 1945* (1982) 114ff pp.18

p.274　*Depressing life*: obituary of Plunket Greene in the *Daily Telegraph*, 9 May 1990

p.274　*Nervous breakdown*: Miriam Gross 'An Interview with Eric Hobsbawm' in *Time and Tide*, autumn 1985, p.54

p.275　*Thirty-eight friends*: Vittorio Vidali *Diary of the Twentieth Congress of the Communist Party of the Soviet Union* (1984) p.18

p.276　*Sun spots*: Dutt quoted in Henry Pelling *The British Communist Party* (1975) p.170

p.276   *Pritt*: see D.N.Pritt *Brasshats and Bureaucrats* (1966) p.189

p.276   *Pollitt*: see John Mahon *Harry Pollitt* (1976)

p.276   *Pollitt not recovering*: Jimmy Reid *Reflections of a Clyde-Built Man* (1976) p.40

p.276   *Closing down CP*: Vittorio Vidali, p.63

p.276   *Reactions*: G.W.Grainger 'The Crisis in the British Communist Party' in *Problems of World Communism*, vol VI, no 2, March – April 1957, pp.8–14; also see the essays in Ralph Miliband and John Saville (eds) *The Socialist Register 1976*

p.277   *CP officials*: Kenneth Newton *The Sociology of British Communism* (1969) fn.11 p.11, fn.11

p.277   *Daly's complaint*: Douglas Hill (ed) *Tribune 40* (1977) p.114

p.277   *Saw for myself*: Peter Fryer *Hungarian Tragedy* (1956) p.7; *a tragedy*, p.9

p.278   *Appeals to loyalty*: Llew Gardner in the *New Statesman*, 29 October 1976

p.278   *Best not leaving*: Henry Pelling, p.180

p.279   *Eden placard*: Alfred Grosser *The Western Alliance* (1980) p.145

p.279   *Khrushchev*: Veljko Micunovic *Moscow Diary* (1980) p.134

p.279   *Party held together*: Mervyn Jones *Chances* (1987) p.117

p.279   *Political trance*: Mervyn Jones 'Days of Tragedy and Farce' in Ralph Miliband and John Saville (eds) *The Socialist Register 1976* p.82

p.280   *Typology*: Nigel Young *An Infantile Disorder?* (1977) p.310; *encounter group*, p.53

p.280   *Line on love*: Philip Toynbee *Friends Apart* (1954) p.10

p.280   *From beginning*: Hall quoted in Ronald Fraser *1968* (1988) p.30

p.280   *Morris*: E.P.Thompson foreword to revised edition of *William Morris: Romantic to Revolutionary* (1977) ix–xi

p.281   *Dictatorship of proletariat*: G.D.H.Cole *William Morris as a Socialist* (1960) p.16

p.281   *Arnold Kettle*: quoted in E.P.Thompson *The Poverty of Theory* (1978) p.75

p.282   *Comprehensive redevelopment*: Raphael Samuel 'Born-again Socialism' in Oxford University Socialist Group *Out of Apathy* (1989) p.41; *the family etc.*, p.52

p.282   *Johnson's proposals*: Paul Johnson 'A Sense of Outrage' in Norman Mackenzie (ed) *Conviction* (1958) pp.202–217

p.282   *Gaitskell song*: Christopher Driver *The Disarmers* (1964) p.61

p.282   *Martyrdom*: Barbara Castle *Fighting All the Way* (1994) p.38

p.283   *Bevan and election*: Philip M.Williams *Hugh Gaitskell* (1982) p.297

p.283   *Attacks on Bevan*: Mervyn Jones *Michael Foot* (1994) p.245

p.284   *Who's Who*: Christopher Driver, p.44

p.284   *Advice to marchers*: David Widgery *The Left in Britain 1956–1968* (1976) p.104

p.284   *Graffiti*: Peggy Duff *Left, Left, Left* (1971) p.116

p.285   *Middle-class*: Richard Taylor 'The Labour Party and CND: 1957–1964' in R.Taylor and N.Young (eds) *Campaigns for Peace* (1987) p.115

p.285   *Not working class*: John Callaghan *The Far Left in Britain* (1987) x

p.285   *Orderly*: Peter Cadogan 'From Civil Disobedience to Confrontation' in R.Benewick and T.Smith (eds) *Direct Action and Democratic Politics* (1972) p.169

p.285   *Role of women*: Mervyn Jones *Chances*, pp.150–151

p.286   *Duff*: *Left, Left, Left*; also Hugh Hebert 'Unarmed Combat' in the *Guardian*, 18 January 1980

p.286   *Macmillan's concern*: David Walker 'Macmillan ordered secret nuclear campaign' in *The Times*, 1 January 1990

p.286   *Moral indignation*: Robert Taylor 'The Campaign for Nuclear Disarmament' in Vernon Bogdanor and Robert Skidelsky (eds) pp.250–251

p.286   *Antiquarianism*: Adam Sisman *A.J.P.Taylor* (1995) p.309

p.286   *Professional politicians*: Mervyn Jones *Chances* p.180

p.287   *Calculating machine*: it is possible Bevan was in fact referring to Attlee, see John Campbell *Nye Bevan and the Mirage of British Socialism* p.293

p.287   *Black and white*: Richard Marsh *Off The Rails* (1978) p.39

p.288   *Attlee silence*: Philip M.Williams (ed) *The Diary of Hugh Gaitskell 1945–1956* (1983) p.333

p.288   *Dalton's help*: Stephen Haseler *The Gaitskellites* (1969) p.36

p.288   *Battle for power*: Williams *Hugh Gaitskell* (1982) p.183

p.289   *The State*: John Strachey *Contemporary Capitalism* (1956) p.246

p.289   *Predicting Thatcherism*: Michael Newman *John Strachey* (1989) p.146

p.289   *Criticism of Crosland*: for example, Anthony Arblaster 'Anthony Crosland: Labour's Last Revisionist' in *Political Quarterly*, vol 48, no 4, 1977, pp.416ff p.289    *Anglo-Saxon economies*: C.A.R.Crosland *The Future of Socialism* xi

p.290    *Anarchist and libertarian*: C.A.R.Crosland, 1956 edition, p.522

p.290    *Old dreams dead*: C.A.R.Crosland, 1956 edition, p.99

p.290    *Revisionism*: Elizabeth Durbin *New Jerusalems* (1985) p.280

p.291    *Patronising*: Kevin Morgan *Harry Pollitt* (1993) p.159

p.291    *Bevan and wealth*: John Campbell, xv, p.363

p.291    *Change mood*: Vernon Bogdanor 'The Labour Party in Opposition, 1951–1964' in Bogdanor and Skidelsky (eds), p.95

p.291    *Luxuries and gadgets*: R.H.S.Crossman *Planning for Freedom* (1964) p.100

p.292    *Glad to see people better-off*: quoted in Lord Windlesham *Communication and Political Power* (1966) p.266

p.292    *Broaden appeal*: David Rubinstein *Socialism and the Labour Party: The Labour Left and Domestic Policy 1945–50* (undated) p.22

p.292    *Bad Godesberg*: William E.Paterson 'The German Social Democratic Party' in William E.Paterson and Alastair H.Thomas (eds) *Social Democratic Parties in Western Europe* (1976) p.185

p.292    *Different manifestoes*: Williams *Hugh Gaitskell* (1982) p.273

p.292    *Suez*: A.J.Davies *We, The Nation: The Conservative Party and the Pursuit of Power* (1995) p.359

p.293    *Name Labour*. Jay's article is reprinted in Douglas Jay *Change and Fortune* (1980) pp.273–275

p.294    *Rationality*: Roy Jenkins on Gaitskell in W.T.Rodgers (ed) *Hugh Gaitskell* (1964) p.126

p.294    *Genesis*: Vernon Bogdanor in Bogdanor and Skidelsky (eds), p.100

p.294    *Nationalisation*: Geoffrey Goodman *The Awkward Warrior* (1979) p.242

p.294    *10 Commandments*: interview with Denis Healey in the *Sunday Times*, 13 July 1980, reprinted in John Mortimer *In Character* (1983) p.197

p.295    *Not from traditional Right*: Peter Shore *Leading the Left* (1993) p.61

p.295    *Remote from reality*: Philip M.Williams (ed) *Diary of Hugh Gaitskell*, p.617

p.295    *Middle-class socialists*: quoted in Peter Shore, p.63

p.295    *Spurs*: see Paul Foot 'Parliamentary Socialism' in Nigel Harris and John Palmer (eds) *World Crisis* (1971) pp.84–85 p.296   *CDS funding*: see, for example, Ben Pimlott *Harold Wilson* (1992) p.245

p.296   *CDS and Europe*: Stephen Haseler, pp.227–236

p.297   *A thousand years*: Hugh Gaitskell *Britain and the Common Market* (1962) p.12

p.297   *History books*: John Barnes 'The Record' in David McKie and Chris Cook (eds) *The Decade of Disillusion* (1972) p.17

CHAPTER ELEVEN
## Harold Wilson's New Britain

p.298   *Men with fire*: Clive Ponting *Breach of Promise* (1989) p.15

p.298   *Maudling to Callaghan*: John Cole *As It Seemed To Me* (1995) p.83

p.301   *Conservative media techniques*: Keith Middlemas *Politics in Industrial Society* (1979) pp.338, 354–355

p.301   *Attlee's visit*: Michael Cockerell *Live from Number 10* (1988) p.40

p.301   *Despair*: Tony Benn *Years of Hope* (1994) p.276

p.301   *Bevan and poetry of politics*: Roy Hattersley 'New Blood' in Gerald Kaufman (ed) *The Left* (1966) p.158

p.301   *Gaitskell and TV*: Philip M.Williams *Hugh Gaitskell* (1982) p.248

p.301   *Wilson and TV*: Michael Cockerell, pp.87ff, 117

p.302   *Wilson's glasses*: Austen Morgan *Harold Wilson* (1992) p.253

p.302   *Wilson's speeches*: John Barnes 'The Record' in David McKie and Chris Cook (eds) *The Decade of Disillusion* (1972) p.19

p.302   *Provincial bounce*: John Beavan 'Lord Wilson of Rievaulx' in the *Independent*, 25 May 1995

p.302   *Industrial technology*: Paul Foot *The Politics of Harold Wilson* (1968) p.148

p.303   *Ears of corn*: Lewis Minkin *The Labour Party Conference* (1980) p.232

p.303   *Excitement*: Tony Benn *Out of the Wilderness: Diaries 1963–67* (1987) p.13

p.304   *Eight firsts*: Denis Healey *The Time of My Life* (1989) p.345

p.304   *Cabinet dissensions*: the bitterness was nothing compared with the venom among Wilson's own staff: for just one (extended) example, see Joe Haines, Wilson's press secretary, and his diatribe against Marcia Williams in *The Politics of Power* (1977) pp.156ff

p.304  *Ambition*: Philip M.Williams (ed) *The Diary of Hugh Gaitskell 1945–1956* (1983) p.46

p.305  *Ridiculous shoestring*: George Brown *In My Way* (1971) p.96

p.306  *Manifesto and social issues*: Michael Hatfield *The House The Left Built* (1978) pp.28–29

p.306  *Governor of Bank*: Harold Wilson *The Labour Governments 1964–1970* (1971) p.37

p.307  *Devaluation papers*: Peter Kellner and Christopher Hitchens *Callaghan: The Road to Number Ten* (1976) p.50

p.307  *Characteristic of system*: Douglas Jay *Change and Fortune* (1980) p.296

p.307  *Knew no economics*: Robert Pearce (ed) *Patrick Gordon Walker: Political Diaries 1932–1971* (1991) p.282

p.307  *Secret US agreement*: see chapter 'The American Connection' in *Clive Ponting*, pp.40–60

p.307  *Get free of America*: George Orwell *Collected Essays, Journalism and Letters, volume 4* (1970) p.426

p.308  *World power*: Giles Radice *Offshore* (1992) p.20

p.308  *Britain's economic power*: Leslie Stone 'Britain and the World' in David McKie and Chris Cook (eds) p.127

p.309  *Idea of planning*: Herbert Morrison *The Peaceful Revolution* (1949) p.85

p.309  *Issue now*: C.A.R.Crosland *The Future of Socialism* (1956) p.501

p.309  *Modernisation committees*: Richard Mayne *Postwar* (1983) p.162

p.310  *Stop-go*: David Marquand *The Unprincipled Society* (1988) p.44

p.310  *DEA in taxi*: George Brown, p.97, though Brown says this was not 'the whole truth'

p.310  *No headquarters*: Geoffrey Goodman *The Awkward Warrior* (1979) p.403

p.311  *Questionnaire*: Peter Sinclair 'The Economy – A Study in Failure' in David McKie and Chris Cook (eds) p.103

p.311  *Wyatt and Brown*: Woodrow Wyatt 'Partying before politics' in *The Times*, 6 May 1993

p.311  *17 'resignations'*: Peter Paterson *Tired and Emotional* (1993) p.241

p.311  *Wilson on Brown*: John Cole, p.57

p.311  *Hadn't run anything*: Tam Dalyell *Dick Crossman: A Portrait* p.48

p.312   *Lack of success*: entry of 11 June 1968 in Richard Crossman *The Diaries of a Cabinet Minister, Volume Three, 1968–70* (1977) p.57

p.312   *Our majority*: Ted Short *Whip to Wilson* (1989) p.70

p.312   *Britain forty-two times*: Clive Ponting, p.160

p.313   *Fred Lee*: Austen Morgan *Harold Wilson* (1992) p.238

p.313   *Independent strategy*: David Howell *British Social Democracy* (1980) p.250

p.313   *Whispering campaign*: Andrew Roth *Sir Harold Wilson* (1977) p.195

p.313   *Artful Dodger*: R.W.Johnson *The Politics of Recession* (1985) p.270

p.313   *Takes six months*: Crosland quoted in Richard Rose *Politics in England* (1980) p.183

p.314   *No Morrison*: Kenneth O.Morgan *Labour in Power 1945–1951* (1984) p.51

p.314   *Unhappy government*: Douglas Jay, p.411

p.314   *Cabinet and leaks*: Tony Benn quoted in Philip Whitehead *The Writing on the Wall* (1985) p.15

p.314   *Hiding things*: Richard Marsh *Off the Rails* (1978) pp.98–99

p.314   *Crossman on Wilson*: entries for 6 December 1964, 13 June 1965, 11 December 1966 and 27 April 1969 in Richard Crossman *The Diaries of a Cabinet Minister, Volume One 1964–66,* (1975) pp.88, 249; *Volume Two 1966–68* (1976) p.169; and *Volume Three 1968–70,* p.459 respectively

p.315   *Manipulator*: Tony Benn *Out of the Wilderness* p.391

p.315   *Trouble with Harold*: Susan Crosland *Tony Crosland* (1982) p.184

p.315   *1967 broadcast*: Ben Pimlott *Harold Wilson* (1993) pp.483–484

p.315   *Wilson's energy*: Muriel Box *Rebel Advocate* (1983) p.200; this book contains an appendix detailing the seventy-eight different subjects on which the Lord Chancellor, Lord Gardiner, spoke to the House of Lords between April 1966 and November 1967 alone, pp.234–235

p.316   *Rich poorer*: Michael Stewart in Wilfred Beckerman (ed) *The Labour Government's Economic Record* (1972) pp.110–11

p.317   *Brought down Rome*: Peter Paterson, p.32

p.317   *Appalling social record*: David Coates *The Labour Party and the Struggle for Socialism* (1975) p.115

p.317   *Swinging Sixties*: Roy Hattersley *Who Goes Home?* (1995) p.24

p.318   *Etiquette*: entry for 22 October 1964 in Richard Crossman, *Volume One* p.29

p.319   *Televising Commons*: Anthony Howard *Crossman: The Pursuit of Power* (1990) pp.281–282

p.319   *Fulton Committee*: Clive Ponting, p.262

p.319   *German and French reorganisation*: see the essays by Pierre Birnbaum and Joachim Hirsch in Richard Scase (eds) *The State in Western Europe* (1980)

p.320   *Rhodesia and oil*: the whole sorry story is told in Martin Bailey *Oilgate* (1979)

p.320   *Too bloody busy*: John Cole, p.215

p.320   *Crumbling*: Michael Pinto-Duschinsky *British Political Finance 1830–1980* (1981) p.160

p.320   *Inner London*: Patrick Seyd and Paul Whiteley *Labour's Grass Roots* (1992) p.15

p.321   *Rich kid's farce*: E.P. Thompson 'An Open Letter to Leszek Kolakowski', reprinted in *The Poverty of Theory* (1978) p.99

p.321   *Transform civilisation*: Tariq Ali *Street Fighting Years* (1987) p.226

p.322   *Czech reform movement*: David Caute *Sixty-Eight* (1988) viii

p.322   *RSSF manifesto*: David Widgery *The Left in Britain 1956–1968* (1976) p.339

p.322   *Powell march*: Widgery quoted in Ronald Fraser *1968* (1988) p.245; also see David Caute, pp.74–76

p.322   *Glossary*: David Widgery, pp.477–505

p.323   *Missionaries*: see Hugh Gaitskell's recollections of Cole in Asa Briggs and John Saville (eds) *Essays in Labour History* (1967) p.15

p.323   *Vast majority*: Perry Anderson 'Components of the National Culture in Robin Blackburn and Alexander Cockburn (eds) *Student Power* (1969) p.223

p.323   *Very surplus*: Perry Anderson *Considerations on Western Marxism* (1976) p.54

p.324   *Group action*: Michael Stewart *Life and Labour* (1980) pp.256–257

p.324   *Thirteen conference defeats*: David Howell, p.246

p.325   *Dog licence speech*: Edward G.Janosik *Constituency Labour Parties in Britain* (1968) p.197

p.326   *Congress House opening*: Henry Pelling *A History of British Trade Unionism* (1976) p.254

p.326   *Conservatives and unions*: V.L.Allen *Trade Union Leadership* (1957) p.150, A.J.Davies *We, The Nation: The Conservative Party and the Pursuit of Power* (1995) pp.286–287. Tony Crosland called this 'a peaceful revolution' in his book *The Future of Socialism*, p.32

p.326   *Vic Feather*: Richard Marsh, p.37

p.326   *Number of unofficial strikes*: Robert Taylor *The Fifth Estate* (1980) p.40

p.327   *Serum*: Professor Turner quoted in Peter Jenkins *The Battle of Downing Street* (1970) p.xii

p.328   *American Democrats*: entry for 22 March 1967 in Richard Crossman, *Volume Two*, p.287

p.329   *Castle's dog*: Barbara Castle *The Castle Diaries 1964–70* (1984) pp.555–556

p.329   *Charter of rights*: Barbara Castle 'Why my reforms were right' in the *Sunday Times*, 13 January 1980

p.330   *Popular support*: Peter Jenkins, p.44

p.330   *Callaghan*: quoted in Ben Pimlott, p.530

p.330   *Basically academics*: Jack Jones *Union Man* (1986) p.204

p.330   *Irritation powder*: Frank Chapple *Sparks Fly!* (1984) p.117

p.330   *Harold and Barbara*: Tony Benn *Office Without Power: Diaries 1968–72* (1988) p.187

p.331   *Peculiar importance*: Philip Ziegler *Wilson* (1993) p.299

p.331   *Lace curtains*: Barbara Castle *The Castle Diaries 1964–70*, p.805

p.332   *Fraction of second*: Tony Benn *Office Without Power*, p.293

p.332   *Public relations*: Kenneth O.Morgan *Labour People* (1987) p.261

CHAPTER TWELVE
## Endings

p.334   *NUT*: Bernard Donoughue *Prime Minister* (1987) p.110

p.334   *Sea-change*: Bernard Donoughue, p.191

p.334   *Never ashamed*: Jim Callaghan quoted in Tony Benn *The End of an Era* (1994) p.42

p.335   *Common sense*: Peter Kellner and Christopher Hitchens *Callaghan: The Road to Number Ten* (1976) p.75

p.335   *Gaitskell on Callaghan*: Philip M. Williams (ed) *The Diary of Hugh Gaitskell 1945–1956* (1983) p.540

p.335   *Zebras and cat's eyes*: James Callaghan *Time and Chance* (1987) p.97

p.336   *Following unions*: Lord Wigg *George Wigg* (1972) p.254

p.336  *Over 50 committees*: Robert Jenkins *Tony Benn* (1980) p.168

p.336  *Wilson missing NECs*: Joe Haines *The Politics of Power* (1977) p.13

p.337  *NEC move left*: see Michael Hatfield *The House the Left Built (1978) passim*

p.337  *Three groups radicalised*: Patrick Seyd *The Rise and Fall of the Labour Left* (1987) pp.47, 74, 139

p.338  *Stagecoach*: 1964 interview with Wilson, quoted in Edward G. Janosik *Constituency Labour Parties in Britain* (1966) p.193

p.340  *IRI's record*: Stuart Holland *The Socialist Challenge* (1975) p.182

p.340  *Party in sight*: Michael Hatfield p.57

p.341  *Idiotic*: David Coates *Labour in Power?* (1980) p.89

p.341  *Incoherence*: Edmund Dell *A Hard Pounding* (1991) p.12

p.342  *No experience*: Denis Healey *The Time of My Life* (1989) p.367

p.342  *No direct experience*: Bernard Donoughue p.54

p.342  *Balance sheet*: Joel Barnett *Inside the Treasury* (1982) p.3

p.342  *Manufacturing decline*: Michael Barratt Brown 'The Growth and Distribution of Income and Wealth' in Ken Coates (ed) *What Went Wrong?* (1979) p.52

p.342  *Majority of three*: David Coates, pp.150–151

p.342  *Around this racetrack*: Bernard Donoughue, p.11

p.344  *Handling of Europe*: Roy Jenkins *A Life at the Centre* (1991) p.342

p.344  *Walking wounded*: Philip Whitehead *The Writing on the Wall* (1985) p.144

p.345  *Campaign v Wilson*: see the chapter 'Dirty Tricks' in A.J.Davies *We, The Nation. The Conservative Party and the Pursuit of Power* (1995) pp.221–256; also see David Leigh *The Wilson Plot* (1988) and Stephen Dorril and Robin Ramsay *Smear!* (1992)

p.346  *Callaghan's tears*: Ben Pimlott *Harold Wilson* (1993) p.685

p.346  *Titanic*: Bernard Donoughue, p.183

p.346  *Fourteen budgets*: David Coates, p.12

p.347  *Moral for spending ministers*: Joel Barnett p.94

p.347  *Father Christmas*: Martin Holmes *The Labour Government, 1974–1979* (1985) p.182

p.347  *Political constraints of full employment*: see Robert Skidelsky The Political Meaning of the Keynesian Revolution' in R.Skidelsky (ed) *The End of the Keynesian Era* (1977) pp.38–39

p.347  *Fossilised*: Martin Holmes, p.58

p.348    *Treasury advice*: Joe Haines, p.42

p.348    *Treasury mis-estimates*: Denis Healey, pp.380–381

p.348    *Suddenness*: Harold Wilson *The Labour Governments 1964–1970* (1971) p.460

p.348    *Restraint of schoolgirls*: James Callaghan, p.428

p.350    *Political bully*: Ian Mikardo *Back-bencher* (1988) p.202

p.350    *Withdraw into citadel*: Stephen Fay and Hugo Young *The Day the Pound Nearly Died* (1978) p.39; there is a detailed account of the crisis in Tony Benn *Against the Tide: Diaries 1973–76* (1989) pp.681–690

p.351    *King Lear*: Edmund Dell, p.261

p.351    *Three co-operatives*: Joel Barnett, p.35

p.352    *£10/£800 million*: Robert Jenkins, p.215

p.352    *1970 election*: David Owen *Time to Declare* (1991) p.158

p.352    *Union domination*: Michael Pinto-Duschinsky *British Political Finance 1830–1980* (1981) pp.221–223

p.352    *NEC seating*: Frank Chapple *Sparks Fly!* (1984) p.105

p.353    *Jones and ACAS*: Jack Jones *Union Man* (1986) p.245

p.353    *Corporate opposition*: Will Hutton *The State We're In* (1995) p.83

p.353    *Anti-intellectualism*: Robert Taylor *The Fifth Estate* (1980) p.91; *insular outlook*, p.224

p.353    *Fringe benefits*: Anthony Crosland *The Future of Socialism* (1956) p.294

p.354    *Centre 42*: see Andrew Davies *Other Theatres* (1987) pp.158–159

p.354    *Men running show*: Barbara Castle *The Castle Diaries 1974–76* (1980) p.309

p.355    *Incomes policies*: Michael Stewart *Life and Labour* (1980) p.195

p.356    *Low wage country*: Robert Taylor, p.135

p.357    *Memory not golden*: Ben Pimlott *Frustrate Their Knavish Tricks* (1995) p.325

p.357    *Radical bookshops*: see Elizabeth-Anne Morgan *An Overview of the Radical Booktrade* (unpublished Sheffield University thesis, September 1981)

p.358    *Servants*: Fred Inglis *Raymond Williams* (1995) p.221

p.358    *Coming decade*: Tariq Ali *The Coming British Revolution* (1972) pp.209, 244; in a letter to me (dated 27 March 1991), Tariq Ali said that he did not write all of this book, and that page 209 was among those not attributable to him. I suppose the reference should therefore read: 'Tariq Ali' *The Coming* . . . etc.

p.358   *Tuesday mornings*: Robert Taylor, p.189

p.359   *Subordinate role*: Philip Whitehead, p.310

p.359   *Women's movement*: see the excellent essay by Sheila Rowbotham 'The Women's Movement and organising for socialism' in the collection *Beyond the Fragments* (1980)

p.359   *Protest's limited life*: Beatrix Campbell *Wigan Pier Revisited* (1984) p.201

p.359   *Clarity*: see the remarks of John Wood, deputy head of the IEA, in Michael Davie 'Men who told Thatcher there was an alternative' in the *Observer*, 24 March 1983. The intellectual origins of the New Right are discussed in Andrew Gamble *Britain in Decline* (1981) pp.143–164

p.360   *Whitehall gentleman*: Ben Pimlott *Hugh Dalton* (1985) p.398

p.360   *We Know Best*: Ferdinand Mount 'Socialism: the package that's past its sell by date' in the *Daily Telegraph*, 13 March 1987

p.360   *Pigeon-keeping*: Roy Hattersley *Choose Freedom* (1987) p.134

p.360   *Plymouth*: Mervyn Jones *Michael Foot* (1993) p.132

p.361   *Bright rooms*: Tony Benn *Years Of Hope* (1994) p.289

p.361   *Ideological stranglehold*: Colin Ward 'Self-help socialism' in *New Society*, 20 April 1978, p.140

p.361   *Big Brother*: Robert Skidelsky 'Fantasy not history' in the *Sunday Times*, 11 January 1987

p.362   *No miracles*: Joel Barnett 'Realism and the socialist way to cut public spending' in the *Guardian*, 25 September 1979

p.362   *Consumers*: *Guardian* editorial 'The spirit of '45, the facts of '79', 8 May 1979

p.363   *Poverty figures*: Frank Field 'The Poor' in Ken Coates, p.146

p.363   *5 per cent too low*: interview in *Denis Healey: The Man Who Did the Dirty Work*, BBC2, 12 October 1989

p.364   *Meeting round clock*: Joel Barnett, p.160

p.365   *Tanks into ICI*: Bernard Donoughue, p.174

p.365   *Passage of time*: James Callaghan, p.537

p.365   *Prostrate*: Frank Chapple, p.150

p.365   *Jenkins plea*: Edmund Dell, p.51

p.365   *Manifesto row*: see Geoff Bish 'Drafting the Manifesto' in Ken Coates, pp.187–206 p.366   *Callaghan's campaign*: David Butler and Dennis Kavanagh *The British General Election of 1979* (1980) p.325

p.367   *Paynter and Annan*: Will Paynter *My Generation* 91972) and Noel Annan *Our Age* (1990)

p.368   *Error to neglect*: Noel Annan, p.449

CHAPTER THIRTEEN
**Towards the Precipice**

p.371   *Germany after 1945*: Eric Hobsbawm in the *Guardian*, 11 July 1988

p.371   *Unqualified pilot*: Roy Hattersley *Who Goes Home?* (1995) p.226

p.371   *Saved Labour Party*: Mervyn Jones *Michael Foot* (1994) p.450

p.372   *Distinctive*: John Biffen 'Ivory tower goes into orbit' in the *Spectator*, 17 December 1988

p.373   *Mentality*: George Orwell *The Lion and the Unicorn* (1982) p.63

p.373   *Ship due north*: R.W.Johnson 'Watership going down' in *New Society*, 30 August 1979, p.462; this essay is not reproduced in the author's collection *The Politics of Recession* (1985)

p.374   *Packaged together*: Graham Turner 'Why Britain's eggheads look down on Mrs Thatcher' in the *Sunday Telegraph*, 10 January 1988

p.374   *Squalid etc.*: Hanif Kureishi 'England, bloody England' in the *Guardian*, 15 January 1988

p.375   *Extreme statement*: *Independent*, 25 October 1988

p.375   *Czechoslovakia*: Timothy Garton Ash 'Czechoslovakia Under Ice' reprinted in his book *The Uses of Adversity* (1989) pp.55–63

p.376   *Brown v intellectuals*: Peter Paterson *Tired and Emotional* (1993) pp.2, 92; *fight with Crossman*, p.115

p.376   *Bring university down*: Jack Jones *Union Man* (1986) p.341

p.376   *First essential*: Richard Crossman 'The Lessons of 1945' in Perry Anderson and Robin Blackburn (eds) *Towards Socialism* (1965) p.146

p.377   *Sun, May 1981*: Mark Hollingsworth *The Press and Political Dissent* (1986) p.58; *Stalin*, p.61

p.377   *Benn as Hitler*: see Tony Benn, *Arguments for Socialism* (1979) p.11; and also the cartoon reproduced in Tony Benn *Office Without Power: Diaries 1968–72* (1988) p.457

p.377   *Benn v peerage*: Tony Benn *Years of Hope: Diaries 1940–92* (1994) pp.356ff

p.378   *Stamps*: Robert Jenkins *Tony Benn* (1980) p.105

p.378   *Forty-four volumes*: Tony Benn *Office Without Power*, pp.397–398

p.378   *Benn and Marx*: Tony Benn *Against the Tide: Diaries 1973–76* (1989) p.12, 692

p.378   *Immatures*: quoted in Robert Harris *The Making of Neil Kinnock* (1984) p.154

p.378   *Bought move*: Martin Holmes *The Labour Government, 1974–1979* (1985) p.42

p.379   *Referendum campaign*: Tony Benn *Against the Tide*, p.465

p.379   *Squash ball*: Bernard Donoughue *Prime Minister* (1987) p.55

p.379   *Castle on Benn*: quoted in Adam Raphael 'Messiah of the militant Left' in the *Observer*, 28 September 1980

p.379   *Silkin/Shore*: John Torode 'The young contenders state their claims' in the *Guardian*, 30 July 1979

p.380   *Watch everybody*: Brian Connell 'A dedication to the idea of accountability' in *The Times*, 18 July 1977

p.380   *Frequently unrepresentative*: Beatrice Webb, diary entry, 19 May 1930

p.381   *Shawcross lifestyle*: Lord Shawcross *Life Sentence* (1995) pp.223–224

p.381   *Crossman at NS*: Mervyn Jones *Chances* (1987) p.230

p.381   *Delete by-line*: letter from Tom Baistow in the *Daily Telegraph*, 16 January 1996

p.382   *Benn on tube*: Tony Benn *Conflicts of Interest: Diaries 1977–80* (1990) p.548

p.382   *Cripps and Cabinet*: James Jupp *The Radical Left in Britain* (1982) p.144

p.383   *Good Samaritan*: Ian Mikardo *Back-bencher* (1988) p.220

p.383   *Benn's meetings and letters*: Tony Benn *The End of an Era: Diaries 1980–90* (1994) pp.45, 123

p.383   *No such thing*: John Carvel *Citizen Ken* (1984) p.212

p.383   *Driberg and Barking*: Francis Wheen *Tom Driberg* (1990) pp.334–335, 377–378

p.384   *Political riff-raff*: Roy Hattersley *Choose Freedom* (1987) p.4

p.384   *Hard men*: David Owen *Time to Declare* (1991) p.158

p.384   *Prima donnaism*: John Cole *As It Seemed To Me* (1995) p.224

p.385   *Building of SDP*: Ivor Crewe and Anthony King *SDP* (1995) p.253

p.385   *90,000 members*: James Hinton *Protests and Visions* (1989) pp.182–183

p.386   *Absence of self-seeking*: James Callaghan *Time and Chance* (1987) p.401

p.387   *Public meeting*: Edmund Dell *A Hard Pounding* (1992) p.106

p.387   *Pax Britannica*: James Hinton, viii–ix

p.387   *Voting for Foot*: Kate Ironside 'How we tried to wreck Labour, by SDP rebels', *Sunday Telegraph* 14 January 1996

p.388   *1981 campaign*: Tony Benn *The End of an Era*, p.500

p.388   *EEC amazed*: Keith Richardson 'Foot shocks his comrades' in the *Sunday Times*, 14 February 1981

p.389   *Saved Labour Party*: Denis Healey *The Time of My Life* (1989) p.484

p.389   *Series of cliches*: Roy Hattersley, p.173

p.390   *Healey replacing Foot*: Denis Healey, pp.499–500

p.390   *Rag, tag*: *Guardian*, 6 June 1983

p.390   *New brand*: Johnny Wright 'Advertising for a change' in *Marxism Today*, January 1985

p.390   *Versus polls*: David Butler and Dennis Kavanagh *The British General Election of 1983* (1984) p.280

p.391   *In the end*: Robert Fox 'Michael Foot's nemesis' in the *Listener*, 16 June 1983

p.391   *Fighting spirit*: Michael Foot *Another Heart and Other Pulses* (1984) p.91; *saw little TV*, p.91

p.392   *Replacing Labour*: Ivor Crewe and Anthony King, p.285

p.392   *Red Ken*: John Carvel, p.208

p.393   *1,000 organisations*: John Carvel, p.208

p.393   *Tatchell saga*: see Peter Tatchell *The Battle for Bermondsey* (1983) passim

p.395   *Bunch of amateurs*: Michael Barratt Brown 'Positive Neutralism Then and Now' in Oxford University Socialist Group *Out of Apathy* (1989) p.84

p.396   *MSF*: Clive Jenkins *All Against the Collar* (1990) pp.16, 129

p.397   *Pit closures*: Mark Adeney and John Lloyd *The Miners' Strike* (1986) p.34

p.398   *Miners' QC*: Michael Crick *Scargill and the Miners* (1985) p.68

p.398   *Might have won poll*: Michael Crick, pp.103, 108

p.398   *Hitler threat*: Lawson quoted in Seumas Milne *The Enemy Within* (1995) p.10

p.399    Seeing files: Tony Benn Out of the Wilderness: Diaries 1963–67 (1988) p.328

p.399    Tapes running out: Stephen Dorril The Silent Conspiracy (1994) p.38

p.399    Gardiner tapped: Tam Dalyell Misrule (1987) pp.123–124

p.400    IRIS: Seumas Milne, pp.434–435

p.400    Press and intelligence: Seumas Milne, pp.262, 381

p.401    Mardy closures: see the moving requiems in the Guardian and The Times, both 21 December 1990

p.401    Membership: Paul Keel 'Labour's lowest membership for 50 years', the Guardian, 30 August 1982

CHAPTER FOURTEEN
## Towards the Middle Ground

p.402    Got to be leader: Michael Cockerell Live from Number 10 (1988) p.287

p.402    Ramsay MacKinnock: Austen Morgan J.Ramsay MacDonald (1987) p.251

p.402    Psychological problem: Barbara Castle Fighting All the Way (1993) p.501

p.403    £10,000 confiscation: Richard Heffernan and Mike Marqusee Defeat from the Jaws of Victory (1992) p.22

p.403    NK and devolution: Caroline Moorehead 'Golden boy with a silver tongue' in The Times, 28/7/80

p.404    Year-long campaign: Roy Hattersley Who Goes Home? (1995) pp.244–245

p.404    1983 sewn up: Clive Jenkins All Against the Collar (1990) pp.209–213

p.404    Most left-wing: 'Who's the leftest of them all?' in The Economist, 11 June 1983

p.404    Purity of party: Neil Kinnock 'Reforming the Labour Party' in Contemporary Record, volume 8, number 3, winter 1994, p.535

p.405    CP revisionists: Heffernan and Marqusee, p.64

p.407    Own instinct: interview with Hobsbawm in Radical History Review, winter 1978–79, p.126

p.408    Changing hats: Lewis Minkin The Contentious Alliance (1992) p.547

p.408   *Must Labour Lose*: contribution of Rita Hinden in Mark Abrams and Richard Rose *Must Labour Lose?* (1960) p.100

p.409   *Strange indeed*: R.W. Johnson *The Politics of Recession* (1985) p.257

p.411   *Hate ghetto*: 'The couturier of designer marxism' in the *Sunday Telegraph*, 25 November 1989

p.411   *Hair cut and suits*: Michael Cockerell 'The Battle for No 10' on *Panorama*, BBC1, 15 June 1987

p.411   *Whitty*: Robert Harris 'Getting the Kinnock Show on the road' in the *Listener*, 3 October 1985

p.412   *Campaign Group and polls*: James Naughtie in the *Guardian*, 23 January 1985

p.412   *Mandelson/Mortimer*: Kathy Myers 'Mandelson's overtures for a Labour victory' in the *Guardian*, 25/11/85

p.412   *NEC subcommittees*: Robert Harris 'Getting the Kinnock Show on the road'

p.413   *1st World War general*: Robert Harris *The Making of Neil Kinnock* (1984) p.164

p.413   *Changed history*: Paul Routledge *Scargill* (1993) p.263

p.413   *Processed cheese*: Tony Benn *The End of An Era: Diaries 1980–90* (1994) p.352

p.414   *Serious mistake*: Bryan Gould *A Future for Socialism* (1989) p.90

p.414   *Failing to consult*: Lewis Minkin, p.656

p.414   *No particular interests*: Ivor Crewe and Anthony King *SDP* (1995) p.463

p.414   *SDP membership*: Ivor Crewe and Anthony King, pp.246–247

p.415   *Ballots*: see Derek Fatchett *Trade Unions and Politics in the 1980s* (1987) pp.3,61,121

p.415   *Unions back*: Keith Harper 'How the unions turned the ballot into a political bullet', the *Guardian*, 3 January 1986

p.416   *Welfare shopping list*: Nicholas Timmins *The Five Giants* (1995) pp.488–489

p.416   *PR in 1987*: Ivor Crewe and Anthony King, p.285

p.417   *Knocking copy*: Margaret Scammell *Designer Politics* (1995) p.140

p.417   *Image problem*: Margaret Scammell, p.243

p.417   *Hands up*: Margaret Scammell, p.151

p.418   *Colour of books*: William E.Paterson 'The German Social Democratic Party' in William E.Paterson and Alastair H.Thomas (eds) *Social Democratic Parties in Western Europe* (1976) pp.185,186 p.418   *112/586*: Colin Hughes and Patrick Wintour *Labour Rebuilt* (1990) p.227

p.418   *Policy committee based*: Hughes and Wintour, p.5

p.418   *Exorcism*: Martin Jacques 'New start for Labour too' in *The Times*, 28 November 1990

p.419   *Basic stance*: Bryan Gould, p.112

p.419   *Hamlet without Prince*: Ferdinand Mount 'Socialism: the package that's past its sell-by date' in the *Daily Telegraph*, 13 March 1987

p.420   *Anti-consumerist*: Beatrix Campbell *Wigan Pier Revisited* (1984) p.227

p.420   *Join us*: Bryan Gould, p.77

p.421   *Political skill*: William Shawcross *Murdoch* (1993 ed) p.414

p.421   *Too many papers*: editorial in the *Sunday Times*, 23 January 1994

p.421   *Frost briefed*: Brian Crozier *Free Agent* (1993) p.287

p.422   *Reviews as package*: Margaret Scammell, p.12

p.422   *Dead generations*: Karl Marx, *The Eighteenth Brumaire of Louis Bonaparte* (1852)

p.422   Negative: Andrew Taylor *The Trade Unions and the Labour Party* (1987) p.291

p.423   *Smiling families*: Eric Shaw *The Labour Party Since 1979* (1994) p.233 fn.5

p.423   *Terrible insularity*: Eric Hobsbawm *Politics for a Rational Left* (1989) p.235

p.423   *1989 Policy Review*: David Marquand *The Progressive Dilemma* (1991) p.201

p.423   *60,000*: Patrick Seyd and Paul Whiteley *Labour's Grass Roots* (1992) p.201

p.424   *Local figures*: Heffernan and Marqusee, pp.333, 335

p.424   *De-energized*: Seyd and Whiteley, p.202

p.425   *Evil woman*: quoted in the *Evening Standard*, 26 November 1990

p.425   *Tunes of glory*: 'Kinnock drops "nonsense" of nationalisation' in the *Sunday Telegraph*, 1 September 1991

p.426   *Since 1979*: David Butler and Dennis Kavanagh *The British General Election of 1987* (1988) p.277

p.426   *Tories still trusted*: Martin J.Smith in 'Neil Kinnock and the Labour Party 1983–92: A Symposium' in *Contemporary Record*, winter 1994, p.567

p.426  *Gap closed*: Martin Linton *Money and Votes* (1994) p.25
p.427  *Conservative finances*: the entire question is discussed at length in the chapter 'Money Matters' in my *We, The Nation: The Conservative Party and the Pursuit of Power* (1995) pp.164–194 and in A.J.Davies 'Opening The Party War Chests' in *Parliamentary Brief*, Vol.4, No.2, November 1995, p.34
p.427  *Hong Kong money*: Chris Blackhurst and Donald Macintyre 'Hong Kong tycoons gave Tories £3.8m' in the *Independent*, 1 March 1996
p.428  *Talking freely*: Barbara Castle *Fighting All the Way* (1993) p.585
p.428  *Gallup law and order*: Jon Sopel *Tony Blair* (1995 ed) p.165
p.429  *Couldn't give it away*: 'Socialism, RIP' in the *Sunday Times*, 12 April 1992
p.429  *Genuinely pleased*: David Own *Time to Declare* (1991) p.810
p.429  *Kinnock's flaws*: quoted in Steven Fielding in 'Neil Kinnock and the Labour Party 1983–92: A Symposium' in *Contemporary Record*, volume 8, number 3, winter 1994, p.591; *not Gaitskell or Wilson*: Steven Fielding, p.589
p.430  *Never let me down*: Margaret Thatcher *The Downing Street Years* (1993) p.858
p.430  *Alliance second place*: John Cole *As It Seemed To Me* (1995) p.422
p.430  *30,000 messages*: Eileen Jones *Neil Kinnock* (1994) p.189


CHAPTER FIFTEEN
**New Worlds, New Labour?**
p.431  *Bowels*: Peter Weiler *Ernest Bevin* (1993) p.70
p.431  *Moral activity*: Andy McSmith *John Smith* (1994 ed) p.320
p.431  *Labour and government*: Blair quoted in the *Evening Standard*, 7 June 1995
p.432  *Sufficient swing*: 'How the Sun won the election' in the *Guardian*, 1 November 1995
p.432  *Buying election*: Meghnad Desai 'Still the economy, stupid' in the *New Statesman*, 1 March 1996, p.16
p.433  *Cumbersome rules*: Andy McSmith, p.185
p.433  *No serious plotting*: Andy McSmith, p.171
p.435  *Straw bawled out*: Anne McElvoy 'The killing of Clause 4', *The Times*, 22 April 1995 p.13

p.435   *Refusing legs*: Andy McSmith, p.325

p.435   *Monklands nepotism*: Editorial 'An abuse of single-party power', the *Guardian*, 21 January 1995

p.436   *Iona visitors*: John Arlidge 'Anger grows as visitors flock to Smith grave', *Independent on Sunday*, 4 June 1995

p.437   *In prison*: Peter Slowe *Manny Shinwell* (1993) p.101

p.437   *Not talking wistfully*: Jon Sopel *Tony Blair* (1995 ed) p.3

p.438   *Smooth performance*: 'Closed Shop, Opening Minds?' in *The Times*, 18 December 1989

p.438   *A bargain*: John Rentoul *Tony Blair* (1995) p.290

p.438   *Gujarati*: Jon Sopel, p.201

p.439   *5% drop*: Kevin Jefferys *The Labour Party Since 1945* (1993) p.134

p.439   *Management and change*: John Harvey-Jones *Making It Happen* (1988) p.122

p.440   *Conservative change*: see A.J.Davies *We, The Nation: The Conservative Party and the Pursuit of Power* (1995) passim

p.440   *Two decisive victories*: David Marquand *The Progressive Dilemma* (1991) p.1

p.440   *Name change*: A.J.Davies *To Build A New Jerusalem* (1992) p.284

p.442   *Sedgefield membership*: John Rentoul, p.313

p.442   *Blair and language*: Patrick Wintour 'How the new boy won the game his way' in the *Guardian*, 22 April 1995

p.443   *Clever thing*: Brian Walden 'Labour must discard its old ideological baggage' in the *Sunday Times*, 19 November 1989

p.443   *3 biggest*: Colin Hughes and Patrick Wintour *Labour Rebuilt* (1990) pp.191–192

p.443   *Idea of modernisation*: John Rentoul, p.213

p.444   *Being brave*: Jon Sopel, p.274

p.444   *Stray cats*: Donald Macintyre 'His course is set for a historic mission' in the *Independent*, 30 December 1995

p.444   *Tory sounding*: Nicholas Timmins *The Five Giants* (1996) p.517

p.445   *Travels light*: Martin Jacques 'Blair Freshener' in the *Sunday Times*, 17 July 1994 p.505

p.446   *Faced with choices*: Barbara Castle *Fighting All the Way* (1994) p.505

p.447   *Positive coverage*: Nicholas Jones 'Taking Tony to the people' in the *Guardian*, 5 June 1995 p.447    *v Sun ads*: Margaret Scammell *Designer Politics* (1995) p.114

p.447    *Telegraph readers*: 'Blair disowns "tax and spend" image' in the *Daily Telegraph*, 26 July 1994

p.449    *Unpleasant thing*: John Rees quoted in 'Should socialists leave the Labour Party?' in *Socialist Review*, 194, February 1996, p.10

p.449    *Legal threat*: Rebecca Smithers 'Blair demands press apology' in the *Guardian*, 21 September 1995

p.450    *Labour Party News*: Steven Fielding 'Volunteers Flocking To Blair's Colours' in *Parliamentary Brief*, vol.4, no.1, October 1995, p.28

p.450    *As Labour moves*: John E.Strafford *The Conservative Party for the 21st Century* (1995) p.4

p.450    *British Youth Council*: Andy Beckett 'Power to the (young) people' in the *Guardian*, 19 June 1995

p.450    *Young Labour*: Peter Mandelson and Roger Liddle *The Blair Revolution* (1996) p.218

p.450    *Labour MP 48*: Margarette Driscoll and Fergus Kelly 'Party people' in the *Sunday Times*, 18 February 1996

p.450    *35% women*: Steven Fielding, p.28

p.450    *Gender gap*: Joni Lovenduski 'Winning Over the Women Defeats the Tories', *Parliamentary Brief*, vol.4, no.1, October 1995, p.27

p.451    *Labour obsession*: Beatrix Campbell 'The intuition Labour lacks' in the *Independent*, 4 October 1994

p.451    *New rulebook*: Andrew Grice 'Row as union fights to keep Labour link', the *Sunday Times*, 10 March 1996

p.451    *No say*: Andy McSmith, p.278

p.451    *German Social Democrats*: Martin Linton *Money and Votes* (1994) p.86

p.451    *Labour finances*: see the *Daily Telegraph*, 19 February 1996

p.452    *Labour lottery*: Jasper Gerard 'Labour to start a party lottery', *Sunday Telegraph* 25 February 1996

p.452    *Thatcher right*: Andrew Grice 'The man with an eye on No 10', the *Sunday Times*, 23 April 1995

p.453    *Bush and taxes*: Bob Woodward *The Agenda* (1995) p.286

p.453    *Deploying language*: Jon Hibbs 'Blair rejects tax and spend' in the *Daily Telegraph*, 23 May 1995, reporting on Blair's Mais lecture

p.453    *Can't get growth*: John Cole *As It Seemed To Me* (1995) p.423

p.454    *Grassroots and public ownership*: Patrick Seyd and Paul Whiteley 'Red in tooth and clause' in the *New Statesman*, 9 December 1994, pp.18–19

p.454    *Decades now*: Byron Criddle 'Old Tory, new Labour, now what?' in *The Times*, 11 October 1995

p.455    *30 minutes*: Peter Mandelson and Roger Liddle *The Blair Revolution* (1996) p.221

p.455    *Differences in income*: Mandelson and Liddle, p.22; *taxation*, p.23

p.455    *No sense of command*: Bob Woodward, p.396

p.456    *Checklist*: Mandelson and Liddle, p.250

p.456    '*Blairspeak*': David Rowan 'Goodbye strike . . .', the *Guardian*, 6 October 1994

p.456    *Moral purpose*: Andy Beckett 'Spinning a Tale', *Independent on Sunday*, 4 February 1996

p.457    *ESOPs*: Bryan Gould *A Future for Socialism* (1989) pp.143ff

p.457    *50 ESOPs*: Clive Woodcock, 'Increasing number of firms learn the Esops lesson', the *Guardian* 2 August 1991

p.457    *British economy*: Will Hutton *The State We're In* (1995) p.21

p.457    *Triple requirement*: Will Hutton, p.298; *MITI*, p.270

p.458    *Drastic recasting*: Will Hutton, p.319

p.458    *Oddity of talk*: 'Stakeholder Capitalism' in *The Economist*, 10 February 1996, p.23

p.459    *Cross-borders*: Martin Walker *The Cold War* (1994) p.334

p.459    *Super-power war*: Martin Walker, p.355

p.459    *Supply side*: Peter Mandelson and Roger Liddle, p.6

p.459    *Central economic ideas*: Vincent Cable 'Freeing the market in ideas' in the *Independent*, 2 December 1994

p.460    *Dunlopillo*: E.P.Thompson *The Poverty of Theory* (1978) p.116

p.460    *Information Act*: Mandelson quoted in *The Times*, 6 March 1996

p.461    *In government*: Margaret Thatcher *The Downing Street Years* (1993) p.579

p.461    *I shall decide*: Tony Benn *The End of An Era: Diaries 1980–90* (1994) p.489

p.462    *Comprehensives failed*: Judith Judd 'Comprehensives have failed, says Blunkett', the *Independent*, 28 February 1996

p.462    *Rapid Response*: Marie Woolf 'Bad news? Labour's abolished it' in the *Independent on Sunday*, 23 April 1995

p.462    *Hecklers*: Margaret Scammell, p.41

p.462  *Eccentricities*: Andrew Roberts 'Farewell to the lords', *Sunday Times*, 11 February 1996

p.463  *Six occasions*: Roy Jenkins in *The Times*, 16 February 1996

p.463  *Possible to link*: Ben Pimlott *Frustrate Their Knavish Tricks* (1995) p.47

CHAPTER SIXTEEN
## Conclusions

p.464  *Where no vision*: Caroline Benn *Keir Hardie* (1992) p.254

p.464  *Don't actually believe*: Miriam Gross 'An Interview with Eric Hobsbawm' in *Time and Tide*, autumn 1985, p.55

p.464  *Most people*: Paul Hirst *After Thatcher* (1989) p.180

p.465  *Sun of Righteousness*: Snowden quoted in Gregory Elliott *Labourism and the English Genius* (1993) p.22

p.467  *God's children*: William Temple *Christianity and Social Order* (1942) pp.14–15

p.468  *Politics deteriorating*: Roy Hattersley quoted in the *Daily Telegraph*, 23 November 1995

p.468  *Socialism by contrast*: speech of Lord Lawson in Keele, reported in the *Guardian*, 1 September 1993

p.468  *Armchair*: Nicholas Timmins *The Five Giants* (1995) p.113

p.468  *Bevan fusion*: Kenneth O. Morgan *Labour People* (1987) p.334

# Select Guide to Further Reading

This select bibliography lists some of the books and articles I found most helpful in writing *To Build A New Jerusalem*. Titles mentioned in abbreviated form in the notes are given in full here. No work is mentioned more than once; if useful in more than one chapter, I have included it in the most important.

Long lists of undifferentiated titles have never seemed of much interest or use. I have therefore grouped the titles under their relevant chapter headings. For a complementary list of titles on the Conservative Party, please see my *We, The Nation: The Conservative Party and the Pursuit of Power* (1995).

Titles of particular use or interest are marked with an asterisk, though this does not necessarily mean I agree with their arguments or interpretations.

The place of publication is London unless specified.

## General
R. Benewick, R.N.Berki and B.Parekh (eds) *Knowledge and Belief in Politics* (Allen & Unwin, 1973)

Asa Briggs *Victorian Cities* (Pelican, 1969)

Asa Briggs *Victorian People* (Pelican, 1965)

David Cannadine *The Pleasures of the Past* (Collins, 1989)

*Peter Clarke *A Question of Leadership: From Gladstone to Thatcher* (Penguin, 1991)

*Michael Cockerell *Live From Number 10* (Faber, 1988)

A.J. Davies *We, The Nation: The Conservative Party and the Pursuit of Power* (Little, Brown, 1995)

Andrew Gamble *Britain in Decline* (Macmillan, 1981)

A.H. Halsey *Change in British Society* (Oxford: University Press, 1981)

J.F.C. Harrison *The Common People: A History from the Norman Conquest to the Present* (Fontana, 1984)

Christopher Harvie *No Gods and Precious Few Heroes: Scotland since 1914* (Edward Arnold, 1981)

E.J. Hobsbawm *Industry and Empire* (Pelican, 1969)

William Keegan and Rupert Pennant-Rea *Who Runs The Economy? Control and Influence in British Economic Policy* (Temple Smith, 1979)

Ross McKibbin *The Ideologies of Class: Social Relations in Britain 1880–1950* (Oxford: Clarendon Press, 1990)

★James Margach *The Abuse of Power: The War between Downing Street and the Media from Lloyd George to James Callaghan* (W.H.Allen, 1978)

James Margach *The Anatomy of Power* (W.H.Allen, 1979)

Arthur Marwick *British Society Since 1945* (Penguin, 1982)

Arthur Marwick *Class: Image and Reality* (Collins, 1980)

Keith Middlemas *Politics in Industrial Society: The experience of the British system since 1911* (André Deutsch, 1979)

Ralph Miliband *Marxism and Politics* (Oxford: University Press, 1977)

Ralph Miliband *The State in Capitalist Society* (Quartet, 1977)

Ferdinand Mount (ed) *The Inquiring Eye: The Writings of David Watt* (Penguin, 1988)

George Orwell *The Collected Essays, Journalism and Letters in four volumes*: *An Age Like This*; *My Country Right or Left*; *As I Please*; and *In Front of Your Nose* (Penguin, 1970)

George Orwell *The English People* (Collins, 1947)

Charles Petrie *The Powers Behind the Prime Ministers* (Macgibbon & Kee, 1958)

★Michael Pinto-Duschinsky *British Political Finance 1830–1980* (USA, Washington: American Enterprise Institute, 1981)

★Ben Pimlott *Frustrate Their Knavish Tricks: Writings on biography, history and politics* (HarperCollins, 1995)

Bernard Porter *Plots and Paranoia: A history of political espionage in Britain 1790–1988* (Unwin Hyman, 1989)

Alan Sked and Chris Cook *Post-war Britain* (Penguin, 1979)

A.J.P. Taylor *A Personal History* (Hamish Hamilton, 1982)

E.P. Thompson *Writing by Candlelight* (Merlin Press, 1980)

Martin Weiner *English Culture and the Decline of the Industrial Spirit 1850–1980* (Cambridge: University Press, 1981)

## General History of the British Labour Movement

Perry Anderson and Robin Blackburn (eds) *Towards Socialism* (Fontana/ New Left Review, 1965)

Perry Anderson *Arguments Within English Marxism* (Verson, 1980)

Joyce M.Bellamy and John Saville (eds) *Dictionary of Labour Biography* (Macmillan, 1972 – series still continuing)

Asa Briggs and John Saville (eds) *Essays in Labour History* (Macmillan, 1967; volume two 1886–1923, Macmillan, 1971; volume three 1918–1939, Croom Helm, 1977)

Gordon Brown and Tony Wright (eds) *Values, Visions And Voices: An Anthology Of Socialism* (Mainstream, 1995)

John Callaghan *Socialism in Britain since 1884* (Oxford: Basil Blackwell, 1990)

David Coates *The Labour Party and the Struggle for Socialism* (Cambridge: University Press, 1975)

Ken Coates and Tony Topham *Trade Unions in Britain* (Faber, 1988)

Margaret Cole *Makers of the Labour Movement* (Longmans, 1948)

A.J. Davies *To Build A New Jerusalem: The Labour Movement from the 1880s to the 1990s* (Michael Joseph, 1992)

Norman Dennis and A.H.Halsey *English Ethical Socialism: Thomas More to R.H. Tawney* (Oxford: Clarendon Press, 1988)

Donald D.Egbert *Social Radicalism and the Arts* (Duckworth, 1970)

Gregory Elliott *Labourism and the English Genius: The Strange Death of Labour England?* (Verso, 1993)

★Hywel Francis and David Smith *The Fed: A History of the South Wales Miners in the twentieth century* (Lawrence & Wishart, 1980)

James Hinton *Labour and Socialism: A History of the British Labour Movement 1867–1974* (Brighton: Wheatsheaf, 1983)

E.J. Hobsbawm *Labouring Men* (Weidenfeld & Nicolson, 1964)

E.J. Hobsbawm *Revolutionaries* (Quartet, 1977)

David Howell *British Social Democracy* (Croom Helm, 1980)

T.A. Jackson *Trials of British Freedom* (Lawrence & Wishart, 1940)

Keith Jeffery and Peter Hennessy *States of Emergency: British Governments and Strikebreaking since 1919* (Routledge & Kegan Paul, 1983)

Tony Lane *The Union Makes Us Strong: The British Working Class, Its Trade Unions and Politics* (Arrow, 1974)

Keith Laybourn *A History of British Trade Unions c.1770–1990* (Stroud: Alan Sutton, 1992)

★Jack Lindsay and Edgell Rickword (eds) *Spokesmen for Liberty* (Lawrence & Wishart, 1941)

David E. Martin and David Rubinstein (eds) *Ideology and the Labour Movement* (Croom Helm, 1979)

Ralph Miliband *Parliamentary Socialism: A Study in the Politics of Labour* (Merlin Press, 1973 ed)

Ralph Miliband and John Saville (eds) *The Socialist Register* (Merlin Press, 1964 – still continuing but now edited by Leo Panitch)

J.P.M. Millar *The Labour College Movement* (National Council of Labour Colleges, 1979)

*Kenneth O. Morgan *Labour People: Leaders and Lieutenants: Hardie to Kinnock* (Oxford: University Press, 1987)

Henry Pelling *The British Communist Party* (A & C Black, 1975)

*Henry Pelling (ed) *The Challenge of Socialism* (A & C Black, 1968)

Henry Pelling *A History of British Trade Unionism* (Pelican, 1976)

Ben Pimlott (ed) *Fabian Essays in Socialist Thought* (Heinemann, 1984)

Ben Pimlott and Chris Cook (eds) *Trade Unions in British Politics* (Longman, 1982)

Charles Poulsen *English Rebels* (Journeyman Press, 1984)

Andrew Rothstein *The House on Clerkenwell Green* (Marx Library, 1983)

Raphael Samuel (ed) *People's History and Socialist Theory* (Routledge & Kegan Paul, 1981)

John Saville 'The Ideology of Labourism' in R.Benewick, R.N.Berki and B. Parekh (eds) *Knowledge and Belief in Politics* (Allen & Unwin, 1973)

John Saville *The Labour Movement in Britain* (Faber, 1988)

Peter Shore *Leading the Left* (Weidenfield & Nicolson, 1993)

Gareth Stedman Jones *Languages of Class: Studies in English working class history 1832–1982* (Cambridge: University Press, 1983)

E.P. Thompson *The Making of the English Working Class* (Pelican, 1968)

E.P. Thompson *The Poverty of Theory and Other Essays* (Merlin Press, 1978)

Neal Wood *Communism and British Intellectuals* (Victor Gollancz, 1959)

Anthony Wright *Socialisms* (Oxford: University Press, 1986)

## General on the International Labour Movement

W. Abendroth *A Short History of the European Working Class* (New Left Books, 1971)

Perry Anderson *Considerations on Western Marxism* (New Left Books, 1976)

★Timothy Garton Ash *The Uses of Adversity: Essays on the Fate of Central Europe* (Cambridge: Granta Books, 1989)

Timothy Garton Ash *We The People* (Cambridge: Granta Books, 1990)

D.S. Bell and Byron Criddle *The French Socialist Party: The Emergence of a Party of Government* (Oxford: Clarendon Press, 1986)

David Caute *The Left in Europe since 1789* (Weidenfeld & Nicolson, 1966)

Fernando Claudin *The Communist Movement From Comintern To Cominform* (Peregrine, 1975)

Milovan Djilas *Conversations with Stalin* (Penguin, 1963)

Alfred Grosser *The Western Alliance: European-American Relations Since 1945* (Macmillan, 1980)

P.S. Gupta *Imperialism and the British Labour Movement, 1914–1964* (Macmillan, 1975)

Stephen Harding, David Phillips and Michael Fogarty (eds) *Contrasting Values in Western Europe* (Macmillan, 1986)

★Eric Hobsbawm *Age of Extremes: The Short Twentieth Century 1914–1991* (Michael Joseph, 1994)

Paul Johnson *A History of the Modern World* (Weidenfeld & Nicolson, 1983)

★Richard Mayne *Postwar: The Dawn of Today's Europe* (Thames & Hudson, 1983)

Sonia Mazey and Michael Newman (eds) *Mitterrand's France* (Croom Helm, 1987)

Veljko Micunovic *Moscow Diary* (Chatto & Windus, 1980)

Keith Middlemas *Power and the Party: Changing Faces of Communism in Western Europe* (André Deutsch, 1980)

Zdelnek Mlynar *Night Frost in Prague: The End of Human Socialism* (C.Hurst, 1980)

Robin Okey *Eastern Europe 1740–1980* (Hutchinson, 1980)

William E.Paterson and Alastair H.Thomas (eds) *The Future of Social Democracy* (Oxford: Clarendon Press, 1986)

William E.Paterson and Alastair H.Thomas (eds) *Social Democratic Parties in Western Europe* (Croom Helm, 1976)

Henry Pelling *America and the British Left: From Bright to Bevan* (A & C Black, 1956)

Donald Sassoon *The Strategy of the Italian Communist Party* (Frances Pinter, 1981)

Richard Scase (ed) *The State in Western Europe* (Croom Helm, 1980)

G.E. Smith, W.E.Paterson and P.H.Merkl (eds) *Development in West German Politics* (Macmillan, 1989)

Norman Stone *Europe Transformed 1878–1919* (Fontana, 1983)

D.W. Urwin and W.E.Paterson (eds) *Development in Western Europe Today* (Longman, 1990)

Martin Walker *The Cold War and the Making of the Modern World* (Vintage, 1994)

Doreen Warriner *Revolution in Eastern Europe* (Turnstile Press, 1950)

## Who Cares About Keir Hardie?

Robert Barltrop *Jack London* (Pluto Press, 1977)

Reg Beer *Matchgirls Strike* (National Museum of Labour History, undated)

★Caroline Benn *Keir Hardie* (Hutchinson, 1992)

Ian Britain *Fabianism and Culture* (Cambridge: University Press, 1982)

H.H. Champion *The Great Dock Strike* (Swan Sonnenschein, 1890, reprinted 1988)

John Cockburn *The Hungry Heart: A Romantic Biography of James Keir Hardie* (Jarrold, 1956)

G.D.H. Cole *James Keir Hardie* (Victor Gollancz, 1941)

Margaret Cole *Beatrice Webb* (Longmans, Green, 1945)

Leonard Cottrell *Madame Tussaud* (Evans, 1951)

George Dangerfield *The Strange Death of Liberal England 1910–1914* (Constable, 1961)

Hamilton Fyfe *Keir Hardie* (Duckworth, 1935)

A.G. Gardiner *Prophets, Priests and Kings* (A.Rivers, 1908)

J. Bruce Glasier *James Keir Hardie: A Memorial* (Labour Press, undated)

J. Bruce Glasier *Keir Hardie: The Man and the Message* (ILP, 1919)

J. Keir Hardie *From Serfdom to Socialism* (George Allen, 1907)

S.G. Hobson *Pilgrim to the Left: Memoirs of a Modern Revolutionist* (Edward Arnold, 1938)

Emrys Hughes *Keir Hardie* (Allen & Unwin, 1956)

Emrys Hughes *Keir Hardie: Some Memories* (Francis Johnson, undated)

Rowland Kenney *Westering* (J.M.Dent, 1939)

Jack London *The People of the Abyss* (Journeyman Press edition, 1978)

David Lowe *From Pit to Parliament* (Labour Publishing Company, 1923)

A.M. McBriar *Fabian Socialism and English Politics, 1884–1918* (Cambridge: University Press, 1966)

Norman MacKenzie (ed) *The Letters of Sidney and Beatrice Webb*: volume 1, *Apprenticeships 1873–1892*; volume II, *Partnership 1892–1912*; volume III, *Pilgrimage 1912–1947* (Cambridge: University Press, 1978)

Norman and Jeanne MacKenzie *The First Fabians* (Weidenfeld & Nicolson, 1977)

James Maxton *Keir Hardie: Prophet and Pioneer* (Francis Johnson, undated)

Kenneth O. Morgan *Keir Hardie: Radical and Socialist* (Weidenfeld & Nicolson, 1975)

Henry Pelling *The Origins of the Labour Party, 1880–1900* (Oxford: Clarendon Press, 1966)

Fred Reid *Keir Hardie: The Making of a Socialist* (Croom Helm, 1978)

Jonathan Schneer *Ben Tillett: Portrait of a Labour Leader* (Croom Helm, 1982)

Frank Smith *From Pit to Parliament: Keir Hardie's Life Story* (Manchester: National Labour Press, undated)

Joan Smith 'Labour Tradition in Glasgow and Liverpool' in *History Workshop*, 17, spring 1984

William Stewart *J.Keir Hardie* (ILP, 1925)

Paul Thompson *The Edwardians* (Weidenfeld & Nicolson, 1975)

John Vincent *The Formation of the British Liberal Party* (Penguin, 1972)

Cedric Watts and Laurence Davies *Cunninghame Graham: A Critical Biography* (Cambridge: University Press, 1979)

Beatrice Webb *My Apprenticeship* (Cambridge: University Press, 1979)

Beatrice Webb *Our Partnership* (Longmans, Green, 1948)

## The Mild–Mannered Desperadoes

Rosemary Ashton *Little Germany: Exile and Asylum in Victorian England* (Oxford: University Press, 1986)

★F.C. Ball *One of the Damned: The life and times of Robert Tressell, author of 'The Ragged Trousered Philanthropists'* (Lawrence & Wishart, 1979)

Asa Briggs *Marx in London* (BBC, 1982)

David Clark *Victor Grayson: Labour's Lost Leader* (Quartet, 1975)

Henry Collins and Chimen Abramsky *Karl Marx and the British Labour Movement* (Macmillan, 1965)

Tom Cullen *Maundy Gregory: Purveyor of Honours* (Bodley Head, 1972)

Andrew Davies *Literary London* (Macmillan, 1987)

Isaac Deutscher *The Prophet Armed: Trotsky 1879–1921* (Oxford: University Press, 1970)

M.M. Drachkovitch (ed) *The Revolutionary Internationals 1917–1943* (USA: Stanford University Press, 1966)

Mary Fels *Joseph Fels* (Allen & Unwin, 1920)

R.G. Gammage *History of the Chartist Movement 1837–1854* (Frank Cass, 1969)

Reg Groves *But We Shall Rise Again* (Secker & Warburg, 1938)

Reg Groves *The Strange Case of Victor Grayson* (Pluto Press, 1975)

H.M. Hyndman *Further Reminiscences* (Macmillan, 1912)

H.M. Hyndman *Record of an Adventurous Life* (Macmillan, 1911)

J.W. Hulse *Revolutionists in London: A Study of Five Unorthodox Socialists* (Oxford: Clarendon Press, 1970)

Prince Kropotkin *Memoirs of a Revolutionist* (USA: New York, 1899)

Nadezhda Krupskaya *Memoirs of Lenin* (Lawrence & Wishart, 1970)

Wilhelm Liebknecht *Karl Marx* (Journeyman Press edition, 1975)

David McLellan *Karl Marx: His Life and Thought* (Paladin, 1973)

Ivan Maisky *Journey into the Past* (Hutchinson, 1962)

L.E. Mins (ed) *Founding of the First International* (Moscow: Co-operative Publishing House, 1935)

Jack Mitchell *Robert Tressell and the Ragged-Trousered Philanthropists* (Lawrence & Wishart, 1969)

*S.S.Prawer *Karl Marx and World Literature* (Oxford: University Press, 1976)

*Reminiscences of Marx and Engels* (Moscow: Foreign Languages Publishing House, undated)

Donald Read and Eric Glasgow *Feargus O'Connor* (Edward Arnold, 1961)

Theodore Rothstein *From Chartism to Labourism* (Lawrence & Wishart, 1983 edition with introduction by John Saville)

Andrew Rothstein *Lenin in Britain* (Communist Party, 1970)

John Saville *1848: The British State and the Chartist Movement* (Cambridge: University Press, 1987)

John Taylor *From Self-Help to Glamour* (History Workshop, 1972)

Robert Tressell *The Ragged Trousered Philanthropists* (Panther, 1965 edition)

Chushichi Tsuzuki *H.M.Hyndman and British Socialism* (Oxford: University Press, 1961)

Barbara Tuchman *The Proud Tower* (Papermac, 1980)

Frances, Countess of Warwick *Afterthoughts* (Cassell, 1931)

Frances, Countess of Warwick *Life's Ebb and Flow* (Hutchinson, 1929)

Kirk Willis 'The Introduction and Critical Reception of Marxist Thought in Britain, 1850–1900' in the *Historical Journal*, 20, 2, 1977

## Socialism and the New Life

R. Page Arnot *William Morris: The Man and the Myth* (Lawrence & Wishart, 1964)

Gilbert Beith (ed) *Edward Carpenter: In Appreciation* (Allen & Unwin, 1931)

Annie Besant *An Autobiography* (Madras: Theosophical Publishing House, 1939)

Annie Besant *Autobiographical Sketches* (Freethought Publishing Company, 1885)

F.G. Bettany *Stewart Headlam: A Biography* (John Murray, 1926)

Robert Blatchford *English Prose And How To Write It* (Methuen, 1925)

Robert Blatchford *Merrie England* (Clarion, 1895)

Robert Blatchford *My Eighty Years* (Cassell, 1931)

Robert Blatchford *The Sorcery Shop: An Impossible Romance* (Clarion Press, 1907)

Florence Boos (ed) 'William Morris's Socialist Diary' in *History Workshop*, 13, spring 1982

Ruth Brandon *The New Women and the Old Men* (Secker & Warburg, 1990)

Asa Briggs (ed) *William Morris: News from Nowhere and Selected Writings and Designs* (Penguin, 1984)

Edward Carpenter *Edward Carpenter 1844–1929: A Restatement and Reappraisal* (Dr. Williams Trust, 1970)

Edward Carpenter *My Days and Dreams* (Allen & Unwin, 1916)

G.D.H. Cole (ed) *William Morris, Prose, Verse, Lectures and Essays* (Nonesuch Press, 1946)

Andrew Davies *The East End Nobody Knows* (Macmillan, 1990)

Barbara Drake *Women in Trade Unions* (Allen & Unwin, 1921)

J. Bruce Glasier *William Morris and the Early Days of the Socialist Movement* (Longmans, Green, 1921)

Philip Henderson (ed) *The Letters of William Morris to his Family and Friends* (Longmans, 1950)

Peter d'A. Jones *The Christian Socialist Revival 1877–1914* (USA: Princeton, 1969)

★Yvonne Kapp *Eleanor Marx, volume 1, Family Life* (Lawrence & Wishart, 1972); *volume 2, The Crowded Years* (Lawrence & Wishart, 1976)

Jack Lindsay *William Morris: His Life and Work* (Constable, 1975)

★Fiona MacCarthy *William Morris* (Faber, 1994)

Paul Meier *William Morris: The Marxist Dreamer*, two volumes (Brighton: Harvester, 1978)

Hannah Mitchell *The Hard Way Up* (Faber, 1968)

William Morris *The Beauty of Life* (Brentham Press, 1974 edition)

William Morris *The Novel on Blue Paper* (Journeyman Press, 1982)

George Orwell *The Road to Wigan Pier* (Penguin edition, 1962)

Linda Parry *William Morris Textiles* (Weidenfeld & Nicolson, 1983)

M.B. Reckitt (ed) *For Christ and the People* (SPCK, 1968)

James Redmond (ed) *William Morris News from Nowhere* (Routledge & Kegan Paul, 1970)

W.Stephan Sanders *Early Socialist Days* (Hogarth Press, 1927)

A.H. Moncur Sime *Edward Carpenter: His Ideas and Ideals* (Kegan Paul, 1916)

Sheila Rowbotham *Hidden from History* (Pluto Press, 1973)

Sheila Rowbotham and Jeffrey Weeks *Socialism and the New Life: The Personal and Sexual Politics of Edward Carpenter and Havelock Ellis* (Pluto Press, 1973)

E.P. Thompson *William Morris: Romantic to Revolutionary* (Merlin Press edition, 1977)

Laurence Thompson *Robert Blatchford: Portrait of an Englishman* (Victor Gollancz, 1951)

Laurence Thompson *The Enthusiasts* (Victor Gollancz, 1971)

John Trevor *My Quest for God* (Labour Prophet, 1897)

Chushichi Tsuzuki *Edward Carpenter 1844–1929: prophet of human fellowship* (Cambridge: University Press, 1980)

Oscar Wilde *De Profundis and other writings* (Penguin edition, 1973)

Stephen Winsten *Salt and His Circle* (Hutchinson, 1951)

## Tho' Cowards Flinch and Traitors Sneer

Margaret Bondfield *A Life's Work* (Hutchinson, undated)

Robert Boothby, John Loder, Harold Macmillan and Oliver Stanley *Industry and the State* (Macmillan, 1927)

Noreen Branson *Britain in the Nineteen Twenties* (Weidenfeld & Nicolson, 1975)

Noreen Branson *Poplarism 1919–1925. George Lansbury and the Councillors' Revolt* (Lawrence & Wishart, 1979)

Philip G. Cambray *The Game of Politics: A Study of the Principles of British Political Strategy* (John Murray, 1932)

Lewis Chester, Stephen Fay and Hugo Young *The Zinoviev Letter* (Heinemann, 1967)

J.R. Clynes *Memoirs*, volume one 1869–1924; volume two 1924–1937 (Hutchinson, 1937)

Joe Corrie *The Road the Fiddler Went* (Glasgow: Forward Publishing Company, undated)

R.E. Dowse *Left in the Centre* (Longmans, 1966)

Lord Elton *The Life of James Ramsay MacDonald* (Collins, 1939)

John Gorman *Banner Bright* (Penguin, 1976)

M.A. Hamilton *J. Ramsay MacDonald* (Jonathan Cape, 1929)

Bob Holton *British Syndicalism 1900–1914* (Pluto Press, 1970)

George Lansbury *The Miracle of Fleet Street* (Labour Publishing Company, 1925)

Keith Laybourn *Philip Snowden: A Biography* (Temple Smith, 1988)

V.I. Lenin *Lenin on Ramsay MacDonald* (Modern Books, 1934)

David Lusted (ed) *Raymond Williams: Film TV Culture* (British Film Institute, 1989)

J. Ramsay MacDonald *Margaret Ethel MacDonald* (Hodder & Stoughton, 1912)

J. Ramsay MacDonald *Wanderings and Excursions* (Jonathan Cape, 1925)

Norman and Jeanne MacKenzie (eds) *The Diary of Beatrice Webb* volume four, 1924–1943 (Virago, 1985)

Ross McKibbin *The Evolution of the Labour Party 1910–1924* (Oxford: University Press, 1974)

David Marquand *Ramsay MacDonald* (Jonathan Cape, 1977)

Austen Morgan *J.Ramsay MacDonald* (Manchester: University Press, 1987)

C.L. Mowat *Britain Between the Wars* (Methuen edition, 1956)

Kingsley Martin *Father Figures* (Hutchinson, 1966)

\*Jeffrey Richards and Anthony Aldgate *British Cinema and Society 1930–1970* (Oxford: Basil Blackwell, 1983)

Robert Skidelsky *Politicians and the Slump: The Labour Government of 1929–1931* (Macmillan, 1967)

Viscount Snowden *An Autobiography*, volume one 1864–1919; volume two, 1919–1934 (Ivor Nicholson and Watson, 1934)

Howard Spring *Fame is the Spur* (Collins edition, 1940)

Julian Symons *The General Strike* (1957; Cresset Library, 1987)

Herbert Tracey *From Doughty Street to Downing Street* (Maclone, Savage, 1924)

*Egon Wertheimer *Portrait of the Labour Party* (G.P.Puttnam, 1929)


## British Revolutionaries in the 1920s

Guy Aldred *John Maclean* (Glasgow: Bakunin Press, 1932)

Francis Beckett *Enemy Within: The Rise and Fall of the British Communist Party* (John Murray, 1995)

Tom Bell *John Maclean: A Fighter for Freedom* (Glasgow: Communist Party, Scottish Committee, 1944)

Tom Bell *Pioneering Days* (Lawrence & Wishart, 1941)

Jack and Bessie Braddock *The Braddocks* (Macdonald, 1963)

Noreen Branson *History of the Communist Party of Great Britain 1927–1941* (Lawrence & Wishart, 1985)

John Callaghan *Rajani Palme Dutt: A Study in British Stalinism* (Lawrence & Wishart, 1993)

William Campbell *Villi the Clown* (Faber, 1981)

Raymond Challinor *John S.Clarke* (Pluto Press, 1977)

Raymond Challinor *The Origins of British Bolshevism* (Croom Helm, 1977)

John S.Clarke *Pen Pictures of Russia Under The 'Red Terror'* (Glasgow: National Workers' Committee, 1921)

Hugo Dewar *Communist Politics in Britain: The Communist Party of Great Britain from its Origins to the Second World War* (Pluto Press, 1975)

R.M. Fox *Smoky Crusade* (Hogarth Press, 1937)

William Gallacher *Revolt on the Clyde* (Lawrence & Wishart, 1978 edition)

James Hinton and Richard Hyman *Trade Unions and Revolution: The Industrial Politics of the Early British Communist Party* (Pluto Press, 1975)

David Howell *A Lost Left: Three Studies in Socialism and Nationalism* (Manchester: University Press, 1986)

P.M. Kemp-Ashraf and Jack Mitchell (eds) *Essays in Honour of William Gallacher* (Berlin: Humboldt University, 1966)

Walter Kendall *The Revolutionary Movement in Britain, 1900–1921* (Weidenfeld & Nicolson, 1969)

George Lansbury *The Miracle of Fleet Street* (Labour Publishing Company, 1925)

L.J. Macfarlane *The British Communist Party* (Macgibbon & Kee, 1966)

Stuart Macintyre *Little Moscows: Communism and Working-Class Militancy in Inter-War Britain* (Croom Helm, 1980)

Stuart Macintyre *A Proletarian Science: Marxism in Britain 1917–1933* (Cambridge: University Press, 1980)

Ian McLean *The Legend of Red Clydeside* (Edinburgh: John Donald, 1983)

*Harry McShane and Joan Smith *No Mean Fighter* (Pluto Press, 1978)

Roderick Martin *Communism and the British Trade Unions 1924–1933* (Oxford: University Press, 1969)

Francis Meynell *My Lives* (Bodley Head, 1971)

Nan Milton (ed) *In the Rapids of Revolution* (Allison & Busby, 1978)

Nan Milton *John Maclean* (Pluto Press, 1973)

Dora B.Montefiore *From a Victorian to a Modern* (E.Archer, 1927)

*Kevin Morgan *Harry Pollitt* (Manchester: University Press, 1993)

Vivien Morton and Stuart Macintyre *T.A.Jackson: A Centenary Publication* ('Our History' pamphlet 73, undated)

Harry Pollitt *Serving My Time* (Lawrence & Wishart, 1940)

B.J. Ripley and J.McHugh *John Maclean* (Manchester: University Press, 1989)

Chanie Rosenberg *1919: Britain on the Brink of Revolution* (Bookmarks, 1987)

Sheila Rowbotham *A New World for Women: Stella Browne Socialist-Feminist* (Pluto Press, 1977)

Mike Squires *Saklatvala: A Political Biography* (Lawrence & Wishart, 1990)

Willie Thompson *The Good Old Cause* (Pluto Press, 1992)

Leon Trotsky *Where Is Britain Going?* (Allen & Unwin, 1926)

Michael Woodhouse and Brian Pearce *Essays on the History of Communism in Britain* (New Park, 1975; reissued 1995)

## The Thirties

Robert Blake *The Conservative Party from Peel to Thatcher* (Fontana, 1985 edition)

Noreen Branson and Margot Heinemann *Britain in the Nineteen Twenties* (Weidenfeld & Nicolson, 1971)

Lord Citrine *Men and Work* (Hutchinson, 1964)

Ronald Clark *JBS: The Life and Work of J.B.S.Haldane* (Oxford: University Press, 1984)

G.D.H. Cole *A History of the Labour Party from 1914* (Routledge & Kegan Paul, 1948)

Sir Stafford Cripps *Can Socialism Come by Constitutional Methods?* (Socialist League, 1933)

Sir Stafford Cripps *The Choice for Britain* (Socialist League, 1933–34)

Margaret Cole and Charles Smith (eds) *Democratic Sweden* (Routledge, 1938)

Judith Cook *Apprentices of Freedom* (Quartet, 1977)

Hugh Dalton *The Fateful Years: Memoirs 1931–1945* (Muller, 1957)

Hugh Dalton *Practical Socialism for Britain* (Routledge, 1935)

Nicholas Davenport *Memoirs of a City Radical* (Weidenfeld & Nicolson, 1974)

Isaac Deutscher *The Prophet Outcast: Trotsky 1929–1940* (Oxford: University Press, 1970)

*Elizabeth Durbin *New Jerusalems: The Labour Party and the Economics of Democratic Socialism* (Routledge & Kegan Paul, 1985)

Ruth Dudley Edwards *Victor Gollancz* (Victor Gollancz, 1987)

Eric Estorick *Stafford Cripps* (Heinemann, 1949)

Michael Foot *Aneurin Bevan 1897–1945* (Paladin, 1975)

Laurence and Helen Fowler (eds) *Cambridge Commemorated: An Anthology of University Life* (Cambridge: University Press, 1984)

St John B.Groser *Politics and Persons* (SCM Press, 1949)

Carmel Haden Guest (ed) *David Guest: A Memoir* (Lawrence & Wishart, 1939)

Wal Hannington *Never On Our Knees* (Lawrence & Wishart, 1967)

*Bob Holman *Good Old George: The Life of George Lansbury* (Oxford: Lion Publishing, 1990)

Hazel Holt and Hilary Pym (eds) *A Very Private Eye* (Macmillan, 1984)

Arthur Horner *Incorrigible Rebel* (Macgibbon & Kee, 1960)

Douglas Hyde *I Believed* (Heinemann, 1950)

Joe Jacobs *Out of the Ghetto* (J.Simon, 1978)

Alan Jenkins *The Thirties* (Heinemann, 1975)

James Jupp *The Radical Left in Britain 1931–1941* (Frank Cass, 1982)

Edgar Lansbury *George Lansbury* (J.Sampson Low, 1934)

George Lansbury *My Life* (Constable, 1928)

S.W. Lerner *Breakaway Unions and the Small Trade Unions* (Allen & Unwin, 1961)

John Lewis *The Left Book Club* (Victor Gollancz, 1970)

John Lucas (ed) *The 1930s: A Challenge to Orthodoxy* (Brighton: Harvester Press, 1978)

Charlotte Haldane *Truth Will Out* (Weidenfeld & Nicolson, 1949)

D.E. McHenry *The Labour Party in Transition 1931–1938* (Routledge, 1938)

Kingsley Martin *Editor* (Penguin, 1969)

Kingsley Martin *Harold Laski 1893–1950: A Political Biography* (Jonathan Cape, 1969 edition)

Naomi Mitchison *You May Well Ask* (Flamingo, 1986)

George Orwell *The Lion and the Unicorn* (Penguin, 1982 edition)

D. Pennington and K.Thomas (eds) *Puritans and Revolutionaries: Essays Presented to Christopher Hill* (Oxford: Clarendon Press, 1978)

★Ben Pimlott *Hugh Dalton* (Jonathan Cape, 1985)

Ben Pimlott *Labour and the Left in the 1930s* (Allen & Unwin, 1986 edition)

Raymond Postgate *The Life of George Lansbury* (Longmans, Green, 1951)

J.B.Priestley *English Journey* (Penguin, 1977 edition)

Kathleen Raine *The Land Unknown* (Hamish Hamilton, 1975)

Philip Rieff (ed) *On Intellectuals* (USA: New York, 1969)

John Ramsden *The Making of Conservative Party Policy* (Longmans, 1980)

Margery Spring Rice *Working-Class Wives, Their Health and Conditions* (Penguin, 1939)

★Jonathan Schneer *George Lansbury* (Manchester: University Press, 1990)

C.H.Rolph *Kingsley* (Victor Gollancz, 1973)

Marion Slingova *Truth Will Prevail* (Merlin Press, 1968)

Pat Sloan (ed) *John Cornford: A Memoir* (Jonathan Cape, 1936)

John Stevenson *Social Conditions in Britain Between the Wars* (Penguin, 1977)

A.J.P. Taylor *English History 1914–1945* (Pelican, 1970)

Hugh Thomas *John Strachey* (Eyre Methuen, 1973)

Ernie Trory *Between the Wars: Reflections of a Communist Organiser* (Brighton: Crabtree, 1974)

Froom Tyler *Cripps: A Portrait and a Prospect* (Harrap, 1942)

Betty D.Vernon *Ellen Wilkinson* (Croom Helm, 1982)
Gary Werskey *The Visible College: A Collective Biography of British Scientists and Socialists of the 1930s* (Free Association Books, 1988 edition)


## Grand Illusions

Dr Friedrich Adler *The Witchcraft Trial in Moscow* (Commission of Enquiry into the Conditions of Political Prisoners, 1936)
David Caute *The Fellow Travellers: A Postscript of the Enlightenment* (Weidenfeld & Nicolson, 1973)
Sir Walter Citrine *I Search for Truth in Russia* (Routledge, 1936)
Dudley Collard *Soviet Justice and the Trial of Radek and Others* (Victor Gollancz, 1937)
Robert Conquest *The Great Terror: A Reassessment* (Hutchinson, 1990 edition)
John Costello *Mask of Treachery* (Collins, 1988)
*H.S. Ferns *Reading from Right to Left* (Canada: University of Toronto Press, 1983)
William Gallacher *The Last Memoirs of William Gallacher* (Lawrence & Wishart, 1966)
William Gallacher *The Rolling of the Thunder* (Lawrence & Wishart, 1947)
Victor Gollancz (ed) *The Betrayal of the Left* (Victor Gollancz, 1941)
Ian Grey *Stalin* (Abacus, 1982)
Richard Griffiths *Fellow Travellers of the Right: British Enthusiasts for Nazi Germany 1933–39* (Constable, 1980)
Paul Hollander *Political Pilgrims: Travels of Western Intellectuals to the Soviet Union, China and Cuba 1928–1978* (Oxford: University Press, 1981)
Robert Rhodes James *Churchill: A Study in Failure* (Pelican, 1973)
John Lehmann *The Whispering Gallery* (Longmans, 1955)
Cecil Day Lewis *The Buried Day* (Chatto & Windus, 1969)
Cecil Day Lewis (ed) *The Mind in Chains* (Muller, 1937)
Margaret MacCarthy *Generation in Revolt* (Heinemann, 1953)
Sylvia R.Margulies *The Pilgrimage to Russia: The Soviet Union and the Treatment of Foreigners 1924–1937* (USA: University of Wisconsin Press, 1968)
Ivor Montagu *The Youngest Son* (Lawrence & Wishart, 1970)
Kim Philby *My Silent War* (Panther, 1969)
D.N. Pritt *The Zinoviev Trial* (Victor Gollancz, 1937)

George Bernard Shaw *The Rationalization of Russia* (USA: Indiana University Press, 1964)

Pat Sloan *Soviet Democracy* (Victor Gollancz, 1937)

*Survey*, issue no 41, April 1962, articles by Hugo Dewar, Alfred Sherman etc.

Christopher Sykes *Nancy: The Life of Lady Astor* (Granada, 1979)

Tatiana Tchernavin *Escape from the Soviets* (Hamish Hamilton, 1933)

Vladimir Tchernavin *I Speak for the Silent* (Hamish Hamilton, 1937)

Edward Upward *The Spiral Ascent: A Trilogy* (Heinemann, 1977 edition)

F.A.Voigt *Unto Caesar* (Constable, 1938)

## New Worlds for Old?

Acton Society Trust *The Men on the Boards* (Acton Society Trust, 1951)

Acton Society Trust *The Worker's Point of View* (Acton Society Trust, 1952)

Paul Addison *The Road to 1945* (Jonathan Cape, 1975)

*Noel Annan *Our Age: Portrait of a Generation* (Weidenfeld & Nicolson, 1990)

Clement Attlee *As It Happened* (Heinemann, 1954)

Corelli Barnett *The Audit of War* (Macmillan, 1986)

Corelli Barnett *The Lost Victory: British Dreams, British Realities 1945–1950* (Macmillan, 1995)

Charles Barr *Ealing Studios* (Cameron & Tayleur, 1977)

Sir William Beveridge *The Pillars of Security* (Allen & Unwin, 1943)

*Robert A.Brady *Crisis in Britain – Plans and Achievements of the Labour Government* (Cambridge University Press, 1950)

Susan Briggs *Keep Smiling Through* (Weidenfeld & Nicolson, 1975)

Trevor Burridge *Clement Attlee: A Political Biography* (Jonathan Cape, 1985)

T.D. Burridge *British Labour and Hitler's War* (André Deutsch, 1976)

Angus Calder *The People's War: Britain 1939–1945* (Panther edition, 1971)

Virginia Cowles *No Cause for Alarm* (Hamish Hamilton, 1949)

Bernard Crick *George Orwell: A Life* (Secker & Warburg, 1980)

Hugh Dalton *High Tide and After: Memoirs 1945–60* (Muller, 1962)

Andrew Davies *Where Did The Forties Go?* (Pluto Press, 1984)

Bernard Donoughue and G.W.Jones *Herbert Morrison: Portrait of a Politician* (Weidenfeld & Nicolson, 1973)

Granville Eastwood *Harold Laski* (Oxford: Mowbray, 1977)

Roger Eatwell *The 1945–1951 Labour Governments* (Batsford, 1979)

T.R. Fyvel *George Orwell: A Personal Memoir* (Weidenfeld & Nicolson, 1982)

★William Harrington and Peter Young *The 1945 Revolution* (Davis-Poynter, 1978)

★Peter Hennessy *Never Again: Britain 1945–1951* (Vintage edition, 1993)

Kenneth Harris *Attlee* (Weidenfeld, 1995 edition)

James Harvey and Katherine Hood *The British State* (Lawrence & Wishart, 1958)

Ian McLaine *The Ministry of Morale* (Allen & Unwin, 1979)

Charles Madge (ed) *Pilot Guide to the British Election* (Pilot Press, 1945)

Leah Manning *A Life for Education* (Victor Gollancz, 1970)

Mass Observation *Peace and the Public* (Longmans, 1947)

Mass Observation *War Factory* (Victor Gollancz, 1943)

Janet Minihan *The Nationalization of Culture* (Hamish Hamilton, 1977)

Lord Moran *Churchill* (Constable, 1966)

Kenneth O. Morgan *Labour in Power 1945–1951* (Oxford: University Press, 1984)

Herbert Morrison *An Autobiography* (Odhams, 1960)

Herbert Morrison *The Peaceful Revolution* (Allen & Unwin, 1949)

J.T. Murphy *Victory Production!* (Bodley Head, 1942)

D. Stark Murray *Why A National Health Service?* (Pemberton, 1971)

Leo Panitch *Social Democracy and Industrial Militancy* (Cambridge: University Press, 1976)

Henry Pelling *The Labour Governments, 1945–1951* (Macmillan, 1984)

D.N. Pritt *The Labour Government 1945–1951* (Lawrence & Wishart, 1963)

J.B. Priestley *Margin Released* (Heinemann, 1962)

A.A. Rogow with Peter Sbore *The Labour Government and British Industry 1945–1951* (Oxford: Blackwell, 1955)

David Rubinstein *Socialism and the Labour Party: The Labour Left and Domestic Policy, 1945–1950* (Leeds: ILP Square One, undated)

Jonathan Schneer *Labour's Conscience: The Labour Left 1945–51* (Allen & Unwin, 1988)

Dudley Seers *The Levelling of Incomes Since 1938* (Oxford: Blackwell, 1951)

Lord Shawcross *Life Sentence: The Memoirs of Lord Shawcross* (Constable, 1995)

Emanuel Shinwell *Lead with the Left* (Cassell, 1981)

Michael Sissons and Philip French (eds) *The Age of Austerity 1945–1951* (Hodder & Stoughton, 1963)

*Peter Slowe *Manny Shinwell: An Authorised Biography* (Pluto Press, 1993)

William Temple *Christianity and Social Order* (Penguin, 1942)

Nick Tiratsoo (ed) *The Attlee Years* (Pinter Publishers, 1991)

Richard M. Titmuss *Problems of Social Policy* (HMSO, 1950)

*James D. Wilkinson *The Intellectual Resistance in Europe* (USA: Harvard University Press, 1981)

Elizabeth Wilson *Only Halfway to Paradise* (Tavistock Publications, 1980)

## With Us or Against Us?

Richard J. Aldrich (ed) *British Intelligence, Strategy and the Cold War, 1945–51* (Routledge, 1992)

V.L. Allen *Trade Union Leadership* (Longmans, Green, 1957)

Christopher Andrew *Secret Service: The Making of the British Intelligence Community* (Sceptre, 1986)

Daniel Bell (ed) *The Radical Right* (USA, New York, 1964)

Carl Bernstein *Loyalties* (Macmillan, 1989)

Aneurin Bevan *In Place of Fear* (Quartet, 1978 edition)

Philip Bolsover *America over Britain* (Lawrence & Wishart, 1953)

Eleanor Bontecou *The Federal Loyalty-Security Program* (USA: Cornell University Press, 1953)

Tom Bower *The Perfect English Spy: Sir Dick White and the secret war, 1935–90* (Heinemann, 1995)

Alan Bullock *The Life and Times of Ernest Bevin.* Volume Two: *Foreign Secretary 1945–1951* (Oxford: University Press, 1983)

John Campbell *Nye Bevan and the Mirage of British Socialism* (Weidenfeld & Nicolson, 1986)

David Caute *The Great Fear: The Communist Purge Under Truman and Eisenhower* (Secker & Warburg, 1978)

Richard Crossman *Planning for Freedom* (Hamish Hamilton, 1964)

Basil Davidson *Special Operations Europe* (Victor Gollancz, 1980)

Anne Deighton (ed) *Britain and the First Cold War* (Macmillan, 1990)

Michael Foot *Aneurin Bevan 1945–1960* (Paladin, 1975)

William Gallacher *The Case for Communism* (Penguin, 1949)

Lord Gladwyn *The European Idea* (Weidenfeld & Nicolson, 1966)

Roy Godson *American Labor and European Politics: The AFL as a Transnational Force* (USA: Crane, Russak, 1976)

Maurice Goldsmith *Sage: A Life of J.D.Bernal* (Hutchinson, 1980)

Martin Harrison *Trade Unions and the Labour Party Since 1945* (Allen & Unwin, 1960)

Douglas Hill (ed) *Tribune 40* (Quartet, 1977)

Fred Hirsch and Richard Fletcher *The CIA and the Labour Movement* (Nottingham: Spokesman Books, 1977)

Mark Hollingsworth and Richard Norton-Taylor *Blacklist! The Inside Story of Political Vetting* (Hogarth Press, 1988)

Mark Hollingsworth and Charles Tremayne *The Economic League: The Silent McCarthyism* (NCCL, 1989)

David Howell *The Rise and Fall of Bevanism* (Leeds: ILP Square One, undated)

Leslie Hunter *The Road to Brighton Pier* (Arthur Barker, 1959)

Rhodri Jeffreys-Jones and Andrew Lownie (eds) *North American Spies* (USA: University of Kansas Press, 1991)

Mark Jenkins *Bevanism: Labour's High Tide* (Nottingham: Spokesman, 1979)

Bill Jones *The Russia Complex: the British Labour Party and the Soviet Union* (Manchester: University Press, 1977)

Karel Kaplan *The Short March* (C.Hurst, 1987)

Jennie Lee *My Life With Nye* (Jonathan Cape, 1980)

Jennie Lee *Tomorrow is a New Day* (Cresset Press, 1939)

David Leigh *The Frontiers of Secrecy* (Junction, 1980)

\*Ian Mikardo *Back-bencher* (Weidenfeld & Nicolson, 1988)

Lewis Minkin *The Labour Party Conference* (Manchester: University Press, 1980)

Janet Morgan (ed) *The Backbench Diaries Of Richard Crossman* (Hamish Hamilton, 1981)

Sallie Pirsani *The CIA and the Marshall Plan* (Edinburgh: University Press, 1992)

Dora Russell *The Tamarisk Tree: Challenge to the Cold War* (Virago, 1985)

Anthony Sampson *Macmillan* (Penguin, 1968)
★ Adam Sisman *A.J.P. Taylor: A Biography* (Sinclair-Stevenson, 1994)
Gordon Stewart *The Cloak and Dollar War* (Lawrence & Wishart 1953)
Don Thomson and Rodney Larson *Where Were You, Brother?* (War on
　Want, 1978)
★Peter Weiler *Ernest Bevin* (Manchester: University Press, 1993)
Francis Williams *Ernest Bevin* (Hutchinson, 1952)
Martin Walker *The Cold War and the Making of the Modern World*
　(Vintage, 1994)


## Expanding Horizons

Mark Abrams and Richard Rose *Must Labour Lose?* (Penguin, 1960)
R.Benewick and T. Smith (eds) *Direct Action and Democratic Politics* (Allen
　& Unwin, 1972)
Tony Benn *Years of Hope: Diaries, Papers and Letters 1940–1962*
　(Hutchinson, 1994)
Vernon Bogdanor and Robert Skidelsky (eds) *The Age of Affluence
　1951–1964* (Macmillan, 1970)
G.D.H. Cole *William Morris as a Socialist* (William Morris Society,
　1960)
*The Communist Answer to the Challenge of Our Time* (Thames Publica-
　tions, 1947)
C.A.R. Crosland *The Future of Socialism* (Jonathan Cape, 1956)
Tom Driberg *Ruling Passions* (Quartet, 1978)
Christopher Driver *The Disarmers: A Study in Protest* (Hodder &
　Stoughton, 1964)
Peggy Duff *Left, Left, Left* (Allison & Busby, 1971)
Peter Fryer *Hungarian Tragedy* (Dennis Dobson, 1956)
Hugh Gaitskell *Britain and the Common Market* (Labour Party, 1962)
Nigel Harris and John Palmer (eds) *World Crisis* (Hutchinson, 1971)
Stephen Haseler *The Gaitskellites: Revisionism in the British Labour Party
　1951–1964* (Macmillan, 1969)
Robert Hewison *In Anger: Culture in the Cold War* (Weidenfeld &
　Nicolson, 1981)
James Hinton *Protests and Visions: Peace Politics In Twentieth-Century
　Britain* (Hutchinson Radius, 1989)
Douglas Jay *Change and Fortune: A Political Record* (Hutchinson, 1980)
★Mervyn Jones *Chances: An Autobiography* (Verso, 1987)

Norman MacKenzie (ed) *Conviction* (Macgibbon & Kee, 1958)

John Mahon *Harry Pollitt* (Lawrence & Wishart, 1976)

Michael Newman *John Strachey* (Manchester: University Press, 1989)

Kenneth Newton *The Sociology of British Communism* (Allen Lane, 1969)

Oxford University Socialist Group *Out of Apathy: Voices of the New Left Thirty Years On* (Verso, 1989)

D.N. Pritt *Brasshats and Bureaucrats* (Lawrence & Wishart, 1966)

W.T. Rodgers (ed) *Hugh Gaitskell* (Thames & Hudson, 1964)

Dora Russell *The Tamarisk Tree: My Quest for liberty and love* (Paul Elek, 1975)

*The Socialist Register 1976* (Merlin, 1976 – essays on '1956' by John Saville, Malcolm MacEwen, Margot Heinemann and Mervyn Jones)

John Strachey *Contemporary Capitalism* (Victor Gollancz, 1956)

Richard Taylor and Colin Pritchard *The Protest Makers: The British Nuclear Disarmament Movement of 1958–1965 Twenty Years On* (Oxford: Pergamon Press, 1980)

Richard Taylor and Nigel Young (eds) *Campaigns for Peace: British peace movements in the twentieth century* (Manchester: University Press, 1987)

E.P. Thompson (ed) *Out of Apathy* (Stevens, 1960)

Philip Toynbee *Friends Apart* (Macgibbon & Kee, 1954)

Vittorio Vidali *Diary of the Twentieth Congress of the Communist Party of the Soviet Union* (Journeyman Press, 1984)

*Francis Wheen *Tom Driberg: His Life and Indiscretions* (Chatto & Windus, 1990)

Philip M.Williams (ed) *The Diary of Hugh Gaitskell 1945–1956* (Jonathan Cape, 1983)

Philip M. Williams *Hugh Gaitskell* (Jonathan Cape, 1979; shortened edition with new material, Oxford: University Press, 1982)

Lord Windlesham *Communications and Political Power* (Jonathan Cape, 1966)

Nigel Young *An Infantile Disorder? The Crisis and Decline of the New Left* (Routledge & Kegan Paul, 1977)

## Harold Wilson's New Britain

Martin Bailey *Oilgate* (Coronet, 1979)

Wilfred Beckerman (ed) *The Labour Government's Economic Record 1964–1970* (Duckworth, 1972)

Tony Benn *Office Without Power: Diaries 1968–72* (Hutchinson, 1988)

Tony Benn *Out of the Wilderness: Diaries 1963–67* (Hutchinson, 1987)

Robin Blackburn and Alexander Cockburn (eds) *Student Power* (Penguin, 1969)

Muriel Box *Rebel Advocate: A Biography of Gerald Gardiner* (Victor Gollancz, 1983)

George Brown *In My Way* (Victor Gollancz, 1971)

John Callaghan *The Far Left in British Politics* (Oxford: Blackwell, 1987)

Barbara Castle *The Castle Diaries 1964–70* (Weidenfeld & Nicolson, 1984)

★Barbara Castle *Fighting All the Way* (Pan, 1994)

David Caute *Sixty-Eight: The Year of the Barricades* (Hamish Hamilton, 1988)

Ken Coates *The Crisis of British Socialism* (Nottingham: Spokesman Books, 1972)

★Susan Crosland *Tony Crosland* (Jonathan Cape, 1982)

Richard Crossman *The Diaries of a Cabinet Minister*, volume one 1964–66 (Hamish Hamilton, 1975); volume two 1966–68 (1976); volume three 1968–70 (1977)

Tam Dalyell *Dick Crossman: A Portrait* (Weidenfeld & Nicolson, 1969)

Wilfred De'Ath *Barbara Castle: A Portrait from Life.* (Clifton Books, 1970)

Stephen Dorril and Robin Ramsay *Smear! Wilson and the Secret State* (Grafton, 1991)

Paul Foot *The Politics of Harold Wilson* (Penguin, 1968)

Ronald Fraser *1968: A Student Generation in Revolt* (Chatto & Windus, 1988)

Geoffrey Goodman *The Awkward Warrior: Frank Cousins, His Life and Times* (Davis-Poynter, 1979)

★Anthony Howard *Crossman: The Pursuit of Power* (Jonathan Cape, 1990)

Edward G.Janosik *Constituency Labour Parties in Britain* (Pall Mall Press, 1968)

Peter Jenkins *The Battle of Downing Street* (Charles Knight, 1970)

Roy Jenkins *A Life at the Centre* (Macmillan, 1991)

Gerald Kaufman (ed) *The Left* (Anthony Blond, 1966)

David McKie and Chris Cook (eds) *The Decade of Disillusion* (Macmillan, 1972)

Richard Marsh *Off the Rails: An Autobiography* (Weidenfeld & Nicolson, 1978)

Austen Morgan *Harold Wilson* (Pluto Press, 1992)

Peter Paterson *Tired And Emotional: the Life of Lord George-Brown* (Chatto, 1993)

Robert Pearce (ed) *Patrick Gordon Walker: Political Diaries 1932–1971* (Historians' Press, 1991)

Ben Pimlott *Harold Wilson* (HarperCollins, 1992)

Clive Ponting *Breach of Promise: Labour in Power 1964–1970* (Hamish Hamilton, 1989)

Andrew Roth *Sir Harold Wilson: Yorkshire Harold Mitty* (Macdonald & Janes, 1977)

Edward Short *Whip to Wilson* (Macdonald, 1989)

Michael Stewart *Life and Labour* (Sidgwick & Jackson, 1980)

Tariq Ali *Street Fighting Years* (Collins, 1987)

David Widgery *The Left in Britain 1956–1968* (Penguin, 1976)

Lord Wigg *George Wigg* (Michael Joseph, 1972)

Raymond Williams (ed) *May Day Manifesto* (Penguin, 1968)

Marcia Williams *Inside Number 10* (Weidenfeld & Nicolson, 1972)

Harold Wilson *The Labour Governments 1964–1970: A Personal Record* (Weidenfeld & Nicolson, 1971)

Peter Wright *Spycatcher: The Candid Account of a Senior Intelligence Officer* (Viking, 1987)

Philip Ziegler *Wilson: The Authorised Life of Lord Wilson of Rievaulx* (Weidenfeld & Nicolson, 1993)

## Endings

Tony Benn *Against the Tide: Diaries 1973–76* (Hutchinson, 1989)

★ Tony Benn *Conflict of Interest: Diaries 1977–80* (Hutchinson, 1990)

★ Joel Barnett *Inside the Treasury* (André Deutsch, 1982)

Nick Bosanquet and Peter Townsend (eds) *Labour and Equality: A Fabian Study of Labour in Power, 1974–1979* (Heinemann, 1980)

David Butler and Denis Kavanagh *The British General Election of 1979* (Macmillan, 1980)

James Callaghan *Time and Chance* (Collins, 1987)

Barbara Castle *The Castle Diaries 1974–76* (Weidenfeld & Nicolson, 1980)

Frank Chapple *Sparks Fly! A Trade Union Life* (Michael Joseph, 1984)

David Coates *Labour in Power? A Study of the Labour Government 1974–1979* (Longman, 1980)

Ken Coates *What Went Wrong?* (Nottingham: Spokesman, 1979)

*Edmund Dell *A Hard Pounding: Politics and Economic Crisis 1974–1976* (Oxford: University Press, 1991)

*Bernard Donoughue *Prime Minister: The Conduct of Policy under Harold Wilson and James Callaghan* (Jonathan Cape, 1987)

Stephen Fay and Hugo Young *The Day The £ Nearly Died* (Sunday Times Publications, 1978)

Robert Fisk *The Point of no Return: The Strike Which Broke the British in Ulster* (André Deutsch, 1975)

Joe Haines *The Politics of Power* (Jonathan Cape, 1977)

Michael Hatfield *The House the Left Built: Inside Labour Policy Making 1970–1975* (Victor Gollancz, 1978)

*Denis Healey *The Time of My Life* (Michael Joseph, 1989)

Stuart Holland *The Socialist Challenge* (Quartet, 1975)

Martin Holmes *The Labour Government, 1974–1979* (Macmillan, 1985)

Clive Jenkins *All Against the Collar* (Methuen, 1990)

Robert Jenkins *Tony Benn: A Political Biography* (Writers and Readers, 1980)

Jack Jones *Union Man* (Collins, 1986)

Peter Kellner and Christopher Hitchens *Callaghan: The Road to Number Ten* (Cassell, 1976)

David Leigh *The Wilson Plot: The Intelligence Services and the Discrediting of a Prime Minister* (Heinemann, 1988)

Will Paynter *My Generation* (Allen & Unwin, 1972)

Barrie Penrose and Roger Courtiour *The Pencourt File* (Secker & Warburg, 1978)

Jimmy Reid *Reflections of a Clyde-built Man* (Souvenir Press, 1976)

Jeremy Seabrook *What Went Wrong?* (Victor Gollancz, 1978)

Patrick Seyd *The Rise and Fall of the Labour Left* (Macmillan, 1987)

Robert Skidelsky (ed) *The End of the Keynesian Era* (Macmillan, 1977)

Tariq Ali *The Coming British Revolution* (Jonathan Cape, 1972)

Robert Taylor *The Fifth Estate: Britain's Unions in the Modern World* (Pan, 1980 ed)

Philip Whitehead *The Writing on the Wall: Britain in the Seventies* (Michael Joseph, 1985)

## Towards the Precipice/Towards the Middle Ground

Jad Adams *Tony Benn: A Biography* (Macmillan, 1992)

Martin Adeney and John Lloyd *The Miners' Strike* (Routledge & Kegan Paul, 1986)

Tony Benn *Arguments for Socialism* (Jonathan Cape, 1979)

Tony Benn *The End of an Era: Diaries 1980–90* (Hutchinson, 1992)

Ian Bradley *Breaking The Mould? The Birth and Prospects of the Social Democratic Party* (Oxford: Martin Robertson, 1981)

David Butler and Dennis Kavanagh *The British General Election of 1983* (Macmillan, 1984)

David Butler and Dennis Kavanagh *The British General Election of 1987* (Macmillan, 1988)

Beatrix Campbell *Wigan Pier Revisited* (Virago, 1984)

John Carvel *Citizen Ken* (Chatto & Windus, 1984)

John Cole *As It Seemed To Me: Political Memoirs* (Weidenfeld & Nicolson, 1995)

*Contemporary Record*: 'Neil Kinnock and the Labour Party 1983–92: A Symposium', volume 8, number 3, winter 1994

*Ivor Crewe and Anthony King *SDP: The Birth, Life and Death of the Social Democratic Party* (Oxford: University Press, 1995)

Michael Crick *Scargill and the Miners* (Penguin, 1985)

Francis Cripps et al *Manifesto: Radical Strategy for Britain's Future* (Pan, 1981)

Brian Crozier *Free Agent: The Unseen War 1941–1991* (HarperCollins, 1993)

Michael De-la-Noy *The Honours System* (Virgin, 1992)

Alan Doig *Westminster Babylon* (Allison & Busby, 1990)

Derek Fatchett *Trade Unions and Politics in the 1980s: The 1984 Act and Political Funds* (Croom Helm, 1987)

Michael Foot *Another Heart and Other Pulses: The Alternative to the Thatcher Society* (Collins, 1984)

Paul Foot *Words as Weapons: Selected Writing 1980–1990* (Verso, 1990)

Bryan Gould *A Future for Socialism* (Jonathan Cape, 1989)

Stuart Hall and Martin Jacques (eds) *The Politics of Thatcherism* (Lawrence & Wishart, 1983)

Stuart Hall and Martin Jacques (eds) *New Times: The Changing Face of Politics in the 1990s* (Lawrence & Wishart, 1989)

Charles Handy *The Age of Reason* (Business Books, 1989)

Robert Harris *The Making of Neil Kinnock* (Faber, 1984)

John Harvey-Jones *Making It Happen* (Collins, 1989)

Roy Hattersley *Choose Freedom* (Michael Joseph, 1987)

Roy Hattersley *Who Goes Home? Scenes from a Political Life* (Little, Brown, 1995)

Richard Heffernan and Mike Marqusee *Defeat from the Jaws of Victory: Inside Kinnock's Labour Party* (Verso, 1992)

Simon Hoggart and David Leigh *Michael Foot: A Portrait* (Hodder & Stoughton, 1981)

Colin Hughes and Patrick Wintour *Labour Rebuilt* (Fourth Estate, 1990)

Mark Hollingsworth *The Press and Political Dissent* (Pluto Press, 1976)

Martin Jacques and Francis Mulhern (eds) *The Forward March of Labour Halted?* (Verso, 1981)

Kevin Jefferys *The Labour Party Since 1945* (Macmillan, 1993)

Clive Jenkins *All Against the Collar: Struggles of a White collar Union Leader* (Methuen, 1990)

Peter Jenkins *Mrs Thatcher's Revolution: The Ending of the Socialist Era (Jonathan Cape, 1987)*

R.W. Johnson *The Politics of Recession* (Macmillan, 1985)

Eileen Jones *Neil Kinnock* (Robert Hale, 1994)

Mervyn Jones *Michael Foot* (Victor Gollancz, 1994)

Ken Livingstone *Livingstone's Labour: A Programme for the Nineties* (Allen & Unwin, 1989)

Martin Linton *Money and Votes* (IPPR, 1994)

Frank I.Luntz *Candidates, Consultants and Campaigns* (Oxford: Basil Blackwell, 1988)

David Marquand *The Progressive Dilemma: From Lloyd George to Kinnock* (Heinemann, 1991)

David Marquand *The Unprincipled Society: New Demands and Old Policies* (Jonathan Cape, 1988)

Seumas Milne *The Enemy Within: The Secret War Against the Miners* (Pan, 1995 edition)

Lewis Minkin *The Contentious Alliance: Trade Unions and the Labour Party* (Edinburgh: University Press, 1992)

David Owen *Time to Declare* (Michael Joseph, 1991)

Paul Routledge *Scargill: The Unauthorized Biography* (HarperCollins, 1993)

Sheila Rowbotham et al *Beyond the Fragments* (Merlin Press, 1980)

★Margaret Scammell *Designer Politics: How Elections are Won* (Macmillan, 1995)

Patrick Seyd and Paul Whiteley *Labour's Grass Roots: The Politics of Party Membership* (Oxford: Clarendon Press, 1992)

Eric Shaw *The Labour Party Since 1979: Crisis and Transformation* (Routledge, 1994)

William Shawcross *Rupert Murdoch: Ringmaster of the Information Circus* (Pan, 1993)

Robert Skidelsky (ed) *Thatcherism* (Chatto & Windus, 1988)

Martin J.Smith and Joanna Spear (eds) *The Changing Labour Party* (Routledge, 1992)

Peter Tatchell *The Battle For Bermondsey* (Heretic Books, 1983)

Andrew Taylor *The Trade Unions and the Labour Party* (Croom Helm, 1987)

Margaret Thatcher *The Downing Street Years* (HarperCollins, 1993)

John Walker *The Queen Has Been Pleased: The British Honours System at Work* (Secker & Warburg, 1986)

## New Worlds, New Labour?

Christopher Bryant (ed) *Reclaiming the Ground* (Hodder & Stoughton, 1993)

Stephen Dorrill *The Silent Conspiracy: Inside the Intelligence Services in the 1990s* (Mandarin, 1994)

Paul Hirst *After Thatcher* (Collins, 1989)

Will Hutton *The State We're In* (Jonathan Cape, 1995)

Nicholas Jones *Soundbites and Spin Doctors: How politicians manipulate the media and vice versa* (Cassell, 1995)

Andy McSmith *John Smith: A Life 1938–1994* (Mandarin, 1994)

Peter Mandelson and Roger Liddle *The Blair Revolution: Can New Labour Deliver?* (Faber, 1996)

Giles Radice *Offshore: Britain and the European Idea* (I.B.Tauris, 1992)

John Rentoul *Tony Blair* (Little, Brown, 1995)

David Smith *From Boom to Bust: Trial and Error in British Economic Policy* (Penguin, 1993)

Jon Sopel *Tony Blair: The Moderniser* (Bantam, 1995)

John E. Strafford *The Conservative Party for the 21st Century* (Bow Group, 1995)

★Nicholas Timmins *The Five Giants: A Biography of the Welfare State* (HarperCollins, 1995)

★David Widgery *Some Lives! A GP's East End* (Simon & Schuster, 1993)

Bob Woodward *The Agenda: Inside the Clinton White House* (Pocket Books, 1995)

A.W. Wright *G.D.H.Cole and Socialist Democracy* (Oxford: Clarendon Press, 1979)

## Newspapers, Magazines and Journals

Rather than devote space to a long list of titles, I suggest that the reader consults the Notes, where 115 different newspapers, magazines and journals are cited.

# Index

Page numbers in **bold** denote major section/chapter devoted to subject.